D0290565

STUDIES IN MACROECONOMIC THEORY

Volume 1

EMPLOYMENT AND INFLATION

This is a Volume in
ECONOMIC THEORY, ECONOMETRICS, AND MATHEMATICAL ECONOMICS

A Series of Monographs and Textbooks

Consulting Editor: KARL SHELL

A complete list of titles in this series appears at the end of this volume.

STUDIES IN MACROECONOMIC THEORY

Volume 1

EMPLOYMENT AND INFLATION

Edmund S. Phelps
Department of Economics
New York University
New York, New York

ACADEMIC PRESS New York San Francisco London
A Subsidiary of Harcourt Brace Jovanovich, Publishers

ACADEMIC PRESS, INC.
111 Fifth Avenue, New York, New York 10003

United Kingdom Edition published by
ACADEMIC PRESS, INC. (LONDON) LTD.
24/28 Oval Road, London NW1 7DX

Library of Congress Cataloging in Publication Data

Phelps, Edmund S.
Studies in macroeconomic theory.

(Economic theory and mathematical economics)
CONTENTS: v. 1. Employment and inflation.
1. Macroeconomics--Addresses, essays, lectures.
I. Title.
HB171.P468 339'.01 78-68344
ISBN 0-12-554001-9 (v. 1)

PRINTED IN THE UNITED STATES OF AMERICA

79 80 81 82 83 84 9 8 7 6 5 4 3 2 1

To Viviana, My Wife

CONTENTS

PREFACE

This volume is a collection of nearly all my scholarly papers at the monetary end of macroeconomics. It excludes reviews and rebuttals of a more topical or polemical nature. It also omits my contributions to a well-distributed 1970 conference volume, although two forerunners of that material are reprinted here to close some of the consequent gap.

The main subject of this retrospective is the development of a microeconomic theory of wage and price decisions and commitments—one which accounts for some features of the modern inflationary process and, at the same time, makes sense of some still accepted elements in the post-classical macroeconomics of Keynes and Phillips. Some staple issues of macroeconomic policy are also studied, and sometimes restudied, from the perspective of this theory. Thus there is more unity of theme, at any rate, than is common in volumes of collected papers.

The essays here have been arranged by topic, each group prefaced by a commentary on the origins and aims of the papers that follow. Some of the papers come in for criticism or correction, but the impulse to repudiate them (and start over) is successfully resisted. The temptation to summarize or restate has also been struggled against, not always so successfully.

Still, no amount of rearranging and explaining of these papers, written intermittently over some twenty years, could produce the kind of integrated exposition nor unity of style expectable from a monograph. An introductory essay was therefore added which, in a short space, consolidates the non-Walrasian theory of wages and prices that is developed piecemeal in many of the subsequent papers.

The assets listed, there come next the liabilities incurred. My first debt is to my coauthors: Edwin Burmeister, Guillermo Calvo, John Taylor, and

Sidney Winter. They worked out the papers I couldn't or wouldn't. It is true that my paper with Winter, having been included already in my 1970 anthology and not existing in an alternate version, is not reprinted here; it is reviewed, however, and recycled in the introductory essay.

My collaboration with Calvo and Taylor through five years together at Columbia went far beyond our two coauthorships. A whole school emerged in which we took up one another's ideas. Certainly I benefited greatly from our long collaboration.

I have finally become aware of how much my emphasis on the expectations of economic actors owes to the influence of two teachers and colleagues, William Fellner and Henry Wallich, during my time at Yale. The subsequent years at Pennsylvania provided the distance needed to develop for myself the expectational approach to wages and prices.

Another acknowledgment is belated beyond repair. When, in 1966, my first two writings on the dynamics and the control of inflation were turned down for publication with discouraging methodicalness, the late Harry Johnson, dashing between *Economica* and the *Journal of Political Economy,* rescued those two papers for timely appearance in major journals. It was not the first nor the last time that Harry gave me energetic assistance and constructive advice. His large presence in our profession is very much missed.

My thanks go also to Karl Shell for bringing this project to the attention of Academic Press. Here were publishers with my taste for photorealism, a second generation of typos thereby averted. In the last doubting days I have taken comfort in their firm belief, however mistaken, that the virtues of this sort of enterprise may outweigh the vice.

INTRODUCTION: DEVELOPMENTS IN NON-WALRASIAN THEORY

A dozen years ago the practicing macroeconomist had still to choose between the Keynesian conception of the money economy, in which the pivotal behavior of money-wage rates was left unexplained, and the Walrasian conception with its imagined economy-wide auctioneer. The former model was altogether too general—no assumption about wages was excluded—and the latter model not general enough. A non-Walrasian conception of the market economy, in which money-wage rates and prices are established in a setting of costly communication and incomplete knowledge, has since grown up to occupy the ground left vacant by Walras and Keynes. Alongside it there has also emerged a theory of contingent commitments and their limits.

The contributions to this literature, my own and others', nevertheless do not provide a unified model. They are not always additive, having been built on varied and sometimes conflicting assumptions. The existing collection of models is without a paradigm case, its conventions and traditions not yet canonized. Some perspective on the progress made to date may therefore be welcome.

The present notes on non-Walrasian macrotheory are not a democratic guide to the populous literature. Neither are they a reminiscence purely of my own ideas in this field. These notes will, however, impart my sense of the direction of non-Walrasian economics, especially its principal stages of development. They may also serve here as an introductory framework within which some, although not all, of my previous papers on the subject can be fit.

At the center of non-Walrasian theory is the plight of its characteristic firms. The non-Walrasian firm has at each moment a current stock of employees and customers. It may also have a non-Walrasian banker but we abstract here from imperfections in the capital market. Each such firm must decide upon its wages and prices, there being no auctioneer (even a local one) to determine them in the standard case. Wage scales are set to recruit or reenlist the desired numbers of employees in each type of job. Prices are set to retain or attract the desired number of customers. Both the planned growth of employees and customers, and the corollary wage and price decisions, depend vitally upon the firm's forecast of other firms' wages and prices—in view of their implications for the competing opportunities of the firm's customers and employees. These unseen expectations are the crux of non-Walrasian behavior.

Any model must posit some rhythm in economic events. It will be supposed here that there is a regular time lag between the point when a firm decides its next prices and wages, on the one hand, and the point or time interval when transactions at those terms take place. Let us suppose, too, that wages and prices are revised at regular intervals in contrast to the notion of continuous review. Both postulates, lead time and longevity, are quite natural to an economic setting in which each transmission of price and wage data is costly, and the more costly the shorter the desired delivery time and the wider the desired delivery area. By giving rise to a period of time over which some or all prices and wages are unresponsive to any shock not previously anticipated, both longevity and lead time *help* to explain why output and employment fluctuations are not completely damped, the effect of the disturbance completely dissipated, in a matter of days or weeks.

I

This view of the dynamic structure in which events occur does not entail a discrete-time formulation; the decision points of firms might form a continuum. But it will be an expository convenience to work with a period model. It is further supposed, to begin with, that all prices and wages have the same regular periodicity and are indeed set synchronously at the start of each period over which they will prevail—equivalently, at the end of the previous period.

The model below portrays a firm's wages and prices to be increasing and inelastic functions of its expectations of the wages and prices currently being decided by other firms—given certain other expectational variables. The wages a firm calculates it must offer to attract or retain a *given* number of employees will be higher, at most proportionately higher, the higher are the wages it expects its competitors in the labor market to be deciding upon for the coming period. Yet such a ceteris paribus rise of "expected wages" will cause the firm to reduce its planned employment, so while the firm will be supposed to raise its own wages in self-defense, it will not raise them proportionately. At the same time the firm will raise its prices to ration the smaller output expected to be producible.

Similarly, a rise of expected prices elsewhere is supposed, other things being equal, to cause the firm to raise its own prices but in smaller proportion, thus to increase its planned number of customers. The resulting reduction in the real incomes and consequent output demanded by its existing customers augured by the rise of "expected prices" may at the same time cause the firm to reduce its planned employment and to reduce its wages accordingly; but it will be supposed here that the predicted gain in the firm's stock of customers outweighs that effect.

To simplify our model we focus the analysis on the representative firm. Its situation, expectations, and consequent behavior represent the average over firms in the economy at large—although no firm takes for granted that its every experience is duplicated, and its reaction replicated, at any other firm. Such a firm's plans for the current period are a function of four subjective variables: the expected wage W^e, the expected price P^e, an expected customer demand price parameter $\tilde{M}^e$, and expected employee productivity J^e; to that list we add its starting stock of employees N_{-1}. The latter state variable indicates both the firm's initial employment position and, since it is representative, the scarcity of initially unemployed workers in the labor market generally. To capture the purely monetary forces affecting the expected "demand price" of customers, let us utilize as a makeshift variable the expected supply of money expressed as a ratio to some shift parameter to which the expected demand for money is proportional—so that an expected doubling of the supply or a halving of the demand-shift parameter would double the size of the makeshift monetary variable, denoted $\tilde{M}^e$.

Thus the representative firm's wage W, its price P, and the associated midperiod level of employment that it plans and expects, N^e, are each a function of the four expectational variables: W^e, P^e, $\tilde{M}^e$, J^e; and of the predetermined state variable denoting the stock of employees on hand in the previous period, N_{-1}. The wage function $\mathcal{W}$ and price function $\mathcal{P}$ have the properties indicated:

$$W = \mathcal{W}(W^e, P^e, \tilde{M}^e, J^e, N_{-1}), \tag{1.1}$$

$$\mathcal{W}_1 > 0,\ \mathcal{W}_2 > 0,\ \mathcal{W}_3 > 0,\ \mathcal{W}_4 > 0,\ \mathcal{W}_5 < 0, \tag{1.1a}$$

$$\mathcal{W}(\cdot) = \mathcal{W}(1, P^e/W^e, \tilde{M}^e/W^e, J^e, N_{-1}) \cdot W^e, \tag{1.1b}$$

$$W^e\mathcal{W}_1/W < 1,\ P^e\mathcal{W}_2/W < 1,\ \tilde{M}^e\mathcal{W}_3/W < 1. \tag{1.1c}$$

$$P = \mathcal{P}(W^e, P^e, \tilde{M}^e, J^e; N_{-1}), \tag{1.2}$$

$$\mathcal{P}_1 > 0,\ \mathcal{P}_2 > 0,\ \mathcal{P}_3 > 0,\ \mathcal{P}_4 < 0;\ \mathcal{P}_5 < 0, \tag{1.2a}$$

$$\mathcal{P}(\cdot) = \mathcal{P}(W^e/P^e, 1, \tilde{M}^e/P^e, J^e, N_{-1}) \cdot P^e, \tag{1.2b}$$

$$W^e\mathcal{P}_1/P < 1,\ P^e\mathcal{P}_2/P < 1,\ \tilde{M}^e\mathcal{P}_3/P < 1. \tag{1.2c}$$

The first-degree homogeneity of these two functions (equations b) is inspired by the neutrality-of-money hypothesis in monetary theory. This homogeneity postulate and the sign conditions on the derivatives (equations a) together imply the aforementioned inelasticity conditions—that the logarithmic derivatives with respect to W^e, P^e, and $\tilde{M}^e$ are each less than one (equations c).

One may use the homogeneity of $\mathscr{W}$ and $\mathscr{P}$ to express (1.1) and (1.2) in terms of the expected real wage, $V^e \equiv W^e/P^e$, and expected effective liquidity, $L^e \equiv \tilde{M}^e/P^e$, since $\tilde{M}^e/W^e$ in (1.1b) is the ratio of L^e to V^e. Hence

$$W = \mathscr{E}^W(V^e, L^e, J^e, N_{-1}) \cdot W^e, \qquad \mathscr{E}_1{}^W < 0,\ \mathscr{E}_2{}^W > 0,\ \mathscr{E}_3{}^W > 0,\ \mathscr{E}_4{}^W < 0, \tag{1.3}$$

$$P = \mathscr{E}^P(V^e, L^e, J^e, N_{-1}) \cdot P^e, \qquad \mathscr{E}_1{}^P > 0,\ \mathscr{E}_2{}^P > 0,\ \mathscr{E}_3{}^P < 0,\ \mathscr{E}_4{}^P < 0. \tag{1.4}$$

Letting lowercase letters denote logarithms—so that $w \equiv \log W$, $\epsilon \equiv \log \mathscr{E}$, and so on—and subtracting from both sides of the equations the lagged value of w and p, respectively, one obtains

$$w_t - w_{t-1} = \epsilon^W(V_t{}^e, L_t{}^e, J_t{}^e, N_{t-1}) + w_t{}^e - w_{t-1}, \tag{1.3$'$}$$

$$p_t - p_{t-1} = \epsilon^P(V_t{}^e, L_t{}^e, J_t{}^e, N_{t-1}) + p_t{}^e - p_{t-1}. \tag{1.4$'$}$$

The functions ϵ^W and ϵ^P may be regarded as the counterparts of the excess-demand functions in Samuelsonian dynamics (1941). A contrast here, however, is that wages and prices are not implied to be stationary when the notional "excess demands" in (1.3′) and (1.4′) are equal to zero. Nor do these equations provide an account of wage and price dynamics until a theory of expectations is introduced into the model.

The economy will be said to be in *equilibrium* if and only if expectations happen to be such as to produce actions that cause those expectations to be fulfilled. The notion of equilibrium as a state of self-confirming expectations can be traced through the literature of game theory, and the Scandinavian school, on back to Cournot. Yet it differs markedly from the Walrasian conception which, making no reference to expectations, identifies equilibrium with market clearing. On the above definition, then equilibrium in the current period requires that *price* and *wage* expectations be a "fixed point":

$$\mathscr{W}(W^e, P^e, \tilde{M}^e, J^e, N_{-1}) = W^e, \tag{1.5a}$$

$$\mathscr{P}(W^e, P^e, \tilde{M}^e, J^e, N_{-1}) = P^e, \tag{1.5b}$$

given $\tilde{M}^e$ and J^e. Let us assume the existence of a fixed point, sufficient conditions for which are derivable from the mathematics of contraction mappings. To check the uniqueness of the solution, use (1.5b), where $\mathscr{P}_2$ is one-signed, to obtain the equilibrium P^e—unique by virtue of (1.2c)—as an increasing function, denoted Ψ, of W^e; then substitute $\Psi(\cdot)$ for P^e in (1.5a) to obtain the equation determining the equilibrium W^e:

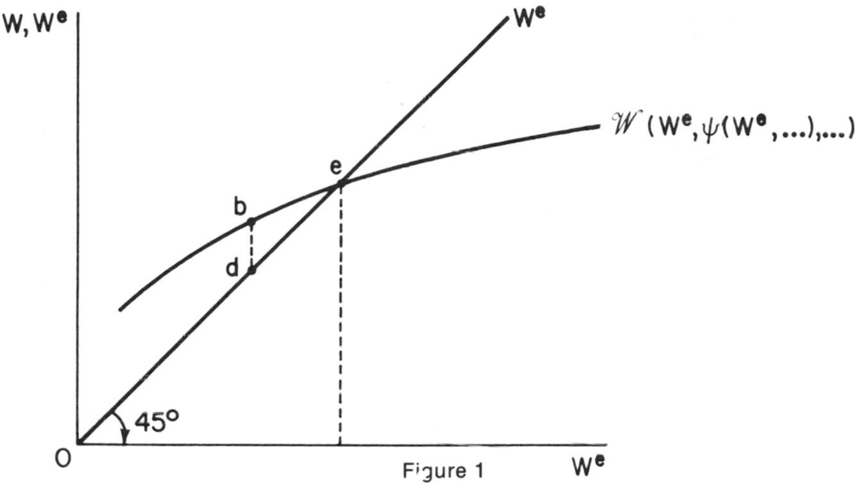

Figure 1

$$\mathscr{W}(W^e, \Psi(W^e, \tilde{M}^e, J^e, N_{-1}), \tilde{M}^e, J^e, N_{-1}) = W^e. \tag{1.6}$$

The solution is illustrated in Fig. 1. Its uniqueness is assured by the inelasticity and sign conditions on the functions $\mathscr{W}$ and $\mathscr{P}$. Once $\mathscr{W}(\cdot)$ has crossed the 45° degree line, the distance between them can only widen. (A similar diagram depicting the determination of the equilibrium price appears in Phelps and Winter, 1970.)

The equilibrium price and wage expectations are equivalently defined by (1.3′), (1.4′), and (1.5). From these relations it follows that, for equilibrium, W^e and P^e must cause V^e and L^e to satisfy

$$\epsilon^W(V^e, L^e, J^e, N_{-1}) = 0, \qquad \epsilon^P(V^e, L^e, J^e, N_{-1}) = 0, \tag{1.7}$$

given $\tilde{M}^e$ and J^e. The first of these equations may be called a condition for equilibrium in the labor market, the second a condition for equilibrium in the goods market. In Fig. 2 the locus of points (L^e, V^e) satisfying the former condition is the curve NN and the locus satisfying the latter condition is the curve GG. Above NN we have $\epsilon^W < 0$ and so $W < W^e$; above GG we have $\epsilon^P > 0$ and thus $P > P^e$. The opposite results occur below these curves. At point a, therefore, $W = W^e$ but $P > P^e$. If P^e rises enough to move (L^e, V^e) down the ray from a to point b then $P = P^e$ but $W > W^e$. If W^e then rises so as to move the system north to point c, both P^e and W^e will still need to be higher for the *general* equilibrium at point e where NN and GG intersect. At points like a and c, the representative firm feels too short of spare capacity to justify to its shareholders supplying the customer demands it would expect to receive if it charged what it expects to be the going price, and so it risks setting a price above the market; but it is

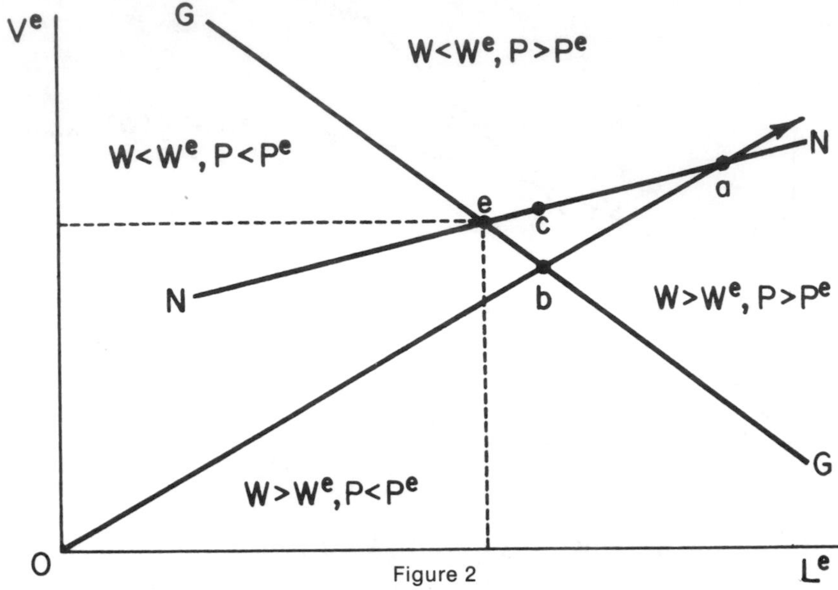

Figure 2

well enough stocked with employees in relation to its prices and wage expectations to want to offer them its expectation of the going wage. At points like *b*, the firm, having better price expectations, reckons it is short of employees and hence sets its wages at a level above what it believes will be the average wage.

What story of employment and unemployment is told by the above non-Walrasian model? Little has been said thusfar about the opportunities and behavior of households; only that household decisions are constrained by scarce access (e.g., limited attention time) to transmissions of wage-price and nonprice data—a fact which firms take into account in setting wages and prices.

One kind of unemployment that the model will generate, in disturbed conditions, can be described as wage-search unemployment. This kind of unemployment is the sole focus on a quite different non-Walrasian model in which the local "market" for jobs is "cleared" at every site. The variety of supply–demand disturbances experienced by firms can generate a wage distribution over labor-market sites; where the money wage is perceived to be comparatively low, however transiently, fewer workers will find that it covers their estimates of the opportunity cost of their working there; to search more intensively for better wages or to relocate for the same purpose, some workers will reject work at the low money wage, opting for temporary unemployment. Thus there will usually be a positive volume of wage-search unemployment even if the economy happens currently to be in non-Walrasian equilibrium—expectations of the average wage being correct though the details of the current wage distribution are not currently known. In such models a perfectly general macroeconomic disturbance, such as an equiproportionate rise of each firm's $\tilde{M}^e$ or J^e, will pull the volume of wage-search unemployment below its current-period equilibrium level if and as long as the consequent rise of wage offers is not understood to be economy-wide and so induces some workers to halt their search.

The present model, however, does not entail that wages are set to clear the market for jobs at every (or any) firm, not even when expectations are appropriate for equilibrium. Wages in relation to product prices are set too high, it will be argued, to clear the labor market with the consequence that, typically, some workers will find themselves "rationed" from gaining employment in the particular firms to which they have had time to apply. In formal terms, the local auction-market solution is (in the present model) a disequilibrium representable by a point like d in Fig. 1, at which, with the corresponding wage and price expectations prevailing, each firm is motivated to raise its wages above the auction level to the point indicated by b; when each firm notices that others have done the same, so no tactical gain in attracting and securing employees has been obtained in compensation for the rise of real labor costs, firms will offer a smaller number of jobs (as well as make further wage and price adjustments) as they grope toward the non-Walrasian equilibrium at point e.

Firms have several motives for setting wages above market-clearing levels:

(i) Because its wages will be set for some significant duration, to enhance their information-value and reduce their transmission costs among other reasons, while its current-period supply of workers (new applicants and initial employees) is stochastic, no firm would maximize expected profits by setting wages so low that no job applicant need ever be turned away—thus bearing all the uncertainty of worker availability—even if all other firms were following that practice. Though in the aggregate the number of jobs ultimately unfilled may equal or exceed the number of workers left unemployed, firms are too heterogeneous in some nonwage dimension to permit use of a clearing house to allocate workers among them in some mechanical fashion.

(ii) Whether or not wages are revised only periodically, the firm desiring a particular assortment of worker skills for production will try to guard against temporary losses of critical skills by paying its employees in excess of their opportunity costs of staying on; though firms cannot in the aggregate pay more than their competitors, the consequent rise in the equilibrium volume of unemployment resulting from job rationing will indirectly deter existing employees from quitting to join the unemployed. Here the heterogeneity of workers with regard to their skills interacts with the heterogeneity of firms to account for the frequency of zero job vacancies among firms.[1]

(iii) Where the piecework system is inapplicable or uneconomic and the monitoring of workers' performance is costlier the more intensively it is conducted, paying its workers more than their reservation wage may be a cost-effective device by which the firm can save some monitoring costs while giving employees an incentive not to get caught shirking.[2] It may also be that an incentive wage is needed to induce greater employee effort when the employee distrusts promises of being rewarded after the fact in the event he makes an extra effort.

(iv) The firm may look with suspicion on a worker attempting to win a job by offering to work for less than current employees are being paid in the same sort of job. If the manager judges quality by price when knowing nothing else, he will fear that the applicant is underqualified and thus worth even less.[3] If the manager believes it is a case of temporary desperation, he will fear that the bargain terms will not last and so will hesitate to make the necessary investment in the overqualified worker that he would not make for a job applicant offering to work at normal terms.

(v) The firm may find that it minimizes labor costs over the long run to avoid a reputation for replacing existing employees with cheaper ones (or better qualified ones at the same pay) in view of the setup costs and other risks which any prospective future employee may have to bear in moving and adjusting to that firm. This does not imply that a firm will find guaranteed-employment contracts to be optimal nor that it will surrender the option to make eventual or period adjustments of general wage scales in response to observed and forecasted changes in normal wages elsewhere and in its own business situation.[4]

The upshot of these arguments for the existence of job rationing is that the representative firm is generally able to increase its employment

[1] The above two considerations, especially the latter, lay behind the model in my 1968 paper on money-wage dynamics. See also the developments by Stiglitz (1974) and Salop (1979).

[2] The supervision model appears in G.A. Calvo (1977).

[3] The fear of buying a "lemon" and its possible consequences are discussed by G. A. Akerlof (1970).

[4] Two distinct slants on contract theory are exemplified by D. F. Gordon (1976) and Calvo-Phelps (1977). See also the references there to C. Azariadis and M. N. Baily.

simply by accepting a larger fraction of job applicants from among the unemployed. Attracting additional employees does not depend upon their mistaking a general rise of money wage rates for a wage rise specific to the firms at which they accept employment nor upon their mistaking a global improvement in the availability of jobs for a local improvement—although recruitment will surely be facilitated by any such misreadings. What is intrinsic to the theory is that when the expectations of firms have induced them to try to raise their wages relative to others' wages, in order to attract employees from one another, the *firms* are disappointed to learn, by inference from their personnel experience if not by direct observation, that other firms' wages have gone up as much as their own. A consequence of that disequilibrium is that firms experience a smaller gain of new personnel and a large attrition of existing personnel then they had planned.

The employment side of the theory, in the simple version we are discussing, may be modeled by the following two equations. The first of these gives the planned employment of the representative firm:

$$N^{e} = \mathcal{N}(\epsilon^{W}(V^{e}, L^{e}, J^{e}, N_{-1}), N_{-1}), \qquad \mathcal{N}_{1} > 0, \quad 1 > \mathcal{N}_{2} \geq 0. \quad (1.8)$$

For simplicity it is supposed, not unreasonably, that the three expectational variables figure in the planned employment function the same way as they figure in the function ϵ^{W} of equation (1.3′). (It would little complicate matters to introduce into the function $\mathcal{N}$ the firms' expectation of current-period unemployment or aggregate employment per firm; but that variable may be a stable function of the variables already appearing in $\mathcal{N}$.) The second of these equations gives the algebraic shortfall of actual employment from the planned level[5]:

$$N^{e} - N = \mathcal{D}(\epsilon^{W}(V^{e}, L^{e}, J^{e}, N_{-1}), N_{-1}), \quad \mathcal{D}(0, N_{-1}) = 0, \quad \mathcal{D}_{1} > 0. \quad (1.9)$$

The degree of disappointment as measured by $\mathcal{D}(\cdot)$ might be supposed proportional to N_{-1} for all $\epsilon^{W}(\cdot)$, the factor of proportionality being an increasing function of the importance of the frictional "inertia" as measured by the size of $\mathcal{N}_{2}$; then $\mathcal{D}_{2}$ would have the algebraic sign of $\epsilon^{W}(\cdot)$. In any case I shall suppose that $\mathcal{D}_{2}$ is small enough in absolute value that

[5] The case $N^{e} > N$ was interpreted in the previous paragraph. To interpret $N^{e} < N$ we should remark that, in view of the investment-type costs of recruiting and training new employees, the firm finding that it has suffered less attrition than it expected to result from its attempt to reduce its relative wage will not discharge remaining employees in the amount of the unexpected improvement of its attrition experience. It will reduce its new hiring by that amount insofar as the unexpected improvement is noticed in time and to the extent that its planned new hiring leaves room for an offsetting reduction. In the event the firm resorts to temporary layoffs, N should be interpreted as including laid-off employees.

$\mathscr{D}_2 \leq \mathscr{N}_2$ (≥ 0) and $\mathscr{D}_2 > \mathscr{N}_2 - 1$ (<0); an extreme example is $\mathscr{N}_2 = \mathscr{D}_2 = 0$. Of course, the function portrays only the mean or systematic part of the employment shortfall; one firm's loss of employees in excess of $\mathscr{D}(\cdot)$ is the other firms' collective gain.

With the foregoing ideas and notation in hand, we can now add to the list of requirements for non-Walrasian equilibrium, heretofore consisting of (1.5a) and (1.5b), the further expectational requirement that $N = N^e$; hence[6]

$$N = \mathscr{N}(\epsilon^W(V^e, L^e, J^e, N_{-1}), N_{-1}). \tag{1.5c}$$

Yet this added requirement puts no new conditions on the expectations (V^e, L^e, J^e) necessary for the occurrence of equilibrium. According to (1.9) above, $N = N^e$ if (and only if) $\epsilon^W(\cdot) = 0$, and the latter was earlier noted in (1.7) to be a condition for the equilibrium requirement that $W = W^e$. Finally, to complete the list of requirements, we may add

$$J = J^e, \tag{1.5d}$$

$$\tilde{M} = \tilde{M}^e. \tag{1.5e}$$

Because the present model does not present functions determining J and $\tilde{M}$, these last two requirements do not enjoy the logical status of the previous three. But a complete model would contain such functions so it seems best, as a general strategy, to let our definition encompass all relevant expectations, not just expectations of those variable which are endogenous in a model that, for pragmatic reasons, is not comprehensive.

From (1.8) and (1.9) it follows that

$$\begin{aligned} N &= \mathscr{N}(\epsilon^W(V^e, L^e, J^e, N_{-1}), N_{-1}) - \mathscr{D}(\epsilon^W(V^e, L^e, J^e, N_{-1}), N_{-1}) \\ &\equiv \mathscr{H}(\epsilon^W(\cdot), N_{-1}), \\ \mathscr{H}_1 &\equiv \mathscr{N}_1 - \mathscr{D}_1 > 0, \qquad 1 > \mathscr{N}_2 - \mathscr{D}_2 \equiv \mathscr{H}_2 \geq 0 \end{aligned} \tag{1.10}$$

If $\epsilon^W(\cdot)$ increases, employment also increases, through disappointingly little. If N_{-1} were larger, employment would be larger by a lesser amount (if at all) though certainly not decreased. Assured that $\mathscr{H}_1$ is everwhere one-signed, we may invert (1.10) to obtain

[6] It would be more congruent with (1.5a) and (1.5b), in which behavioral functions appear on the left and the corresponding expectation on the right, to use in place of (1.5c) the equivalent requirement

$$\mathscr{H}(\epsilon^W(V^e, L^e, J^e, N_{-1}), N_{-1}) = N^e, \tag{1.5c$'$}$$

where the function $\mathscr{H}$ is defined in Eq. (1.10) below.

$$\epsilon^W(\cdot) = \Phi^*(N, N_{-1}), \qquad 0 < \Phi_1{}^* \equiv \mathcal{H}_1^{-1}, \qquad 0 \geq \Phi_2{}^* \equiv -\mathcal{H}_1^{-1}\mathcal{H}_2, \tag{1.11}$$

or equivalently

$$\epsilon^W(\cdot) = \Phi(N, N - N_{-1}), \qquad \Phi_1 = \mathcal{H}_1^{-1}(1 - \mathcal{H}_2) > 0, \qquad \Phi_2 = \mathcal{H}_1^{-1}\mathcal{H}_2 \geq 0. \tag{1.11$'$}$$

The *level* and *growth* of employment are thus a joint indicator of $\epsilon^W(\cdot)$. Substituting (1.11′) into (1.3′) yields the (growth-augmented) Phillips–Lipsey equation generalized to capture arbitrary wage expectations:

$$w - w_{-1} = \Phi(N, N - N_{-1}) + w^{\mathrm{e}} - w_{-1}. \tag{1.12}$$

Much study has gone into the correlations between wage growth and employment level to which (1.12) leads in various scenarios of labor-market *disequilibrium*. On the hypothesis of static expectations, i.e., $w^{\mathrm{e}} = w_{-1}$, there exists a conditionally stable Phillips curve around which the familiar (counterclockwise) Lipsey loop can be generated by a suitable sequence of $\tilde{M}^{\mathrm{e}}$ and J^{e}. On the hypothesis of adaptive expectations regarding the growth of wages, there arises a "statistical" Phillips curve around which a clockwise elliptical loop can be generated—with "stagflation" in late recession and rising wage inflation late in the recovery.[7] Nevertheless the contrasting hypothesis of equilibrium wage expectations, i.e., $w^{\mathrm{e}} = w$, may be a better assumption if firms are playing a many-player game against nature, not the government, and when, after any recent parametric innovations that may have caused errors in W^{e} and a consequent perturbation of employment, firms have had an opportunity to identify and gauge the innovations that have occurred.

In labor-market *equilibrium*, $w = w^{\mathrm{e}}$ and hence $\epsilon^W(\cdot) = 0$. By (1.12) or (1.11), therefore, the equilibrium level of current-period employment, given N_{-1}, is determined by

$$0 = \Phi^*(N, N_{-1}). \tag{1.13}$$

If there is a sequence of equilibria, (1.13) becomes a first-order difference equation determining N_t, $t = 0,1,2,\ldots$. With $\mathcal{H}_2 > 0$, the equilibrium path of N_t resembles a dynamic "multiplier process" which converges montonically to the *stationary* equilibrium level defined by $\Phi^*(N, N) = 0$. Of course, if $\mathcal{H}_2 = 0$, which is not a realistic case, current-period equilib-

[7] The adaptation hypothesis here is $w^{\mathrm{e}} - w_{-1} = \beta(w_{-1} - w^{\mathrm{e}}_{-1}) + w^{\mathrm{e}}_{-1} - w_{-2}$, $0 < \beta < 1$. A diagram of the clockwise motion around the tilted ellipse is shown in Chapter 2 of my 1972 book. Incidentally, the discussion of equilibrium and disequilibrium there, while proceeding without benefit of equations, conforms closely—more than I had remembered—to the present framework.

rium employment is independent of initial conditions, being always equal to the stationary-equilibrium level. (To deal with a setting of steady labor-force growth one can define the steady-state equilibrium employment "rate" to use in place of the stationary equilibrium level.)

Consider now a scenario of *equilibrium* in *both* the labor and product markets. For convenience we take J^e to be constant over the future. Then, if the equilibrium path of N_t is (say) increasing toward its stationary level, the NN curve of Fig. 2 will be shifting downward, thus increasing L^e and reducing V^e; the GG curve will be shifting upward, thus increasing L^e and raising V^e. Hence L^e will be rising, while V^e will rise or fall (or oscillate) toward their respective stationary equilibrium levels. If we take $\tilde{M}^e$ to be constant throughout this equilibrium scenario, P^e will be falling and, we may presume, W^e too. It can be seen, then, that employment and wages trace out a "historical" Phillips curve with a zero point at the stationary equilibrium level of employment: The rate at which P^e falls will be a decreasing function—thus the algebraic rate of inflation will be an increasing function—of the level of employment as the latter recovers, monotonically and asymptotically, to its rest-point value.

Although their accounts are quite different, both the equilibrium and the disequilibrium scenarios warn against the naive supposition that the rate of inflation will necessarily get "better and better" throughout an interlude of economic slack. The equilibrium scenario asserts that the inflation rate tends to recover to its "basic" size, as determined by the trend of $\tilde{M}^e$, as the employment rate recovers to its stationary-equilibrium level—without requiring, as does the disequilibrium scenario, that the recovery travel faster than some speed limit.

II

The non-Walrasian assumptions that wages and prices are determined with a lead time and are subject only to periodic review do not, as noted earlier, require us to adopt a regular period model. Nor do they entail the further assumption, made earlier for pedagogical convenience, that the periodic wage and price decisions of all the firms are synchronized by some unseen hand. It would be an absurd substitution of one *deus ex machina* for another if, having banished the Walrasian auctioneer, we were really to imagine that all firms sing out their wages and prices with every downbeat of some non-Walrasian chorusmaster.

Let us therefore reformulate the theory in the simplest possible non-synchronous setting. A discrete-time model will convey the basic ideas. To minimize complications we drop the frictional role of previous-period employment from the theory, and take $\tilde{M}$ and J to be known parameters which are constant from the present period into the indefinite future. Attention is restricted to the equilibrium path proceeding from arbitrary initial conditions following some disturbance to $\tilde{M}$ or J not anticipated early enough in the past.[8]

Imagine that every wage commitment runs for a "year," but these commitments are staggered symmetrically or uniformly over every such interval. In the semiannual model, then, half the firms set wages at the beginning of one semiannum, and these wages remain in effect for two such periods; the other half set their wages at the beginning of the next period; and so on indefinitely. These two groups of wage rates are so normalized, if necessary, that in the stationary equilibrium of zero wage inflation their levels would be equal.

With regard to prices, it will be supposed that every firm sets new prices at the beginning of each period. There is, in effect, a fall and a spring price list. The present model makes the endogenous price level a function only of the history of money wage rates, given the parameters $\tilde{M}$ and J, so it may be "solved out" of the reduced-form behavioral equation for wages and employment that follows.

Now let $w_v(s)$, $s = (v, v + 1)$, denote the logarithm of the representative wage set in period v. Let $\bar{w}(t)$ denote the logarithm of the geometric average of the two wages, old and new, that coexist in period t; hence

$$\bar{w}(t) = \tfrac{1}{2}w_{t-1}(t - 1) + \tfrac{1}{2}w_t(t). \tag{2.1}$$

Finally, let $\bar{w}_t^{e}(s)$ denote the expectation held at t, $t = (0,1,2, \ldots)$, of $\bar{w}(s)$ for any $s \geq t$. And denote by $\tilde{m}$ the logarithm of our makeshift monetary variable $\tilde{M}$, which is now a known constant. In this clumsy notation, we may write our new-wage function as follows:

$$\begin{aligned} w_t(t) = {} & \tfrac{1}{2}\bar{w}_t^{e}(t) + \tfrac{1}{2}\bar{w}_t^{e}(t + 1) + (\alpha/2)[\tilde{m}_t^{e}(t) - \bar{w}_t^{e}(t) - \lambda] \\ & + (\alpha/2)[\tilde{m}_t^{e}(t + 1) - \bar{w}_t^{e}(t + 1) - \lambda], \qquad 0 < \alpha < 1. \end{aligned} \tag{2.2}$$

Note that $W_t(t)$, the antilog of $w_t(t)$, is homogenous of degree one in $\bar{W}_t^{e}(t)$, $\bar{W}_t^{e}(t + 1)$, $\tilde{M}_t^{e}(t)$, and $\tilde{M}_t^{e}(t + 1)$. The logarithmic derivatives, which are the constant coefficients in the log-linear formulation in (2.2), are all positive fractions adding up to one. Evidently (2.2) is the two-period commitment analog of (1.1)–(1.2) in the one-period commitment model if it is assumed that $P^{e} = \mathscr{P}(\cdot)$ so that P^{e} can be solved out. It may readily be calculated that the constant λ is interpretable as the stationary-

[8] Some precursors in the literature on leap-frogging wages are cited in my paper, "Disinflation without Recession," reprinted in the present volume. The notes here have been much influenced by the extensive theoretical and econometric studies being carried out by John B. Taylor.

equilibrium value of the logarithm of $\tilde{M}$ expressed in wage units—the purchasing power over labor of the demand-adjusted money supply. Equivalently, the stationary-equilibrium value of the logarithm of the money wage, w^*, is $\tilde{m} - \lambda$.

In an equilibrium scenario beginning at $t = 0$,

$$\bar{w}(s) = \bar{w}_t^e(s), \tag{2.3}$$

$$\tilde{m}(s) = \tilde{m}_t^e(s), \qquad \tilde{m}_t^e(s) = \tilde{m}, \quad s \geq t,\ t = 0, 1, 2, \ldots . \tag{2.4}$$

The foregoing four equations yield the following difference equation, in which w_v denotes $w_v(v)$ and w_{-1} is predetermined at $t = 0$:

$$w_t - w^* = (1 - \alpha)[\tfrac{1}{4}(w_{t-1} - w^*) + \tfrac{1}{2}(w_t - w^*) + \tfrac{1}{4}(w_{t+1} - w^*)], \qquad t = 0, 1, 2, \ldots . \tag{2.5}$$

While this equation places a restriction on the paths eligible for equilibrium status, it leaves an infinity of solutions available, all but one of which produce unbounded growth or decline of w_t. It would be quite unrealistic to suppose that our economy would or could follow any of those aberrant paths *indefinitely*. In any case, we shall single out for study the equilibrium path that converges to w^*.

The convergent solution among the equilibrium paths is

$$w_t - w^* = c \cdot (w_{t-1} - w^*), \qquad t = 0, 1, 2, \ldots ,$$
$$0 < c = \frac{1 + \alpha}{1 - \alpha} - \left[\left(\frac{1 + \alpha}{1 - \alpha}\right)^2 - 1\right]^{1/2} < 1. \tag{2.6}$$

The result that $c > 0$ is due to the assumption in (2.2) that $1 - \alpha > 0$; the latter is roughly analogous to the corresponding assumption in the one-period commitment model that $\mathscr{W}(\cdot)$ in (1.6) is an increasing function of W^e, given $\tilde{M}^e$. In the event that $1 - \alpha < 0$, we have $0 > c > -1$ with the convergence of w_t to w^* therefore oscillatory.

With $0 < c < 1$, the convergence of w_t is monotone and asymptotic. So, after a lag, is the corresponding convergence of $\bar{w}(t)$:

$$\begin{aligned} \bar{w}(t + 1) - w^* &= (\tfrac{1}{2} + \tfrac{1}{2}c)(w_t - w^*) \\ &= c \cdot (\tfrac{1}{2} + \tfrac{1}{2}c)(w_{t-1} - w^*) \\ &= c \cdot (\bar{w}(t) - w^*), \qquad t = 0, 1, 2, \ldots . \end{aligned} \tag{2.7}$$

This result implies that if, when the economy has been in stationary equilibrium, there occurs an observed fall of $\tilde{M}$ of J to a new constant level beginning at $t = 0$, so that w_{-1} exceeds the new w^*, then $\bar{w}(t) > w^*$ for all $t \geq 0$. The excess of the average money wage over its stationary value is worked off only in the limit as $t \to \infty$.

It remains to argue that as long as the average money wage is too high for stationary equilibrium, so too will be the money price level; in consequence, the real value of cash balances will be short of its stationary value; invoking the "quantity theory," we then deduce that production will be correspondingly short of its stationary value and, therefore, the profit-maximizing level of employment as well. Letting n denote the logarithm of employment, we may embody this conclusion in the equation

$$n(t) - n^* = \gamma[\tilde{m}(t) - \bar{w}(t) - \lambda], \qquad \gamma > 0, \tag{2.8}$$

whence

$$n(t) - n^* = -\gamma[\bar{w}(t) - w^*], \qquad t = 0,1,2, \ldots . \tag{2.9}$$

It follows that when w_{-1} exceeds w^*, as in the above example, then $n(t) < n^*$ for all $t \geq 0$—absent subsequent shocks that fortuitously decrease the parameter w^* to the level w_{t-1+s} for some $s \geq 1$. Further, the path of n has the same autoregressive structure as $\bar{w}$ along the equilibrium path following a disturbance, i.e.,

$$n(t + 1) - n^* = c \cdot [n(t) - n^*], \qquad t = 0,1,2, \ldots . \tag{2.10}$$

It is worth noting that the equilibrium evolution of the economy traces out a statistical Phillips curve. In the equilibrium scenario just discussed, the rate of wage inflation, even though negative at all times, is rising as the level of employment rises. The rate of wage inflation and the level of employment are positively correlated in the sample space of equilibrium motions. Similar findings from the one-period or synchronous model were reported in the previous section. The charge that contemporary macroeconomic theory does not predict, and hence cannot explain, the "recovery" of inflation to its "basic" rate in the typical course of a business recovery is a false indictment.

We have been discussing a "semiannual" period model in which the "year" is defined to be the length of (every) wage commitment. Several generalizations of this model are easily conceived. There are obvious extensions to the "quarterly" case, say, and, most elegantly, to the continuous case. The analysis of these extended models is still far from having derived all their interesting implications. But a few of their more important properties have become apparent:

(i) While monotone recovery to stationary equilibrium does not occur from all possible configurations of initial conditions regarding the predetermined wages, neither is there any very general tendency for a recovery to overshoot the mark. The semiannual model is a case in point. The potential for oscillations in the manner of Frisch's rocking chair are therefore absent.

(ii) The economy is not generally capable of maintaining employment equal to n^* in the face of arbitrary perturbations of money supply and productivity, $M(t)$ and $J(t)$, even if the behavior of those "forcing functions" has long been foreseen. Because only one cohort of wages is adjusted in each period, the economy lacks the necessary degree of freedom to accommodate such perturbations.

(iii) There does nevertheless exist a unique path of $M(t)$ which, if anticipated at $t = 0$ and beyond, can guide the rate of wage inflation toward an arbitrarily prescribed value without there resulting a temporary deviation of employment from n^* in the process.[9] Readers will understand that this is a theoretical proposition about the implication of a class of models, not a factual proposition.

III

My hope and expectation is that the foregoing kinds of modeling will prove able eventually to explain all, or at any rate most, of the statistical facts with which non-Walrasian theory may be confronted. Already these models can "predict" the statistical Phillips curve, the approximate invariance of employment to steady inflation, and the systematic "persistence" shown in business fluctuations. In addition, several microeconomic phenomena have been illuminated by the theory. It would be naive to believe, on the other hand, that the real world is quite as simple, and as beautiful, as pictured here. There is the possibility that, for dealing with some questions, the theory is critically wrong in some feature or other. It is also true that ever-deeper explanations may be demanded. The theorist's work is never done.

Some deep questions are now being addressed to the above type of models. Why is so fundamental a role ascribed to money and the surface observation that the terms of exchange are expressed, and paid, in units of money—why not a barter-and-credit model? Why a market relationship between worker and firm—why not a more feudal sort of relationship? Answers may be offered, and some are well known. Their compellingness, however, is in the eye of the beholder since no amount of *a priori* reasoning can prove their sufficiency.

One can point to the convenience of money as a unit of account: the cost savings from sending an unconditional message y instead of a function f, and the ways in which unconditional wage and price quotations and term commitments facilitate household and business planning. It would be

[9] Phelps, "Disinflation without Recession," *infra*.

fantastic to assume that, to a close approximation, the economy behaves as if all money prices were retroactively adjusted by transactors in such a way that the transactions taking place were unaffected by current monetary events—particularly the prevailing monetary policy.

The contractual view of the relationship between employer and employee, particularly the hypothesis of tenure, is also open to objections. One can point to disadvantages from job guarantees, or full private insurance against unemployment, which may well outweigh the advantages. If some grounds for dismissal are stipulated in the employment contract, the costs of a quasijudicial hearing will be incurred whenever the firm wishes to discharge employees on grounds other than those protected by the guarantee; alternatively, the workers, who have given up income to get greater job protection, face the "moral hazard" that the firm will defraud them of that protection. If no grounds for dismissal are stipulated, on the other hand, the firm runs a greater risk of bankruptcy and the managers a higher risk of losing their jobs.

The leading polar alternative to the foregoing "monetaristic" models of employment and inflation is the full-indexation model. In this conception there exist long-term arrangements under which all or most money wages are adjusted periodically in strict proportion to the price level reported to have prevailed the previous period. That is, $w_v(t + 1) = w_v(t) + p(t) - p(t - 1), v \leq t < x \leq \infty$, for wage contracts established in period v. An empirical difficulty in such a model is that it provides, at best, only a glacially slow mechanism—the expiration of contracts or the entry of new workers or firms—by which real wages can approximately track the productivity of labor. Another difficulty is that, in a rather general formulation, current prices are likewise indexed to the lagged general price level. But then all prices and wage are either rooted to some aboriginal level, no price moving because no other price has moved, or else the rise of a single price upon expiration of its corresponding contract sets off a steady inflation. As an empirical matter, the full-indexation model imputes too much serial persistence both to the level (and growth) of real wages and to the rate of inflation. Note, however, that this type of model leaves ample sway for central bank stabilization of production owing to the lagged character of the indexation being practiced.

Whatever the realism of indexationist models, and the future of the phenomenon of indexation itself, there is a grain of plausibility in the fundamental premise: Risk-averse workers prefer, and are willing to pay for, some measure of protection against unforeseen reductions of their real wage rates in relation to their forecast of the path of the real wage in their respective occupations. How much protection they are willing to buy depends upon its corollary cost in terms of reduced employment security.[10] The transaction costs and monitoring costs of such insurance should also be borne in mind.

A logically complete macromodel incorporating that premise is well beyond the scope of these introductory notes. A central implication of that premise, however, is that there exists in each period a corresponding lower bound below which an employee's money wage cannot go—at least the money wage paid to employees covered by outstanding implicit contracts. Contracts established in period v provide a constraint on money wage rates paid in period t, as in the following illustration:

$$w_v(t) \geq A(p(t-1), p(t-2), w_v(t-1); v, t). \tag{3.1}$$

A variant of that formulation is

$$w_v(t) \geq B(p(t-1) - p_v{}^e(t-1)) + w_v{}^e(t), B(0) = 0. \tag{3.2}$$

A more general formulation is

$$w_v(t) \geq C(\bar{w}(t-1) - \bar{w}_v{}^e(t-1), \tilde{m}(t-1) - \tilde{m}_v{}^e(t-1), p(t-1) - p_v{}^e(t-1)) + w_v{}^e(t) \tag{3.3}$$

where $C(0, 0, 0) = 0$. In a realistic contract theory, let it be noted, the variable $p(t-1)$ enters the function C with a coefficient smaller than one—the real wage is not fully protected against every rise of the price level—because workers are interested in job protection as well as real wage security and, in such a theory, there is a trade off between those two interests.

The upshot of such a constraint is that the decline of money wages in relation to their trend that results during a business slump may be very much slower, and the slump consequently more protracted, than is predicted by an expectational model without that constraint. In particular, the efforts of the central bank to effect a disinflation by the creation of suitable expectations of future wages and prices may be stymied by such a constraint. Further theoretical research will be required to analyze the severity of these effects. And much empirical research is needed to gauge in quantitative terms the importance of wage constraints, if indeed they are a reality.

This perspective on non-Walrasian theory has identified three stages in its youthful development. There is little doubt that many advances remain to be made. Yet, in a short span of time, some notable progress has been made.

[10] This is the thesis, loosely expressed, of my work with Guillermo Calvo on employment-contingent contracts. There we emphasize that implicit labor contracts must be couched in terms of readily observable data in order to be trustworthy and that, in consequence, there is a trade off between employment security and wage security.

References

Akerlof, G. A. "The Market for 'Lemons': Qualitative Uncertainty and the Market Mechanism," *Quarterly Journal of Economics,* Vol. 84, No. 3 (August 1970).

Calvo, G. A. "Supervision, and Utility and Wage Differentials across Firms," Columbia University Discussion Paper (July 1977).

Calvo, G. A. and E. S. Phelps. "Employment-Contingent Wage Contracts," *Stabilization of the Domestic and International Economy,* ed. K. Brunner and A. H. Meltzer, Carnegie-Rochester Series on Public Policy, Vol. 5, Amsterdam: North-Holland (1977).

Gordon, D. F. "A Neo-Classical Theory of Keynesian Unemployment," *The Phillips Curve and Labor Markets,* ed. K. Brunner and A. H. Meltzer, Carnegie-Rochester Series on Public Policy, Vol. 1, Amsterdam: North-Holland (1976).

Phelps, E. S. "Money-Wage Dynamics and Labor-Market Equilibrium," *Journal of Political Economy,* Vol. 76, No. 4, Part 2 (August 1968).

Phelps, E. S. *Inflation Policy and Unemployment Theory,* New York: W. W. Norton and Co., London: Macmillan and Co., 1972.

Phelps, E. S. "Disinflation without Recession," *Weltwirtschaftliches Archiv,* Band 100, Heft 1 (December 1978).

Phelps, E. S., and S. G. Winter, "Optimal Price Policy under Atomistic Competition," in E. S. Phelps *et al., Microeconomic Foundations of Employment and Inflation Theory,* New York: W. W. Norton and Co., 1970.

Salop, S. C. "A Model of the Natural Rate of Unemployment," *American Economic Review,* forthcoming 1979.

Samuelson, P. A. "The Stability of Equilibrium: Comparative Statics and Dynamics," *Econometrica,* Vol. 9, No. 2 (April 1941).

Stiglitz, J. E. "Alternative Theories of Wage Determination and Unemployment in LDC's," *Quarterly Journal of Economics,* Vol. 88, No. 2 (May 1974).

Taylor, J. B. "Estimation and Control of a Macroeconomic Model with Rational Expectations," *Econometrica,* forthcoming (1979).

Part I
DISEQUILIBRIUM MODELS OF EMPLOYMENT

INTRODUCTION

My earliest paper on wage and employment dynamics, first published in 1968 and reprinted here in the original version, contained most of my non-Walrasian ideas in embryo. The control-theoretic decision problems of the firm and household were not, as they say, fully articulated. Yet the nature of those problems was made clear enough or so I imagined. From the perspective of the more general non-Walrasian model sketched in the Introduction above, the principal limitation of the early paper is its treatment of the firm as a Walrasian price taker in commodity markets; hence the average price faced by the firms, or expected to be faced, takes the role played in the more general model by the expected intensity of customer demands. A treatment of the firm and industry in non-Walrasian competition on the product-market side, in the market for customers, was provided two years later in a paper with Sidney Winter.[1]

The wage dynamics paper dealt with the duration and rhythm of firms' wages in two, mutually exclusive, ways—both framed in terms of "continuous time." Over the more formal stretches of the paper it is assumed that the wages of each firm are under continuous review. No theoretical difficulty would seem to arise if we allowed each firm to adjust its wages discontinuously in the event of a discrete jump of the price level (one engineered, let us say, by the central bank); the speed with which actual wages completed their adjustment to the new equilibrium level would depend upon the quickness with which each firm grasped that the wage increases at other firms had matched its own. But I must have felt that such a disequilibrium process would be too short to be very interesting, and I was uncomfortable with a continuous-time model in which the economy-wide average wage would be subject to discrete jumps. So I assumed that each firm would adjust its wages gradually in the desired direction; then firms in deciding upon their own rate of wage change will want to form expectations of the rate at which other firms are changing

[1] E. S. Phelps and S. G. Winter, "Optimal Price Policy under Atomistic Competition," in Phelps *et al.*, *Microeconomic Foundations of Employment and Inflation Theory*, New York: W. W. Norton and Co., 1970.

their wages, although it is permissible to suppose (if we like) that firms always know the current level of the average wage across other firms.

A quite different view of the timing of wage decisions surfaces at other points of the paper. There it is assumed that each firm subjects its wage scales to periodic review—once a year, say—and that these decision points of firms are staggered evenly over any such interval of calendar time. The wage commitment of firms whose turn has come will overlap with earlier wage commitments until they come up for review and, eventually, with the subsequent wage commitments that will take their place. In the continuous-time framework, then, the economy-wide average wage cannot take jumps no matter how sharply each firm revises its wages once its decision point arrives. In the event of a drop in prices, the limited durability of wage commitments blocks any possibility of a quick cascade of firms' wages to a lower trend path. The resulting recession of employment away from its stationary equilibrium level is thereby lengthened and deepened. In fact, although the point may have been overlooked in the paper, the process of adaptive expectations may be dispensed with since, in the event of an unforeseen drop in prices, even the subsequent equilibrium scenario with overlapping wage commitments must generate a recession along the way to the new stationary equilibrium.

This broad conception of the determination of money wage rates has had to struggle against two opposing—and conflicting—schools. The older of these, the Keynesian or New England school, protests any model claiming that downward adjustments of money wage rates are equally as consistent with the "employment relation" as upward adjustments. I now give a little more credence (than did my earliest work) to the notion of some overarching quasi-contractual restraint against a firm's imposing, at the scheduled review time, a cut of its money wage scales—absent any sharp fall of its employment rolls that it can point to, of course—*if* it is not demonstrable to the employees that similarly situated workers are accepting such wage cuts. Yet such quasi-contractual boundaries on wage behavior are a far cry from Keynesian "money illusion" since there may be an analogous restraint against not raising money wages at least as much as the rise of money wages that other similarly situated workers are demonstrably receiving. The hypothesis of such an unwritten *most-favored-nation clause* has not so far been brought to any formal sort of empirical test. And as a theoretical proposition it suffers, I suspect, the same controversiality that besets the choice criterion known as *minimax regret*.

Another school of thought questions why any risk-averse employees would join a firm, except for a wage premium the firm would find unprofitable to pay, without a commitment from the employer to adjust the money wage in proportion to the latest index of the cost of living and to guarantee them employment in the bargain. Since this criticism is addressed in later papers collected in this volume, a brief response may suffice here: The firm will ordinarily value the right to dismiss an employee and, for practical reasons, employees' protection of the real value of their wages may jeopardize their employment security beyond its worth; moreover, the indexation of money wages to observable data would pose nuisance costs and would be worth less to the extent that, owing to similar considerations, the employee's expenditure commitments have been fixed in money terms. That said, we should still entertain any realistic contract-theoretic formulation in which there are lower bounds on a firm's money wage decisions because it must "show cause" in terms of observable data that do not yet (and cannot generally) bear out the anticipations of the firm causing it to want to reduce wages (or raise them less than other firms have been doing). Some work by Guillermo Calvo and me, contained in the last group of papers in this volume, is directed toward just such a theory.

The next paper in the present group was my second effort at a theory of employment fluctuations. It was a troubling feature of the preceding work that every rise of employment is tied up with a decline of the real wage. Though a comparable non-Walrasian treatment of commodity markets—as in the Phelps–Winter paper cited earlier or the more general non-Walrasian framework sketched in the Introduction—would avert the theoretical necessity of such an association, this essay looked for a quite different escape route. The map left of the way out is pretty well indecipherable, even to me. But what I must have meant is simple enough, however problematic.

Suppose that the government, say, has taken off the auction-like commodity market an unexpectedly large quantity of goods the previous period, thus leaving a below-average starting stock of inventory this period. The real rate of interest between this period and next period will be thereby increased. That effect can (tenably) be supposed to increase the supply of labor at each current-period real wage, since households weigh the going money wage for current-period employment not just against the (expected) price level in the current period but also against the discounted price level in subsequent periods over which saved portions of current wage income will finally be spent.

To this point the argument is a forerunner of the model by Robert Lucas and Leonard Rapping in which it is shown that a rise of the expected real rate of return to saving may elicit an increase in the utility-maximizing supply of labor at each real wage in terms of current goods.[2] If

[2] R. E. Lucas and L. A. Rapping, "Real Wages, Employment, and Inflation," in Phelps *et al.*, *Microeconomic Foundations of Employment and Inflation Theory,* New York: W. W. Norton and Co., 1970.

that were all to my argument we would obtain the Lucas–Rapping result that employment is increased and the current-period real wage is thus pushed down.

It is further argued, though, that the reduction of the starting stock of finished inventories raises the demand for labor at each current real wage and that, in principle, the demand for labor may increase more than the supply so as to cause a rise of the current-period real wage. If this argument is correct, then, the rise of employment which is induced by the disturbance to inventories need not spell a reduction of the current real wage. Evidently the wage-interest frontier has been shifted up by the depletion of speculative inventory holdings so that the rise of the real interest rate, which is a reflection of the loss of inventories, does not entail a fall of the current real wage.

My survey paper heralding the new microeconomics in employment and inflation theory closes this group. It advertised some of the contributions scheduled for a 1969 conference out of which came the volume *Microeconomic Foundations of Employment and Inflation Theory* in 1970. Among the ideas it surveyed from the conference volume is the notion of the Phelps–Winter firm. Hoping that the main findings in my work with Winter are well summarized in the survey paper, and wanting to minimize the overlap of the present collection with the conference volume, I have chosen to omit the Phelps–Winter paper from the essays here. Nevertheless that paper occupies a key place in my conception, and I hope that of others, of the non-Walrasian economy. The concept of the "customer" is formalized and the firm's optimal pricing policy derived. The analysis shows the existence of a gap between the real wage and the marginal product of labor. There is a sense in which firms may be said to maintain spare capacity since a surge of customer demands may elicit increased production even if money wages keep up with prices. The assumption in the Phelps–Winter paper that the firm's price continuously clears the market makes it formally dissimilar to my wage-dynamics paper. That assumption is not ideal since, to give one reason, fluctuations in the firm's price might cause some degradation of the information value of that price in attracting and keeping customers. In reality we should expect to observe to varying degree the analog of job rationing in non-Walrasian product markets, namely, the practice of giving priority to regular customers when capacity is short.

The 1969 survey paper also introduced my parable of the archipelego economy in which each island has its own auction-type market for migrant workers. The idea here is reminiscent of my earlier treatment of the non-Walrasian firm which must set its wages without foreknowledge of the wage changes that other firms are going to make. Yet the image of local auction markets for labor was a deviation from that earlier conception. The convenient view that the unemployed consist only of workers rejecting local market-clearing wages to search for better wages, not primarily of people looking for job openings at wages within a range they have correctly estimated, was taken over from the conference-volume paper by Armen Alchian (also surveyed). While I never produced a detailed model built on the basic idea, some rigorous developments along this line were achieved in a series of subsequent papers by Robert Lucas, of which the nearest in spirit to my parable is probably his paper with Edward Prescott.[3]

The patent unrealism of the view that unemployment is wholly voluntary (Pareto optimal or not) is a troubling feature of such models (some versions do not even mention labor, referring only to outputs) although not a fatal one for some strategic purposes. Models with clearing markets and imperfect communication among them are certainly efficient devices to illuminate the reactions of output and employment to various "private" disturbances—unannounced disturbances of firms' and households' opportunities and preferences such as a change in the labor force or in liquidity preference.

A more serious limitation of such models, however, is their failure to take realistic account—realistic in my view—of the consequences of "public" disturbances. In particular, these models are apt to mislead us about the effects of central bank actions on output and employment. If we imagine that each period the money supply is adjusted after the labor markets have cleared and closed, how can an unanticipated change of the money supply alter employment in the current period? Firms and workers have already been contracted for the period. If instead we suppose that the new money supply is predetermined (and observable) or preannounced on the eve of each period's labor auctions, it might be wondered whether the central bank's monetary policy, thus anticipated, could have any real effects. This latter puzzle arises in any model in which all wages and price are regularly determined afresh. If the Hume–Patinkin quantity theorem were applicable to equilibrium money wages and money prices and the actors of the model knew it, would they not have the sense to mark up their expectations of the upcoming period's general price level and general wage level in proportion to the new money supply?

In a complex model, one complicated enough to tax the econometric sophistication of most of the actors who people it, the answer to that neutrality question is a conditional no. For suppose that the central bank's

[3] R. E. Lucas and E. C. Prescott, "Equilibrium Search and Unemployment," *Journal of Economic Theory,* Vol. 7 (February 1974).

announcement of its money-supply target serves a signaling function; for example, that the private actors rightly believe that the higher the money supply is, the higher must be the best-informed estimate of the money supply necessary to prevent (on the average) a deficiency of aggregate demand at the wage level the bank wants to engineer (which is, therefore, the wage level the actors should expect). Then firms experiencing a rise of their own costs, but not sure of the extent to which other firms (especially in other industries) have experienced the same cost rise, may take the increase of the money supply as a signal to expect generally higher prices and to reduce employment (if at all) less than they would otherwise do. Or firms may take the money-supply increase to be a sign that the central bank aims to neutralize a rise of the demand for money, of which firms themselves have little or no independent forecast. In either case, the increase of the money supply, though observed beforehand, would make an active difference for the current level of employment.

However it is possible, on Muth's hypothesis of rational expectations, to exclude that "activist" argument. On that hypothesis, all firms and workers would know that the increase of real costs was general and they would expect generally lower money wages in the absence of an increase of the money supply—lower by just enough to prevent (on the average) a deficiency of demand without an increase of the money supply. In such a world, rushing in with more (or less) money in response to events about which all private actors can be assumed to be as well informed as the central bank would do nothing to stabilize employment. Its only function would be to put under social control the extent to which money prices would rise and money wages fall. This is the conclusion to which Lucas and others were led.

The adoption of models in which all prices and wages are free to be redetermined each period (or continuously) leads us into a methodological trap. If the model is simple enough to be analytically manageable the temptation is to "infer" that the world modeled is also transparent enough to be grasped by all its inhabitants; who among them will play central banker is indeterminate. It may be that, as a methodological device, the postulate of rational expectations will prove to be irresistable—whatever our doubts over its substantive reliability. If so we had better reject for stabilization policy analysis those models in which it is assumed that in every period or moment every wage is free for decision and revision.

MONEY-WAGE DYNAMICS AND LABOR-MARKET EQUILIBRIUM

If the economy were always in macroeconomic equilibrium then perhaps the full-employment money-and-growth models of recent vintage would suffice to explain the time paths of the money wage and the price level. But since any actual economy is almost continuously out of equilibrium we need also to study wage and price dynamics under arbitrary conditions.

The numerous Phillips-curve studies of the past ten years have done this with a vengeance in offering countless independent variables in numerous combinations to explain wage movements. But it is difficult to choose among these econometric models, and rarely is there a clear rationale for the model used. This paper presents a modest start toward a unified and empirically applicable theory of money-wage dynamics. At the same time it tries to capture the role of expectations and thus to work into the theory the notion of labor-market equilibrium.

I. Evolution of the Phillips Curve and its Opposition

Keynes' *General Theory* (1936) and virtually all formal macroeconomic models of the postwar era postulated a minimum unemployment level—a full-employment level of unemployment—which could be maintained with either stable prices or rising prices. In this happy state, additional aggregate demand would produce rising prices and wages but no reduction of unemployment. The full-employment quantity of unemployment was identified as "frictional" and "voluntary"; and frictional unemployment was (mistakenly) assumed to be unresponsive to demand.[1] Hence there was no need to choose between low unemployment and price stability.

* This study was supported by a grant from the National Science Foundation.

[1] A monetary economy can choose among different levels of frictional unemployment that correspond to different levels of aggregate demand and job vacancies. In fact, therefore, there is no unique full-employment quantity of frictional unemployment.

Reprinted by permission from *The Journal of Political Economy*, Vol. 76(4), Part II, July/August 1968.

This doctrine depended on Keynes' notions of money-wage behavior. At more than minimum unemployment, a rise (fall) of demand and employment would produce a once-for-all rise (fall) of the money wage, prices constant; a rise (fall) of the price level would cause a rise (fall) of the money wage in smaller proportion. Hence, in a stationary economy at least, his theory did not predict the possibility of a secular rise of money-wage rates at normal unemployment rates—let alone wage rises exceeding productivity growth—only the one-time "semi-inflation" (Keynes, 1936, p. 301) of prices and wages during the transition to minimum unemployment.

This doctrine was quickly disputed by Robinson (1937, pp. 30–31), who wrote of a conflict between moderately high employment and price stability. Dunlop (1938) suggested that the *rate of change* of the money wage depends more on the *level* of unemployment than upon the rate of change of unemployment, as Keynes had it. After the war, Singer (1947), Bronfenbrenner (1948), Haberler (1948), Brown (1955), Lerner (1958), and many others wrote that at low albeit above-minimum unemployment levels there occurs a process of "cost inflation," "wage-push inflation," "income inflation," "creeping inflation," "sellers' inflation," "dilemma inflation," or the "new inflation"—a phenomenon which was attributed to the discretionary power of unions or oligopolies or both to raise wages or prices or both without "excess demand."[2]

I believe this customary attribution of cost inflation to the existence of such large economic units to be unnecessary and insufficient. Like the theory of unemployment, the theory of cost inflation requires a non-Walrasian model in which there is no auctioneer continuously clearing commodity and labor markets. Beyond that, it is not clear to me what monopoly power contributes. An increase of monopoly power—due, say, to increased concentration—will raise prices relative to wages at any given unemployment rate and productivity level; but once, at the prevailing unemployment rate, the real wage has fallen (relative to productivity) enough to accommodate the higher markup, this process will stop and any continuation of inflation will depend on other sources.[3]

[2] Some wage-push theorists like Weintraub (1959) appear to treat inflation as almost spontaneous, virtually independent of the unemployment rate over any relevant range, and hence not induced by aggregate demand. I once tested the hypothesis that the 1955–57 inflation was more of this character than were the two earlier postwar inflations, making the assumption that autonomous "wage push" or "profit push" would be uneven in its sectoral incidence, so that the coefficient of correlation between sector price changes and sector output changes would (if the hypothesis were true) be algebraically smaller in the 1955–57 period than it was earlier (1961). It was algebraically smaller, but the statistical significance of the decline was impossible to determine. Incidentally, Selden's correlation test (1959) wrongly attributes significance to the positivity of the coefficient in 1955–57 instead of to the magnitude of the decline.

[3] The answer of Ackley (1966) and Lerner (1967) that corresponding to every unemployment rate and productivity level there is a natural real wage that is irreducible

Similarly, I doubt that the existence of labor unions is remotely sufficient to explain the cost inflation phenomenon. Whether the unions significantly exacerbate the problem—whether they increase that unemployment rate which is consistent with price stability—is, however, a difficult question. The affirmative answer frequently starts from the theory, set forth by Dunlop (1950), that a union, to maximize its utility, seeks to "trade off" the real wage rate against the unemployment of its members, raising the former (relative to productivity) until the gain from a further real wage increase is offset by the utility loss from the increase in unemployment expected to result from it. At an unemployment level below the unions' optimum, the unions then push up wage rates faster than productivity. But firms pass these higher costs on to consumers, so the real wage gains are frustrated, and as long as the government maintains the low unemployment level the rounds of inflation will continue.

I have trouble applying such a model to the American economy. Almost three-quarters of the civilian labor force do not belong to unions. This fact casts doubt on the quantitative importance of the model. And perhaps the fact goes much deeper. If the union members whom the unions make unemployed have no good prospect of future union employment, they will be inclined to seek employment elsewhere. If, at the other extreme, the union unemployment is shared in the form of a short workweek, this unemployment—while real enough to the extent that members do not "moonlight"—does not add to the official unemployment rate as it is measured. Certainly the unions *participate* in the cost inflation process, and they may even increase a little the volume of unemployment consistent with price stability. But I should think that a union must offer its membership a frequency of employment opportunities that is roughly comparable to that elsewhere in order to thrive and that appreciably reduced employment opportunities require a greater wage differential between union and other employment than is commonly observed.[4]

Phillips' successful fitting of what we now call the Phillips curve (1958) to a scatter diagram of historical British data deprived the discussions of some of their institutional color, but epitomized the new concept of cost inflation—if by that term we mean (as I think most of the aforementioned writers intended) *that kind of inflation which can be stopped only by a reduction of the employment rate* through lower aggregate demand and which

despite structural changes, so that money wages will keep pace with prices until unemployment is allowed to increase, seems to me to be terribly implausible. In any case, if this paper is right, cost inflation theory does not require any such "double monopoly" argument.

[4] It is certainly likely, however, that an *increase* of union power, even if localized, will raise the average money-wage level at any constant unemployment rate (see Hines, 1964).

thus raises a cruel dilemma for fiscal and monetary policy.[5] The Phillips curve portrayed the rate of wage change as a continuous and decreasing function of the unemployment rate, with wage increases exceeding typical productivity growth at sufficiently low albeit above-minimum unemployment rates. Hence, if prices are tied to marginal or average costs, the smaller the level at which aggregate demand sets the unemployment rate the greater is the *continuing* rate of inflation.

Strikingly, Phillips found that the nineteenth-century data pointed to a trade-off between wage increases and unemployment in the same way as contemporary data. Lipsey's sequel (1960) showed a statistically significant Phillips-curve relation for the subperiod 1861–1913. In fact, this early Phillips curve was *higher* (by about one percentage point) than the Phillips curve he fitted to the period 1929–57.[6] Apparently the cost inflation tendency, if real, is not "new" in history; in Britain anyway it may be no worse than it used to be.

But is the Phillips trade-off real, serious, and not misleading? I shall discuss briefly two challenges to the Phillips curve to which this paper is relevant. The first is the question of whether the slope of the wage increase-unemployment relation is great enough to pose a serious dilemma for aggregate demand policy. Though proponents of an American Phillips curve had tough sledding at first—numerous other variables were held to be important (Bowen, 1960; Bhatia, 1962; Eckstein and Wilson, 1962)—Perry's synthesis (1964) of much of this early work left a quantitatively important role for the unemployment rate (as well as for the profit rate and the rate of change of prices) in explaining money-wage movements in U.S. manufacturing. But in 1963 Bowen and Berry (1963) found that the *decrease* of the unemployment rate was far more important than the level of the unemployment rate in contributing to wage increases. The recent study of annual long-term wage data by Rees and Hamilton (1967) also showed a negligible (and statistically insignificant) relation between the steady-state unemployment rate and the rate of wage increase (though

[5] By contrast, in the pure "demand inflation" of Keynes and the classics, a reduction of the price trend could be achieved without cost to output and employment, since aggregate demand is necessarily superfluous to begin with. "Demand inflation" may be worth preserving, since a regime of "mixed inflation" is conceivable.

My earlier paper (1961) contains a fairly complete taxonomy of inflations (see also Fellner, 1959). Incidentally, the occasional definition of cost inflation as an autonomous upward shift of the Phillips curve is very awkward and does not imply the "policy dilemma" with which inflation analysts were concerned in the fifties.

[6] At a constant price level and an unemployment rate of 2 per cent, Lipsey's (1960) 1862–1913 regression (his equation [10]) predicts a 2.58 per cent wage increase annually, while the 1929–57 regression (his equation [13]) predicts a 1.65 per cent annual increase. At the same 3 per cent productivity growth in both periods, for example, price stability would have permitted smaller unemployment in the latter period. But Lipsey's Table 2 (p. 30) is evidence of the early Phillips curve's underestimation of the wage increases after World War II.

wage-change effects on prices feed back strongly on wages in their equation). This evidence strongly supports the neo-Keynesian revival led by Sargan (1964) and Kuh (1967) who make the level of the unemployment rate, together with productivity and the price level, determine the *level* of the money wage.[7] The underlying theory is apparently that a rise of aggregate demand creates "bottlenecks" and hence a rise of wage rates in certain areas and skills at the same time that it increases employment; once these bottlenecks have melted away and employment has reached its new and higher level there is no longer upward wage pressure. On this theory, money-wage increases go hand in hand with employment growth and not intrinsically with a high level of the employment rate.

Less frontal in a way but having equally profound policy implications is the second issue of the so-called stability of the Phillips curve. Continental economists like von Mises (1953, pp. 418–20) always emphasized the role of expectations in the inflationary process. In our own day, William Fellner and Henry Wallich are most closely associated with the proposition that the maintenance of too low an unemployment rate and the resulting continued revision of disappointed expectations will cause a runaway inflation. These ideas are reflected in the modern-day models of steady, "anticipated" inflation, begun by Lerner (1949), which imply (or assume) that high inflation confers no benefits in the form of higher employment if (or as soon as) the inflation rate is fully anticipated by firms and workers.[8] Recently, Friedman (1966) and I (1967) have sought to reconcile the Phillips hypothesis with the aforementioned axiom of anticipated inflation theory. I postulated that the Phillips curve, in terms of percentage price increase (or wage increase), shifts uniformly upward by one point with every one point increase of the expected percentage price increase (or expected wage increase). Then the *equilibrium* unemployment rate—the rate at which the actual and expected price increases (or wage increases) are equal—is independent of the rate of inflation. If one further postulates, as Friedman and I did, an "adaptive" or "error-correcting" theory of expectations, then the persistent underestimation of price or wage increases which would result from an unemployment level consistently below the equilibrium rate would cause expectations continually to be revised upward so that the rate of inflation would gradually increase without limit; and, similarly, a very high, *constant* rate of inflation, while "buying" a very low unemployment rate at first, would require a gradual rise of the unemployment rate toward the equilibrium rate as expectations

[7] If the *real* wage rate were made a rapidly increasing function of the employment rate, the Kuh-Sargan model could then produce (cost) inflation at low, yet above-minimum, unemployment rates.

[8] Lerner (1967) now recants. A paper of mine (1965) on anticipated inflation contains many of the references. Two recent money-and-growth models which study the consequences of alternative anticipated price trends are those by Tobin (1965) and Sidrauski (1967).

of that inflation developed. Therefore, society cannot trade between steady unemployment and steady inflation, on this theory. Society must eventually drive (or allow) the unemployment rate toward the equilibrium level or force it to oscillate around that equilibrium level.[9]

This paper is addressed primarily to these two issues. The next section offers a theory of why, given expectations, both the level of unemployment *and* the rate of change of employment should be expected to explain money-wage movements. The following section presents a theory of the influence of expected wage changes upon the Phillips curve. Some econometric tests of the predictions of these theories are reported in a statistical appendix.

II. "Turnover" and "Generalized Excess Demand"

For most of this section, until I try to accommodate other factors, I shall deal only with a more or less "atomistic" labor market in which there is no collective bargaining between unions and firms. But I exclude any Walrasian auctioneer to clear the labor market—the labor market is never properly cleared in this model—and I do not require that commodity markets be cleared. Firms may be said to have some dynamic monopsony power in that they need to pay a higher wage the faster they wish to attract labor, other recruitment activities held constant.

The model postulates considerable variety in the kinds of jobs and workers and postulates imperfect information about their availabilities.[10] Firms must incur "search costs" to find round pegs to fill round holes, and unemployed workers must also expend money and energy to find suitable employment. As a consequence, positive unemployment and positive job vacancies tend to persist in a growing labor market and even under stationary labor supply because of the turnover or attrition of firms' employment rolls. Total vacancies can be positive for every kind of job and total unemployment can be positive for every type of worker because

[9] On certain assumptions regarding preferences and other matters, I showed that society (or the world) would choose between an "overemployment" route *down* to the equilibrium employment rate (thus leaving a heritage of a high Phillips curve corresponding to inflationary expectations) and an "underemployment" route *up* to the equilibrium employment rate on the basis of "time preference." The role of time preference is illuminated by Friedman's (1966) characterization of "the true trade-off" (p. 59) as one between "unemployment today and unemployment at a later date"; there is such an intertemporal trade-off in the model under discussion if one holds eventual inflation rates constant, in the same way that the Fisherian trade-off between consumption today and consumption tomorrow holds subsequent wealth or capital constant. But there remains at any moment of time a statical trade-off between unemployment and inflation (with the expected inflation rate a parameter), analogous to the statical trade-off between consumption and capital formation (with initial capital stock a parameter) which lies at the roots of the intertemporal trade-off.

[10] Works by Stigler (1962), by Alchian and Allen (1964, xxxi), and by Holt and David (1966) contain some economics of such labor markets.

of spatial mismatching among jobs and people. In the formal model I shall exclude serious bottlenecks in one or more kinds of labor in order to speak aggregatively of "the" wage rate, "the" unemployment rate, and "the" vacancy rate as if they were pretty much uniform over the spectrum of workers and jobs.

As defined here, "aggregate unemployment," denoted U, consists of both those individuals without employment who are actively seeking a job (at going real wage rates) and the more passive without work who would accept a job opportunity (at the going rate) were it known to them. "Aggregate job vacancies," denoted V, consist both of those jobs which employers are actively seeking at a cost to fill and of the quantity of unfilled jobs that would be filled if and only if workers presented themselves without recruitment cost to the firm. Though it is doubtful that "active" unemployment and vacancies are equivalent, respectively, to "passive" unemployment and vacancies in their consequences for wage rates, I merge these active and passive components for simplicity.[11]

Letting N denote the number of persons employed, we have as a definition of labor supply, L, the relation

$$L = N + U. \tag{1}$$

Labor demand, N_D, is defined by

$$N_D = N + V. \tag{2}$$

L may depend upon the usual factors like the real wage rate, income, wealth, and demographic factors; N_D may depend on the technology, the product wage (net of interest and "depreciation" on the investment outlays to process and train a new employee), the degree of monopoly power, and, if prices do not clear the commodity markets, upon aggregate demand as well.

The concept of "excess demand" for labor, denoted X, is usually defined as

$$X = N_D - L, \tag{3}$$

when

$$X = V - U. \tag{4}$$

The usual excess-demand theory of money-wage dynamics states that the proportionate rate of change of the money wage is proportional to the excess demand *rate*, denoted x. The latter is excess demand per unit of labor supply, and hence equal to the excess of the vacancy rate, v, over the unemployment rate, u:

$$x = v - u, \quad x = X/L, \quad v = V/L, \quad u = U/L. \tag{5}$$

[11] Econometric analysis by Simler and Tella (1967) shows total unemployment to explain wage movements better than active or "measured" unemployment alone.

The modal rationale for the simple Phillips-curve relation between wage change and the unemployment rate is that, at least in sectors or economies with little or no unionization, the unemployment rate is a good proxy for the excess-demand rate and that the latter largely explains wage movements (apart from aggregation phenomena like changes in the employment mix).[12] Even if excess demand were the sole determinant of wage changes—this paper seeks to generalize that theory and to make it accommodate the influence of expectations—it is not obvious that the unemployment rate is a good proxy for it. What if, at times, the vacancy rate in (5) enjoys a life of its own, moving independently of the unemployment rate? (I shall later discuss the evidence on this.) Lipsey's paper (1960) brilliantly deduces from a model of employment dynamics a well-behaved relationship between the vacancy rate (hence the excess-demand rate) and the *steady* unemployment rate. I shall show, however, using a similar model, that in the non-steady-state case the unemployment rate is an inadequate indicator of the excess-demand rate and that the rate of change of employment constitutes an essential additional indicator for inferring the excess-demand rate.[13]

The excess-demand explanation of wage movements is unlike the law of gravity in that this explanation itself calls for an underlying explanation. When we try to rationalize it, however, its restrictiveness becomes clear. It implies that a one-unit increase of the vacancy rate always has the same

[12] The most extensive exposition is Lipsey's (1960). In criticizing the reliance solely on the unemployment rate which this rationale promotes, Perry (1966) wrote, "If the rate of wage change is proportional to the amount of excess demand which in turn is measured by unemployment, there is no room for other variables" (p. 22). I believe his abandonment of the excess-demand theory *on this ground* was mistaken. This paper adduces three explanatory variables from what is essentially an excess-demand theory.

[13] These two points can perhaps be understood simply from the following exercise: Draw a non-negatively sloped labor supply curve and a non-positively sloped labor demand curve in the customary real wage-employment plane. Consider now the locus of points corresponding to a given unemployment rate; this iso-unemployment-rate curve will lie to the left of the supply curve and will also be non-negatively sloped. It is immediately obvious that if the demand curve is negatively sloped, or the supply curve positively sloped, then not all points on the locus represent equal algebraic excess demand; in particular, as we move down this locus from its intersection with the demand curve, vacancies and excess demand increase despite constancy of the unemployment rate. Thus the latter is not necessarily a sufficient proxy for excess demand. (This demonstration in no way contradicts the proposition that, *vacancy rate constant*, excess demand is decreasing in unemployment. The zero-vacancy, on-the-demand-curve case is a familiar example. This paper tries to get away from the supposition that we are always "on the demand curve," even the Keynesian demand curve arising from excess supply in commodity markets.)

However, as we consider situations of higher vacancies, the unemployment rate unchanged, we should expect the rate of increase of employment likewise to be higher as employers seek to reduce vacancies through greater recruitment. The *two* pieces of information—the unemployment rate, and the rate of increase of employment—may together constitute a satisfactory proxy, or a better proxy, for excess demand.

wage effect as a one-unit decrease of the unemployment rate. Second, the excess-demand theory implies that most of the time, in the neighborhood of "equilibrium" (see Part III), vacancies will equal unemployment and that a *disequilibrium* rise of wage rates requires vacancies to exceed unemployment. That vacancies almost never exceed unemployment[14] may be due in part to the behavior of unions, as conceded earlier, and in part to the existence of "unemployables" and the resistence to money-wage cuts in sectors and trades where the market calls for them. But I suspect that a part of the reason is the inaccuracy of the excess-demand theory on its own terms.

I shall now describe and try to rationalize a *generalized* excess-demand theory of money-wage movements, one which is less restrictive than the simple excess-demand theory but which admits it as a special case. Elements of this approach have previously been discussed by James Duesenberry[15] (1958, pp. 300–9). Until Part III, where expectations are introduced, I hold constant the rate at which each firm expects *other* firms to change over time the wage they pay their labor. For ease of exposition, it is assumed simply that each firm expects the wage paid elsewhere to be constant for the near future.

An important element of this theory is the cost to the firm of its "turnover rate." Given a constant differential between the firm's wage rate and the wage rates paid by other firms, a fall of the unemployment rate will tend to increase the quit rate experienced by the firm. Unless the firm's employment was excessive to begin with, the increase of its quit rate will impose costs: The firm must either allow its output to decrease, thus losing profits, or incur the recruitment, processing, and training costs of replacing the departing workers (or choose some combination of these two losses). At a sufficiently high quit rate corresponding to a low unemployment rate, the firm will want to increase the differential between the wage it pays and the average wage paid elsewhere, on the ground that the savings from lower turnover costs will more than pay for the extra wage bill. As all firms attempt to raise this differential, the general wage index rises.[16] (The theory will work in reverse as well: There presumably exists a sufficiently high unemployment rate such that the quit rate is low enough to induce the firm to want to pay a wage below that paid by others on the ground that the wage savings will more than pay for the extra turnover costs.) Thus one role of unemployment in this theory stems from its effect upon quit rates rather than from any supposed underbidding for jobs by unemployed workers.

Undoubtedly job vacancies also play a part. First of all, the quit rate may depend upon both the unemployment rate and the vacancy rate since

[14] Ross (1966, p. 98) reports American evidence that only at an unemployment rate as low as 2.5 per cent does the vacancy rate equal the unemployment rate.

[15] I have also benefited from a conversation on this subject with Professor Duesenberry, but he is not responsible for deviations and errors on my part.

[16] For impressive empirical support of this part of the theory, see Eagly (1965).

these two variables together can be supposed to affect accession rates and hence the expected duration of unemployment by anyone contemplating quitting. Second, when a firm finds it has unfilled jobs it will respond with some combination of additional recruitment expenditures and an attempted increase of the differential between the wage it pays and the wage paid elsewhere, in order to facilitate recruitment and encourage workers to seek employment at the firm as they learn of the higher differential.[17] The magnitude of the desired differential *on this account*, for the ith firm, depends presumably upon the number of vacancies in the firm, V_i, the size of the unemployment pool, U, the number of workers employed elsewhere, $N - N_i$, and the size of the labor force, L.

Let Δ_i^* denote the ith firm's desired wage differential as defined by

$$\Delta_i^* = \frac{w_i^* - w}{w}, \tag{6}$$

where w is the average wage paid by all firms and w_i^* is the wage rate which the ith firm wishes to pay. Then the above theory states that

$$\Delta_i^* = j^i(u, v, U, V_i, N - N_i, L). \tag{7}$$

Suppose now that j^i is homogeneous of degree zero in the last four variables. Then we may write

$$\Delta_i^* = k^i(u, v, v_i), \quad v_i = V_i/L, \tag{8}$$

if we neglect the small discrepancy (in the atomistic case) between N/L and $(N - N_i)/L$. Now if all firms are much alike, we can express the *average* desired wage differential, denoted Δ^*, as a function of both the unemployment rate and the aggregate vacancy rate, $v = \Sigma v_i$ (as given in [5]):

$$\Delta^* = m(u, v), \quad u, v > 0, \tag{9}$$

where I shall suppose

$$m_1 < 0, \quad m_2 > 0, \tag{9a}$$

$$m_{11} \geqq 0, \quad m_{22} \geqq 0, \quad m_{12} \leqq 0. \tag{9b}$$

Before discussing the postulated shape of the m function, let us take the last step:

$$\frac{\dot{w}}{w} = \lambda\Delta^* \quad (\lambda \text{ a positive constant, } \dot{w} \equiv dw/dt). \tag{10}$$

[17] Of course the firm will be tempted to pay the higher wage differential only to new workers—and only for a short time! But this tendency will be inhibited considerably if potential recruits know the long-run costs of joining a firm that engages in such sharp practices. I suppose, as an approximation, that new and old workers in a firm receive the same wage.

This assumes, as mentioned earlier, that each firm expects the wage rate paid by other firms to be constant at least for the duration of the wage negotiated. The rationale of (10), stated loosely, is that the average wage rate will rise (fall) if all firms want to pay a wage higher (lower) than other firms.[18] It is assumed here that firms in the aggregate adjust their wage only gradually in the direction of the average desired differential; otherwise v and u would be implied to adjust instantaneously to make $\Delta^* = 0$ continuously. The gradualness might come from the administrative and psychic cost of changing wage rates that causes wage rates to be changed only intermittently or periodically; if these wage negotiations are staggered across firms or across workers, then the average wage will move more or less smoothly as indicated. In addition, perhaps uncertainty of the firm that the "desired" wage differential, if instituted, would have the desired effect upon turnover costs will induce a cautious, gradual response in the individual firm's wage decision.

As for the postulated shape of the m function, the signs of the derivatives in (9a) are of course fundamental to the theory. The excess-demand theory, which is a special case, assumes that the second derivatives are zero with $m_2 = -m_1 = \text{constant} > 0$. My weaker restrictions on the second derivatives in (9b) are inessential; they affect only the curvature of the augmented Phillips curve which I shall derive. The inequality $m_{11} \geqq 0$, meaning that Δ^* decreases with the unemployment rate at a non-increasing rate, vacancy rate constant, is plausible if, as the data suggest (Eagly, 1965), the quit rate is likewise convex with respect to the unemployment rate. The inequality $m_{22} \geqq 0$ assumes "rising marginal costs" to the firm of filling vacancies by means other than raising its wage differential. Finally $m_{12} \leqq 0$ makes sense if it takes a larger increase of the firm's wage differential to facilitate the filling of some fraction of a given increment in its vacancies the smaller is the unemployment pool from which workers can conveniently be drawn. The curve labeled $m(u, v) = 0$ in Figure 1 gives the combinations of u and v that make $\Delta^* = 0$. Its slope, being $-m_2/m_1$, is necessarily positive, but the size of that slope and the curvature are indeterminate and of no qualitative consequence. To the right of this locus $\Delta^* > 0$, and to the left $\Delta^* < 0$.

In the United States and most other countries, satisfactory vacancy data are still unavailable. I shall couple the above model with a theory of labor turnover or employment dynamics, along lines suggested by Lipsey (1960), in order to derive testable implications of relations among easily observable data.

The absolute time rate of increase of the aggregate number of persons employed, denoted $\dot{N} = dN/dt$, consists of the number of persons hired

[18] Stability of the average wage is consistent with some positive differentials if there exist firms content with negative ones. What counts for the average wage movement is the weighted *average* desired differential, Δ^* (in relation to the ex post, actual, weighted average differential, say Δ, which necessarily equals zero).

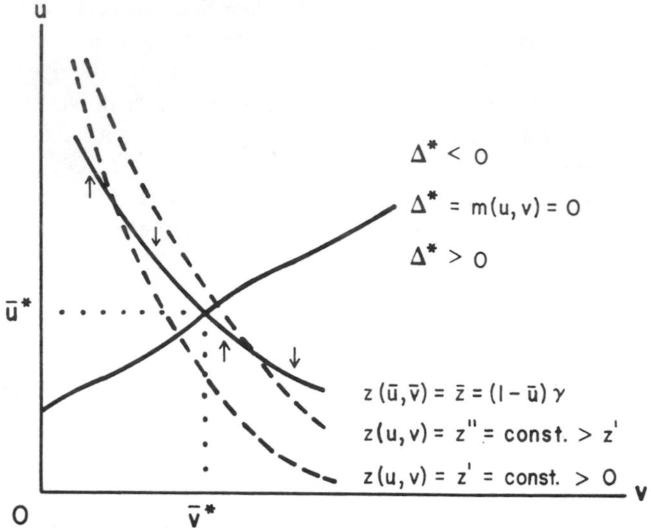

FIG. 1.—Relations between vacancy and unemployment rates

per unit time from the unemployment pool, denoted R, less the departures (due to death and retirement) per unit time of employed persons from the labor force, denoted D, and the quitting of employees to join the unemployed in search of new jobs, denoted Q. This accounting ignores involuntary terminations and layoffs, which I shall not treat, and it assumes that entrants to the labor force first enter the unemployment pool before being hired. Of course, the accessions and separations of employed persons who transfer directly from one firm to another cancel out and do not add to $\dot{N}$. That is,

$$\dot{N} = R - D - Q. \tag{11}$$

I shall make the variables on the right-hand side of (11) depend *in the aggregate* only upon unemployment (or employment), vacancies, and the labor supply. While the hire and quit rates of the individual firm depend upon its actual wage differential, the weighted average actual differential across all firms must be constant (being equal to zero), so one expects wage differentials to wash out in the aggregates.[19]

I shall suppose that D is proportional to employment, δ being the factor of proportionality. (This neglects any effect of a real wage change on people at the retirement margin.) To eliminate scale effects (rightly or not), I shall take new hires and quits to be homogeneous of degree one in

[19] Perhaps the dispersion of the wage differentials has some effect upon R and Q.

unemployment, vacancies, and the labor supply. Hence

$$\dot{N} = R(U, V, L) - \delta N - Q(U, V, L), \quad R(U, V, L) = LR(u, v, 1), \quad Q(U, V, L) = LQ(u, v, 1). \tag{12}$$

Equivalently, defining $z \equiv \dot{N}/L$,

$$z = R(u, v, 1) - \delta(1 - u) - Q(u, v, 1) = z(u, v); \quad u, v > 0, \tag{13}$$

where I shall suppose

$$z_1 > 0, \quad z_2 > 0 \tag{13a}$$

$$-z_2^{-2}\left\{\left[z_{11} + z_{12}\left(\frac{-z_1}{z_2}\right)\right]z_2 - \left[z_{21} + z_{22}\left(\frac{-z_1}{z_2}\right)\right]z_1\right\} > 0. \tag{13b}$$

Thus the absolute rate of change of employment per unit labor supply is a function of the same two variables that determine Δ^* and in so doing influence the rate of wage change.

What is the logic of the z function, in particular the role of the vacancy rate in that function? We ordinarily think of the level of labor input as determined by output which in turn depends upon aggregate demand and productivity. There probably is a fairly tight relationship between man-hours and output (given productivity); but N is measured by the number of persons employed. In a labor market that is at least moderately tight, the firm will respond *initially* to an increase of aggregate demand (which increases job vacancies) by lengthening hours worked per worker (including overtime), by more intensive use of "buffer" or "cushion" employees ("hoarded" labor), by calls for extraordinary efforts on the part of employees, and perhaps by raising prices to reduce output demanded. But these measures do not eliminate the job vacancies, and finding new employees to fill new jobs takes time.[20] Firms will choose to take time for two reasons: because marginal recruitment costs are positive, it may pay the firm to wait for suitable persons to present themselves for employment; and because there may be "rising marginal recruitment costs,"[21] it will pay the firm to smooth its recruitment efforts over time.

Now the properties of the z function. The assumptions on derivative signs in (13a) are, unlike those in (13b), fundamental to the theory. It is

[20] Some of the new employees wanted can be acquired virtually instantaneously so that the response of N to aggregate demand is not entirely the gradual or continuous response that I have postulated. Incidentally, since a raise of price will not appreciably reduce output demanded, prices will go on rising.

[21] That is, the additional recruitment or search costs necessary to increase by one the expected number of recruits per unit time may be greater if the firm is aiming at 500 recruits in a week than if it is aiming for only ten. This is a short-run cost curve in which we hold constant the size of the firm and its personnel office. Large firms are not implied to suffer disadvantages in recruitment.

assumed that, the unemployment rate constant, the higher the vacancy rate the greater is the rate at which firms will acquire unemployed workers, that is, $R_2 > 0$. A higher vacancy rate will induce more intensive recruitment, and it will increase the probability that any unemployed person contacting a firm will find a job open. This increase of accessions may itself induce more quits, as suggested in the paragraph preceding (6), so that $Q_2 > 0$ is possible. But it would be strange to find that the higher vacancy rate reduced employment growth on balance; any increase of quits will stimulate partially offsetting extra recruiting. Hence I postulate that $R_2 > Q_2 \geqq 0$, so that $z_2 = R_2 - Q_2 > 0$, for all u and v.

Clearly $R_1 > 0$ since, vacancy rate constant, the higher the unemployment rate the greater is the flow to the firm of unemployed workers who can fill open jobs and the easier is recruitment. Since an increase of unemployment discourages quitting, $Q_1 < 0$. Hence $z_1 = R_1 + \delta - Q_1 > 0$.

Consider the dashed curves labeled z = constant in Figure 1. Each depicts the locus of (u, v) combinations giving a particular value of z. The slope of such curves at any point is $-z_2/z_1 < 0$; as the unemployment rate is reduced an increase of the vacancy rate is required to keep z constant. These z contours as drawn display strict convexity or "diminishing marginal rate of substitution," meaning that as the unemployment rate is reduced the vacancy rate increases at an increasing rate along any contour. This convexity is the content of (13b).

The best rationale for this convexity is the presumption that $z_{21} = R_{21} - Q_{21} > 0$. This states that an increase of the vacancy rate has greater effect on employment growth the greater the unemployment rate. The primary basis for that assumption is that recruitment will be more difficult the smaller is unemployment (indeed totally unsuccessful in the aggregate at zero unemployment), so that $R_{21} > 0$. It is plausible also that an increase of the vacancy rate has less effect, if it has any, upon quits the less tight the labor market, so that $Q_{21} \leqq 0$. (Since $z_{12} = z_{21}$ an equivalent view is that changes of the unemployment rate have greater impact upon z the greater the vacancy rate.) Secondly, we should expect $z_{11} = R_{11} - Q_{11} \leqq 0$ on the two grounds that, vacancy rates constant, an increase of the *employment* rate reduces new hires at an increasing rate and that it increases quits at an increasing rate (or at least at non-decreasing rates).[22] Thirdly, and most controversially, it might be argued that $z_{22} = R_{22} - Q_{22} \leqq 0$. $R_{22} < 0$ could result from a rising marginal recruitment cost schedule; given the unemployment rate, the new hire rate (R) might even approach an upper bound as the vacancy rate increased without limit. My guess is that $Q_{22} \geqq 0$, but I know of no evidence or presumption in its favor. In any

[22] If quits *per employee* is linear in the employment rate, given the vacancy rate, then $Q(u, v, 1)$, that is, quits per unit labor supply, will be strictly convex with respect to the employment rate.

case, (13b) shows that the algebraic signs of second derivatives suggested here are merely *sufficient* for convexity of the z contours.[23]

We can now combine (9), (10), and (13) to obtain an augmented Phillips curve in terms of the easily observed variables u and z. Since z_2 is one-signed, (13) implicitly defines v as a single-valued function of u and z, say,

$$v = \psi(u, z), \tag{14}$$

when

$$\frac{\dot{w}}{w} = \lambda m[u, \psi(u, z)] = f(u, z), \tag{15}$$

which is our augmented Phillips curve. Since to every (u, z) pair there corresponds a unique v, there exists a derived Phillips-like relation between $\dot{w}/w$ and (u, z) pairs.

We can establish the properties of f after determining how v varies with u and z.

$$\begin{aligned}
\psi_1 &= \frac{-z_1[u, \psi(u, z)]}{z_2[u, \psi(u, z)]} < 0; \\
\psi_2 &= \frac{1}{z_2[u, \psi(u, z)]} > 0; \\
\psi_{11} &= -z_2^{-2}\left\{\left[z_{11} + z_{12}\left(\frac{-z_1}{z_2}\right)\right]z_2 - \left[z_{21} + z_{22}\left(\frac{-z_1}{z_2}\right)\right]z_1\right\} > 0; \\
\psi_{22} &= -z_2^{-3}z_{22} \gtreqless 0 \quad (?); \\
\psi_{21} &= -z_2^{-2}\left[z_{21} + z_{22}\left(\frac{-z_1}{z_2}\right)\right] < 0 \quad (?).
\end{aligned} \tag{16}$$

The last two inequalities are based on the conjectures discussed in connection with (9b), while the first three inequalities follow from (13a) and (13b).

Now we can deduce the following restrictions on the augmented Phillips curve:

$$\begin{aligned}
f_1(u, z) &= \lambda(m_1 + m_2\psi_1) < 0; \\
f_{11}(u, z) &= \lambda(m_{11} + m_{12}\psi_1 + m_{22}\psi_1^2 + m_{22}\psi_{11}) > 0; \\
f_2(u, z) &= \lambda m_2\psi_2 > 0; \\
f_{22}(u, z) &= \lambda(m_{22}\psi_2^2 + m_2\psi_{22}) \gtreqless 0 \quad (?); \\
f_{21}(u, z) &= \lambda[(m_{21} + m_{22}\psi_1)\psi_2 + m_2\psi_{21}] < 0 \quad (?).
\end{aligned} \tag{17}$$

The first result states that every constant-z Phillips curve is negatively sloped: Decreased unemployment directly adds pressure on wage differentials, and this effect is reinforced by the concomitant increase of vacancies

[23] It might be thought that the convexity of the R contours and convexity of the Q contours would suffice to imply convexity of the z contours, but the former two convexities are neither necessary nor sufficient for the latter convexity.

which is deducible from the constancy of z in the face of decreased unemployment. The second result states that this constant-z relation between the rate of wage change and the unemployment rate is strictly convex, as the Phillips curve is ordinarily drawn; as the unemployment rate is decreased by equal amounts the vacancy rate must increase at an increasing rate to keep z constant, by virtue of (13b), which implies $\psi_{11} > 0$, so that even in the simple excess-demand case (in which the second derivatives in [9b] are equal to zero) the rate of wage increase itself increases at an increasing rate. As for the third result, $f_2 > 0$, the higher is employment growth, the unemployment rate constant, the higher must be the vacancy rate and hence the greater the upward pressure on the money wage. Thus the association between high employment growth and high wage gains is consistent with the excess-demand or generalized-excess-demand theory of the Phillips curve. The convexity of this relation between wage change and z is not certain since it involves the problematical ψ_{22}. Finally, there is a negative interaction between u and z, meaning $f_{21} < 0$, if my guess is right that z_{21} is strongly positive; this interaction means that a given increase of z signifies a greater increase of the vacancy rate the smaller is the unemployment rate.

The variables u and z cannot go their own way for long since a high (low) z implies a falling (rising) u. There is, therefore, some interest in the "steady-state" Phillips curve that relates the rate of wage increase to alternative, *constant* values of the unemployment rate. Let us take the proportionate rate of growth of the labor supply to be a non-negative constant, γ. Then, corresponding to any *steady-state* unemployment rate, to be denoted $\bar{u}$, there is a steady $\bar{z}$ and a steady $\bar{v}$ which obey the relation

$$\bar{z} = z(\bar{u}, \bar{v}) = \frac{N}{L}\frac{\dot{N}}{N} = \frac{N}{L}\frac{\dot{L}}{L} = (1 - \bar{u})\gamma, \quad \gamma \geqq 0. \tag{18}$$

If $\gamma > 0$, then clearly $\bar{z}$ must be higher the smaller $\bar{u}$. This relation also yields a locus of steady-state $(\bar{u}, \bar{v})$ points, which is shown in Figure 1 by the solid, downward sloping curve intersecting (from below) the broken-line iso-z contours. This locus is negatively sloped and flatter than the z contours, for as steady-state $\bar{u}$ is decreased, $\bar{v}$ must increase not only enough to keep z constant but to increase z to the required level implied by (18). Referred to the *vertical axis*, the slope is

$$\frac{d\bar{v}}{d\bar{u}} = \frac{-(z_1 + \gamma)}{z_2} < 0, \tag{19}$$

and, at least for sufficiently small γ, the locus will be convex like the z contours:

$$\frac{d^2\bar{v}}{d\bar{u}^2} = -z_2^{-2}\left\{\left[z_{11} + z_{12}\left(\frac{-z_1 - \gamma}{z_2}\right)\right]z_2 - \left[z_{21} + z_{22}\left(\frac{-z_1 - \gamma}{z_2}\right)\right](z_1 + \gamma)\right\} > 0 \quad (?). \tag{20}$$

It is not surprising, therefore, that our steady-state Phillips curve, $f[\bar{u}, (1 - \bar{u})\gamma]$, is negatively sloped and steeper than the constant-z Phillips curves:

$$\frac{\partial f[\bar{u}, (1 - \bar{u})\gamma]}{\partial \bar{u}} = f_1 - f_2\gamma < 0. \tag{21}$$

Also we find

$$\frac{\partial^2 f[\bar{u}, (1 - \bar{u})\gamma]}{\partial \bar{u}^2} = f_{11} - f_{12}\gamma - (f_{21} - f_{22}\gamma)\gamma > 0 \quad (?), \tag{22}$$

so there is some presumption of convexity (and certainly for small enough γ).

I note in passing that the steady-state Phillips curve is higher the greater the labor force growth rate, that is, $\partial f/\partial \gamma > 0$ for $\bar{u} < 1$. The reason is that faster growth of the labor supply requires a larger z and hence a larger vacancy rate to hold steady any given unemployment rate. This is an interesting testable implication of the theory. (The relationship may help to explain the aforementioned improvement in Britain's Phillips curve.)

Are there direct tests of the above theory of the augmented Phillips curve?[24] Quarterly British vacancy data have been prepared by Dow and Dicks-Mireaux (1958). Their study shows a scatter diagram of U and V points which, after 1950 or so, cluster around a convex, negatively sloped curve like the z contours or the steady-state locus in Figure 1. This is encouraging support for the *long-run* implications of (13) and (18). But my theory denies a strict and simple short-run relation between the unemployment rate *level* and the vacancy rate level. (Otherwise, the unemployment rate would suffice as an indicator of generalized excess demand.) In its unadulterated form, the employment dynamics model here implies that unemployment and vacancy levels together determine the rate of change of employment and, hence, given γ, the *rate of change* of the unemployment rate. The differential equation is

$$-\dot{u} = z(u, v) - (1 - u)\gamma. \tag{23}$$

This says that if, at the prevailing u, v exceeds the corresponding $\bar{v}$ on the steady-state locus, so that $z > \bar{z} = (1 - u)\gamma$, then u will be falling (and vice versa if v is less than the corresponding $\bar{v}$). See the arrows in Figure 1.

The British data, despite being quarterly, offer a striking example that u can fall because v is high even though v is falling, which supports the emphasis on the level of v, rather than its rate of change, as a determinant of $\dot{u}$. After a sharp rise of vacancies that reduced unemployment, the latter went on falling in the second half of 1955 when vacancies had leveled off and proceeded to fall (Dow and Dicks-Mireaux, 1958, Fig. 1*B*, p. 3).

[24] All of the empirical evidence to be cited was consulted after I had arrived at an almost identical model in an earlier unpublished manuscript so that this evidence permits a real test of the model.

Indeed, the early postwar years in general showed a long-run trend of falling unemployment coinciding with falling vacancies. On the other hand, cyclical turning points usually occurred in the same quarter, so perhaps one should not totally neglect the rate of change of vacancies as a determinant of unemployment movements.

In the United States one has to make do with the Help-wanted Advertising Index, Series 46, in *Business Cycle Developments* (U.S. Department of Commerce). In a recent study of this index, Cohen and Solow (1967) in effect regressed the value of this index on the unemployment rate and the "new hire rate." Now (23) implies that v is a decreasing function both of u and $\dot{u}$, since points above the steady-state locus will be associated with falling u. It is of some interest, therefore, that the new hire rate which may be a proxy for $-\dot{u}$ entered positively in that regression and the unemployment rate negatively; further, study of the residuals showed vacancies to be underestimated by this regression in cyclical phases of falling unemployment.[25]

A hasty study of the monthly data on aggregate unemployment and vacancies in Australia also appears to give some support to the present model.[26] After dividing U and V by a geometrically rising series that approximates the growth of the labor supply, I used a standard program to deseasonalize the resulting unemployment and vacancy rates. One of the best regression results was the following:

$$\log v_t = 9.76 - \underset{(44.10)}{0.95} \log u_t - \underset{(2.40)}{0.35} \log (u_{t+1}/u_t), \quad \bar{R}^2 = .925, \quad \text{DW} = 0.15, \tag{24}$$

where the numbers in parentheses are t-ratios and v_t and u_t denote an average of the seasonally adjusted percentage vacancy rate and unemployment rate, respectively, in month t and month $t + 1$ (multiplied by 100). Both coefficients have the predicted signs and are highly significant. The serial correlation is fearsome, but that is partly due to the monthly averaging. When only even-numbered observations were run, the Durbin-Watson statistic rose to 0.35 and the t-ratio for $\log (u_{t+1}/u_t)$ rose to 3.17, with no appreciable change in the coefficients. When the regression is turned around to make $\log (u_{t+1}/u_t)$ the dependent variable, the t-ratios

[25] Cohen and Solow (1967) wrote: "The residuals [from this regression] progressively underestimated [the help-wanted index] in the course of upswings and overestimated during downswings, the error getting worse in the course of each one-way movement" (p. 109). Apart from the progressivity, this constitutes additional support for the theory. As for the progressivity, the authors suggest that "formal advertising is treated as something of a last-resort method of recruitment." This means, I take it, that the help-wanted advertising index is not a totally satisfactory measure of job vacancies.

[26] I am grateful to Peter Burley of Princeton University for providing me with these data and to Arthur Donner and Steven Salop for carrying out these and other calculations made for this paper.

remained significant but $\bar{R}^2$ plummeted, perhaps because the rate of change of unemployment is subject to considerable measurement error. On the whole, I think these explorations offer some hope of very good results from a complete analysis.

I shall now try informally and briefly to open the model to some other factors. The "bottleneck" theory also helps to explain why wage increases should be associated with rapidly *increasing* employment. An economy adjusted to one level of aggregate demand, with its peculiar structure, cannot adapt instantaneously to a higher aggregate demand level with its new structure; certain types of labor will be in excess demand, and this will drive up the general wage index. Hansen's model (1957) emphasizes that excess supplies of other types of labor, even if they sum to a figure in excess of the total of excess demands, need not hold down the wage index if wages are stickier downward than upward. In the usual bottleneck theory, however, the resulting change in wage structure will dissolve the bottlenecks, so that a low *level* of unemployment is not *ultimately* or *persistently* inflationary. It takes another slump and the passage of time if major bottlenecks are to reappear. Such a theory, therefore, seems to fit in with "ratchet inflation" of the sort analyzed by Bronfenbrenner (1954).

Lipsey attributed the influence of $\dot{u}$ in his regressions to an aggregation phenomenon (1960, pp. 21–23). To the extent that each sector of the economy has a simple and strictly convex Phillips curve of its own, the simple macro Phillips curve will shift upward with an increase in the sectoral inequality of unemployment rates. Lipsey suggested that these inequalities are worse in upturns than in downturns, so that a negative $\dot{u}$ tends to be more inflationary than a positive $\dot{u}$ at the same u. In any case, changes in the structure of vacancy and unemployment rates may be important.

What about unions? As a starting point, one might suppose the union to maximize the welfare of its members. In that case the union's wage objectives will be determined by real income opportunities outside the union. It will examine the wage differential between union jobs and jobs that members could get elsewhere, weighing also the expected time required to get jobs elsewhere, hence unemployment rates and vacancy rates in the relevant areas and occupations. The average wage differential desired by unions thus depends upon our pervasive u and v. At sufficiently small unemployment rates or large vacancy rates, the unions, just like individuals and firms, desire incompatibly large wage differentials, and the general index of wage rates will therefore rise.[27] But this is only a possible

[27] This ties in somewhat with Keynes' (1936) emphasis on the relative wage: "Every trade union will put up some resistance to a cut in money-wages [since such reductions 'are seldom or never of an all-round character']. But . . . no trade union would dream of striking on every occasion of a rise in the cost of living" (pp. 14–15). See also Hicks (1955). I should think, however, that the desired relative wage is dependent on labor market conditions.

start. It is not clear to me how unions regard the interests of new members. And Paul Weinstein has suggested to me that the union leadership will be constrained in its wage policy by the need to support financially its administrative bureaucracy.

Finally, the explanation of the influence of the change of employment (or unemployment) upon wage increases is sometimes expectational. Ball (1964) suggests that firms and workers extrapolate the unemployment trend and set wages on the basis of the projected unemployment rate. Let us now try to introduce expectations into the model.

III. Expectations and Macroequilibrium

In Part II it was postulated that each firm expects other firms as a whole to hold their wage rates constant. In that case, it is natural for the firm to assume that an increase in its wage rates would assist it in attracting new employees and in discouraging quitting, since it would expect any increase of its wage to increase its wage differential. But in the general case the firm will have to forecast wage changes elsewhere in order to estimate the employment effects of its wage decision. This assumes that frequent wage negotiation with employees is sufficiently costly that wage contracts run for something like a year.

A simple derivation of the result I want—too glib a derivation as we shall see—might go like this. Let each firm expect with certainty that the average wage paid elsewhere will change at a certain proportionate rate over the life of the firm's wage contract. Consider now a firm whose immediate and prospective vacancy rate (v_i) in relation to labor market conditions (u and v) is such that, in the absence of wage changes elsewhere, it would want to keep its present wage rate to maintain its expected wage differential at its present actual level; this firm is in equilibrium in the sense that its actual wage differential equals its desired differential. But if the firm in fact expects the average wage elsewhere to be increasing at the rate of 2 per cent annually and it expects other firms to pass on the higher costs through a 2 per cent rise of prices annually, then it will want to raise its wage rates by 2 per cent annually; for it will calculate that it can raise its prices by 2 per cent without loss of customers and thus leave unchanged its real position, that is, its real sales, its product wage and vacancy rate, and its competitiveness in the labor market. As for the disequilibrium case, if its vacancy rate and labor market conditions are such that in the absence of expectation of wage changes elsewhere it would want to raise its wage by 1 per cent, say, it will, under the above expectations, want in fact to raise its wage by 3 per cent for the next year. Upon averaging over firms we are then led to the proposition that we must add the expected rate of wage change, denoted $\dot{w}^e/w$, to the rate of wage change that would occur under stationary wage expectations, in order to determine the actual rate of wage change per annum:

$$\frac{\dot{w}}{w} = \lambda\Delta^* + \frac{\dot{w}^e}{w} = f(u, z) + \frac{\dot{w}^e}{w}. \tag{25}$$

The result is quite natural. By "equilibrium," following Hayek, Lindahl, Harrod, and others (using varied terminology), we generally mean a path along which the relevant variables work out as people think they will. A necessary labor-market condition for what might be called a *macroequilibrium* in terms of the relevant averages and aggregates is therefore equality of the expected and actual rate of change of the average wage rate:

$$\frac{\dot{w}}{w} = \frac{\dot{w}^e}{w}. \tag{26}$$

Hence macroequilibrium entails

$$f(u, z) = \Delta^* = m(u, v) = 0, \tag{27}$$

meaning that "generalized excess demand," as measured by $m(u, v)$, be equal to zero. Any other result would be disturbing! But note that this equilibrium admits a rising or falling average money wage. Further, there is no clearing of the labor market in any ordinary sense.

This result needs interpretation and defense. First there is a matter of dating the variables. Imagine that wage negotiations are annual and are evenly staggered (across firms) over the year. Consider a firm negotiating at the beginning of the calendar year. Suppose it expects average wage rates *in the future* to rise steadily at the rate of 2 per cent over the year. Then if the wage index is 100 at the beginning of the year, the firm will expect the index to stand approximately at 101 by midyear. By raising its wage by just 1 per cent, the firm can expect to maintain on the average over its new contract its past average competitiveness with other employers over the old contract. Thus if the wage index stood at 100 throughout last year and our firm is content with its past wage differential, we appear to get only a 1 per cent wage rise resulting from a 2 per cent expected rise of the index. The resolution of this puzzle consists of defining $\dot{w}^e/w$ as the expected rate of change of the index from six months prior to the firm's wage negotiation to six months after the wage negotiation, so that it is centered on the date of the firm's wage decision. In our example, therefore, the "expected rate of wage change" so defined is really only 1 per cent. If, in the following year, the expected *future* rate of wage change (2 per cent) is unaltered and this year's expectations are borne out —so that the index will next year be expected to rise from approximately 101 (at last midyear) to approximately 103 (at the next midyear)—our firm must then raise its wage by 2 per cent if it expects to stay as competitive as before with other employers. This matter is possibly of some econometric significance, since the above example suggests that a perfect proxy for the expected *future* rate of wage change will tend to enter a regression equation resembling (25) with a less-than-unitary coefficient; it is only the expected rate of wage change as I defined it that is predicted to enter such an equation with a unitary coefficient.[28]

Why should the expected rate of wage change enter in (25) rather than expected price change? I believe the expectation of price increases affects money wages only through its effects on expected vacancy rates and the expected unemployment rate. *Given the latter*, a rise of the expected rate of inflation will have little or no effect upon the wage increase which a firm grants if it expects other firms to hold the line on the money-wage rates they pay; in particular, the threat of an employee expecting a rise of the cost of living to quit in search of another job will be empty if it is not expected that other firms' wages will rise with the cost of living. Whether Keynes was right that unions too are interested only in *relative* wages I do not know, but I gather that cost-of-living clauses are not very widespread in this country and have never ranked very high among union objectives.

If (25) is to be really satisfactory, however, it must hold when the expected price trend is flat as well as in the case (discussed above) where producers can expect to pass on their wage increase in higher prices with impunity. Probably (25) *is* too simple; a full analysis requires a theory of the optimal price dynamics of the firm. Yet I am prepared to defend it as a tolerable approximation along the following lines. Continue to abstract from productivity growth and consider a firm at wage-setting time. The vacancy rate of this firm, v_i, and the values of u and v which determine its desired differential must be taken as expected averages over the life of the wage contract. Though the firm will be concerned more with the near future than it will be with the less certain far future, let us imagine the firm thinks simply in terms of its mid-contract prospects, say v_i^e, u^e, and v^e, and its desired mid-contract differential, Δ_i^*, which is a function of these prospects. I shall evaluate the firm's v_i^e at the wage it expects it will need to maintain the competitiveness it enjoyed, as measured by its past mid-contract differential Δ_i, over the last contract period. Hence, if the desired differential $\Delta_i^* = k^i(u^e, v^e, v_i^e)$ is equal to the previous differential, Δ_i, *when the expected rate of wage change is zero*, it will not alter its wage rate; for in this situation maintenance of its former wage will yield it an expected

[28] The left-hand side variable is likewise the rate of change of the actual wage index expressed at annual rates. If wage negotiations are evenly distributed over the year, the firms setting wages in January, by raising their wage rates 1 per cent, will raise the index by one-twelfth of 1 per cent from its December level and hence by 1 per cent at an annual rate. Where annual wage negotiations are unevenly distributed over the year (producing some seasonality), one may want to work with the actual one-year rates of change of the index (for example, January-to-January), in which case the "expected rate of wage change" is an average of twelve figures centered (respectively) on each of the twelve months in the one-year interval.

vacancy rate at mid-contract with which it is content. As a second situation, suppose now that, *other things equal*, the firm expects a 1 per cent rate of wage increase (as defined earlier, from mid-contract to mid-contract). In this situation it does not expect to be able to raise its prices by an additional 1 per cent without loss of customers. Therefore when the firm evaluates its vacancy rate at the 1 per cent higher wage it will find its expected vacancy rate smaller in this second situation, so that its $\Delta_i^* = k^i(u^e, v^e, v_i^e)$ is less than its previous average wage differential, Δ_i. This means that while the firm may raise its wage it will raise it less than 1 per cent in order to reduce its expected differential. To the extent that this second situation is general among firms, we will have a smaller $m(u^e, v^e)$. Firms will recruit less so that z and hence $f(u, z)$ will both be smaller. Thus a *ceteris paribus* rise of $\dot{w}^e/w$ in (25), to the extent that businesses do not expect to be able to shift the expected wage costs onto buyers, will be partially offset by a resulting fall of z and $f(u, z)$ so that $\dot{w}/w$ is not implied to rise by an equal amount.

But other things, like productivity and the demand for the firm's product, need not be equal. As I argued earlier, if the firm expects to be able to raise its price in proportion to its wage rates without loss of prospective sales—because, say, other firms are expected to raise their prices in that proportion and aggregate demand is not expected to change—then neither the expected product wage implied by the firm raising its wage rate just enough to maintain its previous competitiveness nor the expected quantity of its output demanded (all at mid-contract) will change, so its expected vacancy rate, v_i^e, will not change; thus the firm will in this case match the expected rate of wage change, adding or subtracting the wage change it would have chosen under stationary expectations. Another example of interest is the expectation by the firm of growth in the marginal and average productivity of its labor together with expected growth of its output demanded (at present prices) at a rate equal to the expected rate of wage change. Such a change in the firm's situation will leave its expected vacancy rate unchanged from its previous mid-contract level, when this is evaluated at the wage expected to be necessary to keep its wage differential at its previous mid-contract level. Hence, the firm will raise its wage by just the amount of the expected rate of wage change if it likes its previous differential—by more (less) if that previous differential is too low (high). In all cases, the firm is imagined notionally to increase its wage by the amount it expects is necessary to keep its past average competitiveness, to make an optimal price adjustment, and then to evaluate its expected vacancy rate at the implied product wage and expected demand for its product; if the desired differential calculated at that hypothetical vacancy rate is equal to its past average differential, it goes ahead with the "competitive" wage increase; if the desired differential is greater (less), the firm will increase its wage by more (less) than the expected or competitive amount.

The mathematics of all this becomes simple if we shrink the contract period to zero to avoid dating complications. Suppose that each firm adjusts continuously its wage in such a way as to make the absolute rate of change of its expected wage differential, Δ_i^e, proportional to the difference between its desired differential and its present differential:

$$\dot{\Delta}_i^e = \lambda_i(\Delta_i^* - \Delta_i), \tag{28}$$

where

$$\Delta_i^e = \frac{w_i - w^e}{w^e},$$

$$\Delta_i^* = \frac{w_i^* - w^e}{w^e},$$

and $w^e = w$ at the current moment, though $\dot{w}^e = \dot{w}$ if and only if the average wage change is correctly forecast. Calculation of the derivative $\dot{\Delta}_i^e$ and its substitution in (28) yields

$$\frac{\dot{w}_i}{w_i} = \lambda_i \Delta_i^* \frac{w}{w_i} - \lambda_i \Delta_i \frac{w}{w_i} + \frac{\dot{w}^e}{w}. \tag{29}$$

For firms as a whole we have $\Delta_i = 0$ and $w/w_i = 1$ on the average. Hence, for the rate of change of the average wage in terms of average Δ^* and average λ we obtain (25). But the use of a continuous-time analysis which treats wage rate changes as costless really deprives the role of wage expectations of its rationale.[29]

I shall briefly point out some implications and needed qualifications of this model.

One implication seems to be that a guidepost policy can be successful if it causes firms to expect other firms to raise their wages at a lower rate. In this respect there seems to be some advantage in a numerical guidepost standard like 3.2 per cent wage growth.

The model has implications for the requirements of equilibrium. Our equilibrium condition (27) together with the differential equation (23) that links $\dot{u}$ to u and z imply that corresponding to every initial unemployment rate is an equilibrium time path, $u^*(t)$. Any such time path satisfies

$$f\left[u^*, (1 - u^*)\frac{\dot{L}}{L} - \dot{u}^*\right] = 0. \tag{30}$$

It is easy to show that if the rate of labor-supply growth, $\dot{L}/L$, is equal to a non-negative constant, γ, each equilibrium path (corresponding to each initial u) converges to a *steady-state equilibrium* in which $\dot{u}^* = 0$. The

[29] A continuous-time model with a set-up cost of changing the wage rate at any time—rather than periodic wage negotiations—might offer some interesting contrasts to the analysis here, though I would not expect differences in steady-state behavior.

steady-state equilibrium value of the unemployment rate, denoted by $\bar{u}^*$, is determined by

$$f[\bar{u}^*, (1 - \bar{u}^*)\gamma] = 0. \tag{31}$$

Corresponding to $\bar{u}^*$ is some steady-state equilibrium vacancy rate, $\bar{v}^*$, which is given by the relation $m(\bar{u}^*, \bar{v}^*) = 0$.

Consider now alternative steady-state equilibria corresponding to different rates of wage increase but having the same productivity growth. It is clear that each of these steady-state equilibria must have the same unemployment rate. This conclusion requires simply that γ, on which $\bar{u}^*$ depends, be invariant to the nominal trend of money-wage rates in any steady-state equilibrium. That requirement is satisfied if the labor supply is perfectly inelastic with respect to all economic variables. It is also satisfied if the growth of labor supply depends only upon real variables and the latter are invariant, in steady-state equilibrium, to the rate of change of nominal wage rates. (For example, constancy of steady-state markups over time would leave the rate of growth of the real wage independent of the nominal wage trend.) Thus the locus of steady-state equilibrium points in Figure 2 is a vertical (dashed) line at $\bar{u}^*$. This locus might be called the *equilibrium* steady-state Phillips curve.

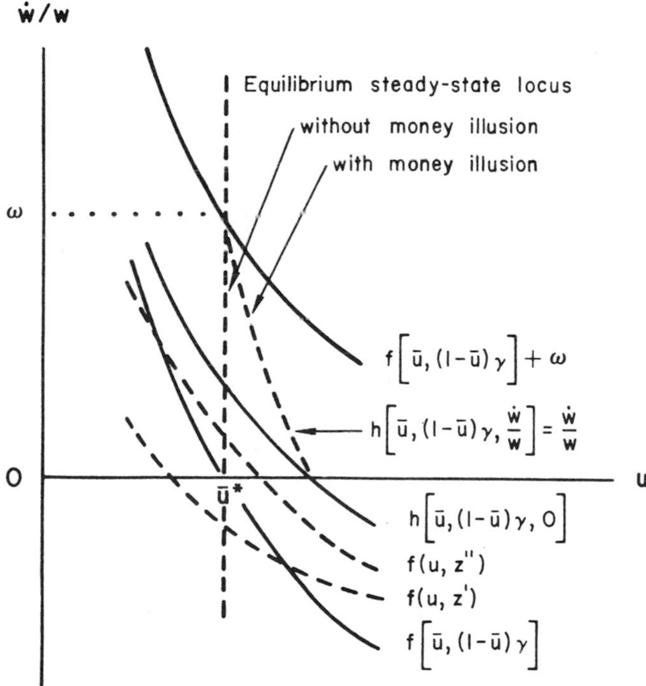

FIG. 2.—Augmented Phillips curves and equilibrium steady-state loci

Clearly this result fits the theory of anticipated inflation. For it implies that an economy experiencing and anticipating 10 per cent money-wage growth (and corresponding inflation rate) would not, in a steady state, have an unemployment rate different from what it would have if it were experiencing and anticipating a much smaller rate of wage increase.

What if higher money-wage growth in one steady state is matched by higher productivity growth? It is sometimes held that an economy can maintain a steady-state equilibrium—and thus a steady state with a stationary price trend (as well as any other trend)—with a smaller steady unemployment rate the faster its productivity growth. This is obvious on the usual Phillips curve analysis where no expectational variables are introduced; and it is also valid if the expected rate of wage change in my model is replaced by the expected rate of price change. But our theory denies this proposition if it is assumed that steady wage growth eventually generates the expectation of that growth. Then the difference in rates of wage increase consistent with price stability between rapid-productivity-growth and slow-productivity-growth situations does not permit a favorable difference in steady unemployment rates, since the difference in $\dot{w}/w$ will be matched by an equal difference in $\dot{w}^e/w$. Indeed the proposition in question could be reversed in a more general model: If rapid productivity growth and resulting obsolescence of plants strike firms unevenly and thus make greater demands for labor mobility and flexible skills, the steady-state equilibrium unemployment rate may very well be higher the faster is the growth of productivity. (But *given* productivity growth, $\bar{u}^*$ is still independent of the expected nominal wage trend.)

It is worth pointing out that because a rise of the rate of growth of the labor force will increase the value of z and hence the vacancy rate needed to maintain any given unemployment rate and because equilibrium $\bar{u}^*$ must then fall to accommodate a higher $\bar{v}^*$, the steady-state unemployment rate is higher the faster the labor supply grows. From (31) we calculate that

$$\frac{d\bar{u}^*}{d\gamma} = \frac{-(1 - \bar{u}^*)f_2}{f_1 - f_2\gamma} > 0. \tag{32}$$

Thus rapid economic growth from any source appears to increase the equilibrium steady-state unemployment rate.

Given the rates of labor force and productivity growth, therefore, the model implies that $\bar{u}^*$ is a constant, independent of $\dot{w}/w$ and $\dot{w}^e/w$. It is clear from (30) and (31) that if the unemployment rate is maintained at any constant level other than $\bar{u}^*$ a disequilibrium will result, since every equilibrium path converges monotonically to $\bar{u}^*$. For example, if $u = \bar{u} < \bar{u}^*$, $\bar{u}$ a constant, then $f[\bar{u}, (1 - \bar{u})\gamma] > 0$, so that $\dot{w}/w > \dot{w}^e/w$. What are the consequences of such a disequilibrium? To answer this we need some theory of expectations. Suppose we adopt the adaptive-expectations theory, first used by Cagan (1956), according to which $\dot{w}^e/w$ tends toward $\dot{w}/w$. Then $u = \bar{u} < \bar{u}^*$ implies $\dot{w}^e/w$ will be rising. But every one-point increase of $\dot{w}^e/w$ makes $\dot{w}/w$ one point higher if $u = \bar{u}$ is maintained. As a consequence, $\dot{w}^e/w$ and hence $\dot{w}/w$ will be increasing without limit as long as $u = \bar{u}$. The result of this is hyperinflation. The same explosive spiral must eventually result if the unemployment rate, while possibly variable, is bounded below $\bar{u}^*$, that is, $u(t) \leqq \bar{u}^* - \epsilon$, for all t, ϵ = constant > 0.

Suppose we are convinced that steady, non-accelerating inflation at some moderate rate is possible in this country at a steady unemployment rate of 4 per cent. In the present model this implies $\bar{u}^*$ equals 4 per cent.[30] Is it plausible that, as the above model predicts, wages and prices would spiral upward at an ever accelerating rate if aggregate demand consistently maintained the unemployment rate at 3.5 per cent? One might argue that it is not plausible on the "money-illusion" ground that an unemployment rate as high as 4 per cent is consistent with a moderate and steady rate of inflation, because some of those firms which would like to reduce substantially their wage differentials prefer to accept below-optimal profits or even dismiss some employees rather than impose money-wage cuts on their employees, and because some employees would rather quit than suffer the indignity of a money-wage cut; this means that the average money wage can be rising at the expected rate of wage change even when the "true" average desired wage differential, Δ^*, is negative. But money-wage cuts are occasionally appropriate for a firm which wants a lower wage differential only when the expected rate of wage change is moderately low. On this argument, therefore, a 3.5 per cent unemployment rate might also be consistent with equilibrium if the expected rate of wage change were high enough that a firm could reduce its expected relative wage by the amount desired without having to impose a money-wage cut.

Formally, the introduction of this "money illusion" (or resistance to money wage cuts) necessitates the more general wage-change function,

$$\frac{\dot{w}}{w} = h\left(u, z, \frac{\dot{w}^e}{w}\right), \tag{33}$$

where, for those values of $1 - u$, z and $\dot{w}^e/w$ low enough to raise the wage-cut obstacle for one or more firms, the derivative $\partial h/\partial(\dot{w}^e/w)$ is less than one, increasing in both $\dot{w}^e/w$ and z and decreasing in u; for values of $1 - u$, z and $\dot{w}^e/w$ sufficiently large that the wage-cut constraint is not binding for any firm, the derivative $\partial h/\partial(\dot{w}^e/w)$ is a constant equal to one as in the original formulation.

This variant of the model implies that the locus of steady-state equilibrium points is vertical only for $\dot{w}^e/w$ equal to or exceeding some positive level, ω in Figure 2, that is sufficiently high to circumvent the money-illusion problem. As $\dot{w}^e/w$ is reduced by equal successive amounts, the

[30] Note that the unemployment rate required to keep average money-wage rates in pace with productivity in the American economy, perhaps 6 per cent, will exceed the American $\bar{u}^*$ if, as seems likely, the expected rate of change of the money wage exceeds the rate of growth of productivity.

steady-state curve $h[\bar{u}, (1 - \bar{u})\gamma, \dot{w}^e/w]$ shifts down by smaller amounts so that, in this range, the locus of steady-state equilibrium points, where $\dot{w}/w$ equals $\dot{w}^e/w$, is negatively sloped, meaning that the $\bar{u}$ necessary for equilibrium is a decreasing function of $\dot{w}^e/w$. A dashed curve in Figure 2 depicts this money-illusion version of the equilibrium steady-state Phillips curve.

This variant of the model admits the possibility that a 3.5 per cent unemployment rate may be a sustainable equilibrium level too, like 4 per cent, though only at a higher rate of wage increase. Nevertheless, there exists some unemployment rate, perhaps 3 per cent, such that maintenance of the unemployment rate at a level below that rate would require a disequilibrium accelerating spiral of wages and prices. Such a revision of the model appears to reinforce the earlier hypothesis that faster labor force growth worsens the unemployment-inflation trade-off if the faster labor force growth would tend to depress the rate of growth of real wage rates. It *could* reverse the earlier hypothesis that productivity growth increases the steady-state unemployment rate necessary for price stability (or any steady-state equilibrium) if productivity growth tended to raise the rate of growth of real wage rates.

Another qualification of the model may be appropriate, though probably it has only short-run significance. The above model takes expectations of wage change, vacancy rates, and so on, to be certain. One may feel intuitively that a mean expected wage increase of 5 per cent has less of an impact on the firm's wage increase than a 5 per cent increase that is expected with certainty, that in response to the former the firm will "hedge" with a less-than-competitive wage increase to reduce the variance of its prospective profits distribution at some cost to mean expected profits. Then $\dot{w}^e/w$ will have a less-than-unitary coefficient if changes in $\dot{w}^e/w$ are accompanied by increases of the dispersion of $\dot{w}^e/w$ (which die out if the new $\dot{w}^e/w$ stabilizes), even though the constant-dispersion coefficient is really unitary. If firms do behave in this manner, the slope of the equilibrium steady-state locus will be underestimated to the extent that high wage growth expectations are not intrinsically more uncertain than low wage growth expectations once they become habitual. Much as I would like to be able to justify this intuition, I find a rational basis for it altogether elusive thus far. In particular, from the point of view of employment effects alone, maintenance of a firm's competitiveness or even an increase of its competitiveness would seem to offer minimum risk of high recruitment expense and excessive quitting. On the other hand, firms may act on similar intuitions whether rational or not.

I have been considering modifications of the simple model that bear on its implication of explosive hyperinflation or hyperdeflation at all unemployment rates different from some unique steady-state equilibrium rate. I have registered skepticism regarding the hypothesis that the greater uncertainty temporarily attaching to extreme or outlying wage expectations serves to moderate the otherwise explosive wage change movements, thus lending the economy the *appearance* of non-explosiveness. Perhaps another factor that makes a 4 per cent unemployment rate or even a 3 per cent rate appear to be permanently sustainable without forever mounting inflation is that expectations are not always "adaptive" in the way usually specified. When the standard expectations model predicts a rate of wage increase of, say, 6 per cent per year, employers may "switch off" that model, suspend the adaptation of their expectation to events, and place their faith in Washington or Providence to prevent wage increases beyond, say, 5 per cent.[31] But such bounds on expectations would eventually give way if Washington broke faith by continuing to permit wage increases outside the bound; so the point relates only to the statistical appearance of non-explosiveness.

IV. Summary

A generalized excess-demand theory of the rate of change of the average money-wage rate has been developed for frictional labor markets that allocate heterogeneous jobs and workers without having perfect information and market clearance by auction. There are two explanatory variables: the vacancy rate and the unemployment rate. The unemployment rate and the rate of change of employment (per unit of labor supply) are shown to be joint proxies for the vacancy rate. Hence generalized excess demand can be regarded as a derived function of the unemployment rate and the rate of change of employment. This relationship is the augmented Phillips curve. Some of its properties are deduced. The steady-state Phillips curve that relates the rate of wage increase to the steady unemployment rate is also derived.

The expected rate of wage change is then added to the Phillips function —to the excess-demand term—to obtain the rate of wage increase under non-stationary expectations in a no-money-illusion world. Equilibrium entails equality between the actual and expected rates of wage change. The steady-state equilibrium locus is implied to be a vertical line at a unique steady-state equilibrium unemployment rate. This is consistent with the usual theory of anticipated inflation. But if there are downward money-wage rigidities, then, up to a point, every one percentage point increase of the expected rate of wage change produces *less* than a one percentage point increase of the actual rate of wage change. The steady-state equilibrium locus will then have the characteristic negative slope of the Phillips curve in the range of large unemployment rates. But at sufficiently small (steady) unemployment rates, equilibrium is impossible, and, under the adaptive expectations theory, an explosive hyperinflation will result.

[31] I believe I owe this point, or one very close to it, to G. L. Bach.

Statistical Appendix

For this occasion I have been able to carry out only a few experiments with American data. I have used a quarterly model which, upon summation over four quarters to avoid seasonality and to reduce noise and measurement error, yields a model where all variables are essentially four-quarter rates of change and four-quarter averages. The four-quarter rate of wage change, based on unpublished U.S. non-farm average hourly compensation data of the Bureau of Labor Statistics and the civilian and non-civilian "potential" labor force, were generously supplied by N. J. Simler. The variable $\bar{E}_t$ denotes the four-quarter average employment rate. I have usually worked with the level and rate of change of E rather than with the rate of change of employment per unit labor supply as in the model. Where appropriate, the variables are expressed as percentages. The regressions cover third-quarter 1953 to second-quarter 1964. Figures in parentheses are t-ratios.

A natural starting point is the regression

$$\frac{\dot{w}}{w_t} = \underset{(2.78)}{-3.55 + 0.71\bar{E}_t} - \underset{(2.76)}{0.66\bar{E}_{t-1}} + \underset{(6.73)}{0.73\frac{\dot{w}}{w_{t-1}}}, \quad \bar{R}^2 = .698, \qquad \text{(A.1)}$$

where E is the global Simler-Tella adjusted employment rate. This can be interpreted as a *simple* Phillips curve combined with adaptive expectations or as an *augmented* Phillips curve in which $(\dot{w}/w)_{t-1}$ is simply extrapolated by firms. In the latter case it may make some sense to introduce $[(\dot{p}/p) - (\dot{w}/w)]_{t-1}$, where p is a price index, as an additional indicator of the discrepancy between the vacancy rate and its steady-state value in the following way:

$$\begin{aligned}\frac{\dot{w}}{w_t} = {} & -9.26 + \underset{(3.11)}{1.11\bar{E}_t} - \underset{(3.14)}{1.00\bar{E}_{t-1}} + \underset{(1.58)}{0.21\left(\frac{\dot{p}}{p} - \frac{\dot{w}}{w}\right)_{t-1}} \\ & + \underset{(6.88)}{0.80\frac{\dot{w}}{w_{t-1}}}, \quad \bar{R}^2 = .709. \qquad \text{(A.2)}\end{aligned}$$

Use of the z-like rate of change variable, $C_t = (\bar{N}_t - \bar{N}_{t-1})/\bar{L}_t$, leads to a minor improvement in the fit:

$$\begin{aligned}\frac{\dot{w}}{w_t} = {} & -10.92 + \underset{(1.65)}{0.13\bar{E}_t} + \underset{(3.20)}{1.06C_t} + \underset{(1.67)}{0.22\left(\frac{\dot{p}}{p} - \frac{\dot{w}}{w}\right)_{t-1}} \\ & + \underset{(6.83)}{0.79\frac{\dot{w}}{w_{t-1}}}, \quad \bar{R}^2 = .711. \qquad \text{(A.3)}\end{aligned}$$

Since the length of the work week, H, is also a good proxy for the vacancy rate, like C, it is not surprising that its introduction detracts from the power of C:

$$\begin{aligned}\frac{\dot{w}}{w_t} = {} & -51.3 + \underset{(2.76)}{0.19\bar{E}_t} + \underset{(1.49)}{0.49C_t} + \underset{(3.56)}{8.61\bar{H}_t} \\ & + \underset{(3.17)}{0.40\frac{\dot{p}}{p_{t-1}}} + \underset{(3.57)}{0.45\frac{\dot{w}}{w_{t-1}}}, \quad \bar{R}^2 = .778. \qquad \text{(A.4)}\end{aligned}$$

This equation implies a very steep equilibrium steady-state Phillips curve.

On the other hand, the conjunction of the augmented Phillips curve and adaptive expectations yields

$$\frac{\dot{w}}{w_t} = \underset{(2.34)}{-5.07 + 1.19\bar{E}_t} - \underset{(1.75)}{1.69\bar{E}_{t-1}} + \underset{(1.09)}{0.56\bar{E}_{t-2}} + \underset{(6.82)}{0.75}\frac{\dot{w}}{w_{t-1}}, \quad \bar{R}^2 = .700. \quad (A.5)$$

The E coefficients have the right signs and are largely significant. When the price change variable is introduced, $\bar{E}_{t-2}$ loses all significance and the twice-lagged price change variable has the wrong sign:

$$\frac{\dot{w}}{w_t} = -14.94 + \underset{(2.31)}{1.41\bar{E}_t} - \underset{(1.34)}{1.49\bar{E}_{t-1}} + \underset{(0.46)}{0.26\bar{E}_{t-2}} + \underset{(0.77)}{0.12}\left[\frac{\dot{p}}{p} - \frac{\dot{w}}{w}\right]_{t-1} + \underset{(1.29)}{0.18}\left(\frac{\dot{p}}{p} - \frac{\dot{w}}{w}\right)_{t-2} + \underset{(6.91)}{0.82}\frac{\dot{w}}{w_{t-1}}, \quad \bar{R}^2 = .718. \quad (A.6)$$

Introduction of the workweek did not appear to help.

Use of civilian non-agricultural employment to form a new employment rate, E', led to somewhat different results. While

$$\frac{\dot{w}}{w_t} = -3.96 + \underset{(3.05)}{0.88\bar{E}'_t} - \underset{(3.18)}{0.80\bar{E}'_{t-1}} + \underset{(1.14)}{0.13}\left(\frac{\dot{p}}{p} - \frac{\dot{w}}{w}\right)_{t-1} + \underset{(5.25)}{0.77}\frac{\dot{w}}{w_{t-1}}, \quad \bar{R}^2 = .712 \quad (A.7)$$

is not very different from (A.2), the following gives a smaller coefficient for $(\dot{w}/w)_{t-1}$ and a higher $\bar{R}^2$ than (A.5):

$$\frac{\dot{w}}{w_t} = -35.26 + \underset{(5.70)}{2.76\bar{E}'_t} - \underset{(5.35)}{4.31\bar{E}'_{t-1}} + \underset{(4.66)}{2.06\bar{E}'_{t-2}} + \underset{(5.49)}{0.59}\frac{\dot{w}}{w_{t-1}}, \quad \bar{R}^2 = .809. \quad (A.8)$$

The introduction of hours worked yields

$$\frac{\dot{w}}{w_t} = -41.5 + \underset{(4.11)}{2.48\bar{E}'_t} - \underset{(4.00)}{3.73\bar{E}'_{t-1}} + \underset{(3.75)}{1.79\bar{E}'_{t-2}} + \underset{(1.48)}{4.84\bar{H}_t} - \underset{(1.04)}{3.89\bar{H}_{t-1}} + \underset{(5.59)}{0.60}\frac{\dot{w}}{w_{t-1}}, \quad \bar{R}^2 = .810. \quad (A.9)$$

Introduction of the price change variables yields the mysterious equation

$$\frac{\dot{w}}{w_t} = -42.70 + \underset{(6.01)}{2.87\bar{E}'_t} - \underset{(5.35)}{4.22\bar{E}'_{t-1}} + \underset{(4.54)}{1.96\bar{E}'_{t-2}} - \underset{(0.39)}{0.05}\left(\frac{\dot{p}}{p} - \frac{\dot{w}}{w}\right)_{t-1}$$

$$+ \underset{(1.79)}{0.19}\left(\frac{\dot{p}}{p} - \frac{\dot{w}}{w}\right)_{t-2} + \underset{(4.86)}{0.59}\frac{\dot{w}}{w_{t-1}}, \quad \bar{R}^2 = .820, \qquad \text{(A.10)}$$

or, equivalently, apart from rounding errors,

$$\frac{\dot{w}}{w_t} = -42.55 + \underset{(3.95)}{0.61\bar{E}'_t} + \underset{(5.80)}{2.25(\bar{E}'_t - \bar{E}'_{t-1})} - \underset{(4.52)}{1.95(\bar{E}'_{t-1} - \bar{E}'_{t-2})}$$

$$- \underset{(0.39)}{0.05}\left(\frac{\dot{p}}{p} - \frac{\dot{w}}{w}\right)_{t-1} + \underset{(1.79)}{0.19}\left(\frac{\dot{p}}{p} - \frac{\dot{w}}{w}\right)_{t-2} + \underset{(4.85)}{0.60}\frac{\dot{w}}{w_{t-1}}, \quad \bar{R}^2 = .819. \qquad \text{(A.11)}$$

Finally, for whatever curiosity value it may have, I computed

$$\frac{\dot{w}}{w_t} = -56.55 + \underset{(4.04)}{2.42\bar{E}'_t} - \underset{(3.48)}{3.38\bar{E}'_{t-1}} + \underset{(3.23)}{1.62\bar{E}'_{t-2}}$$

$$+ \underset{(1.64)}{6.14\bar{H}_t} - \underset{(0.91)}{3.55\bar{H}_{t-1}} - \underset{(0.21)}{0.04}\frac{\dot{p}}{p_{t-1}} + \underset{(1.07)}{0.21}\frac{\dot{p}}{p_{t-2}}$$

$$+ \underset{(4.71)}{0.66}\frac{\dot{w}}{w_{t-1}} - \underset{(1.65)}{0.22}\frac{\dot{w}}{w_{t-2}}, \quad \bar{R}^2 = .824. \qquad \text{(A.12)}$$

The reader can calculate the equilibrium steady-state Phillips relations on the natural assumption that $\dot{p}/p = \dot{w}/w - \rho$ where ρ is invariant to the steady-state level of E.

I have not begun to test the many hypotheses which the present model suggests, such as the various non-linearities and interaction terms. Work of this sort probably requires more careful data construction. But I believe that several of the main features of the model have received some support from these empirical results.

References

Ackley, G. "The Contribution of Guidelines," in G. P. Shultz and R. Z. Aliber (eds.). *Guidelines, Informal Controls, and the Market Place*. Chicago: Univ. of Chicago Press, 1966.

Alchian A. A., and W. R. Allen. *University Economics*. Belmont, Calif.: Wadsworth Publishing Co., 1964.

Ball, R. J. *Inflation and the Theory of Money*. London: Allen & Unwin, 1964.

Bhatia, R. J. "Profits and the Rate of Change of Money Earnings in the United States, 1935–1959," *Economica*, XXIX (August, 1962), 255–62.

Bowen, W. G. *Wage Behavior in the Postwar Period*. Princeton, N.J.: Indus. Relations Sec., 1960.

Bowen, W. G., and Berry, R. A. "Unemployment Conditions and Movements of the Money Wage Level," *Rev. Econ. and Statis.*, XLV (May, 1963), 163–72.

Bronfenbrenner, M. "Postwar Political Economy: The President's Reports," *J.P.E.*, LVI (October, 1948), 373–91.

———. "Some Neglected Implications of Secular Inflation," in K. K. Kurihara (ed.). *Post-Keynesian Economics*. New Brunswick, N.J.: Rutgers Univ. Press, 1954.

Brown, A. J. *The Great Inflation, 1939–51*. London: Oxford Univ. Press, 1955.

Cagan, P. H. "The Monetary Dynamics of Hyperinflation," in M. Friedman (ed.). *Studies in the Quantity Theory of Money*. Chicago: Univ. of Chicago Press, 1956.

Cohen, M. S., and Solow, R. M. "The Behavior of Help-Wanted Advertising," *Rev. Econ. and Statis.*, XLIX (February, 1967), 108–10.

Dow, J. C. R., and Dicks-Mireaux, L. A. "The Excess Demand for Labor: A Study of Conditions in Great Britain, 1946–56," *Oxford Econ. Papers*, X (February, 1958), 1–33.

Duesenberry, J. S. *Business Cycles and Economic Growth*. New York: McGraw-Hill Book Co., 1958.

Dunlop, J. T. "The Movement of Real and Money Wage Rates," *Econ. J.*, XLVIII (September, 1938), 413–34.

———. *Wage Determination under Trade Unions*. New York: A. M. Kelley, 1950.

Eagly, R. V. "Market Power as an Intervening Mechanism in Phillips Curve Analysis," *Economica*, XXXII (February, 1965), 48–64.

Eckstein, O., and Wilson, T. "The Determinants of Money Wages in American Industry," *Q.J.E.*, LXX (August, 1962), 379–414.

Fellner, W. J. "Demand Inflation, Cost Inflation, and Collective Bargaining," in P. D. Bradley (ed.). *The Public Stake in Union Power*. Charlottesville: Univ. of Virginia Press, 1959.

Friedman, M. "Comment," in G. P. Shultz and R. Z. Aliber (eds.). *Guidelines, Informal Controls, and the Market Place*. Chicago: Univ. of Chicago Press, 1966.

Haberler, G. "Causes and Cures of Inflation," *Rev. Econ. and Statis.*, XXX (February, 1948), 10–14.

Hansen, B. "Full Employment and Wage Stability," in J. T. Dunlop (ed.). *The Theory of Wage Determination*. New York: St. Martin's Press, 1957.

Hicks, J. R. "Economic Foundations of Wage Policy," *Econ. J.*, LXV (September, 1955), 389–404.

Hines, A. G. "Trade Unions and Wage Inflation in the United Kingdom 1893–1961," *Rev. Econ. Studies*, XXXI (October, 1964), 221–52.

Holt, C. C., and David, M. H. "The Concept of Job Vacancies in a Dynamic Theory of the Labor Market," in *The Measurement and Interpretation of Job Vacancies: NBER Conference Report*. New York: Nat. Bureau Econ. Res., 1966.

Keynes, J. M. *The General Theory of Employment, Interest and Money*. London: Macmillan Co., 1936.

Kuh, E. "A Productivity Theory of Wage Levels—an Alternative to the Phillips Curve," *Rev. Econ. Studies*, Vol. XXXIV (October, 1967).

Lerner, A. P. "The Inflationary Process—Some Theoretical Aspects," *Rev. Econ. and Statis.*, XXXI (August, 1949), 193–200.

———. "Inflationary Depression and the Regulation of Administered Prices," in *The Relationship of Prices to Economic Stability and Growth*. Compendium of papers submitted to panelists appearing before the Joint

Economic Committee (85th Cong., 2d sess.). Washington: Government Printing Office, 1958.

Lerner, A. P. "Employment Theory and Employment Policy," *A.E.R.: Papers and Proc.*, LVII (May, 1967), 1–18.

Lipsey, R. G. "The Relation between Unemployment and the Rate of Change of Money Wage Rates in the United Kingdom, 1862–1957: A Further Analysis," *Economica*, XXVII (February, 1960), 1–31.

Mises, L. von. *The Theory of Money and Credit*. New Haven, Conn.: Yale Univ. Press, 1953 ed.

Perry, G. L. "The Determinants of Wage Rate Changes and the Inflation-Unemployment Trade-off for the U.S.," *Rev. Econ. Studies*, XXXI (October, 1964), 287–308.

———. *Unemployment, Money Wage Rates and Inflation*. Cambridge, Mass.: M.I.T. Press, 1966.

Phelps, E. S. "A Test for the Presence of Cost Inflation in the United States 1955–57," *Yale Econ. Essays*, I (Spring, 1961), 28–69.

———. "Anticipated Inflation and Economic Welfare," *J.P.E.*, LXXIII (February, 1965), 1–17.

———. "Phillips Curves, Expectations of Inflation and Optimal Unemployment over Time," *Economica*, XXXIV (August, 1967), 254–81.

Phillips, A. W. "The Relation between Unemployment and the Rate of Change of Money Wage Rates in the United Kingdom, 1861–1957," *Economica*, XXV (November, 1958) 283–99.

Rees, A., and Hamilton, Mary T. "The Wage-Price-Productivity Perplex," *J.P.E.*, LXXV (February, 1967), 63–70.

Robinson, J. *Essays in the Theory of Unemployment*. New York: Macmillan Co., 1937.

Ross, A. M. "Guideline Policy," in G. P. Shultz and R. Z. Aliber (eds.). *Guidelines, Informal Controls, and the Market Place*. Chicago: Univ. of Chicago Press, 1966.

Sargan, J. D. "Wages and Prices in the United Kingdom: A Study in Econometric Methodology," in P. E. Hart, G. Mills, and J. K. Whitaker (eds.). *Econometric Analysis for Economic Planning: Sixteenth Symposium of the Colston Research Society*. London: Butterworths, 1964.

Selden, R. T. "Cost-Push versus Demand-Pull Inflation, 1955–57," *J.P.E.*, LXVII (February, 1959), 1–20.

Sidrauski, M. "Rational Choice and Patterns of Growth in a Monetary Economy," *A.E.R.: Papers and Proc.*, LVII (May, 1967), 534–44.

Simler, N. J., and Tella, A. "Labor Reserves and the Phillips Curve" (Minneapolis: University of Minnesota, 1967 [mimeographed]).

Singer, H. W. "Wage Policy in Full Employment," *Econ. J.*, LVII (December, 1947), 438–55.

Stigler, G. J. "Information in the Labor Market," *J.P.E.*, LXX (suppl.; October, 1962), 94–105.

Tobin, J. "Money and Economic Growth," *Econometrica*, XXXIII (October, 1965), 671–84.

U.S. Department of Commerce. *Business Cycle Developments* (monthly).

Weintraub, S. *A General Theory of the Price Level, Output, Income Distribution and Economic Growth*. Philadelphia: Chilton Co., 1959.

SHORT-RUN EMPLOYMENT AND REAL WAGE IN COMPETITIVE MARKETS

THIS PAPER EXPLORES the effects upon aggregate employment and the real wage rate of a decline of aggregate demand in two economies in which the commodity market is competitive. In the first economy, all goods just produced are supplied to the market perfectly inelastically, the costs of storage being too great to warrant the holding of stocks at any non-negative market price. In the second type of economy, holding costs are low enough that producers will carry over some stock into the next market period when the current market price is low enough on the speculation that future sales will be possible at a higher price. This latter model has been studied by Edwin Mills [7, (chapter 4)] and Edward Zabel [**9**], and it will be supposed here that firms follow the optimal production and sales policies derived by Zabel [**9**].

Consider a decrease of aggregate demand for commodities which does not prevent the continued *existence* of a full-employment equilibrium. Under what conditions concerning the dynamics of the system will the fall of aggregate demand cause involuntary unemployment, at least transitionally? In particular, is a failure of money wages immediately to fall in proportion to the price level (at any given level of employment) a necessary condition for involuntary unemployment? That is, will involuntary unemployment occur only if the fall of aggregate demand causes a rise of the real wage rate? This is the principal question to be studied in this paper.

1. A "TEXTBOOK" MODEL AND THE EVIDENCE

The usual textbook answer to the above question is in the affirmative. On the market-clearing assumption, each competitive firm will reckon that, within any reasonable range, it can sell as much of the commodity as it likes without significantly reducing the price. To maximize profits, it is argued, firms will produce up to the output level at which marginal cost equals price or, equivalently, where the marginal productivity of labor equals the "product wage" or real wage in an aggregative model. Thus output will fall and employment will fall only if price falls faster than marginal cost at the initial output rate; equivalently, output will decline only if the real wage rises above the marginal productivity of labor at the initial employment level.

Let us specify, as textbooks usually do, continuous production through time with final output resulting instantaneously from the application of the primary variable input, labor. Output is never stored, all output being instantaneously auctioned at the price that clears the market.

* Manuscript received October 22, 1966, revised September 8, 1967.

[1] This research was supported by a National Science Foundation grant for study by the author of price and wage behavior.

Reprinted by permission from *International Economic Review*, Vol. 10(2), June 1969.

For any given money supply, one can construct an "aggregate demand curve" in the price-aggregate output plane. This indicates, for any output level, the price level necessary for equality of *ex ante* investment and saving and equality of the supply and demand for real cash balances. It is negatively sloped by virtue of the Pigou (cash-balance) and Keynes (interest-rate) effects.

For any given money wage rate, there is also an upward-sloping "aggregate supply curve" in the same diagram. This upward-sloping curve is simply the "industry" (or economy) marginal cost curve. It shows, for any price level, the output producers would like to supply, which is the output they *will* supply on the market-clearing assumption (provided there is no positive excess demand in the labor market). The counterpart to our economy being "on" the aggregate supply curve is its being "on" the labor demand curve where marginal productivity equals the real wage rate.[2]

Imagine that the economy is initially in full-employment equilibrium, so that the money wage rate is such that the real wage rate implied by equality of aggregate demand and supply clears the labor market. And now suppose that the aggregate demand curve shifts downwards, say by 10 percent at the full-employment output level, due possibly to a reduction of investment demand or to a fall of the money supply—without any change in technology and in labor supply. Then the new full-employment equilibrium requires a 10 percent lower money wage and the price level, with no change in real wage rate, employment and output. Whether unemployment will arise (at least temporarily, in the transition to the new equilibrium) depends solely upon whether the real wage rate rises in response to the decline in aggregate demand, and hence upon labor market dynamics.

Let us suppose that the labor market is not instantaneously cleared, so that excess supply (or demand) may exist. If wage bargains are struck in real terms, money wages will fall *pari passu* with the price level so that the real wage and employment will stay at their full-employment levels. If wage bargains are struck in money terms and if price and wage changes are not expected, it is plausible to hypothesize that

$$\frac{\dot{w}}{w} = f(E)\,, \quad f(0) = 0\,, \quad f'(E) > 0\,, \tag{1}$$

where w is the money wage and E is excess demand for labor. If E is monotonically decreasing in the real wage rate then

$$\frac{\dot{w}}{w} = g\left[\left(\frac{w}{p}\right)^* - \frac{w}{p}\right], \quad g(0) = 0\,, \quad g'(\,\cdot\,) > 0\,, \tag{2}$$

where $(w/p)^*$ is the full-employment, equilibrium real wage. Since money wages fall slowly relative to the fall of price, it is obvious that the fall of demand must raise the real wage rate. (If the real wage were not to rise, the money wage would not fall; but the latter must fall by 10 percent to maintain the real wage.) In terms of the diagram, the shift of the demand curve drives the system downward along the aggregate supply curve, thus

[2] For such a diagram, see for example, McKenna [6].

raising the real wage rate and causing unemployment; this induces a fall of the money wage, hence a downward shift of the supply curve, thus driving the system downward along the demand curve until employment and the real wage have returned to their full-employment levels.

Hence, in the above model, there is a perfect negative correlation between employment and the real wage rate due to the diminishing marginal productivity of labor. Keynes' *General Theory* also supposed diminishing returns and postulated that competition would drive price toward marginal cost with some lag (during which the commodity market would not be cleared) so that the real wage rate would tend to equality with the marginal productivity of labor. He concluded that in the downswing, when the money wage rate was falling, the real wage rate would rise; and that in the upswing the real wage rate would fall.

John Dunlop [2], working with British data, and L. Tarshis [8], using American data, argued that this proposition was not borne out by the experience of the thirties. Though reliance on the government's cost-of-living index, which gave excessive weight to food expenditures, had led most economists in Britain to believe that real wages had risen significantly between 1930 and 1932, Dunlop's revised indices failed to show any marked tendency of the real wage rate index to lie above its long-run trend path, especially in the mid-thirties.

These findings drew a cautious response from Keynes [3]. He observed that the theory implied a countercyclical rise of the product wage rather than of the real wage. Nevertheless employment fell in the consumption goods sector as well so that, with respect to that sector, the problem remains. He also pointed to a League of Nations study by James Meade which reached conclusions concerning real wage movements in several countries in conformity with the theory. The wage and price series used by William Phillips and Richard Lipsey also show a significant rise of the real wage rate index in the early thirties.[3] On the other hand, the product wage series for United States manufacturing recently constructed by Edwin Kuh does not show any countercyclical movement in the product wage rate in the thirties that is obvious to the naked eye.[4]

The subject needs econometric analysis. In the depression of the thirties, there was undoubtedly a decline in the rate at which the marginal labor productivity schedule was shifting upwards. Second, the marginal productivity schedule, though downward sloping, may have been almost flat at least in the relevant range. Thus it may be that no pronounced rise of the real wage rate above the *historical trend path* should have been expected even on the basis of the theory.

But the former argument has less force with respect to the outset of a

[3] See Lipsey [5].

[4] Kuh [4] reported the absence of a statistically significant regression relation between the rate of change of the product wage and the rate of change of unemployment. Such a relation, if there is any theoretical presumption in its favor, would be considerably obscured by lags in the adjustment of employment to the quantity of labor demanded in a state (at a given real wage).

depression or to a short recession—to intervals of time too short for the fall of investment to have reduced the marginal productivity schedule below its trend path. Thus short recessions will be accompanied by detectable upward "blips" of the real wage rate, according to the above market-clearance model, on the natural assumption that productivity growth tends to be comparatively smooth, never taking downward blips which would appreciably forestall the real wage blips. Yet we do not consistently find such behavior in our series of real and product wage. Even if, in the depression of the thirties, real wages tended to move qualitatively in the expected way (which is by no means established), the shorter postwar recessions do not seem to be accompanied systematically in the downswing (or just prior to it) by an abnormal rise of the real wage.

If that is the case, how must the above economic model be modified? Keynes, in his response to Dunlop, emphasized that his theory of unemployment did not fundamentally require a rise of the real wage. Keynes meant that even if money wages fall instantaneously in proportion to the price level there could and would be involuntary unemployment, at least temporarily, as a result of the fall of aggregate demand. The difference between the above model and Keynes' thinking, I believe, centers on the postulate of equilibrium in commodity markets.

Let us retain the postulate of equilibrium commodity prices however. Is it really true in that case that all realistic competitive models can generate involuntary unemployment from a decline of aggregate demand only if that decline causes an increase of the real wage rate?

2. A DISCRETE-TIME MODEL WITH PROHIBITIVE STORAGE COSTS

In both of the following models, each period begins with bids from consumers and offers from producers in the commodity market for the "starting stock" of goods, y_t. These result in the establishment of a market-clearing price, p_t, in period t, a certain intentional storage of commodities by producers, x_t, and a certain quantity of commodities sold and consumed $(y_t - x_t)$. Then the labor market opens and establishes a money wage, w_t, (paid at the end of the period) and a certain volume of employment in the production of commodities for sale or for storage in the next period. Production is denoted q_t and the "starting stock" at the beginning of next period satisfies $y_{t+1} = q_t + x_t$. Once given p_t, firms and labor form a common subjective probability distribution of the market price in future periods. Firms are postulated to maximize the expected value of the present discounted value of the sequence of profits over an infinite time horizon.

In the first model, marginal storage costs, $h'(x)$, and the discounted mean expected price, $\alpha\bar{p}_{t+1}$, are supposed to satisfy $\alpha\bar{p}_{t+1} < h'(0)$ in every period, with $h''(x) \geq 0$, so that storage is never optimal at any $p_t \geq 0$. Then the firm need merely maximize, in each period, the expected value of next period's profits. Thus, assuming an interior maximum to exist, every firm will equate marginal cost to mean expected price. Hence, letting $C'(q_t)$ denote marginal cost,

$$C'(q_t) = \bar{p}_{t+1} ,$$

where $\bar{p}_{t+1}$ is the mean price expected (in period t) to prevail in period $t + 1$. Using

$$C'(q_t) = \frac{w_t}{\phi'(N_t)} \tag{4}$$

where N_t denotes employment in period t and $\phi'(N)$ labor's marginal productivity, we obtain

$$\phi'(N_t) = \frac{w_t}{\bar{p}_{t+1}} . \tag{5}$$

Thus aggregate employment in every period will be such as to equate marginal productivity to the "expected real wage rate," $w_t/\bar{p}_{t+1}$.

Suppose that in period $t - 1$ the labor market were in equilibrium. Suppose that $\bar{p}_t = p_{t-1}$, and suppose that $\bar{p}_{t+1} = p_t$ if $p_t = \bar{p}_t$. Then if in fact $p_t = \bar{p}_t$, we will observe $w_t = w_{t-1}$, since constancy of the money wage will maintain the labor market in equilibrium, labor supply and demand not having changed.

Consider now the case $p_t < \bar{p}_t$. The price is less than was expected. Let the number $k > 0$ (not necessarily a parameter) describe how the expected real wage adjusts to this event:

$$\frac{w_t}{\bar{p}_{t+1}} = k\frac{w_{t-1}}{p_{t-1}} \left[= k\frac{w_{t-1}}{\bar{p}_t} \right] . \tag{6}$$

If firms and workers think only in real terms, if workers look only at the mean expected price rather than the dispersion (or if the dispersion of the probability distribution has in some relevant sense remained unchanged), *and if the wage were equilibrating*, we would find that $k = 1$, that the money wage would satisfy

$$\frac{w_t}{w_{t-1}} = \frac{\bar{p}_{t+1}}{\bar{p}_t} ; \qquad k = 1 , \tag{7}$$

so as to keep the expected real wage constant. But we should entertain the possibility that $k > 1$, that the money wage falls insufficiently. In that case, employment and production will fall, with involuntary unemployment occurring.

But a rise of the expected real wage need not produce a rise of the *current* real wage in the sense of w_t/p_t. Using

$$\frac{w_t}{p_t} = \frac{w_t}{\bar{p}_{t+1}} \frac{\bar{p}_{t+1}}{p_t} \tag{8}$$

and (6) we obtain

$$\frac{w_t/p_t}{w_{t-1}/p_{t-1}} = k\frac{\bar{p}_{t+1}}{p_t} . \tag{9}$$

Now if $\bar{p}_{t+1} = p_t$, the current real wage will rise, like the expected real wage.

But the current real wage will *fall* if $\bar{p}_{t+1}/p_t < k^{-1}$. Thus if the fall of the current price below the expected level causes producers and workers to expect that prices will fall further in the next period—if the price decline is extrapolated—the current real wage may fall simultaneously with the fall of employment.

Three objections to the applicability of this point will be briefly considered. It might be argued that extrapolative expectations are exceptional at best, that a more reasonable assumption is the "adaptive" one that the expected price, $\bar{p}_{t+1}$, will lie somewhere between p_t and $\bar{p}_t$, so that $\bar{p}_{t+1}/p_t > 1$; the notion here is that the "normal" mean price $\bar{p}$ adjusts sluggishly to deviations of the actual price from the "normal." But if p is the money price level rather than the real (relative) price of one among many commodities, then it is plausible that it is the expected *rate of change* of money price that adapts to "deviations." In this case, if price falls when the expected rate of change was zero, the rate of change expected next period will be negative also (though algebraically greater than the current actual rate of change), so that $\bar{p}_{t+1}/p_t < 1$; here it is the normal rate of change that adjusts sluggishly.[5] Of course, expectations mechanisms other than adaptive ones deserve consideration.

A second objection is that the above analysis would appear to be of practical importance only where the period of production is long. If production takes only a day, it seems unlikely that inter-period rates of expected price change will be appreciable and hence unlikely that any large discrepancy between the current real wage and the expected real wage would arise. Yet even where the production period is short, employers will look ahead at expected real wage rates in more distant periods if there are hiring and firing costs. In recognition of these costs, employers who expect money wage stickiness in the face of a prospective downward price trend may hire considerably less labor than would have to be hired to equate labor's marginal product to next period's expected real wage. Thus we may observe a fall of employment below its full-employment path despite little rise (or even a fall) of the current real wage, even in competitive economies with market-clearing prices, whether or not the production period is long.

A third objection is that the "current real wage" as defined above has no relevance to the well-being of the worker, so that the model merely warns against using an inappropriate real wage index. But this is the kind of index usually employed so it is the perverse behavior of that kind of index that we are seeking to explain (under market-clearing prices). It is clear that the index w_t/p_{t+1} also can behave perversely if actual price declines are less than expected or, as in a more general model, if staggered labor inputs are required at various dates in advance of the final outputs, so that expectations of prices far in the future can affect the "current" real wage.

3. A DISCRETE-TIME MODEL WITH ECONOMICAL STORAGE

In the previous model, employment will fall if and only if the *expected* real wage rate rises. In the following model, a fall of aggregate demand can

[5] For an empirical application, see Cagan [1].

reduce both employment and the expected real wage rate as well as the current real wage rate. In this model, the quantity of labor demanded depends not only on the expected real wage rate but also upon the quantity of final goods voluntarily carried over by producers for speculative reasons.

As before, each identical firm is supposed to maximize the present value of the sequence of expected profits from its sales and production policies. We postulate now that the subjective probability distribution of future prices in each period, $\psi(p)$, is "stationary"; the distribution is the same for all future periods and is invariant to the current price. Let y denote next period's starting stock, x denote the current stock after the current period's sales and q denote current output. Then $y = x + q$. Variable production costs, $C(q)$, are a positive, increasing and convex function of output. Holding costs are taken to be a positive, increasing, convex function of inventories held, $h(x)$, so that $h(x) > 0$, $h'(x) > 0$, $h''(x) > 0$. Rising marginal holding costs are fundamental to the results here; these are physical storage costs (made up of wages and rents), the opportunity costs of tying up funds in stocks being already taken into account by the discount factor, α, $0 < \alpha < 1$. That the individual firm faces rising marginal holding costs evidently requires conditions causing firms to do their own storage rather than to use a perfect market for storage.

This model is one of several studied by Zabel. The firm's production and sales problems are represented by the equations

$$f(x) = \max_{y \geq x} [-C(y-x) + \int_0^\infty R(y; p)\psi(p)dp] , \tag{10}$$

where

$$R(y; p) = \max_{0 \leq s \leq y} [ps - h(y - s) + \alpha f(y-s)] , \tag{11}$$

s being the amount sold next period (from the quantity y made available from production this period and initial inventory).

These equations may be interpreted as follows. Current production costs are paid out at the beginning of the next period, when sales are made; for simplicity of notation, outlays and receipts at the beginning of next period are undiscounted, those two periods hence being discounted once, and so on. The cost of holding x this period is a bygone, independent of y, and hence is omitted from the maximand in (10); expenses for the holding of stocks into the next period are paid out at the beginning of the current period. All receipts and outlays are expressed in money terms.

We shall confine our attention to the case in which $\alpha\bar{p} > h'(0)$. If this inequality did not hold, then $\alpha\bar{p} - p \leq h'(0)$ for all $p \geq 0$ so that inventories would never be carried over, even at a zero curent price. (Zabel considers all cases.) In our case, some storage is optimal at a sufficiently small positive price.

The nature of Zabel's results can be illustrated by Figure 1. We have let $\bar{R}(y)$ denote $\int_0^\infty R(y; p)\psi(p)dp$, so that $\bar{R}'(y)$ can be interpreted as the "marginal expected discounted maximized revenue" of starting stock. On the assumption that $C'(0) < \bar{R}'(0)$, the optimal production level, $y^* - x$, equates marginal cost to this "marginal revenue" concept.

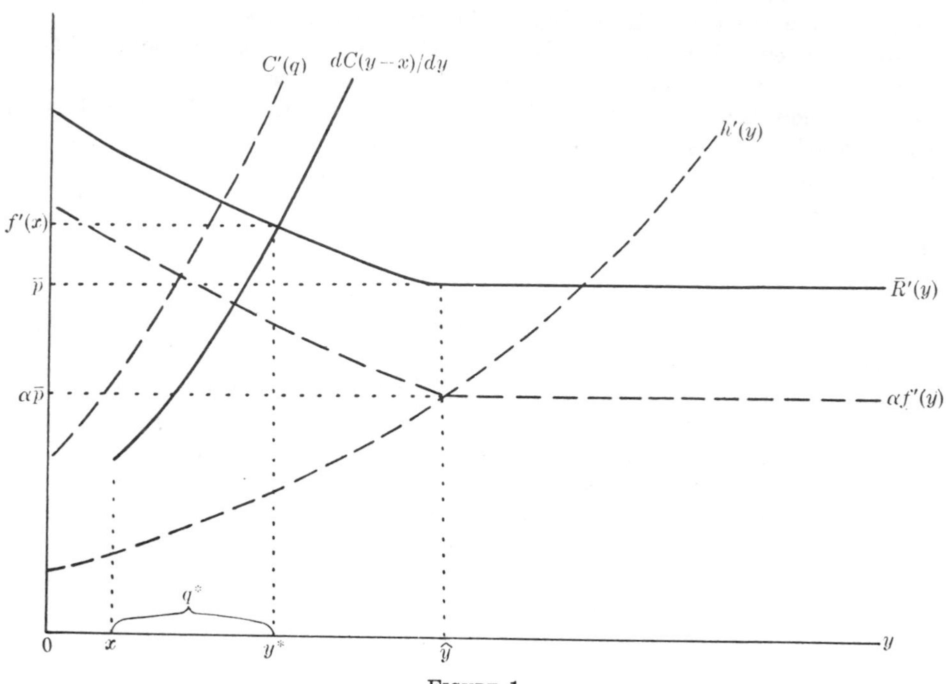

FIGURE 1
MARGINAL REVENUE AND MARGINAL COST

The crucial feature of Figure 1 for our purposes is the marginal revenue segment which lies above $\bar{p}$ and slopes downward. Marginal revenue will exceed expected price at sufficiently low stock levels because the firm has the option to carry over some of the stock into future periods if the market price is "low" next period in the expectation that future sales will be possible at a higher price. By selling little when price is below the expected mean and selling much when price is high, the firm can expect average revenue over time to be in excess of mean price.

This segment is downward sloping. For the greater the starting stock, the greater are expected future costs (for expected storage will be greater and marginal holding costs are rising) so that storage of each extra unit of starting stock is decreasingly likely as starting stock is increased. But clearly marginal revenue cannot be less than the mean expected price for, at worst, the firm can sell each marginal unit of starting stock at the market price, the expectation of which is $\bar{p}$. At $y \geq \hat{y}$, where $h'(\hat{y}) = \alpha\bar{p}$, it is certain that marginal starting stock will be sold. Thus the marginal revenue curve also contains the horizontal segment of height $\bar{p}$. (If no finite $\hat{y}$ exists, the curve is asymtotic to $\bar{p}$ and the propositions below are somewhat simplified.)

This argument will now be elaborated. For y such that $\alpha f'(y) > h'(y)$, the optimal sales policy is shown by Zabel to be

$$s^*(y;p) = \begin{cases} y & \text{if} \quad p > \alpha f'(0) - h'(0) \\ \pi(y;p) & \text{if} \quad \alpha f'(0) - h'(0) \geq p \geq \alpha f'(y) - h'(y) \\ 0 & \text{otherwise} \end{cases} \tag{12}$$

where π satisfies

$$p + h'(y - \pi) - \alpha f'(y - \pi) = 0 \, . \tag{13}$$

If $\alpha f'(y) \leq h'(y)$, sales will occur even at a zero price. When $p = 0$, sales will be the amount $y - \hat{y}$ which ensures $\alpha f'(\hat{y}) = h'(\hat{y})$ or equivalently $\alpha \bar{p} = h'(\hat{y})$; thus there is an upper bound, $\hat{y}$, on the amount of starting stock which will be carried over into the subsequent period.

As (12) shows, if price is "high," meaning $p > \alpha f'(0) - h'(0)$, then all starting stock will be sold. Hence $ds^*/dy = 1$ and marginal revenue will be the conditional price expectation for price in this range. If price is in the "medium" range, there will be some storage and some sales. The optimal carryover of stock, $y - \pi$, is independent of y [by (13)] so that, in this range too, $ds^*/dy = 1$. Hence, again, marginal revenue of starting stock for price in this range is the conditional price expectation. But for a "low" price, meaning $0 \leq p < \alpha f'(y) - h'(y)$, nothing will be sold so that in the event of such prices $ds^*/dy = 0$. Thus marginal revenue is smaller the greater is y since storage is greater and the value of marginal holding costs is therefore higher. Thus marginal revenue is decreasing when $\alpha f'(y) > h'(y)$ since then price may fall in this third, sell-nothing range.

Zabel shows that, for $\alpha f'(y) > h'(y)$,

$$\bar{R}'(y) = z[\alpha f'(y) - h'(y)] + (1 - z)\left[\frac{\int_{\alpha f'(y) - h'(y)}^{\infty} p\psi(p)dp}{1 - z}\right] \tag{14}$$

where

$$z = \int_0^{\alpha f'(y) - h'(y)} \psi(p)dp \tag{15}$$

denotes the probability of a "low," sell-nothing price. Differentiation of (14), with attention to cancellations, yields (using Zabel's result that $f''(y) \leq 0$)

$$\bar{R}''(y) = z[\alpha f''(y) - h''(y)] < 0 \tag{16}$$

for $\alpha f'(y) > h'(y)$. For $\alpha f'(y) \leq h'(y)$, $\bar{R}'(y) = \bar{p}$ as indicated previously.

This downward slope of the marginal revenue curve has important consequences for the effect of the current price—through its effect on the current carryover, x, —upon optimal output. Suppose that $C'(0) < \bar{R}'(0)$; otherwise there would never be positive output. Then, as one can see from Figure 1, an increase of x shifts rightward the dC/dy curve with the consequence that optimal starting stock increases—but by less than x in the range where

$y^*<\hat{y}$. Thus optimal output is a decreasing function of initial stock (in the x range small enough to make $y^* < \hat{y}$). Zabel obtains

$$\frac{dy^*}{dx} = \frac{C''(y^* - x)}{C''(y^* - x) - \bar{R}''(y^*)}, \tag{17}$$

which is less than one when $\bar{R}''(y^*) < 0$, and

$$\frac{dq^*}{dx} = \frac{\bar{R}''(q^* + x)}{C''(q^*) - \bar{R}''(q^* + x)}, \tag{18}$$

which is negative when $\bar{R}''(y^*) < 0$.

Suppose that p_{t-1} lies either in the high, sell-everything range, so that $x_{t-1} = 0$, or in the medium, sell-something, store-something range, so that $x_{t-1} > 0$. In the former case, a sufficient fall of price ($p_t < p_{t-1}$) will cause $x_t > 0$ and hence $x_t > x_{t-1}$; in the latter case, any fall of price will cause $x_t > x_{t-1}$ (since, in the medium range, any fall of price increases the optimal storage level, independently of starting stock). Then, if $y^*_{t-1} < \hat{y}$, so that firms are on the downward sloping marginal-revenue-curve segment, output will be smaller in period t—even though the marginal cost schedule and the expected price distribution have not changed, or, equivalently, even though the expected real wage rate, $w/\bar{p}$, associated with any volume of employment and the marginal productivity schedule have not changed. Thus a fall of aggregate demand may, by reducing the current price and increasing the current optimal carry-over of stock, cause a reduction of optimal output and employment even without a change of the expected real wage.

However, the decline of price will raise that *current* real wage which must be offered workers *for any given volume of employment*. Since the fall of price is regarded as temporary, the labor supply schedule in terms of the money wage rate will not fall in response to the current price decline. Yet the *equilibrium* current real wage rate need not rise. The fall of labor demand and of employment will cause a fall of the money wage if the labor supply schedule is positively sloped. It is possible for the equilibrium money wage to fall proportionately more than current price, so that the real wage rate falls. This requires, of course, that the money marginal-revenue-productivity-of-labor schedule fall proportionately more than price. To show the possibility of that result, we calculate the following, for price in this store-something, sell-something range:

$$\frac{\partial(MRP)}{\partial x} = \frac{\partial[\phi'(N)\bar{R}'(\phi(N) + x)]}{\partial x} = \phi'(N)\bar{R}''(\phi(N) + x) \tag{19}$$

$$\frac{\partial(MRP)}{\partial p} = \phi'(N)\bar{R}''(\phi(N) + x)\frac{dx}{dp} = \frac{\phi'(N)\bar{R}(\phi''(N) + x)}{\alpha f''(x) - h''(x)} \quad \text{[by (13)]} \tag{20}$$

$$\frac{\partial(MRP)}{\partial p}\frac{p}{(MRP)} = \frac{p\bar{R}''(\phi(N) + x)}{\bar{R}'(\phi(N) + x)[\alpha f''(x) - h''(x)]} \tag{21}$$

$$= \frac{pz[\alpha f''(y) - h''(y)]}{\bar{R}'(y)[\alpha f''(x) - h''(x)]} \quad \text{[by (16)]}.$$

By (10) and (13) we have

$$\frac{p}{R'(y)} = \frac{\alpha f'(x) - h'(x)}{f'(x)} \quad \text{if} \quad y = y^* , \tag{22}$$

which, like z, is less than one; hence if the elasticity in (21) is to exceed one in the neighborhood of y^*, the desired result, we require the ratio of the bracketed terms to exceed one (sufficiently). This does not seem impossible as $f''' - h''' < 0$ is presumably possible. This possibility is supported upon deriving $f''(x) = \bar{R}''(y^*)(dy^*/dx)$, whence

$$\frac{\alpha f''(y^*) - h''(y^*)}{\alpha f''(x) - h''(x)} = \frac{\bar{R}''(y^*)}{\alpha \bar{R}''(y^*) \dfrac{dy^*}{dx} - h''(x)} \tag{23}$$

whose reciprocal is

$$\alpha \frac{dy^*}{dx} - \frac{h''(x)}{\bar{R}''(y^*)} = \alpha \frac{dy^*}{dx} - \frac{h''(x)}{\alpha f''(y^*) - h''(y^*)} . \tag{24}$$

Our contention is that this reciprocal could be substantially less than one so that the elasticity in (21) could exceed one. We see that the first term on the righthand side of (24) is less than one. The second term is positive, when taken with the minus sign, but could be very small. Thus it appears to be theoretically possible for the money marginal-revenue-productivity-of-labor schedule to shift downward (at least in the neighborhood of the optimal employment level) as much or more, proportionately, as the current price when aggregate demand falls. As a consequence, a fall of demand can, in this model, induce a simultaneous fall of employment and the *current* real wage rate (as well as the expected real wage rate). Even if the current real wage rises, the employment decline can substantially exceed the decline predicted by marginal productivity considerations alone.

It might seem easier to suppose that the fall of current price leads, in cobweb fashion, to an equal proportionate fall of "expected prices," of the labor supply schedule in money terms and of future expected money holding costs. Noting that optimal output in Zabel's model is homogeneous of degree zero in these money magnitudes, we would find that the current real wage rate would fall unambiguously with a fall of price if and only if the expected real wage fell. (Such an approach, incidentally, would make more plausible the assumption of a constant nominal rate of interest which is implicit in the constancy of α.) But if firms' price and wage expectations responded to current price in this fashion, a fall of current price would fail to motivate additional speculative inventory holding, and hence fail to reduce labor demand, for prices next period would not be expected to return to former, high levels.

One clearly wants to relax the assumption of stationarity in expectations while not going in the direction of the preceding possibility.[6] Adaptive ex-

[6] Zabel has considered cobweb and adaptive expectations in as yet unpublished materials. But his analysis is excessively microeconomic from the present point of view; holding costs and production costs are invariant to revisions of price expectations in Zabel's analysis.

pectations in terms both of level and rate of change of price may be attractive.

There is another weakness in the model from a macroeconomic point of view. If the expected real rate of interest is held constant (by monetary policy), the expectation of a price recovery or rise ($\bar{p} > p$) will raise the money interest rate and reduce α, just enough in fact to nullify the stimulus to stock building created by a price decline. Thus the present model requires that the expected real rate of interest decline with a fall of aggregate demand if an increase of carryover, and the other effects which that produces, are to take place. This is not an unreasonable requirement. Provided that the decrease of the demand for commodities is accompanied predominantly by an increase of the demand for money rather than for bonds and other debt instruments, the fall of aggregate demand will reduce the real rate of interest at any given level of output when the money supply is held constant. (The fall of output induced by the resulting speculative inventory building will then cause a further fall of the real interest rate, given the money supply. If the fall of price inspires "easy money" through government purchase of securities, the real interest rate will fall still further.) It is possible, therefore, that the money interest rate will rise very little or not at all in the present model when aggregate demand falls.

Note lastly that while we have been discussing a fall of labor demand and employment, the decline of labor demand will cause involuntary unemployment if the money wage responds insufficiently in the current period to an excess supply of labor. Thus it can be shown that the appearance of involuntary unemployment can coincide with a fall of the current real wage rate—or, if technical progress admitted, with a real wage rate rise which is smaller than the rate of growth of productivity. Of course, it is always true in neoclassical theory, and has not been denied in this paper, that involuntary unemployment can arise only if the wage exceeds its *equilibrium* value. The point has been that a fall of aggregate demand can reduce the equilibrium (expected and/or current) real wage rate so that even if the money wage falls in proportion to the current price level, there may be a fall of employment and, transitionally, the appearance of involuntary unemloyment.

I have explored here certain aspects of what may be called neoclassical employment theory. Such theory may have considerable relevance for highly commercialized, primarily agricultural economies.

University of Pennsylvania, U.S.A.

REFERENCES

[1] CAGAN, P., "The Monetary Dynamics of Hyperinflation," in M. Friedman, ed., *Studies in the Quantity Theory of Money* (Chicago: University of Chicago Press, 1956).

[2] DUNLOP, J. T., "The Movement of Real and Money Wage Rates," *Economic Journal*, XLVIII (September, 1938), 413-34.

[3] KEYNES, J. M., "Relative Movements of Real Wages and Output," *Economic Journal*, XLIX (March, 1939), 34-51.

[4] KUH, E., "Unemployment, Production Functions and Effective Demand," *Journal*

of Political Economy, LXXIV (June, 1966), 238-49.

[5] LIPSEY, R. G., "The Relation between Unemployment and the Rate of Change of Money Wage Rates in the United Kingdom, 1862-1957: A Further Analysis," *Economica*, XXVII (February, 1960), 1-31.

[6] MCKENNA, J. P., *Aggregate Economic Analysis* (New York: Dryden, 1955; third edition, 1969).

[7] MILLS, E. S., *Price, Output and Inventory Policy* (New York: John Wiley and Sons, 1962).

[8] TARSHIS, L., "Changes in Real and Money Wage Rates," *Economic Journal*, XLIX (March, 1939), 150-54.

[9] ZABEL, E., "A Dynamic Model of the Competitive Firm," *International Economic Review*, VIII (June, 1967), 194-208.

THE EMERGING MICROECONOMICS IN EMPLOYMENT AND INFLATION THEORY

It is notorious that the conventional neoclassical theory of the supply decisions of the household and of the firm are inconsistent with Keynesian employment models and with the post-Keynesian economics of inflation. Why should a fall of aggregate demand[1] reduce output and employment? Relentless application of textbook principles to either a competitive industry or a pure monopoly shows that output and employment in the corn industry will fall, given the technology and fixed factors, only if there is a rise of the product wage—the wage in terms of corn.[2] Why should a fall of demand raise product wage rates? The Keynesians, while postulating money wage "stickiness," never articulated a labor model in which the absence of automatic wage escalator clauses (tying money wage rates to the price level) could be explained. Further, it is widely agreed that product wage rates do not unerringly move "countercyclically" if they have any such tendency at all. What, then, is the appropriate theory of industry prices and outputs? Similarly, why should inflation (or unexpected inflation) be said in post-Keynesian economics to "buy" an increase of output and employment? Firms might be thought, neoclassically, to require lower product wage rates to produce more while households would be unlikely to respond with a corresponding increase of labor supply if real wage rates were to fall. It seems clear that macroeconomics needs a microeconomic foundation.

Now there has emerged the necessary kind of microeconomic theory of production, labor supply, wage and price decisions—a body of theory which is not restricted to conditions of neoclassical intertemporal equilibrium. The theory is different from some other efforts to buttress Keynes in that it sticks doggedly to the neoclassical postulates of lifetime expected utility maximization and net worth maximization, it makes no appeal to faulty perceptions (money illusion) and it does not plead that price setters economize on their decision-making time. Despite these abstractions, the new theory manages to deepen our understanding of traditional Keynesian economics and to adduce new hypotheses about macroeconomic behavior. It offers reasons why money wage rates are "sticky" in the face of price-level movements—why money wage rates (and thus prices) do not quickly respond by enough to keep employment and output at their equilibrium levels when aggregate demand changes.[3] It explains the stickiness of prices when money production costs move, so that real wage rates are not implied necessarily to rise when employment falls despite diminishing marginal productivity. The new theory generates a momentary steady-

* The author's work in this area is being supported by the Brookings Institution, for which he is preparing a monograph on public policy towards inflation and unemployment.

[1] By "aggregate demand" I mean (throughout) a schedule in the price-real income (or output) plane. This schedule may be vertical or, under Keynes or Pigou effects, negatively sloped.

[2] Aggregate demand can make absolutely no difference to any competitive firm's output except through the market-clearing prices and wage rates. In the monopoly case, there is the obvious elasticity qualification.

[3] Hence the previously advertised title of this paper, "Economics of the Absent Escalator."

Reprinted by permission from *American Economic Review*, Vol. 59(2), May 1969.

state Phillips curve relation between the employment level and the rate of wage (or price) change; the rate of change of employment (or output) also frequently figures in the general Phillips relation. Finally, the crucial role which the new theory assigns to expectations, especially expectations of wage and price change, together with the notion of adaptive expectations has led most of the new theorists to the hypothesis that the Phillips curve is like a "predetermined" or "state" variable: today's Phillips curve may be largely inherited but tomorrow's curve will depend upon how the economy behaves today—in such a way, to be precise, that steady inflation will not "buy" a permanent (non-vanishing) reduction of the unemployment rate.[4]

The theoretical departure that is common to this otherwise neoclassical analysis is the removal of the Walrasian postulate of complete information. In the Walrasian economy, all transactions take place under complete information on the part of each buyer and seller about his alternatives. As a consequence, the Walrasian economy satisfies the two conditions for economic equilibrium.

The first of these conditions is that there is no nonprice rationing. There exists no buyer who, knowing he could make both himself and some seller better off by paying a higher price in return for more of the seller's product, is yet somehow frustrated from overbidding because the seller is (at least temporarily) ignorant of his bid. Similarly, no seller is frustrated form underbidding. This condition can also be expressed by saying that prices clear markets.[5]

[4] This hypothesis, known variously as the "permanent unemployment thesis" or the "strong expectations hypothesis," should not shock scholarly economists. Fellner and Wallich argued it in this country more than ten years ago, and von Mises before them. The novelty in the work reviewed here in this connection is its explicitness about the expectational and learning mechanisms involved.

The market-clearance condition means only that every price is market-clearing among the set of people who know the price. It means that every firm knows how much output those buyers who know his price are willing to buy from him at various prices he might set, and analogously for sellers to the firm. The second condition for equilibrium is that each household (and each firm if there are interfirm transactions) always knows the market-clearing prices of every firm now and in the future. There is perfect knowledge of current prices in the stringent sense that if a price were to change somewhere in the economy, every household would know the new price immediately. This requires there be no cost to learning or to advertising these prices.[6] The equally stringent condition that future market-clearing prices are known is best interpreted as a matter of perfect foresight or intuition.[7]

[5] That prices clear markets follows from the maximization postulate that no buyer or seller would knowingly pass up an opportunity for improvement together with the informational postulate that the firm knows its purchase and sale opportunities. In the case of a monopolist firm that sets price (nondiscriminatorily), market clearance means simply that the monopolist operates "on" his demand curve; he never rations buyers and he never produces in excess of quantity demanded at the price he sets because he knows his maximum sales at every price. Similarly, the monopsonist firm setting price operates "on" his supply curve. In the competitive case, where buyer and seller act as if the price necessary to effect a purchase or a sale were independent of the quantity purchased or sold, market clearing means that supply equals demand.

[6] It is not simply that the household thinks it knows all the prices and it happens to be right in the prevailing economic state; the weaker concept of non-Walrasian equilibrium involves the correctness of expectations.

[7] The analytical construct of a comprehensive futures market to determine all future prices in advance, so that future prices are placed on a par with current prices, falls to the ground in an economy with a positive birth rate. For the present members of the economy, to achieve economic efficiency, will want to be able to trade later with the yet unborn members of the economy who cannot as yet enter into futures contracts.

On the high ice-clad slopes of the Walrasian equilibrium economy, the question of a connection between aggregate demand and the employment level is a little treacherous.[8] Only one path of aggregate demand will produce the path of the price level and money-wage level that people foresee. But we may ask what difference it would make if people were spontaneously to foresee inflation (of prices and money wage rates equally) rather than a stationary price and wage level, so that aggregate demand must be steadily increased to validate these expectations. Would the inflationary scenario be one of higher employment than in the stationary-price story? The answer is that there is no necessary connection between the rate of anticipated inflation and the level of employment. Employment, investment, and other real supplies and demands will be invariant to the difference in the anticipated price trend if all foreseen relative prices, including foreseen real rates of interest, are likewise invariant. The two tools of fiscal and monetary policy give the government enough degrees of freedom to validate and sustain a "pure" or "neutral" inflation in which real interest rates are insulated from the expectations of inflation.[9]

I shall briefly discuss here the three types of disequilibrium models to be found in the new microeconomics under incomplete information. I start with the labor market side.

I. *Labor Markets and Money Wage Behavior*

Search Unemployment and Effective Labor Supply. A paper by George Stigler [13] has emphasized that labor markets are characterized by seriously incomplete information on the part of the worker concerning current wage rates elsewhere in the economy, so that a certain amount of "search unemployment" is normal. Armen Alchian has pointed out that, on a reasonable expectational hypothesis, the quantity of search unemployment and thus the level of employment will vary with aggregate demand through its effect on sampled money wage rates [1].[10] Specifically, an increase of aggregate demand will reduce search unemployment by causing the searcher to mistake a general rise of money wage rates for a lucky sampling of a high relative money wage offer which he believes he should accept.

Perhaps the simplest model would be a picture of the economy as a group of islands between which information flows are costly: to learn of the wage paid on an adjacent island, the worker must spend the day traveling to that island to sample its wage instead of spending the day at work. Imagine, only for simplicity, that total labor supply—the sum of employment and (search) unemployment—is a constant for every household, independent of real wage rates, expected real interest

[8] If one wishes to discuss money prices and inflation in the Walrasian economy, one needs to suppose that, even in the fully informed Walrasian economy, peoples' IOU's would not be completely trusted and that the government—or a few firms (banks) under government regulation—monopolize the manufacture of currency.

[9] Three qualifications to this conclusion may be mentioned: The expected capital loss on real money balances may substitute for taxation of income so that if taxes are not assumed to be lump-sum, there will be a substitution effect favoring employment and saving. Second, if legal or technological factors prevent money (or some components of money) from bearing interest, the opportunity costs of holding money will be greater under anticipated inflation and one could imagine that the resulting additional nuisance of managing transactions balances would shorten the workday a little or divert secondary household workers from the labor market. Third, there may be "distribution effects" on labor supply if the inflation was not anticipated as early as the signing of the oldest outstanding contract expressed in money terms.

[10] Mention should also be made of Leijonhufvud's new book [6] which views money wage stickiness in much the same way.

rates, and so on. Suppose, also, that labor is technically homogeneous in production functions and indifferent among the many heterogeneous jobs of producing a variety of products. Producers on each island are in pure competition in the labor market as well as in the interisland product markets. Each morning, on each island, workers "shape up" for an auction that determines the market-clearing money wage and employment level. To start with, imagine a very stationary set-up in which there is no taste change and no technical change, with constant population size.

Initially, wage rates are moving as has been expected, and it is believed that unsampled wage rates (on other islands) are equal to the sampled (own-island) one. The economy is thus in a kind of non-Walrasian equilibrium in which wage rates are correctly guessed—though a change of some island's wage would not be immediately learned. For simplicity, suppose that money wages have been expected to be stationary. Now let aggregate demand fall. If the decline of derived demand for labor were understood to be general and uniform across islands, money wage rates (and with them prices) would fall so as to maintain employment and the real wage rate (provided that a new equilibrium exists). But suppose that workers on every island believe the fall of demand is at least partly island-specific due to their island's individual product mix. It is natural then to postulate that workers' expectations of money wage rates elsewhere (on other islands) will "adapt" less than proportionally to the unforeseen fall of sampled money wage rates. To the extent that the island-specific component of the wage change is believed to be enduring enough to make search for a better money wage rate seem worthwhile, the acceptance wage on each island will fall less than proportionally to product prices; some workers will refuse employment at the new (lower) market-clearing money wage rates, preferring to spend the time searching for a better relative money wage elsewhere.[11] Effective labor supply thus shifts leftward at every real wage rate, real wage rates rise and profit maximizing output and employment fall.

A pioneering paper by Charles Holt [4] and a closely related one by the present author [10] discuss the generation of a Phillips curve from models of imperfect information in labor markets. More about these models later. In fact, the faint shape of a Phillips curve relation between the steady unemployment rate and the rate of wage change can be seen to emerge from the ultra-simple island model. If the government were to manipulate aggregate demand to keep the average money level constant at its new lower level, the search unemployed would be disappointed at finding money wage rates equally low elsewhere and would hence revise downward their expectations of the mean wage elsewhere relative to sampled wage rates; search would become less attractive and effective labor supply would shift rightward.[12] To prevent the market-clear-

[11] I assume that workers differ in age, and hence differ in their appraisal of the lifetime gain from a specified expectation of wage-rate improvement, or that workers differ in the "adaptability" of their wage expectations, so that each island's effective labor supply curve is upward sloping.

[12] Is there a nonsteady-state path of return to steady-state equilibrium along which the expectations of wage rates by searchers are continuously validated? The answer is apparently no if expectations are identical across workers (and not only in that case). To confirm the expectations of the hopeful searchers, money wage rates must rise. To confirm the expectations of nonsearchers with like expectations (but older people), money wage rates cannot rise by as much—for there was an expectation of a change in wage relatives as well as the possibility of some return to normal money wage levels. (There might exist odd configurations of heterogeneous expectations which could be validated.) The nonsteady-state equilibrium paths of my recent paper [10] could be viewed as paths which make the wage rates move in conformity with the expectations by the employed of the trend of wage rates elsewhere.

ing employment rate from rising, therefore, the government would have to continue to reduce money wage rates by contracting aggregate demand (or by holding the aggregate demand function steady if aggregate demand is independent of the price level). This action would be effective on the hypothesis that every unexpected decrease of sampled money wage rates produces a less than proportional decrease of expected money wage rates elsewhere. Then each day, there is some rate of decline of money wage rates that would keep sampled money wage rates equal to a constant fraction of expected money wage rates elsewhere. Thus some continuing decline of money wage rates (of the right magnitude) accompanies the maintenance of the specified volume of search unemployment.[13]

Clearly, the "required" rate of decrease of money wage rates is larger the greater is the shortfall of actual wage rates from expected wage rates. It is also true that the volume of search unemployment is larger the greater is this shortfall. Hence we deduce a Phillips-like relation between the steady level of unemployment and the algebraic rate of increase of money wage rates. In this relation, the expected long-run trend rate of money wage increase figures as a parameter. If workers look backward and see that money wage rates are steadily falling and adapt their expectations of the general wage trend accordingly, an ever accelerating rate of decrease of wage rates will occur if the search unemployment level is maintained.

In the above story, every steady state of positive unemployment is one of disequilibrium in the sense that sampled wage rates are continually and systematically different from (less than) what they were expected to be.[14] Steady-state equilibrium occurs only at zero unemployment. To escape this implication, it is necessary to introduce structural change, like "real" microeconomic product-demand shifts, relative cost shifts, or perhaps (simple) population growth.[15] Then the islands where money wage rates are above the average money wage rates expected elsewhere will be numerous enough relative to the islands where wage rates are below expected wage rates elsewhere that the equilibrium steady unemployment rate (at which, on average, money wage rates move as expected) will be positive. There will be enough job "vacancies"—as defined by the quantity of labor that would be demanded at expected mean wage rates elsewhere minus actual employment where wage rates are "high"—in relation to the quantity of search unemployment that a kind of equilibrium "in the large" is possible in which, while individual searchers and nonsearchers may be disappointed or delighted, the mean rate of change of money wage rates is equal to the average expected trend rate of change.[16,17] In the

[13] A rigorous argument that the rate of wage decline is constant—or simply asymptotically constant—is undoubtedly difficult.

[14] If the expected long-run trend rate of money wage change is, say, 4 percent, a small enough steady unemployment rate will be associated with rising money wage rates; but they will be rising at less than 4 percent, so that the same overestimates of wage rates elsewhere will exist and disappointment will occur.

[15] G. C. Archibald has been looking into the kinds of continuing sequences of structural change required to keep the steady-state equilibrium unemployment rate positive.

[16] If every area is searched (in equilibrium), the equilibrium so defined seems also to be characterized by equality of mean wage levels elsewhere with the actual mean wage level, on the average over workers. If easterners do not search the West, believing wage rates drastically lower there, then that characterization need not hold (whether or not westerners search the East).

[17] Note that in the kind of economy I have been sketching, wage rates will be high and falling where vacancies are defined to be present, while in sectors where wage rates are below expected wage rates elsewhere (the current loci of the unemployment) wage rates will be low and rising. These rates of change, I believe, need not characterize more thoroughly non-Walrasian markets where each firm is an island.

model so extended, "overemployment" is possible. It results when, starting from the equilibrium level of search unemployment, money wage rates rise faster than expected. Such unexpected rises induce some of the search unemployed to stop search earlier, to accept employment at the sampled wage rates (and some employed to postpone search)—if, as hypothesized before, every unexpected wage increase produces a less than proportional increase of mean expected money wage rates elsewhere.[18]

In summary, the search unemployment model suggests a wage change equation in which the Phillips relation is one element. The rate of wage change is connected to the level of the unemployment rate, the rate of change of employment and the expected trend rate of increase of wage rates —the latter entering the equation with a unitary coefficient. The first of these latter variables reflects the expected rate of wage improvement from search, and the second of these variables measures the rate of change in this expected improvement.[19]

Holt's paper presents a richly detailed model of job search, including on-the-job search by employed workers. In his model, the rate of overall wage increase is a weighted average of the rate at which unemployed persons reduce their acceptance wage (as they learn about the wage distribution they are sampling from) and the rate at which employed persons improve their wage rates by moving from low-wage to high-wage jobs. The smaller the steady-state unemployment rate, the larger is this weighted-average rate of wage change. The way in which a rise of general wage rates reduces the unemployment rates is also discussed. The effect of expectations of general trend rates of change in wage rates seems to be abstracted from in Holt's paper.

The present author's recent paper on wage dynamics and labor market equilibrium emphasizes the economics of wage setting and recruitment by the firm which is in an incompletely informed labor market. Here each firm is a kind of island having transient, dynamical monopsony power at each point in time: a rise of its wage offers relative to those elsewhere will increase the speed with which its employment roll will increase. Each firm will pay a higher wage relatively to its expectations of money wage rates elsewhere the smaller is the expected unemployment rate and the larger is its own expected job vacancy rate.[20] If expectations of going money wage rates elsewhere are "static," then, when all (or most) firms pay more than they believe wage rates elsewhere to be—a situation of "generalized excess demand" in which vacancies are high and unemployment low—recruitment results are disappointing, there is learning of actual wage rates elsewhere, and conse-

[18] Just as the average length of search is shortened, one might expect that fewer people would quit in order to search when money wage rates are rising unexpectedly fast. It seems to be the case, however, that quit rates are higher the smaller is the unemployment rate. To accommodate that generally accepted hypothesis, it is apparently necessary to add that quit rates depend upon the unemployment rate because the latter reflects expectations of the time required to find employment. This introduces nonmarket-clearing factors.

[19] I should mention two weaknesses, neither necessarily serious, which are peculiar to the above search-unemployment model. First, a fall of aggregate demand may fail to produce the expectation of finding better relative money wage rates elsewhere, and thus fail to increase search unemployment, if workers observe that the cost of living has fallen in proportion to sampled money wage rates (or in greater proportion) and if they take those consumer prices to be some indication of general wage rates. (This suggests that price-level stickiness has a novel role to play in search unemployment.) Second, if an unforseen inflation is marked by an abnormally low expected real rate of interest, the search-shortening effect of the unexpectedly high wage rates sampled could, in principle, be offset by the reduced discounting of the future wage gain expected from continued search.

[20] Measured at the expected going wage.

quently general wage rates float upwards. It is argued that unemployment and vacancies together determine the rate of change of employment as well as that of money wage rates, given expectations of the long-term trend rate of change of money wage rates elsewhere, so that the unemployment rate and the rate of change of employment are interpretable partly as joint proxies for generalized excess demand in Phillips curves. But even with zero generalized excess demand, it is maintained, money wage rates will change at a rate equal to the expected rate of change of average money wage rates elsewhere. On the hypothesis of adaptive expectations, faster growth of aggregate demand cannot achieve a permanent reduction of the unemployment rate below its equilibrium steady-state level. Further, faster productivity growth would not improve (and might worsen) the equilibrium unemployment rate.

A new paper by Dale Mortensen [8] combines and further develops some of the notions of Holt and myself, obtaining a logically complete and rigorous model of the labor market. This important paper sustains and illuminates most of the foregoing propositions about wage and employment dynamics in models of imperfectly-informed labor markets.

"Wait" Unemployment, Nonmarket Clearance and Stochastic Factors. A recent paper by Donald Gordon and Allan Hynes [3] explores the implications of probabilistic demands (of unknown mean frequency) for a service in a statistical-decision-theoretic model of optimal price setting by the seller. The paradigm there is the pricing (or rental-setting) problem of the manager of a group of apartments. But Gordon and Hynes rightly insist that such a model has much to offer as a description of labor markets as well.

The authors maintain that every wage contract between employer and employee is, at least implicitly, a contract for some finite duration of time. The labor supplier whose service is, for the moment, not in demand at his standard wage will, if he reduces his wage enough to become employed, take the risk of having to reject an offer of employment at his standard wage in the near future. The supplier who faces a stochastic demand will want to set his wage high enough that, if he has correctly estimated the (stationary) demand distribution, he will be intermittently unemployed due to stochastic fluctuations in demand. Such a model certainly sheds light on the sporadic unemployment of artisans, lawyers and actors for whom a contract now will preclude new employment for some time.

When there is an increase of the mean frequency of demand, due to a change of aggregate demand, say, idle suppliers will accept employment at standard rates. But as the unusual frequency of demands persists, suppliers will adaptively revise their expectations of the mean demand frequency and raise their standard wages accordingly. Employment in excess of the equilibrium level, at which mean demand frequencies are correctly estimated, thus generates a succession of wage increases (in excess of the normal trend rate of increase). But as suppliers find that steady escalation of their fees is not enough to return them to their objectively optimal average idleness, wage rates will accelerate. Gordon and Hynes conclude that their model too denies the possibility of a stable trade-off between employment and inflation.

Probably the idea of a buffer stock of free time can be applied more broadly to labor markets. The employer who cannot recruit and train labor costlessly may be willing to employ—i.e., pay wages to—a buffer stock of idle or near-idle workers to insure his being able to meet randomly high demands for his products. Further, the employer who faces a stochastic supply of labor—at each wage, how many employees will quit tomorrow and how many unemployed will seek and accept jobs?—may find it optimal, frequently or even normally, to set his wage *above* the market-clearing level.[21]

The Neoclassicial Speculative Labor Supply Model. The most neoclassical of the disequilibrium models drops the postulate of perfect foresight, while retaining the other informational postulates of the Walrasian system. All current prices are market clearing and are universally known.

Consider an economy initially in Walrasian equilibrium: thus far the future has been correctly guessed. For simplicity, suppose that the expected price trend has been level. Now let aggregate demand increase so as to produce an unexpected rise of market-clearing product prices. If we abstract from speculative inventory accumulation and the use of goods in process in some industries, firms' production and employment will be unchanged if current real wage rates are unchanged (provided there is no change of the demand elasticities perceived by firms). The unforeseen price rise can increase the willingness of firms to hire labor only by somehow reducing market-clearing real wage rates. Now why should this occur? Why should the behavior of labor supply cause money wage rates to rise less than proportionally to the rise of the current price level?

The explanation offered is in part that workers will speculate on the future return of the price level toward its original level. Workers will "adapt" their expectations of the future price level, on this hypothesis, only partially in response to the unexpected rise of the current price level.

[21] Then it is not just the worker's expectation of money wages elsewhere but also his expectations of the number of job vacancies and the number of unemployed looking for them that will determine his reservation wage and quit decision.

Hence, if workers expect to spend any increment of money wages partly on future consumption goods, a rise of money wage rates in proportion to the current price level would make additional labor supply more attractive. Thus the labor supply curve shifts rightward at every real wage rate. Therefore real wage rates fall and employment is increased.[22]

This rationale for money wage stickiness was briefly discussed in 1952 by James Tobin [15] though the entire focus there was on the possibility of "underemployment" arising from an unforeseen fall of the general price level. Robert Lucas and Leonard Rapping [7] have now produced an intertemporal lifetime utility-maximization model of household labor supply, involving present and future consumption and leisure which rigorizes this kind of analysis.

Out of the Lucas-Rapping model comes not only a theory of money wage stickiness but a Phillips curve relation between the rate of price change and the employment rate. If aggregate demand is manipulated by the government in such a way as to keep the price level constant at its new and higher (and unforeseen) level, workers will (on the above adaptive-expectations hypothesis) successively revise upwards their expectations of future consumption-goods prices; these revisions will gradually reduce labor supply (at every real wage), thus driving money wage rates up and driving profit maximiz-

[22] Even if workers did not save, one could build a model arriving at the same result in which employment during the current period produces output during the current period while wages are received at the end of the period and spent over the next period. But it is hard to believe that the lag of wage payments behind wage accruals is long enough for this mechanism to be effective in stimulating employment; and if the average lag of output behind the application of labor input is equally long one would need to introduce asymmetrical expectations as between the individual firm's own future price and the future general level of prices.

ing output and employment back toward their steady-state equilibrium levels.[23] But there is some rate of continuing unforeseen price increases, a rate which is able to keep the expected future price level equal to a constant fraction of the actual price level—if each unforeseen increase of the current price level induces a constant and less than proportional increase of the expected price level—which can thus induce households to maintain their labor supply at the given "overemployment" level. But note that the required rate of inflation is constant rather than ever accelerating, only if what might be called the "expected normal long-run trend rate of price change"—set equal to zero in this exposition—fails to adapt to the actual trend of the price level. In the Lucas-Rapping formulation of the price-change (or wage-change) equation, the expected long-run trend rate of price enters with a unitary coefficient.[24]

II. *Price and Output Dynamics*

In the above models, there was postulated to be complete information on the part of all buyers about all goods prices. If a firm were to change its commodity price, the full effect of this change on the quantity demanded of the firm's commodity would be felt instantaneously. In that kind of model, inducing the firm to produce more—to move down its demand curve expressed in wage units as it were —requires a fall of product wage rates or, more loosely, of real wage rates. No one believes that production fluctuations can be accounted for completely, if at all, by such countercyclical real wage rate movements. More sophisticated views of pricing which dispense with various Walrasian informational postulates can avert the implication that real wage rates must so behave if aggregate demand changes are to have output effects.[25] They can also rationalize a kind of excess capacity phenomenon as a normal accompaniment, like unemployment, of the non-Walrasian economy.

Customer Search, Optimal Pricing, and Output Supply. Recent work by Sidney Winter and myself [11] analyzes a model in which, because of sluggishness in the diffusion of information, the firm finds itself at every moment having at least transient monopoly power: it will not instantaneously lose all its customers if it raises its price nor gain the whole market if it cuts its price.[26] Yet over time the effect of such a price variation will be more appreciable as information on price differentials becomes more diffused through the

[23] One might ask, is there some nonsteady-state path of employment back to steady-state equilibrium, a path along which new and current expectations are validated? No, not generally, I should think, for the path that ratifies price expectations need not presumably ratify expectations of money wage rates.

[24] It must be emphasized that the unforeseen rise of the price level causes workers to believe that an additional dollar of money wage earnings offers increased command over future goods only if the unforeseen price increase causes a rise of the expected real rate of interest—the money rate plus the expected rate of decrease of future consumption-good prices. The latter is assumed to increase when there is an unexpected increase of the current price level; but this assumes that the regressive effect—future prices are expected to regress to their expected long-term trend—overcomes the extrapolative effect—the long-term trend rate of increase may be adapted upward. Is that assumption generally appropriate? As for the money rate of interest, there is no reason to suppose that it invariably falls by the amount of the expected rate of decrease of future prices. But what of an inflation that is triggered by open market purchases or credit expansion? A considerable literature suggests that inflationary episodes are frequently associated with a depression of expected real rates of interest. Perhaps Lucas-Rapping are right for the opposite reasons: unexpected price increases may be typically extrapolated, money interest rates may typically rise (if at all) by less than the expected rate of future price increase and the income effect of the resulting fall of expected real interest rates induces an increase of labor supply.

[25] In a manner of speaking, the derived demand for labor can be shown to shift like the effective supply of labor.

[26] The analogy to the Phelps-Mortensen attention to the dynamical monopsony power of the firm in labor markets should be clear.

market. I shall restrict attention here to the special case in which the firm is asymptotically competitive; it knows that setting a price permanently above the expected "going price" in the economy for comparable goods would ultimately cost it its entire market share, while setting a price permanently below the going price would ultimately capture a huge number of customers. In such an economy, we can imagine a non-Walrasian equilibrium in which, on the product side, for every firm, the inflow of newborn customers just matches the outflow of customers; the firm believes therefore that its price is just competitive, being equal to prices charged elsewhere; likewise, its customers believe they are being charged the going price elsewhere.

There are two obvious theorems about "markups" (over marginal cost) in that equilibrium. The first propostion is that the firm does not fully exploit its transient monopoly position. It produces beyond the point where marginal cost equals instantaneous marginal revenue because it estimates that a temporary rise of price, while bringing a larger cash flow for the immediate future, would be offset in the future by the resulting erosion of its market share. The second proposition is that the firm produces less than that output rate at which its marginal costs would equal the equilibrium going price. To obtain the larger cash flow which greater sales at the going price would seem to offer, the firm would have temporarily to reduce its price in order to attract additional customers. Provided the expected real rate of interest is positive, there is some gap between marginal cost and price which is small enough that the present sacrifice of cash flow entailed by a small temporary price cut (remember the firm is already producing too much from a myopic view) is not worth the discounted future increase of cash flow which the resulting customer gain would bring.[27]

There is a kind of excess capacity in this equilibrium state. If we think of the array of "machines," each of which can produce a unit of output but which generally differ in their labor requirements, then some of the more labor intensive of these machines will be idle even though, at the going product wage, some revenue would be left over as rent for these machines if their output could find a buyer without the aforementioned costs. There may be excess capacity in another sense: it can happen that output increases are obtainable from an increase of aggregate demand without any decline of product wage rates.[28]

To see that in principle real wage rates can move procyclically, we note that, given the parameters controlling the expected rate of response of customer flow to a change in the firm's price, the firm's optimal price is homogeneous of degree one in the height of its instantaneous demand curve, the money wage rate and the expected going price elsewhere.[29] Its optimal output is homogeneous of degree zero in these variables. Now suppose that an increase of aggregate demand produces an isoelastic upward shift of the firm's demand curve and that money wage rates happen to rise in the same proportion. If the firm's expectation of the going price at competing firms is unchanged or is revised upwards in smaller proportion to the rise

[27] The same propositions can be deduced if the firm is in an analogous position in the labor market, having at every moment some transient monopsonistic power yet being an asymptotically competitive buyer of labor.

[28] Nevertheless, there need be no excess capacity in the sense of depressed output at the equilibrium employment level. Decrees to cut price relative to marginal costs would increase national output only if an increase of real wage rates would increase the quantity of labor supplied.

[29] For this exercise, I postulate a Walrasian and competitive labor market in which the firm is a wage taker.

of its own demand, then it is possible that the firm will want to raise its price less than proportionally to its instantaneous "demand price," meeting the additional quantity demanded with greater output (and greater employment). To raise its price in full proportion to the rise of the demand price at the intitial equilibrium output would be to neglect its belief that such a price increase would worsen its competitiveness.[30] The disequilibrium result, then, is a rise of real wage rates and an increase of output and employment.[31] In the symmetrical situation of a fall of demand and of money wage rates, producers let their markups increase, failing to realize that they must cut price further if they are to maintain their competitiveness. Thus the price level may fall by less than the money wage rate level despite the fall of output and employment.[32]

A Phillipsian relation between the output level (relative to capacity) and the rate of price increase results if each firm continuously adjusts upwards its price as it learns that it is not experiencing a net loss of customers from its higher price and as money wage rates keep pace with the general price level. The now familiar qualification must again be made: the long-run trend rates of increase of money wage rates, of demand, and of the going price elsewhere expected by the firm figure as parameters in any such steady-state Phillips relation. As these expected trend rates adapt to perceived trends, the Phillips relation floats upward.

Inventories, Excess Capacity, and Stochastic Demand. Still another model of economic fluctuations in output emerges from recent analyses of optimal pricing and/or production by the supplier of a good under conditions of uncertainty about future price or demand. The uncertainty attaches to the profitability of leaving some output unsold in the present when a choice must be made between selling the output in the present or in the future.

Edward Zabel [17] has studied a model of production and sales by a perfectly competitive firm that can store its output under increasing marginal storage costs. In the simplest version, the firm has a stationary subjective probability distribution of the market price in each future period. The occurrence of an abnormally low price will normally cause the firm to sell relatively little and to increase its inventory. If the money wage facing the firm is constant and if the firm's inventory holdings were not already large, the increase in their quantity will reduce the firm's optimal output; for with rising marginal holding cost, it is more likely now than last period that any increase of output (relative to last period's) would end up being sold next period for the mean expected price—rather than being held for a somewhat higher expectation of revenue on chance of an abnormally high price subsequently—since marginal holding costs of inventory have increased with the increase in inventory held. Whether total output in this competitive economy will fall depends upon the response of money wage rates. If we postulate a positively sloped labor supply curve against money wage rates (which is plausible

[30] Formally, the output effect in this situation can be viewed as the result of a *ceteris paribus* fall of the prices which the firm believes other firms to be changing. Such a fall will cause it to reduce its markup, being grateful for whatever additional output is demanded as a result.

[31] D. H. Robertson seems to have had the clue to this process when he wrote: ". . . the stimulus of rising prices is partly founded in illusion . . . [the business leader] is spurred on . . . by imaginary gains at the expense of his fellow business men. It is so hard to believe at first that other people will really have the effrontery or the good fortune to raise their charges as much as he has raised his own" [11].

[32] This result is a possibility, not a necessity, in the model. Further, I believe that it is a less likely result if the firm has transient monopsony power. In an unforeseen inflation, the tendency to underestimate going wage rates may tend to dampen the firm's wage increase relative to its price increase.

since expected mean future prices levels are constant, though the expected real interest rate has increased since Zabel holds the money interest rate constant), aggregate output and employment will fall. In a recent note, I looked into the question of whether money wage rates could be depressed proportionally more than the current price of goods, so that "measured" real wage rates are not generally implied to move countercyclically [9]. This appears to be a possibility. Note finally that adaptations by firms of their expectations of the mean price when actual prices continue to deviate from the expected mean price will produce a Phillips phenomenon —with the usual qualifications about the "stability" of the trade-off.

Previous work by Oscar Lange [5] and by Robert Clower [2] was addressed to the problem of the ignorant monopolist facing a stationary demand curve. The aforementioned paper by Gordon and Hynes analyzes the monopolist who faces a stochastic demand curve. Their paper fits the problem of the owner of an apartment building who must offer one-year leases on his apartments. Simplifying somewhat, they imagine that the owner sets a rental on vacant apartments each day or period. The owner does not aim to set the rental so low that there would be a high probability of no vacancies each day. A higher rental is superior for the usual buffer-stock reason.

An increase of mean demand will at first reduce the vacancy rate. Rentals on vacant apartments are sticky because the increase of mean demand is mistaken for a random deviation. As this experience with the below-equilibrium vacancy rate continues, the owner will begin to "adapt" his subjective estimate of the mean demand at his current rental, raising his rentals accordingly. If aggregate demand is steadily increased so as to permit the below-equilibrium vacancy rate to continue, the upward adjustments of apartment rentals continues as owners grope for the mean of the distribution. This is the temporary Phillips relation at work. But owners eventually learn that they must raise rentals faster than they have been doing if they are to succeed in restoring their vacancy rates. Gordon and Hynes declare that there cannot be a stable law of disequilibrium price dynamics for the same reason that one cannot have a stable law for use in predicting individual stock price movements. When others learn the law, it is no longer descriptive. Their point goes deep but just how deep we cannot pursue here.

True "User Cost" and Neoclassical Speculative Capital Utilization. Following Keynes and Sidney Weintraub [16], there has been a revival of interest in the consequences of (true) "user cost." That term refers to the fact that some machinery deteriorates faster the greater the speed with which it is run and the greater the number of shifts per day (because maintenance opportunities are thereby reduced). Paul Taubman and Maurice Wilkinson [14] have looked into the consequences of user cost for the optimal output and investment decisions of the competitive firm, generally under static expectations.

The concept of user cost together with adaptive expectations may be capable of offering an additional reason why unforeseen price movements can cause output changes despite unchanged product wage rates. Let all product prices and money wage rates rise unexpectedly and in the same proportion. Suppose that prices and wages are adaptively expected to regress gradually in the direction of their previous level. Consider now the producer who can neither sell his existing capital nor buy additional capital. It is then obvious that the firm will want to add shifts and speed up its machinery since marginal money quasi-rent from so doing increases in proportion to current prices and wage rates, while the money shadow-price of capital utilization, which reflects future expected quasi-rents, increases in smaller proportion.[33] Thus the process of unforeseen inflation can produce a rightward shift of output supply and labor demand through user cost.[34] But, once again, increasing inflation is presumably necessary to maintain the disequilibrium.

III. *Conclusions*

There is a common thread running through all these models. Each one postulates that the actors of the model have to maximize as best they can under incomplete information about the future or even about the present situation outside their respective sampled domains. Lacking the desired knowledge, the actors (at least implicitly) form expectations of the state of the economy—over space and over time. The supply prices of outputs and of labor services and the demand prices for labor are linear-homogeneous in known and expected prices (including expected mean demand prices in the stochastic case)—present and future; and quantity decisions are homogeneous of degree zero in these variables. On adaptative or more general error-correcting expectational hypotheses, a change of aggregate demand alters the relations between known or sampled prices and expected prices. The implied alteration of expected relative prices—of expected wage rates elsewhere relative to sampled rates, of expected mean future demand prices relative to current demand prices, of expected real rates of interest, etc.—causes a change in quantity decisions, hence employment and output. If public policy maintains a disequilibrium in which expectations on average are systematically in error, learning causes expectations to be revised—and with them the supply and demand prices for labor services and the supply prices of outputs. It seems to be widely believed that maintenance of the disequilibrium, and thus the regeneration of these expectational errors, requires or would cause explosiveness in the rates of change of actual prices.

[33] This assumes, in Lucas-Rapping fashion, that the money rate of interest at which current quasi-rents can be lent has not fallen, if at all, by as much as (or more than) the expected rate of decline of future prices and wage rates.

[34] Taubman and Wilkinson are verifying and further developing this hypothesis in a forthcoming manuscript

REFERENCES

1. A. Alchian, "Information Costs, Pricing, and Resource Unemployment," forthcoming in E. S. Phelps, A. Alchian, C. C. Holt, *et al., Microeconomic Foundations of Employment and Inflation Theory* (New York, 1969).
2. R. W. Clower, "Some Theory of an Ignorant Monopolist," *Econ. J.*, Dec., 1959.
3. D. F. Gordon and A. Hynes, "On the Theory of Price Dynamics," forthcoming in *Microeconomic Foundations of Employment and Inflation Theory, op. cit.*
4. C. C. Holt, "Job Search, Phillips' Wage Relation and Union Evidence: Theory and Evidence," forthcoming in *Microeconomic Foundations of Employment and Inflation Theory, op. cit.*
5. O. Lange, *Price Flexibility and Full Employment* (Bloomington, 1944).
6. A. Leijonhufvud, *Keynesian Economics and the Economics of Keynes* (New York, 1968).
7. R. E. Lucas and L. A. Rapping, "Real Wages, Employment and Inflation," forthcoming in *Microeconomic Foundations of Employment and Inflation Theory, op. cit.*
8. D. T. Mortensen, "A Theory of Wage and Employment Dynamics," forthcoming in *Microeconomic Foundations of Employment and Inflation Theory, op. cit.*
9. E. S. Phelps, "A Note on the Real Wage-

Employment Relation in Zabel's Competitive Inventory Model," *Int. Econ. Rev.* (forthcoming).
10. ———, "Money-Wage Dynamics and Labor-Market Equilibrium," *J.P.E.*, July-Aug., 1968, Part II.
11. E. S. PHELPS AND S. G. WINTER, JR., "Optimal Price Policy under Atomistic Competition," forthcoming in *Microeconomic Foundations of Employment and Inflation Theory, op. cit.*
12. D. H. ROBERTSON, *Money* (Cambridge, 1929).
13. G. J. STIGLER, "Information in the Labor Market," *J.P.E.*, Oct., 1962, Part II.
14. P. TAUBMAN AND M. WILKINSON, "User Cost, Capital Utilization and Investment Theory," Pennsylvania discussion paper, 1968.
15. J. TOBIN, "Money Wage Rates and Employment," in S. E. Harris, ed., *The New Economics* (New York, 1952).
16. S. WEINTRAUB, *Price Theory* (New York, 1949).
17. E. ZABEL, "A Dynamic Model of the Competitive Firm," *Int. Econ. Rev.*, June, 1967.

Part II
MACROEQUILIBRIUM EMPLOYMENT

INTRODUCTION

This group of papers gives closer scrutiny than do the previous papers to the idea of the "natural" rate of unemployment. My association with that concept goes back to my 1967 essay on optimal inflation control, collected here in the fourth group of papers, which gave the idea an algebraic formulation. There I dubbed the concept the "warranted" rate of unemployment because, in the model there, it is that unemployment level which is called for *if* the public's expectations of the rate of inflation are to be met. Since a characteristic of Roy Harrod's "warranted rate of growth" was that it might be manipulated if otherwise it would cause harm, I thought I had hit upon a value-free term. But Milton Friedman's catchy term for the same idea, though derived from a different model, was the easy winner. Not that I (nor Friedman) was the first to conceive or utilize the idea: Hayek, Mises, Fellner, and Wallich all talked and wrote about it in earlier decades, and the latter two taught it to me. It runs in the blood of economists between the Danube and the Rhein.

What I have sometimes called the *natural rate hypothesis* consists of two propositions. The first states that a given degree of disequilibrium in the labor market—as measured by the excess of the actual rate of wage inflation over the expected rate—could be maintained or exceeded indefinitely only if the expected rate of wage inflation, and therefore the actual rate, were made to increase without bound. Of course there are upper and lower bounds on the expected rate of price inflation, and thus the expected rate of wage inflation, that a monetary economy can accommodate, so this formulation is a little odd. To put the proposition another way, any disequilibrium in the labor market must eventually vanish and the course of employment must converge to its equilibrium path as long as the rate of change of aggregate demand—we may think here of the growth rate of the money supply—stays within certain bounds outside of which monetary equilibrium ceases to be possible. Subject to that proviso, then, expectations tend to be equilibrating.

The second proposition states that, with regard to any equilibrium scenario, the addition of a fixed number of points to the percentage growth rates of wages and prices will not have any permanent effect upon the equilibrium path of employment. In a model in which there is no overhang of previously set money-wage rates and money prices, there will not result even a temporary alteration of the equilibrium path of employment. In particular, the equilibrium steady-state rate of unemployment to which the equilibrium path of the unemployment rate converges under essentially stationary conditions is invariant to the addition of k points to the steady rate of wage and price inflation. The equilibrium steady-state unemployment rate, if inflation-invariant, is called the "natural" rate. Any stimulus to employment that would otherwise have been produced by the faster growth of aggregate demand generating the faster inflation is offset by the necessarily equal rise of the expected rate of wage inflation prevailing in this equilibrium state.

The upshot of the natural rate hypothesis is that monetary and fiscal policies engineering faster growth of aggregate demand will make no permanent difference for the rate of unemployment: The equilibrium unemployment rate will not be permanently affected, and the actual unemployment rate will converge to its equilibrium path. Likewise, the deliberate gearing down of the growth rate of aggregate demand will not produce a permanent reduction of employment, only a transient depression however protracted. The acknowledged existence of boundary rates of inflation and deflation qualify this conclusion a little. And there may, of course, be political limits to the inflation and deflation that can be engineered without there resulting changes in the institutional setting that might affect the equilibrium rate of unemployment.

The two papers in this group expressed my attitude toward the natural rate hypothesis. I was amazed, on the one hand, that it met not just empirical skepticism but methodological resistance as well—as if the hypothesis were a violation of basic tenets in economic theory. I had thought the shoe was on the other foot, although anyone would have been aware that the hypothesis would not be widely accepted until better empirical evidence and tests on its behalf could be provided. The tide was finally turned with the publication of the paper by Thomas Sargent[1] in which he pointed out the inappropriateness in typical time-series studies of adopting (without modification) the adaptive expectations hypothesis for the purpose of testing the natural rate hypothesis.

I did not, on the other hand, delude myself that the natural rate hypothesis was the inescapable implication of high economic theory. How could one be sure that in the true expectations-generalized Phillips equa-

[1] T. J. Sargent, "A Note on the 'Accelerationist' Controversy," *Journal of Money, Credit and Banking*, Vol. 3, No. 3 (August 1971).

tion, say

$$w - w_{-1} = \phi(N, N_{-1}; \ldots) + w^{e} - w_{-1},$$

such variables as the expected rates of price and wage inflation and indeed certain policy parameters did not figure importantly after the semicolon in the ϕ function? We know the quantity theorem of Hume and Patinkin to be inexact in the most general of monetary models. The natural rate hypothesis deals more generally with the effects of changes in the growth rate as well as the initial level of the money supply.

The first of the papers in this section discusses a few of the many qualifications to which the natural rate hypothesis is no doubt subject. Some of these were cited in my 1968 paper on wage dynamics and new ones were entertained in my 1972 book.[2] Today it is common to emphasize above all that faster inflation, even when anticipated, erodes the value of money as a unit of account in terms of which we record and store our observations of wages and prices. While this point has long been recognized in the balance sheets of costs and benefits from inflation, I imagined that it would cause lower unemployment to result from higher inflation—owing to a human tendency to underestimate the power of compound growth, the more so the faster the growth rate. But some economists incline to the view that it would cause higher unemployment to result from higher inflation—because, knowing they are confused, people will feel they have more to gain from searching for better wages and prices.

The other paper in this group inquires into the theoretical possibility that ordinary monetary and fiscal actions by the government influence directly the path of employment in steady-state equilibrium, independently of how they may alter the expected rate of inflation and independently of whether such an alteration has the effect (contrary to the natural rate hypothesis) of changing the equilibrium employment level. Changes in public expenditures and taxation as well as open-market operations to change the money supply are generally agreed to have a variety of effects on real variables—real wealth and liquidity, saving, and real rates of interests—in nearly every model of intertemporal equilibrium. It would be surprising, therefore, if these "real effects" did not have ramifications for the equilibrium state of the labor market.

[2] E. S. Phelps, *Inflation Policy and Unemployment Theory,* New York: W. W. Norton and Co., 1972, pp. 52–57.

THE 'NATURAL RATE' CONTROVERSY AND ECONOMIC THEORY

The Significance of the Natural Rate Controversy

In the field of macroeconomic policy there are important divisions within the profession over inflation objectives, over the feasibility and desirability of alternative instruments to secure them, and the benefits that would be gained thereby. In part, these criticisms may be traceable to the generally increased expressiveness and outspokenness on social issues; but the criticisms being expressed also imply intensified doubts about the reliability, insight and utility of many accepted descriptions of how an economy like that in America or Canada works.

The recent dispute over the Phillips Curve occupies a prominent place on this battle-front. Ten years ago the Phillips Curve replaced the orthodox "Keynesian" supposition of a "flat" relationship between the rate of price change and the level of employment. If low unemployment were maintained by monetary and fiscal policies, it would be accompanied by some inflation – the larger the inflation rate the lower the unemployment rate, according to the negatively sloped curve.

Today the opposition to the Phillips Curve comes at the opposite flank to those who argue the fundamental importance of expectations of price and wage changes. With a looseness that is pardonable in battle-front coverage, one may say that the enemy is now the hypothesis of a natural rate of unemployment. That hypothesis states that a permanent step-increase of the inflation rate will bring only a temporary fall of the unemployment rate below the natural rate. A permanent reduction of the unemployment rate to a figure below the natural level would require an ever increasing inflation rate.

There are political overtones to this dispute that parallel the political aspects of some of the other issues being discussed these days. Economists from both sides have noted that, at least when inflation is maintained at a low rate, the social and institutional factors at work in the labour markets produce too much unemployment, especially among unskilled and minority workers. Phillips Curve proponents contended that aggregate demand policies favouring moderate inflation would largely solve this problem. If the natural rate hypothesis is tolerably accurate, however, then we need important reforms in the workings of our labour and product markets and perhaps in the private institutions that operate in these markets.

It goes without saying that the monetary and fiscal policy-makers have also had a lively interest in the Phillips Curve dispute. Its outcome is likely, at least in America where balance of payments considerations are less binding, to influence the path of inflation, up or down, that they will regard as most desirable. Please note, however, that one can be an inflationist, as I am, without holding out much hope that anyone's "long-run Phillips Curve" is anything but very steep,

Reprinted by permission from *Inflation and the Canadian Experience,* Industrial Relations Centre, Queen's University, Kingston, Ontario, 1971.

perhaps even exactly vertical, at some moderately low rates of unemployment. Conversely, there are some who prefer zero inflation, properly measured, even if such price stability proves to be obtainable only at a large price in terms of unemployment.

From the political and macropolicy points of view, however, it must surely be said that the bad news is pretty much in. If we have learned anything from the past 24 months it is that the econometrician's "medium-run Phillips Curve 1965-1970" is awfully steep at the unaccustomedly high inflation rates of that period. Econometricians continue to fit lagged "long-run Phillips Curves" containing lagged wage change and price change variables. They still (whatever they are worth) exhibit the traditional negative slope of that curve as conceived by Phillips. But what a slope! Certainly the recent inflationary episode has brought home how little unemployment reduction we can expect to be purchasable from even a 6 percent rate of inflation per annum. Small differences in the steepness of a "long-run Phillips Curve" can make only small differences for scientific economic policy, a point that last-ditch defenders of the Phillips Curve sometimes appear to overlook.

For the future, therefore, it seems to me that the significance of the dispute between exponents of the natural rate hypothesis and defenders of the Phillips Curve hypothesis will lie in the area of economic theory. Here at least there is special significance in the question of the long-run economic consequences of alternative inflation rate targets. If a higher long-run average inflation rate is found to have little or no effect on the average unemployment rate over the long run, that fact would be remarkable confirmation of highly standard economic theory over alternative theories, some articulated, some not, some departing radically from the standard, some only marginally.

Reading Kuhn's book, *The Structure of Scientific Revolutions,* put me in mind of the present skirmishes over the Phillips Curve. As Kuhn describes so tellingly, the hypotheses and descriptions that constitute the prevailing paradigm for research scientists is a tough cat to kill – not the fragile creature of Popper's diffident scientist. The normal description or theory is finally relinquished only when there is an attractive alternative to move to – and then only slowly. Until that time, the prevailing paradigm cannot be budged. There is an earlier example of this phenomenon from the very area of unemployment and inflation that we are talking about in the postwar period when numerous writers asserted the risks of cost-push inflation in times of high aggregate demand and correspondingly high employment. Yet as the formal construct used for teaching purposes and, I think, to a large extent for policy-making purposes, the orthodox Keynesian concept of a flat Phillips Curve (up to the point beyond which an inflationary gap would occur) continued to rule in normal economics. The orthodox theory continued to be defended on an *ad hoc* basis against acknowledged deviations of the data from the strict predictions of that theory. It was always possible to insist that the orthodox theory left room for random stochastic disturbances – the animal spirits of Jimmy Hoffa, crop failures, or vicissitudes in the degree of monopoly power. By treating the anomalies of 1937, 1946, 1950 and 1956 as unsystematic, or random, it was possible to cling to the orthodox viewpoint. It was not until the arrival of Phillips' paper and its official recognition on these shores by Samuelson and Solow that the orthodox left-hand-L or inflationary gap dogma was finally abandoned.

Now it is the Phillips Curve that constitutes orthodoxy. Again certain facts appear to be flatly inconsistent with the orthodox view. How can the Phillips men explain the co-existence of 6 percent inflation per annum this summer in America with a measured unemployment rate that is about 5 percent and is still rising? The downward momentum of employment in the past few months may make matters worse for the Phillips Curve hypothesis than they appear; for if the *rate of change* of aggregate demand has a positive influence upon the rate of inflation then the current unemployment rate of 5 percent would correspond to a somewhat higher inflation rate if the economy were stable at the present unemployment rate. The rise of the inflation rate during 1969 is another plus for the natural rate hypothesis: it demonstrates vividly the influence of upwardly adapting inflation expectations when the economy is sitting above the natural employment level or even falling gently down to that level. A modified Phillips Curve theory which gives less weight to past price or wage changes than the natural rate hypothesis has a harder time explaining the acceleration of prices in 1969.

Once again we find *ad hoc* defences of the orthodox view, this time from the orthodox Phillips Curvers. It has been an education, and I am not being entirely facetious, to watch the inventiveness of the defenders of the orthodox theory. We have learned in the past two years that the structure of the labour market has changed so that an unemployment rate of 4 percent in America constitutes a much more taut labour market in 1970 than it did in the 1950's. Therefore, less of the inflation in 1969, say, is to be attributed to expectations of inflation than one would have thought, and more is to be attributed to the tautness of the labour market in Phillips Curve fashion. We have also been alerted to the possibility that when the Nixon administration forswore the policy option of moral suasion, whatever the utility of that option might have been then, or at some time in the future, corporations in a number of industries seized the opportunity to raise their mark-ups and thus exacerbated the inflation in the first half of 1969. Another pertinent observation made by Phillips Curve defenders is the unexpected growth of the labour force, particularly women, that accompanied the increased tightness of the labour market during 1968 and 1969. If the Phillips Curve were to be measured in terms of employment per unit of population, instead of the unemployment rate, a flatter short-run curve could perhaps be fitted to the data – but not necessarily a flatter long-run curve.

While it is not dwelt upon by Kuhn, it might be added that the defenders of orthodoxy are sometimes tempted to employ tactics of careless misunderstanding and kidding of the dissenters. I was a little stunned by one man's capsule characterization of the natural rate hypothesis: "We have a pregnancy model of inflation where there is no way to be just a little bit pregnant, at least not for very long. So we must set aggregate demand policies to eliminate inflation, for anything less is ruin."[1] The natural rate hypothesis means that macroequilibrium at the same old natural rate of unemployment is just as conceivable at 5 percent inflation as at zero percent – a great deal easier to conceive these days in fact. Another ploy is to suggest that "long-run" trade-offs are of no relevance for policy: something will turn up. A defender of the Phillips Curve writes: " . . . the trade-off . . . may not be 'permanent'; but it lasts long enough for

1. George Perry, "Inflation and Unemployment", *Annual Conference on Savings and Residential Financing*, May 7-8, 1970, p. 5.

me".[2] This is an expression of personal time preference regarding economic policy, not a refutation of the natural rate hypothesis, and it comes most strangely from growth theorists who a decade ago plugged for more abstemious capital deepening and wore their hair shirts proudly. The other tactic I notice is a tendency to associate the natural rate concept and the models supporting it solely with Milton Friedman. Because he is too extreme on exponential money growth and unmanaged exchange rates, the natural rate hypothesis must also be far out. In fact, Friedman is neither the earliest nor a particularly persuasive exponent of the natural rate hypothesis. He is the most extreme.

There is, however, an important and highly curious dissimilarity between the recent crisis for the Phillips Curve and the characteristic overthrow of a scientific paradigm described by Kuhn. While the Phillips Curve defenders willingly wear the mantle of orthodoxy – they are at least the ones on the defensive – they are not in fact legitimate standard-bearers of normal economic theory. It is really the natural rate hypothesis that depends, however precariously, upon the current paradigm of normal economic science – not just "neoclassical" economics but the post-neoclassical economics (all right, neo-neoclassical economics) of behaviour under risk and uncertainty. I refer of course to the normal postulate of the maximization by each individual of the mathematical expectation of his lifetime utility relative to his perception of the constraints or his Bayesian estimates of those constraints. In this set-up, the individual compares benefits to opportunity costs and his subjectively "optimal policy" or best strategy depends upon his subjective probability distributions of real quantities and relative prices (including, strictly, the leisure cost of acquiring real liquidity). The normal paradigm leads naturally to the natural rate hypothesis – making certain approximations discussed below, and confining the hypothesis to inflation rates that are not too extreme.

It is of considerable importance to economic theory, therefore, for us to determine the degree of accuracy (or inaccuracy) of the natural rate hypothesis. With this end in mind I will devote the next section of this paper to a discussion of some of the ways in which I believe that recent Phillipsian tests of the natural rate hypothesis need improvement.* To be very Kuhnian, though, I should say that the continual re-estimation and refurbishing of Phillips Curves to rebut or incorporate criticism is likely to be a dying industry. The basic notion of a short-run trade-off will undoubtedly survive; it has already survived from Hume's day. So far as the long-run consequences of alternative inflation paths are concerned, however, I suspect that it will become customary to start with the paradigm of utility maximization. Then the question will be, in what qualitative ways might the presence of this or that feature in the particular time and place, various factors "outside" the neoclassical paradigm, cause one to want to qualify the natural rate hypothesis? This will appear to the profession as a tidier, more illuminating and more fruitful way to think about the longer-run consequences of alternative inflation policies. The outcome of this rethinking will not include any "stable" or ahistorical "long-run Phillips Curve" at all. I will illustrate this thought in the last section.

---

2. Robert M. Solow, *Price Expectations and the Behaviour of the Price Level* (Manchester: Manchester University Press, 1970), p. 17.

***This section, now econometrically obsolete, has been deleted.**

The Natural Rate Hypothesis and Economic Theory

I maintained in the first section of this paper that normal economic theory leads naturally to the hypothesis of the natural rate of unemployment. Yet the natural rate hypothesis should be understood as an approximation for it deliberately neglects feedbacks upon the unemployment rate from variables that are explicitly recognized in the normal theoretical framework. I shall give a few examples of places where approximations clearly have to be made in arriving at the natural rate hypothesis before proceeding to the question of whether or not the normal theoretical paradigm that is used for arriving at the natural rate hypothesis is itself only a very rough approximation to economic reality.

Approximations made. A more general concept than the natural unemployment rate is the unemployment rate that would prevail in a particular specified macroeconomic equilibrium. I shall say that the system is in macroequilibrium if the actual rate of inflation is equal to the average expected rate of inflation – where we are averaging over people. Strictly speaking, this notion of macroequilibrium also requires that the actual rate of increase of the mean money wage rate be rising at the average expected rate of increase, as indicated in the previous section. The macroequilibrium is a steady-state equilibrium if the rate of inflation in question is constant over time and when by virtue of some underlying stationarity in the system, the unemployment rate corresponding to that equilibrium is also constant over time.

In principle, there could be a different steady-state equilibrium unemployment rate corresponding to each different steady rate of inflation. The natural rate hypothesis in these terms states that, to a first approximation, the macroequilibrium unemployment rate is independent of the rate of inflation when there is macroeconomic equilibrium. Yet, as I have suggested, normal economic theory does not promise any exact invariance.

The slippage between the exact implications of the normal theory on the one hand, and the natural rate hypothesis on the other, arise from the fact, a fact perfectly well representable in the normal theory, that monetary, fiscal, and calculational efficiencies in any real life economy being described are a good deal less than "100 percent".

Consider the matter of monetary efficiency. Because some kinds of money do not bear interest – more aptly, it is administratively too expensive to pay interest to holders of some kinds of money like coin and currency – a higher rate of actual and expected inflation has for some time been recognized to be equivalent of an increase in the "tax" on money-holding. Like other taxes, a tax on liquidity has both a substitution effect and an income effect. The substitution effect makes people devote more of their time to economizing on their cash balances and hence to spend less of their time engaged in market employment or in leisure. Firms at the same time will be driven to divert some of their work force to activities that economize on the holding of non-interest bearing cash balances. The upshot presumably is on this account some decline in the macroequilibrium employment level. Whether the macroequilibrium unemployment rate per unit measured labour force would be increased is, however, somewhat problematic.

The income effect of an increase in the tax on liquidity is normally to reduce the demand for leisure and to reduce the demand for consumption – if other tax rates are held constant. This tends by itself to increase the natural employment level and to increase the fraction of net national product that goes for capital formation. These effects, too, will presumably have some influence upon the natural employment level.

It is, of course, open to the fiscal authorities to nullify that income effect by an appropriate decrease in the ordinary taxation rate under their jurisdiction (upon consent of the legislature). To the extent that ordinary tax rates are reduced so as to tend to nullify the income effect of the increased tax on liquidity, we have a lessening of the substitution effect of those taxes "in return" for the substitution effect from the increased tax on liquidity. Presumably, the reduction of these ordinary tax rates will have substitution effects tending to reduce the demand for leisure – we know, for example, that income taxation is a subsidy to leisure taking – and this tends to increase the natural employment level and thus to offset the opposite substitution effect upon the macroequilibrium employment level of the increased tax on liquidity. The net effect after the substitution of one tax for another is not clear to me, and I imagine that in the range of moderate alternative inflation rates the net effect, whatever it is, is not quantitatively important. (This does not mean that the net effect for "economic welfare" is not important.)

It may be that the inability of people to make exact corrections for the trend rates of change of money prices and money wage rates is a more important source of error in the natural rate hypothesis. In comparing an automobile price today with a different price on a different automobile six months earlier, the householder may fail to make adequate correction for the trend in the general price level even though he understands full well that there is such a trend and even though he has estimated the trend rate correctly. How many executives, professionals and professors would appreciate that in a steady regime of 5 percent inflation per year an offer of $24,000 this year is not as good "relative to the market" as an offer of $22,500 last year (assuming 3 percent growth of the mean real wage per annum). On this line of thinking it is plausible to hypothesize that the higher the steady rate of inflation in macroequilibrium, the smaller is the equilibrium amount of leisure and the smaller is the equilibrium amount of consumption – with obvious implications for the natural employment level and the level of investment in the economy. Of course, if the steady inflation rate were great enough then some other unit of account might be devised to replace the medium of exchange for that purpose.

The above remarks on the difficulties of logarithmic calculations may remind the reader of money illusion, but I take it that money illusion refers to the difficulties of a perceptual and perhaps psychological nature in adjusting to a higher or lower level of money prices and money wage rates. There may very well be such money illusion and if so, while one would expect that a higher price level would eventually come to be adjusted to, the tendency of the price level to continue to rise might very well cause a permanent gap between reality and perceptions to persist. Sometimes economists label money illusion as irrational and appear to draw the conclusion that it is unlikely to be found to any marked degree in human behaviour. I think that we have to be prepared to concede that human behaviour is not wholly rational at all times, so that, in principle, we should be prepared to allow considerable room for money illusion in our predictions of the consequences of truly important social and economic public policies. I am, however, inclined to agree with those theorists who believe that, so far as our formal models are concerned, the postulate of money illusion should be the very last resort, something that should be appealed to only when all the other factors we can think of appear to be grossly inadequate in explaining behaviour.

Hysteresis factors. Let me turn now to some more fundamental defects of our normal theoretical paradigm with the natural rate hypothesis in mind – leaving money illusion aside. Normal economic theory proceeds on the assumption that people behave "as if" they had an infinite amount of time available to them to make a mental note of every price quotation they perceive and to decide in the light of their prices and their income what their best decision is. In fact, taking mental stock of such signals as the ideal receiver would be aware of, and making the appropriate decision on the basis of the information stored, takes time and energy. It is perfectly possible, therefore, that we could have the outward appearance of a macroequilibrium in the economy, even though the actual rate of inflation exceeded the rate of inflation on whose expectation people operate. Some discrepancy between actual and expected inflation rates may be possible without any consequent revision of the expected inflation rate. This discrepancy might be of the same size no matter what the expected inflation rate that prevails. Hence, we might have a pseudo-equilibrium at 6 percent inflation per annum when people expect 4 percent inflation, but not when people expect 3 percent inflation; and likewise we might have a pseudo-equilibrium at 3 percent inflation when people expect inflation at 1 percent per annum – but not when they expect no inflation. This leads to the notion of the natural rate of unemployment as a band, not a point. Somewhere in the centre of that band is the "true" macroequilibrium unemployment rate but the unemployment rate can be maintained at either side of the true macroequilibrium rate so long as the resulting discrepancy between the actual and expected inflation rates is not "noticeable".

Such a generalization implies that there is indeed a "long-run" historical Phillips Curve but one heavily infused with the notion of the natural rate. At any moment in history, a "long-run" Phillips Curve cuts through "the" natural unemployment rate, considered as a point, with the characteristically negative slope but only within some band roughly centred on the natural rate. At some unemployment rate critically below the natural rate the long-run Phillips Curve becomes perfectly vertical; and at some unemployment rate critically above the natural rate, the long-run historical Phillips Curve again becomes perfectly vertical.

I believe that such a construction might be of considerable help in estimating the long-run effects of alternative inflation policies. It would help to meet a criticism – there is no way of telling for sure whether it is in fact a valid criticism – of the opponents of the natural rate hypothesis who say they find no evidence of steady or constant decline of the algebraic inflation rate when aggregate demand is bringing about an unemployment rate in the neighborhood of 5.5 or 6 percent. It might be that the "natural band" spans a range of unemployment rates running from about 4 percent in the U.S. economy to 6 percent.

I am not empowered by my fellow formulators of the natural rate hypothesis to make this concession to their antagonists, but it ought to be pointed out that even if this concession were to be welcomed by all, it would still leave the "message" of the natural rate hypothesizers very much the same. It would then be the case that the smallest unemployment rate in the band – 4 percent in my numerical illustration above – would have the "upside" properties of the natural rate of unemployment. If the monetary and fiscal authorities were to maintain the unemployment rate below that minimal figure in the band then, for the duration of that policy, the actual inflation rate would steadily increase – without bound if we assumed that the band is a vertical strip in Phillips Curve space. In the neighbourhood of that unemployment rate, aggregate demand policies which increase the inflation rate by a notch would bring only a "temporary" reduction of the rate of unemployment.

One might wonder what determines the height of the historical Phillips Curve inside the band where it exhibits a negative slope. The answer is the past history of experience with inflation and whatever other current and past events determine the expected rate of inflation when aggregate demand maintains unemployment inside the band. For example, governmental exhortations which reduce the expected rate of inflation would shift down the long-run Phillips Curve inside the band. To take another example, an episode of noticeable inflation in excess of expectations would shift up the negatively sloped historical Phillips Curve segment inside the band; consequently if it were desired to return to some unemployment rate inside the band after the disequilibrium excursion to the left of the band, we would find that the old unemployment rate would upon its restoration correspond to a higher steady inflation rate than was associated with it before the excursion. This is an illustration of the concept of "hysteresis" which refers to the dependence of a relationship between two variables upon the behaviour of one or both of them over the past.

Let me turn now to some other respects in which the normal theoretical paradigm may be an inadequate description of economic behaviour and accordingly mislead us about the natural rate hypothesis. So far as I know, normal economic theory gives no satisfying account of the existence, let alone the behaviour, of labour unions in the economy. As I understand it, the rarefied economics of perfectly frictionless markets and perfect certainty leave no room for a coalition of workers to form against some employer or employers and other workers that cannot be "blocked" by some other coalition. If one wants to introduce labour unions into an economy of certainty and perfect information, it is necessary (I am not saying reprehensible) to invoke "purely sociological" causal factors for the existence and survival of those unions. Happily, the progress that has been made in the past few years in thinking about markets operating under imperfect information offer some opportunities for economic explanations of the creation and survival and functions of labour unions. One of the functions served by a labour union presumably is to collect, analyze, disseminate and otherwise utilize information about the labour market beyond the ken or observation of any one labour union member. It may very well be, therefore, that the net effect of the presence of labour unions in an economy is to reduce somewhat the macroequilibrium unemployment rate that goes with any specified rate of actual and expected inflation. The present question for us is whether or not the operation of labour unions accords with or goes against the natural rate hypothesis.

A certain amount of unemployment can perhaps be attributed to the search by nonunion workers for union jobs, these jobs being relatively better-paying than the nonunion jobs typically open for blue-collar and low-skilled workers.

Finding a union job may be something like hitting the jackpot compared to finding vacancies in nonunion jobs for many members of the labour force. The presence of a high wage differential between union and nonunion work may have other and rather subtle effects upon the general macroequilibrium unemployment rate. It may be that many workers have feelings of resentment, a kind of dog-in-the-manger attitude, that causes them to be less committed to steady employment in the nonunion sector, less inclined to hold a job for a long time, more inclined to take time off, socializing in the neighbourhood or "hustling" or whatever, because of frustration and dissatisfaction with the absence of opportunity for relatively high-paying jobs for which there is no visible absence of qualification.

When aggregate demand creates a boom, an episode of disequilibrium inflation and high employment, there will be a tendency for some workers who had not belonged to unions to find union jobs during the boom. What will be the situation when equilibrium is re-established at some higher rate of inflation? With the ranks of the labour union now swollen because of the preceding boom, it is reasonable to suppose that the labour unions will have to set *relative* wage rates somewhat lower for the sake of the employment of their membership than they would have if the number of union members had not so increased. There seem to be two effects of this that suggest that the unemployment rate in the new equilibrium will be lower than in the old equilibrium attainable before the boom. First of all, there are now more workers who have the relatively greater job security that goes or that may go with belonging to a union. Second, with the equilibrium wage in union jobs now smaller relative to the wage in nonunion jobs in macroequilibrium there will tend to be less unemployment of the sort which is attributable to the union-nonunion wage differential. Again, we have here a hysteresis effect: the historical time-path to the prevailing macroequilibrium has a persisting influence upon the relationship between the new equilibrium unemployment rate and the corresponding rate of inflation.[4]

What other hysteresis effects upon the equilibrium unemployment rate might be expected to result from a boom of the sort I have described? After a boom, the economy may be left richer in material capital, in government debt, charge accounts, many things. Each of these may be expected to have some influence upon the unemployment rate that corresponds to the new macroequilibrium at the higher inflation rate. Of a long list of historical residues that would or might be left from such a boom, one of the most important for the matter of the equilibrium unemployment rate is job experience.

When people are engaged in sustained work of a kind which they have not experienced before, they change in a number of ways which are probably quite relevant to the equilibrium unemployment rate. For example, punctuality is about the most important habit any worker can acquire in the majority of jobs. For many of the people who are in the most-frequently-unemployed group, learning to be "reliable" and learning to work with other people are necessary attributes for continuation in the job. A successful experience in holding a job is also likely to increase the commitment of a person to steady job-holding. In addition, there may be a learning phenomenon going on for managers and supervisory personnel in addition to the experience they acquire in supervising

4. See Robert E. Hall, "Unionism and the Inflationary Bias of Labor Markets", University of California Discussion Paper, January 1970.

inexperienced and unassimilated members of the labour force. In these simple ways, it may be that a boom leads to the reduction of the equilibrium unemployment rate.

A boom also leaves effects upon the skills possessed by the members of the labour force. Many workers during a boom rise to more demanding jobs in the skill hierarchy than they could ordinarily qualify for in a less tight labour market. The upgrading of many workers that occurs during a boom may lead to a general rise in an average "quality" of the labour force. But for the behaviour of the macroequilibrium unemployment rate, what is crucial is the effect upon the differential between the skills of the skilled and the skills of the least skilled. A sudden general increase in the productivity of us all would not augur any reductions of the equilibrium unemployment rate if the history of past decades is any guide. Since it is the least skilled members of the labour force who tend to be the greatest beneficiaries of upgrading – the people with the top skills have nowhere else to go – it is plausible to suppose that the boom tends to make the labour force more homogeneous in terms of skills and this tendency would cause the macroequilibrium unemployment rate to be smaller.

The theme of these last two considerations, the operation of labour unions and the acquisition of job experience and better skills, has been that an increase of the steady rate of inflation may very well have some permanent effect in the downward direction upon the macroequilibrium unemployment rate, contrary to the natural rate hypothesis. Note however that these considerations do not necessarily lead to the re-establishment of a non-historical or "stable" Phillips Curve. What would happen, one may ask, if the monetary and fiscal authorities decided to restore the original rate of inflation? Would the economy then move back down a stable negatively sloped long-run Phillips Curve? I suppose that examples of hysteresis effects are possible such that a reversion to the original equilibrium state would be possible. It is more likely, however, that the re-establishment of the original and lower rate of inflation would not cause the economy to travel back down the way it came, or, to borrow a title by Thomas Wolfe, "You can't go home again".

Re-establishment of the original inflation rate would, I suspect, leave the corresponding equilibrium unemployment rate smaller than it was originally. Let me give an example. Suppose that the original macroequilibrium unemployment rate was 5 percent. Let the boom take the unemployment rate down to 3 percent, at the end of which an unemployment rate of 4 percent becomes equilibrating at some higher rate of inflation. If now it is desired to go back to the original rate of inflation one might need to drive the unemployment rate up to 6 percent – another 2 point discrepancy – for a length of time as long as the previous boom. Upon re-establishment of the original rate of inflation, what is the final equilibrium unemployment rate corresponding to it? Is it 5 percent, the original equilibrium unemployment rate? My guess is that it is somewhere between 5 percent and 4.5 percent, the latter being an average of the unemployment rate in the boom and the unemployment rate in the slump. Essentially, one is inserting into a price change equation not just the current employment level, perhaps one or two lagged employment levels, and an expected inflation rate proxy; one is also assigning some role to the sum of all past employment. It is like those learning-by-doing models in which the cumulative serial number on today's batch of output plays a role in determining the cost of producing that output. In a more refined model, one would want to introduce some attenuation or "depreciation" of past employments insofar as their influence is not inherited but rather dies with their direct beneficiaries.

The thoughts set out in this section are enough to illustrate the inadequacy of the natural rate hypothesis as an exact economic law. Really, this is just a reflection of the inadequacy of the normal paradigm of economic theory. It is important to note that in no way do they resuscitate any "long-run" Phillips Curve of an ahistorical and stable character.

MONEY, WEALTH, AND LABOR SUPPLY

We ordinarily think—at least I usually think—of the macroequilibrium level of employment as a constant, independent of practically everything. The concept of macroequilibrium is neoclassical, having nothing to do with Keynesian aggregate demand, and it conjures up vertical lines in (p, Y) and (E, Y) diagrams. The Phillips Curve diagram represents the macroequilibrium employment level as the absicca of the point where the actual inflation rate—the ordinate of the curve—equals the expected inflation rate; if the latter is zero, the macroequilibrium employment level is that at which the Phillips Curve corresponding to expectations of price stability intersects the horizontal employment axis. The natural rate hypothesis advanced by Lerner, Fellner, Phelps and Friedman goes as far as to propose that this equilibrium level of output is invariant to the expected rate of inflation. The counterhypothesis of some writers that the Phillips Curves indexed by successively greater expected inflation rate mark off successively higher equilibrium employment levels is one route (not necessarily a valid route) to denying that macroequilibrium is invariant to monetary and fiscal policies.

With this paper I propose to go back to square one and ask the question: How do monetary and fiscal actions by the government affect the macroequilibrium level of employment corresponding to any given rate of expected inflation? Consider, say, the Phillips Curve that is indexed by a zero expected rate of inflation. Does an open-market purchase by the monetary authorities shift this Phillips Curve, and thus affect the associated macroequilibrium employment level, and if so in what way? Does a change in the rate of taxation shift the curve? A change in the level of government expenditure?

Students of monetary theory may be reminded by these questions of the famous nonneutrality theorem of Lloyd Metzler [1] according to which an open-market purchase reduces the rate of interest by hastening the course of capital deepening. Metzler adduced a reverse Pigou Effect from such an open-market operation that retards consumption. Perhaps the major point

From *Journal of Economic Theory,* Vol. 5(1), August 1972.

of this brief paper is that the same operation has a reverse Pigou Effect on the volume of labor supply. But the consequences of fiscal shifts upon aggregate supply are also examined.

All this must seem very raffiné. We rightly conceive of monetary and fiscal actions as useful in moderating or precipitating movements of output and employment *away* from equilibrium. When economic activity exceeds the equilibrium level, and expectations of inflation are not too small, we want monetary or fiscal policy (or both) to play the role of dampening the disequilibrium. When expectations of inflation are judged too high (low), we may elect to use fiscal and monetary policy to create a disequilibrium that will correct those expectations. We do not ordinarily conceive of stabilization policy as adjusting supply.

So let me explain the motivation of this paper, thus perhaps to encourage the reader's interest: This was to be the prolegomenon to a much harder paper in which expectations of income, price and wage movements are "rational"—statistically unbiased rather than mechanically adaptive. If monetary or taxation policy is to be effective in such a model, it must have the effect of moving the equilibrium levels of output and employment. For in that kind of model the expectation in each period is that the system will land on macroequilibrium—plus white noise. Such a paper is probably still worth developing; but in view of its intrinsic difficulties, and the novelties necessitated by the consideration of the present piece, I doubt now that I will follow that original plan. I am inclined now to view the system as capable of operating in disequilibrium despite rational expectations, owing to the lengthiness of wage and price contracts so that a somewhat different sequel is called for. I trust, however, that this thought does not deprive the present paper of interest. We have long needed a policy treatment of aggregate supply that is symmetrical to the literature on aggregate demand.

I. Equilibrium Effects of Monetary Operations

I begin with a case that Metzler was not concerned to analyze: the consequences for "real" variables of an open-market purchase when the government leaves its tax rates unchanged.

A. *Fixed Tax-Rate Case*

The theory of how an increase of the money supply through an open-market purchase will affect the price level and the "real" variables of the economy—wealth, saving, the rate of interest, and so on—was first developed by Metzler. It is a tribute to that paper that 20 years later it is still a staple of graduate reading lists—indeed more needed than ever as a corrective to the oversimplifications of some quantity-theorists of the price level. (Of course, its own oversimplifications help explain its durability in the classroom.)

We shall suppose, with Metzler, that the central bank is the only money-creating bank in the economy and there is no government interest-bearing bonds—save possibly, "index bonds" which are homogeneous with equities in private portfolios.

The Metzler system can be portrayed thus:

$$L = L(r, Q), \qquad L_r < 0, \qquad L_Q > 0 \tag{1}$$

$$C(\bar{K} + L - \bar{J}, r) + \dot{K} = Q, \qquad C_{\bar{K}} > 0 \tag{2}$$

$$Q = Q(\bar{K}, N) > 0, \qquad Q_K\bar{K} + Q_N N = Q \tag{3}$$

$$r = Q_K(\bar{K}, N) > 0, \qquad Q_{KK} < 0, \qquad Q_{KN} > 0 \tag{4}$$

$$N = \text{const} > 0. \tag{5}$$

Here L denotes the real value of the money supply (central bank deposits), Q the rate of output, r the rate of return to holders of capital, $\bar{K}$ the capital stock at the given moment of time, $\dot{K}$ its time derivative—the rate of investment, $\bar{J}$ the portion of the capital stock owned by the central bank (net of any government index bonds outstanding), and N the equilibrium level of employment.

Metzler saw that the money supply increase consequent upon an open-market purchase of capital can by itself have no effect on the system other than to raise the price level proportionally to the money supply. But the operation also has the effect of a capital levy for the private sector then owns less capital by the amount of the increase in $\bar{J}$, the additional capital purchased by the bank. This reduces the rate of consumption at any level of r (and corresponding L).

Looking at the medium run, which is essentially the Metzler perspective in terms of the present model, the reduction of consumption adds to the pace of capital formation so that at any date in the future K is higher than it otherwise would be. This depresses r so that L is increased, meaning that the price level is raised less-than-proportionally to the increase in M. This is Metzler's nonneutrality theorem. The induced rise in L dampens the reduction of C (for any given K) produced by a given rise of J.[1]

[1] What of the very long run, a domain of Schumpeter, Ramsey, Solow and Swan? Will the capital stock increase without limit, settle at a higher stationary-state figure than otherwise would have been approached, or sink back to some unaltered stationary state? The first appears the most likely. The initial stationary state (J^*, K^*) must be

Let us now treat labor supply more symmetrically with consumption demand, replacing (5) with

$$N = N(\bar{K} + L - \bar{J}, v), \qquad N_{\bar{K}} < 0, \qquad N_v > 0 \tag{5'}$$

and adding

$$v = Q_N(\bar{K}, N) > 0, \qquad Q_{NN} < 0. \tag{6}$$

It is clear that the short-run effect of an open market purchase is to increase labor supply, thus to increase N and reduce v, by virtue of its augmentation of $\bar{J}$. Consequently r is *increased*, Q is increased and hence L also is increased. In the longer run there may be some tendency for r to recede, for if the increase of J and Q combine to increase $\dot{K}$, the capital–labor ratio will tend to grow.

B. *Balanced-Budget Case*

We have seen that, when fiscal policy is described by a fixed rate of taxation, an open-market purchase is nonneutral in the short run, raising equilibrium employment and affecting output and factor rewards accordingly. The explanation is simply the reverse wealth effect of the open-market operation on the demand for leisure and hence labor supply. At least over the longer run, however, it is more natural to conduct the analysis, as did Metzler, under the assumption of a balanced budget. Then an open-market purchase entails a reduction of tax rates to offset the increase in central bank earnings, and corresponding increase in the consolidated government revenue, from an increase in the portion of capital claims held by the bank.

Let the system of taxation be described by a flat rate of income tax, t, applicable to income from holdings of government index bonds, if any, to private wages and profits and to the bank's earnings alike. Let us also introduce a fixed level of real government purchases, G, primarily for later use.

---

one where, whenever realized, the government budget is balanced. An increase in $\bar{J}$ throws the budget into surplus by the amount r *times* the increase in J. An increase of capital also tends, through income taxation, to increase the surplus. An increase of $\bar{J}$ increases $\dot{K}$ while, let us assume, an increase of $\bar{K}$ decreases $\dot{K}$. Then the rest point of the full system

$$\dot{J} = f(J, K), f_1 > 0, f_2 > 0$$

$$\dot{K} = g(J, K), \qquad g_1 > 0, g_2 < 0$$

is a saddle point. The fixed tax-rate assumption is therefore inappropriate to long-run analysis.

The new system, to be interpreted below, is represented as follows:

$$C + \dot{K} + G = Q \tag{7}$$

$$Q = Q(\overline{K}, N) > 0 \tag{8}$$

$$r = Q_K(\overline{K}, N) = \psi(v) > 0, \qquad Q_{KK}(\overline{K}, N) < 0, \qquad \psi'(v) < 0 \tag{9}$$

$$v = Q_N(\overline{K}, N) > 0, \qquad Q_{NN}(\overline{K}, N) < 0 \tag{10}$$

$$t = Y(J, Q; G), \qquad Y_J < 0, \qquad Y_Q > 0 \tag{11}$$

$$C = F(\overline{K}, L, J, r, v, t; G), \qquad F_K > 0, \qquad F_L > 0, \qquad F_J < 0 \tag{12}$$

$$N = H(\overline{K}, L, J, r, v, t; G), \qquad H_K < 0, \qquad H_L < 0, \qquad H_J > 0, \tag{13}$$

$$H_v + \psi'(v)\, H_r > Q_{NN}\,, \qquad H_t < 0$$

$$L = L(Q, r, t, \overline{K} - J; G), \quad L_Q > 0, \quad L_r < 0, \quad L_t \gtrless 0, \quad L_K > 0. \tag{14}$$

Here r and v are before-tax profit and real-wage rates, respectively.

The balanced-budget tax-rate function, Y, should not need comment. The consumption–demand and labor supply functions raise the question of the treatment of "wealth effects." It is clear that if there existed perfect futures markets in all goods, including labor services, then the present discounted value of the tax reductions (present and future) associated with the balanced-budget tax rate reduction would just offset the reduction in private holdings of capital (the increase in J) consequent upon an open-market purchase—as calculated at any initial set of household resource allocation programs. There would thus be no net wealth effect. We would then have $H_J = 0$. There would be a substitution effect from the reduction of the flat income tax rate which effect would favor employment and saving: $H_t < 0$, $C_t > 0$. Yet these substitution effects would in a sense be anomalous, for with such perfect futures markets, or their Arro-Debreu contingent-claims generalization, there would be no obstacle to the use of the technically superior device of lump-sum taxation rather than income-geared taxation.

However, owing to the irremediable absence of comprehensive futures markets, especially in human services, reasons arise why a net wealth effect is to be expected. These are the same reasons that make complete futures markets in labor services inoperable.

First, the fact of mortality makes the recipients of the more distant reduction in tax liabilities different people. Only if all these successors were heirs whose inheritances could be reduced by those living at present in the amount of the tax reductions, and likewise their heirs' bequests, *et seq.*, could one expect that the tax liability reductions of the distant future would receive their present-value weight.

Second, an individual—even an immortal—cannot borrow against his expected tax liability reduction at as favorable a rate of interest as he can obtain for the purpose of purchasing tangible capital. A given expected future after-tax reward to human capital goes at a larger discount than an equal mathematical expectation of after-tax reward (of the same future date) to nonhuman capital. One reason for this that there is a lesser "moral hazard" that the borrower purchasing a tangible capital good will waste his asset in relatively unprofitable uses, thus diminishing stream from it, than there is that the owner of human capital will let down his efforts to utilize effectively that capital; in the latter case the borrower can default usually without fear that his wages will be garnisheed while the tangible assets of bankrupt firms can be seized by creditors; and human capital is always subject to the temptations of leisure or less onerous employment while the idleness of a tangible capital good does not offer an equivalent temptation to its owner. Hence, owing to the interest-rate differential, if the individual does borrow against the prospective decrease in tax liabilities (at the initial household resource allocation plan), and he might have to in order to approximate to his allocation program, available liquid resources will still suffer a net decline: the loss of marketable nonhuman wealth—the capital-levy part of the open-market purchase—exceeds the increment in borrowed funds, for a net wealth effect.

Third, with reference to the individual who has enough nonhuman capital to do so, he can do better by maintaining his consumption program in the face of the capital levy, thus in effect borrowing from himself and repaying that debt steadily out of the subsequent diminutions in tax liability. But the old consumption plan will no longer maximize the expectation of his lifetime utility. In the quaint terms used by Pigou [3, 4], the private holdings of capital claims extinguished by the open-market purchase had an *amenity value* that the expected stream of tax savings lacks. The latter is less "liquid" in the sense of being riskier: The individual's wage-earning power may fall so he may never get to see the tax savings he would otherwise have enjoyed, while the individual's holdings of capital claims (including government index bonds, if any), being cheaply diversifiable, pose less risk of loss. As Donald Nichols [2] has noted, the high tax rates that go with a low or negative J—i.e., that go with large net government indebtedness—offer the individual a kind of after-tax income insurance. There is the presumption, I believe, that if the government, by its capital levy through an open-market purchase and resulting reduction of the income tax rate, should reduce this insurance then people will seek to compensate by earning more income (and by saving more to build up future income, as Pigou theorized). In this way individuals can regain (or at least approach) the same degree of security against a deprivation of consumption standards that they had before.

Fourth, the reduction of the income tax rate necessary to rebalance the budget after an open-market purchase leaves a pure substitution effect favoring future consumption at the expense of present consumption *and* present leisure. This is from the rise of the after-tax profit or rate of interest. This is an unambigously positive effect from the tax rate reduction because the reduction in tax collections is offset by the elimination of the earnings on the capital no longer privately held. Last, but not necessarily least, there is additionaly the pure substitution effect upon labor supply of the rise in the after-tax wage rate resulting from the tax rate reduction.

For these four reasons it seems reasonable to assume that

$$\partial H/\partial J = H_J + Y_J H_t > 0,$$

where $H_J > 0$, $Y_J < 0$ and $H_t < 0$ (as of a balanced budget). It likewise is reasonable to suppose that

$$\partial C/\partial J = F_J + Y_J F_t > 0$$

though the short-run aggregate supply effect to be deduced does not in any way depend upon it. I shall return to some of the paradoxical consequences of all this shortly.

Lastly, note that "outside money," L, which is a component of "outside wealth," $L–J$, enters with a partial derivative having the usual sign.

It remains to discuss the liquidity preference function. It is necessary only to note that an increase of the tax rate may increase real cash balances by reducing the rate of return on capital claims. Consequently

$$\partial L/\partial J = L_K(-1) + Y_J L_t < 0.$$

The pertinent supply subset from the system (7–14) may be reduced as follows:

$$L = L[Q(\bar{K}, N), Q_K(\bar{K}, N), Y(J, Q(\bar{K}, N); G); \bar{K}–J; G] \qquad (15)$$

$$N = H[\bar{K}, L, J, Q_K(\bar{K}, N), Q_N(\bar{K}, N), Y(J, Q(\bar{K}, N); G); G] \qquad (16)$$

in which we seek the solution for the equilibrium L and N as functions of the parameter J (and the parameter G to be considered below). A graphical analysis can bring out the interesting features of the solution quite clearly (Fig. 1).

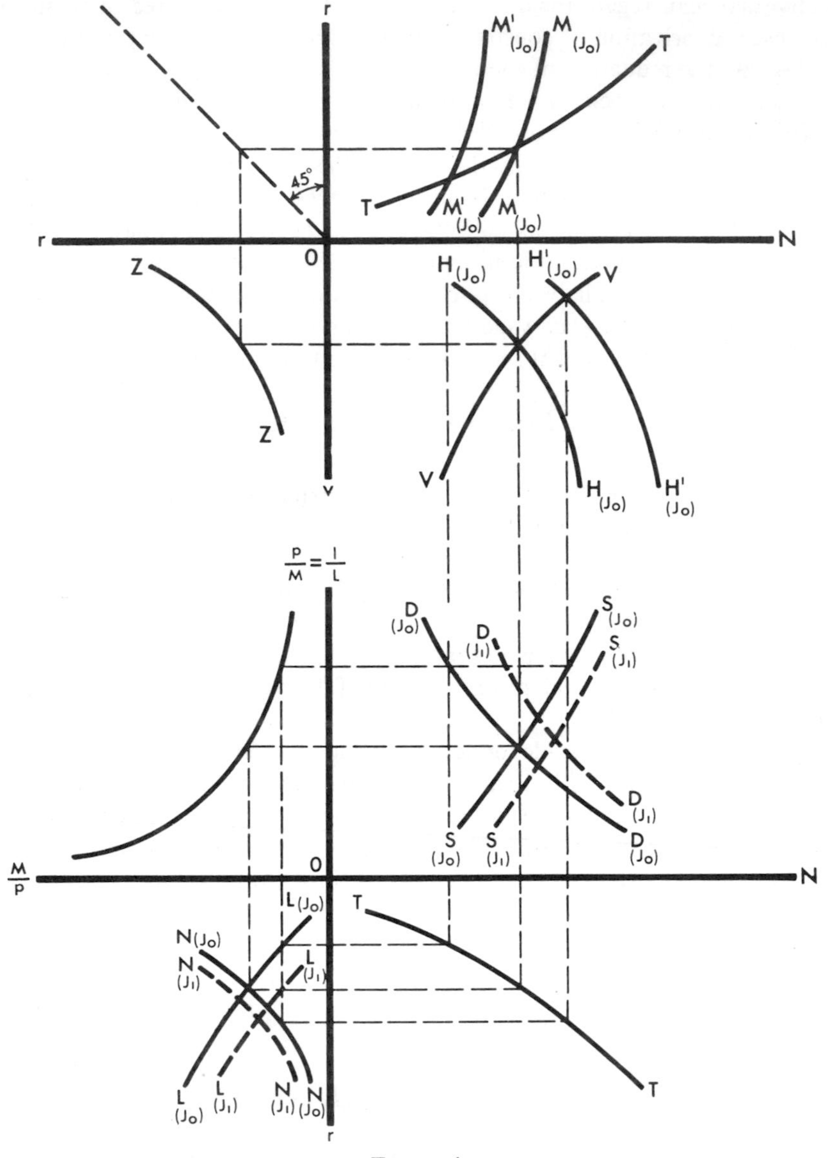

FIGURE 1

The combinations of L and N which satisfy (15) are represented by the DD curve in the lower panel. This curve is downward sloping if and only if the positively sloped MM curve (in the upper panel) which depicts (14)—it is essentially the familiar Hicksian LM curve—is steeper than the positively sloped TT curve depicting (9). This is because a decrease of L shifts MM leftward to $M'M'$, reflecting the reduced Q and N that is then possible for any r if (14) is to be satisfied.

The combinations of L and N which satisfy (16) are represented by the SS curve in the lower panel. This curve is upward sloping provided that $H_v + \psi'(v)\, H_r > Q_{NN}$ so that the "labor demand curve," VV is "more negatively sloped" than the "labor supply curve," HH, if the latter is negatively sloped at all. Then a rightward shift of HH to $H'H'$ due to a decrease of L increases N and reduces v.

The equilibrium L and N occur where DD and SS intersect. How does this equilibrium shift with an open-market purchase that increases J? Because $\partial H/\partial J > 0$, the increase of J must shift SS to the right, tending to increase L (decrease p/M). Because $\partial L/\partial J < 0$, the increase of J must shift DD to the right, tending to decrease L (increase p/M). This shift follows because, at a higher J, additional cash balances are available to support a larger Q and N at any given r. Therefore the open-market operation unambiguously increases equilibrium output and employment, and raises the equilibrium (before-tax and after-tax) rate of interest.

Note that "liquidity" as measured by L will be increased if the SS shift—which raises Q, and hence the demand for real balances—outweighs the upward shift of DD which, while indirectly inducing a rise of Q as well, has the *direct* effect of reducing the demand for real balances via the reduction of the portfolio motive, K–J, and the tax-rate reduction which increases the after-tax rate yield on capital.

Yet the after-tax (and, insofar as it is relevant, the before-tax) rate of return on capital claims is up as the result of the open-market purchase. Thus the opportunity costs of being liquid are increased and, in that sense, liquidity is decreased. This accords with the appropriate overall view of the matter: The open-market purchase constitutes *dis*intermediation for it increases the risks of a fall in the return to total privately owned capital, "human" and "tangible." That paradoxical conclusion arises from viewing the monetization of capital claims as wiping out a certain degree of income insurance offered by high income tax rates. Any induced rise of real (outside) cash balances appears to be merely the partial compensation induced by the resulting increase of labor supply. It should be noted, in conclusion, that in the long run the same disintermediation tending to increase labor supply may also diminish consumption demand. This would stimulate capital deepening, tending to restore the rate of interest while further increasing aggregate supply.

II. Monetary Effects of an Expenditure Increase

Consider now a balanced-budget increase of government expenditure. If we make the heroic (Keynesian) assumption that the object of the extra public expenditure, when provided free to the populace and financed by taxation, does not affect directly the demand for leisure, then we are left with the income-tax rate substitution effect, $H_t Y_G < 0$. Then HH and SS shift leftward. On the other hand, if the increase in expenditure is a regrettable necessary (unsought military attack which is desired to be repulsed), then possibly $\partial H/\partial G > 0$. In that case, SS may shift rightward on balance.

Looking at liquidity preference, the increase of G financed by a balanced-budget tax increase reduces the demand (by the private sector) for real cash balances at any level of Q and N; a larger fraction of any total real expenditure, Q, is now spent by the public sector whose cash needs do not figure in L. On this account, MM shifts rightward, for the same L can now "finance" a larger Q (and N) at any given r; to this extent DD shifts rightward.

The upshot is that if SS shifts leftward less than DD shifts rightward, or *a fortiori* shifts rightward, then equilibrium employment is increased. In either case, L is decreased.

It is unnecessary to say that the subject of the effects of monetary and fiscal policies needs further study. The purpose of the present exercise has been primarily to show that it should not be supposed that the macro-equilibrium levels of employment and output are invariant, even approximately, to shifts in monetary and public expenditure operations.

References

1. L. A. Metzler, Wealth, Saving and the Rate of Interest, *J. Polit. Econ.* **59** (1959), 93–116.
2. D. A. Nichols, Private Wealth and the Government Debt, (Mimeographed) FFR 6820*(rev.), Social Systems Research Institute, University of Wisconsin.
3. A. C. Pigou, The Classical Stationary State, *Econ. J.* **53** (1943), 342–352.
4. A. C. Pigou, Economic Progress in a Stable Environment, *Economica* **14** (1943), 180–190.

Part III

WELFARE ANALYSIS OF ANTICIPATED INFLATION: LIQUIDITY AND SAVING

INTRODUCTION

The papers in this third group study the welfare economics of inflation in an equilibrium context. They are in the spirit of natural rate doctrine: Whatever the benefits and costs that would accrue if the rate of inflation, actual and expected, were higher or lower, a different unemployment rate would not be among them. If the new equilibrium path is transiently affected by the overhang of wage or price commitments made before new inflation rate was anticipated, the transient benefits and costs thus generated are neglected. The studies also abstract from the one-time benefits and costs arising from any disequilibrium episode in the transition from one equilibrium to the other. In short, these are exercise in full-employment economics. It is not typically imagined, though, that we are effectively choosing among full-fledged golden-age patterns in which all variables (capital stock, labor supply, public debt, etc.) have reached their postulated steady-state tracks.

I had noticed sometime in 1963 an implication in the writings of Martin J. Bailey and Milton Friedman that may have been overlooked. If anticipated inflation is markedly worse than price stability, fiscal considerations aside, then by the same argument there must be some sufficiently small anticipated rate of deflation that is better. The expectation of deflation, in creating an expected real rate of return to money holding closer to the real rate of return from holding claims to capital goods, would reduce the costly diversion of people's activity from productive efforts into efforts to economize on cash balances; the consequent rise in the real value of cash balances would seemingly cost society nothing to maintain—no new coins and notes need be printed and replaced—and if so there would be no social losses to set against the social gains from the deflation. The best deflation rate, then, would be one making the real rate of return on money equal to the real rate of return on capital—at which point there could be said to be "full liquidity." The latter notion emerged, I think, in a conversation with Paul Samuelson, who alludes to it in his 1964 memorial tribute to D. H. Robertson. The same idea was independently discovered by Alvin Marty in the course of his 1964 review of the work by Gurley and Shaw.

My 1965 exposition of the case for full liquidity had nevertheless to meet two difficulties. If the real rate of return on money were equal to the real rate on capital, no wealth-holder would want to acquire ownership claims to capital. And if the increase of real cash balances resulting from anticipated deflation had a Pigou effect on consumption, economic growth would suffer unless some countervailing actions were taken. A solution to the former problem was drawn to my attention by William Brainard: Full liquidity could be obtained with something less than complete equalization of the expected real rates of return in view of the setup cost of financial transactions. The application to anticipated inflation by Robert Mundell of Metzler's model of liquidity and real interest provided a convenient vehicle for discussing the latter problem: To preserve economic growth while achieving full liquidity the government could accompany the central bank's program of money-supply reduction with a fiscal program of budgetary surplus. The opportunity frontier between liquidity and growth (as represented by the real rate of interest), as well as the social preference between these two desiderata, could be laid out in the Metzler plane; the optimum on that frontier is the fiscal target.

The theoretical framework in this first essay on the welfare economics of anticipated inflation was adopted again in my subsequent papers on the "inflation tax." Taxation and money-supply creation through open-market operations constitute two tools of government, independent and distinctive in their effects. The opposing framework, in which the growth of the money supply is tied rigidly to the growth of the public debt, presents quite a different picture. While the last section of my 1965 paper took up a problem of that second-best type, the leading models in that vein were developed by others. Their principal finding, that budgetary deficits encourage capital deepening, hinges on the one-tool assumption which makes deficits inflationary; but deficits are not inherently inflationary in the two-tool economy.

In many of its theoretical details, however, the 1965 model was deficient for a realistic appraisal of the welfare costs and benefits of anticipated inflation and deflation. In particular, the rise of taxes that would be necessary to insulate the course of real interest rates from a move to deflationary full liquidity would add to the deadweight losses produced by proportional or graduated taxation. The welfare gains from fuller liquidity might be offset or outweighed by the welfare losses from the steeper taxation. One wants to know, therefore, by how much tax revenues must be increased to insulate the real rate of interest when faster anticipated deflation (or slower anticipated inflation) is brought about. My 1973 paper calculated the answer: By the amount of the increase that results in the area of the rectangle under the demand curve for real cash balances. The "inflation tax" is just the seigniorage earned by the central bank—which will be positive at zero inflation and even at full liquidity since the money interest rate must be positive if wealth-holders are to be willing to buy capital, as explained in the above discussion of the 1965 paper.

This paper goes on to utilize this result for the purposes of framing the choice of the anticipated inflation rate as a problem in optimal taxation. One finding is that the optimal tax mix will not generally let the holding of real balances go scot-free of taxation—full liquidity would be as suspect as the proposal for "full wages." Beyond that, exact results are difficult to achieve. Whether this sort of analysis makes positive anticipated inflation optimal from a fiscal standpoint is, of course, an empirical question. Such an outcome is a reasonable bet, though, if the demand for real balances is quite interest-inelastic.

The final paper in this group explores the fiscal and monetary arithmetic of steady anticipated inflation in a balanced-growth setting. I and my coauthor, Edwin Burmeister, thought it a merit of our paper that it entertained more than one hypothesis as to which variable, money or public debt, is the driving autonomous force determining the price level. In another view, the taxonomic approach is the source of intellectual litter. Of course, no author should be required to embrace all hypotheses equally. It is hard to see, though, why we should make a virtue of our uneasiness with complexity and uncertainty.

The balanced-growth models offer an opportunity to test whether the above formula for the "inflation tax," obtained in the short-run setting of my 1973 paper, holds good in the long run as well. The balanced-growth analysis *appears* to reach a contrary conclusion. But the difference in results is wholly due to the unnatural assumption in the steady-state analysis that the central bank refund its seigniorage directly to the public in the form of lump-sum transfer payments rather than turn it over to the treasury. The latter alternative is the sensible one, especially if the treasury would have to inflict additional deadweight losses to replace with extra tax collections the revenue no longer turned over by the central bank. The misstep in assumptions is corrected and the necessary recalculations made in a forthcoming note by Alvin Marty in the *Journal of Money, Credit and Banking*. Of course, most of the results (other than the inflation-tax calculation) survive the change.

Thus the view of the "inflation tax" as just the seigniorage earned by the central bank holds good over both the long and short run in the two-tool monetary and fiscal model.

ANTICIPATED INFLATION AND ECONOMIC WELFARE

I. INTRODUCTION

It was once believed that a fully anticipated inflation has no effect upon the allocation of resources. While this proposition was reiterated as late as 1949 by Lerner, it met with an objection by Friedman:[2] If holders of money receive no interest on their deposits (or if the rate of interest on money is fixed) then the expectation of inflation—by leading to a higher nominal rate of interest on other (earning) assets—will widen the spread between the rate of interest on money and that on other assets and hence increase the incentive to "economize" on money. People will be driven to reallocate their resources—for example, to take more trips to the bank—in an inefficient way.

Friedman's argument was later formalized by Bailey,[3] who proposed to measure the "cost" of inflation (per unit time) by the area under the demand curve for real-money balances (displayed as a function of the nominal rate of interest) between the initial and the new level of real-money holdings, the new equilibrium level being smaller than the initial as a consequence of the rise in the equilibrium nominal rate of interest. Bailey joined Friedman in condemning inflation in view of this cost.

There the matter lay until Robert A. Mundell[4] demonstrated, in the context of the Metzler flexible wage-price model,[5] that the expectation of inflation does not raise the nominal rate of interest on earning assets by the full amount of the expected rate of inflation. Rather, as the nominal interest rate rises and people seek to reduce their money holdings, prices move to a higher equilibrium level, reducing the real value of these holdings

[1] I should like to acknowledge helpful discussions with William C. Brainard and Paul A. Samuelson on the subject of this paper. Ronald Bodkin and Harry G. Johnson suggested several improvements of earlier drafts.

[2] Milton Friedman, "Discussion of the Inflationary Gap" (revised), in his *Essays in Positive Economics* (Chicago: University of Chicago Press, 1953), pp. 253–57.

[3] Martin J. Bailey, "The Welfare Cost of Inflationary Finance," *Journal of Political Economy*, LXIV (April, 1956), 93–110.

[4] "Inflation and Real Interest," the *Journal of Political Economy*, LXXI (June, 1963), 280–83.

[5] Lloyd G. Metzler, "Wealth, Saving, and the Rate of Interest," *Journal of Political Economy*, LIX (April, 1951), 93–116.

and thus stimulating greater saving at given levels of the real rate of interest and real income (the "Pigou effect"). The increased desire to save reduces the equilibrium real rate of interest and thereby prevents the nominal rate of interest from rising above its initial level by the full amount of the expected rate of inflation.

By implication the cost of inflation in Mundell's model cannot be measured as Bailey proposed because *ceteris* are not *paribus:* the real rate of interest has fallen. Mundell concludes that the expectation of inflation confers "benefits" or "evils" depending apparently upon whether the rise of saving and investment associated with the fall of the real interest rate is good or bad. The upshot is that the welfare analysis of inflation appears to lack definite conclusions.

Nevertheless, definite welfare conclusions can be drawn. It will be shown in this paper that Mundell's analysis refers only to an exogenous expectation of inflation to which the government makes no fiscal or monetary response. Using a Metzler-like model having fiscal and monetary controls over consumption and investment demand, I show that whether the real interest rate falls or rises when inflation becomes expected depends entirely upon the government's use of these fiscal and monetary controls. Should the expectation of inflation be induced by inflationary government policies the real rate of interest still need not fall: the government has the latitude to induce inflationary expectations by (fiscal) means which raise the real rate of interest, or by (monetary) means which reduce the real rate of interest. Thus, the expectation of inflation, even when that expectation is induced and sustained by the government, will depress the real rate of interest, as Mundell concluded, only if the government desires that to happen.

Since there is no necessary connection between the expected rate of inflation and the real rate of interest, it can be shown that, as Friedman and Bailey argued, the expectation of inflation in excess of a certain rate (which may be negative) has an unambiguously ill effect upon "feasible welfare" provided the government finds it infeasible to pay interest on money at a suitable rate. But it will also be shown that the expectation of inflation need have no effect upon welfare if the government is able to pay the appropriate rate of interest on money.

Finally, I reconcile my results with William S. Vickrey's well-known argument that in some circumstances an anticipated inflation would be desirable.[6] A summary of my principal results concludes the paper.

II. CONSEQUENCES OF THE EXPECTATION OF INFLATION WITHOUT GOVERNMENT ACTION

I postulate that wages and prices are perfectly flexible, that the economy is able in each period to achieve a full-employment equilibrium, and that the supply of labor is pefectly inelastic so that equilibrium employment is fixed and independent of the other variables.

I treat the banking system as a unit, henceforth referred to as "the bank." I suppose that the economy divides its wealth between only two assets, non-interest-bearing "money" and equity "shares" (claims upon capital goods). Initially I suppose that the government owns no shares. Hence the equilibrium real value of the privately held shares, E, in any period equals the real value of the economy's capital after the investment of

[6] "Stability through Inflation," in *Post-Keynesian Economics*, ed. K. K. Kurika (New Brunswick, N.J.: Rutgers University Press, 1954), pp. 89–122.

the current period.[7] Real private wealth is therefore $W = E + M/p$, where M is the amount of money held and p is the price level.

I further suppose that there is no uncertainty concerning the prospective rise of the price level and the prospective real rate of return on shares. There is thus no speculative demand for money or shares; the motive for holding money is entirely the transaction demand, and, as Baumol and Tobin have shown, this demand will be well defined and interest elastic.

The demand for real money holdings is taken to be a function of the nominal rate of interest, i (this is the prospective nominal yield on shares), and the aggregate volume of planned transactions during the period. Presumably, the greater the yield on shares, the smaller is the amount of money that people are willing to hold, relative to transactions. Since currently planned transactions depend mainly upon the volume of current production and the latter is a datum if resources are fully employed, production can be suppressed from the demand function, which can be written $M = pL(i)$, $L_i < 0$.

The supply of money, which is determined by the fiscal and monetary authorities, I initially take as given, hence $M = M_o$.

The market in which these two assets (money and shares) are traded for one another will be in equilibrium—a "portfolio" equilibrium—when the price level and prospective nominal yield on shares equate the demand and supply of money:

$$\frac{M_o}{P} = L(i). \qquad (1)$$

[7] I have in mind a model in which the capital stock changes by discrete amounts in every period, or planting season, as it were.

Now if ρ, the expected relative rate of price inflation, is zero, then the nominal rate of interest, i, and the real rate of interest, r, are equal. Therefore, the LM curve labeled $\rho = 0$ in Figure 1 is the locus of pairs of the real (as well as the nominal) interest rate and real-money holdings that satisfy the equilibrium requirement of equation (1) when there is a zero rate of expected inflation.

The amount of capital invested, I, in any period is equal to private saving (unconsumed production), S, plus public saving (the government budgetary surplus). The latter is simply net taxes T, since government expenditures are omitted. Hence $I = S + T$. All taxes are assumed to be lump sum.

Private saving is assumed to depend on the real rate of interest (the real prospective yield on shares), real private wealth, and taxes. Real pretax income is suppressed since it is assumed constant. Hence $S = S(r, W, T)$. It is further supposed that an increase of wealth will decrease desired private saving, $S_W < 0$; that a rise of taxes reduces saving but by less than the amount of the tax, $-1 < S_T < 0$ and that an increase of the real return on shares will not decrease saving (if it decreases it at all) by as much as it decreases investment, $S_r > I_r$. Public saving is initially assumed constant: $T = T_o$.

The prospective real rate of return on investment (shares) is assumed to be inversely related to the volume of investment, which gives us the relation $I = I(r)$, $I_r < 0$.

Equilibrium of the whole system requires in addition to equation (1) that the real rate of interest and real wealth be such as to equate the corresponding level of investment to the corresponding level of saving:

$$I(r)=S\left(r,E+\frac{M_o}{p},\ T_o\right)+T_o. \quad (2)$$

The IS curve in Figure 1 is the locus of pairs of the real interest rate and real money holdings that satisfy this equilibrium requirement. The slope of the curve is positive because a rise of the real interest rate reduces investment and so requires an increase of the real value of money holdings (inducing a decline of desired saving) in order to maintain equality of desired saving and investment.

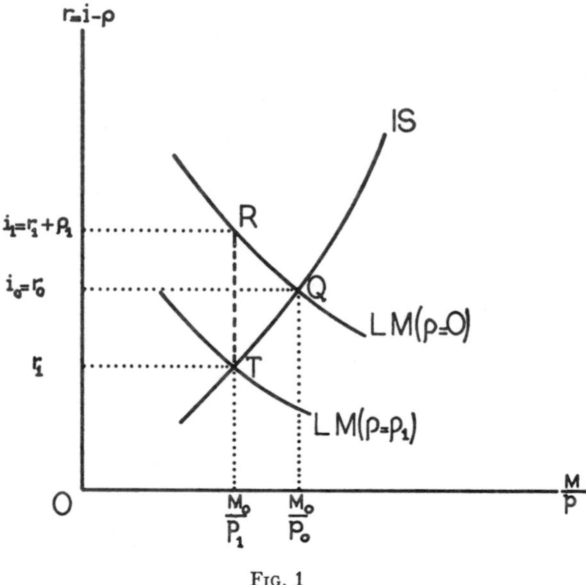

FIG. 1

If no inflation or deflation is expected, then the intersection at Q of this IS curve with the LM curve for $\rho = 0$ determines the equilibrium nominal and real interest rate, $i_o = r_o$, and the equilibrium real value of money holdings, M_o/p_o (that is, the equilibrium price level, p_o).

In general, however, the expected nominal rate will exceed the real rate (to a first approximation) by the expected relative rate of change of the price level between this period and the next one. Letting ρ denote the expected rate of inflation we have

$$r=i-\rho. \quad (3)$$

The expectation of a rising price level raises the nominal yield of shares at each real rate of interest (real yield on shares); this decreases the quantity of real money balances demanded, increases the quantity of shares (hence capital) demanded, and thereby causes the price level to be bid higher. To the extent that the resulting decline of the real value of money holdings stimulates additional saving, additional investment will take place, driving down the real yield on shares and thus lessening the ultimate rise of the nominal rate of interest. Equilibrium is reached when the real value of cash balances has declined sufficiently that money holdings are no longer in excess supply.

With reference to Figure 1, let ρ be positive and equal to $\rho_1 = RT$. Then the

LM curve for $\rho = \rho_1$ will lie below the LM curve for $\rho = 0$ by the amount ρ; because $\rho > 0$, it takes a lower r to keep $L(i) = L(r + \rho)$ constant at any specified M/p. The new equilibrium is at T where the real interest rate is r_1 and the real value of the money supply is M_o/p_1. The point R indicates the new nominal interest rate $i_1 = r_1 + \rho_1$.[8]

III. CONSEQUENCES FOR POLICY OPPORTUNITIES OF THE EXPECTATION OF INFLATION

The foregoing results, obtained by Mundell, describe the effects of a spontaneous change of the expected rate of price change, with the government making no response to the change of expectations or being itself responsible for the change of expectations.

The monetary and fiscal authorities need not, however, acquiesce to the new equilibrium shown above. Investment and the real interest rate could be restored to their "original" levels by open-market sales of securities by the central bank or by a tax reduction; alternatively the authorities could restore real money holdings and the nominal interest rate to their original levels by the opposite steps; or the authorities could bring about some different equilibrium lying either between or outside these two possible equilibria.

Should the government induce the expectation of inflation by the way it employs one of its two tools (say, taxes), it still needs not accept the particular change of equilibrium shown above; the government's other tool (say, open-market purchases) gives it latitude in choosing what the new real interest rate and investment level shall be.

I now analyze the separate effects of these two government tools and go on to deduce the consequences for policy opportunities of the expectation (spontaneous or induced) of inflation.

TAX POLICY

A change of taxes changes by an equal amount the algebraic budgetary surplus (which may be positive or negative) of the government. Since there are just two assets, money and shares, any change of the surplus must be "financed" by an equal and opposite change of the money supply.

A change of taxes has three points of impact upon the model: A change of T has an "income effect" upon consumption demand, hence available total saving, as shown in the right-hand side of equation (2); a change of T changes M and thus has an "asset effect" (or a "Lerner effect") upon private saving, again as shown in equation (2); and finally, a change of M has monetary effects through equation (1).

Consider first the impacts of the change of M, holding T constant. M appears in equations (1) and (2) only as a ratio to p; in other words, it is only the real value of money holdings, not their nominal size, that affects behavior. Therefore, if there existed initially an equilibrium with real money balances M_o/p_o, then, when the reduction of the algebraic surplus increases the money supply from M_o to M', there must exist a new equilibrium with the same r, E, and so on but with a price level, p', that makes the real value of money holdings the same as initially. Moreover, since for every given M there is a unique equilibrium, p' must be the only possible equilibrium price level. It follows that

[8] Clearly one could alternatively represent the new equilibrium as the result of an upward shift of the IS curve considered as a function of the nominal rate of interest. A rise of ρ requires an equal rise of i if any given M_o/p is to continue to satisfy eq. (2).

the new equilibrium, holding T fixed, does not differ from the original equilibrium, except for equiproportionate changes in M and p, since only a change of M/p can change the behavior of the economy.

Hence, taking as given the expected rate of inflation, any effects of the tax cut are due solely to its "income effect" upon consumption demand. This is a well-known story: The tax cut stimulates consumption and hence requires a reduction of real balances (to stimulate private saving) if any given real rate of interest is to continue to satisfy the investment-saving equality in expression (2). Hence the *IS* curve shifts to the left. The *LM* curve remains fixed.

Therefore, given the rate of expected inflation, a tax reduction results in a higher rate of interest (both real and nominal so as to satisfy equation [3]) and therefore a smaller level of real-money holdings and a smaller level of investment. It follows that, by suitable tax policy (shifts of *IS*) the government can bring about an equilibrium anywhere on the given *LM* curve.

MONETARY ACTIONS

In the present model, monetary actions are confined to open-market operations—the exchange of money (the bank's liabilities) for shares.

Open-market transactions can be viewed as having two impacts: the impact of the change in E, interpreted now as privately held shares (total shares issued less the bank's holdings), and the impact of the equal and opposite change of M. A change of M, keeping the bank's holdings of shares constant, has no effect on the interest rate (real or nominal, given ρ) nor any other real magnitude, only an effect upon the price level, which must change in the same proportion as M. Any "real" effect of open-market operations must therefore arise from the impact of the change in privately held shares. Indeed, as Metzler explained, open-market purchases of shares have the same effect as a capital levy payable only in shares.

A reduction of privately held shares (due to an open-market purchase) evidently has no effect upon the demand for real money holdings at any given interest rate since that demand is based upon transactions needs. But the loss of securities does increase the quantity of real money holdings needed at any interest rate to produce the private wealth total that will equate desired saving to investment. Hence the *IS* curve shifts to the right. Since M/p must increase by the amount of the decrease of E, the shift at any real interest rate is equal to the amount of shares purchased.[9] Hence the intersection of the *IS* curve with the *LM* curve moves downward and rightward along *LM*.

An open-market purchase therefore results in a lower rate of interest (nominal and real), therefore in greater real money holdings (as well as greater nominal holdings), and in a greater rate

[9] Because T, which is held constant, signifies net government receipts, its constancy implies that the government reduces taxes by the amount of the earnings from the shares purchased by the bank. The Metzler model implies that tax reduction has no effect upon consumption demand if it is matched by equal loss (to the private sector) of interest earnings due to a reduction of privately held shares, given total real wealth and the rate of interest. Mundell and Horwich have pointed out that this implies that the tax reduction must not be offered as a reduction on property-tax rates or corporate-tax rates; otherwise it will be "capitalized" by the market and hence raise the market value of property (shares). A stronger point should be made: Only if the tax reduction is considered transitory rather than permanent will the tax reduction fail to be "capitalized" to some degree and hence fail to stimulate consumption demand.

of investment. In these respects it is similar to a tax increase.

Note that both open-market action and tax variation work by shifting the *IS* curve and leave unchanged the *LM* curve, given the expected rate of inflation. The government can employ either a tax reduction or an open-market sale to raise the real rate of interest; it can employ either a tax increase or an open-market purchase to reduce the real rate of interest. Note, however, that these actions have different price effects. A tax reduction raises the price level; in fact, since M/p falls, p must rise proportionately more than M. An open-market sale, while also reducing M/p, reduces the price level; since M/p falls by an amount less than $(1/p_o)\Delta M$, the amount of money withdrawn by the bank, p, must fall.

It is immediately clear that if the expected rate of inflation is completely exogenous the government can use either the fiscal or the monetary tool to raise or lower the real interest rate. Any point on the *LM* curve for $\rho = \rho_1$ can be chosen by the government. Mundell's result that the real interest rate must fall assumes the absence of any government response to the shift of the *LM* curve.

The conclusion is no different if the expectation of inflation is induced by inflationary government actions rather than exogenous. Just as the government can maintain a stationary price level by fiscal-monetary policies that produce either a high or a low real rate of interest, the government can also engineer a rising price trend combined with a high or low real rate of interest.

Suppose (without loss of generality) that to induce a certain expected rate of inflation the government desires to raise the price level a certain amount (above) what the price level would be if the government took no action). To raise the price level the government must either reduce taxes or engage in open-market purchases. The former action shifts the *IS* curve to the left while the latter shifts it to the right. Hence the tax reduction will accomplish the desired inflation with a higher real rate of interest than will the open-market purchase. But the difference between these two resulting real interest rates does not exhaust the range of choice. If the government should desire a higher real rate than would result from tax reduction alone, it should engage in open-market sales (which reduce the price level) together with additional tax reductions (to keep the price level constant at the desired level) until the real rate of interest reaches the desired level. In short, the government can choose among the points on the *LM* curve that prevails in an anticipated inflation as easily and in just the same way as it chooses among the points on the (different) *LM* curve that prevails under stationary price expectations.

Thus the government can choose what kind of inflation to have: an inflation with high saving and a low real rate of interest—brought about by open-market purchases—or an inflation with low saving and a high real rate of interest—brought about by low taxes.[10] This

[10] Note that a permanent change of tax rates has an effect upon the path of the price level from period to period that a once-for-all change in the supply of money due to an open-market transaction does not have. If the government sets the tax level so as to run a deficit ($T < 0$) then, since the money supply will be increasing over time while the real value of money holdings will be constant from period to period (if the *IS* and *LM* curve remain the same over time) the price level will be increasing over time in proportion to the changing money supply. The monetary authority can cause inflation—through continual increases of the money supply—only if it engages in fresh open-market purchases each period. A permanent change of taxes causes a

proposition is the analogue for a flexible price model of the familiar proposition for inflexible price models that the government, by its use of fiscal and monetary controls, can control both the level of employment and the rate of interest; in a flexible price model, it is the rate of inflation and the (real or nominal) rate of interest which can be independently controlled.

I conclude that the expectation of inflation—even when that expectation is deliberately induced and sustained by the government—will depress the real rate of interest, as Mundell maintained, only if the government allows that to happen.

The pairs of values of the real interest rate and real money holdings which the government may feasibly bring about by taxation and open-market operations are represented by the *LM* curve; this curve constitutes the "opportunity locus" for these policy instruments. The effect of anticipated inflation upon "feasible welfare"—the maximum welfare attainable through tax and open-market policies under the given monetary arrangements and institutions—depends therefore only upon the resulting downward shift of this opportunity locus in relation to community preferences. I now proceed to analyze the welfare effects of anticipated inflation.

IV. CONSEQUENCES FOR FEASIBLE WELFARE OF ANTICIPATED INFLATION

In the present model, welfare can be considered a function of the amount of time spent economizing on money holdings and the investment-consumption mix (that is, the degree to which the economy's investment approximates to the "optimum" level).

Clearly the economy can invest so much of its output as to leave too little available for present consumption; or it can invest so little as to leave too little income available for consumption in the future. Therefore welfare depends upon the level of investment, given the present capital stock, employment, and time spent in husbanding money holdings.

Given time spent in production and the amounts of output invested and consumed respectively, welfare will depend upon the amount of time left for leisure. The greater the number of deposits and withdrawals at the bank made by individuals in order to keep a greater share of wealth in the forms of earning assets (shares), the smaller is the amount of time left for leisure; hence, given the public's distaste for this activity, the greater the number of these trips to the bank, the smaller will be the community's welfare.

The twofold dependence of welfare upon investment and leisure can be expressed in terms of the real interest rate and real money holdings on our simplifying—but not crucial—supposition that the community is determined to devote a fixed amount of time to production. On this supposition, the amount of output invested is an inverse function of the real rate of interest. Therefore, given employment and given time spent economizing on money (hence given leisure), welfare can be represented as a function of the real rate of interest: As the real rate is decreased (investment increased) welfare first increases and then eventually decreases when investment becomes excessive. Thus, there is an optimal real rate of interest, say r^*, corresponding to the optimal rate of investment.

Also, the amount of time spent in economizing on money instead of spent

---

change in the trend of prices over time (as well as a change in the level of prices in the first period), while an open-market transaction causes a change of the price level only in the current period.

in leisure can be represented as a function of real money holdings, since the greater equilibrium real money holdings, the smaller must be the nominal rate of interest, and therefore the smaller the incentive to economize on money. Therefore, given employment and given the real rate of interest (hence investment), welfare can be represented as a function of the real value of money holdings: As real money holdings are increased (the nominal interest rate decreased) welfare increases until the nominal rate of interest has fallen to a point near zero where the incentive to economize on money is nil. When the incentive to economize on money is nil, meaning that all transactions balances are held in the form of money, I shall say that there is "full liquidity." Assuming that it costs the government nothing to increase real balances (at least in the neighborhood of full liquidity), the optimal level of liquidity is at full liquidity. I denote this liquidity optimum m^*. It is represented in Figure 2 by the quantity of real balances demanded when $\rho = 0$ and $r = 0$ (that is, when the nominal interest rate is zero).

The optimal real rate of interest, r^*, may not be as small as the nominal interest rate required to produce full liquidity. Suppose that it is not. Then the optimum is at point (r^*, m^*) which lies above the LM curve for $\rho = 0$. Any point $(r, M/p)$ different from this optimum entails a below-optimal level of welfare.

Suppose now that $\rho = \rho_o = 0$ and that the government is committed to sustaining the expectation of a stationary price level by keeping the price level stationary. Then the LM curve for ρ_o is the opportunity locus of points from which the government must be content to choose if it is committed to sustain stationary price expectations. Let (r_*, m_*) be the best point on this opportunity locus. Then the government, if it seeks the greatest level of welfare feasible, will choose those fiscal and monetary actions (among all actions which keep the price level stationary) that cause the IS curve to intersect the LM curve at this point. Trivially, this point is inferior to (r^*, m^*).

Suppose now that the community expects rising prices $(\rho = \rho_1 > 0)$ and that the authorities commit themselves

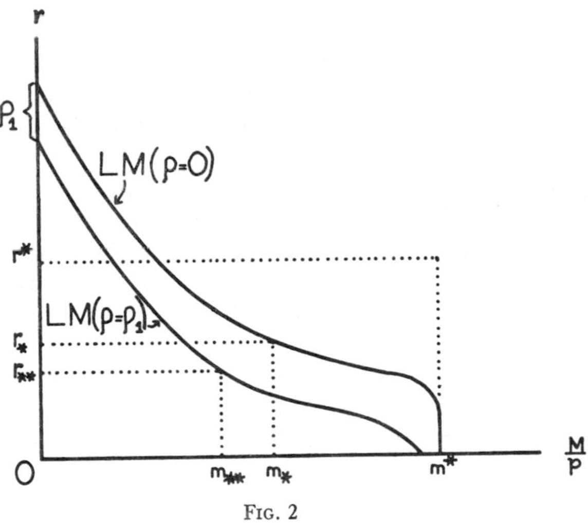

FIG. 2

to sustaining this expectation. Then the new *LM* curve for ρ_1 becomes the locus of policy opportunities. This locus is clearly inferior to the previous locus, for any real interest rate that can be achieved on the first locus can be achieved (if at all) on the second locus only at a smaller level of liquidity—with a greater short fall of liquidity from optimal liquidity. Hence (r_{**}, m_{**}), the best feasible equilibrium on the ρ_1 locus, is inferior to (r_*, m_*). The expectation of inflation reduces feasible welfare below that attainable when a stationary price trend is expected.[11]

We have finally arrived at a familiar proposition: Anticipated inflation is unambiguously bad. From this proposition it is sometimes concluded that, should the expectation of inflation develop, anti-inflationary measures ought to be introduced in order to induce the expectation of "stable prices." I shall make three remarks on this conclusion.

First, should the government rely solely upon monetary tightening to curb the price trend (in the hope that people will thereby learn not to expect inflation) while sticking to the same fiscal course, it is possible that the cure will be worse than the disease. Surrender of the equilibrium at (r_{**}, m_{**}) in favor of tighter money will, until the community revise its price expectations, place the economy higher up on the *LM* curve: Real money holdings will fall below m_{**} and, while the real interest rate will rise above r_{**}, the net effect of this alternation is to place society in a worse position since the former position was the best feasible on the *LM* curve.

[11] Another proof that (r_*, m_*) is better than (r_{**}, m_{**}) is the following: The first locus permits $(r_{**}, \dot{m})$ where $\dot{m} > m_{**}$ and this is better than (r_{**}, m_{**}). If (r_*, m_*) is preferred to $(r_{**}, \dot{m})$, it must also be better than (r_{**}, m_{**}). It is not possible, however, to measure how much better it is. Only if $r_{**} = r_*$ could we make use of Bailey's measure of the welfare cost of the inflation.

Similarly, should the government rely solely upon fiscal tightening (an increased surplus) to arrest the price rise, then (given an unchanged course of action by the monetary authority) the equilibrium at (r_{**}, m_{**}) will give way to one with a lower real rate of interest and, despite greater real money holdings, welfare will here also fall below the feasible level—until the desired effect upon the *LM* locus finally develops.

The lesson of this, of course, is that monetary and fiscal policies must be used jointly to bring about a moderation of the price trend together with maintenance of feasible welfare. We require both monetary and fiscal tightening—open-market sales (which lower the price level and raise the nominal interest rate) and an increase of the surplus (which lowers and slows the price level while reducing the nominal interest rate) in such proportions that the real rate of interest remains at r_{**} until the *LM* curve begins to shift rightward. In this way the economy can be guided along some optimal expansion path from (r_{**}, m_{**}) to (r_*, m_*).

Our second remark is that there is nothing optimal in this model about stationary price expectations. The same logic as demands the elimination of inflation in favor of price stability also demands the abandonment of price stationarity in favor of an appropriate rate of price deflation. The optimal expansion path does not end at (r_*, m_*) but continues over to (r^*, m^*), the grand optimum. To realize any point on this stretch of the expansion path it is necessary to bring about a certain rate of expected deflation, that is, a certain value of $\rho < 0$.

What rate of expected deflation is necessary to bring about equilibrium at the optimum (r^*, m^*)? Here there is "full liquidity." Hence the spread between the nominal (and real) yields of money and shares must be approximately zero. Since the nominal yield on money is zero, the nominal rate of interest, therefore, must be approximately equal to zero.[12] This means that the expected rate of deflation must approximate the real rate of interest r^*, the real rate that is optimal when there is full liquidity. In short $\rho \cong -r^*$ is required to cause the *LM* curve to pass through the point (r^*, m^*).

In this optimal equilibrium there is no incentive to exchange money for shares in order to economize on money. Transactions balances consist only of money; there would be no purpose in increasing liquidity if that were possible. Moreover, the investment level is chosen solely with regard to intertemporal consumption preferences rather than with regard also to the consequences for liquidity of the implied nominal rate of interest. By manipulating ρ the government would be able to break the link between the nominal interest rate (liquidity) and the real rate of interest (investment) and therefore achieve simultaneously both full liquidity and the investment optimum.

This route to the optimum seems rather awkward, however. It might be argued that the process of teaching the community to expect deflation is uncertain and slow at best. The deflationary method of attaining the grand optimum depends upon a tendency of the community to extrapolate recent price trends into the future. But it is conceivable that price expectations are "adaptive" in too stabilizing a fashion—that, the expected price level next period is a positively weighted average of the current and each past price level so that the expectation of a price fall could not be induced by the policy act of making prices fall.

Fortunately there is another method of attaining the optimum, one suggested by Friedman and others,[13] and this is the subject of my third remark. I supposed from the start that money bore no interest. This placed money at a greater disadvantage relative to shares when the nominal interest rate (yield on shares) rose. Planned deflation, which people will eventually anticipate, is a device for making non-interest-bearing money bear a positive real rate of return. If $\rho \cong -r = -r^*$, both money and shares will bear approximately the same real (and the same nominal) rate of return. The trouble with any expected price trend that is less deflationary—especially any inflationary trend—is that it creates an excessive spread between the nominal (and hence also the real) rates of return on money and shares; clearly it is on this spread between the nominal interest rate on shares and that on money (until now supposed to be zero) that the demand for real money holdings depends. The greater this spread, the greater will be the community's socially inefficient efforts to economize on money.

Suppose now that the government pays interest (in money) to holders of money. Let μ denote the (own) rate of interest on money. The spread between the nominal rates of interest on shares and money is now $i - \mu = r + \rho + \mu$. Therefore the real money demand function is

$$\frac{M}{p} = L(r + \rho - \mu). \qquad (1')$$

Money is no longer at a potential disadvantage relative to shares. If $\mu > 0$,

[12] It is not necessary to drive the nominal interest rate all the way to zero in order to eliminate the incentive to switch transactions balances in and out of money. Provided even one such transaction has a finite disutility the *LM* curve will possess a vertical slope closed to the horizontal axis (that is, for very small nominal interest rates).

[13] See, for example, Milton Friedman, *A Program for Monetary Stability* (New York: Fordham University Press, 1960).

money has an inherent attraction beyond its utility in making transactions. If ρ should rise, the government can prevent the effect of that rise upon the LM curve, hence its effect upon real money balances and the real interest rate, by raising μ by an equal amount. Indeed, in a laissez faire banking system in which it is legal to pay interest on deposits, the advent of inflationary expectations would presumably lead profit-maximizing banks to raise the interest rates they pay to depositors enough to maintain the spread between the yields on money and shares and thus maintain their deposits and earnings in real terms. This seems a significant qualification to the usual welfare analysis of inflation and to the analysis by Mundell: Such analysis has little relevance to economies in which the rate of interest on a large portion of the money supply fluctuates with other yields so as to keep most interest differentials roughly invariant to the expected rate of inflation.[14]

More importantly, the government can now achieve the optimum through control of μ rather than by efforts to control ρ. It can narrow the spread between the nominal (or real) rate of interest on shares and that on money by raising the own rate of interest on money rather than by attempting to lower the expected nominal rate of interest on shares (the real rate plus the expected rate of change of prices). Taxation and open-market operations can be used to bring about the desired price level and the desired real rate of interest on shares while the bank raises their own rate of interest on money toward the nominal rate of interest on shares, reducing the spread sufficiently to eliminate the incentive to economize on money.

By this method, then, the government can achieve the optimum without having to attempt to influence the rate of expected change of the price level. The economy is not restricted to maximizing the welfare level that is feasible under any given rate of expected algebraic inflation. The economy's full potential welfare can be achieved through the device of paying interest on money.

My analysis has led to the conclusion that anticipated inflation and even insufficient deflation is bad unless its ill effects are neutralized by the payment of a suitable interest rate on money. But there is a qualification: I analyzed only the case in which the optimum point (r^*, m^*) lay above the LM curve for $\rho = 0$; we supposed, in other words, that r^* was so high that if $\rho = 0$ and $\mu = 0$ then, when $r = r^*$, the cost of holding money, $i - \mu = r + \rho - \mu = r^*$, would have been too high to permit full liquidity. It was for this reason that we required either a positive μ or a negative ρ to realize both the optimal r and an $i - \mu$ small enough to induce full liquidity.

But it is possible that the optimum point lies on the LM curve for $\rho = 0$, that is, somewhere on the vertical stretch of LM where $M/p = m^*$. The meaning of this case is that r^* is so small that, when $\rho = 0$, $\mu = 0$, the cost of holding money, $i - \mu = r + \rho - \mu = r^*$, is small enough to insure full liquidity.

In this second case there is no need to introduce a negative ρ or positive μ to shift the LM curve upward; that curve already intersects the optimum point. Hence, to realize the optimum, it suffices to adopt a fiscal-monetary policy that is neither inflationary nor deflationary (in order to keep ρ equal to zero) and that causes the IS curve to intersect the LM curve for $\rho = 0$ at the point (r^*, m^*). There is no need here for deflation or interest on money.

Further, just as a stationary price

[14] For a fuller discussion of the significance of bank interest payments see Vickrey, pp. 112–13.

trend is consistent with optimality in this case without need for interest on money, a moderate rate of anticipated inflation may be harmless. While a positive ρ will produce an LM curve below that for $\rho = 0$, this new LM curve will still intersect the optimum point if ρ and r^* are small enough. This is because the LM curve for $\rho = 0$ is vertical for some distance over the point $M/p = m^*$ (meaning that there is a finite range of smaller nominal interest rates consistent with full liquidity). Hence an LM curve slightly below that for $\rho = 0$ will also have a vertical stretch over the point $M/p = m^*$; the two curves will coincide near the horizontal axis and hence may coincide at the optimum point if the latter is close to the horizontal axis.

Our conclusion, therefore, is that anticipated inflation above a certain critical rate is bad unless offset by the payment of interest on money. The critical rate may be negative (deflation required in the absence of interest on money), or it may be positive. The critical rate is negative if and only if the optimal real interest rate is sufficiently high that equality of the nominal interest rate with that real rate (implying $\rho = 0$) would prevent full liquidity; that is, if and only if the optimum point (r^*, m^*) lies above the LM curve for $\rho = 0$.

The reader may feel that in fact the optimum point lies well above the LM curve for $\rho = 0$, that is, that r^* is so high that we require for full liquidity either anticipated deflation or interest on money. But this is less certain if we recognize that there may be a speculative as well as a transaction demand for money.

Suppose there is a speculative demand for money. Optimal liquidity occurs when the cost of holding money $(i - \mu)$ is small enough to induce full liquidity—to cause all individuals to hold all their transactions balances in the form of money. Let m^* denote the level of real money holdings when the cost of holding money is just small enough to induce full liquidity. A "difficulty" in this case, and it is not a real one, is that if the cost of holding money is reduced further there may be a larger speculative demand (the transactions demand is already satiated) so that the level of real money holdings corresponding to this reduced cost of holding money may be larger than m^*. Hence there may be a whole range of values of real money holdings, $M/p \geq m^*$, all of which correspond to equilibria of full liquidity. This is illustrated in Figure 3 (see Sec. V), where, rather than a single optimum point, there is an "optimum line": Any point on the horizontal line stretching rightward from the point (r^*, m^*) is a point of optimal investment and full liquidity.

The important difference which a speculative demand makes pertains to the position of (r^*, m^*) relative to the LM curve for $\rho = 0$. When there is only a transaction demand for money, m^* is equal to the value of M/p at which the LM curve reaches the horizontal axis; hence the point (r^*, m^*) is either on the LM curve (if r^* is very small) or above the LM curve. But when there is a speculative demand for money as well, then full liquidity—all transactions balances held in the form of money—can occur without there also occurring liquidity satiation—the demand for money equal to total wealth. In other words, the value of M/p at which the cost of holding money is just small enough to produce full liquidity may be smaller than the value of M/p corresponding to liquidity satiation. Hence m^* need not be the horizontal intercept of the LM curve for $\rho = 0$; rather, m^* may be to the left of this intercept. As a consequence, if r^* is rather small, the point (r^*, m^*) may be below the LM curve for $\rho = 0$ (this is shown in Fig. 3). There are, therefore, three cases to be considered.

If the point (r^*, m^*) lies above the LM curve for $\rho = 0$ then either anticipated deflation or positive interest on money is needed to shift up the LM curve so that it will intersect (r^*, m^*) or any other point on the optimum line.

If the LM curve for $\rho = 0$ passes through (r^*, m^*) then, to realize optimal investment and liquidity, it suffices to adopt a fiscal-monetary policy that is neither inflationary nor deflationary (in order to keep ρ equal to zero) and that causes the IS curve to intersect the LM curve for $\rho = 0$ at the point (r^*, m^*).

If the point (r^*, m^*) lies below the LM curve for $\rho = 0$ then the optimum line must stretch rightward from that point, reaching the LM curve at some $M/p > m^*$, $r = r^*$. As has been explained, this point is also an optimum. Hence, for an optimum it suffices to adopt a non-inflationary, non-deflationary, fiscal-monetary policy that makes the IS curve intersect the LM curve at this point, where $r = r^*$.

In the latter two cases, therefore, neither deflation nor interest on money is required for an optimum. Further, in the last case, a moderate rate of anticipated inflation is harmless. In that case there is a range of anticipated inflation rates which, while they produce LM curves below the one for $\rho = 0$, still allow the LM curve to pass through or above (r^*, m^*), and hence still allow an optimum to be achieved without payment of interest on money.

I am not sure which is the empirically relevant case. But I can say that the presence of a speculative demand for money increases the likelihood that the last case is the relevant one, hence increasing the likelihood that optimal investment and liquidity can be achieved without deflation or interest on money and can be achieved even with a moderate rate of inflation (without paying interest on money).

I have concluded that anticipated inflation, at least if it is excessive, reduces feasible welfare if no interest is paid on money. But what of Vickrey's well-known argument that anticipated inflation may be desirable? I append a final section in which our respective analyses are reconciled. The analysis below differs from that above in that I now suppose, with Vickrey, that the bank is restrained from buying the quantity of shares it would like to buy.

V. THE ANALYSIS UNDER A MONETARY RESTRAINT

Vickrey supposes that there is a speculative demand for money. Further, he supposes that, when $\rho = 0$, there is some rate of interest, say $\check{\imath}$, such that at any $i < \check{\imath}$, everyone expects a negative yield on shares (including the capital loss). Hence the LM curve exhibits a so-called liquidity trap as shown in Figure 3. At any interest rate below a critical level, everyone is happy to sell all his shares; the demand for real money is equal to real total wealth; liquidity preference is "absolute."

However, such a phenomenon in no way impairs the power of the monetary authority to bid for shares and hence to drive down the nominal rate of interest to any desired level short of zero. At the kink in the LM curve, shareholders will have sold all their remaining shares to the bank; thereafter, the price offered by the bank for new shares determines the equilibrium rate of interest.

Yet, in Vickrey's model, the bank is unable to establish a "low" real rate of interest, if that should be desired. The reason is that the monetary authority is supposed to be unable to purchase the total stock of private shares. If, for example, all open-market operations in private claims were illegal (and no other debt such as government bonds existed for purchase or sale) then, should fiscal policy be committed to price stationariness (or to any other price trend) there would be just one possible equilibrium real rate of interest—where the *IS* curve corresponding to the required fiscal policy intersects the associated *LM* curve. In Figure 3, r^0 denotes the lowest r^* and $M/p \geq m^*$; r^* is lower than r^0. All points on this optimum line are points of full liquidity.

In this situation, the government seems unable to drive the real interest rate to the optimal level. But Vickrey proposes a solution through inflation. He would have the government contrive a program of announced inflation in order to shift the *LM* curve downward on the belief that a lower real rate of interest would then be feasible.

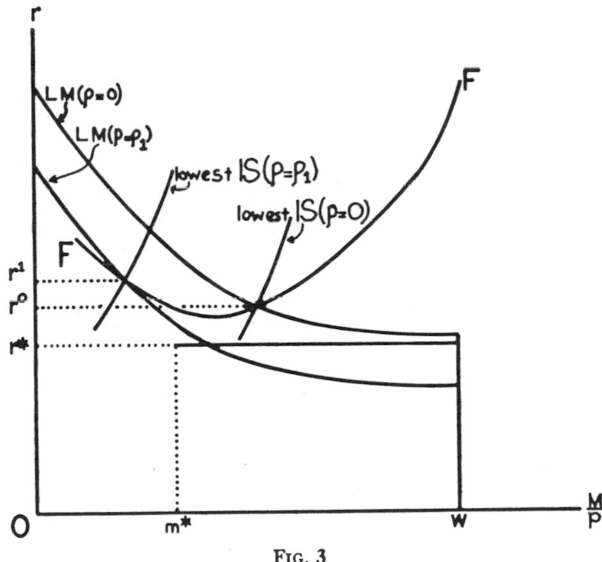

FIG. 3

real rate of interest that the monetary authority can bring about when the fiscal authorities are committed to a stationary price trend; it corresponds to the lowest (furthest right) *IS* curve attainable by the monetary authority, given the constraint on fiscal action.

Vickrey's next step is to suppose that, as is surely conceivable, the optimum entails a real rate of interest that is smaller than the lowest real rate of interest capable of realization by the monetary authorities in a stationary-price economy.[15] Accordingly, in Figure 3, an optimum occurs at any point where $r =$

How is this inflation to be generated? The bank can cause a rising price trend only by repeated open-market purchases from period to period. But this route is evidently closed by Vickrey's assumption of a restraint on bank holdings of shares. The only apparent alternative is fiscal policy.

To raise the price level and hence to induce the expectation of inflation by means of taxation the government must,

[15] "If a level trend of prices is considered a sine qua non, a high [nominal] interest rate also implies a high real rate of interest which in turn may discourage . . . capital formation to an undesirable extent" (*ibid.*, p. 98).

on the usual stability condition, reduce taxes (increase the deficit). This shifts the *IS* curve in Figure 3 to the left for reasons explained earlier. The *LM* curve will shift downward by the amount of the expected rate of inflation that the new price trend induces. But notice that, as Figure 3 illustrates, the resulting real rate of interest, r^1, is not necessarily lower than r^0. If and only if the downward shift of *LM* exceeds the upward shift of *IS* will the real rate fall. Thus there is no guaranty that this fiscal effort to achieve a lower real rate of interest will be successful.

In Figure 3 I have drawn the curve *FF*, which is the locus of points of intersection of every "lowest *IS* curve," each one corresponding to some rate of anticipated inflation, with the *LM* curve that corresponds to the same rate of anticipated inflation. This curve is the boundary of the policy opportunity set: Through monetary tightening it will be possible to achieve any point on or above this frontier; but the constraint on monetary ease makes it impossible to achieve any point below *FF*.

I have demonstrated that the government may be unable to reduce the real interest rate through fiscally induced inflation. The government's only tool for sustaining inflation, namely, the deficit, may raise the real rate of interest on balance (and reduce liquidity in addition) and therefore reduce welfare. This is the result where *FF* is downward-sloping as it may be in the left-hand range; it is the result shown in the diagram. But *FF* may be upward-sloping—the *LM* shift predominating—in which case Vickrey's result occurs; the diagram shows *FF* to be upward-sloping to the right, where *LM* is very flat, as Vickrey supposed.

Even if the real rate does fall (*FF* upward-sloping in the relevant range), however, there is no necessity that welfare will thereby be increased, since liquidity also falls. If the new and smaller liquidity level still exceeds or equals full liquidity—so that all transactions balances are held only in the form of money—liquidity reduction is of no consequence for welfare; then, since the real rate was originally above the optimum level by assumption, welfare will be increased if the reduction of the real rate is of the "right" magnitude. But if the new liquidity level is less than "full," the reduction of liquidity accompanying the fall of the real interest rate may reduce welfare. In any case it is always possible to go so far along *FF* that welfare begins to fall. Somewhere on the *FF* boundary there may be constrained optimum. (This is the case in Fig. 3 where the unconstrained optimum lies below *FF*.) The real interest rate associated with this constrained optimum may or may not be lower than r^0, the lowest real rate consistent with non-inflationary fiscal policy, so that a fall of the real rate below r^0 may or may not increase welfare.

To summarize: Inflation through fiscal means does not insure an increase of welfare in this case. A fiscally induced inflation may fail to reduce the real rate, may reduce welfare even if it succeeds, and cannot—if the restraint on the monetary authority is sufficiently binding—make feasible the optimum.

To assure feasibility of the optimum or even a desirable reduction of the real rate of interest the government needs a third tool. A negative own rate of interest on money—a tax on money holding—is such a tool.

Suppose the government maximizes monetary ease subject to the restraint on the bank. Let the government choose that fiscal policy consistent with price stability, so that $\rho = 0$. The resulting *IS* curve—the "lowest *IS*" for $\rho = 0$—may, as in Figure 3, lie to the right of the point (r^*, m^*) and hence intersect the optimum line connected to that point. If this *IS* curve lies to the left, let the government choose a sufficiently tighter fiscal policy to shift the *IS* curve to the right so as to intersect somewhere with the optimum line. In either case the *LM* curve that corresponds to the *IS* curve chosen will intersect the *IS* curve somewhere on *FF*. By hypothesis, *FF* lies everywhere above the optimum line. The problem therefore is to make the *LM* curve intersect the chosen *IS* curve where the latter intersects the optimum line. This can be achieved by levying a tax on money. Let μ continue to denote the own rate of interest on money; then $-\mu$ is the tax rate on money. Just as the introduction of a positive own rate on money shifts the *LM* curve (corresponding to a given ρ) upward by the amount μ, the introduction of a tax on money will shift the *LM* curve downward by the absolute value of μ. Hence it is only necessary to set the tax rate on money so as to shift the *LM* curve down from its intersection with the chosen *IS* at *FF* to an intersection with *IS* at the point where the chosen *IS* curve intersects the optimum line.

Hence, by establishing a negative own rate of interest on money and by adopting a sufficiently tight fiscal policy, the government can secure full liquidity and the optimal real rate of interest. Given the third tool of negative interest on money, the "price" of the monetary restraint, if binding, is only that a deflationary fiscal policy may be required to bring down the real rate of interest. In the present model there are no welfare effects of deflation, given that optimal levels of investment and liquidity are achieved; in particular, full employment is assumed to result whatever the price trend.

VI. CONCLUSIONS

If fiscal and monetary policies are effective and unconstrained, there is no necessary connection between the rate of anticipated inflation and the real rate of interest (hence investment and growth). The government can engineer a high-investment or a low-investment inflation in the same way that it can engineer high or low investment and keep the price level stationary.

If the government has unconstrained power to buy and sell claims on wealth (shares, in our model) and has the power to pay interest on money, considerations of investment and liquidity offer no basis for choosing among anticipated price trends: The desired levels of investment and liquidity can be achieved with any anticipated price trend. But if the government cannot pay interest on money, anticipated inflation in excess of some critical rate (which may be negative) will prevent attainment of the optimum; attainment of the desired levels of investment and liquidity may require a deflationary mix of fiscal and monetary policies.

If, in addition to being unable to pay interest on money, the government faces a constraint on the quantity of private wealth it can monetize, the optimum may not be attainable; in that case, attainment of a constrained optimum (the best feasible investment-liquidity combination) may require a rising anticipated price trend, as Vickrey argued, or a falling anticipated price trend. But if the government can tax money holdings (thus making the own rate of interest on money negative) it can achieve the optimum whether or not there is a constraint on open-market operations; however, if this constraint is binding, attainment of the optimum by means of fiscal policy and the taxation of money holdings may entail a falling price level.

INFLATION IN THE THEORY OF PUBLIC FINANCE

Summary

What are the essential features of the thought-experiment one has in mind when he speaks of the "tax-like effect" of an increase in the anticipated rate of inflation? Various authors have had various experiments in mind and thus arrived at differing measures of the revenue from inflation.

The present author proposes that inflation-tax analysis be carried out along now-standard lines—namely, by the method of differential tax analysis employed by Wicksell, Ramsey, Boiteux, Musgrave and virtually every contemporary.

The implementation of this approach in a model of money and inflation requires that the treasury adjust its deficit so as to maintain *invariant* the sum-of-income-effects from the combined operations of the branches of government in the face of a rise in the anticipated inflation rate.

The results of the analysis are as attractive as the method.

There exists a series of papers that might be called the "Chicago discussion" of the optimum rate of inflation—alias rate of growth of the money supply.[1] This discussion is identified by its use of several distinctive assumptions: (1) The economy being modelled is in equilibrium so that the expected rate of inflation is equal to the actual rate of inflation; (2) The equilibrium unemployment rate is independent of the expected inflation rate (the natural rate hypothesis); (3) The economy is closed, or other countries adapt their inflation rates, or else the economy's exchange rate can be continuously adjusted without significant cost; (4) Stabilization of the economy (around equilibrium) is not made easier or harder by increased inflation; (5) Any costs surrounding the discrete changes of individual prices and wage rates are disregarded; (6) It is impossible, inconvenient, or otherwise too costly to pay own-interest on some or all kinds of money.

The effect of these assumptions is to focus attention on the consequences of inflation for liquidity and saving. Does an increase of the inflation rate

* This paper benefitted at several points from discussions of the author with M. J. Bailey, E. Burmester, A. L. Marty, and J. E. Stiglitz.

[1] See, for example, the papers by Friedman, Bailey, Marty, Mundell, Tobin, and myself listed in the bibliography.

Reprinted by permission from *Swedish Journal of Economics,* Vol. 75(1), January–March, 1973.

perform like a tax to restrain consumption demand and thus release resources for capital formation or public use? And, if so, how does the deadweight welfare cost of this tax compare with that of other tax instruments that restrain consumption to the same degree? This paper will be in that same tradition. It will view the consequences of, and the optimization of, inflation from the important, though limited-vision, standpoint of fiscal and monetary efficiency.

Despite the agreement on purposes, the Chicago discussion has not yet reached a consensus on how to measure the costs and benefits of inflation. In particular, there is some disagreement over the concept of the "inflation tax".[1] As a consequence of the conceptual differences, different *measures* of the "proceeds" of the inflation tax have been derived.

Early in the discussion, Friedman (1948) and later Bailey (1956) identified the inflation tax revenue as the *rate of inflation* multiplied by the real value of the (outside) quantity of money, $\pi M/p$. Influenced by the balanced-growth Tobin paper (1965), Marty in 1967 proposed to mesaure the inflation tax by the *rate of growth of the money supply* time real balances, $(\pi + g)M/p$—where g is the real *growth* rate. Working outside the monetary-and-real-balanced-growth framework, Friedman, in 1971, also endorses the "total" inflation tax as the money-supply growth rate times real balances, that is, $(\dot{M}/M)M/p$. In my inflation policy book, I used the nominal interest rate multiplied by real balances, $(\pi + r)M/p$—where r is the real *interest* rate (see Phelps, 1972).[2] Needless to say, these various measures generally differ from one another, and not by inessential constants, save in the case of a stationary state with zero real rate of interest.

One objective of this paper is to clarify the kind of hypothetical policy experiment in terms of which, I believe, the inflation tax ought to be defined; and then go on to find a formula for inflation tax revenue within a specified (or largely specified) general-equilibrium model.[3]

Another point is that, despite the agreement on purposes, the Chicago discussion has not thus far produced a consensus on the policy "implications". Followers of the discussion have witnessed a Jekyll–Hyde alternation between inflationism and deflationism. At times deflation is championed on the ground that it promotes monetary efficiency. If, at zero inflation rate, the nominal interest rate is too high for full liquidity, then attainment of the latter requires that monetary policy engineer deflation to get the money interest rate down.

[1] I have even heard it said, at a recent conference, that the term "inflation tax" had no meaning. The difficulty is that the various authors using the term have not meant the same thing by it.

[2] In this concept, the proceeds of the inflation tax are metaphorical in the sense that the tax does not produce a visible flow of currency into the treasury like that produced by ordinary taxes or a currency printing press in the treasury basement. However, as shown below, the proceeds of the tax as conceived here are measured in terms of the "saving" in *other* (nonmetaphorical) tax revenues.

[3] My book does present a derivation of the formula cited (p. 187) but it is not as clear probably as the one presented in this paper, it is not as general, and it is marred by a typographical error (third line from the bottom, p. 187).

If it is objected that deflation coupled with the resulting enlargement or real cash balances would boost consumption, it is replied that ordinary taxes could be increased if it were desired to neutralize the income and wealth effects of inflation upon saving (Marty, 1963; Phelps, 1965; Friedman, 1969).

At the same time, inflation has often been upheld for its usefulness as a "tax" with which to hold down the claim of private consumption upon scarce resources, and thus promote capital deepening and growth (Mundell, 1963; Tobin, 1965). If it is objected that inflation would reduce liquidity, it is replied that every (acceptable) tax poses deadweight allocative distortions and even collection costs so that the optimal mix of taxes might very well entail a steep rate of inflation (Bailey, 1956; Phelps, 1972).

In his latest contribution to the discussion, Professor Friedman (1971) has sought to exorcise the latter, inflationist tendency. First he argues that if the economy of his model is growing, the budgetary deficit of his government might actually *fall* in real terms if there were a shift from zero inflation to a positive inflation rate. There is no treasury borrowing or lending in the Friedman model. Hence, given the rate of governmental expenditure and benefit payments, any reduction of the real deficit must imply an increase of ordinary taxes. The intended import of this proposition, presumably, is that where a reduction of the real deficit occurs the inflation has failed to substitute for ordinary taxes and therefore the inflation has not generated tax proceeds or "inflation revenue".

Next, Friedman argues that, upon specifying a demand-for-money function with a kink at full liquidity, it is mathematically possible that no conflict exists between maximum monetary efficiency and the maximum deficit: The real deficit is maximized (and hence ordinary tax collections minimized) *and* liquidity is maximized at the same rate of deflation.

In fact, from the standpoint of traditional public finance theory, Friedman's contention that inflation may fail to operate like a tax is an utter *non sequitur*. His complete model cannot even speak on the question of the tax-like effect of inflation because it lacks a consumption function and labor-supply function. "What is the purpose of taxation anyway?", Kermit Gordon asked Yale graduate students years ago, and the question is apposite once again. Noting that the object of federal taxes certainly wasn't the wherewithal to make outlays—as Gordon had already observed, the federal government could borrow the money—those students explained that the role of taxes (net of transfers) was to protect the rate of economic growth: If public expenditures were unaccompanied by positive net taxes, the resources diverted to public use would come mainly from the capital goods sector; there would be no fiscal restraint on consumption or leisure to accomodate the public expenditure so as to spare capital formation.

In performing an analysis of the inflation tax without a consumption function (and labor supply function), therefore, Professor Friedman has given us Hamlet without the Prince. The omission is no less fatal if, for some reason such as default risk, the treasury were unable to borrow from the public. For to demonstrate within his model that inflation does not operate like a tax to restrain consumption, he would have to argue that what he identified as the "total yield" from inflation (it is the treasury deficit) possesses an income effect (or wealth effect) upon consumption demand and labor supply that is comparable to the income effect (or wealth effect) of the ordinary non-metaphorical taxes.

Section I of this paper will explore the inflation tax from the approach that is in the central tradition of public finance theory from Wicksell (1896) to Musgrave (1959). This is the *differential taxation* approach in which *total* net tax "revenue" (as well as public expenditures) is held constant as one tax is substituted for another. It is essential to grasp that the very concept of total tax revenue is derived solely from the postulated consumption and labor-supply functions. This approach leads to the happy result that, as in the usual tax theory, the revenue from the inflation tax is simply the excess of the consumer's price over the producer's price (that is, price including tax less marginal cost) *times* the amount produced and purchased—just like the revenue from any other sort of tax. Hence, in the case where liquidity is costless, it is equal to the money rate of interest times real cash balances.

In the model employed here, where there are no lump sum taxes, the treasury must drive a wedge between price and marginal cost for one of more goods if it is to obtain its prescribed revenue. There is, therefore, the same presumptive conflict between full liquidity and the desire for revenue that exists between "full effort" or "full saving" and the requirements of revenue. Should liquidity be spared by setting the inflation tax at zero? Section II addresses the question of the optimal inflation tax within the optimal differential-taxation framework begun by Ramsey (1927) and Boiteux (1956). Under simplifying but not uncustomary assumptions, the answer obtained from an illustrative model is that the optimal inflation tax is positive. That is, the money interest rate is optimally positive.[1] This result, it may be added, *depends* upon the concept of total tax revenue, defined in terms of income effects in demand functions, introduced in Section I.

I. The Inflation Tax: Concept and Measure

I shall work with a model of the aggregate type familiar in macroeconomics. In this model we may think of government policy as being executed by three agencies or branches. This does not mean that each agency decides upon its intruments or controls in decentralized fashion. To the contrary, each agency is conceived here as calculating the actions it must take in full knowledge of

[1] Chapter 6 of my book gives a lengthy discussion of this topic but it does not present an example of an exact development as given here.

those actions by the other agencies which are entailed by their concerted pursuit of specified government policy objectives.

The expenditure-and-transfer branch sets the level and composition of real government expenditures (outlays of the resource-absorbing type) and real government benefits (cash transfer payments and subsidies *excluding* interest on the government debt). These programs we shall take as exogenous, as functions only of time, denoted t. So if G denotes the real value of expenditures and B the real value of benefits, then, for the sake of emphasis, we might write

$$G = \gamma(t) \geqslant 0, \ B = \beta(t) \geqslant 0 \tag{1}$$

where it is understood that G and B are to be read as $G(t)$ and $B(t)$ respectively. At each t, γ and β are "constants", independent of taxes and inflation and so on, but they may move arbitrarily over time.

The treasury sets the method of financing these government outlays, plus the interest on government debt held by the public. It can deficit-finance by selling interest-bearing debt in the bond market, and it can tax-finance without limits "in the relevant range". I shall consider only the simplest case, that in which a tax on wage income is the only available tax of the ordinary kind—that is, apart from the "inflation tax". I shall further suppose that the maturity of the debt is so short that its market value is sufficiently well approximated by its par value, its value at maturity. Thus if D denotes the cumulated net sum of money borrowed by the treasury over the past, D is also equal to the nominal market value of the current stock of interest-bearing debt issued by the government. The current rate of borrowing, the algeraic deficit, is the time-derivative of D, denoted $\dot{D}$. Let p denote the price level and D^* denote the debt held by the public. For every t then, the treasury's financial constraint is

$$T + \dot{D}/p = G + B + i_D D^*/p \tag{2}$$

where i_D is the nominal interest rate on government debt. The "theory" of the treasury's selection of $\dot{D}/p$, subject to (2), is that this selection represents the government's final control over the rate of national investment. In analogy to (1), therefore, we might postulate that the deficit is to be chosen so as to make the rate of investment equal to some arbitrary and exogenous function of time, say $\alpha(t)$. This approach, taken in the paper by Burmeister and Phelps, would be entirely in the *spirit* of the present paper; but the approach actually followed here is slightly different, as will be seen. Let me also mention that while the treasury deficit is an effective instrument to control the rate of growth, the relationship is not one-to-one: The monetary authorities also have some "fiscal" influences upon consumption and saving, and hence upon the growth rate for a given treasury deficit.

The third government agency in the model is the central bank. The central bank sets the timepath of the money supply, and it can do so independently of the treasury. The rate of new money creation need not equal the rate of treasury borrowing. If M denotes the money supply set by the central bank, then money creation in the sense of $\dot{M}$ is not a function of $\dot{D}$—as it would be if, say, the bank were required to support the rate of interest on government debt. Actually, as in nearly all of the well-known equilibrium theories, we will conceive of the control variable of the bank as the *level* of M; at any time t the desired level can be achieved by an "instantaneous" open-market purchase or sale of government debt from or to the public. For every t, then, we have the asset-constraint relation

$$M = D - D^* \tag{3}$$

As in the usual theory also, we shall suppose that for every price-level timepath that might be desired from the current time forward, there is some corresponding selection of the current money supply and subsequent growth that will generate that prescribed price-level path at the current time (or soon enough).[1] In this connection, there is no *logical* need, though there may be an emotional need, to choose a particular theory of money such as the Cambridge-k theory, nor to discuss the class of admissable theories, etc.; any theory is fine for which it is true that $M(t)$ can be chosen, subject to (3), so as to realize each one from the alternative inflation objectives being considered. We may represent the alternative price-level programs which it will be the bank's responsibility to engineer in the following way:

$$p(t) = \phi(t; \pi) \tag{4}$$

Here π is a shift-parameter that we may interpret as the desired rate of inflation—that is, the inflation-rate planned by the government.

We are now in a position to inquire into the trade-off between an increase of inflation, with its tax-like effects, and in increase in the rate of taxation of wage incomes. This is the method of differential tax analysis, introduced Wicksell (1898) and employed by Musgrave (1959) and other contemporaries. The method treats as a "constant"—variable *over time*, perhaps, but invariant *at each moment*—the sum of tax revenues. The effect of this constancy, presumably its methodological purpose, is to keep the sum of the *income effects* upon demands for leisure and consumption goods generally *invariant* to a variation of the mix of taxes. The substitution effects of such a tax shift are thus starkly revealed.

The problem for us now is to implement this traditional approach in a model of the monetary economy where consumer demands for goods involve the real

[1] Thus I am disregarding the dynamic obstacles to full controllability that might exist in a model containing various lags. This seems fair enough in the present context of long-run inflation planning. Further, the requirement may be somewhat stronger than needed in view of the later equation (12).

value of cash balances and of interest-bearing debt, and involve the real returns on these assets—all of which are potentially affected by the (anticipated) inflation rate. The solution consists of requiring, in the event of an increase of the inflation rate planned by the government, that the treasury and central bank jointly hold invariant their aggregated algebraic contributions to net spendable income and spendable wealth as these appear in household demand functions.

We posit consumption-demands and manhour-supply (leisure-demand) functions of the following form:

$$C = C(\tilde{Y}, W; \ldots; N; t), C_1 > 0, C_2 \geqslant 0 \tag{5}$$

$$H = H(\tilde{Y}, W; \ldots; N; t), H_1 < 0, H_2 \leqslant 0 \tag{6}$$

where real net spendable potential income, $\tilde{Y}$ is given by

$$\tilde{Y} = \overline{Y} + B + i_D D^*/p - T - \pi(M/p + D^*/p) \tag{7}$$

and real net spendable wealth (real marketable net worth) is given by

$$W = K + D/p(= K + M/p + D^*/p) \tag{8}$$

In (8), K is the real market-value of the capital stock, and D/p is so-called "outside wealth" added by the government to households' net worth. In (7), $\overline{Y}$ is *potential* pretax real income,

$$\overline{Y} = r_K K + w\overline{H}, \tag{9}$$

where $\overline{H}$ is maximum manhours, the amount that would be worked if leisure demand were zero. In (5) and (6), N denotes current population size. The space after the semicolon in these functions contains the relative aftertax goods prices, such as the real rate of interest and wage rate; their *substitution effects* upon consumption and leisure are outside the inquiry of this section.

The difference between $\overline{Y}$ and $\tilde{Y}$ is the government's overall fiscal contribution to, or subtraction from net spendable income. It is the sum of the income effects of the operations by the central bank (its debt-holding and its inflation) and the treasury (its wage taxation). A proper differential tax analysis requires that at current t, this overall fiscal subtraction be held *invariant* to a change in the current mix of taxes—in our case, to a change in the inflation rate or inflation "tax". Formally, if the bank shifts π then the treasury is required to make such compensatory adjustment of T as needed to continue satisfying

$$T + \pi M/p - (i_D - \pi)D^*/p = \theta(t), \tag{10}$$

where θ at any t is a "constant", independent of the tax mix, the price level, inflation rate and so on; it is given exogenously as a "forcing function" of *time only*, a wondrous dynamic parameter. To repeat, the lefthand side of

(10) may be thought of as overall net revenue, and (10) insists that all of our hypothetical variations in the mix of taxes, corresponding to variations of the inflation rate, must yield the same timepath of overall net revenue—for Wicksell's sake if not for mine.

Now the concept of the inflation tax is the "saving" that inflation permits in the volume of (wage) taxes that have to be collected, T, in order that the government achieve a certain sum-of-income-effects, as prescribed by θ (t) in (10), and a certain prescribed sum-of-wealth-effects total. So we will be returning to (10). But first we have to attend to the wealth effects. The treatment of these will make the system determinate and thus yield a specific and definite *measure* of the inflation tax.

Because the government's operations have wealth effects as well as income effects (not to mention substitution effects) upon consumption and leisure demands, a proper differential tax analysis requires that the overall fiscal contribution to wealth be held *invariant* to a change of the inflation rate. For if an increase of the (anticipated) inflation rate were allowed to result in a "flight" from money and bonds, the *wealth effect* of the resulting fall in the real value of outside wealth would act like a "wealth tax" to depress consumption and leisure even if the treasury adjusted T as dictated by (10) in order to avoid a net *income effect* of the increased inflation rate. Thus we require that

$$\frac{M}{p}+\frac{D^*}{p}=\Delta(t), \tag{11}$$

an exogenous function of time, independent of π. I leave it to the reader to show that $\theta(t)$ is the time-derivative, $\dot{\Delta}(t)$; consequently, if the central bank can contrive to satisfy (11) at time zero, then the treasury, in satisfying (10), will insure that (11) holds for all subsequent $\pm$ as well.

Let us imagine that the central bank announces its plans for a faster rate of inflation beginning at "time zero", that the public believes the bank, and that faster anticipated inflation does indeed ensue. What are the implications of this new plan for the central bank in view of (11)? According to (3), $D^*(0)+M(0)=D(0)$ is *given* as a predetermined result of past treasury financing. Equation (11) insists that $D(0)/p$ is also a given, equal to $\Delta(0)$. Thus $p(0)$ is implied to be held "constant", that is, invariant to the increase of π—though, of course, the rate of change of $p(t)$ at $t=0$ is not invariant. To avoid a wealth effect from the increase of π, the price level must not jump at $t=0$:

$$p(0)=p_0>0, \text{ a given} \tag{12}$$

Has the government enough tools to engineer such a potential experiment? If π is to be increased, the treasury will have its hands full adjusting $T(0)$ in obedience to (10). We know also that, whatever the theory of money we like, the central bank will need "faster growth" of the money supply to support a faster anticipated rise of the price level. The solution to the problem is that, as indicated above, $M(0)$ is not the same as $\dot{M}(0)$. The initial level of p can be controlled by an adjustment of the initial level of M, which is a free variable at the $t=0$ end point. As we shall show shortly, a one-time open market sale at $t=0$ to reduce $M(0)$ will enable $p(0)$, and thus $D(0)/p(0)$, to be held invariant to the increase of π. Thereupon the growth rate of $M(t)$ can be increased to accomodate the faster growth of $p(t)$.

We are finally ready to measure the inflation tax, at least in the short run at $t=0$. Upon substituting (3), (11) and (12) into (10) we obtain

$$T+i_D M/p_0=\theta(t)+(i_D-\pi)\ \Delta(t) \tag{13}$$

Increased inflation substitutes for wage-tax revenue insofar as it enlarges the *seignorage* (the second term on the left) received by the government from the central bank's exchange of interestless cash for earning assets from the public and, further, insofar as it reduces the real rate of interest on government debt, $i_D-\pi$. The latter effect may be quite important, but I will assume it away in what follows.

In the simplest case we can examine, the real rate of interest on government debt is equated by the market to the real rate of return on capital and the latter is a predetermined function of the inherited stock of capital goods at $t=0$:

$$i_D-\pi=r_K=\varrho,\ a \text{ given} \tag{14}$$

Then (13) may be written

$$T+(\varrho+\pi)M/p=\theta(0)+\varrho\ \Delta(0)\ (\text{at } t=0) \tag{15}$$

The "revenue from the inflation tax" is simply its contribution to the government's *seignorage* or monopoly-rents as the supplier of money, iM/p. The inflation tax here is simply a tax on *liquidity*, and the *tax rate* is $i=\varrho+\pi$, the opportunity cost (paid by households) of leasing liquidity.

To determine the behavior of $M(0)$ in (15), and thus the change in the revenue from the liquidity tax, when π is increased, we need a concrete theory of money. Let us suppose the demand function,

$$M/p_0=L(Y,r_K+\pi,K+D/p) \tag{16}$$

Then

$$\frac{-dT}{d\pi}=\frac{d}{d\pi}\left(\frac{iM}{p}\right)=\frac{M}{p_0}+iL_2+iL_1\frac{dY}{d\pi} \tag{17}$$

Let us disregard the output change, $dY/d\pi$, due to the substitution effects of the change in tax rates. Then $d(iM/p)/\pi$ is positive if, and only if, the demand for real balances is interest-inelastic.

To close this section, I wish to consider the two propositions in Friedman's recent paper. The question is whether these propositions about *his* concept of the inflation tax carry over to the concept, and corresponding measure, of the inflation tax developed here. In this discussion, I will use the demand-for-money function in (16).

Friedman's first proposition is that inflation tax revenue might actually fall in a shift to positive inflation from zero inflation, or, for that matter, from negative inflation. As we just showed in (17), such a possibility exists here too. This is because the inflation tax here is essentially $i_D L$, not πL. As a corollary, the inflation-tax-maximizing π could occur at negative π. This is not surprising for $i_D = 0$ is the natural floor such that a higher π imposes a tax, not $\pi = 0$. But it must be said that Professor Friedman, of all economists, is the last from whom we would expect it to be argued that the liquidity preference function is interest-elastic (in the neighborhood of $\pi = 0$). We may take it as agreed by even the worst "elasticity pessimists" that, say, a doubling of the nominal interest rate—from two to four per cent or from five to ten per cent—would not, in any advanced economy of which we have knowledge, lead to a halving of the real value of the money supply or any reduction close to that.

Friedman's second proposition, that there may be no conflict between full liquidity and inflation-tax-revenue maximization is *not true* of the inflation tax concept here. At least, it is not supportable if we adopt his own assumptions regarding the demand for money or, so far as I can see, any plausible alternative to them. If, with Friedman, we identify full liquidity (sometimes called liquidity satiation) as occurring if and only if $i \leqslant 0$, and if we assume, again with Friedman, that

$$L(Y, 0, K + D_0/p_0) < \infty, \tag{18}$$

then the revenue from the inflation tax, $i_D M/p_0$, must be non-positive at full liquidity. At *any* inflation rate too large for full liquidity, but not so large that $M/p = 0$, inflation tax revenue is positive. Hence there *is* a conflict between acquiring revenue and achieving full liquidity.

Now if it were desired, as a mathematical exercise, to erase the above conflict, one could postulate that the liquidity preference function has a "kink" at some *positive* i_D not too large to be inconsistent with full liquidity. The latter could indeed be attained at a sufficiently small, yet positive, i_D, if there were no precautionary demand for money, only a transactions-demand with positive set-up brokerage costs for each bond transaction however small. The point was argued in Phelps (1965). Then if the demand curve for real balances in the $(i_D, M/p)$ plane were everywhere interior, except at the kink, to the equilateral hyperbola which passes through the kink, the proceeds of the inflation tax would actually be maximized at the kink. But this construction requires that the demand for money have an interest-elasticity greater than one in a small neighborhood above the kink. The picture is not believable. And the assumption that interest rates below the kink would not bring a (gross) social gain from increased precautionary liquidity—albeit at a cost in lost inflation revenue—is not plausible.

In the next and last section, the household utility functions postulated do not produce such kinks so that we are faced with the conflict between the desire for revenue and the attainment of full liquidity.

II. Optimizing the Revenue from Inflation

The aim here is to present a model of the optimal tax mix—with emphasis upon the optimal inflation tax—in the tradition begun by Ramsey (1927) and Boiteux (1956, for example). Present-day writers have found a reasonably general analysis sufficiently arduous that they have often worked in teams—Bradford/Baumol (1970), Diamond/Mirrlees (1971) and Stiglitz/Dasgupta (1971). In view of the analytical difficulties it will be expedient to choose a model of the simplest kind merely to illustrate the applicability of optimal tax theory to the question: What is the best inflation rate from the point of view of public finance?

I shall take the view that liquidity is prized as a "consumer durable". It is rented by households to obtain useful services from it in a world of imperfect information. For example, the more liquid is the household (given wealth), the more economical it is for the household to take advantage of fortuitous bargains that may come its way; even the holding out for a better job offer might be facilitated by increased liquidity. Putting it quite simply, the quality of what is purchased (on the average over time) with a given average money outlay per unit of time and at a given "price level" is enhanced by an increase of liquidity. At a positive rental rate—the opportunity cost of liquidity, the nominal rate of interest—the consumer will balance the marginal utility of liquidity against its price (rental). Ordinarily the optimal tax literature refers to economies of identical households; but the presence of heterogeneity in tastes and talents—to which the imperfect information must ultimately be attributed—precludes that assumption in a literal sense. To get on with the analysis I appeal to something like the representative household. Averaging over households, I (dare to) write average utility as a function of aggregate goods consumed, C, the real value of personal saving, S, the real value of money holdings, L, and aggregate manhours, H:

$$U = U(C, S, L, H), \tag{19}$$

$$U_C > 0,\ U_S > 0,\ U_L > 0,\ U_H < 0$$

I posit the usual convexity conditions and assume that households' utility maxima are interior ones. Clearly this is only one of several possible models of the demand for, and efficiency-functions of, real cash balances. Other models, and a discussion of them from the point of view of the optimum inflation tax, are presented in my recent book.

For simplicity I select a short-run framework—the capital stock is a predetermined state variable at the current moment. There are just two taxes, the inflation tax and a proportional wage tax, again to maximize simplicity. To simplify factor pricing, I let capital and manhours be perfect substitutes in production, with constant marginal returns to each factor. Government expenditure, G, is fixed as before. Liquidity is socially costless in the sense that it does not require labor or capital for its production or maintenance. Aggregate gross final output, Y, is

$$Y = \bar{w}H + (\bar{r} + \delta)K = C + G + \dot{K} + \delta K$$

$$\delta,\ \bar{w},\ \bar{r} = \text{constants} > 0 \tag{20}$$

where K is capital and δ the rate of depreciation. I treat $\bar{w}$ as the before-tax wage and $\bar{r}$ as the real rate of interest.

Wage taxes are to be adjusted to inflation so as to achieve, or preserve invariant, a prescribed rate of change of the value of government indebtedness, $\dot{\Delta}$, as explained in Section I. Let Z denote real wage income before tax, $\bar{w}H$, and let t denote the wage tax rate. Using

$$D/p = \Delta \tag{21}$$

$$G + B + (\bar{r} + \pi)(D/p - L) - tZ - \pi D/p = \dot{\Delta}\,(= \dot{D}/p - \pi D/p) \tag{22}$$

we obtain

$$tZ + iL = \gamma + \beta + \bar{r}\Delta - \dot{\Delta} = a \text{ given} \tag{23}$$

The reader will recognize this as equation (10) or (15). The lefthand side is overall net revenue, and it is constrained to follow an exogenous timepath. The corresponding budget constraint for households is

$$C + S = (1 - t)Z + (r + \delta)K + \bar{B} + i(\Delta - L) - \pi\Delta - \delta K \tag{24}$$

or equivalently

$$C + S + iL = (1 - t)Z + \bar{r}W + B \tag{25}$$

where

$$W = K + \Delta,\ S = \dot{W} \tag{26}$$

Households will be supposed to maximize their utility functions subject to similar budget constraints. Disregarding any externalities, we then say, for every t and i satisfying (23), that C, S, L and Z (that is, H) are such as to maximize U in (19), subject to (25). The necessary first-order conditions for and interior maximum of the Lagrangian expression

$$\mathcal{L}(C, S, L, Z; t, i) = U(C, S, L, H) - \lambda[C + S + iL - (1-t)Z - rW - B] \tag{27}$$

are

$$\begin{aligned} &U_C = U_S = \lambda \\ &U_L = U_C i \qquad D \\ &U_H = -U_C(1-t)\bar{w} \\ &\text{or } U_Z = -U_C(1-t) \end{aligned} \tag{28}$$

With this information we can calculate some relationships between the households' *maximized* utility, say U^*, and the tax rates t and i facing them. If we write

$$V(t, i) = U^*[C(t, i), S(t, i), L(t, i), Z(t, i)] \tag{29}$$

we have

$$\begin{aligned} V_t(t, i) &= U_C^* \partial C/\partial t + U_S^* \partial S/\partial t + U_L^* \partial L/\partial t + U_Z^* \partial Z/\partial t \\ V_i(t, i) &= U_C^* \partial C/\partial i + U_S^* \partial S/\partial i + U_L^* \partial L/\partial i + U_Z^* \partial Z/\partial i \end{aligned} \tag{30}$$

Using (28) we can obtain

$$\begin{aligned} V_t(t, i) &= U_C^*[\partial C/\partial t + \partial S/\partial t + i\partial L/\partial t - (1-t)\partial Z/\partial t] \\ V_i(t, i) &= U_C^*[\partial C/\partial i + \partial S/\partial i + i\partial L/\partial i - (1-t)\partial Z/\partial i] \end{aligned} \tag{31}$$

But differentiation of the budget identity in (24) yields

$$\begin{aligned} &Z + [\partial C/\partial t + \partial S/\partial t + i\partial L/\partial t - (1-t)\partial Z/\partial t] = 0 \\ &L + [\partial C/\partial i + \partial S/\partial i + i\partial L/\partial i - (1-t)\partial Z/\partial i] = 0 \end{aligned} \tag{32}$$

whence

$$\begin{aligned} V_t(t, i) &= -U_C^* Z \\ V_i(t, i) &= -U_C^* L \end{aligned} \tag{33}$$

For an optimum mix of taxes the government must choose t and i, subject to (23), so as to maximize $V(t, i)$. The necessary first-order conditions for a maximum of the Lagrangian

$$\psi(t, i) = V(t, i) + \mu[tZ + iL - \bar{R}] \tag{34}$$

are

$$\begin{aligned} V_t(t, i) &= -\mu\, \partial/\partial t[tZ + iL] \\ V_i(t, i) &= -\mu\, \partial/\partial i[tZ + iL] \end{aligned} \tag{35}$$

whence, using (33)

$$\frac{\partial R/\partial t}{Z}=\frac{\partial R/\partial i}{L}=\frac{U_c^*}{\mu} \tag{36}$$

where $R=tZ+iL$ (total revenue).

The second-order conditions insure that, at a maximum, $\partial R/\partial t$ and $\partial R/\partial i$ and μ are positive. (If $\bar{R}$ were the maximum feasible revenue, the economy would be taxed "to capacity" with $\partial R/\partial i=\partial R/\partial t=0$.)

The formula in (36) may be quite useful for fiscal planning. Ramsey and Boiteux made use of the symmetry of the Slutsky substitution effects along compensated, constant $V(t,\ i)$, demand curves to obtain another formula. Noting, as earlier, that the increases in real income, I, necessary to compensate for an increase of t or i are

$$(\partial I/\partial t)_{\bar{V}}=-Z,\ (\partial I/\partial i)_{\bar{V}}=-L \tag{37}$$

we write

$$\begin{aligned}\frac{\partial R}{\partial t}&=\left\{t\left[\left(\frac{\partial Z}{\partial t}\right)_{\bar{V}}-Z\frac{\partial Z}{\partial I}\right]+i\left[\left(\frac{\partial L}{\partial t}\right)_{\bar{V}}-Z\frac{\partial L}{\partial I}\right]+Z\right\}\\ \frac{\partial R}{\partial i}&=\left\{t\left[\left(\frac{\partial Z}{\partial i}\right)_{\bar{V}}-L\frac{\partial Z}{\partial I}\right]+i\left[\left(\frac{\partial L}{\partial i}\right)_{\bar{V}}-L\frac{\partial L}{\partial I}\right]+L\right\}\end{aligned} \tag{38}$$

By the symmetry $(\partial L/\partial t)_{\bar{V}}=(\partial Z/\partial i)_{\bar{V}}$, we have

$$\begin{aligned}\frac{\partial R}{\partial t}&=\left\{t\left(\frac{\partial Z}{\partial t}\right)_{\bar{V}}+i\left(\frac{\partial Z}{\partial i}\right)_{\bar{V}}+Z\left[1-\left(\frac{\partial Z}{\partial I}+\frac{\partial L}{\partial I}\right)\right]\right\}\\ \frac{\partial R}{\partial i}&=\left\{t\left(\frac{\partial L}{\partial t}\right)_{\bar{V}}+i\left(\frac{\partial L}{\partial i}\right)_{\bar{V}}+L\left[1-\left(\frac{\partial Z}{\partial I}+\frac{\partial L}{\partial I}\right)\right]\right\}\end{aligned} \tag{39}$$

hence

$$\frac{1}{Z}\left[t\left(\frac{\partial Z}{\partial t}\right)_{\bar{V}}+i\left(\frac{\partial Z}{\partial i}\right)_{\bar{V}}\right]=\frac{1}{L}\left[t\left(\frac{\partial L}{\partial t}\right)_{\bar{V}}+i\left(\frac{\partial L}{\partial i}\right)_{\bar{V}}\right]=\frac{U_c^*}{\mu}-1+\left(\frac{\partial Z}{\partial I}+\frac{\partial L}{\partial I}\right) \tag{40}$$

For a small amount of revenue to be collected, we may say that Z and L are to be cut back in the same proportion relative to what they *would be* for the same $\bar{V}$ at $t=i=0$. This is Ramsey's formula.

In the analysis of (40) it is often assumed that there are no cross-substitution effects (independent demands): That is, $(\partial L/\partial t)_{\bar{V}}=(\partial Z/\partial i)_{\bar{V}}=0$. Then the rule is

$$\left(\frac{\partial Z}{\partial t}\frac{t}{Z}\right)_{\bar{V}}=\left(\frac{\partial L}{\partial i}\frac{i}{L}\right)_{\bar{V}} \tag{41}$$

Now $(\partial Z/\partial t)_{\bar{V}}<0$ of course, like $(\partial L/\partial i)_{\bar{V}}$.

Therefore $i > 0$ if and only if $t > 0$. Since t or i or both must be positive for raising $\bar{R}$ of revenue, both liquidity and wages are optimally taxed at positive rates. It is only in the limiting case where $(\partial Z/\partial t)_{\bar{V}} = 0$, meaning that the compensated labor supply curve is perfectly inelastic, that all taxation would optimally fall on labor (within the context of the present model).

To put (41) in terms of the after-tax factor-price elasticities, write the after-tax real wage as $v = (1-t)\bar{w}$. Thus v is the wage to "consumers" and w the wage to producers; similarly, i is the price of liquidity to consumers and zero is the price to "producers". Then, noting that $dv/v = -(t/1-t)\, dt/t$, we obtain

$$\frac{\dfrac{t/(1-t)}{1}}{\left(\dfrac{\partial Z}{\partial v}\dfrac{v}{Z}\right)_{\bar{V}}} = \frac{\dfrac{1}{1}}{\left(\dfrac{\partial L}{\partial i}\dfrac{i}{L}\right)_{\bar{V}}} \tag{42}$$

The numerators are interpretable as the "specific" tax on a unit of real wages and liquidity respectively when expressed as a ratio to the consumer prices of these "commodities", $(1-t)$ and i respectively. Tax rates, thus expressed, are optimally made proportional to the reciprocals of the corresponding elasticities. This harks back to Ramsey's results and appears to be consistent with Stiglitz–Dasgupta (especially p. 164, bottom).

III. Some Conclusions

Evidently, quite different thought-experiments can be considered when we ask the question: How and when does faster inflation substitute for (or in some sense supplement) other conventional forms of taxation? A merit of the approach taken here over that taken by Marty and Friedman is that it focuses attention on the effects of inflation upon households' demands for consumption and leisure—hence upon investment and growth; money creation is like a tax, not merely a surrogate for a tax, only insofar as its consequences (faster expected inflation, higher money interest rates) have income-effects that restrain household demands for goods like any other tax. A merit of the approach here over that used by Tobin is that it employs the method of differential tax analysis in which the sum of the income effects from inflation and ordinary tax instruments is held invariant to a variation in their mixture; for this purpose, it is the central bank that should be made the source of the inflation and the treasury left the freedom to make compensating variations in the deficit. Another merit is that the traditional approach proposed here produces traditional kinds of results: Inflation yields revenue by driving a wedge between "consumer's price" and "producer's price". The rate of growth is not relevant.

It does not follow, of course, that liquidity should be taxed "like everything else"; some other tax might conceivably dominate the inflation-taxation of liquidity. Nevertheless, a simple optimal-tax model has been displayed (where a wage tax is the alternative source of revenue) that does have the property that, unless there is non-independence of commodity demands of a special sort, it will be optimal to tax liquidity. And if, as so often maintained, the demand for money is highly interest-inelastic, then liquidity is an attractive candidate for heavy taxation—at, least from the standpoint of monetary and fiscal efficiency.

References

Bailey, M. J.: Welfare cost of inflationary finance. *Journal of Political Economy 64*, 93–110, April 1956.

Baumol, W. & Bradford, D.: Optimal departures from marginal cost pricing. *American Economic Review 60*, 265–83, June 1970.

Boiteux, M.: Sur la question des monopoles publics astreints a l'equilibre budgetaire. *Econometrica 24*, 22–40, January 1956.

Burmeister, E. & Phelps, E. S.: Money, public debt, inflation and real interest. *Journal of Money, Credit and Banking 3*, 153–182, May 1971.

Diamond, P. A. & Mirrlees, J. A.: Optimal taxation and public production. *American Economic Review 61*, 8–27, 261–278, March–June 1971.

Friedman, M.: Discussion of the inflationary gap. In *Essays in Positive Economics* (ed. M. Friedman), University of Chicago Press, Chicago, 1953.

Friedman, M.: The optimum supply of money. In *The Optimum Supply of Money and other Essays* (ed. M. Friedman), Aldine, Chicago, 1969.

Friedman, M.: The revenue from inflation. *Journal of Political Economy 79*, May–June 1971.

Marty, A. L.: Growth and the welfare cost of inflationary finance. *Journal of Political Economy 75*, February 1967.

Marty, A. L.: Gurley and shaw on money in a theory of finance. *Journal of Political Economy 69*, 56–62, February 1961.

Mundell, R. A.: Inflation and real interest. *Journal of Political Economy 71*, 280–83, June 1963.

Musgrave, R. A.: *The Theory of Public Finance*, especially Part III. McGraw–Hill, New York 1959.

Phelps, E. S.: Anticipated inflation and economic welfare. *Journal of Political Economy 73*, 1–17, January 1965.

Phelps, E. S.: *Inflation Policy and Unemployment Theory*. W. W. Norton and Co., New York, 1972.

Ramsey, F. P.: A contribution to the theory of taxation. *Economic Journal 37*, 47–61, March 1927.

Stiglitz, J. E & Dasgupta, P.: Differential taxation, public goods, and economic efficiency. *Review of Economic Studies 38*, 151–174, April 1971.

Wicksell, K.: *Finanztheoretische Untersuchungen und das Steuerwesen Schweden's*. Jena, Germany, 1896.

MONEY, TAXATION, INFLATION AND REAL INTEREST

INTRODUCTION*

THIS PAPER studies three neoclassical growth models in which the government has both a fiscal and a monetary instrument with which to control the demand for capital and the supply of saving. In these equilibrium models, there is no inherent relationship between the inflation rate and the economy's capital intensity as measured, say, by the real interest rate or the capital-labor ratio. It is shown here, for each of these models, that capital intensity is invariant to the inflation rate if and only if net real government indebtedness is insulated from the rate of inflation through suitable compensatory action either by the central bank or by the government treasury. Thus the conditions for the "neutrality" of changes in money and public debt are clarified. But not every degree of capital intensity can be engineered because the assets available for monetization by the bank are finite and because the viability of money sets an upper bound on the money rate of interest. (The liquidity trap never stands in the way of a low real interest rate, by virtue of the inflation possibility, though the money interest rate cannot be driven to zero.) The choice set from which the government can select real-money/capital or money-interest/real-interest combinations is fully drawn for one of our models.

The second contribution is to the equilibrium theory of the inflation rate. Consonant with the canon in static models that the price level is homogeneous of degree one in the *liquid* and *interest-bearing* obligation of the government

* Burmeister's research for this paper was supported by the National Science Foundation and Phelps' research was supported by the Brookings Institution.

EDWIN BURMEISTER *is associate professor of economics and* EDMUND PHELPS *is professor of economics at the University of Pennsylvania.*

together, *not* in either money or government bonds *singly*, our models show that if the central bank follows a "real" behavioral rule in its market operations, the growth of the treasury's nominal debt will ultimately equalize the rate of increase of both assets and thus govern the rate of inflation. If instead the treasury follows a "real" rule, the central bank's money operations will ultimately govern the growth rate of both assets and thus govern the rate of inflation. But, only if the "real" rule pursued is wholly "illusion-free," being independent of the *rate of change* of the price of goods as well as the price *level*, will the resulting inflation rate be neutral toward the "real" variables.

The third contribution is for the allocation consequences of selection within the choice set. Though a higher inflation rate, at each capital intensity, produces a higher money interest rate and a consequent diminution of monetary efficiency, it also yields larger relief from income (and other ordinary) taxation and hence permits an improvement in "fiscal" efficiency.[1]

Each of our models is confined to equilibrium time-paths. One strength of that feature is that our results are not dependent upon the exact dynamics that need to be specified in disequilibrium models. Another is that for the purposes of economic policy there is hardly any interest in discussing the various equilibria that exist for the contemplation of policymakers if we do not also suppose that the government possesses the necessary stabilization techniques for steering from one equilibrium to another. Once that capacity to equilibrate at wish within the choice set is postulated, there is no longer any interest in the stability of private behavioral relations when unassisted by stabilizing government policies. It should be acknowledged, nevertheless, that we focus here entirely on steady-state equilibrium paths. This proved difficult enough for a single paper.

The pertinent literature has ballooned in the past five years. Mundell had held that a rise of anticipated inflation would increase capital intensity [12]. Phelps contended that the connection depended upon the fiscal-monetary mix by which the inflation was generated [14]. The possibility of jointly controlling "growth" and inflation was shown in the static Metzler model, with due respect to the instantaneous choice set, but the sustainable choice over time was not explored.

The issue then rose again in terms of growth models. Tobin, and subsequently Sidrauski, argued that more inflation led to greater capital intensity and that the treasury determined the inflation rate through its rate of deficit spending [23, 19]. Rose claimed that the central bank determines the rate of inflation, the treasury being powerless to have a permanent effect on the inflation rate [16]. It was left unclear whether the central bank's money creation, like the treasury's, would also increase capital intensity if the anticipated inflation were supposed, contrary to Rose, to have no employment effects; but the analyses of Metzler, Patinkin [13], and Samuelson [17] prepared us to

[1] We are ignoring the welfare effects associated with moving along a path from one equilibrium to another.

expect a capital-deepening effect, since open-market operations have inhomogeneous effect upon *private holdings* of public debt, capital, and money.

The welfare aspects of choosing the rate of anticipated inflation from the point of view of monetary efficiency were discussed by Friedman [5] and Bailey [1], and the concept of "full liquidity" discussed by Marty [9], Phelps [14], and Samuelson [18]. The implications of inflation for the deficit appropriate to a given volume of investment—or, similarly, for the volume of private saving that goes with a given deficit—have been examined by Bailey [1] and Lovell [7], as well as by earlier writers on "forced saving."

I. Models of Anticipated Inflation and Capital Intensity

The models below contain either one or two (homogeneous) earning assets in addition to non-interest-bearing money. We postulate that the per capita demand for money is a function only of per capita money income, per capita money wealth, and the common expected yield on earning assets. We further assume money demand (m^d) always equals the actual money supply (m) so that the equilibrium condition

$$m^d = G(y, pw, i) = m \tag{1}$$

is always satisfied[2] where:

$n \equiv \dot{L}/L =$ rate of growth of the labor force;
$m \equiv M/L =$ per capita money stock;
$p \equiv$ price of output in terms of money as *numeraire*;
$y \equiv pF(K, L)/L$
$\quad \equiv pf(k) =$ net per capita money income;
$k \equiv K/L =$ capital-labor ratio;
$w \equiv$ real per capita private wealth;
$\pi \equiv$ expected inflation rate (equals actual $\dot{p}/p$)[3]
$i \equiv$ expected money yield on earning assets, e.g. capital's expected yield $= f'(k) + \pi$;
$r \equiv$ real rate of interest $= f'(k)$;
$x \equiv m/p =$ per capita real money balances.

Absence of "money illusion" requires that (1) be homogeneous of degree one in its first two arguments. Consequently we may write

[2] This equation could in principle be derived by aggregating the money demand functions of individuals having identical tastes, income, and wealth. More forthrightly, it may be assumed that the aggregate relationship will be of the same form as the individually-determined demand function.

[3] Throughout this paper we shall make the assumption of *perfect myopic foresight* so that $\pi = \dot{p}/p$ for all t.

$$m/p = G(y/p, w, i) \tag{2}$$

where we suppose $G_1 > 0$, $1 > G_2 > 0$,[4] and $G_3 < 0$ for variables in the relevant ranges. Wealth will generally be defined differently for each of the models we will discuss below. But, in all instances we can find a function

$$x = g(k, i), \tag{3}$$

describing the equilibrium per capita real cash balances at various levels of capital stock and yield, (with $g_1 > 0$, $g_2 < 0$), and another function

$$i = \varphi(k, x), \tag{4}$$

which determines the yield necessary to maintain equilibrium with various portfolios of cash and real capital (with $\varphi_1 > 0$, $\varphi_2 < 0$).[5] In addition, the functions (2), (3), and (4) will depend upon the policy parameters of our models, and partial derivatives with respect to these parameters enable us to study comparative statics.

In *all* that follows, we shall suppose that the capital-labor ratio is bounded away from zero,[6] i.e.,

$$k \geqq \epsilon > 0.$$

We suppose also that $g(k, i)$ has the property that, given any $0 < \epsilon \leqq k < \infty$ and for all feasible values of the policy parameters we will consider, there exists a finite value $\bar{\imath} = \bar{\imath}(k)$ such that

$$g[k, \bar{\imath}(k)] = 0. \tag{5}$$

Since

[4] The condition $1 > G_2$ simply means that an extra dollar of wealth will not *all* be held in the form of money balances.

[5] Equation (3) and (4) are derived directly from (2). For example, to derive (3) for Model A discussed below, we write (2) in the implicit form $H(k, x, i) \equiv x - G[f(k), x + (1 - \alpha)k, i] \equiv 0$ where real per capita private wealth, w, is $x + (1 - \alpha)k$; see equation (14). Total differentation of H gives $dH = dx - G_1 f'(k)\, dk - G_2[dx + (1 - \alpha)\, dk] - G_3\, di \equiv 0$. Since

$$\partial H/\partial x = 1 - G_2 > 0,$$

the existence of (3) is proved, and by direct calculation $\partial x/\partial k \equiv g_1 = G_1 f'(k)/(1 - G_2) > 0$ and $\partial x/\partial i \equiv g_2 = G_3/(1 - G_2) < 0$.

Equation (4) for Model A is derived in exactly the same manner. Equation (37) for Model B2 is analogous to equation (3) for Model A. We emphasize that in all instances such equations provide *equilibrium relationships*.

[6] While we make this assumption for mathematical reasons, it is certainly realistic on economic grounds because no one would argue that an economy with a capital-labor ratio near zero would behave as described here.

$$i = f'(k) + \pi, \tag{6}$$

this assumption states that corresponding to any finite, positive value of the capital-labor ratio, k, there exists some rate of price inflation at which the per capita demand for real money balance is zero. In other words, given a fixed k, we assume there exists a yield $\bar{\imath}(k)$ sufficiently large as to satisfy (5). With such a high yield on the alternative asset, no money balances are desired and the economy resorts to "barter" or some commodity money. We derive

$$\bar{\imath}'(k) = -g_1/g_2 > 0$$

from equation (5), i.e., $\bar{\imath}$ is an increasing function of k.[7] We further postulate that the equation

$$\bar{\imath}(k) = f'(k) + \theta - n \tag{7}$$

has a root denoted by $\underline{k}$ (which is obviously unique). Thus for all $k \leqq \underline{k}$, the equilibrium demand for real per capita money balances is zero.

The existence of a liquidity trap is a further issue. For any fixed value of k, (4) determines i as a function of x alone; of course,

$$\bar{\imath} \equiv \varphi(\underline{k}, 0)$$

is implied by the above discussion. However, consider *any* fixed value of $k \in [\epsilon, \infty)$, and from (4) we deduce that there exists a function

$$i = i(x), \qquad \bar{\imath} \equiv i(0), \tag{8}$$

with $i'(x) < 0$. *Note that (8) is an equilibrium condition derived from the assumption $m^d = m$.* Now as i approaches zero, we shall assume that x approaches infinity.

In other words, with k *fixed* at a positive and finite value, we assume that the *only* value of per capita real money balances consistent with equilibrium is infinity. The interested reader can convince himself that our approach is indeed analogous to and consistent with a traditional Keynesian liquidity trap.

Finally, we impose the following commonly-invoked regularity conditions on the per capita production function $f(k)$:

[7] Actually we could allow $\bar{\imath}'(k) = 0$ without significantly altering our analysis. The implication $\bar{\imath}'(k) > 0$ is derived by differentiating (5) and using the assumptions $G_1 > 0$, $1 > G_2 > 0$, and $G_3 < 0$, but one might wish to alter these conditions to weak inequalities (e.g., $G_1 \geqq 0$), at least for some extreme ranges of the variables, as for example at $x = 0$. See footnote 5.

$$f(k) > 0, \quad 0 < k < \infty; \quad f(0) = 0; \quad f(\infty) = \infty;$$

$$f'(k) > 0, \quad 0 < k < \infty; \quad f'(0) = \infty;$$

$$f'(\infty) = 0; \quad f''(k) < 0, \quad 0 < k < \infty.$$

The latter conditions, while not indispensable, serve to avoid difficulties which might arise at boundaries.

Before turning to an analysis of our specific models, we emphasize that we do not pretend to have captured every important feature of a monetary economy. Money is a mediating entity necessary because barter is not efficient and capital markets are not perfect or frictionless. Our demand for money function, equation (2), is quite traditional; it implies a trade-off between transactions demand and opportunity cost, and hence money demand is a function of real per capita money income, real per capita *private* wealth, and the expected money yield on earning assets. Clearly this "explanation," although consistent with econometric estimates, fails to deal adequately with such issues as the structure of financial markets, financial institutions, and other complications. Moreover, we have skirted the problem of "inside" versus "outside" money as we did not wish to derive a complete descriptive theory of government decisions and their interaction with financial intermediaries.

Our definition of real per capita disposable income involves a related question. Essentially we again follow economic and accounting tradition; real per capita disposable income equals real per capita output (minus exhaustive government expenditures) plus the real value of the government deficit minus the inflation rate times the real per capita value of assets (money and bonds) privately held. We then assume per capita (physical) consumption is a constant fraction of real disposable income so defined, a relationship which again is supported by econometric evidence for the steady-state comparisons we wish to analyze. But if people are *not* indifferent to the distribution of assets—for example, to the percentage of government bonds held by the central bank—and if, as a result, consumption habits are substantially different than we have described them, then our conclusions would need modification. But some of the subtle ways by which money and liquidity could affect consumption demand can be introduced in our models via changes in the propensity to consume $(1 - s)$.

Thus the models we present below are based on quite conventional economic assumptions, and to the extent the issues just raised are important, our results could be misleading in some respects. However, we do not believe that our main conclusions, described both in the Introduction and in Part II, are sensitive to these issues, and our tentative explorations of alternative assumptions support this belief. Nevertheless, one cannot be certain, and any contribution would be welcome that helps clarify these questions.

Model A

The following model, like the early model of Metzler's, contains one earning asset, capital, which the Central Bank can purchase with money of its creation. The main features of this version were suggested by Hahn [6], and we have introduced little modification of them. In this model the government always owns a *constant* fraction α of the capital stock, $0 \leqq \alpha < \bar{\alpha} \leqq 1$, where $\bar{\alpha}$ will be defined precisely later. The selection of some exogenous $\alpha \in [0, \bar{\alpha})$ is nevertheless a matter of government choice. Constancy of α means that the government must purchase capital at the flow rate $\alpha\dot{K}$ for all points in time. We assume the nominal money stock increases at the exogenous *constant* rate θ, which is again a matter of government policy choice, but we may conceptually identify two distinct roles by writing

$$\theta = \dot{M}/M = \dot{M}_1/M + \dot{M}_2/M; \tag{9}$$

here we interpret $\dot{M}_1/M$ as the flow rate of money transfer payments by the Treasury, while $\dot{M}_2/M$ is the rate of change in the money supply required to purchase capital at the flow rate αK, thereby keeping α constant. Consequently, we have

$$\dot{M}_2 = \alpha p\dot{K},$$

or equivalently,

$$\begin{aligned}(\dot{M}_2/M)(M/pL) = (\dot{M}_2/M)x &= \alpha\dot{K}/L \\ &= \alpha(\dot{k} + nk).\end{aligned} \tag{10}$$

Further assumptions are needed regarding the government's use of its capital and the savings behavior of individuals when $\alpha > 0$. Suppose *all* the rentals received on the capital stock owned by the government, αK, are distributed to the public as transfer payments over and above, i.e., not included in $\dot{M}_2$. Then one component of net disposable income is

$$\begin{aligned}\alpha F_K K + (1 - \alpha)F_K K + F_L K &= F_K K + F_L K \\ &= F(K, L).\end{aligned} \tag{11}$$

However, $Y(\alpha) \equiv$ *real net disposable income* is determined by *adding* $d(M/p)/dt$ and *subtracting* $\dot{M}_2/p = \alpha\dot{K}$ from (11), i.e.,

$$Y(\alpha) = F(K, L) + d(M/p)/dt - \alpha\dot{K}. \tag{12}$$

This definition is plausible since $\dot{M}_1/p$ are transfer payments which *add* to disposable income, while $\dot{M}_2/p$ represents a trade of money for capital.

Furthermore, our basic flow equilibrium condition is

$$\dot{W}(\alpha) = sY(\alpha) \tag{13}$$

where

$$\begin{aligned} W(\alpha) &= (1-\alpha)K + M/p \\ &= \text{real private wealth.}^{8} \end{aligned} \tag{14}$$

Manipulation of (12), (13), and (14) yields the differential equation[9]

$$\dot{k} = \frac{sf(k) - [(1-\alpha)n + s\alpha n]k - (1-s)(\theta-\pi)x}{(1-\alpha) + s\alpha}. \tag{15}$$

Likewise we may derive an equation for $\dot{x}$, given below, and conclude that $\dot{x} = 0,\ x \neq 0$, whenever

$$x = h(k;\theta,\alpha) = g[k, f'(k) + \theta - n; \alpha]. \tag{16}$$

Moreover, it is easy to show that under our assumptions the curve $h(k;\theta,\alpha)$ shifts downward and to the right with an increase in either θ or α.[10]

In summary, we may derive a differential equations system[11]

$$\left.\begin{aligned} \dot{k}(k,x;\theta,\alpha) &= \{sf(k) - \xi k - (1-s)[f'(k) + \theta - \varphi(k,x;\alpha)]x\}/ \\ &\qquad [(1-\alpha) + s\alpha] \\ &\text{and} \\ \dot{x}(k,x;\theta,\alpha) &= [f'(k) + \theta - n - \varphi(k,x;\alpha)]x \end{aligned}\right\} \tag{17}$$

[8] Our approach thus follows Tobin [22, 23]. We are also assuming that individuals are *indifferent* in their concept of real net disposable income no matter whether (i) they own the entire capital stock and receive all rental payments $F_K K$ directly, or alternatively, (ii) the government owns a fraction α of the capital stock, but since all rental income is turned back to the public as transfers, they still receive exactly the same total income.

[9] Differentiating (14) and equating the result with (13) gives

$$sY(\alpha) = (1-\alpha)\dot{K}\,(+dM/p)/dt;$$

the latter together with $\dot{K}/L = \dot{k} + nk$ and equation (12) implies (15).

[10] See Burmeister and Dobell [2, pp. 191–92]. (The expression for $\dot{k}$ in (87) on p. 192 of [2] should be divided by $[(1-\alpha) + s\alpha]$.)

[11] This form of the $\dot{k}$ equation is derived by substituting equation (4) into equation (6) and then substituting the resulting expression for $-\pi$ into (15).

To derive the $\dot{x}$ equation, differentiate $x \equiv M/pL$ which gives $\dot{x} = (\dot{M}/M - \dot{p}/p - \dot{L}/L) = (\theta - \pi - n)$; then substitute $-\pi$ as above. See Burmeister and Dobell [2], pp. 167–69 and 189–92.

where

$$\xi \equiv (1 - \alpha)n + s\alpha n.$$

The system (17) is written in a form which explicitly indicates that θ and α enter as government policy parameters which are subject to choice, but which are assumed constant except for our comparative static comparisons. We shall spare the reader cumbersome mathematical details and simply *assume* the existence of an equilibrium point $(k^*, x^*) > (0, 0)$ for $\alpha \neq 0$, $\alpha \in (0, \bar{\alpha})$.[12]

We have already stated that the curve $x = h(k; \theta, \alpha)$, along which $\dot{x} = 0$, $x \neq 0$, shifts downward and to the right for increases in either θ or α. Now define

$$\gamma(k; \alpha) \equiv [sf(k) - \xi k]/(1 - s)n \tag{18}$$

where $\xi \equiv (1 - \alpha)n + s\alpha n$. The expression (18) gives the value of x when $\dot{k} = 0$ and $\dot{x} = 0$, $x > 0$. Clearly

$$\left.\frac{\partial \gamma}{\partial \alpha}\right|_k = k > 0. \tag{19}$$

Likewise, $d\tilde{k}/d\alpha = -n(1 - s)/sf''(\tilde{k}) > 0$, where $\tilde{k}$ is the root to $sf'(k) - \xi = 0$ and is the value of the capital-labor ratio where the γ curve is at a maximum for a given α. Consequently the curve $\gamma(k; \alpha)$ shifts upward and to the right for increases in α. Equilibria are represented by the intersections of the γ and h curves.

All the features discussed above are illustrated in Figure 1. The policy

[12] See Burmeister and Dobell [2; pp. 173–77] for a proof of uniqueness in a model with $\alpha = 0$ and with one additional assumption. They also show the following result (footnote 32, p. 192): "Observe that k is determined by the intersection of the curves $\bar{\imath}(k)$ and $j'(k) + \theta - n$, where $\bar{\imath}(k)$ is the solution to $0 = g[k, \bar{\imath}(k); \alpha]$ and where $\bar{\imath}'(k) > 0$. Hence

$$0 = g_1\, dk + g_2\, d\bar{\imath} + g_\alpha\, d\alpha,$$

or

$$\left.\frac{\partial \bar{i}}{\partial \alpha}\right|_{k,\theta} = -g_\alpha/g_2 < 0.$$

The latter means that the $\bar{\imath}(k)$ curve shifts *downward* with an increase in α implying the stated conclusion."

"Finally if there is to exist a root $(k^*, x^*) > (0, 0)$ for any fixed θ, it is necessary to restrict our attention to $\alpha \in [0, \bar{\alpha})$ where $\bar{\alpha}$ is defined as the root to $k(\bar{\alpha}; \theta) = k^{***}$ and k^{***} satisfies $sf(k^{***}) - \xi k^{***} = 0$. It is important to realize that $\bar{\alpha}$ may be substantially less than one, depending, of course, upon the function $f(k)$ and the exogenous parameters θ, s, δ, and n."

For similar reasons very high values of θ may preclude the existence of an equilibrium point $(k^*, x^*) > (0, 0)$. We return to this important issue in a later section where we discuss the set of feasible steady-state equilibria points, or the choice set. Note that g_α may be calculated from (2) with $w = (1 - \alpha)k + x$; we find $g_\alpha = -kG_2/(1 - G_2) < 0$.

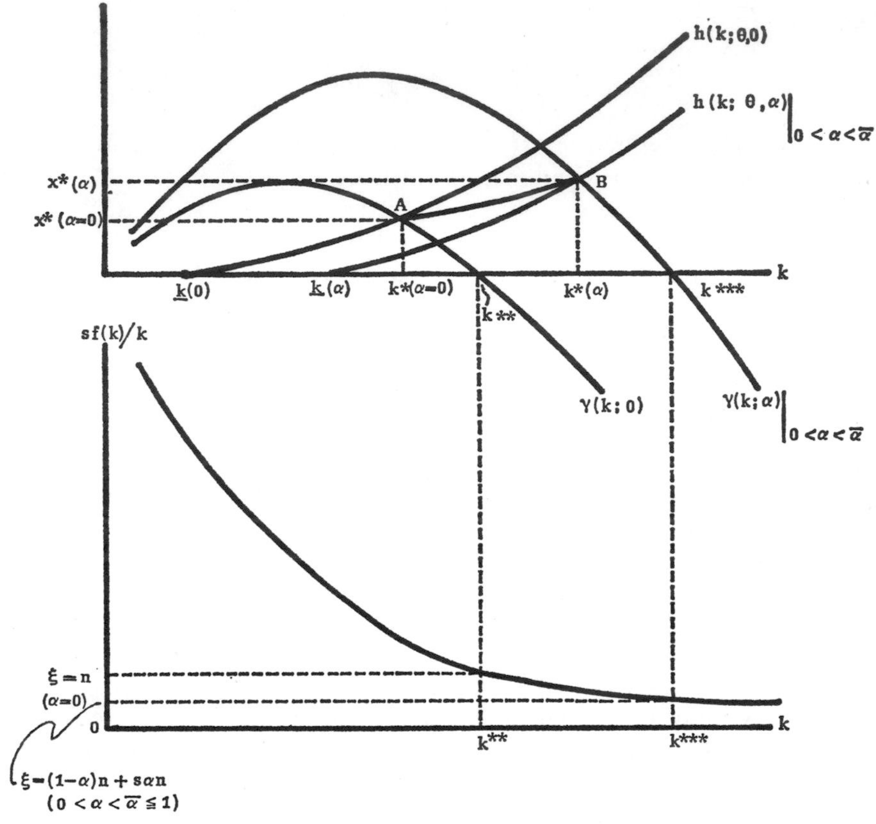

FIG. 1. For a *fixed* θ, *any* point on the *AB* curve represents a feasible (k^*, x^*) equilibrium corresponding to a value of α satisfying $0 \leqq \alpha < \bar{\alpha} \leqq 1$.

implications are immediately evident. For example, suppose the government insists upon zero inflation in equilibrium which necessitates fixing $\theta = n = \dot{L}/L$. If $\alpha = 0$, the equilibrium point (k^*, x^*) is completely determined and no further government "control" is possible. For illustrative purposes, suppose the equilibrium point *A* depicted in Figure 1 is possible with $\alpha = 0$ and $\theta = n$. By choosing a value of $\alpha \in (0, \bar{\alpha})$ *a whole locus of equilibrium points is now possible*. For example, any point on the curve labelled *AB* in Figure 1 is now a feasible equilibrium position.[13] (In Figure 1 it has been assumed that $\alpha < \bar{\alpha}$.)

[13] The proper slope of the *AB* curve in Figure 1 is not immediately evident either graphically or intuitively. However, it is clear that any root k^* must satisfy

$$\Psi(k^*, \theta, \alpha) \equiv sf(k^*) - \xi k^* - (1 - s)ng[k^*, f'(k^*) + \theta - n; \alpha] = 0,$$

and the fact that (k^*, x^*) is unique implies $D^* \equiv \partial\Psi(k^*; \theta, \alpha)/\partial k^* < 0$. Consequently we find

A more complete discussion of the set of feasible steady-state equilibria points $(k^*, x^*) > (0, 0)$ will be deferred to Part II. However, our analysis already provides the following theorem.

THEOREM 1:

Let the real per capita net debt in equilibrium be denoted by $\Omega^* = x^* - \alpha k^*$. Further let θ be fixed and assume $\alpha \in [0, \bar{\alpha})$. Then for any feasible equilibrium value of the capital-labor ratio k^*, there corresponds one and only one value of the real per capita net debt Ω^*. The exact relationship is

$$\Omega^* = \gamma(k^*; 0) = [sf(k^*) - nk^*]/(1 - s)n$$

where $\gamma(k; \alpha)$ is defined by (18). Furthermore, if k^{**} is feasible, then $k^* = k^{**}$ *if and only if* $\Omega^* = 0$ where k^{**} is the "no money" Solow equilibrium for which $sf(k^{**}) - nk^{**} = 0$.

Proof:

Equilibrium prevails if and only if $sf(k^*) - \xi k^* - (1 - s)nx^* = 0$, where $\xi = (1 - \alpha)n + s\alpha n$. Substituting $x^* = \Omega^* + \alpha k^*$ into the latter and simplifying yields the conclusion. Q.E.D.

We have noted that the government may pursue policies which stabilize the system; thus we have an immediate corollary of Theorem 1:

Corollary:

Any stabilizing policy for which

$$\lim_{t\to\infty} k^t = k^{**} \Rightarrow \lim_{t\to\infty} \Omega^t = 0.$$

Conversely, *any* stabilizing policy for which

$$\left.\frac{\partial k^*}{\partial \alpha}\right|_\theta = [g_\alpha - (1 - s)nk^*]/D^*,$$

which is clearly positive because g_α is negative. Since $x^* = g[k^*, f'(k^*) + \theta - n; \alpha]$, we may calculate

$$\left.\frac{\partial x^*}{\partial \alpha}\right|_\theta = [g_1 + g_2 f''(k^*)]\partial k^*/\partial\alpha + g_\alpha,$$

and while the first term of the latter expression is clearly positive, g_α is negative. Therefore an increase in α, for any fixed θ, may either increase or decrease x^*.

However, observe that $g_\alpha^* = -k^*G_2/(1 - G_2)$, where G_2 represents the partial derivative of the demand for real per capita money balances with respect to real per capita private wealth. We may anticipate that G_2 is very near zero, in which case it is likely that $\partial x^*/\partial\alpha|_\theta$ is positive, as implied by the upward-sloping *AB* curve in Figure 1.

$$\lim_{t\to\infty} \Omega^t = 0 \Rightarrow \lim_{t\to\infty} k^t = k^{**}.$$

Such stabilizing policies have been discussed by, e.g. [2, 4, 6, 21]; likewise the Corollary applies to models which are stable because of disequilibrium adjustment mechanisms, as in [2, 6, 16, 20].

Model B

In this model we postulate a third asset, interest-bearing government bonds.[14] We also suppose that there is absolutely no difference (in the eyes of the portfolio managers) between holding physical capital versus bonds; that is, everyone views capital and bonds as having exactly the same uncertainty characteristics. Consequently, if both assets are to be held in portfolios their yields must be equal:

$$i = f'(k) + \pi. \tag{20}$$

Unlike Model A, the Treasury no longer finances its deficit by note issue; i.e., in the notation of the previous model, $\dot{M}_1 \equiv 0$. The government deficit is financed by borrowing. The Central Bank creates money by asset purchases. For expositional convenience we consider only the two polar cases: Case B1 in which the Central Bank holds no capital, and Case B2 in which it holds no government bonds. Of course, combinations of these cases could be studied as long as a selection rule is specified. For example, a linear combination of Cases B1 and B2 is clearly admissible.

We use the following notation:

D = the money value of the outstanding government debt (bonds)
D_{CB} = the money value of government debt held by the Central Bank
K_{CB} = the quantity of capital owned by the Central Bank
$\Delta \equiv D/pL$ = real per-capita government debt
G = government (exhaustive) expenditures in money terms
$\equiv \gamma p f(k) L$ where $\gamma \in [0, 1)$ is an exogenous constant
T = money taxes
Def. = the money value of the government deficit
$\equiv G + rD - T - r(D_{CB} + pK_{CB})$
$\equiv \dot{D}$
Ω = the per capita real value of government net indebtedness
$\equiv (D - D_{CB} + M - pK_{CB})/pL$
$\equiv \Delta - \Delta_{CB} + x - k_{CB}$
$\omega \equiv \dot{\Omega} + n\Omega$

[14] It is assumed that the maturity of the debt is finite and that our equations describe situations in which all the debt has been turned over at least once at the current i. All debt therefore sells at par.

$\delta =$ a policy parameter
$\equiv \dot{D}/pL \equiv$ Def.$/pL$
$\theta \equiv \dot{M}/M =$ a policy parameter (as before).

All the other notation is the same as that employed in the previous sections. In particular, M is still the stock of money, now solely M_2. Moreover, the demand for money function and its properties remain as described by equations (1) to (5) above.

Equilibrium steady-state values of the variables are denoted by asterisks as superscripts, e.g., k^*. Only points $(k^*, x^*) > (0, 0)$ will be considered, and we shall ignore the cumbersome details of the conditions which insure existence.[15] We also define steady-state equilibrium by the properties

$$0 = \dot{\Delta} = \dot{x} = \dot{k}.$$

We now wish to explore the implications of various government policies upon the equilibrium steady-state value of the capital-labor ratio k^*. We define the following additional notation:

$\tilde{y} =$ real per capita disposable income
$\equiv f(k) + \dot{D}/pL - \gamma f(k) - \pi(M + D - D_{CB})/pL.$
$c =$ per capita (physical) consumption
$\equiv C/L.$

Our consumption function is of the simple form

$$c = (1 - s)\tilde{y} \tag{21}$$

where $s \in (0, 1)$ is the average and marginal propensity to consume.[16]

Of course,

$$F(K, L) \equiv \dot{K} + C + \gamma F(K, L), \tag{22}$$

and from (21) and (22) we deduce

$$\dot{k} = (1 - \gamma)f(k) - (1 - s)\tilde{y} - nk$$

or, using our definitional identities and straightforward calculation,

$$\left.\begin{aligned} \dot{k} &= s(1 - \gamma)f(k) + (1 - s)\pi(M + D - D_{CB})/pL - (1 - s)\delta - nk \\ &= s(1 - \gamma)f(k) - nk - (1 - s)[\delta - \pi(x + \Delta - \Delta_{CB})]. \end{aligned}\right\} \tag{23}$$

In steady states we have the relations

[15] See Burmeister and Dobell [2; pp. 173–77] for one example of such considerations.
[16] Thus again our approach is in the recent tradition [4, 19, 23].

$$\left.\begin{aligned} \pi &= \theta - n, \qquad (x > 0, \dot{x} = 0) \\ \Delta^* &= \frac{\delta}{\theta} \end{aligned}\right\} \tag{24}$$

upon using $\dot{\Delta} = \delta - (\pi + n)\Delta = 0$.

Hence we can express the fundamental steady-state equation for Model B:[17]

$$0 = s(1 - \gamma)f(k) - nk - (1 - s)[\delta - (\theta - n)(x + \Delta - \Delta_{CB})]. \tag{25}$$

We can see how the root of (25) is related to ω (and thus to Ω) as follows. Using $\dot{M} = \dot{D}_{CB} + p\dot{K}_{CB}$, we find the relation

$$\omega = \delta - \pi(\Delta + x - \Delta_{CB})$$

which shows how δ must be adjusted to π in order to keep $\dot{\Omega}$ invariant to π.[18] Substituting this in (25) and using $\dot{\Omega} = \omega - n\Omega$, we have

$$0 = s(1 - \gamma)f(k) - nk - (1 - s)[n\Omega + \dot{\Omega}].$$

Hence, *if* $\dot{\Omega} = 0$ in steady states, then steady-state k is invariant to π if Ω is held invariant to π. The only step remaining is to show that the steady-state conditions require $\dot{\Omega} = 0$.

Case B1: $K_{CB} \equiv 0$.

When the Central Bank holds no capital, it is clear that $M \equiv D_{CB}$, and $\dot{M} = \dot{D}_{CB}$ is a flow equilibrium condition. Consequently

$$(D - D_{CB})/pL = D/pL - x = \Delta - x,$$

and from (24) we find

[17] In greater detail, we have $(1 - \gamma)f(k) - c = \dot{K}/L = \dot{k} + nk$, and substituting $c = (1 - s)\tilde{y}$ and the definition of y into the latter together with the steady-state conditions (24), we derive (25) by direct algebraic manipulations.

[18] The derivation is

$$\begin{aligned} \dot{\Omega} &= \frac{\dot{D}}{pL} - (\pi + n)\Delta - \frac{\dot{D}_{CB}}{pL} + (\pi + n)\Delta_{CB} \\ &\quad + \frac{\dot{M}}{pL} - (\pi + n)\frac{M}{pL} - \frac{\dot{K}_{CB}}{L} + n\frac{K_{CB}}{L} \\ &= \delta - (\pi + n)(\Delta - \Delta_{CB} + x) - nk_{CB}, \end{aligned}$$

so the definition of Ω and $\omega \equiv \dot{\Omega} + n\Omega$ imply $\omega = \delta - \pi(\Delta - \Delta_{CB} + x)$.

$$[(D - D_{CB})/pL]^* = (\delta/\theta) - x. \tag{26}$$

Substituting (26) into (25) gives us

$$s(1 - \gamma)f(k) - nk - (1 - s)\delta n/\theta = 0.^{19} \tag{27}$$

Note that the simplicity of Model B1 is due to the fact that x does not appear in (27).

Now define

$$H(k) \equiv s(1 - \gamma)f(k) - nk; \tag{28}$$

$\dot{k} = 0$ if and only if k satisfies

$$H(k) = (1 - s)\delta n/\theta \tag{29}$$

where δ and θ are government policy parameters. A typical situation is illustrated in Figure 2a where $\delta/\theta > 0$ and k^{***} represents the solution to

$$H(k) = s(1 - \gamma)f(k) - nk = 0 \tag{30}$$

and may be called the Solow-root.

There are several facts immediately evident from Figure 2a, e.g., there are at most two steady-state equilibria (k^*, x^*) and (k^{**}, x^{**}). However, we now prove a result exactly analogous to Theorem 1 for Model A and which is not immediately evident.

THEOREM 2:

Consider Model B1 (with $K_{CB} = 0$) and suppose we restrict our attention to the relevant choice set. The steady-state equilibrium capital-labor ratio k^{***}, defined by (30), prevails iff $\delta = 0$ iff $\Omega^* = 0$. The exact relationship between steady-state values of Ω and k is

$$\Omega^* = [s(1 - \gamma)f(k^*) - nk^*]/(1 - s)n. \tag{31}$$

Proof:

Examination of (27) shows that it suffices to prove that $\delta = \theta\Omega^*$. More-

[19] More specifically, we have:

$$\begin{aligned} &s(1 - \gamma)f(k) - nk + (1 - s)\pi(x + \delta/\theta) - (1 - s)\delta \\ &= s(1 - \gamma)f(k) - nk + (1 - s)\pi x + (1 - s)[(\theta - n)\delta/\theta - \delta] \\ &= s(1 - \gamma)f(k) - nk + (1 - s)\pi x - (1 - s)n\delta/\theta = 0. \end{aligned}$$

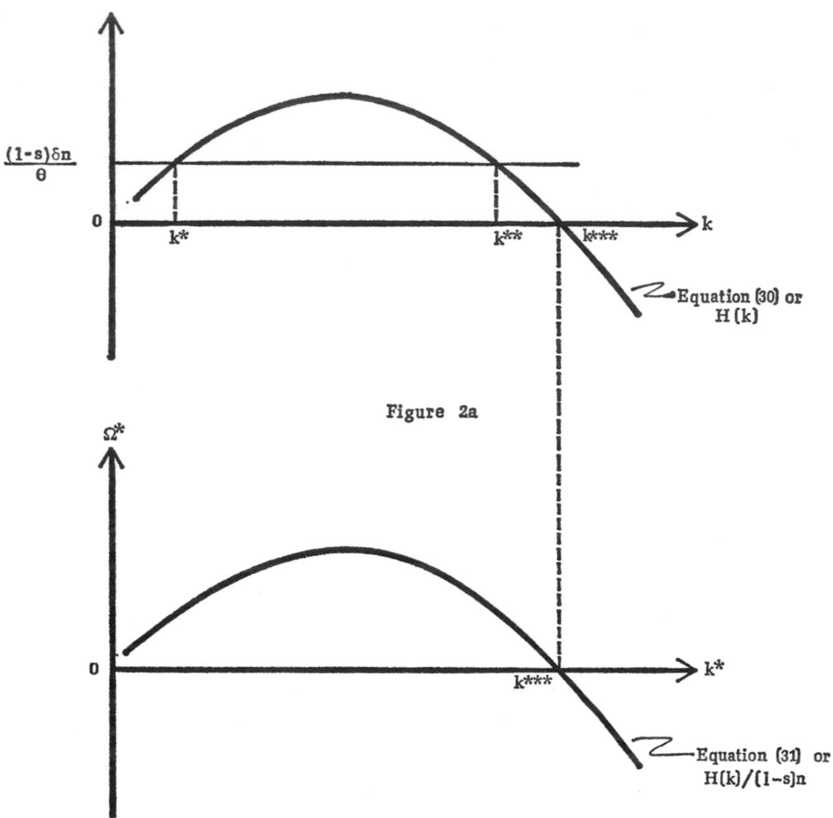

FIG. 2b.

over, when $K_{CB} \equiv 0$, $M \equiv D_{CB}$ and consequently $\Omega = D/pL \equiv \Delta$. Thus (24) implies $\delta = \theta\Omega^*$. Q.E.D.

Theorem 2 is illustrated by Figure 2b. A Corollary analogous to that of Theorem 1 is obvious, and we need not state it here.

Case B2: $D_{CB} \equiv 0$.

We now will examine the polar case in which the Central Bank holds some physical capital, but its holdings of government bonds is identically zero. In this case it is clear that a flow equilibrium condition for the Central Bank is

$$\dot{M} = p\dot{K}_{CB} . \tag{32}$$

Now substitution of $D_{CB} = 0$ and $\Delta^* = \delta/\theta$ into (25) gives

$$s(1 - \gamma)f(k) + (1 - s)(\theta - n)(x + \delta/\theta) - (1 - s)\delta - nk = 0. \tag{33}$$

Note that unlike Model B1, the variable x does not drop out of the equation determining steady-state value(s) of the capital-labor ratio(s). Hence k^* *is* influenced by the equilibrium demand-for-money function

$$x \equiv M/pL = G[f(k), w, i; \gamma] \tag{34}$$

where, now, real per capita private wealth is,

$$w \equiv k - k_{CB} + \Delta + x \tag{35}$$

with $k_{CB} \equiv K_{CB}/L$.[20]

We require the following result.

LEMMA:

$$k^*_{CB} = \theta x/n.$$

Proof:

$$\dot{k}_{CB}/k_{CB} = \dot{K}_{CB}/K_{CB} - n \quad \text{or} \quad \dot{k}_{CB} = 0, \qquad k_{CB} \neq 0, \Rightarrow \dot{K}_{CB}/L = nk^*_{CB}.$$

But, from (32) we find $\dot{K}_{CB}/L = (\dot{M}/M)(M/pL) \equiv \theta x$, implying the conclusion. Q.E.D.

The above Lemma, together with (24), implies that w in steady-state equilibrium is given by

$$w = k - \theta x/n + \delta/\theta + x. \tag{36}$$

We must now check that the equilibrium condition (34) can be solved for x to give a function

$$x = \Gamma(k; \theta, \delta, \gamma, n, s) \tag{37}$$

which determines steady-state equilibrium values of x for assigned values of k. To this end we define the implicit function

$$\begin{aligned} \Phi(k, x) &\equiv G[f(k), w, i; \gamma] - x = 0 \\ &= G[f(k), k - \theta x/n + \delta/\theta + x, f'(k) + \theta - n; \gamma] - x = 0 \end{aligned} \tag{38}$$

and calculate

$$\partial\Phi/\partial x = G_2(-\theta/n + 1) - 1. \tag{39}$$

[20] The latter observation is related, if not identical to the issues of "neutrality" and "dichotomy"; see, e.g., Modigliani [11] and Patinkin [13].

Now $0 < G_2 < 1$ by assumption, so certainly $G_2 - 1 < 0$. Consequently *for all* $\theta \geqq 0$, $\partial\Phi/\partial x$ given by (39) is strictly negative, implying the existence of (37). We may also note that if G_2 is small, then negative values of θ are admissible without violating the necessary inequality

$$\partial\Phi/\partial x < 0.$$

Below we will find that the sign of $\Gamma'(k; \cdot)$ is crucial, and we calculate that result now by differentiation of (38):

$$d\Phi = G_1 f'(k)\, dk + G_2[dk - (\theta/n)\, dx + dx] + G_3[f''(k)\, dk] - dx = 0 \quad (40)$$

which implies

$$\begin{aligned} dx/dk &\equiv \Gamma'(k; \cdot) \\ &= [G_1 f'(k) + G_2 + G_3 f''(k)]/[G_2(+\tfrac{\theta}{n} - 1) + 1]. \end{aligned} \quad (41)$$

Clearly our assumptions $G_1 > 0$, $G_2 > 0$, $G_3 < 0$ and (39) <0 imply that $\Gamma'(k, \cdot) > 0$ and hence

$$(n - \theta)\Gamma'(k; \cdot) \quad \begin{Bmatrix} > 0, & n > \theta \\ = 0, & \theta = n \\ < 0, & n < \theta \end{Bmatrix}. \quad (42)$$

We now return to our main objective, namely determining k^*('s). To this end we substitute (37) into (33), thereby obtaining

$$s(1 - \gamma)f(k) - nk + (1 - s)(\theta - n)\Gamma(k; \cdot) - (1 - s)n\delta/\theta = 0. \quad (43)$$

As before, (43) has a simple interpretation: any steady-state equilibrium $(k^*, x^*) > (0, 0)$ must have a capital-labor ratio satisfying equation (43).

Now define

$$\Lambda_1(k) \equiv s(1 - \gamma)f(k) - nk \quad (44)$$

and

$$\Lambda_2(k) \equiv (1 - s)(n - \theta)\Gamma(k; \cdot) + (1 - s)n\delta/\theta. \quad (45)$$

Clearly (43) is satisfied if and only if

$$\Lambda_1(k) = \Lambda_2(k), \quad (46)$$

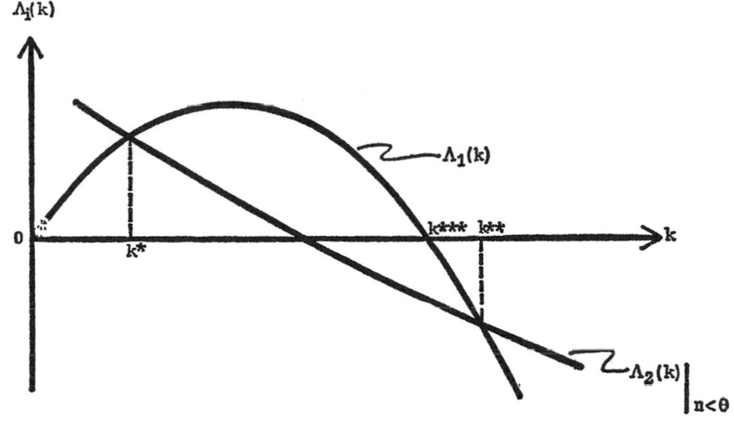

Figure 3a

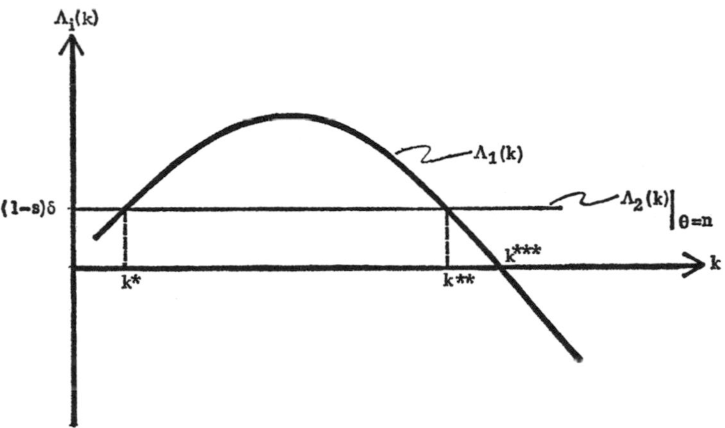

FIG. 3b.

and it is the latter equilibrium condition which is depicted in Figures 3a and 3b. Note that (42) determines the slope of the $\Lambda_2(k)$ curve because $\Lambda_2'(k) = (1 - s)(n - \theta)\Gamma'(k; \cdot)$.

One observation is immediately evident from the preceding discussion and Figure 3b:

Unlike Model B1, $\delta = 0$ implies the Solow-point capital-labor ratio k^{***} only in the special case where $\theta = n$ and $\dot{\pi}^* = 0$ (no inflation or deflation). Moreover, in this case an increase in δ from $\delta_1 > 0$ to $\delta_2 > \delta_1 > 0$ increases k^* and decreases k^{**} (see Figure 3b).

Despite this observation, however, our main theorem remains valid, as we shall now prove.

THEOREM 3:

Consider Model B2 (with $D_{CB} \equiv 0$) and suppose we restrict our attention to the relevant choice set. The steady-state equilibrium capital-labor ratio k^{***}, defined by (30), prevails if and only if $\Omega^* = 0$. The exact relationship is identical to equation (31) stated in Theorem 2.

Proof:

Equation (43) may be written as

$$\Lambda_1(k) + (1 - s)[(\theta - n)x - n\delta/\theta] = 0, \tag{47}$$

where $D_{CB} \equiv 0$. Moreover, $D_{CB} \equiv 0 \Rightarrow \Omega = D/pL + M/pL - K_{CB}/L$, and using (24) and the preceding Lemma, we derive

$$\Omega = \delta/\theta + x - \theta x/n$$

or

$$-(1 - s)n\Omega = (1 - s)(\theta - n)x - (1 - s)n\delta/\theta. \tag{48}$$

Equations (47) and (48) together imply

$$\Omega^* = \Lambda_1(k^*)/(1 - s)n = [s(1 - \gamma)f(k^*) - nk^*]/(1 - s)n,$$

which is identical to (31). Q.E.D.

The content of Theorem 3 is again illustrated by Figure 2b. Moreover, if we set $\gamma = 0$, Figure 2b also describes the relationship between Ω^* and k^* in Model A.[21]

Model C

It will be instructive to consider now a model in which the Central Bank takes as its assignment the setting of the money rate of interest rather than the rate of growth of the money supply. This more "Keynesian" formulation is the one adopted by Tobin [23]. Its rationale might be that the Central Bank takes its primary responsibility to be the maintenance of monetary efficiency by keeping the opportunity costs of money balances small.

It will be convenient to use the structure of Model B, changing only the roles of some variables from parameters to unknowns and vice versa. Hence $i = \iota \equiv$ the money interest rate target (= a policy parameter). For $x > 0$, we have again

[21] Recall that Ω^* represents real per capita net government indebtedness. Also the reader is warned that the exogenous parameter γ should not be confused with the function $\gamma(k; \theta, \alpha)$.

$$\dot{M}/M = n + \pi. \tag{49}$$

Our equation for steady-state k remains

$$0 = s(1 - \gamma)f(k) - nk - (1 - s)\left[\frac{\dot{D}}{pL} - \pi(x + \Delta - \Delta_{CB})\right] \tag{50}$$

or

$$0 = s(1 - \gamma)f(k) - nk - (1 - s)[n\Omega + \dot{\Omega}]. \tag{51}$$

It is possible to show, as in Case B, that in steady states $(\dot{\Omega})^* = 0$ for polar cases, so that invariance of k^* implies invariance of Ω^*.

To determine π and Δ we again require some rule for $\dot{D}$. One possible rule is

$$\frac{\dot{D}}{D} = \lambda \equiv constant \geqq 0, \qquad D > 0 \text{ for all } t. \tag{52}$$

Thus, using

$$\frac{\dot{\Delta}}{\Delta} = \frac{\dot{D}}{D} - n - \pi, \tag{53}$$

we find the steady-state inflation rate (where $\dot{\Delta} = 0, \Delta > 0$) is

$$\pi = \lambda - n. \tag{54}$$

Consider now the case where $K_{CB} \equiv 0$ so that $x = \Delta_{CB}$, where Δ_{CB} denotes the real per capita government debt held by the Central Bank. Then, writing $\dot{D}/pL$ in the form $\lambda\Delta$, (50) and (54) imply

$$0 = s(1 - \gamma)f(k) - nk - (1 - s)n\Delta. \tag{55}$$

To determine x, given Δ, we need only use

$$x = G[f(k), k + \Delta, \iota] \tag{56}$$

where now real private wealth is $k + x + (\Delta - \Delta_{CB}) = k + \Delta$. It follows that x and k depend only on Δ, given the exogenous policy parameter ι. To close the system we use

$$\iota - \pi = f'(k). \tag{57}$$

Equations (54)–(57) determine the unknowns π, k, Δ, and x. The absolute price level p is therefore proportional to the initial debt D.

The above argument shows that the steady-state deficit is positively associated with the rate of inflation. But if we consider

$$\frac{\dot{D}}{D} = \lambda \geqq 0. \qquad D < 0, \tag{59}$$

then inflation is associated with a *surplus* greater than $-\lambda D > 0$. In this case the Central Bank requires $K_{CB} > 0$ in order to create money. We leave it to the interested reader to analyze this case.

It may be objected that treating $\dot{D}/D$ as a policy parameter is unappealing. But $\dot{M}/M$ is equally so. The natural rationale for θ and equally for λ is the wish of the corresponding agency to maintain the desired rate of inflation. The only noteworthy difference between Model B and C is that in the latter case the remaining agency aims for a certain liquidity through control of the interest rate, while in the former the other agency aims to control the consumption-investment mix through the deficit. But this difference could be removed by assigning to the Central Bank the objective of maintaining a specified real rate of interest.

Another possibility is that the Treasury will desire to control net deadweight indebtedness, Ω, while the Central Bank controls the money interest rate—for "growth" and "liquidity" objectives, respectively. M and D are then dependent variables, so that from one point of view p is indeterminate. But the rate of inflation is a determinate by-product. An increase of the money rate of interest necessitates an equal rise of the inflation rate.

It will be obvious by now that in all the models presented here, the changes in the common rate of growth of money and debt produce equal changes in the inflation rate—it matters not which asset's growth rate is (explicitly or implicitly) exogenous. Such increases are not *intrinsically* non-neutral for the capital-labor ratio or, equivalently, the real rate of interest: the real interest rate will be invariant if Ω is kept invariant, which requires compensation for capital gains or losses on certain paper asset holdings. But such changes are never truly neutral on the real economic system as a whole if (as here) money bears no own-interest. Hence the set of opportunities for policy choice is of importance.

II. The Choice Set and Welfare Considerations

In all of the models we have discussed, an important policy question concerns the set of feasible steady-state equilibrium points. Clearly there may exist welfare trade-offs between x^* and k^*, an issue we elaborate upon below, but it is meaningless to examine equilibria which are not economically feasible. Since we have implicitly assumed throughout this paper that our models are somehow stabilized, perhaps via direct government action, we restrict our attention to feasible *steady-state* equilibria. For simplicity we shall confine our discussion to Model A, although the same general argument may be applied to our other models.

For the reader's convenience we remind him of several results derived earlier; in particular

$$\gamma(k; \alpha) \equiv [sf(k) - \xi k]/(1 - s)n \tag{60}$$

where

$$\xi \equiv (1 - \alpha)n + s\alpha n$$

and where $k^{**}(\alpha)$ is defined as the unique root of

$$\gamma(k; \alpha) = 0. \tag{61}$$

We may calculate

$$dk^{**}/d\alpha = -(1 - s)nk^{**}/[sf'(k^{**}) - \xi] > 0; \tag{62}$$

equation (62) is strictly positive because $[sf'(k^{**}) - \xi]$ is negative.

Also recall that $\underline{k}(\theta, \alpha)$ was defined by equation (7); it is a root to

$$g[k, \bar{\imath}(k)] \tag{63}$$

where

$$\bar{\imath}(k) = f'(k) + \theta - n. \tag{64}$$

Hence, we derived a curve

$$h(k; \theta, \alpha) \equiv g[k, f'(k) + \theta - n; \alpha] \tag{65}$$

along which $\dot{x} = 0$, $x \neq 0$. Moreover, as is immediately evident from Figure 1, a necessary condition for the existence of *any* point $(k^*, x^*) > (0, 0)$ is

$$\underline{k}(0, 0) < k^{**}(0).^{22} \tag{66}$$

We assume that equation (66) is always satisfied, for otherwise the feasible set would be null.

[22] We are imposing the restriction $\dot{M}/M \equiv \theta \geqq 0$.

We also stated that the h curve shifts to the right with increases in either α or θ, i.e.,

$$\partial \underline{k}(\theta, \alpha)/\partial(\cdot) > 0 \tag{67}$$

and

$$\partial h/\partial(\cdot)\big|_{k} > 0 \tag{68}$$

where $(\cdot)$ represents θ or α. Finally, we proved that

$$d\tilde{k}/d\alpha > 0 \tag{69}$$

where $\tilde{k}$ is the unique root to $sf'(k) - \xi = 0$; (62) and (69) together imply that the curve $\gamma(k; \alpha)$ shifts upward and to the right with increase in α.

Now let $\theta = 0$ be *fixed* and define

$$\bar{\alpha} \equiv \sup\{\alpha \mid 0 \leqq \alpha \leqq 1; \underline{k}(0, \alpha) < k^{**}(\alpha)\}. \tag{70}$$

LEMMA:

No $\alpha > \bar{\alpha}$ is consistent with $(k^*, x^*) > (0, 0)$ equilibrium *for any* $\theta \geqq 0$.

Proof:

Consider the inequality

$$\underline{k}(0, \bar{\alpha}) < k^{**}(\bar{\alpha}); \tag{71}$$

clearly (71) is implied by (70). Now the right-hand side of (71) is fixed, while the left-hand side of (71) *increases* with θ; see (67). Thus we must have $\alpha \in [0, \bar{\alpha}]$. Q.E.D.

For convenience we first postulate $\bar{\alpha} = 1$. We now turn to a discussion of Figure 4 depicting the set of feasible steady-state equilibria when $\bar{\alpha} = 1$. There are several important observations which we now enumerate and prove:

i. The curve AB, analogous to the curve AB in Figure 1, is upward sloping. *Proof:* It is easily verified that $f'(\hat{k}) = n$ at point P, i.e., $\hat{k}$ is the Golden Rule capital-labor ratio. Further, $i \to 0$ as $k \to \hat{k}$ along the curve $h(k; 0, 1)$ since $i \equiv f'(k) + \theta - n$. Thus $k = \hat{k}$ represents a liquidity trap as discussed earlier and we conclude that $h(k; 0, 1)$ is asymptotic to $k = \hat{k}$. Also $k(0, 0) < \underline{k}(0, 1)$ is implied by (67), and this fact together with (69) proves the stated conclusion.

ii. The line $\Omega^* = 0$ is consistent with the Solow no-money point S where $k = k^{**}(0)$. To the left of the $\Omega^* = 0$ line, the government is a net debtor and any equilibrium capital-labor k^* is less than $k^{**}(0)$. Conversely, to the right

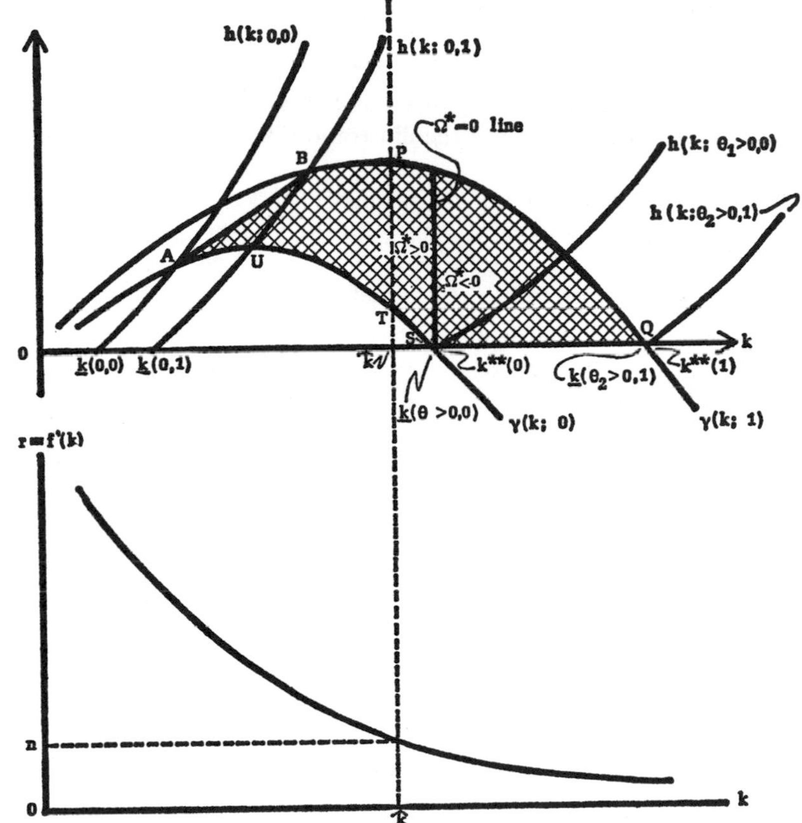

FIG. 4. The case of $\bar{\alpha} = 1$; the set of feasible steady-state equilibria points $(k^*, x^*) > (0, 0)$ is the interior of the region *ABPQSTUA*.

of the $\Omega^* = 0$ line the government is a net creditor and any $k^* > k^{**} > 0$. *Proof:* See Theorem 1.

iii. At any equilibrium point (e.g., *T*) where $k = \hat{k}$, the slope of the curve $d\Omega^*/dk = -1$, implying that real private wealth $w = x + (1 - \alpha)k$ is maximized. The result is attributed to Solow and von Weizsäcker [13].

Proof: It suffices to show,

$$\left.\frac{dx}{dk}\right|_{k=\dot{x}=0} = \gamma'(k^*,0) = [sf'(k) - n]/(1 - s)n = -1 \qquad \text{iff}$$

$$f'(k) = n \qquad \text{iff } k = \hat{k}, \text{ (see Theorem 1)}.$$

iv. Sustainable per capita consumption is maximal anywhere on the line *PT*.

Proof: Familiar Golden Rule.

v. Per capita consumption is zero at Q. *Proof:* Substituting $x = 0$ into (17) and solving for $\dot{k} = 0$ gives $sf(k) = nk$, which implies $c = 0$ because $f(k) \equiv c + \dot{k} + nk$.

vi. One would normally expect that the Solow-point S would lie to the left of $k = \hat{k}$; we have not drawn the illustration in this way merely for convenience.

vii. Both points S and Q are positions of "barter" discussed earlier; in these cases no one wants to hold money balances in his portfolio because θ is so high that $i = \bar{\imath}$.

viii. Any point interior to the region defined by $ABPQSTUA$ is feasible.

Proof: Clearly point A is feasible, and by increasing α from 0 to 1, we can attain any point on AB. Now keep α fixed at zero, and increase θ from 0 to θ_1; this procedure sweeps out points on the curve $AUTS$. Likewise keep α fixed at 1, and increase θ from 0 to θ_2, thereby attaining points on the curve BPQ. Finally, by changing both θ and α (both satisfying $0 < \theta_1 \leqq \theta \leqq \theta_2$ and $0 \leqq \alpha \leqq 1$) so as to maintain the equality

$$\underline{k}(\theta, \alpha) = k^*(\alpha),$$

we can deduce that any point on SQ is feasible. Note the latter is possible only because $\bar{\alpha} = 1$ by assumption.

Finally, since all our curves shift continuously with the parameters θ and α, any point interior to the stated region is feasible. We exclude the boundaries for mathematical convenience and to insure that every equilibrium point satisfies $(k^*, x^*) > (0, 0)$ with strict inequality.

It remains to discuss the situation when $\bar{\alpha} < 1$, in which case we must restrict our attention to $\alpha \in [0, \bar{\alpha}) \subset [0, 1]$. In this instance the set of steady-state equilibria points is somewhat more complicated to determine, but the general method remains the same. The crucial difference is that we must now determine the locus of intersections of the curves $\gamma(k; \alpha)$ and $h(k; 0, \alpha)$ for all $\alpha \in [0, \bar{\alpha})$; this locus is the curve AQ in Figure 5. We leave it as an exercise for the reader to deduce the other properties of Figure 5.

At this point we address ourselves to some welfare aspects of the feasible choice set. It might seem, at least to those unfamiliar with the inflation literature, that society should be equally pleased with all points on any vertical, for example the stretch TP in Figure 4, on the ground each point corresponds to the same steady-state per capita consumption level. But the increase of x along any vertical corresponds to a decrease of the money interest rate: the increase of required α must be accompanied by a decrease of θ to prevent an increase of k; with the real rate of interest unchanged and the inflation rate smaller, the money interest rate, $i = f' + \theta - n$, must be smaller. The implied reduction of the opportunity cost of holding money balances is commonly regarded as a social gain exhibited by added leisure for example (see Phelps [14]). Thus

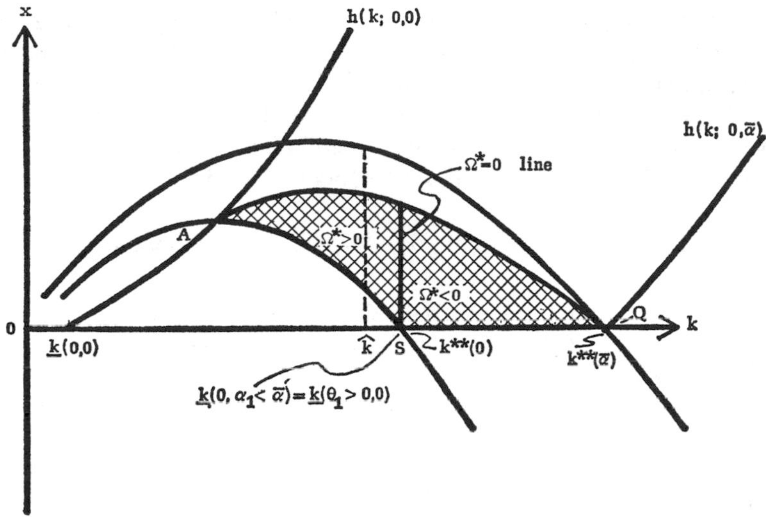

FIG. 5. The case of $\bar{\alpha} < 1$; the set of feasible steady-state equilibria points $(k^*, x^*) > (0, 0)$ is the interior of the region *AQSA*. Other properties of the set remain similar to those discussed in detail for the case $\bar{\alpha} = 1$ illustrated by Figure 4.

the conventional conclusion is to regard the northern boundary, *ABP*, as the efficient frontier (skirting the issue of whether the set contains that boundary)—without regard, of course, to the transition costs of increasing k from one level to another nor the frictional transition costs, outside the scope of this model, from increasing x by means of decreasing the expected algebraic inflation rate.

There are other considerations in judging the superiority of the frontier in relation to interior points. This is not an appropriate place for a comprehensive discussion, but one new conclusion emerges from the formal model behind the choice set: a movement down any vertical stretch within the choice set corresponds to an increase of the inflation rate and a decrease in the per capita pace of asset acquisition by the Central Bank, αnk; both of these have effects upon the per capita budgetary deficit, the per capita government debt in private hands and hence upon the "tax rate," τ, defined as *taxes per unit of taxable income*. If we recall that lump-sum taxes raise awkward questions of practical attainability at least as serious as the problem of paying own-interest on money, we see that the effect of the x selection in the choice set affects fiscal efficiency as much as monetary efficiency. The "tax rate" just defined seems to be a fair measure of the strength of the substitution effects from positive taxes, though it must be acknowledged that these effects are not expressed in the behavioral functions, the supply of labor L, and the private supply of saving per unit disposable income, s. Despite this shortcoming, a brief investigation of the tax-rate effect of x for given k will probably prove to be not totally misleading for a proper analysis.

In the present context, Model A, the real deficit per head is $\dot{M}_1/pL$,[23] and this may be thought of as the *shortfall* between real bank earnings *plus* taxes per head and real government expenditures per head, here conveniently set equal to zero. Hence each dollar increase of the deficit is a dollar reduction of positive taxes per head when public expenditures are appreciable and the deficit is smaller. From (9) and (10) of Model A we find

$$\dot{M}_1/pL = (\dot{M}_1/M_1)(M_1/M)(M/pL) = \theta x - n\alpha k(> 0). \tag{72}$$

Now consider any fixed k on the northern boundary ABP (or, for that matter $ABPQ$). By Theorem 1, Ω must then be constant as well. Then, recalling $\Omega = x - \alpha k$, we have

$$\dot{M}_1/pL = (\theta - n)x + n\Omega. \tag{73}$$

As we move downward from the boundary with k held constant, θ is increased and x decreased: the derivative of (73) with respect to θ is

$$x + (\theta - n)(dx/d\theta)\Big|_{k(\theta,x) = \text{const.}} = [1 + (dx/d\theta)(\theta/x) - (n/x)(dx/d\theta)]x. \tag{74}$$

The first term reflects the deficit increase entailed by faster growth of p and M_1; it is the ordinary-tax relief needed to offset the implied increase of the inflation-tax, the latter being measured by πx. But the increase of θ (and accompanying decrease of α which keeps k and Ω constant) reduces x so that, for sufficiently large $(\theta - n)$ the effect on the deficit is reversed. However, even for small n, the derivative remains positive as long as the Cagan–Sidrauski-like elasticity satisfies $(dx/d\theta)(\theta/x) > -1$, an elasticity implicitly involved in their treatment of stability. (See Cagan [3] and Sidrauski [19].)

In terms of the tax rate, we have, as a definition, for the simple case at hand,

$$\tau = \frac{\gamma f(k) + \dot{M}_1/pL}{f(k) - r\alpha k} \tag{75}$$

where γ denotes government expenditures as a fraction output, $\gamma = 0$ here. Note that $\dot{M}_1/pL$ are gifts over and above the recycling of the Central Bank's interest earnings; but its holdings of interest-bearing assets make a difference to taxable income (though not to disposable income) since households do not pay tax on the "gifts" financed by the bank's earnings if those "gifts" take the form of an appropriately calculated reduction of tax rate or if they are "nontaxable" for any other reason. (Thus $r\alpha k$ is a subtraction from the bottom, not an addition to the top.)

[23] $\dot{M}_1$ is gifts *over and above* the gifts of the government financed out of $r\alpha k$.

We see then that the compensating *decrease* of α that accompanies the increase of θ has a reinforcing effect (for $\tau > 0$) of reducing the tax rate by *broadening* the tax base, $f(k) - \alpha rk$, from which taxes must be raised to cover the *excess* of expenditures over the deficit provided the latter is positive. We see then that there may be some allocative advantages from an increase of the equilibrium inflation rate that might outweigh the disadvantages stemming from the associated rise of the money rate of interest.

Literature Cited

1. Bailey, Martin J. "Welfare Cost of Inflationary Finance," *Journal of Political Economy,* 64 (April, 1956), 93–110.
2. Burmeister, Edwin and A. Rodney Dobell. *Mathematical Theories of Economic Growth.* New York: Macmillan, 1970.
3. Cagan, Philip. "The Monetary Dynamics of Hyperinflation," in *Studies in the Quantity Theory of Money,* Milton Friedman, ed. Chicago: University of Chicago Press, 1956.
4. Foley, Duncan K., Karl Shell and Miguel Sidrauski. "Optimal Fiscal and Monetary Policy, and Economic Growth," *Journal of Political Economy,* 77 (July–August, 1969), 698–719.
5. Friedman, Milton. "Discussion of the Inflationary Gap," in *Essays in Positive Economics.* Chicago: University of Chicago Press, 1953.
6. Hahn, F. H. "On Money and Growth," Journal of Money, Credit and Banking, 1 (May, 1969), 172–88.
7. Lovell, Michael C. "A Keynesian Analysis of Forced Saving," *International Economic Review,* 4 (September, 1963), 247–64.
8. Levhari, David and Don Patinkin. "The Role of Money in a Simple Growth Model," *American Economic Review,* 58 (September, 1968), 713–53.
9. Marty, Alvin. "Gurley and Shaw on Money in a Theory of Finance," *Journal of Political Economy,* 69 (February, 1961), 56–62.
10. Metzler, Lloyd. "Wealth, Saving and the Rate of Interest," *Journal of Political Economy,* 59 (April, 1951), 93–116.
11. Modigliani, Franco. "The Monetary Mechanism and its Interaction with Real Phenomena," *Review of Economics and Statistics,* 45 (February, 1963), 79–107.
12. Mundell, Robert. "Inflation and Real Interest," *Journal of Political Economy,* 71 (June, 1963), 280–83.
13. Patinkin, Don. *Money, Interest, and Prices,* 2nd ed. New York: Harper & Row, 1965.
14. Phelps, Edmund S. "Anticipated Inflation and Economic Welfare," *Journal of Political Economy,* 73 (February, 1965), 1–17.
15. ———. *Fiscal Neutrality Toward Economic Growth,* New York: McGraw-Hill, 1965.
16. Rose, H. "Unemployment in the Theory of Growth," *International Economic Review,* 7 (September, 1966), 260–82.

17. SAMUELSON, P. A. "Reflections on Central Banking," in *Collected Scientific Papers.* Cambridge, Massachusetts: MIT Press, 1966.

18. ———. "D. H. Robertson," *Quarterly Journal of Economics,* 77 (November, 1963), 796–810. Also in *Collected Scientific Papers.* Cambridge, Massachusetts: MIT Press, 1965, 517–36.

19. SIDRAUSKI, MIGUEL. "Inflation and Economic Growth," *Journal of Political Economy,* 75 (December, 1967), 796–810.

20. STEIN, JEROME L. "Money and Capacity Growth," *Journal of Political Economy,* 74 (October, 1966), 451–65.

21. STEIN, JEROME L. and KEIZO NAGATANI. "Stabilization Policies in a Growing Economy," *Review of Economic Studies,* 36 (April, 1969), 165–83.

22. TOBIN, JAMES. "A Dynamic Aggregative Model," *Journal of Political Economy,* 63 (April, 1955), 103–115.

23. ———. "Money and Economic Growth," *Econometrica,* 33 (October, 1965). 671–84.

Part IV
INFLATION PLANNING

INTRODUCTION

The welfare economics of anticipated inflation is an analysis of where we would like to be if we were already there. It can be only an ingredient in thinking about where we want to go from here. In the present group of papers the selection of an inflation policy is properly viewed as a problem in optimal dynamic control from given initial conditions. For convenience the assumption of a natural rate of unemployment is maintained throughout. The first two of these studies adopt the premise of the adaptive-expectations hypothesis: Expectations of excessive inflation can be purged only at the cost of a slump in output and employment; the contrivance of a boom must produce rising expectations of inflation in the process. The third and last essay explores, with some misgivings, a more hopeful formulation.

The criterion of choice in the 1967 paper is Frank Ramsey's intertemporal utilitarianism. If we do not discount the utility of any future generation relative to any preceding one, the optimal path of the expected inflation rate approaches asymptotically the optimum rate of anticipated inflation. The optimum anticipated inflation rate was that identified with full liquidity. Unless the expected inflation rate was already at the latter optimum from the beginning, therefore, unemployment must be driven above its natural rate and allowed to return only in the limit. The optimal time path, then, was a dreary prospect. Generations would have to suffer unnaturally high unemployment to win for future generations an increase of liquidity—although the former sacrifices, roughly commensurate with the latter benefits, might be quite small. This deflationism was enough, though, to cast me as Lucifer in the struggle for the souls of central bankers. My own uneasiness with this position and my ambivalence toward the utilitarianism underlying it are described in the next paper.

The criterion of choice in the following paper, written a decade later, is the "maximin" standard associated with John Rawls. The conception of the optimum anticipated rate of inflation is a more sophisticated one that takes into account the uses of a moderately high money rate of interest for the purposes of tax revenue and of central bank stabilization.

It is remarkable, to me at least, that a qualitative feature of the utilitarian solution turns up in this radically different problem: When expectations of inflation are dangerously high, an optimal inflation policy seeks to reduce those expectations despite the consequence of temporarily fewer jobs for the present generation of workers. The reason involves the risks for future generations of seeking to maintain a perilous status quo ante.

Are the hardships of "planned slump" truly necessary when initial expectations of inflation are excessive in the eyes of all the participants in the economy? One would hope that, with monetary statesmanship, disinflation could be devised without the cost of a disequilibriating departure from the natural rate. This question is the subject of the last essay in the present group.

In the previous models where all wages are set synchronously, either periodically or continuously, the institution of a monetary policy aiming to reduce expectations of inflation induces a recession in the process because the central bank, if not so counterproductive as to conceal its intentions, lacks credibility and must earn it by carrying out its threats; only the visible evidence of slower growth in the money supply, sales, prices, and so on will cause expectations of price and wage inflation to subside. But what if the situation were dire enough to lend credibility to the central bank? There are theoretical settings, whether or not real-world ones, in which no wage and price setter would have reason to bet that other wage and price setters are not anticipating the central bank's execution of its plan and not also anticipating the generality of that anticipation; in that case each wage and price setter will predict success for the central bank's plan and adjust his own wages and prices accordingly. The central bank would be expected to crown its success by carrying out its announced plans rather than jeopardize its credibility for the future.

However, in models where wage setting is staggered over the year (or more generally the common interval between periodic wage review), there is another dimension to the problem of disinflation without recession. One might even suspect that the previous wage commitments still outstanding at the current time would completely predetermine the path of future wages if henceforth the money supply is always to be chosen to underwrite full employment. This turns out not to be so in the expectational model of wage determination studied in the third essay. There are infinitely many sequences of present and future money supplies—and corresponding sequences of the average money wage—that are consistent with the same full-employment or nonrecession path of employment, even though (as supposed) those sequences and employment consequences are forecast perfectly from the present time forward. Nevertheless, to achieve asymptotically any particular steady rate of wage inflation without a deviation of employment from its steady-state equilibrium level the central bank must thread the needle: Too gradual a deceleration of the money supply in the effort to eliminate inflation—to take the simplest example—will produce excessive upward pressure on current new wage commitments (in anticipation of much higher future wages) in relation to the current money supply (which, by hypothesis, is not being sharply increased). Too sharp a deceleration of the money supply to expunge inflation, on the other hand, will not grant enough room for new wage commitments to catch up with their latest predecessors.

It would be agreeable to leave matters at that. Everything is possible within the feasible set. There exists the possibility of curbing excessive inflation without recession, although not without a measure of skill and luck, and not as quickly as one would like. Yet doubts arise at the level of the model. A too thorough list of reservations is recited in the paper itself. Throwing incautiousness to the winds, I had better emphasize here a point on which I may have been too sanguine in the paper: the model is based on an expectational theory of money-wage determination unbridled by quasi-contractual restraints that never look forward, but only backward to observable and quantifiable data. The idea of tax-based income policy rests on the assumption that such restraints exist and it will be necessary to compensate people for the risks they apprehend, realistically or not, in allowing those restraints to be trespassed.

PHILLIPS CURVES, INFLATION EXPECTATIONS, AND OPTIMAL EMPLOYMENT OVER TIME

This article is a study of the "optimal" fiscal control of aggregate demand. It presents a dynamic macroeconomic model from which is derived the optimal time-path of aggregate employment. Given this employment path and the initially expected rate of inflation, the time-path of the actual rate of inflation (positive or negative) can also be derived. If I am right about the dynamic elements, the problem of optimal demand is sufficiently difficult to justify some drastic simplifications in this first analysis: a closed, non-stochastic economy is postulated in which exogenous monetary policy immunizes investment against variations in capacity utilization in such a way as to keep potential capital intensity constant over time. But despite these limitations, I believe that the analysis introduces some important desiderata for national and international policy towards aggregate demand.

The principal ingredients of the model are the following: first, a sort of Phillips Curve in terms of the rate of price change, rather than wage change, that shifts one-for-one with variations in the expected rate of inflation; second, a dynamic mechanism by which the expected inflation rate adjusts gradually over time to the actual inflation rate; third, a social utility function that is the integral of the instantaneous "rate of utility" (possibly discounted) at each point in time now and in the future; last, a derived dependence (from underlying considerations of consumption and leisure) of the rate of utility at any time upon current "utilization" or employment—the decision variable under fiscal control —and upon the money rate of interest, hence, given the real rate of interest, upon the expected rate of inflation. An optimal utilization or employment path is one which maximizes the social utility integral subject to the adaptive expectations mechanism that governs the shifting of the Quasi-Phillips Curve.

The choice problem just sketched is dynamical: an optimal utilization policy by the government must weigh both the current benefits and the consequences for future utility possibilities of today's utilization decision. By contrast, the conventional approach to the employment-

[1] This article was written during my tenure of a Social Science Research Council Faculty Research Grant in the Spring of 1966 at the London School of Economics. I am very grateful to numerous economists there and at the Universities of Cambridge, Essex and York for their helpful comments on oral presentations. David Cass and Tjalling Koopmans of Yale University kindly scrutinized certain technical aspects of a preliminary and more extensive version of this article to which I shall make occasional reference: "Optimal Employment and Inflation Over Time", Cowles Foundation Discussion Paper No. 214 (August 1966). Any errors and other defects in this article are my responsibility.

Reprinted by permission from *Economica*, Vol. 34(3), August 1967.

inflation problem—if there is a conventional approach—is wholly statical.[1] I shall briefly describe that approach and show where I believe it goes wrong. Then I shall summarize the conclusions of the dynamical approach and attempt an intuitive explanation of them for those readers who do not wish to study the model in detail.

Visualize a diagram on which we represent the locus of unemployment-inflation combinations available to the government *when the expected rate of inflation equals zero* by a characteristically shaped Phillips Curve.[2] This curve is negatively sloped, strictly convex (bowed in toward the origin) and it intersects the horizontal axis at some unemployment ratio, say u^*, $0 < u^* < 1$. The quantity u^* measures the "equilibrium" unemployment ratio, for it is the unemployment rate at which the actual rate of inflation equals the expected rate of inflation so that the expected inflation rate remains unchanged. Now superimpose on to the diagram a family of social indifference curves, negatively sloped (at least in the positive quadrant) and strictly concave, and suppose that one of these indifference curves is tangent to the Phillips Curve at some unemployment ratio, say $\mathring{u}$, smaller than u^*. The quantity $\mathring{u}$ measures the (statical) optimum in the conventional approach. The inequality $\mathring{u} < u^*$ stems from the customary (though not unanimous) judgment that there is some reduction of unemployment below u^* that is worth the little inflation it entails.

But if the statical "optimum" is chosen, it is reasonable to suppose that the participants in product and labour markets will learn to expect inflation (and the concomitant money wage trend) and that, as a consequence of their rational, anticipatory behaviour, the Phillips Curve will gradually shift upward (in a uniform vertical displacement) by the full amount of the newly expected and previously actual rate of inflation. Now if the recalculated "optimal" unemployment ratio does not change in the face of the shift, greater inflation will result than before and the pattern will repeat as expectations are continually revised upwards; there will occur what is popularly called a "wage-price spiral" that is "explosive" or "hyper-inflationary" in character. It is more likely that the upward displacement of the Phillips Curve will cause the policy-makers to "take out" the loss in the form of an increase in the unemployment ratio as well as some increase in the rate of inflation. The rate of inflation will continue to increase as long as the unemployment ratio is smaller than u^*, so that the actual rate of inflation exceeds the expected rate with the consequence that the Phillips Curve is rising; but as the statically "optimal" $\mathring{u}$ approaches

[1] A recent example of the approach I have in mind is R. G. Lipsey, "Structural and Deficient-Demand Unemployment Reconsidered", in A. M. Ross (ed.), *Employment Policy and the Labor Market*, Berkeley, 1965. See also A. M. Okun, "The Role of Aggregate Demand in Alleviating Unemployment", in *Unemployment in a Prosperous Economy*, A Report of the Princeton Manpower Symposium, May 13-14, 1965, Princeton, N. J., pp. 67-81.

[2] The classic reference of course is W. A. Phillips, "The Relation Between Unemployment and the Rate of Change of Money Wage Rates in the United Kingdom, 1861-1957", *Economica*, vol XXV (1958), pp. 283-99.

u^*, a stationary equilibrium will be asymptotically reached in which $\dot{u} = u^*$ and there is equality between the expected and actual rates of inflation. Even though a state of steady inflation is eventually achieved, it is likely to be a very high rate of inflation—much higher than the policy-makers myopically bargained for. Thus the conventional approach goes wrong in implicitly discounting future utilities infinitely heavily.[1] (This is not the only amendment to the conventional approach that I shall make.)

The dynamical approach recognizes that any optimal time-path of the unemployment ratio must approach the steady-state equilibrium level, u^*; perpetual maintenance of the unemployment ratio below that level (perpetual over-employment) would spell eventual hyper-inflation and ultimately barter, while perpetual maintenance of unemployment above that level (perpetual under-employment) would be wasteful of resources. The policy trade-off is not a timeless one between permanently high unemployment and permanently high inflation but a dynamic one: a more inflationary policy permits a transitory increase of the employment level *in the present* at the expense of a (permanently) higher inflation and higher interest rates in the *future* steady state. Optimal aggregate demand therefore depends upon society's time preference.

If there is no time discounting of future utilities, future considerations dominate and society should aim to achieve asymptotically the best of all possible steady states, namely the one in which the (actual and expected) inflation rate is low enough, and hence the money interest rate (the cost of holding money) is low enough, to satiate the transaction demand for liquidity by eliminating private efforts to economize on cash balances. If that steady state is not realizable immediately at the equilibrium unemployment ratio, because the initially expected rate of inflation is too high, society should accept under-employment in order to drive down the expected rate of inflation to the requisite point and thus permit an asymptotic approach to the desired steady state. If society has a positive discount rate, it will pay to trade off an ultimate shortfall of

[1] Of course, my criticism is founded also upon the postulated "instability" of the Phillips Curve. In fact, a situation of sustained "over-employment"—more precisely unemployment less than u^* by a non-vanishing amount— has been supposed to produce an explosive spiral through its effects upon the Phillips Curve. On my assumptions, the only *steady-state* Phillips Curve is a vertical line intersecting the horizontal axis at u^*. Now some econometric work over the past ten years might suggest that, especially on a fairly aggregative level, the Phillips Curve is a tolerably stable empirical relationship. But these studies probably estimate some average of different Phillips Curves, corresponding to different expected rates of inflation and of wage change which have varied only over a small range. Further, some writers have found the actual rate of inflation to have a weak influence on wage change and this may be explained by the view that the actual rate of inflation is a proxy, but a very poor one, for the expected rate of price or wage change. See, with reference to British data, R. G. Lipsey, "The Relation Between Unemployment and the Rate of Change of Money Wage Rates in the United Kingdom, 1862-1957: A Further Analysis", *Economica*, vol. XXVII (1960), pp. 1-31; and, with reference to American data, G. L. Perry, "The Determinants of Wage Rate Changes and the Inflation-Unemployment Trade-off in the United States," *Review of Economic Studies*, vol. 31 (1964), pp. 287-308.

liquidity in the future steady state—to accept an ultimately higher rate of inflation and hence a higher cost of holding money—for higher employment in the present; the steady state chosen will be more inflationary the greater the discount rate. If that ultimately desired steady state does not now obtain at equilibrium unemployment because the initially expected inflation rate is *too high*, under-employment must still be accepted in order to drive down the expected inflation rate. But, symmetrically, if the initially expected rate of inflation is *below* the ultimately tolerated rate of inflation, *over-employment* is optimal to drive up the expected inflation rate. (In both cases, unemployment gradually approaches the equilibrium level as the expected inflation rate approaches the ultimately desired level.) Clearly, over-employment is more likely to be appropriate the greater is the discount rate; optimal employment in the present is an increasing function of the discount rate. Thus optimal employment policy in this dynamic model depends to an important extent upon time preference.[1]

Now for the construction, defence and analysis of the model. In this publication I confine myself to the simplest version with an infinite decision-making horizon, a smooth utility function and an equilibrium "utilization" ratio that is independent of the rate of inflation (as in the above discussion).

I. Possibilities and Preferences

In this part the model is developed and the optimization problem stated. The solution will be discussed in Parts II and III.

A. *The "virtual" golden age, utilization and interest.* To make the money rate of interest a stationary function of employment or utilization, to make only consumption, not investment, vary with utilization—both in order to simplify preferences—and to make the marginal productivity of labour rise at the same constant proportionate rate for every employment or utilization ratio—in order that the notion of a stationary family of Phillips Curves in terms of prices have greater plausibility—I postulate that the economy, thanks to a suitably chosen monetary policy and to the nature of population growth and technological progress, is undergoing "virtual" golden-age growth. By this I mean that actual golden-age growth *would be observed* in the economy if the employment-labour force ratio or utilization ratio were constant. (Golden-age growth is said to occur when *all* variables change exponentially, so that investment, consumption and output grow at the same rate which may exceed the rate of increase of labour.)

[1] If the Phillips Curve shifts upward with a one point increase of the expected inflation rate by less than one point, then the steady-state Phillips Curve will be negatively sloped. But it will be steeper than the non-steady-state Phillips Curves which is all that is required to justify a dynamical analysis and to make the discount rate important. It is true, however, that the criticism of the statical approach loses more of its force and the discount rate is less important the less steep is the steady-state curve in relation to the non-steady-state curves. A case of a negatively sloped steady-state Phillips Curve is analysed in my preliminary paper, "Optimal Employment and Inflation Over Time," *op. cit.*

To generate virtual golden-age growth I suppose that the homogeneous labour force (or competitive supply of labour) is homogeneous of degree one in population and homogeneous of degree zero in the real wage, disposable real income per head and real wealth per head.[1] Hence, whenever the latter three variables are changing equiproportionately, the labour supply will grow at the population growth rate, say γ. More general assumptions are apt to impair the feasibility of golden-age growth.

As for production, let us think in terms of an aggregate production function which exhibits constant returns to scale in capital and employment with technical progress, if any, entering in a purely labour-augmenting way, so that output is a linear homogeneous function of capital and augmented employment (or employment measured in "efficiency units"). Suppose further that the proportionate rate of labour augmentation is a non-negative constant $\lambda \geqslant 0$. Then augmented labour supply will grow exponentially at the "natural" rate, $\gamma + \lambda > 0$, whenever the real wage rate, disposable real income per capita and real per capita wealth grow in the same proportion.

As for capital, we require that the capital stock grow exponentially at the rate $\gamma + \lambda$. Then output will grow exponentially, as will investment and hence consumption, at the rate $\gamma + \lambda$ for any constant augmented employment-capital ratio—which I shall call the *utilization ratio*. This implies that the government, by monetary actions I shall assume, always brings about the right level of (exponentially growing) investment necessary for exponential growth of capital at the natural rate.

On these assumptions there is virtual golden-age growth: at any *constant* utilization ratio, output, investment, consumption, capital, augmented employment and, under marginal productivity pricing, real profits and real wages will all grow exponentially at the natural rate, while the marginal and average product of labour and, under marginal productivity pricing, the real wage rate, real income per capita and real wealth per capita will all grow at the rate λ. Disposable real income per head will also grow at rate λ on plausible assumptions (e.g., a constant average propensity to consume) such that the taxes per head necessary for the exponential growth of consumption per head also grow at rate λ. Thus the labour supply will grow at rate γ, like population and employment. The marginal product of capital and the equilibrium competitive real interest rate will be constant over time. (If the augmented employment-capital ratio is changing over time, most of these variables will not be growing exponentially; it is only population, labour augmentation, capital and investment that grow exponentially, come what may.)

[1] Taxes will be lump-sum. Labour supply is supposed independent of the real and money rates of interest. I neglect the difference between wealth and capital, i.e., the government debt. This is acceptable if the wealth-capital ratio is constant over time. While this will not occur in my model, that ratio will become asymptotic as any golden-age path is approached. I suggest therefore that the error is small enough to be neglected safely.

While the monetary authority (the Bank) is postulated to guide investment along its programmed path, the fiscal authority has control over consumption demand and hence, given the programmed investment demand, aggregate demand and employment. Since employment is the decision variable in the present problem, fiscal devices are the policy instruments by which consumption demand and thus employment are controlled. I postulate unrealistically that the Fisc levies "lump-sum" taxes (taxes having no substitution effects) on households for this purpose.

The monetary instruments by which the Bank keeps investment on its programmed path are assumed to be devices like open-market operations which operate through the rate of interest or directly upon the demand for capital. The Bank must be alert therefore to adjust interest rates in the face of changes in aggregate demand or utilization engineered by the Fisc. If the real interest rate equals or is closely tied to the marginal productivity of capital, then clearly the real rate of interest will be higher the greater is the utilization ratio, since investment is to be kept on the exponential path appropriate to virtual golden-age growth.[1] Now to the details.

The real rate of interest is the money rate of interest minus the expected rate of inflation. I assume here that expectations of the current price trend are held unanimously and certainly by the public (but not necessarily by the policy-makers who, from this point of view, lead an unreal existence). If we let i denote the money rate of interest and let r denote the real rate of interest, we obtain

(1) $i = r - x, \quad 0 \leqslant i < i_b,$

where x is the expected rate of algebraic *deflation*. Thus $-x$ is the expected rate of inflation.[2] Equation (1) says, therefore, that as x becomes algebraically small, i.e., as inflation becomes expected, the money rate of interest becomes high, given the real rate of interest; for given the physical or real yield on capital, the prospects of high nominal capital gains on physical assets (and hence on equities) produced by the

[1] We do usually observe that interest rates are relatively high in "good times", but evidently they are not sufficiently high or high soon enough to prevent procyclical variations of investment expenditures. Possibly the reason is that business fluctuations are too sharp and imperfectly foreseen to permit the monetary authorities to stabilize investment. But if fiscal weapons were used effectively to control consumption demand, as they are assumed to be in this article, then the Bank's job of controlling investment would be much facilitated. It must be admitted, however, that the whole question of optimal fiscal and monetary policy in the presence of exogenous stochastic shocks and policy lags is beyond the scope of this article.

It should also be mentioned that the exclusive assignment of investment control to the monetary authority is inessential to this article. Indeed, it might be more realistic to suppose that investment was controllable in the desired manner through fiscal weapons. But then one could not identify the real rate of interest even loosely with the pre-tax marginal product of capital so there would be no simple interpretation of the shape of the $r(y)$ function in equation (2).

[2] I know that I owe the reader an apology for inflicting this notation on him. I have chosen to work in terms of expected deflation in order to emphasize its resemblance to capital in the well-known problem of optimal saving, a problem having some similarity to the present one.

expectation of inflation will induce people to ask a high interest rate on the lending of money, while borrowers will be prepared to pay a high rate since the loan will be expected to be repaid in money of a lower purchasing power.

Since no one will lend money at a negative money rate of interest when he can hold money without physical cost, the money rate of interest must be non-negative. Further, it is assumed that there is a constant, i_b, to be called the "barter point", such that at any money interest rate equal to or in excess of it money ceases to be held so that the monetary system breaks down; this is because such a high money rate of interest imposes excessive oppertunity costs on the holding of non-interest-bearing money instead of earning assets like bonds and capital.

As indicated previously, the real rate of interest will be taken to be an increasing function of the utilization ratio, denoted by y:

$$(2) \quad r = r(y),\ r(y) > 0,\ r'(y) > 0,\ r''(y) \geqslant 0,$$
$$0 < \mu \leqslant y \leqslant \bar{y} < \infty.$$

Consider the bounds on the utilization ratio. If positive employment is required for positive output then, by virtue of diminishing marginal productivity of labour, there is some small utilization ratio, denoted by μ, such that output will be only large enough to permit production of the programmed investment, leaving no employed resources for the production of consumption goods. Since negative consumption is not feasible, no value of y less than μ is feasible. The value μ is a constant by implication of the previous postulates. In the other direction, there is clearly, at any time, an upper bound on (augmented) employment arising from the supply of labour function and the size of population. This explains the upper bound $\bar{y}$ which, quite plausibly in view of the previous assumptions, is taken to be a constant.

Consider now the $r(y)$ function itself in the feasible range of the utilization ratio. The postulate that $r(y) > 0$ for all feasible y is perhaps not unreasonable; it could be relaxed. The curvature of $r(y)$ is of greater importance. (The later Figure 2 gives a picture of this function.) On the view that r is equal to the marginal product of capital, one is in some difficulty, for there are innumerable production functions that make the marginal product of capital a strictly *concave* (increasing) function of the labour-capital ratio, e.g., the Cobb-Douglas. Fortunately, I do not really require convexity of $r(y)$; $r''(y) \geqslant 0$ is overly strong for my purpose which, it will later be clear, is the concavity of U in y in (8). (Even the latter concavity could probably be dispensed with by one more expert than the present author in dynamic control theory, though probably the solutions would be somewhat affected.) I shall later indicate the minimum requirement on $r''(y)$. Moreover, there are countless production functions which make $r''(y) \geqslant 0$; for example, any production function which makes the marginal-product-of-labour curve linear or strictly convex in labour (which is not customary in textbooks) will suffice and even some concavity is consistent with (2).

Finally, a word about the use of the ratio of augmented labour to capital as a strategic variable in the model. Since capital is growing like $e^{(\gamma+\lambda)t}$ while employment is multiplied by $e^{\lambda t}$ to obtain augmented employment, it can be seen that, if N denotes employment and K denotes capital, then, with suitable choice of units,

$$y = \frac{e^{\lambda t} N}{K} = \frac{e^{\lambda t} N}{e^{(\gamma+\lambda)t}} = \frac{N}{e^{\gamma t}}.$$

Hence the definition of the utilization ratio used here does not imply a neo-classical model with aggregate "capital" in the background. Only neo-classical *properties* like diminishing marginal productivities need to be postulated and these are much more general than the neo-classical model. The previous relation shows that we could as well define the utilization ratio as the employment-population ratio (since population is growing like $e^{\gamma t}$) which, in the present model, is a linear transformation of the augmented employment-capital ratio. Thus the utilization ratio here measures not only the intensity with which the capital stock is utilized (the number of augmented men working with a unit of capital) but also the utilization of the population in productive employment.

B. *Inflation, utilization and expectations.* I am going to postulate that the rate of inflation depends upon the utilization ratio and upon the expected rate of inflation. In particular, the rate of inflation is an increasing, strictly convex function of the utilization ratio. When the expected rate of inflation is zero, the rate of inflation will be zero when the utilization ratio equals some constant y^* between μ and $\bar{y}$, will be positive for any greater utilization ratio and negative for any smaller utilization ratio. As $\bar{y}$ is approached, the rate of inflation approaches infinity. Finally, every increase of the expected rate of inflation by one point will increase by one point the actual rate of inflation associated with any given utilization ratio. Remembering that $-x$ is the expected rate of inflation, one therefore may write

$$\begin{aligned} \dot{p}/p &= f(y) - x, \qquad \mu \leqslant y \leqslant \bar{y}, \\ f'(y) &> 0, f''(y) > 0, f(\bar{y}) = \infty, f(y^*) = 0, \quad \mu < y^* < \bar{y}, \end{aligned} \tag{3}$$

where p is the price level and $\dot{p}$ its absolute time-rate of change so that $\dot{p}/p$ is the rate of inflation. Thus we must add the expected rate of inflation to the function $f(y)$ to obtain the actual rate of inflation. For every x we have a Quasi-Phillips Curve relation between $\dot{p}/p$ and y. The relationship is pictured in Figure 1.

I believe there can be no real question that, if the somewhat Phillipsian notion of the $f(y)$ function is accepted, the expected rate of inflation must be added to it as in (3) if, as assumed, the supply of labour is independent of the real and money rates of interest and hence independent of the expected rate of inflation. If the matter were otherwise, every steady state of fully anticipated inflation would be associated with different "levels" of output, employment and the real wage. Note that no assumption of any kind concerning the formation of expectations

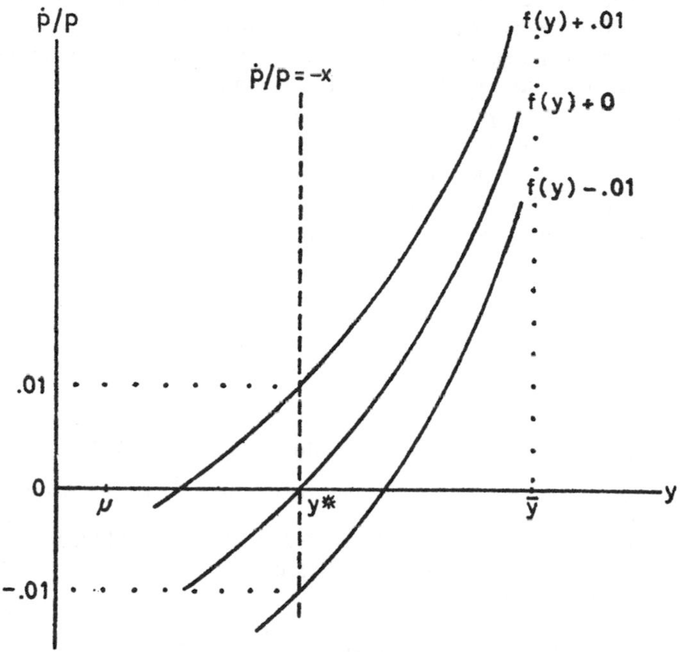

FIGURE 1. QUASI-PHILLIPS CURVES FOR $-x = \cdot 01, 0, -\cdot 01$.

has yet been made here; no assumption of perfect foresight or the like is implied in the formulation of this inflation function.

The concept of the function $f(y)$ is more vulnerable to criticism. From the usual Phillips Curve standpoint, we have to regard the utilization ratio as a proxy for the ratio of employment to labour supply and to neglect rising marginal cost. And of course the simple Phillips Curve itself is recognised to be an inadequate description of wage behaviour.

Looking at Figure 1 or equation (3) we see that y^* can be regarded as the *equilibrium* utilization ratio, for at $y = y^*$ (and only there) the actual rate of inflation will equal the expected rate of inflation. Mathematically, $\dot{p}/p = -x$ at $y = y^*$ since $f(y^*) = 0$. The diagram likewise shows that all the points on the vertical dashed line intersecting y^* are equilibrium points. Without intending normative significance, we may refer to $y > y^*$ as "over-utilization" and refer to $y < y^*$ as "under-utilization", merely from the point of view of equilibrium.

When there is over-utilization, the actual rate of inflation exceeds the expected rate, and *vice versa* when there is under-utilization. In either of these situations there will presumably be an adjustment of the expected rate in inflation. I shall adopt the mechanism of "adaptive expectations" first used in this context by Phillip Cagan.[1] The (algebraic) absolute time-rate of increase of the expected rate of inflation will be supposed to be an increasing function of the (algebraic) excess of the actual rate of inflation over the expected rate, being equal to zero when the latter excess equals zero. Symbolically, if $(\dot{p}/p)^e$ denotes the expected rate of *inflation*, the postulate is

$$\frac{d}{dt}\left(\frac{\dot{p}}{p}\right)^e = a\left[\frac{\dot{p}}{p} - \left(\frac{\dot{p}}{p}\right)^e\right]$$

or, in terms of the expected rate of *deflation*,

$$(4)\quad \begin{aligned} &-\dot{x} = a\left(\frac{\dot{p}}{p} + x\right), \\ &a(0) = 0, a'(\ ) > 0, a''(\ ) > \frac{-a'(\ )f''(\ )}{f'(\ )f'(\ )}. \end{aligned}$$

Concerning the curvature of the function $a(\dot{p}/p + x)$, it might be thought to be linear or it might be conjectured to be strictly convex for positive $\dfrac{\dot{p}}{p} + x$ and strictly concave for negative $\dfrac{\dot{p}}{p} + x$. All I am requiring is that the function not be "too concave" in the feasible range of y; in particular, it must not be more concave then the f function is convex, loosely speaking.

Substitution of (3) into (4) yields $-\dot{x} = a[f(y) - x + x] = a[f(y)]$. If we let $G(y)$ denote $-a[f(y)]$, then, by virtue of (3) and (4) we may write

$$(5)\quad \begin{aligned} &\dot{x} = G(y), \quad \mu \leqslant y \leqslant \bar{y}, \\ &G(y^*) = 0, \quad G'(y) < 0, \quad G''(y) < 0. \end{aligned}$$

Thus, when $y = y^*$, the actual and expected inflation rates are equal so that there is no change in the expected rate of inflation. When $y > y^*$, so that the actual inflation rate exceeds the expected rate, the expected rate of inflation will be rising or, equivalently, the expected rate of *deflation* will be falling. The opposite results hold when $y < y^*$. Note that as y is increased, the rate at which the expected rate of *inflation* is increasing over time will increase with y at an increasing rate.

In order to determine the path of x over time as a function of the chosen y path, we need to know the (initial) x at time zero, $x(0)$, which we take to be a datum:

$$(6)\quad x(0) = x_o.$$

We have to consider the admissible values of x_o in view of the upper and lower bounds on the money interest rate given in (1). First, for our analytical problem to be interesting, we require that x_o not be so algebraically small—that the initially expected *inflation* rate not be so great—that no feasible y decision by the Fisc can save the monetary system from breaking down in the first instant; that is, x_o must be sufficiently large algebraically that $i = r(y) - x_o < i_b$ for sufficiently

[1] P. Cagan, "The Monetary Dynamics of Hyperinflation," in M. Friedman (ed.), *Studies in the Quantity Theory of Money*, Chicago, 1956, pp. 25-117.

small $y \geqslant \mu$. Hence we require that $r(\mu) - x_o < i_b$ (or, in later notation, $x_o > x_b(\mu)$).

As for the non-negativity of the money interest rate, by analogous reasoning I should require only that x_o not be so large—that the initially expected deflation rate not be so great—that there is no y that will permit the Bank to make the real rate of interest low enough to induce the programmed volume of investment; that is, x_o must be sufficiently small that $i = r(y) - x_o \geqslant 0$ for sufficiently large $y < \bar{y}$, hence that $r(\bar{y}) - x_o \geqslant 0$. But I have to confess that I do not take seriously the non-negativity constraint in my analysis. To justify this neglect I want somewhat stronger assumptions that will prevent the constraint from becoming binding when an optimal policy is followed. The constraint will not be binding initially if $r(\mu) - x_o \geqslant 0$, since the chosen y must be at least as great as μ. If, further, we postulate that $r(\mu) - \hat{x}(y^*) \geqslant 0$, where $\hat{x}(y^*)$ is a "satiation" concept later defined, then the constraint will not be binding in the future either, for our solution will be seen to imply that the optimal $x(t) \leqslant \max\,[x_o, \hat{x}(y^*)]$ for all t. I believe these conditions are fairly innocuous (as well as over-strong) and that it is wise not to complicate the problem at this stage by serious consideration of the non-negativity constraint.

C. *Utilization, liquidity and utility*. The problem of the Fisc is to choose a path $y(t)$, $t \geqslant 0$, or, equivalently, a policy function, $y(x, \ldots)$ subject to (5), (6) and the information in (1), (2) and (3). For this the Fisc requires preferences. I shall follow Frank Ramsey in adopting a "social utility function" that is the integral over time of the possibly discounted instantaneous "rate of utility".[1]

On what variables should the (undiscounted) rate of utility, U, at any time t be taken to depend? I am going to suppose that the only two basic desiderata are consumption and leisure. On this ground I write the twice-differentiable function

(7) $U = \varphi(i, y) = \varphi[r(y) - x, y]$

where

(a) $\varphi_2 > 0$ for $y < y^0$, $y^* < y^0 < \bar{y}$,
$\varphi_2 < 0$ for $y > y^0$,
where $\varphi_2(i, y^0) = 0$ for all i, y^0 a constant.
$\varphi_{22} < 0$ for all y.
$\lim_{y \to \mu} \varphi = -\infty$, $\lim_{y \to \bar{y}} \varphi = -\infty$.

(b) $\varphi_1 = \varphi_{11} = \varphi_{12} = 0$ for $i \leqslant \hat{\imath}$, $0 \leqslant \hat{\imath} < i_b$,
$\varphi_1 < 0$, $\varphi_{11} < 0$, $\varphi_{21} = \varphi_{12} \leqslant 0$ for $i > \hat{\imath}$,
where $\varphi_1(\hat{\imath}, y) = 0$ for all y, $\hat{\imath}$ a constant.
$\lim_{i \to i_b} \varphi = -\infty$.

[1] F. P. Ramsey, "A Mathematical Theory of Saving," *Economic Journal*, vol. 38 (1928), pp. 543-59. For a discussion in a different context of the axiomatic basis for such a utility function, see T. C. Koopmans, "Stationary Ordinal Utility and Impatience", *Econometrica*, vol. 28 (1960), pp. 287-309.

It should be noted that the function φ is taken to be determined up to a linear transformation so that the assumptions on the signs of the second partial derivatives are meaningful. Figure 2 shows the contours of constant U.[1] Now the explanation.

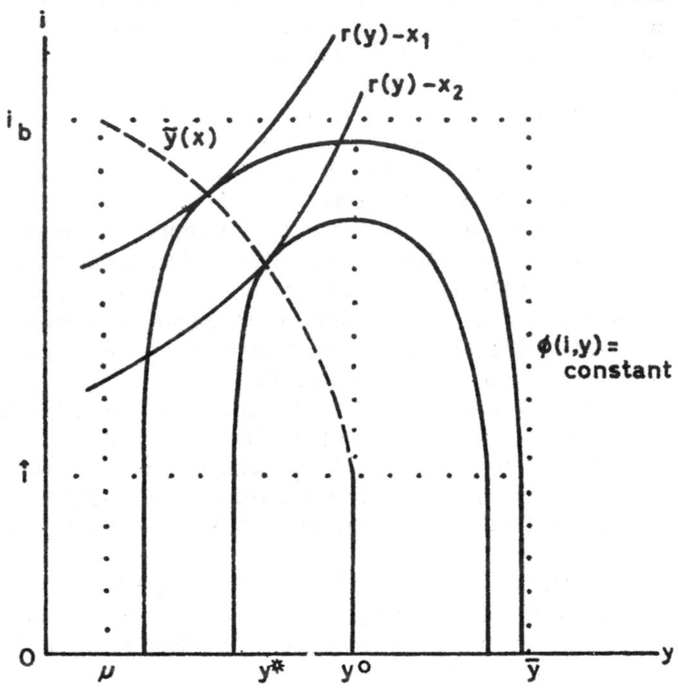

FIGURE 2: CONTOURS OF CONSTANT ϕ (i,y), THE INTEREST RATE FUNCTION AND THE FUNCTION $\mathring{y}$ (x).

Consider first the dependence of the rate of utility upon utilization *for a fixed money rate of interest*. That is, consider (7a). Clearly, as y is increased, there will be more output, assuming always positive marginal productivity of labour, so that, given exogenous investment, there will be more consumption. In addition, there will be a reduction of involuntary unemployment, at least in a certain range. But, on the other hand, there will also be a reduction of leisure. Further, a discrepancy between y and y^* implies the failure of expectations to be realized,

[1] The assumptions in (7) guarantee strictly diminishing marginal rate of substitution above $\hat{\imath}$ and to the left of y°. But for convexity to the right of y° we require that φ_{21} not be "too negative." Fortunately the contours are of no interest to the right of y° so we need not bother to place a lower bound on φ_{21}.

which suggests that people will have wished they had made different decisions.[1]

To make order out of this tangle of conflicting influences on the utility rate, I suggest the following view. Suppose for the moment that there were a perfect homogeneous national labour market. Then y^* would be the market-clearing utilization ratio at which the gain from a little more income (or consumption) was just outweighed by the loss of leisure necessary to produce it; thus the utility peak would be at y^*. Since consumption is strictly concave in y while effort increases linearly with y, we would expect the curve to be strictly concave everywhere, i.e., dome-shaped. Moreover, as y approaches μ, so zero consumption is approached, the rate of utility can reasonably be supposed to go to minus infinity; similarly, as y approaches $\bar{y}$, it is perhaps natural to suppose that the rate of utility again goes to minus infinity (although nothing in the solution hinges on this strong assumption). In such a world, what permits the Fisc to coax employment in excess of y^* is the failure of people to predict the magnitude of the inflation; in this world, some real normative significance attaches to "over-utilization" or "over-employment",

But in the real world, where there are countless imperfections and immobilities among heterogeneous sub-markets for different skills of labour in different industries, an additional consideration is operative. In such a world, there is substantial involuntary unemployment in some (presumably not all) sectors of the economy and among certain skill categories of labour even in utilization equilibrium; the point y^* is characterized by a balance between excess demand in some sectors and excess supply in others. In view of this and the social undesirability (*ceteris paribus*) of involuntary unemployment, I have supposed in (7) that the dome-shaped utility curve reaches a peak at some constant y^0 greater than y^* but less than $\bar{y}$; but the rate of utility does decline with y beyond this point as the involuntary over-employment in some labour markets and other misallocations by individuals (due to their failure to expect the resulting inflation) become increasingly weighty.[2] I shall indicate later the effect of making $y^0 = y^*$ contrary to my postulate. Note that y^0 is a constant independent of the money interest rate; this simplifying assumption seems advisable for consistency with the earlier postulate that the supply of labour is independent of the money interest rate.

I have discussed (7a)—that is, the profile of φ against utilization for a given money rate of interest. (A diagram of the relation between U and y *for a given* x will be shown later.) Consider now the dependence of the

[1] With aggregate investment being fixed, people cannot save too much or too little in the aggregate. But they can work too much or too little as a consequence of incorrect expectations.

[2] In polling people to determine y° the Fisc does not reveal to people that the level of the money rate of interest depends upon their social choice of y; y° is, like y^* earlier, a utility peak at any *fixed* money interest rate. With regard to the y° peak, labour turnover and perhaps labour hoarding are also relevant.

rate of utility on the money interest rate *for a given utilization ratio*. The money rate of interest measures the opportunity cost of holding money in preference to earning assets since, in the absence of own-interest on money, the money interest rate measures the spread between the yield on earning assets and the yield on money. After a point, an increase of the money interest rate increases incentives to economize on money for transactions purposes by means of frequent trips to banks and the like. I shall suppose for simplicity that these time-consuming efforts fall on leisure rather than on labour supply as indicated earlier. As the money rate of interest approaches the "barter point", i_b, these activities become so onerous that money ceases to be held and the monetary system breaks down. At a sufficiently small (but positive) money interest rate, $\hat{\imath}$, or at any smaller interest rate, incentives to economize are weak enough to permit a state of "full liquidity" in which all transactions balances are held in the form of money.[1]

Thus, concerning the relation between φ and i for given y, I suppose that the curve is flat in the full-liquidity range, $0 \leqslant i \leqslant \hat{\imath}$, negatively sloped and strictly concave for greater i and that the curve approaches minus infinity as i approaches i_b. I do not care how close $\hat{\imath}$ and i_b are to one another as long as they are separated. By making the curve go to minus infinity I insure that the optimal policy is not one producing the breakdown of the monetary system. I have now explained (7b) except for the condition that $\varphi_{21} = \varphi_{12} \leqslant 0$. This means that an increase of the money interest rate (outside the full-liquidity range) decreases or leaves unchanged the marginal utility of utilization; this seems reasonable since both an increase of i and of y imply a reduction of leisure, making leisure more or at least not less valuable at the margin.

It is clear from Figure 2 that, given the dependence of the interest rate on utilization, neither the value of y such that $i = \hat{\imath}$ (full liquidity) nor $y = y^0$ is generally a statical optimum, i.e., gives the maximum current rate of utility. The decision to make $i = \hat{\imath}$ may cost too much in terms of under-utilization while the decision $y = y^0$ may entail too high an interest rate. As Figure 2 shows, the static optimum is at $\tilde{y}$ which is an increasing function of x up to y^0. If the Fisc sought to maximize the current rate of utility (which it is not optimal to do), it would (except in the case of a no-tangency, full-liquidity solution) equate the marginal rate of substitution, $-\varphi_2/\varphi_1$, to the slope of the i-function, $r'(y)$, taking out any gain from a downward shift of the i-function—of an increase of x—in the form of greater y and smaller i; for all x greater than or equal

[1] A formal analysis of interest and "full liquidity" is contained in my paper, "Anticipated Inflation and Economic Welfare", *Journal of Political Economy*, vol. 73 (1966), pp. 1-13. That paper deliberately neglects the steps necessary to establish the desired expected inflation rate in the particular case where, as here, no interest can be paid on money; it is entirely comparative statics, unlike the present paper. Incidentally, it is assumed there too that the lost time from economizing on money is "taken out" in the form of a leisure reduction rather than a labour-supply reduction (in order to facilitate diagrammatic analysis). The present paper does not assume knowledge of that paper.

to some large x, say $\hat{x}(\tilde{y})$, $\tilde{y}$ is identical of y^0 and $i \leqslant \hat{\imath}$ (full liquidity) as the diagram shows.

We need now to describe the rate of utility as a function of x and y, i.e., taking both the direct effect and the indirect effect through i, given x, of a change of y. From (2) and (7) wc obtain

$$
\begin{aligned}
(8)\quad & U = U(x,y), \quad 0 \leqslant r(y) - x < i_b, \quad \mu \leqslant y \leqslant \bar{y} \\
& U_y = \varphi_1 r'(y) + \varphi_2 > 0 \text{ for } y < \tilde{y}(x) \\
& U_y < 0 \text{ for } y > \tilde{y}(x), \quad \mu < \tilde{y}(x) \leqslant y^0, \\
& \text{where } U_y(x,\tilde{y}) = \varphi_1 [r(\tilde{y}) - x]\, r'(\tilde{y}) + \varphi_2 [r(\tilde{y}) - x, \tilde{y}] = 0. \\
& U_{yy} = \varphi_{11} r'(y) r'(y) + 2\varphi_{21} r'(y) + \varphi_{22} + \varphi_1 r''(y) < 0 \text{ (for all } y). \\
& U_{yx} = -\varphi_{11} r'(y) - \varphi_{21} \left\{\geqslant\right\} 0 \text{ as } x \left\{\begin{matrix} < \\ \geqslant \end{matrix}\right\} \hat{x}(y) \text{ or } i \left\{\begin{matrix} \geqslant \\ \leqslant \end{matrix}\right\} \hat{\imath}. \\
& \tilde{y}'(x) = -U_{yx}/U_{yy} \geqslant 0. \\
& \lim_{y \to \mu} U = -\infty, \quad \lim_{y \to \min[y_b(x),\, \bar{y}]} U = -\infty \\
& \text{where } r(y_b) - x = i_b, \ y_b'(x) > 0\cdot \\
(b)\quad & U_x = U_{xx} = U_{xy} = 0 \text{ for } x \geqslant \hat{x}(y) \\
& U_x = -\varphi_1 > 0, \ U_{xx} = \varphi_{11} < 0, \ U_{xy} = -\varphi_{11} r'(y) - \varphi_{12} < 0 \\
& \qquad \text{for } x < \hat{x}(y), \\
& \qquad \text{where } r(y) - \hat{x} = \hat{\imath}, \ \hat{x}'(y) > 0. \\
& \lim_{x \to x_b(y)} U = -\infty \text{ where } r(y) - x_b = i_b, \ x_b'(y) > 0. \\
(c)\quad & U(\hat{x}, y^*) = \varphi(\hat{\imath}, y^*) = \hat{U}.
\end{aligned}
$$

Let us first interpret the new notation before looking at the diagrams. The function $\tilde{y}(x)$ has already been explained; it denotes the y at which the rate of utility is at a maximum with respect to y, taking into account the influence of y upon i, given x. The quantity y_b, also an increasing function of x, is that value of y which, given x, is just large enough to cause a breakdown of the monetary system by virtue of its causing $i = i_b$ through the $r(y)$ function; of course, x may be large enough to make $y_b > \bar{y}$ in which case y_b is irrelevant; it will be relevant if x is so negative that the economy is teetering on the edge of barter. The quantity $\hat{x}$, which is an increasing function of y, is that value of x just sufficiently great, given y, to permit full liquidity, to permit $i = \hat{\imath}$; since an increase of y entails a higher r, i.e., $r'(y) > 0$, we shall need greater x to maintain $i = \hat{\imath}$ the higher is y; of course, any $x > \hat{x}(y)$ is also consistent with full liquidity, as $\hat{x}$ is the *minimum* x consistent with full liquidity. The quantity x_b, which is certainly negative even for large y, is that value of x so small algebraically that, given y, $i = i_b$ so that the monetary system breaks down; since $r'(y) > 0$, an increase of y causes an algebraic increase of x_b for we then need a smaller expected *inflation* rate to save the economy from barter. Finally, as a matter of notation, $\hat{U}$ denotes the rate of utility at equilibrium utilization and full liquidity, i.e., at $y = y^*$ and $x \geqslant \hat{x}(y^*)$; $\hat{U}$ is the maximum *sustainable* rate of utility.

Figure 3 illustrates the dependence of the utility rate on y, allowing for the interest effect of utilization, for two particular values of x:

first, $x = \hat{x}(y^*)$ so that there will be full liquidity at $y = y^*$ (and at smaller y); second, $x = x_1 < \hat{x}(y^*)$, i.e., at a smaller x. I have supposed for the sake of definiteness that x_1 is so small—very negative—that when $x = x_1$ full liquidity is not realizable even at very small y so that the two curves never coincide; and that $x_b(y^*) < x_1$ so that the right-hand asymptotic lies to the right of y^*.

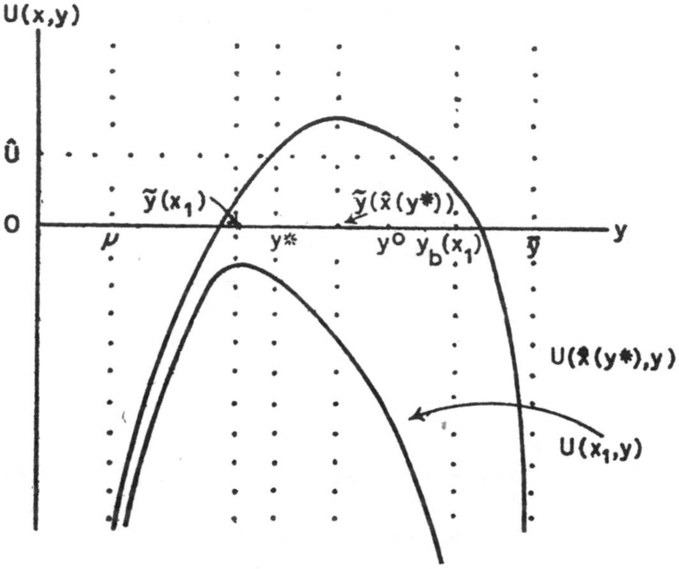

FIGURE 3.—DEPENDENCE OF THE UTILITY RATE ON THE UTILIZATION RATIO WHEN $x=x(y^*)$ AND WHEN $x=x_1$.

Both curves are strictly concave since $U_{yy} < 0$. (It can now be pointed out that $r''(y) > 0$ is unnecessarily strong for U_{yy} everywhere, let alone for $U_{yy} < 0$ in the neighbourhood of $\tilde{y}$ as consideration of Figure 2 will show. One can simply postulate $U_{yy} < 0$ noting that this prohibits $r''(y)$ from being excessively negative.) Both curves reach a peak—the static optimum—left of y^0 since $x < \hat{x}(y^0)$ in both cases. The top curve reaches a peak to the right of y^* because at $y = y^*$ there is full liquidity, so $\varphi_1 = 0$ (right-hand as well as left-hand derivative), while $\varphi_2 > 0$ because $y^0 > y^*$, so that $U_y[\hat{x}(y^*), y^*] > 0$, i.e., the curve must still be rising at y^*. For purposes of illustration it was assumed that $y_b[\hat{x}(y^*)] \geqslant \bar{y}$ so that the right-hand asymptote is $\bar{y}$. The lower curve, corresponding to a much smaller x, has the same shape but reaches a peak, $\tilde{y}(x_1)$, to the left of y^*. This is because, in the case illustrated (if x is very small), the marginal gain from higher utilization at $y = y^* < y^0$ is not worth the concomitant increase of interest rate because the interest rate is already so high in this case. [It should be remarked that the portion of the solution (discussed later) which can be regarded as "deflationist" is not in any way dependent upon the fact that, for sufficiently small x, $\tilde{y}(x) < y^*$; deflation (or at least $y < y^*$) can be optimal even for x much higher than the aforementioned value, i.e., even when the static optimum is always above y^*.] Looking at the right-hand asymptote, this reflects the fact that for sufficiently small x, $y_b(x) < \bar{y}$. I have assumed for definiteness that $y_b(x_1) > y^*$, but the reverse inequality is certainly possible. Note finally, for completeness, that $y_b(x)$ approaches μ asymptotically as x falls and approaches $x_b(\mu)$.

Figure 4 illustrates the dependence of the utility rate on x for two given values of y: first, $y = y^*$ so that there will be full liquidity at $x \geqslant \hat{x}(y^*)$; second, $y = y_1 < y^*$. Both curves are, loosely speaking, reverse images of the curve (not drawn but fully discussed) of φ against i since, with y fixed, every one point increase of x is a one point decrease of i. Both curves are concave, strictly concave outside the full-liquidity range. Consider the former curve. It is assumed for illustration only that $\hat{x}(y^*) > 0$, meaning that, in equilibrium, deflation is necessary for full liquidity. As x is decreased—the expected *inflation* rate increased—

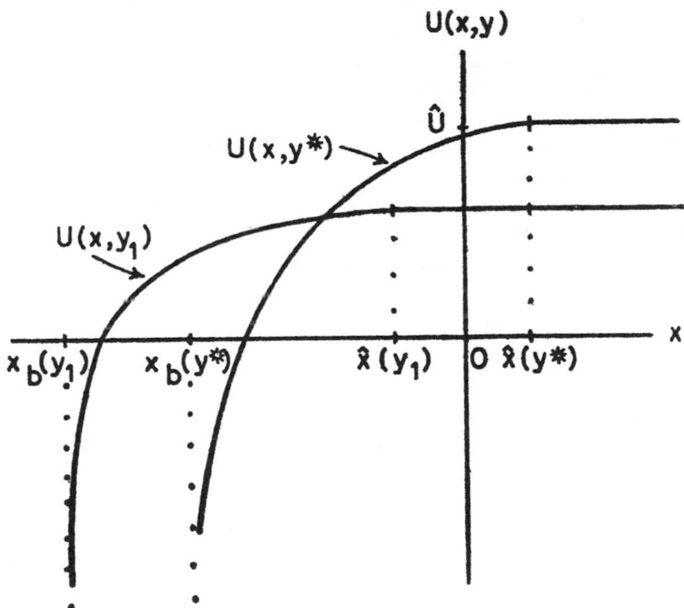

FIGURE 4.—DEPENDENCE OF THE UTILITY RATE ON EXPECTED RATE WHEN $y = y^*$ AND WHEN $y = y_1$.

the money rate in interest is increased (at a constant rate) so the rate of utility falls—at an increasing rate by virtue of the strict concavity of φ in

i. As x approaches $x_b(y^*)$, so that i approaches the barter point, the rate of utility goes to minus infinity. The other curve, corresponding to a smaller y, has the same shape. However, because y is smaller in this case and therefore i is smaller for every x, the critical rate x_b which drives the system into barter is algebraically smaller than in the previous case; i.e., a higher expected *inflation* rate is consistent with $i < i_b$ when y is smaller. Similarly, a smaller algebraic deflation rate, namely $\hat{x}(y_1)$, is needed for full liquidity. Note that since $y_1 < y^* < y^0$, full liquidity ($i \leqslant \hat{\imath}$) in this case gives a lower rate of utility than does full liquidity in the previous case where $y = y^*$. While it is of no significance, these considerations imply that the two curves cross: at algebraically very small x, $y^* > y_1 > \tilde{y}(x)$ so that $y^* > y_1$ actually reduces the rate of utility in that range of x.

Before (8) is utilized, some defence of it and consideration of alternatives is in order. Consider the poor German worker of the early 1920s. He was not in the market for equities so that for him the real interest rate was zero; or, rather, for him the real interest rate was only the convenience yield of holding a stock of consumer durables (cigarettes, bottled beer, etc.) which we might regard as becoming rapidly negligible as this stock is increased. It could be argued that for such people the appropriate utility-rate function is better described by $U = \psi(-x, y)$ on the ground that the opportunity cost of holding money is simply the expected rate of inflation. If we make assumptions like $\psi_{21} < 0$ in the spirit of (7) we can still arrive at (8). There is little to be gained except simplicity from this approach at the cost of neglecting altogether the role of the real rate of interest for those people who participate in the capital market and who own a substantial amount of the wealth.

Another issue is my omission of the *actual* inflation rate from (7). Observe that, by virtue of (3) which makes the inflation rate a function of x and y, the utility rate must ultimately depend on x and y, as in (8). We could write

$$U = \psi(\dot{p}/p, i, y) = \psi[f(y) - x, r(y) - x, y]$$

and still obtain some version of (8). The issue therefore revolves only around the shape of the function in (8).

I have already given full weight to the loss of utility arising from a discrepancy between the actual and expected rates of inflation. It is in large part this discrepancy that motivates opposition to inflation. It is not really inflation *per se* that many economists oppose but rather an unexpectedly high rate of inflation. Nevertheless it might be argued that it is of no consolation to fixed-income groups to guess correctly the current rate of inflation if they did not *anticipate* when they contracted their fixed money incomes the bulk of the inflation that has occurred in the intervening time!

On one interpretation, this is a distributional argument: the real incomes or real wealth of widows and orphans on previously contracted fixed incomes will be eroded to socially undesirable levels by inflation. My grounds for omitting the actual inflation rate, from this point of view, must be that the government has other means than the depressing of the utilization ratio to rectify tolerably the distribution of income.[1]

To the extent that appropriate redistribution efforts still leave such groups too poor, there is certainly a case for introducing the actual rate of inflation into the utility-rate function, ψ. But it is enormously difficult to introduce it appropriately. For if the actual and expected inflation rates should be equal for a long time then the actual rate of inflation deserves less and less weight over time; for eventually the inflation will have become a *fully anticipated* one. Thus an appropriate utility-rate function must be a non-stationary function. No simple possibilities satisfy me. But I wish to point out that since the optimal path in my model produces asymptotically a steady rate of algebraic inflation, hence an asymptotically anticipated inflation, and since the rate of an anticipated inflation makes no difference distributionally (apart from its liquidity effect already recognized), the asymptotic properties of the solution here are immune to criticism from this point of view.

The actual inflation rate has another influence which, it could be argued, is time-independent and hence persisting for all time. This is the nuisance cost of adjusting price lists up or down. If the rate of inflation is 20 per cent. or —20 per cent. per annum, every firm in every industry will have to revise its price lists very frequently, which again has its leisure or production costs. This suggests giving the actual rate of inflation a weak role in the utility-rate function. $\psi(\quad)$ can be made a dome-shaped function of $\dot{p}/p$. The concavity of U in y would be threatened a little—precautions would be needed to insure that $U_{yy} < 0$ everywhere—but not much of (8) would be lost. The main difference is that instead of having a U maximum in the x plane for all $x \geqslant \hat{x}(y)$ we would have a unique, non-flat peak in Figure 4, since too high an expected rate of deflation would cause too high an actual deflation rate from the point of view of price lists. I shall mention in the next section an instance where it would be useful to introduce such a modification.[2]

My greatest reservations centre on the stationarity of the utility-rate function in (7). Suppose that $\lambda = 0$. Due to virtual golden-age growth, aggregate consumption and leisure will be growing at rate γ, like population, at any constant utilization ratio. Since the "pie" is getting bigger over time, should not U be made to depend upon t ? Fortunately, however, *per capita* consumption and *per capita* leisure, which depend only on i and y—will be constant so that the use of a stationary utility-

[1] On another view the government has a moral obligation to valididate the expectations held by groups who have contracted for fixed incomes (whether or not they are poor), even to the extent that if inflation has occurred recently the government now owes these groups a little deflation. The government of my model treats such obligations as "bygones", worrying only about the consequences of current deceptions, not past ones.

[2] This price-list consideration perhaps ought also to enter in a complicated, non-stationary way since a high, *steady* rate of inflation might eventually call forth institutional changes in the nature of money or perhaps even some system of "compounded prices".

rate function is not wholly unreasonable. The real issue here is "discounting".

More serious difficulties arise when $\lambda > 0$. Then a constant i and y imply exponentially growing consumption per head and constant leisure per head (by virtue of the labour supply function's properties). In this case it does seem a little strange that time should not appear as an argument of the utility-rate function. But I believe that examples of underlying utility functions could be found such that time would not appear in the derived utility-rate function φ in (7).

I shall however allow the rate of utility to be "discounted" at a non-negative rate in the usual multiplicative way. No solution to our problem in its present formulation will exist if there is negative discounting.

In deciding which of two (x,y) paths to take—actually $x(t)$ alone suffices to describe a path—the Fisc is postulated to compare the integrals of the possibly discounted rates of utility produced by the two paths. Hence the "social utility", W, of a path (x,y) is given by

$$(9) \quad W = \int_0^\infty e^{-\delta t} U(x,y)\, dt, \qquad \delta \geqslant 0,$$

where t is time, $e^{-\delta t}$ is the discount factor applied to the rate of utility t years hence, and δ is the rate of utility discount. (It is understood in (9) that $x = x(t)$, $y = y(t)$.) The case $\delta = 0$ will receive special consideration in a moment.

The optimization problem of the Fisc can now be stated as: maximize (9) subject to (5) and (6). The "optimal policy" is the function $y = y(x)$ which gives the greatest feasible W. Given $x(0) = x_0$, there is an optimal path $x = x(t)$ which describes the state of the system at each time. From this information one can also derive $y = y(t)$, since $\dot{x}(t)$ gives $y(t)$ by (5).

In the case $\delta = 0$, there may be many feasible paths which cause the integral in (9) to diverge to infinity, which give infinite W; intuitively, it is unreasonable to regard all of these paths as "optimal" so that a different criterion of preferences and of optimality is wanted in this case. Such a criterion will be described briefly in the next section, which also gives the solution to the zero-discount case. (Nevertheless the above formulation of the mathematics of optimization is essentially correct.) The subsequent section gives the solution to the case of a positive utility discount rate.

II. Optimal Policy when no Utility Discounting

The optimality criterion now widely used by economists to deal with no-discount, infinite-horizon problems of this sort has been called the "over-taking principle". A path $[x_1(t), y_1(t)]$ is said to be preferred or indifferent to another path $[x_2(t), y_2(t)]$ if and only if one can find a time T^0 sufficiently large that, for all $T > T^0$,

$$\int_0^T U(x_1, y_1)\, dt \geqslant \int_0^T U(x_2, y_2)\, dt.$$

The former path is preferred because it eventually "overtakes" the latter path. A feasible path is said to be *optimal* if it is preferred or indifferent to all other feasible paths. If one then obtains a solution to the maximization problem now to be described, this solution is the optimum in this sense.[1]

The above optimality criterion justifies the use of a device first employed by Ramsey in his analysis of the somewhat analogous problem of optimal saving over time: choose the units in which the utility rate is measured in such a way that $\hat{U} = 0$, i.e., $U[\hat{x}(y^*), y^*] = 0$. This is merely a linear transformation of the function U that will not affect the preference orderings implied by the integral comparisons just described. Now go ahead with the problem

$$(10) \qquad \begin{array}{ll} \underset{y}{\text{Max}}\ W = \displaystyle\int_0^\infty U(x,y)\,dt, & \hat{U} = 0, \\ \text{subject to } \dot{x} = G(y), & x(0) = x_0. \end{array}$$

The divergence problem cannot now arise. This is not to say, however, that an optimal policy will exist for all x_0.

Readers familiar with the Ramsey problem will recognize (10) as rather like the "optimal saving" problem. There x is "capital" and y is "consumption".[2] There is a zero-interest capital-saturation level in Ramsey that is analogous to our liquidity satiation level, $\hat{x}(y)$; his income—the maximum consumption subject to constant capital—is analogous to our y^*. His solution was the following. If initial capital is short of capital saturation, consume less than income, driving capital up to the saturation level; if initial capital exceeds the saturation level, consume more than income, driving capital down to the saturation level; if initial capital equals the capital-saturation level, stay there by consuming all capital-saturation income. Thus capital either equals for all time or approaches asymptotically and monotonically the capital-saturation level while consumption either equals or approaches asymptotically (and monotonically) the capital-saturation level.

The solution to the problem here is similar in part. If $x_0 < \hat{x}(y^*)$ it is optimal to make $y < y^*$ for all t, causing x to rise and approach $\hat{x}(y^*)$ asymptotically, while y approaches y^* asymptotically and monotonically. In other words, if the economy "inherits" an initially expected algebraic deflation rate that is insufficient for full liquidity when the utilization ratio is at its equilibrium value, then, for an optimum, the Fisc must engineer under-utilization for all time so as to cause a gradual, asymptotic movement of the expected deflation rate up to the level consistent with full liquidity and equilibirum utilization; in the limit, as time

[1] See, for example, "The Ramsey Problem and the Golden Rule of Accumulation" in E. S. Phelps, *Golden Rules of Economic Growth*, New York, 1966, and the references cited there.

[2] Some differences are that his utility rate was independent of capital; his investment-consumption relation, G, depended upon capital; utility was everywhere increasing in consumption; and $G^I(y) = -1$ in his case.

increases, under-utilization vanishes and a full-liquidity equilibrium is realized.

If $x_0 = \hat{x}(y^*)$ then $y = y^*$ is optimal for all t, and therefore $x = \hat{x}(y^*)$ for all t. Should the economy inherit the minimum expected deflation rate consistent with full liquidity at equilibrium utilization, then equilibrium utilization with full liquidity is optimal for all time. The case $x_0 > \hat{x}(y^*)$ will be discussed later.

What will be remarkable to those steeped in the statical approach is that, when $x_0 \leqslant \hat{x}(y^*)$, over-utilization is not optimal whether or not x is large enough to make $\tilde{y}(x) > y^*$. Further it can be shown that optimal y is always smaller than $\tilde{y}$ even when $\tilde{y} < y^*$.

Analogous to the Ramsey-Keynes equation that gives optimal consumption as a function of capital is the following equation that describes optimal utilization as a function of the current expected deflation rate.[1]

$$(11) \quad U(x,y) + G(y)\frac{U_y(x,y)}{-G'(y)} = 0.$$

For purposes of diagrammatics it is helpful to write $U = V(x,\dot{x}) = V[x, G(y)]$, which we may do since $G(y)$ is monotone decreasing in y, and then to express (11) in the form

$$(12) \quad V(x,G) - G\,V_G(x,G) = 0$$

where $V_G = \dfrac{U_y(x,y)}{G'(y)}, \qquad V_x = U_x,$

$$V_{GG} = \frac{U_{yy}\,G' - G''\,U_y}{G'G'G'}, \qquad V_{Gx} = \frac{U_{yx}}{G'(y)}.$$

If we think of $\dot{x} = G(y)$ as "investment", then (12) says that the optimal policy equates the rate of utility to investment multiplied by the (negative) marginal utility of investment, V_G; this is essentially the Ramsey-Keynes rule.

From the information above on derivatives we see that V *increases* as G is increased [i.e., as y is decreased from $\tilde{y}$ or $y_b(x)$, whichever is smaller] up to $G(\tilde{y})$ whereupon V then decreases, going to minus infinity as G approaches $G(\mu)$. Only this latter decreasing region, where $V_G < 0$ or $U_y > 0$, is of relevance; in that region, $V_{GG} < 0$ unambiguously.

In Figure 5 the solid curve depicts the possibly realistic case of x_o great enough that $\tilde{y}(x_o) > y^*$, so that $G[\tilde{y}(x_o)] < 0$, but not great enough for full liquidity when $y = y^*$, i.e., $x_o < \hat{x}(y^*)$. Thus the solid utility curve, for $x = x_o$, has a peak left of the origin but it passes under the origin, since $U(x_o,y^*) < \hat{U} = 0$. The tangency point, at (V_o, G_o), shows the optimal initial $G(y)$ and hence the optimal y. Since optimal $G(y) > 0$ (i.e., $y < y^*$), x will be increasing and the V curve will therefore shift up and possibly to the left; as this process occurs, the tangency

[1] For a simple derivation, in which the differentiability necessary for the Euler condition is not assumed, see R. E. Bellman, *Dynamic Programming*, Princeton, 1956, pp. 249-50.

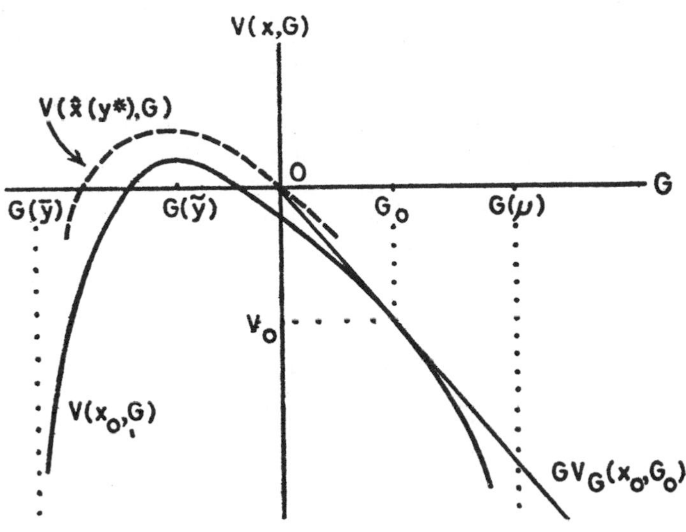

FIGURE 5.—THE NO-DISCOUNT UTILIZATION OPTIMUM WHEN $x_0 < \hat{x}(y^*)$.

point approaches the origin, so that $y = y^*$ and $x = \hat{x}(y^*)$ in the limit.[1] The dashed curve represents the asymptotic location of the V curve. Just as equilibrium utilization is approached only asymptotically, it can be shown that full liquidity ($i \leqslant \hat{\imath}$) is approached only asymptotically. (This follows from $r'(y) > 0$ and the results that $U_y > 0$ along the optimal path.)

The case $x_o = \hat{x}(y^*)$ is now obvious. Here we are in long-run equilibrium to begin with, as shown by the dashed V curve in Figure 5. The tangency point occurs at the origin so $y = y^*$ is optimal initially; this means that the equality $x(t) = \hat{x}(y^*)$ continues so that $y = y^*$ continues to be optimal for all t.

Consider now the case $x_o > \hat{x}(y^*)$. Since there cannot be *more* than full liquidity when $y = y^*$, i.e., $U(x_o, y^*) = \hat{U}$ even when $x_o > \hat{x}(y^*)$, the tangency point continues to be at the origin. Yet the implied policy $y(t) = y^*$, $x(t) = x_o > \hat{x}(y^*)$ for all t *cannot be optimal*. For there is a "surplus" of expected deflation here; i.e., $i < \hat{\imath}$ when $y = y^*$. Since V reaches a peak to the left of y^*, there are clearly policies of at least temporary over-utilization ($y > y^*$) which will permit $U > \hat{U}$ for at

[1] The reader may have noticed a second tangency point with $G < 0$. Pursuit of that policy would lead asymptotically to $y = y^*$ with $x = \tilde{\hat{x}}$ where $\tilde{y}(\tilde{\hat{x}}) = y^*$; since $\tilde{\hat{x}} < \hat{x}(y^*)$, such a policy must cause W to diverge to minus infinity so that it cannot be optimal.

least a while and yet allow $U = \hat{U}$ forever after; this is because $x = \hat{x}(y^*) < x_o$ is sufficient for $U(x,y^*) = \hat{U}$. In other words, there is room for a "binge" of at least temporary over-utilization while all the time enjoying full liquidity and while never driving x below $\hat{x}(y^*)$.

But it cannot be concluded that over-utilization is optimal when $x_o > \hat{x}(y^*)$. For no such temporary or even asymptotically vanishing binge of over-utilization can satisfy (12), which is a necessary condition for an optimum; in terms of Figure 5, there is no way that such a policy can satisfy the necessary tangency condition.

Since neither $y > y^*$, $y = y^*$ nor $y < y^*$ is optimal, the inescapable conclusion is that there exists no optimum in this case. An intuitive explanation is the following. For every binge that you specify which makes $x(t)$ approach $\hat{x}(y^*)$ (as y approaches y^*), I can, by virtue of the strict concavity of the V curve, specify another binge that makes x approach $\hat{x}(y^*)$ more slowly which will be even better. There is no "best binge" (or even set of "best binges") just as there is no number closest to unity yet not equal to it. Hence there is no path preferred or indifferent to all other feasible paths.

There are at least four avenues of escape from this disconcerting situation. Let us first ask, how did Ramsey avoid it? He could avoid it (actually he never recognized it) by postulating that the net marginal product of capital became negative beyond the capital saturation point so that there was an immediate and positive loss from having too much capital. (This is fair enough if capital depreciates even in storage.) In our model there is no immediate loss from having "too high" an expected deflation rate; $i < \hat{\imath}$ is as good as $i = \hat{\imath}$. To introduce a loss we need to suppose that U in (8) is strictly concave in x, reaching a peak and falling off thereafter. As mentioned earlier, this postulate could be justified by the price-list consideration that it is a nuisance to have to reduce prices with great frequency. (But a previous footnote indicates my uneasiness with this consideration.) Alternatively one could make assumptions leading to $G_x(x,y) < 0$, as is done in the preliminary version of this paper.

Another avenue of escape is the introduction of a positive utility discount, as I have done in the next section. Then there will be a "best binge" so there will be an optimum for all x_o (in the admissible range).

A third avenue is to employ a finite-time horizon. Then any binge must come to an end at the end of some given number of years. There will be a "best binge" and an optimum will always exist. The unpublished version of this paper contains such a model.

The fourth avenue of escape is to postulate that $y^0 = y^*$ so that $\tilde{y}(x) \leqslant y^*$ for all x and therefore the V peak cannot occur to the left of the origin. I find this unsatisfactory although some readers may not. The reader can now work out this case using a diagram like Figure 5. If $x_0 > \hat{x}(y^*)$, under-utilization is optimal as before; if $x_0 \geqslant \hat{x}(y^*)$, equilibrium utilization is optimal. Anyone who wants to go as far as postulating $y^0 < y^*$ will encounter problems of the non-existence of an optimum.

Some of the qualitative results of this section may be expressed by the following "policy function" derived from (12):

$$(13) \qquad y = y(x), \qquad x \leqslant \hat{x}(y^*),$$
$$\text{where } y'(x) \{\gtreqless\} 0 \text{ as } x \{\lesseqgtr\} \hat{x}(y^*),$$
$$y(x) \begin{cases} = y^* \text{ if } x = \hat{x}(y^*), \\ < y^* \text{ if } x < \hat{x}(y^*), \end{cases}$$
$$\lim_{x \to xb(\mu)} y(x) = \mu.$$

Let us turn now to the mathematically more congenial case of a positive discount.

III. Optimal Policy When Positive Utility Discounting

Our problem now is

$$(14) \qquad \underset{y}{\text{Max}}\ W = \int_0^\infty e^{-\delta t}\, U(x,y)\, dt, \qquad \delta > 0,$$
$$\text{subject to } \dot{x} = G(y), \quad x(0) = x_0.$$

A mathematical analysis, in which (14) is a special case, is contained in the preliminary version of this paper. I shall describe the solution here.

The optimal path of the variable $x(t)$ either coincides with or monotonically approaches (from every x_0) a "long-run equilibrium" value, x^*, which is uniquely determined by

$$(15) \qquad \delta = \frac{-U_x(x^*, y^*)\ G'(y^*)}{U_y(x^*, y^*)}.$$

It is easy to see from (15), the inequality $G'(y) < 0$ and the observation that an optimal path would never make $U_y(x,y) < 0$, that $U_x(x^*,y^*) > 0$. This and (8) yield the result that $x^* < \hat{x}(y^*)$. Thus, in the long run, there will be less than full liquidity when there is positive discounting of future utility rates. This is because the current gain from high utilization always offsets the *discounted* future loss due to a short fall from full liquidity.

If $x_o < x^*$, so that the expected deflation rate is below its long-run optimal value, then, to drive $x(t)$ monotonically toward x^* we require $y < y^*$, i.e., under-utilization; $y(t)$ will approach y^* only asymptotically as $x(t)$ approaches x^*. If $x_o = x^*$, then $y = y^*$ is optimal for all t. If $x_o > x^*$, then, to drive $x(t)$ monotonically toward x^* we require $y > y^*$, i.e., over-utilization; but, again, $y(t)$ will approach y^* asymptotically. (It does not appear that the path $y(t)$ is necessarily monotonic but this is of little importance.)

This last result—the optimality of over-utilization in some circumstances—is of considerable interest. The previous section laid a possible foundation for a "deflationist" policy when the initially expected deflation rate was insufficient for full liquidity with equilibrium utilization; more precisely, under-utilization was optimal in that circumstance so that the actual rate of *inflation* resulting would be less than the expected rate, though it need not be negative initially [or even asymptotically if $\hat{x}(y^*) \leqslant 0$]. Moreover, an "inflationist" policy of over-utilization, though it might be better than any under-utilization policy, was never optimal for there could never exist an over-utilization optimum. We see here that, when there is a positive utility discount, over-utilization will be optimal when $x_o > x^*$; since $x^* < \hat{x}(y^*)$, this embraces the case $x_o = \hat{x}(y^*)$, i.e., the case in which there would be full liquidity at equilibrium utilization.

The greater is the utility discount rate, the smaller algebraically will be the equilibrium deflation rate. Differentiation of (15) yields

$$(16) \quad \frac{dx^*}{d\delta} = \frac{[U_y(x^*,y^*)]^2}{[U_{yx}(x^*,y^*)U_x(x^*,y^*) - U_{xx}(x^*,y^*)U_y(x^*,y^*)]G'(y^*)} < 0,$$

since the denominator is unambiguously negative for all $x^* < \hat{x}(y^*)$, hence for $\delta > 0$. This indicates that, given some x_o, we are more likely to find over-utilization initially optimal ($x_o > x^*$) the larger is the utility discount rate.

Nevertheless one cannot, by choosing sufficiently large δ, make x^* arbitrarily small (algebraically), not even as small as $x_b(y^*)$. It is the inequality $\tilde{y}(x^*) > y^*$ that lies behind the optimality of $y > y^*$ when $x_o > x^*$. It can be shown that x^* cannot be made larger than $\tilde{x}(y^*)$, where $\tilde{x}$ is defined by $\tilde{y}(x) = y^*$; for as δ goes to infinity, the derivative $U_y(x^*,y^*)$ in (15) goes to zero (while $U_x(x^*,y^*)$ stays finite), indicating that x^* approaches the value such that $U_y(x,y^*) = 0$, hence approaches the value $\tilde{x}(y^*)$.

The value $\tilde{x}(y^*)$ is precisely the level of x to which the myopic, statical approach would drive $x(t)$. That approach, which maximizes the current rate of utility at each time, leads to a policy $y = \tilde{y}(x)$; under that policy, equilibrium is realized only when (asymptotically) $x = \tilde{x}(y^*)$ so that $\tilde{y}(x) = y^*$. Thus the statical approach and the case of an infinitely high discount rate lead to the same equilibrium value of x. Indeed, it can be shown that infinite utility discounting makes $U_y(y,x) = 0$ always, which means $y = \tilde{y}(x)$, so that the statical approach and infinitely heavy discounting lead to identical policies throughout time.

But optimal behaviour in the limit as δ goes to infinity is of little interest. Given any (finite) value of δ, the dynamic approach yields different results from the statical policy $y = \tilde{y}(x)$. First, since $U_y(x,y) > 0$ along any dynamically optimal path, the optimal $y < \tilde{y}$ for all x. Second, and this needs emphasis, even if x_o is such that $\tilde{y}(x_o) > y^*$, so that myopic maximization of the initial rate of utility would call for $y > y^*$, the truly optimal $y < y^*$ if (and only if) $x_o < x^*$. Thus, if the currently expected rate of inflation is 2 per cent. while the long-run equilibrium (asymptotically optimal) expected inflation rate is less, say 1 per cent., then under-utilization is optimal whether or not the current utility-rate curve peaks to the right of y^*. This theme is essentially a repetition of a theme of the previous section: a dynamical approach can lead to an optimal policy that is qualitatively different from that of a myopic, statical approach. In particular, a "deflationist" policy of under-utilization (and hence a rise of x over time) may be optimal even when myopic maximization of the current rate of utility calls for over-utilization (and hence a fall of x over time).

The above results may be summarized in a qualitative way as follows.

$$
\begin{aligned}
& y = y(x) \\
(17)\quad & \text{where } y(x) \begin{cases} > y^* \text{ if } x_o > x^*, \\ = y^* \text{ if } x_o = x^*, \\ < y^* \text{ if } x_o < x^*, \end{cases} \\
& \lim_{x \to xb(\mu)} y(x) = \mu, \quad y(x) < \tilde{y}(x) \text{ for all } x, \\
& \text{with } \tilde{x} < x^*(\delta) < \hat{x}(y^*) \text{ for all } \delta > 0, \quad x^{*\prime}(\delta) < 0.
\end{aligned}
$$

Once again we may ask, what if $y^0 = y^*$? Then $\tilde{y}(x) \leqslant y^*$ for all x. In this event, $y < y^*$ when $x_o < x^*$ as above. And if $x_o \geqslant x^*$, then $y = y^*$; hence there is no over-utilization, because there is no gain to be had in the present (from over-utilization) that is worth a discounted future loss (from a reduction of future liquidity).

IV. Concluding Remarks

The principal theme here has been that, within the context of the above model, a tight fiscal policy producing "under-utilization", and hence producing an actual algebraic inflation rate that is smaller than the currently expected inflation rate, is optimal if and only if the currently expected inflation rate exceeds the asymptotically optimal inflation rate. The latter is determined by liquidity considerations and by social time preference (the utility discount rate), not by the strength of preferences for high or low utilization (at a given rate of interest). If the utility discount rate is zero, the asymptotically optimal inflation rate is simply the maximum expected inflation rate consistent with full liquidity (at equilibrium utilization). If there is positive discounting of future utility rates, the long-run inflation rate exceeds the full-liquidity rate and is greater the larger is the discount rate. From this point of view, therefore, what characterizes the advocates of a "high-pressure" policy of over-utilization is their implicit adoption of a large utility discount. In favouring high utilization today at the cost of high inflation in the eventual future equilibrium, they reveal high "time preference".

Dynamical models of this sort are a methodological step forward from the statical approach to optimal aggregate demand discussed at the outset of this article. But it would be premature to base policy on the particular model employed here. Among a host of needed extensions, the following stand out. Inflation should be made to depend upon the change of utilization, as well as the level. Investment should be made endogenous and possibly even optimized simultaneously with aggregate demand. And where it is appropriate to assume fixed or only occasionally adjustable exchange rates, balance-of-payments considerations should be introduced; from this viewpoint, the model's greatest relevance may be for a nation's optimal objectives in the international co-ordination of aggregate demand and price trends among countries.

University of Pennsylvania.

INFLATION PLANNING RECONSIDERED

It is not an event—the purist might say that it is not a non-event—likely to attract wide notice. It is nevertheless the tenth anniversary of my first essay on the theory of inflation planning (Phelps, 1967) and the fifth anniversary of my book on the same subject (Phelps, 1972a). In the last five years my thoughts on welfare economics, and on the welfare economics of inflation in particular, have not stood still. To mark the numerical occasion therefore I would like to reformulate my earlier theory.

I

An intention of my paper on "optimal unemployment over time" was to tease a faction of the profession over an apparent incongruity. Most or all of those economists who took a hard line on economic growth seemed inconsistently soft on inflation. Those who, embracing the inter-generational utilitarianism of Frank Ramsey (1928), urged fiscal austerity to achieve *capital saturation* (in the limit) showed no similar relish for the sacrifices that might be required to reach *liquidity satiation* (Ramsey's model is described below). If it is utilitarian–optimal to build up the nation's capital stock to the Golden Rule state of full investment, the implied curtailment of present consumption notwithstanding, why is it not also utilitarian–optimal to work down the economy's inflationary expectations (on which the cost of money depends) to the level needed for full liquidity, despite the transient sacrifices of consumption and jobs?

Later I realized that the incongruity was reciprocated by the other camp. Those economists advocating the painful extirpation of inflationary expectations, on the ground that a steady state of expected price stability (if not price deflation) is the best steady state achievable, were "speaking" utilitarianism—with or without knowing it. Yet when it came to fiscal policy towards investment and growth, those same economists viewed the notion of the Golden Rule state as an intellectual toy of the effete East having no possible normative significance. If consumers in their sovereign wisdom wish to discount the utilities of their heirs in relation to their own, and thus stop short of accumulating capital to the zero-interest saturation point, then austerity-taxation to "force" the return on capital below that discount rate would not be right.

To draw a close parallel between the two problems, optimal inflation and optimal growth, it was of course necessary to structure the former like the latter. In Ramsey's problem of national saving, textbook version, the labour force is constant from generation to generation and we may imagine that the employment rate is perfectly stabilized by (neutral) monetary policy.[1] The division of national income between consumption and net investment is the object of fiscal control. Up to the point of capital saturation, national

Reprinted by permission from *Economica*, Vol. 45(2), May 1978.

income is an increasing function of the capital stock. Hence income is rising or falling according as consumption is smaller or larger than income.

The current rate of "enjoyment" or "utility" is an increasing function of the current rate of consumption. If fiscal policy keeps consumption *equal* to income, therefore, income and the rate of utility will be constant in the resulting steady state. This sustainable or steady-state utility is smaller the lower is initial income. If fiscal policy instead keeps consumption *below* income as long as the economy falls short of maximum income, then income and the rate of utility will sooner or later reach or approach their *maximum* sustainable levels. Short of capital saturation there is always available an eventually *permanent gain* in the rate of utility, but only in return for a *sacrifice* of consumption over the near term.

As I set up the inflation problem, the labour supply is again a constant but we are to think of monetary policy as stabilizing the capital stock.[2] The variable under fiscal control is taken to be the level of employment through the effect of tax collection on aggregate consumption demand. Equivalently we may regard the control variable as the rate of inflation, since, on Phillips' hypothesis, the inflation rate is an increasing function of the employment rate—at given inflationary expectations. The expected rate of inflation becomes the state variable in place of national income in the Ramsey problem. On Cagan's hypothesis of adaptive expectations, the expected inflation rate is rising or falling according to whether the actual inflation rate is currently higher or lower than the expected rate: if the former, unemployment is unnaturally low, and if the latter, unemployment is unnaturally high. The equilibrium unemployment rate—the rate at which the actual inflation rate equals the prevailing expected inflation rate—is hypothesized to be independent of the expected inflation rate and is called the natural rate of unemployment.[3]

The rate of utility is reducible to a function of the current employment level and the current money rate of interest, because the output of consumption goods, the other variable on which utility evidently depends, is also a function of employment and, perhaps, of the money interest rate. Up to the natural level of employment and a bit beyond, utility is higher the greater is the level of employment—at any given money rate of interest. Up to the point of liquidity satiation, real cash balances and perhaps consumption too are larger and hence utility is larger the lower is the money rate of interest—at any given level of employment. Of course, the interest rate is lower, at given employment, the lower is the expected rate of inflation. Thus the rate of utility at given employment is larger the lower is the expected rate of inflation.

So the structure of the two problems is similar in essentials. If fiscal policy keeps employment *equal* to its natural level, the expected rate of inflation and every other pertinent variable will be preserved in a steady state. The resulting sustainable rate of utility will be smaller the farther the shortfall from full liquidity. If fiscal policy instead keeps employment *below* the natural level as long as the expected inflation rate is too high for liquidity satiation (at the natural rate), inflationary expectations will decline towards the point where the money interest rate is low enough to permit liquidity satiation (at the natural rate of employment) and hence the rate of utility will sooner or later reach or approach its *maximum* sustainable level. Short of liquidity satiation there is available an eventually *permanent gain* in the rate of utility, but only in return for a near-term *sacrifice* of consumption and employment.[4]

Will a society wish to make such a sacrifice when there is a permanent gain available in return? That is, will it wish to invest in capital when the economy is not saturated with capital, or to invest in disinflationary unemployment when the economy is not satiated with liquidity? The answer depends upon the society's inter-generational choice criterion—if it has one. The *utilitarian* answer, from Ramsey to von Weizsäcker, is Yes: whenever a permanent gain can be had for a transient sacrifice—no matter that each generation is transient too—the (proper) utilitarian society, which does not discount the utilities of future citizens relatively to present ones, *will* make such sacrifices as to inch optimally toward that ideal steady state where there are no more sustainable gains left to achieve.

As long as the expected inflation rate is too high to yield liquidity satiation at the natural employment level, then it is utilitarian–optimal to bring it down. In the problem as I set it up, that objective calls for a fiscal policy of slack aggregate demand to drive actual inflation below expected inflation and thus force unemployment above its natural rate. Gradual recovery of employment to its natural level is to be promoted as inflationary expectations recede toward their destination. In the utilitarian analysis, the only real problem is the calculation of the particular trajectory that is optimal—best on the sum-of-utilities criterion—among the infinitely many paths that reach or approach the ideal steady state. It should be said in fairness to the utilitarian viewpoint that the magnitude of the sacrifice that it is optimal to impose on, say, the present generation might be small. The sacrifice indicated is largely a matter of the distance that the expected inflation rate has to cover.

II

The 1967 essay was never intended as a plea for deflation. For all I knew then, steady inflation might be justified. The essay was intended to provoke thought by showing the fearsome implications for inflation policy—in a model plainly rigged to be like Ramsey's capital model—of the utilitarianism so frequently accepted in matters of "growth". After having my fun with the growth-utilitarians, I learned that satirical intentions, unless delivered with the heavy hand of a Swift, are apt to be missed. I soon found myself cast as a theoretician of disinflation through planned slump.[5]

Anxious not to share responsibility for a decade of economic slack, I set about a more circumspect analysis of inflation planning during 1970. But how to avoid the clarion call, unmistakable in the earlier paper, for a forced march to full liquidity? One escape would have been to jettison the utilitarian criterion. But until I was influenced by John Rawls—via the wall of our adjoining offices that year, but too late to help—I knew of nothing with which to replace utilitarianism. The only way out that I saw was to revise the structure of the model. Certainly the old structure left room for improvement.

The basic alteration presented in the 1972 book consisted in revising upward from full liquidity the expected inflation rate that would be judged best in a comparison of steady states of differing constant inflation. Some moderate rate of steady inflation, like 5 per cent per annum, was deemed better than the much lower (perhaps negative) inflation rate necessary for liquidity satiation. The presumption that liquidity should not go untaxed any more than any other consumer good in a world without lump-sum taxation was one argument for that revision. Hence money interest rates should exceed the quasi-zero level that would be required for ideal liquidity, just as consumer prices should generally exceed the (marginal social cost) levels required for "ideal outputs". The other argument for a moderately inflationary target was that, with interest rates moderately high, there would be less liquidity around to grease the skids in the event of unintentionally booming demand; and in an incipient slump, the central bank would have more room to manoeuvre money interest rates to lower levels.[6]

With the structure of the model thus altered, the Bentham–Ramsey follower could countenance and even espouse inflation in moderation, despite the grim natural-rate hypothesis that higher employment would not be among its benefits. It is only the *excess* expected rate of inflation that should be the utilitarian object of extinction. Estimates and models of the best inflation rate would of course remain in some dispute. Yet one could at least *question* the utilitarian optimality of any tight-demand policy aiming ultimately at "price stability"—if (as postulated) such a policy would take a toll in unnaturally low employment and consumption—to say nothing of more Draconian policies.

Apropos Draconian measures, it should be added that the kind of disinflationary programme embarked upon in the United States in 1969 (and again in 1974) is a far cry from the sort of counter-inflationary technique I had modelled. In my analysis, any planned disinflation would be spearheaded by austere fiscal policy to compress consumption spending and employment, while monetary policy would have the task of insulating investment demand from the consequent decline of prospective profits and sales. If, contrariwise, the imposed slump were to set back the growth of capital as it set back the growth of the price level, the future generations on whom would fall the burden of eventually making up the lost investment might not be grateful on balance for its predecessors' misguided sacrifices. What can be the rationale, utilitarian or other, for a counter-inflationary policy that leaves a legacy of lost capital, broken families and disaffection for productive work that is worse than the inflationary expectations that the next generation would otherwise inherit? The next section is a development—not the only one possible—of this point.

III

The foregoing revision of the model nevertheless left intact a characteristic conclusion of intertemporal utilitarian analysis. When the expected inflation rate currently exceeds the best steady-state inflation rate, the "optimal" monetary–fiscal policy should seek to reduce expected inflation by contriving a slump of employment. The lingering uneasiness I felt over this feature of the solution was manifested in my hallucinatory interrogation before the revolutionary tribunal (p. 262 of the book). But is there a way out of it?

Any lasting escape will surely require a fundamental reform of the inter-generational choice criterion applied to the model; I shall be considering a reform of that kind below. It is however worth noting that a certain extension of the model may, under appropriate initial conditions, win a temporary reprieve even when sticking to the utilitarian criterion of choice.

Consider the more general utilitarian problem in which the authorities are to control both the rate of unemployment and the rate of capital formation, so as to maximize the inter-generational sum of utilities. Thus the central bank is to optimize the rate of investment, not simply to insulate it from what the "fisc" is doing. The simplest possible story is this: the rate of utility depends only upon the rate of consumption, and net potential output depends upon the two state variables, capital stock and the expected rate of inflation. Consumption is what is left over from net potential output after subtracting net capital formation and slack capacity. The capital stock is rising or falling according to whether the volume of net capital formation is positive or negative. The expected rate of inflation is falling or rising according to whether the amount of slack capacity is positive or negative.

There are then two ways in which a generation can "invest" for the sake of future generations. It can allocate some of its potential output to "slack" in order to reduce the expected rate of inflation, or it can allocate some of its net potential output to net capital formation in order to enlarge the capital stock (or it can do both). Either form of investment entails a sacrifice of the current generation's consumption. There is also the possibility of investing in capital while "disinvesting in inflation". That means an excess of actual output over consumption while actual output also exceeds potential output (negative slack).

In this world where capital and expected inflation are both subject to optimal control, it is still true that the utilitarian solution restrains consumption below potential income, keeping positive the *sum* of investment in capital formation *and* investment in slack, as long as potential income falls short of the maximum sustainable level of consumption—roughly, the Golden Rule (or best-steady) level of net potential output at which having and maintaining more capital or less expected inflation would do no good. But that observation leaves open the mix of investments between slack and capital formation. To determine that mix we need the efficiency condition stating that the rates of return to each of the two kinds of investment must first be brought into equality and then kept equal along the optimal path.

We arrive now at the point that, even though the expected inflation rate initially exceeds its best steady-state level, the capital stock may well fall so short of *its* best steady-state level that the rate of return to investing in decreased inflationary expectations, while positive, is beneath the rate of return to investing in captial (when these return rates are calculated at the utilitarian–optimal rate of consumption). In that case, the optimal monetary–fiscal policy proceeds to engineer negative slack in the interests of greater capital formation at the expense of worsening inflationary expectations—until the inequality in rates of return is rectified. Only when that latter equality is realized will disinflation through positive slack become utilitarian-optimal.[7]

Thus a positive rate of return to investment in disinflation does not suffice to establish that it is best for the utilitarian society to invest in positive disinflationary slack. While such a condition is necessary, it is also necessary that this rate of return be at least as large as the rate of return on the best of other investment opportunities. This point led me, in an appraisal of the American Government's counter-inflationary Game Plan of 1969–1971, to a semi-serious suggestion:

> Suppose that the reduction of production and employment resulting from the drive to reattain stable prices [is] wholly temporary. Even so, it would be improper to weigh dollar for dollar any future benefits of that price stability against those irretrievable losses of economic benefits in the present. The Congress and the Bureau of the Budget [now the OMB] do not let public agencies have money for capital projects which can be justified only at a zero or negligible [real] rate of interest. This investment in price stability demanded by the Federal Reserve, borne by us at the cost of substantial unemployment, should also be subject to a similar interest-rate test. [Phelps, 1972b, p. 223]

It should be kept in mind however that the reprieve from disinflation via slack which this extended utilitarian model holds out is limited and temporary. The argument is that investment in disinflation can be counted out *if* and *as long as* its rate of return is inferior to that on capital. It is not denied that if, for example, the former rate of return is initially positive the utilitarian–optimal plan calls for *eventual* disinflation—once the rates of return are equalized—in order to carry that rate of return, alongside the rate on capital, finally to zero.

We should also re-emphasize the assumption that the Central Bank and the fisc are reliable utilitarian partners. The fiscal contraction of consumption may in some cases be based on the understanding that the Central Bank will fill in the resulting gap with increased investment. The monetary stimulus to investment spending may likewise be based on the understanding that the fiscal authorities will not seize upon the increased public revenues to increase government expenditures or to reduce tax rates. There are undoubtedly economies in which some kind of second-best non-cooperative model will appear to be more realistic, although the source of the non-cooperation may raise conceptual difficulties.

IV

I confessed above to a satirical element in my first essay on inflation planning. I wonder now whether it was not also a satire, muted and perhaps unconscious, of utilitarianism itself. And if my Golden Rule Fable for Growthmen was a satire, it too was directed at the utilitarian enthusiasm for growth, not at neoclassical capital theory as Mrs Robinson thought. (What struck me as laughable about the Solovians was not their delightful science but their falling over themselves to reach the Golden Rule state—there to live happily ever after.) Though I was not an explicit and consistent critic of utilitarianism in the 1960s, it frequently seemed to me that utilitarianism gave very odd results.

If we abandon utilitarianism, what shall we put in its place? And will that reform of the ethical choice criterion in the optimal inflation model succeed in averting the awful conclusion that inflationary expectations must sooner or later be brought down to the steady-state ideal?

The leading reform candidate is surely the inter-generational version of Rawls' "maximin" criterion. According to that criterion, an inequality among the respective utilities scored by each generation is justified if and only if it serves to raise the utility scored by the generation with the least utility—the minimum utility over all generations. It is this inter-generational minimum utility that the maximin-optimal fiscal–monetary policy strives to maximize. It follows from this criterion and our model that it would be wrong of monetary–fiscal policy to reject the available steady state of equal utilities over generations in favour of a disinflationary policy that lowered the utility of the generation living now for the sake of raising the utilities consequently available to future generations. (I exclude here the possibility that the present generation would earn so large a "derived utility" from the prospect of their successors' benefits that they would feel compensated for their sacrifice.)

The implications of applying this maximin criterion in place of the utilitarian one to my 1972 model, with its constraint that monetary policy keep the capital stock on an even keel, are obvious. If the current expected rate of inflation should happen to exceed the best ideal steady-state expected inflation rate, then live with it—pursue that aggregate demand policy which tends to equate the actual rate of inflation to the current expected rate and thus tends to keep the unemployment rate equal to its macro-equilibrium level.[8] Thus the present generation, particularly its least well-off contributors, do not sacrifice for future generations, particularly their least well-off, who, even without that sacrifice, will be as well-off as they.

Introducing joint monetary–fiscal control of both capital formation and the expected inflation rate, along the lines of the previous section, may very well alter the maximin-optimal policy towards inflation and unemployment. Yet, as I shall suggest, this revision of the basic model leaves intact the anti-disinflationism of the maximin moral.

Suppose as before that the rate of return to disinflation, while positive, is less than the rate of return to capital formation. Then every generation can have a higher (equal) utility than would be afforded by steady-state maintenance of both the current capital stock and inflationary expectations. The maximin-optimal monetary–fiscal policy will seek to tighten taxation, thus to make room for greater capital formation, and at the same time to ease money and raise employment by so much as actually to raise the consumption enjoyed by the present generation. By this device the present generation is permitted to share equally with future generations the higher equalized utility made possible by establishment of an efficient mix of the two state variables on which utility possibilities depend, the size of the capital stock and the expected rate of inflation. In contrast to the utilitarian solution in this case, the expected rate of inflation never turns around to head for its ideal steady-state level. Once the two rates of return are brought into equality, the maximin-optimal monetary fiscal policy locks the economy in the corresponding steady state.[9]

In the opposite case, where the rate of return to disinflation is initially higher than the rate of return on capital and both rates are positive, the analogous solution is apparently to drive down the expected inflation rate while at the same time decreasing the rate of capital formation by so much as actually to increase the rate of consumption (and of utility) enjoyed by the present generation. The maximin-optimal monetary–fiscal policy is evidently to "trade off" some of the initial capital for an improvement of inflation expectations in the interests of a higher equalized utility than would be available with the *status quo*.

Yet I doubt that this solution should be accepted as genuinely Rawlsian. If, in the spirit of Rawls, we identify the utility of any generation as the prospects for self-realization of its least advantaged members and if the latter would be hit hard by planned unemployment, it is far from clear that society can "compensate" them (in any fitting Rawlsian sense) for the loss of jobs by lavishing them with added public grants and public services. A more generous dole for productive citizens is not in Rawls' vision of economic justice.

V

Have we then found in the maximin criterion, or at any rate in Rawls' version of it, a kind of amulet to ward off any and all future temptations to commit "planned slump"? Or may events sometimes loose a malevolent force even stronger than the Rawlsian charm? I shall argue tentatively and intuitively that the introduction of uncertainty into the theory of optimal inflation policy reopens the door to contingencies under which no class of workers in the generation affected could legitimately claim exemption from underemployment—if no other precaution to protect subsequent generations would work as surely.

Let us assume, in analogy with all the certainty cases studied above, that the only available strategy to reduce the public's subjective mean expectation of the rate of inflation is to engineer unnaturally high unemployment. It is supposed that in an economy beset by random disturbances, a tighter fiscal policy will work "on average" to reduce inflationary expectations; it will do this by reducing the true *expected value* of the actual rate of inflation, even though the outcome in any particular instance need not be a fall of the inflation rate—owing to supply shocks, demand shifts and the like. Moreover, the subjectively expected rate of inflation, the rate in the minds of the public, may be subject to random impulses of its own. Consequently, what we are calling the (subjectively) expected rate of inflation may fail to fall over any definite interval of time despite the tighter fiscal policy.

The other allowance for uncertainty we need to make is to replace the utility scored by a generation, heretofore the career opportunities of the least advantaged in the workforce, by the *expected utility* of such workers. I believe it will serve our purpose reasonably well to identify this expected utility as the probability that a member of this worst-off class will not suffer a broken, interrupted, delayed or otherwise impaired career. The higher the unemployment rate that a generation plans for itself, the lower will be this probability and hence the smaller will be that generation's expected utility in the eyes of the *ex ante* Rawlsian scorer. The "Rawlsian" criterion thus implied is *equal chances* save in those situations where unequal chances would improve the chances of all.

In the certainty model, with capital either fixed or having the lower rate of return, the maximin policy sought to preserve the *status quo* by planning actual inflation equal to expected inflation. In the uncertainty model, the risks of such a strategy are the crux of the problem. A demand policy that sought regularly to maintain the existing expected rate of inflation, whatever it might currently be, by supplying just enough additional aggregate demand to produce an actual rate of inflation that is (in an expected value sense) precisely equal to the expected inflation rate, would invite the aimless drift of the expected inflation rate, up or down. If the actual inflation rate turned out to exceed the expected rate, the latter would be revised upwards as long as the chance discrepancy continued. If the expected inflation rate spontaneously increased, the fortunate matching of the actual inflation rate with the *former* expected inflation rate would serve only to attenuate the increase of the latter, and then only until the actual inflation rate was aimed at the new level of the expected rate. Hence a demand policy that promotes the *status quo ante*, whatever it is, runs the risk that the expected inflation rate will go from bad to worse.

Consider then the following contingency. The expected inflation rate facing the present generation is so high that if "we" were to permit ourselves an aggregate demand stance intended to pass along that same inflationary expectation to the next generation, and so give ourselves the prospect of the natural level of employment, we would add to the probability—expectations of inflation being labile—that the next generation would experience a monetary collapse and therefore suffer abnormally high unemployment. In that situation, I contend, it would not be Rawls-optimal of the present generation to conduct "business as usual", offering its representative least-advantaged worker the normal chance of employment. By doing so it would reduce to a level lower than its own the conditional probability that the next generation's representative least-advantaged worker will find employment, and that would violate the standard of equal chances.

Now it would seem that we have "proved" too much. If the expected rate of inflation of the present generation is always a certainty, while the next generation's expected rate of inflation is uncertain and so exposes the latter generation to the risk that it will face unsupportable hyperinflationary expectations, it would seem that the present generation ought always to sacrifice some employment for the sake of the following generation that is asymmetrically at risk. If so, *every* generation would have to plan for unnaturally high unemployment in order to pull up the probability of employment conditionally forecast for the least advantaged of the next generation and pull down the corresponding probability for the least advantaged of the current generation to the point where these two probabilities were equalized. And if that were so, the expected rate of inflation would tend always to be falling in an expected-value sense, bouncing up again only on the occasion of an unanticipated inflationary disturbance.

The fancied difficulty is dispelled by recalling that there was a Keynes as well as Bresciani-Turoni. The next generation could be exposed to a downside risk as well as the upside one. If that generation inherits too low an expected rate of inflation it may find itself unable (or at least hard-put) to aim for the natural rate of unemployment. It is possible that there will exist no "full-employment" or natural-rate equilibrium at a non-negative money rate of interest and positive price level, and the radical (institutional or fiscal) surgery then indicated may be insufficiently effective or timely. Once that consideration is brought in, it is clear that it is not Rawls-optimal for a generation to plan to bequeath to its successor an expected inflation rate that is lower than its own, or even *as* low, if its own expected inflation rate is so low (perhaps negative) that such a plan, taking account of the risk that it will fall short, would place the next generation in jeopardy.

We seem then to have come full circle. When the expected rate of inflation is low, the current generation ought to take monetary–fiscal steps that will be likely to increase it; when the expected inflation rate is too high, the current generation must aim to reduce it. The fateful implication of the latter event, that the least-advantaged workers will be subjected to a higher probability of unemployment than would be promised by (a policy aiming for) the natural rate of unemployment, is of no moment. Sometimes people are asked to accept additional risks for the sake of others who would otherwise stand in even greater peril. (A somewhat similar result has been obtained in a study of the maximin accumulation of risky capital; see Calvo, 1977.) The wisdom—now conventional?—of my 1972 book appears to be "good Rawls" as well as "sound utilitarianism".

The principal difference between the utilitarian and maximin analyses, I conclude, must be purely quantitative though not unimportant. The maximin criterion advises us to steer the expected inflation rate towards the safest waters, somewhere in the middle between the Scylla of monetary collapse through hyperinflation and the Charybdis of Keynesian disaster that (greater) expectations of inflation could prevent. The utilitarian criterion focuses on the average, with no special attention to the probabilities of worst outcomes. (Stochastic utilitarian programming is insightfully treated in Merton, 1975.) One suspects, consequently, that the utilitarian criterion would have us aim much closer to what would be the best steady-state rate of inflation in a world of certainty than would the maximin criterion. If that is correct, and if this best rate of inflation corresponds to a money rate of interest perilously close to the Keynesian danger-point at zero, the maximin criterion beckons us to higher ground, that is to higher inflation and interest rates, than does the utilitarian criterion—certainly higher than the latter criterion when no account is taken of uncertainty.

To decide whether or not the maintenance of expectations of moderate inflation is really important as a cushion against the chance encounter of Keynesian difficulties, consider the following. Imagine that the oil shock of late 1973 had come in a setting of price stability, full employment and money interest rates on the order of, say, 1 or 2 per cent per annum. Could central banks then have eased interest rates enough to maintain full employment—had they wanted to? I am doubtful that they could have, although the question raises issues too complex to enter into here. If not, could fiscal policy have come to the rescue—assuming again the willingness to maintain full employment? Presumably a deep cut in profit taxation could have saved the day, but it could not be taken for granted that a legislative consensus on such a measure would develop promptly enough (if at all). It is a reasonable inference, then, that the inflationary expectations prevailing in 1973 provided valuable room for monetary manoeuvre in 1974. The fact that central banks did not take advantage of it does not refute the contention.

None of this means that I feel I have the whole truth about optimal inflation or have expressed it all in this paper. At least one qualification seems essential. It has to do with planning for unnaturally high unemployment.

If it should turn out that the operation of the inflation policy envisaged here would on occasion entail planned unemployment seriously above the natural rate, we might well want to consider whether there is not available some better technique of reducing inflationary expectations. The kind of aggregate demand policy studied here may be considered "optimal" only if the optimum it produces is good enough compared with the optimum producible by some other kind of "institution", to use a broad term.

ACKNOWLEDGMENTS

Portions of this paper were presented in abbreviated form at the Athens Conference on the Political Economy of Inflation and Unemployment, October 1976.

APPENDIX: TECHNICAL NOTES

The following notes on the stochastic "maximin" problem of the last section are not intended to be wholly rigorous.

Let n and x denote the planned employment rate and the expected rate of inflation in period t, and let n_{-1} and x_{-1} denote the corresponding rates in period $t-1$. The model posits that the (conditional) mathematical expectation of x, given x_{-1} and a choice of n_{-1}, is

$$(\text{A1}) \qquad E_{-1}x = x_{-1} + n_{-1} - n^*, \qquad 0 < n^* < 1,$$

where n^* is the natural rate of employment. The random deviation of x from $E_{-1}x$ is governed by a twice-differentiable distribution function,

$$F(x - E_{-1}x)$$

with

$$(\text{A2}) \qquad F'(x - Ex) > 0 \qquad \text{for all } x, \text{ say.}$$

Any employment planning rule, $n = n(x)$, is constrained by

$$(\text{A3}) \qquad n = \begin{cases} n_K < n^*, & \text{if} \quad x < x_K (> -\infty) \\ n_B < n^*, & \text{if} \quad x \geq x_B (< \infty), \qquad x_B > x_K. \end{cases}$$

A somewhat intuitive representation of our maximin problem is

$$(\text{A4}) \qquad \underset{n_{-1}}{\text{maximize}}\, E_{-1}n(x) \quad \text{s.t.} \quad n_{-1} \geq E_{-1}n(x) \quad \text{and given} \quad x_{-1}.$$

A less "heuristic" approach will be indicated in a moment.

Let us then maximize with respect to n_{-1} the Lagrangean corresponding to (A4), viz.

$$\text{(A4a)} \quad \int_{-\infty}^{\infty} n(x)F'(x-x_{-1}-n_{-1}+n^*)\,dx + \mu\left\{\int_{-\infty}^{\infty} n(x)F'(x-x_{-1}-n_{-1}+n^*)\,dx - n_{-1}\right\}$$

or equivalently

$$\text{(A4b)} \quad (1+\mu)\left[n_K F(x_K-x_{-1}-n_{-1}+n^*)+\int_{x_K}^{x_B} n(x)F'(x-x_{-1}-n_{-1}+n^*)\,dx + n_B\{1-F(x_B-x_{-1}-n_{-1}+n^*)\}\right]-\mu n_{-1}$$

where μ is the Lagrange multiplier and $n(x)$ is the (unknown) maximin planning rule. The upper bound, 1, on n_{-1} is disregarded. Of course, this maximization is possible only when $x_K \leq x_{-1} < x_B$. The first-order condition for a maximum is

$$\text{(A5)} \quad (1+\mu)\left[-n_K F'(x_K\ldots)-\int_{x_K}^{x_B} n(x)F''(x\ldots)\,dx + n_B F'(x_B\ldots)\right]-\mu=0.$$

There are two classes of outcome. If x_{-1} is close enough to x_K then $\mu=0$ and the derivative in the square brackets is zero. Hence $E_{-1}n(x)$ attains its unconstrained maximum and, except in the borderline case,

$$n_{-1} > E_{-1}n(x).$$

In this class of outcomes it is obvious that $dn_{-1}/dx_{-1}=n'(x_{-1})=-1$. The reason is that a rise of x_{-1} simply displaces leftward the curve showing $E_{-1}n$ as a function of n_{-1} by the amount of the rise of x_{-1}. Further

$$\max_{n_{-1}} E_{-1}n(x)$$

is locally independent of x_{-1}.

If x_{-1} is higher, then $-1<\mu<0$ and the derivative in the square brackets is negative; the *unconstrained* maximum of En occurs where

$$n_{-1} < E_{-1}n.$$

In this case, therefore, n_{-1} is constrained to lie on the 45° line where

$$E_{-1}n = n_{-1}.$$

It follows that $-1<dn_{-1}/dx_{-1}<0$ (since a rise of x_{-1} displaces leftwards the curve depicting $E_{-1}n$ as a function of n_{-1} by the amount of the rise of x_{-1} while the aforementioned derivative at the 45° line is finite and negative.)

A more rigorous approach proceeds to maximize the infimum of the conditionally expected n's over time. The maximized infimum will be some (unknown) function of x_{-1}, say $m(x_{-1})$. Then, for $x_K \leq x_{-1} < x_B$,

$$\text{(A6)} \quad m(x_{-1})=\max_{n_{-1}}\left[\min\left\{n_{-1},\ \int_{-\infty}^{\infty} m(x)F'(x-x_1-n_{-1}+n^*)\,dx\right\}\right]$$

and

$$\text{(A7)} \quad m(x_{-1})=\max_{n_{-1}}\left[\left[\int_{-\infty}^{\infty} m(x)F'(x-x_{-1}-n_{-1}+n^*)\,dx + \lambda\left\{\int_{-\infty}^{\infty} m(x)F'(x-x_{-1}-n_{-1}+n^*)\,dx-n_{-1}\right\}\right]\right].$$

The first-order condition for a maximum of the Lagrangean in (A7) is

$$\text{(A8)}\qquad (1+\lambda)\left\{-\int_{-\infty}^{\infty} m(x)F''(x-x_{-1}-n_{-1}+n^*)\,dx\right\}-\lambda=0.$$

To interpret the Lagrange multiplier, λ, note that

$$\text{(A9)}\qquad m'(x_{-1})=(1+\lambda)\left\{-\int_{-\infty}^{\infty} m(x)F''(x-x_{-1}-n_{-1}+n^*)\,dx\right\}.$$

whence $\lambda=m'(x_{-1})$.

The analysis of (A7) and (A8) is now like that of (A4) and (A5). If x_{-1} is close enough to x_K then $m'(x_{-1})=0$, $E_{-1}m(x)$ is maximized without bind from the constraint, and $dn_{-1}/dx_{-1}=-1$ as before. If x_{-1} is so high as to make the constraint in (A7) binding, so that

$$n_{-1}=E_{-1}m(x),$$

then

$$-1<m'(x_{-1})=n'(x_{-1})<0.$$

The curve depicting $E_{-1}m(x)$ as a function of n_{-1} shifts laterally to the left, point for point, with each rise of x_{-1}.

The extended utilitarian problem of Section III, details aside, is

$$\underset{\{I,Z\}}{\text{maximize}}\int_0^{\infty} U\{C(t)\}\,dt,$$

given K_0 and X_0, and subject to

$$\text{(A10)}\qquad C+I+Z=P(K,X),\quad \dot K=I,\qquad \dot X=-\beta Z/P(K,X)$$

where $U'(C)>0$ and

$$U\{P(K^*,X^*)\}=0,\qquad P(K^*,X^*)\equiv\max P(K,X).$$

The Ramsey–Keynes equation for $I+Z$, easily derived from Bellman's equation, is

$$\text{(A11)}\qquad 0=U(C)+U'(C)\{P(K,X)-C\}.$$

If we write the problem as

$$\text{(A10}'\text{)}\qquad \max_{\{X,K\}}\int_0^{\infty} U\{P(K,X)-\dot K+\dot XP(K,X)\beta^{-1}\}\,dt$$

and use the Euler conditions

$$\text{(A12)}\qquad 0=\frac{\partial U}{\partial K}-\frac{d}{dt}\frac{\partial U}{\partial \dot K}=\frac{\partial U}{\partial X}-\frac{d}{dt}\frac{\partial U}{\partial \dot X},$$

we obtain

$$\text{(A13)}\qquad -\frac{dU'(C)}{dt}\frac{1}{U'(C)}=\left(1-\frac{Z}{P}\right)P_K=\frac{-P_X+\beta^{-1}P_K\dot K}{P\beta^{-1}}$$

whence

$$\text{(A14)}\qquad -\beta P_X=CP_K$$

along the efficient interior-optimum path. Equations (A11) and (A14) may be written as

$$\text{(A15a)}\qquad 0=U(-\beta P_X/P_K)+U'(-\beta P_X/P_K)\{\dot K-\dot XP(K,X)\beta^{-1}\}$$

$$\text{(A15b)}\qquad -\beta P_X-P_KP=\{-\dot K+\dot XP(K,X)\beta^{-1}\}P_K.$$

They give the trajectory of (K, X) which both satisfies the Euler conditions and approaches the Golden Rule rest-point, (K^*, X^*). The locus shows X to be a function of K, a decreasing function at least for C near $P(K^*, X^*)$.

If X_0 is less than the X corresponding to K_0 on this efficient trajectory, the optimal policy trades away increased X for increased K as fast as possible, while always adhering to (A11), until the efficient locus is reached. One may think of some (negative) lower bound on Z as limiting the speed of the adjustments.

NOTES

[1] Other interpretations of Ramsey's spare model are possible. Readers of the original version may recall that, while the population is indeed stationary, the supply of labour is treated as an endogenous variable with the supply of saving. Here I follow the simpler textbook version.

[2] To be accurate, the model postulated an underlying Golden Age in which labour supply and capital stock are both growing exponentially at a non-negative rate. A different treatment of monetary policy is discussed in Section III.

[3] It may have been their unreadiness to accept this natural rate hypothesis, a notion long implicit in works by Fellner, Lerner and Wallich, in place of the empiricist Phillips Curve that accounts for the unwillingness of some utilitarian economists to accept the long-run optimality of deflationary full liquidity.

[4] As the utility function is specified here, it is possible that a small contraction of employment would reduce the interest rate required to stabilize net capital formation by so much as to leave the rate of utility undiminished or even increased. In that event all generations could be given increases in utility compared with the immediately available steady-state utility obtainable at the natural level of employment. But this phenomenon could arise only at high expected inflation rates if, given the money interest rate, the marginal utility of employment is strictly positive at the natural rate.

[5] After the elections of 1969, for example, I was named to President-Elect Nixon's Task Force on inflation. In fact, in that council I favoured only the provisional step of returning to the natural rate of unemployment, then gauged to be about 5 per cent or a little more, so as to end the *rise* of inflation. But this limited proposal was ultimately swept into a "gradualist" program of *dis*inflation—not unlike the one actually carried out, under the "Game Plan", between 1969 and 1971. It may have been a resulting apprehension of being implicated in the ensuing recession that accounts for the severity with which I criticized the Council of Economic Advisers (Phelps, 1972c).

[6] The second argument, which was originated by William Vickrey, appealed to random variations in the *IS* curve and thence employment, not necessarily to those in inflation (actual or expected). However, I realize now that it foreshadows the theory of optimal inflation control in a stochastic setting that is discussed below in Section V.

[7] It follows, from the aforementioned initial conditions, that the capital and expected inflation variables describe a loop before heading towards their point of rest. Such a loop, and a somewhat similar model may be found in Van Order (1975, pp. 369–380).

[8] That recommendation is not without precedent. The proposal was made as early as 1967 at the Montauk Point Conference of the American Bankers Association by M. J. Bailey: see his comment on the optimal rate of growth of money (Bailey, 1968). My puzzled reaction to Bailey on p. 884 of that journal shows that I had not thought of the maximin criterion.

[9] The position of this rest-point is determined by the initial conditions prevailing at the advent of the maximin criterion. In this respect and in some others the solution resembles the findings for the (different) maximin problem analysed in Phelps and Riley (1978).

REFERENCES

BAILEY, M. J. (1968). Comment on the optimal rate of growth of money. *Journal of Political Economy*, **76,** 874–876.

CALVO, G. A. (1977). Optimal maximin accumulation with uncertain future technology. *Econometrica*, **45,** 317–328.

MERTON, R. C. (1975). An asymptotic theory of growth under uncertainty. *Review of Economic Studies*, **42,** 375–393.

PHELPS, E. S. (1967). Phillips curves, expectations of inflation and optimal unemployment over time. *Economica*, **34,** 254–281.

—— (1972a). *Inflation Policy and Unemployment Theory*. New York: Norton.

—— (1972b). Unreasonable price stability. In *The Battle Against Unemployment* (A. M. Okun, ed.), pp. 214–223. New York: Norton.

—— (1972c). Economics and government. *American Economic Review*, **62,** 533–539.

—— and Riley, J. G. (1978). Rawlsian growth. *Review of Economic studies*, **45**.

Ramsey, F. P. (1928). A mathematical theory of saving. Economic Journal, **38,** 543–559.

Van Order, Robert (1975). A model of optimal growth and stabilization. *International Economic Review*, **16,** 369–380.

DISINFLATION WITHOUT RECESSION: ADAPTIVE GUIDEPOSTS AND MONETARY POLICY

Keynes' doctrine held that the monetary authorities in a market economy are better placed than the uncoordinated decision makers of the private sector for the task of restoring and maintaining "full" employment. Although the authorities might anticipate a shock to aggregate demand or (we may add) aggregate supply no better than the "market," well-tutored central bankers could counteract such a shock more reliably—short of some distant "long run"—than would the unguided practitioners of industrial wage policy, each of them left to wondering what normal wage practice is going to be. The task of employment stabilization will actually be easier to the extent that prevailing labor practice, supported by monetary policy itself, promotes constancy, or constancy of the path, of the average money wage.[1]

Milton Friedman's doctrine stood Keynes on his head: The ordinary mechanisms of the market would serve to stabilize employment as well as central bankers can. Indeed the market would do it better if private decision-makers could count on constancy, or constancy in the growth, of the stock of money. The difficulty they have heretofore experienced in anticipating the central bank's reaction to disturbances, "however well intentioned," has been the largest obstacle to greater economic stability.[2]

This paper will not weigh Friedman's k percent rule for monetary growth against policy rules of the "Keynesian" feedback type. In the present times the contest between these two strategies could hardly be more starkly irrelevant. My aim is rather to come to grips with their shared steady-state limitations: Both types of stabilization rules are geared to some "desired" rate of wage inflation—each in its own way, as elabo-

[1] See Keynes (1936). Keynes' preference for a "stable" course of the money wage is expressed in Chapter 19. Allusions to the conjectural problem in noncooperative decision-making appear occasionally, and that consideration presumably accounts for his distrust of wages as a stabilizer. Perhaps the unwritten chapter, "The Distinction between a Cooperative Economy and an Entrepeneur Economy," was intended to make this more explicit.

[2] See Friedman (1956, especially Chapter 4; 1959). Friedman might well cite the astonishing deceleration of money over the fall and winter of 1974–1975. What labor market would have accelerated wages in that situation?

Reprinted by permission from *Weltwirtschaftliches Archiv*, Vol. 100(2), December 1978.

rated in Appendix A. Either monetary rule may entail costly adjustments unless the wage structure of the economy to which the rule is introduced is quickly adaptable or perchance already adapted (by the accident of past wage behavior) to the specific rate of wage inflation for which the new policy is designed.

In the 1970s the countries lacking a central synchronous mechanism of national wage setting have constituted a laboratory for experimental confirmation of the difficulty. When introduced into economics conditioned to high or moderate inflation, monetary policies better fitted to already lower inflation have tended to produce a slump in the process of reducing the inflation. Nor have the gradualist attempts at monetary counterinflation generally escaped the problem of unemployment. This is the "crisis" of both Keynesian and Friedmanian policies.

Why is it that in most market economies the efforts of the monetary authorities to reduce inflation appear to be so problematic? In the traditional answers, only seeing is believing. The earliest theory is that, as long as the business outlook remains normal, firms will not dare to lessen wage increases unless they see other firms doing so. The outlook for sales and employment will not worsen unless business conditions actually decline. Recession is thus the very modus operandi of counterinflationary monetary policy.

A newer theory is that wage setters do not at first believe the central bank will finally be willing to carry out its intention to institute slower monetary growth—perhaps only because each one doubts that the bank's intended action is predicted by others and therefore doubts that wages will slow as he suspects is necessary for the bank to follow through. Hence forecasts of sales and unemployment linger at their normal levels. And firms, believing that the others are encouraged to do the same, consequently proceed to push up wages at the customary rate—at least until events have significantly worsened the outlook. If the bank remains firm, then, the average money wage will begin outrunning the money supply and above-equilibrium unemployment will develop. Only then, when the recession is felt, may wage inflation tend to weaken. But so may the resolve of the monetary authorities! The recession-or-inflation dilemma for the central bank gives some grounds for the initial belief that the bank will relent—that any resulting recession would be too short-lived to warrant an appreciable anticipatory revision of wage behavior.

The capsule model below will permit a formal analysis. Let M_t, W_t, and N_t denote, respectively, the money supply, the average money wage, and the level of employment in period t. And let F_vX_t denote the popular forecast at the start of period v of any variable X_t in period t, $v \leq t$. The macroequilibrium or "full" employment level—being inflation-invariant it is also the "natural" level—will be denoted N^*. The full-employment quantity of money in wage units, the value of M_t/W_t needed for $N_t = N^*$, will be denoted Ψ, a function of N^* and other parameters. In this notation the reduced-form model is

$$\log N_t - \log N^* = \mu[\log M_t - \log W_t - \log \psi], \qquad \mu > 0, \tag{1}$$

$$\log W_t = \log F_t W_t + \phi \cdot (\log F_t N_t - \log N^*), \qquad \phi > 0. \tag{2}$$

The employment equation is stylized Keynes. The other one, after substraction of $\log W_{t-1}$ from both sides, may be recognized as (a log-linearization of) the expectations-generalized Phillips equation for the rate of wage change:

$$g_t = F_t g_t + \phi \cdot (\log F_t N_t - \log N^*), \qquad g_t \equiv \log W_t - \log W_{t-1}, \quad F_t g_t \equiv \log F_t W_t - \log W_{t-1}. \tag{2'}$$

It should be emphasized that (2) describes the average money wage in period t in an economy of *one-period wage commitments,* all wages being preset at the end of the previous period on the basis of full information about the past and popular beliefs about the future.[3]

The oldest formal analysis asserting that counterinflationary policy breeds recession makes the mechanical assumption of "adaptive expectations" regarding the endogenous variables—here, wages and employment. In brief: Suppose the period before t was one of macroequilibrium, so that $g_{t-1} = F_{t-1}g_{t-1}$ and $N_{t-1} = F_{t-1}N_{t-1}$. Therefore $F_{t-1}N_{t-1} = N^*$ by (2′) and $\log M_{t-1} - \log W_{t-1} = \Psi$ by (1). If expectations are merely adaptive or error-correcting, then $F_t g_t = F_{t-1}g_{t-1}$ and $F_t N_t = F_{t-1}N_{t-1}$, there having been no errors in the previous period needing correcting. Therefore $F_t N_t = N^*$ too and consequently, by (2′), $g_t = g_{t-1}$. Hence a "counterinflationary" decision by the central bank to set $k_t \equiv \log M_t - \log M_{t-1} < g_{t-1}$ implies $\log M_t - \log W_t < \log M_{t-1} - \log W_{t-1}$ and $N_t < N_{t-1}$. If the same k is maintained over subsequent periods, the lapse from macroequilibrium employment could (in principle) be quite prolonged.[4]

The newer theory (sketched earlier) instead makes (limited) use of "rational expectations." It postulates (with Muth) that the public's forecasts of the *endogenous* variables of the model are based on perfect

[3] The closest single reference seems still to be Phelps (1968). Readers of that paper will recall, however, that it argues for a richer ϕ term than the one with which eq. (2) contents itself and it foreshadows the growing emphasis on "overlapping" wage commitments.

[4] Adaptive expectations won widespread favor following its successful application in Cagan (1956). A recent empirical defense of autoregressive expectations is in Feige and Pearce (1976).

knowledge of that model, and are thus "rational" (costs apart) relative to that model.[5] Hence

$$\log F_tN_t - \log N^* = \mu \cdot (\log F_tM_t - \log F_tW_t - \log \psi), \tag{3}$$
$$\log F_tW_t = \log F_tW_t + \phi \cdot (\log F_tN_t - \log N^*). \tag{4}$$

Therefore, from (1) through (4),

$$\log W_t = \log F_tW_t = \log F_tM_t - \log \psi, \tag{5}$$
$$\log N_t - \log N^* = \mu \cdot (\log M_t - \log F_tM_t). \tag{6}$$

Now suppose the central bank resolves at the end of $t - 1$ to slow the growth of money in period t, while the skeptical public bets on money growth more like the past. Then $F_tM_t > M_t$ with the result that $\log W_t > \log M_t - \log \psi$ and so $N_t < N^*$.

Such arguments hypothesize an initial frictional cost to counterinflation and proceed to attribute the friction to the incapacity of the public generally to anticipate fully and promptly the central bank's new course, and to anticipate the generality of that anticipation. But the explanation is as puzzling as the hypothesis to be explained! For suppose the central bank, in a setting described in part by Equations (1) and (2), were to broadcast its intentions to adopt a new counterinflationary policy. If the monetary authorities were to publicize their conditional forecast of its consequences in the event its effects were generally anticipated and believed to be so, and if the public showed that these conditional consequences would be widely welcomed, what reason would wage-setters (and other economic agents) have not to expect the bank to carry out the intended policy? What reason would any agent have to believe that others would not expect the bank to pursue the new policy? If none, what reason would agents have not to anticipate the conditionally forecasted effects of the new policy?

We can conceive reasons in particular situations:[6] There might be a strong faction favoring somewhat *less* counterinflation than the new policy seeks, in which case the life of the announced plan is uncertain. The conditional forecast of the effects of the policy might be too uncertain or disputed to inspire their confident expectation, in which case the policy will not be anticipated to work (and will not work) as intended. (The latter

[5] See Muth (1961), Lucas (1972), and Sargent and Wallace (1975).

[6] Elsewhere I have argued that there may exist political–economic circumstances in which the public *does* have reason to doubt the central bank's determination and the bank expects to cure the public of its misapprehension. Then an underemployment disequilibrium, with $N_t < F_tN_t = N^*$, might occur and persist. But the case under discussion is not one of those situations. There is, by hypothesis, no group opposing the central bank's anti-inflationary aims. See Phelps (1978).

point needs to be taken seriously in the more complex theoretical settings that appear later in this paper.) There are other potentially applicable objections. Yet I think it is worthwhile to suspend our disbeliefs until we have some picture—of course, I cannot draw the whole picture—of how much (or how little) there is to disbelieve.

This paper will build a series of rational-expectations models with which to study the requirements of counterinflationary policy without recession—in circumscribed conditions where it is not apparently "irrational" of the public to anticipate that policy, if such can be found. The rational expectations extend to the policy variable as well as the endogenous ones—in a sense, the policy is endogenized—although not necessarily without some institutional aids. The main novelty, though, is the introduction of *overlapping multiperiod "contracts"* into the process of money-wage behavior to which rational expectations must apply.

The questions to be resolved are these: Does there exist a monetary program which, accompanied by rational expectations (and possibly aids thereto), could reduce the rate of wage inflation to the extent desired? If so, do initial conditions regarding outstanding wage contracts permit the rate of wage inflation to be reduced slowly or quickly, as one likes, or is there a unique path to the final target rate? If the latter is true, what is the character of that path and the complexity of the policy and forecasting rules needed to place and keep the economy on target?

I. One-Period Contracts

Of course, these questions are trivial to resolve in the *one-period wage-contract* model containing Equations (1) through (4). On our hopeful assumption of extended rational expectations we add

$$\log F_t M_t = \log M_t, \qquad t = 0, 1, 2, \ldots . \tag{7}$$

Then, for every $t \geq 0$,

$$\log W_t = \log M_t - \log \psi, \tag{8}$$

$$\log N_t = \log N^*. \tag{9}$$

By choice of the suitable sequence $\{M_t\}$ any desired path $\{W_t\}$ of the average money wage may be engineered without lapsing from the full-employment level, N^*. In particular, it is possible to reach the target, $\log W_t - \log W_{t-1} = g^*$, in any and every period, beginning immediately at $t = 0$. Or, if desired, the achievement of the target may be approached gradually.

Needless to say, the introduction of moving parameters N_t^* and Ψ_t

would present no essential complication provided that these parameters were always forecasted correctly; it would be understood that planned changes in M_t through time were intended to counter these parameter movements in such a way as to keep W_t on its planned path and simultaneously to maintain $N_t = N_t^*$ for all t. On the other hand, recognizing that ψ_t and perhaps also N_t^* are functions of the expected rate of inflation, and thus of $\log F_t W_{t+1} - \log W_t$, will add to the econometric and analytical tasks of finding the money-supply path required to support full employment along the planned path of wages: Paradoxically, an accommodative (one-time) lift of the money supply at $t = 0$ might be needed if the new-found prospects for disinflation would touch off an extensive flight out of goods into money.[7] It is possible that such arcane considerations may make the central bank's plan more difficult to explain to the public and thus impair its credibility. But this not necessarily so. The task of the central bank is to break the public's habit of predicting future wage inflation from current movements in the stock of money and to inculcate instead the public's prediction of the money supply from the intended and forecasted course of the average money wage.

Those who take heart from these findings (as I do) will nevertheless sense that something is amiss. If disinflation without recession were within such easy reach, more central banks would have grasped it by now! What then is the source of the trouble, absent the psychological and political barriers earlier excluded, that the present model leaves out of account? I suggest that the trip wire for disinflationary policy, at least when nothing else has stood in the way, is an institutional feature of most national labor markets that equation (2) neglects. This is the phenomenon of *staggered wage-setting* for a multiperiod duration and the consequent coexistence in every period of *overlapping wage "contracts."*[8]

The crucial complication which the dynamics of contractual wages pose for counterinflationary planning is this: The new money-wage commitments made in the current period must be figured to "catch up" with old wage commitments still outstanding (and hence subsequent to the expiring ones)—and even to "overtake" old wage commitments that are anticipated to have some "catching up" or "overtaking" of their own to do. But forecasting the sequence of future wages warranted by the government's new inflation objective is fraught with difficulty. Errors in such

[7] See Mundell (1963). The above ground is well covered, with different emphasis, in Sargent and Wallace (1973).

[8] Perhaps the earliest study to identify leap-frogging wages and prices as a major problem is Fellner *et al.* (1961). Aspects of such dynamic processes have been modeled in Akerlof (1969), Phelps, "Money-Wage Dynamics," (*op cit.*, especially Appendix 1 of the 1970 version), Ross and Wachter (1973), Fischer (1977), Taylor (1976), and Baily (1976).

calculations, by either firms or the central bank, may disappoint the hopes for disinflation or full employment or both. If firms calculate correctly the catch up appropriate to full employment while the bank underestimates it, the consequent deficiency in the growth of money will produce a decline of employment—even if firms somehow anticipate the under-provision of money![9] If the bank calculates the warranted catch up correctly but firms overestimate it, the consequence will be a shortfall of disinflation from the plan and probably a deline of employment—for even if the bank anticipates the excessive catch up, it may hesitate to underwrite mistakes in full.

A successful strategy of counterinflation must therefore clear the difficult, but I think not insurmountable, hurdle of calculating (and promulgating) the path of wages and the corresponding course of the full-employment money supply that will lead to the ultimate target rate of wage inflation. The next three sections illustrate the possibility of such calculations in the simplest abstract settings.

II. Two-Period Contracts

The reader is to think of unindexed one-year wage "contracts" in the context of a semiannual period model. At the start of each period or semiannum, money-wage rates must be reset for roughly half of the jobs in the economy and these rates will stick for two periods; a period later wage rates for the other jobs are reset and last for the next two periods, and so on indefinitely. These two groups of wage rates are so normalized that in a stationary state of zero wage inflation their mean levels would be equal. The normalization is akin to seasonal adjustment.

Let $W_v(s)$ denote the mean wage rate set in contracts of "vintage" v and prevailing in period s, $s = (v, v + 1)$. As stated, $W_v(v + 1) = W_v(v)$ and, in a stationary state, $W_v(v) = W_{v+1}(v + 1)$ for all v. In this notation, the new-wage function with which I replace equation (2) is[10]

[9] The firms setting new wages will not forego their catch up by the whole of the amount needed to offset the bank's error, but only by an amount which anticipates the impending decline of sales and rise of unemployment. Incidentally, an abrupt switch to the final growth rate of money implied by the final inflation objective might produce a bulge of unemployment and a slow decline of inflation, both vanishing in the limit, that look like "adaptive expectations" at work when the real difficulty is the inconsistency of the monetary policy with the aims of reduced inflation without recession.

[10] Equation (10) is in the spirit of my "Money Wage Dynamics" (*op. cit.*, especially pp. 697–700). See also Taylor, *op. cit.*, which takes up the econometrics of a model containing a similar equation.

$$\log W_t(t) = \tfrac{1}{2}\log F_t\bar{W}(t) + \tfrac{1}{2}\log F_t\bar{W}(t+1) + \tfrac{1}{2}\phi(\log F_tN_t - \log N^*) + \tfrac{1}{2}\phi(\log F_tN_{t+1} - \log N^*), \tag{10}$$

where $\bar{W}(t)$ is the geometric average of the old and new wage rates in period t, .

$$log\ \bar{W}(t) \equiv \tfrac{1}{2}\log W_{t-1}(t) + \tfrac{1}{2}\log W_t(t), \tag{11}$$

and $F_v\bar{W}(t)$ is its forecast at the start of period $v(\leq t)$. These primitive forms are adopted only for their expediency. A minor convenience of (10) and (11) is that they permit arbitrarily fast or slow steady-state growth of wages at the same "natural" or inflation-independent N^*, owing to their log-linearity. (Other functional forms would not have this nice property.)

Substituting (11) into (10) and using $W_t(t+1) = W_t(t)$ we obtain

$$\log W_t(t) = \tfrac{1}{2}\log F_tW_t(t) + \tfrac{1}{2}[\tfrac{1}{2}\log W_{t-1}(t) + \tfrac{1}{2}\log F_tW_{t+1}(t+1)] + \tfrac{1}{2}\phi(\log F_tN_t - \log N^*) + \tfrac{1}{2}\phi(\log F_tN_{t+1} - \log N^*). \tag{12}$$

Invoking rational expectations, we also have

$$\log F_tW_t(t) = \log W_t(t) \tag{13}$$

whence, by (12) and (13),

$$\log W_t(t) = \tfrac{1}{2}\log W_{t-1}(t) + \tfrac{1}{2}\log F_tW_{t+1}(t+1) + \phi[\log F_tN_t - \log N^*) + (\log F_tN_{t+1} - \log N^*)]. \tag{14}$$

So the (mean) wage in the current new contracts is a symmetrical geometric average of the (mean) wages in the previous and succeeding contracts over the relevant span. This formulation, with which one might have started, provides the difference equation we have to study. It will be convenient to write it in simpler notation:

$$w_t = \tfrac{1}{2}w_{t-1} + \tfrac{1}{2}F_tw_{t+1} + \phi\cdot(F_tn_t - n^* + F_tn_{t+1} - n^*), \quad t = 0, 1, 2, \ldots, \tag{14}$$

where w_t denotes $\log W_t(t) = \log W_t(t+1)$, n_t denotes $\log N_t$, and so on.

In this notation, we now seek the wage path or paths $\{w_t^* | t = 0, 1, 2, \ldots\}$ having the property that the target rate of wage growth, denoted g,* is reached in finite t or else asymptotically and meeting the following necessary conditions: (1) the path is supported by a monetary plan $\{m_t^* | t = 0, 1, 2, \ldots\}$ correctly and always anticipated to maintain full employment, so that $F_tn_s = F_tF_{t+1}n_s = \cdots = F_tF_sn_s = F_sn_s = n_s = n^*$ for every $s \geq t$ and $t \geq 0$, and (2) the path, when so accompanied, is itself correctly and always anticipated, so that $F_tw_s = F_tF_{t+1}w_s = \ldots$

$= F_t F_s w_s = w_s = w_s^*$, again for every $s \geq t$ and $t \geq 0$. Such a path must therefore satisfy

$$w_t^* = \tfrac{1}{2} w_{t-1}^* + \tfrac{1}{2} w_{t+1}^*, \qquad t = 0, 1, 2, \ldots ; \quad w_{-1}^* = w_{-1}, \quad \text{a datum.} \tag{15}$$

In the cases of particular interest, inflation has been going on, so that $w_{-2} < w_{-1}$, and the objective is to reduce it. Nothing essential will be lost if we often focus attention on $g^* = 0$.

Equation (15) describes an inflation-smoothing process to which there is only one solution corresponding to a specified g^*. For each $t \geq 0$, w_t^* must make $w_t^* - w_{t-1}^* = w_{t+1}^* - w_t^* = g$, a constant. If $g^* = 0$, for example, this desired growth rate is therefore obtainable if and only if there is a one-time catch up making $w_0^* - w_{-1} = w_1^* - w_0^* = \cdots\cdot =$ $w_t^* - w_{t-1}^* = \cdots = g^* = 0$. Hence, if $w_{-1} > w_{-2}$, so that $w_0^* > w_{-2}$, the average wage $\bar{W}(t)$ rises just once, at $t = 0$.

That solution may be verified by subtracting $\frac{1}{2} w_t^*$ from (15) to obtain

$$w_t^* - w_{t-1}^* = w_{t+1}^* - w_t^*, \qquad \text{i.e.,} \qquad g_t^* = g_{t+1}^*, \qquad (t = 0, 1, 2, \ldots) \tag{15'}$$

so that g_t^* is a constant, subject to choice. Or we may write Eq. (15) in the canonical form, adding 1 to all subscripts,

$$w_{t+2}^* - 2\, w_{t+1}^* + w_t^* = 0, \tag{15''}$$

and establish that the corresponding characteristic equation has both roots equal to one, so that $w_t^* = C_0 1^t$, $C_0 = w_{-1}$.

There is left an interpretive matter of some importance. Suppose that the government, having calculated the desired path of wages, announces only the appropriate *monetary* plan to be followed by the central bank:

$$m_t = \log \psi + w_{-1}, \qquad (t = 0, 1, 2, \ldots), \quad m_t \equiv \log M_t. \tag{16}$$

It might do so, we may imagine, on the premise that the "market" can be relied to establish $w_t = \log \bar{W}(t) = w_{-1}$ for all $t > 0$ if the bank is counted on to provide that constant money supply which, at the constant solution level of the average wage (viz., $W_{-1}(0)$), would maintain full employment. It is not then possible, in theory, that the market will somehow hit upon a rational-expectations path other than our desired wage path with the result that full employment is not maintained?

Appendix B shows that the only other rational-expectations solutions are all explosive and consequently imply a behavior of the economy that must eventually become infeasible, economically or politically or both. No such path could be realized indefinitely, therefore, and so none could serve as a tenable scenario on which decision-makers might base their expectations of future wages. However, that proposition does not remove the possibility that myopic wage setters, unaware the economy was on a collision course, might mysteriously form expectations that steadily proved to be correct until the collision or its eventual prediction.

Fortunately, we need not ponder further the issue of whether the market would have the wit to avoid expecting, and thus turning into a temporarily self-fulfilling prophecy, any of those undesired wage paths. The practical point that needs making is that the government, to play it as safely as possible, had better do more than preannounce and follow the "right" monetary policy. It would be prudent and helpful to announce also the path of wages appropriate to its goal. This precaution although it cannot be "proved" to succeed, would help to instill the right expectations and thus promote the likelihood that the initial catch-up of new wages at $t = 0$ will not overshoot the mark.

III. Three-Period Contracts

In this case each year is divided into three periods. The wage contracts are again equally distributed, one year in duration, and their wages "seasonally" normalized as before. The corresponding new-wage function in any period t, analogous to (11), is

$$\log W_t(t) = \tfrac{1}{3}\log F_t W(t) + \tfrac{1}{3}\log F_t \bar{W}(t+1) + \tfrac{1}{3}\log F_t \bar{W}(t+2) + \tfrac{1}{3}\phi[\log F_t N_t + \log F_t N_{t+1} + \log F_t N_{t+2} - 3\log N^*], \quad (17)$$

$$\equiv \tfrac{1}{3}\log \bar{W}_{t-2}(t) + \tfrac{1}{3}\log W_{t-1}(t) + \tfrac{1}{3}\log W_t(t). \quad (18)$$

Hence

$$\log W_t(t) = \tfrac{1}{3}\{\log F_t W_t(t) + [\tfrac{1}{3}\log W_{t-2}(t) + \tfrac{2}{3}\log F_t W_{t+1}(t+1)] + [\tfrac{2}{3}\log F_t W_{t-1}(t) + \tfrac{1}{3}\log F_t W_{t+2}(t+2)]\} + \tfrac{1}{3}\phi[\log F_t N_t + \log F_t N_{t+1} + \log F_t N_{t+2} - 3\log N^*]. \quad (19)$$

Then, by rational expectations, specifically equation (13), we have[11]

$$w_t = \tfrac{1}{2}[\tfrac{1}{3}w_{t-2} + \tfrac{2}{3}w_{t-1} + \tfrac{2}{3}w_{t+1} + \tfrac{1}{3}w_{t+2}] + \tfrac{1}{2}\phi[F_t n_t + F_t n_{t+1} + F_t n_{t+2} - 3n^*], \qquad t = 0, 1, 2, \ldots . \quad (20)$$

The path or paths that meet the necessary conditions of full employment and full anticipation therefore satisfy, for $t = 0, 1, 2, \ldots$,

$$w_t^* = \tfrac{1}{6}w_{t-2}^* + \tfrac{2}{6}w_{t-1}^* + \tfrac{2}{6}w_{t+1}^* + \tfrac{1}{6}w_{t-2}^*; \quad w_{-2}^* = w_{-2}, w_{-1}^* = w_{-1}. \quad (21)$$

Again we are especially interested in situations where $w_{-3} < w_{-2} < w_{-1}$

[11] The *average* $Fn - n^*$ has a smaller impact upon the new w_t in (20) than is true in (14′) because the weight (viz. $\tfrac{1}{3}$) accorded its indirect expectations effect via $F_t W_t(t)$ in (19) is smaller than is the case in (12) for the reason that $W_t(t)$ is a smaller component of $\bar{W}(t)$ when there are three overlapping wages rather than two.

and it is desired that $g_t^* \equiv w_t^* - w_{t-1}^*$ be brought down, in finite time or in the limit, to some ultimate g^* less than $w_{-1} - w_{-2}$.

To find the desired solution to (21) it is convenient to put it in canonical form,

$$w_{t+4}^* + 2\,w_{t+3}^* - 6\,w_{t+2}^* + 2\,w_{t+1}^* + w_t^* = 0, \qquad w_{-2}^* = w_{-1}, w_{-1}^* = w_{-1}, \tag{22}$$

and exploit its symmetry and homogeneity as follows. First subtract and add w_{t+3}^*, w_{t+2}^*, and w_{t+1}^* to obtain essentially the *same* equation in terms of the growth rates:

$$g_{t+4}^* + 3\,g_{t+3}^* - 3\,g_{t+2}^* - g_{t+1}^* = 0, \qquad g_{-1}^* = w_{-1} - w_{-2}, g_t^* \equiv w_t^* - w_{t-1}^*. \tag{22'}$$

Adding and subtracting g_{t+3}^* and g_{t+2}^* then yields, subtracting 2 from the subscripts, the same equation again in terms of acceleration:

$$a_{t+2}^* + 4\,a_{t+1}^* + a_t^* = 0, \qquad a_t^* \equiv g_t^* - g_{t-1}^*. \tag{22''}$$

The general solution of (22″) for a_t^* is given by

$$a_t^* = C_1 b_1^{\,t} + C_2 b_2^{\,t}, \qquad -1 < b_1 = -2 + 3^{1/2} < 0, \qquad b_2 = -2 - 3^{1/2} < -1, \tag{23}$$

where (b_1, b_2) are the roots of the characteristic equation. There are no initial conditions of acceleration constraining C_1 and C_2—only w_{-2} and w_{-1} are current and predetermined at $t = 0$. The algebraic acceleration at $t = 0$ appropriate to the desired long-run target determines only that $C_1 + C_2 = a_0^*$. However, if $C_2 \neq 0$ then $a_t^* \to C_2 b_2^{\,t}$ which, since $b_2 < -1$, is an undamped oscillatory motion precluding any approach toward the steadystate g^*. So any eligible solution must show $C_2 = 0$ and $C_1 = a_0^*$, whence

$$a_t^* = a_0^*\, b_1^{\,t}, \qquad -1 < b_1 = -.268 < 0. \tag{24}$$

The required sequence of accelerations is alternating in sign, damped, and converging to zero.

It remains to find the value of a_0^* that generates the sequence $\{g_t^* \mid t = 0, 1, 2, \ldots\}$ approaching the target g^*. From (24) and the definition of a_t^* we have

$$g_t^* = g_{-1}^* + a_0^*(1 + b_1 + b_1^{\,2} + \cdots + b_1^{\,t}) = g_{-1}^* + a_0^* \cdot \frac{1 - b_1^{t+1}}{1 - b_1}. \tag{25}$$

Hence a_0^* will give $g_t^* \to g^*$ as $t \to \infty$, as desired, if and only if

$$a_0^* = (1 - b_1)(g^* - g_{-1}^*). \tag{26}$$

With $g^* - g_{-1}^*$ less than zero, for example, equal to $-g_{-1}^* < 0$, a_0^* must therefore be negative.

With this key result in hand, we may express the solutions for the wage variable and its "derivatives" as functions of *time* or as functions of the appropriate *state variables* in each period. From (24), (25), (26) and the definitions of a_t^* and g_t^* we can obtain the time series, for $t = 0, 1, 2, \ldots,$

$$g_t^* = g^* - b_1^{t+1}(g^* - g_{-1}), \tag{27}$$

$$\begin{aligned} w_t^* &= w_{-2} + g_{-1}(1 + b_1 + b_1^2 + \cdots + b_1^{t+1}) \\ &\quad + g^*(1 - b_1)[1 + (1 + b_1) + \cdots + (1 + b_1 + b_1^2 + \cdots + b_1^t)] \\ &= w_{-1} + g_{-1}(b_1 + b_1^2 + \cdots + b_1^{t+1}) \\ &\quad + g^*(1 - b_1)[1 + (1 + b_1) + \cdots + (1 + b_1 + b_1^2 + \cdots + b_1^t)] \end{aligned} \tag{28}$$

Hence $g_t^* - g^*$ vanishes in the limit as $t \to \infty$. In the special case where the objective is to expunge *all* the wage inflation we also have (in the limit)

$$w_\infty^* = \frac{1}{1 - b_1} w_{-1} + \frac{-b_1}{1 - b_1} w_{-2}, \qquad g^* = 0. \tag{28a}$$

(Indeed, if $g^* = 0$ it follows from (28) that w_t^* lies between w_{-2} and w_{-1} for every $t \geq 0$, as will become clear.)

It is especially useful to express the solution in terms of the appropriate relation between the variable described and its relevant past values. By (27),

$$g_t^* = b_1 g_{t-1}^* + (1 - b_1) g^*, \tag{27'}$$

and therefore

$$\begin{aligned} w_t^* &= w_{t-1}^* + b_1(w_{t-1}^* - w_{t-2}^*) + (1 - b_1)g^* \\ &= w_{t-2}^* + (1 + b_1)(w_{t-1}^* - w_{t-2}^*) + (1 - b_1)g^* \\ &= (1 + b_1)w_{t-1}^* + (-b_1)w_{t-2}^* + (1 - b_1)g^*. \end{aligned} \tag{28'}$$

Hence $W_t(t)$ is made a Cobb–Douglas function of $W_{t-1}(t - 1)$ and $W_{t-2}(t - 2)$ with positive exponents $1 + b_1$ and $-b_1$, respectively. If $g^* = 0$, then $\min(w_{t-2}^*, w_{t-1}^*) < w_t^* < \max(w_{t-2}^*, w_{t-1}^*)$. In that case it follows that $\min(w_{-2}, w_{-1}) < w_t^* < \max(w_{-2}, w_{-1})$ for all $t \geq 0$.

When $g^* = 0$, how does the *average* money wage, $\bar{W}(t)$, behave? Let us suppose $w_{-3} < w_{-2} < w_{-1}$. Then the finding in (28′) that $w_0^* > \min(w_{-2}, w_{-1}) = w_{-2}$ implies $w_0^* > w_{-3}$; this initial catch-up makes $\bar{W}(0) > \bar{W}(-1)$. And since $w_1^* > \min(w_{-1}, w_0^*) = w_0^* > w_{-2}$ there is a second stage of (limited) catch-up making $\bar{W}(1) > \bar{W}(0)$. So the full-employment monetary plan must anticipate these *increases* of the *average wage* in the *first two periods*. But $w_2^* < \max(w_0^*, w_1^*) = w_1^* < \max(w_{-1}, w_0^*) = w_{-1}$ so that $\bar{W}(2) < \bar{W}(1)$. In subsequent periods $w_3^* > w_2^* > w_0^*$, hence $\bar{W}(3) > \bar{W}(2)$, and $w_4^* < w_3^* < w_1^*$, hence $\bar{W}(4) < \bar{W}(3)$. How far does $\bar{W}(\infty)$ drop back? The reader may check, using (27′) and (28′), that when $g^* = 0$

$$\log \bar{W}^*(t + 2) = (1 + b_1) \log \bar{W}^*(t + 1) + (-b_1) \log \bar{W}^*(t), \quad t = 0, 1, 2, \ldots, \tag{29}$$

that is, the average money wage obeys the same autoregressive formula as the new wage beginning with the third period of the disinflation program (in $t = 2$). Since $\bar{W}^*(0) < \bar{W}^*(1)$, it follows that $\bar{W}^*(0) < \bar{W}^*(t) < \bar{W}^*(1)$ for all $t \geq 2$. After two periods of rise, the average wage retreats in a see-saw struggle, never giving up any of the first gain but never retaking the whole of the second gain.

Two brief comments on these results. While g_t^* approaches g^* only asymptotically, unlike our findings in the previous model, it is striking to see that the upward trend or momentum of wages is halted after just two periods. The anticipation that w_{-1} will be succeeded by a lower w_2^* and that all subsequent w_t^* will likewise be smaller than w_{-1} serves also to lessen sharply the wage increases agreed upon in the first two periods. The great mistake of "gradualist" programs of disinflation is that, when instituted, they promise continuing (albeit dwindling) money-supply growth for many periods ahead and consequently invite anticipatory wage increases at first that are excessive in relation to the money-supply increases initially provided. Steady deceleration of the money stock finally yields too much money in the future and hence too little money in the present.

The other comment is that the correct behavior of wages, given the correctly preannounced path of the money supply, evidently requires considerable sophistication on the part of wage setters—especially those who "go first" in the adjustment process—in the absence of expert advice on which they feel they can rely. Yet the adjustment process is rather simply described by (27′) and (28′). Each new wage is to be the appropriately weighted average of the wage settlements in the periods intervening since the contracts now expired were drawn up. This suggests the use of what might be called *adaptive guideposts*. The appropriate average of new wages in each periods is a function of—is to be adapted to—the pattern of outstanding wages at that time. This function, with its constant coefficients, is stable from period to period, and extraordinarily robust against changes in the structure of the economy. By contrast, the *fixed guidepost*, as its architects understood, made no allowance (or was mute on the allowance to be made) for catch-up wage increases.[12] However, discus-

[12] In the situation for which it was constructed, such as the early 1960s in the U.S., a provision for catch-up may not have been much needed.

sion of the implementation of the scheme investigated here is left for the concluding section.

IV. z-Period Contracts

If annual contract dates are distributed uniformly over z periods, $z < \infty$, then

$$\log W_t(t) = \frac{1}{z} \sum_{s=0}^{z-1} \log \bar{W}(t + s) + \frac{1}{z} \phi \sum_{s=0}^{z-1} (\log F_t N_{t+s} - \log N^*), \quad (30)$$

$$\log \bar{W}(t) = \frac{1}{z} \sum_{s=0}^{z-1} \log W_{t-s}(t), \quad (31)$$

whence

$$\begin{aligned} w_t = \frac{1}{z} \Bigg[& \frac{1}{z} w_{t-z+1} + \frac{2}{z} w_{t-z+2} + \frac{3}{z} w_{t-z+3} + \cdots + \frac{z-1}{z} w_{t-z+(z-1)} \\ & + F_t w_t + \frac{z-1}{z} F_t w_{t+z-(z-1)} + \frac{z-2}{z} F_t w_{t+z-(z-2)} + \cdots \\ & + \frac{1}{z} F_t w_{t+z-1} \Bigg] + \frac{1}{z} \phi \, [F_t n_t + F_t n_{n+1} + \cdots + F_t n_{t+z-1} - zn^*] \end{aligned} \quad (32)$$

and, by rational expectations ($w_t = F_t w_t$),

$$\begin{aligned} w_t = \frac{1}{z-1} \Bigg(& \frac{1}{z} w_{t-z+1} + \frac{2}{z} w_{t-z+2} + \cdots + \frac{z-1}{z} w_{t-z+(z-1)} \\ & + \frac{z-1}{z} F_t w_{t+z-(z-1)} + \frac{z-2}{z} F_t w_{t+z-(z-2)} + \cdots + \frac{1}{z} F_t w_{t+z-1} \Bigg] \\ & + \frac{1}{z-1} \phi [F_t n_t + F_t n_{t+1} + \cdots + F_t n_{t+z-1} - zn^*]. \end{aligned} \quad (33)$$

Once again our interest narrows to the class of paths meeting the necessary conditions of continuing full employment and fulfilled expectations. By (33), such paths satisfy

$$\begin{aligned} & w^*_{t+z-1} + 2w^*_{t+z-2} + 3w^*_{t+z-3} + \cdots + (z-1)w^*_{t+z-(z-1)} - z(z-1)w_t^* \\ & \quad + (z-1)w^*_{t-z+(z-1)} + (z-2)w^*_{t-z+(z-2)} + \cdots + 2w^*_{t-z+2} + w^*_{t-z+1} = 0, \end{aligned} \quad (34)$$

which is the generalization of (22). And again we are looking for a path in this class having the desired property that the excess wage inflation vanishes, at least in the limit.

The existence and uniqueness of the desired solution to (34) have been shown by my colleague G. A. Calvo. A somewhat detailed proof is contained in Appendix C. The gist of the argument is the following: The characteristic equation for (34),

$$b^{z-1} + 2b^{z-2} + \cdots + (z - 1)b^1 - z(z - 1)b^0 \\ + (z - 1)b^{-1} + \cdots + 2b^{-z+2} + b^{-z+1} = 0 \quad (35)$$

has $2z - 1$ terms and $2z - 2$ roots, $(b_1, b_2, \ldots, b_{2z-2})$. Owing to the zero-sum of its coefficients, one of these roots, say b_1, is equal to one; and that unitary "root" can be shown to occur twice, so set the last root, b_{2z-2}, equal to one also. All the other $2(z - 2)$ roots come in pairs, each pair having the property that one root is the reciprocal of the other in the pair; for if $b = b_i$ satisfies (35) then so does $b = b_i^{-1}$ by virtue of the symmetry of this equation about its center. But of these roots, half must have absolute values greater than one (there are none having absolute value of one other than b_1 and b_{2z-2}) and those $z - 2$ roots do not qualify for an eligible solution since to accord any of them nonzero weight in the solution for w_t^* would produce explosive behavior. The root b_{2z-2} may be disqualified for the same reason. That leaves $(z - 1)$ qualifying roots in all, namely $(b_2, b_3, \ldots, b_{z-1})$, each less than one in absolute value, and $b_1 = 1$. Because there are $z - 1$ predetermined wages $(w^*_{-1}, w^*_{-2}, \ldots, w^*_{-(z-1)})$, there are just enough data to determine (with zero degrees of freedom) the $(z - 1)$ coefficients in the appropriate formula for w_t^*. This sketches Calvo's proof.

The problem now is the calculation of the required w_t^* as a function of the current wage data. To that end it is natural to try the method used above for the case $z = 3$. Thus, a rearrangement of the terms in (34) yields the growth-rate equation

$$\begin{aligned} g^*_{t+z-1} &+ (1 + 2)g^*_{t+z-2} + (1 + 2 + 3)g^*_{t+z-3} + \cdots \\ &+ (1 + 2 + \cdots + z - 2)g^*_{t+z-(z-2)} \\ &+ (1 + 2 + \cdots + z - 1)g^*_{t+z-(z-1)} \\ &- (1 + 2 + \cdots + z - 1)g^*_{t-z+z} \\ &- (1 + 2 + \cdots + z - 2)g^*_{t-z+(z-1)} - \cdots \\ &- (1 + 2)g^*_{t-z+3} - g^*_{t-z+2} = 0, \end{aligned} \quad (34')$$

which generalizes (22′). A rearrangement of these terms yields the acceleration equation

$$\begin{aligned} a^*_{t+z-1} &+ [1 + (1 + 2)]a^*_{t+z-2} + \cdots + [1 + (1 + 2) \\ &+ (1 + 2 + 3) + \cdots + (1 + 2 + \cdots + z - 2)]a^*_{t+z-(z-2)} \\ &+ [1 + (1 + 2) + (1 + 2 + 3) + \cdots \\ &+ (1 + 2 + 3 + \cdots + z - 1)]a^*_{t-(z-1)} \\ &+ [1 + (1 + 2) + \cdots + (1 + 2 + \cdots + z - 2)]a^*_{t-z+z} \\ &+ \cdots + [1 + (1 + 2)]a^*_{t-z+4} + a^*_{t-z+3} = 0, \end{aligned} \quad (34'')$$

which generalizes (22″).

Few could resist pausing over the austere natural beauty of these equations!

> What immortal hand or eye
> could frame thy fearful symmetry?

The coefficient patterns made by (34), (34′), and (34″) also evoke Pascal's Triangle with which he studied combinatorials:

1	1	1	1	1	1	1
1	2	3	4	5	6	
1	3	6	10	15		
1	4	10	20			
1	5	15				
1	6					
1						

The coefficients of (34) are like the second row or column, those of (34′) like the third, and those of (34″) like the fourth. But so far I know of no work on equations with row-drawn coefficients—only Pascal's binominal expansions using the northwest diagonals.

Unfortunately, (34″) seems to be the end of the road: There is no way of getting successive equations in the third, fourth, . . . , $(z - 1)st$ difference of w_t^*, the last of which would be advantageous like (22″)—because the coefficients in (34″), while still symmetrical, do not add up to zero like those in (34) and (34′). Yet (34′) tells us something of interest: The same difference equation (having the same coefficients) applies to the excess-growth-rate variable, $g_t^* - g^*$. Such an equation, together with existence and uniqueness, implies that the desired solution makes $g_t^* - g^*$ a linear function of the predetermined excess growth rates (of the still surviving wages), *viz.*, $g_{t-1}^* - g^*, g_{t-2}^* - g^*, \ldots, g_{t-z+2}^* - g^*$. This was the form of the solution for the case $z = 3$ shown in (27′).

Consider, for illustration, the quarterly case $z = 4$. Assume that the solution, for $t \geq 0$, is of the form

$$g_t^* - g^* = b_1 (g_{t-1}^* - g^*) + b_2 (g_{t-2}^* - g^*), \quad g_{-1}^* = g_{-1}, g_{-2}^* = g_{-2}. \qquad (36)$$

First-differencing this equation implies that, for $t \geq 1$,

$$a_{t+1}^* = b_1 a_t^* + b_2 a_{t-1}^*, \qquad a_{-1}^* = a_{-1}, \qquad (37)$$

which may be inserted into the acceleration equation (34″) with $z = 4$. This "method of undetermined coefficients" yields

$$a_{t+1}^* = \frac{-(b_1 + 4)b_2 - 4}{(b_1 + 4)b_1 + b_2 + 10} a_t^* + \frac{-1}{(b_1 + 4)b_1 + b_2 + 10} a_{t-1}^*. \qquad (38)$$

Equating the first coefficient to b_1 and the second to b_2, I calculated the approximations

$$b_1 = -.425, \qquad b_2 = -.1195. \tag{39}$$

It can be confirmed that (36), with these coefficients, makes $g_t^* \to g^*$ in a damped oscillatory manner. Since the rule expressed by (36) and (39) satisfies (34″), thus also (34), and since there exists a unique solution to (34) having the property that $g_t^* - g^*$ vanishes, this rule is the only desired solution.

To express this solution in terms of the level of each period's new wages, as did (28′), we deduce from (36) and the definition $g_t = w_t - w_{t-1}$ that

$$w_t^* = (1 + b_1)w_{t-1}^* + (b_2 - b_1)w_{t-2}^* + (-b_2)w_{t-3}^* + (1 - b_1 - b_2)\, g^*, \tag{40}$$

whence, by (39),

$$w_t^* = .575\, w_{t-1}^* + .305\, w_{t-2}^* + .120\, w_{t-3}^* + 1.5445\, g^*. \tag{41}$$

The case $z = 5$ would be of only marginal interest and try the patience of author and reader alike. For practical purposes we want at least $z = 12$, the monthly model, and better yet the daily model, say $z = 250$, or maybe $z = 365$. There surely exist computerized methods to calculate the desired solutions to these high-order difference equations.

Pending those results, I would conjecture that the z period case has a solution

$$w_t^* = (1 + b_1)w_{t-1}^* + (b_2 - b_1)w_{t-2}^* + \cdots + (b_{z-2} - b_{z-3})w_{t-z+2} + (-b_{z-2})w_{t-(z-1)}^* + (1 - b_1 - b_2 - \cdots - b_{z-2})g^* \tag{42}$$

in which the first $z - 1$ coefficients (of the predetermined wages) are positive fractions that form a declining sequence summing (of course) to one—with the last of these coefficients going to zero as z goes to infinity; and the last coefficient is greater than 1 but less than some upper bound smaller than, at least not much larger than, 2.

V. Summary and Appraisal

This paper has explored the requirements of counterinflation *cum* full employment in the simplest of models with symmetrically overlapping wage contracts of uniform length. Each such counterinflationary program, if unerring, was shown to have exact implications for the course of successive new wage commitments from period to period. For the cases in which wage commitments are staggered evenly over $z = 2, 3$, and 4 subperiods, I found the qualitative structure and actually calculated the time series and the functional relation that each period's new wage is required to satisfy along the trajectory to the (final) target rate of wage inflation. If all wage contracts are for a year and all wages so contracted, the warranted growth rate of new wages from subperiod $i - 1$ to subperiod i, denoted g_i^*, will satisfy the relation

$$g_i^* - g^* = \beta_1(g_{i-1} - g^*) + \beta_2(g_{i-2} - g^*) + \cdots + \beta_{z-2}(g_{i-z+2} - g^*),$$

where g^* is the target rate and g_{i-s} is the actual growth rate s periods before i. The general result due to Calvo showed the existence and uniqueness of the desired trajectory no matter how finely subdivided the contract length over which wage commitments are staggered is—months, weeks, or days.

The paper also considered the institutional tools and aids for effecting the counterinflationary plan in the face of decentralized wage and price determinations. The two devices discussed are the adoption by the central bank of a *dynamic monetary program* which is calculated to maintain full employment insofar as the average wage approximates its warranted path, and the institution of some form of *indicative wage planning* to guide and promote the growth of wages along that warranted path. The aid of the latter device notwithstanding, the central bank would be advised to announce beforehand the shape (over the near term at any rate) of its intended monetary program—understood as a contingency plan that will adjust appropriately to the vicissitudes of the (full-employment) demand for real cash balances—lest the "market" misconstrue the early growth of the money stock (to accommodate early wage catch-ups and lessened inflation expectations) as a sign of the program's likely failure and perhaps abandonment. It would also be useful of the government to preannounce the prospective wage-growth guides for the whole near-term future so that wage-setters and wage bargainers will anticipate the slower wage growth in prospect several months ahead, once the early bulge of catch-ups is over.

I need hardly mention the practical difficulties that would beset actual implementation of the scheme studied here in many or most real-life economies: the fact that wage contracts are not evenly staggered;[13] the worse fact that some contracts run for three years or longer while at the

[13] If contracts are unevenly distributed over quarters of a year, yet all contracts are annual, the coefficients β in the previous equation would be seasonally dependent. In that setting, it would be natural to express a quarter's wage guidepost in terms of the year-over growth rate of wages allowable in the quarter, $w_i^* - w_{i-4}$.

other extreme we find piecework and day-labor; the skimpiness of the wage data from which to construct numerical wage guides; the need to correct for midlife wage increases in price-indexed contracts. (The prevalence of fully escalated contracts would render the scheme unworkable.) There would arise too the familiar gamut of problems in steering aggregate demand along that course which, if wages behave according to plan, would support full employment—that is, the natural rate of unemployment.

It is, however, the stability or viability of the scheme, the practical difficulties of engineering aside, with which I am primarily concerned at this stage. Does the indicated solution to disinflation without recession truly exist? Or would the scheme, if initiated, founder on the rocks of natural self-interest, human error, or other chance disturbances?

The psychological and political prerequisites for such a counterinflationary program were touched on in my introductory discussion. The former of these prerequisites is the common expectation that future wages are going to behave according to the full-employment counterinflationary plan. (Although expectations are not inherently and faultlessly rational, I am equally sure that they are not invariably and irremediably adaptive.) The latter prerequisite is broad political support for nonrecessionary counterinflation and even a consensus for the particular inflation target of the counterinflationary plan to be undertaken. (My reading of mathematical politics is that such a consensus is not generally impossible.) If we call these two prerequisites Faith and Hope, what about Charity? Is some departure from self-interest a necessity too? Does the scheme need a generous amount of Luck for good measure? If so, the program would be unlikely to enlist the necessary Faith and Hope either.

I can give neither a general "proof" nor a disproof of the stability of the scheme. Two points at issue seem to me to be central to that question, however, and these will be briefly discussed.

It was shown in Section III that the new wage commitments made in the third period of the counterinflationary program must rise so little (or actually fall) as to lower the prospective relative wage of workers under those new contracts in comparison to what the relative wage had been in the first two periods of the program. If events were to proceed according to plan up to that third period, could firms and workers be counted on to enact such a prospective relative-wage reduction? What would motivate the warranted reduction?

I would begin my answer with a reminder that, in principle, the counterinflationary plan is consistent with the equations of the model and the latter purport to describe in a rough and ready way the outcome of "maximizing" behavior by workers and firms. It is true, though, that the implicit theoretical framework does not admit the (conceivable) phenomenon called hysterisis or irreversability, as might arise from habit formation, nor the (conceivable) phenomenon called money illusion. "Vulgar economics," the term we use when we are on the other side, posits either or both of these phenomena to argue that relative wages would not be so reduced. The irreversibility of relative wage gains lies behind the theory of "ratchet inflation." (The irreversibility of *real* wage gains may lie behind the model so popular now in Britain.)

My own presumptions lean toward the assumption of "ordinary" maximizing behavior in this instance at any rate. Because it is the easiest to describe, take the worst case in which the target rate of wage inflation is zero, so that *money* wages set in the third period under the counterinflationary program must actually fall: I claim that any firm setting a one-year wage that period would lower that wage on the justification that the wage in the old contract was visibly outsized—because the counterinflationary program had not been anticipated a year earlier and the rise of other wages in the first two periods under the new program was consequently overpredicted—and must therefore be scaled down to the new realities if the affected jobs are not to be cut back. Of course, this may need explaining to workers. A function of the wage guideposts is to assist in such explanations. Nevertheless it might be prudent to set the target rate of wage inflation high enough that the windfall relative-wage gains resulting from the first months of unanticipated wage-disinflation can be reversed without the necessity of reversing any past money-wage gains.

We may now complete the argument: If the desired scenario could be counted on beginning with the third period, conditional on events' going according to plan up to that time, then firms setting wages in the first and second period of the counterinflationary program could expect to regain their customary relative-wage positions (over the lives of their new contracts) by means of more modest money-wage catch-ups than theretofore owing to the new anticipation of even more sharply slower money-wage growth (if not actual money-wage reductions) to be shown by contracts set in the third period and beyond. It is apparent, then, that in the counterinflationary transition the restoration of relative-wage positions as contracts expire must rely less completely than before on "front-loading" through money-wage increases and rely more on the anticipation of slackening money-wage gains in the subsequent contracts which present ones will overlap. In an economy where credit facilities are well developed and after-tax real rates of interest are typically less than 5% annually, this largely temporary shift away from front-loading would not have an important effect on the supply of labor at existing real annual wages and thus upon the prospective real wages that firms are driven to pay. The major issue, with which I have tried to deal, is the confidence of firms and workers that the wage agreements made later in the year (in other contracts) are going to be low enough to deter present money-wage catch-ups in excess of those warranted by the counterinflationary full-employment program.

The other issue, and perhaps the more worrisome, is the difficulties that may arise from chance errors and other disturbances. Suppose, for example, that the natural rate of unemployment increases and the rise is not inferred in time for the central bank to prevent a more-than-warranted rise of money wages. Once the problem is discovered, ought the bank to support the new natural rate and thus ratify the elevation in wages? If so, ought the bank also to ratify any and all instances of wages' overshooting their warranted growth so as to support the natural rate through thick and thin?

A tenable answer to the first of these questions is Yes: A regime in which the wage level follows a random walk with a determinate trend rate (or term structure of trend rates) at the desired figure is not such a bad system. However that may be, answering the second question is a great deal more problematic. If full employment were underwritten by the central bank regardless of any departure of wages from the warranted path, and if that were known to be the case, there would be nothing to render determinate the market's expectations of future wage growth—unless it be the wage guideposts. But the guideposts may be viewed as being merely the government's prediction of that unique course of wages which will lead to the target among the set of paths that could prove surprise-free and consistent with the maintenance of full employment. If the central bank stood ready to support full employment whatever the course of wages, *any* expectation of wages that the public might hold would be consistent with full employment; indeed there would be an infinity of wage paths such that if the public were doggedly to maintain the expectation of any of those paths, that path would occur—whether or not it was the unique path leading to the government's target rate of wage inflation. Without monetary "teeth" for the counterinflationary program, the guideposts could function only as propaganda around which it might be hoped that otherwise arbitrary beliefs would coalesce. And that fragile authority might be lost if, in the event that wages went off the track, the public found some other expectational rule that seemed to work better.

Ratification by the central bank of deviations from the guideposts, therefore, would place at risk the credibility of the counterinflationary program. Should wage expectations become more inflationary than the indicative wage plan, it would be prudent of the central bank to penalize them through tightening of money—assuming that the guidepost calculations were still believed to be sound. In such an event, though, the guideposts themselves would have to be modified to take into account the prospective deviation from full employment imposed by the monetary discipline. Again, it is not necessary nor obviously appropriate that wages be made to return to their originally planned path; it would be satisfactory to approach the target rate of wage inflation from the new and unplanned wage base. But it would make no sense, except as a rough approximation, for the guideposts to continue to be calculated as if full employment were still being supported by the central bank in every period including the near term. Of course, a study of adaptive guideposts for such special contingencies is well beyond the scope of the present paper.

Someone said of Disraeli, I think, that he wished he were as confident of anything as Disraeli was of everything. At the risk of seeming too diffident, I have identified the two issues which bar outright assurance (at least my assurance) that the counterinflationary scheme analyzed here would, if welcomed and adopted, work as well as hoped and intended. Yet the complete success of the plan has been shown to be a theoretical possibility. And it is only the comparative success of the plan with which we ought to be concerned. I do believe that the counterinflationary program set out here would work a great deal better, at much less cost in unemployment especially, than the alternative method of planned slump to which our ingenuity has so far been limited. In my scheme of values, rather little would be risked by trying it—if disinflate we must. I venture to suggest that much of the opposition to the plan will be aroused more by its goals than by its imperfections. The program envisioned here aims soon to stabilize wages on a level or rising path, leaving the price level to be buffeted by supply shocks and exchange-rate disturbances. There is still a branch of opinion in favor of sacrificing the stability of wages and employment on the altar of stable prices.

Appendix A: Friedman's and "Keynesian" Rules Compared

Friedman's rule is of the form $F_tM_t = a\ (1 + k)^t$ where a and k are to be selected for all time at $t = 0$, M_t is the quantity of money supplied in period t, and F_tM_t is the money supply planned and forecasted at the start of that period, before the current disturbances occur. Hence, for $t = 0, 1, 2, \ldots,$

$$log\ F_{t+1}M_{t+1} = \log F_tM_t + k, \qquad k = \text{constant}. \tag{A1}$$

Let W_t denote the average money-wage set (perhaps predeterminedly at the end of period $t - 1$) for period t, and let $F_v X_t$ denote the start-of-period-v forecast of the value of variable X in any period $t \geq v$. In this notation, Keynesian stabilization policy may be characterized by the rule

$$\begin{aligned} \log F_{t+1}M_{t+1} = {} & \log F_t M_t + g^* \\ & + [\log F_{t+1}P^s_{t+1}(F_t W_t) - \log F_t P_t (F_t W_t)] \\ & - [\log F_{t+1}P^d_{t+1}(F_t M_t) - \log F_t P_t^d (F_t M_t)], \\ g^* \equiv {} & \log W^*_{t+1} - \log W_t^* = \text{constant}. \end{aligned} \tag{A2}$$

Here g^* is the growth rate of the path of the desired money wage, $W_t^* = W_0 \ (1 + g^*)^t$. P_t^s (W) denotes the supply price of "full-employment" aggregate output in period t when calculated at a money wage level of W, and P_t^d (M) denotes the demand price for the full-employment output in period t calculated at the specified money supply M. The intent of this rule is to accommodate exogenous forces driving (up or down) the supply and demand prices in just such a way as to make the money wage necessary and sufficient for full employment (i.e., macroequilibrium) grow along the desired path, $W_0 \ (1 + g^*)^t$; monetary policy, insofar as it is successful, relieves wage setters of adjusting to shocks—they have only their own mistakes and any micro imbalances to correct.

To see how (A2) may lead to a feedback rule, and to compare further the two rules, consider the case in which productivity, labor supply, and the full-employment "velocity" of money are random-walk variables, with or without trends, so that for all t and every W and M,

$$\begin{aligned} \log F_{t+1}P^s_{t+1}(W) - \log P_t^s(W) &= \log F_t P^s_{t+1}(W) \\ &\quad - \log F_t P_t^s(W) \equiv \lambda_s = \text{const.}, \\ \log F_{t+1}P^d_{t+1}(M) - \log P_t^d(M) &= \log F_t P^d_{t+1}(M) \\ &\quad - \log F_t P_t^d(M) \equiv \lambda_d = \text{const.}, \end{aligned} \tag{A3}$$

if the supply and demand prices are unbiasedly forecast.

Then the appropriate Friedman rule sets k to satisfy

$$k = \log \, (W_{t+1}/W_t)^* + \lambda_s - \lambda_d, \tag{A4}$$

where the first term on the right is interpretable as the desired average rate of growth of the money wage (corresponding to the desired rate of inflation, given λ_s and λ_d). If this desired wage trend is set equal to g^* for purposes of comparison, then, by (A3),

$$\begin{aligned} k = g^* & + [\log F_t P^s_{t+1}(F_t W_t) - \log F_t P_t^s(F_t W_t)] \\ & - [\log F_t P^d_{t+1}(F_t M_t) - \log F_t P_t^d(F_t M_t)]. \end{aligned} \tag{A5}$$

By using (A5) to substitute for g^* in (A2) we may express the Keynesian rule as

$$\begin{aligned}\log F_{t+1}M_{t+1} = {} & \log F_tM_t + k \\ & + [\log F_{t+1}P^s_{t+1}(F_tW_t) - \log F_tP^s_{t+1}(F_tW_t)] \\ & - [\log F_{t+1}P^d_{t+1}(F_tM_t) - \log F_tP^d_{t+1}(F_tM_t)], \end{aligned} \tag{A6}$$

or, by (A3), in the form of the error-response or feedback rule

$$\begin{aligned}\log F_{t+1}M_{t+1} = {} & \log F_tM_t + k + [\log P_t{}^s(F_tW_t) \\ & - \log F_tP_t{}^s(F_tW_t)] - [\log P_t{}^d(F_tM_t) - \log F_tP_t{}^d(F_tM_t)] \end{aligned} \tag{A7}$$

The first bracketed expression signifies the unanticipated increase the previous period in the supply price of full-employment output attributable to unexpected productivity decreases and labor-force growth; the second bracketed expression signifies the unanticipated decrease in the demand price of full-employment output owing to unexpected decrease of "velocity" and unexpected growth of full-employment output.

An implication of (A7) is that the Keynesian money supply follows a random walk *with trend rate equal to Friedman's k.* The Friedman rule, on the other hand, makes the money wage required for full employment follow a (essentially identical) random walk *with trend rate equal to the Keynesians' g^**. In respect to these fixed trend rates, therefore, the two types of rules are similar—and similarly rigid.

Appendix B: Multiple Rational-Expectations Solutions

If we use $\bar{W}(t)$ as defined by (11) in place of W_t appearing in (1), we have

$$n_t - n^* = \mu[m_t - \tfrac{1}{2}w_{t-1} - \tfrac{1}{2}w_t - \log \psi]. \tag{B1}$$

Then (14′), (16), (B1), and perfect foresight imply

$$w_t = \tfrac{1}{2}w_{t-1} + \tfrac{1}{2}w_{t+1} + \phi\mu[(w_{-1} - \tfrac{1}{2}w_{t-1} - \tfrac{1}{2}w_t) + (w_{-1} - \tfrac{1}{2}w_t - \tfrac{1}{2}w_{t+1})]. \tag{B2}$$

Letting $\tilde{w}_t$ denote $w_t - w_{-1}$, we may express (B2) as

$$-A\tilde{w}_{t+1} + \tilde{w}_t - A\tilde{w}_{t-1} = 0, \qquad A = \frac{1 - \phi\mu}{2(1 + \phi\mu)} = \frac{1}{1 + \phi\mu} - \frac{1}{2}. \tag{B3}$$

The parameter restrictions $0 < \phi\mu < \infty$ imply

$$-\tfrac{1}{2} < A < \tfrac{1}{2}. \tag{B4}$$

Clearly the path $\tilde{w}_t = 0$ is necessarily a solution of (B3), regardless of the value of A. This is the desired path, as explained in the text. Are there any other solutions?

If $\phi\mu = 1$, whence $A = 0$, then (B3) shows that $\tilde{w}_t = 0$ is the only solution. If $\phi\mu \neq 0$, the two roots of the characteristic equation associated with (B3) are

$$b_1, b_2 = \tfrac{1}{2}[A^{-1} \pm (A^{-2} - 4)^{1/2}] = (1 \pm (\phi\mu)^{1/2})^2 \cdot (1 - \phi\mu)^{-1}. \quad \text{(B5)}$$

By virtue of (B4) these roots are real and by the symmetry of (B3) they are reciprocals, $b_2 = b_1^{-1}$. Consequently, with $0 < \phi\mu$, one root must have absolute value greater than 1. If $\phi\mu < 1$, whence $0 < A < \frac{1}{2}$, there is a positive root greater than 1; then there are nonoscillatory explosive solutions. If $\phi\mu > 1$, whence $0 > A > -\frac{1}{2}$, there is a negative root less than -1; then there are undamped oscillatory solutions.

Appendix C: Existence and Uniqueness of the Desired Trajectory

Defining $n = z - 1$ we have

$$0 = b^{-n} + 2b^{-(n-1)} + \cdots + nb^{-1} - (n + 1)\, nb^0 + nb^1 + \cdots + 2b^{n-1} + b^n = P(b) \quad \text{(C1)}$$

for the characteristic equation associated with (34) in the text.

It is obvious that 1 is a root. From the fact that $P'(1) = 0$ and $P''(1) > 0$, it follows this root has multiplicity 2.

We next show that, other than 1, there are no other roots on the unit circle. Suppose that $\cos\theta + i\sin\theta$ is a root. Then, in view of (C1) we must have

$$\cos(-n\theta) + 2\cos(-(n - 1)\theta) + \cdots + n\cos(-\theta) + \cdots + 2\cos((n - 1)\theta) + \cos(n\theta) = (n - 1)n. \quad \text{(C2)}$$

But the right-hand side of (C2) is clearly an upper bound for the left-hand side. Thus (C2) implies that all the cosine expressions there are equal to 1; hence θ is a multiple of 2π and therefore $\cos\theta + i\sin\theta = 1$.

By the symmetry of (C1), if b is a root then b^{-1} is also a root. Therefore, because (C1) has $2n$ roots and only two lie on the unit circle, $n - 1$ roots have absolute value less than 1. Denote these roots $b_2, b_3, \ldots, b_n$. To simplify the exposition, suppose that these roots have multiplicity 1. Then any solution of (34) making the growth rate, $w_t^* - w_{t-1}^*$, convergent to g^* must be of the form

$$w_t^* = C_0 1^t + C_1 t 1^t + C_2 b_2{}^t + \cdots + C_n b_n{}^t \quad \text{(C3)}$$

and C_1 must be set equal to g^*. Since there are n predetermined wage data there is a solution and it is unique.

ACKNOWLEDGMENTS

I am much indebted to my colleague Guillermo Calvo for his advice at several points and especially for the important general theorem he contributed to Section IV and Appendix C. The theoretical framework here partially reflects my research with Calvo and John Taylor under a grant from the National Science Foundation. My collaborators do not bear responsibility however for the particulars of the model employed nor its uses here. The preliminary version of this paper, under the title "Checking Contractual Inflation without Causing Recession," was presented at the Konstanzer Seminar in June 1977. This final version was prepared for the Monetary Conference of Central Banks at Baden, Austria in September 1977, and is reprinted here by their permission.

References

Akerlof, G. A. "Relative Wages and the Rate of Inflation." *Quarterly Journal of Economics,* Vol. 83 (August 1969).

Baily, M. N., "Contract Theory and the Moderation of Inflation by Recession and by Controls," *Brookings Papers on Economic Activity,* Vol. 7 (December 1976).

Cagan, P. H., "The Monetary Dynamics of Hyper-Inflation," *Studies in the Quantity Theory of Money* M. Friedman (ed.), Chicago: University of Chicago Press, 1956.

Feige, E. L., and D. K. Pearce, "Economically Rational Expectations: Are Innovations in the Rate of Inflation Independent of Innovations in Measures of Monetary and Fiscal Policy?" *Journal of Political Economy,* Vol. 84 (June 1976).

Fellner, W. J. *et al., The Problem of Rising Prices.* Paris: Organization for European Economic Cooperation, 1961.

Fischer, S., "Long-Term Contracts, Rational Expectations, and the Optimal Money Supply Rule", *Journal of Political Economy,* Vol. 85 (February 1977).

Freidman, M., *Essays in Positive Economics.* Chicago: University of Chicago Press, 1956.

Friedman, M., *A Program for Monetary Stability.* New York: Fordham University Press, 1959.

Keynes, J. M., *The General Theory of Employment, Interest and Money.* London: Macmillan and Co., 1936.

Lucas, R. E., "Econometric Testing of the Natural Rate Hypothesis," *The Econometrics of Price Determination,* O. Eckstein (ed.), Washington, D. C.: Federal Reserve System, 1972.

Mundell, R. A., "Inflation and Real Interest," *Journal of Political Economy,* Vol. 71 (June 1963).

Muth, J. F., "Rational Expectations and the Theory of Price Movement," *Econometrica,* Vol. 29 (July 1961).

Phelps, E. S., "Money-Wage Dynamics and Labor-Market Equilibrium," *Journal of Political Economy,* Vol. 76, Part 2 (August 1968).

Phelps, E. S., "Commodity-Supply Shock and Full-Employment Monetary Policy", *Journal of Money Credit and Banking,* Vol. 10 (May 1978).

Ross, S. A., and M. L. Wachter, "Wage Determination, Inflation, and the Industrial Structure" *American Economic Review,* Vol. 63 (September 1973).

Sargent, T. J., and Wallace, N., "The Stability of Models of Money and Growth with Perfect Foresight," *Econometrica,* Vol. 41 (November 1973).

Sargent, T. J., and N. Wallace, "Rational Expectations, the Optimal Monetary Instrument, and the Optimal Money Supply Rule," *Journal of Political Economy,* Vol. 83 (April 1975).

Taylor, J. B., "Estimation and Control of a Macroeconomic Model with Rational Expectations," *Econometrica,* forthcoming 1979.

Part V
IDENTIFYING DISTURBANCES OF THE PRICE LEVEL

INTRODUCTION

The optimum policy response to an unforeseen deviation of the inflation rate generally depends on the causes which are inferred to be at work. That would not be the case only if optimal policy were so perfectly automated that all the data bearing on a causal inference already figured in the policy function and that function was already optimized. To be concrete about it, the monetary authorities *might* want to contract the money supply if the rise of inflation were thought to be attributable to some financial innovation raising the velocity of money, for example, and to expand the money supply if the rise of inflation were thought to be due to some supply shock reducing the productivity of capital and labor—for reasons involving the contrasting effects of these two shocks on certain other variables, such as employment and wages. It is not denied, of course, that there are risks in acting on the wrong inference, risks of overreacting, and so on.

The papers in this group discuss hypotheses about the causes of the rise in the rate of inflation in two historical episodes. The earlier of these papers reports some results from my doctoral dissertation on the American inflation between 1955 and 1957.[1] Those years are best remembered now for their invention of "wage push." The notion of *induced* wage push, in which the rate of wage-push inflation is treated as endogenous to the prevailing economic situation, found its apotheosis in the Phillips curve. In an era in which computers had just begun to make regressions less laborious to run, most economists merely took for granted the existence of such a historical relationship—with a possible exception for the 1930s; what made Phillips's scatter diagram striking was the absence of any clear shift of the historical relationship over a century of British wage and unemployment data.

My own study was directed more toward the hypothesis of an exogenous or autonomous wage push operating particularly, or with peculiar strength, in the 1955–1957 period. Its contribution, if there is one,

[1] E. S. Phelps, "A Test for the Presence of Cost Inflation in the U.S. Economy, 1955–57," *Yale Economic Essays*, Vol. 1, No. 1 (January 1961).

was to work out—more laboriously than any regression ever run—the effect of an *uneven* cost-push disturbance upon the correlation between the Δp's and Δq's in a multisector (three-sector) model. The analysis formalizes and refines what any trained observer would do in trying to infer whether the prices going up fastest are being pulled up by demand or pushed up by costs.

The later paper here discusses the surge of inflation in America between 1972 and 1974. Its theme is that the popular and monistic theory of the price level according to which only the supply of money matters—never the supply of goods, and not even the demand for money—was only a brief stopover on the way to a more comprehensive and sensible theory. (The title of this conference paper, first presented in Tokyo, was borrowed from the Mr. Moto series by J. P. Marquand.)

It appears that eclecticism never made anyone famous. The paper might nevertheless have served a useful purpose: to call attention to the range of important supply shocks that had recently occurred and to the consequent *possibility* that an increase of the money supply would be needed to offset their effects upon money wages and employment. The fact that this kind of analysis was left underdeveloped, and had no discernible impact upon policy-making, is another story—one recounted in the supply-shock sequel contained in the next group of papers.

A TEST OF THE COST INFLATION HYPOTHESIS: 1955–1957[1]

We are all familiar with the arguments for a cost-push interpretation of the 1955–1957 inflation. During that period output grew too slowly and unemployment was too high, it is argued, for the inflation to be attributable simply to demand. Second, had demand been responsible, prices would have led rather than lagged wages, and labor's share in national income would not have increased, as it did, so markedly. Evidence of this aggregative character has much merit, but it is not conclusive. Counterexplanations of the behavior of these aggregates could be offered.

A second approach focuses on the individual industry or firm. This is an excellent way of learning about the institutions in question, but such an investigation cannot answer the cost push question by itself for it neglects interindustry relations. For example, if strong demand elsewhere were to attract resources away from a particular industry, the observer of the industry in isolation might wrongly identify it as a source of cost push.

For these reasons, many economists are not yet ready to reject the traditional demand-pull interpretation of the 1955–1957 inflation (as well as the other postwar inflations preceding it). Therefore, it may be useful to perform a new test of the traditional demand-pull hypothesis—a test which is comparatively nonaggregative, but which takes into account the interactions among markets. I would like now to describe such a test, indicate briefly the theoretical basis for the test, and finally to state my findings using this test.

The test is this: Adopt as a base period some interval of time over which it is assumed there was no cost inflation. Over this time interval, prices and outputs in the various industries will have changed due to changes in tastes, technology, and resource availabilities. Let us compute the coefficient of correlation between the proportionate price changes and the weighted proportionate output changes, where the weights measure the relative importance of the output in G.N.P.

Now turn to the period of time which is suspected of cost inflation

[1] Read at the annual American meeting of the Econometric Society, December 1959.

(here 1955–1957). Compute the corresponding correlation coefficient. If the correlation coefficient observed for the suspect period is significantly lower than the corresponding coefficient for the base period, then we may reject the null hypothesis that there was no cost inflation (only demand pull) during the suspect period.

This test may be intuitively plausible if one thinks of a two-commodity economy whose prices and outputs are determined by supply and demand. Suppose there is a change in tastes in favor of commodity *A* and away from commodity *B;* we would expect (and we would be right) that the price and output of commodity *A* would rise and the price and output of good *B* would fall. Movement along supply curves, in short, produces a positive correlation of prices and output changes. Suppose, on the other hand, that cost push (say, an autonomous increase in the supply price of labor) takes place in industry *A*. As before, the price of *A* would increase, but its output would decline. In industry B, output would rise (due to consumer substitution) and so would price, but not so much as in *A*. Price and output changes are negatively correlated in this case. Now it follows that if price and output changes in this simple world are the product of a mixture of movements along supply curves and movements along demand curves, then the greater the former, the lower algebraically the observed, net resultant coefficient of correlation.

Is there any basis for this proposition (concerning the sign of the correlation coefficient) in an economy with any number of commodities? To determine the sign of the correlation coefficient in a model in which there are present the usual interrelations among the labor and commodity markets is quite impracticable unless certain simplifications are made. The major simplification in the models I have constructed is that they are structured in such a way that real income (which equals the real value of the aggregate output here) is invariant to the changes in demand patterns and cost patterns.

In the model employed for studying the sign of the coefficient associated with a change in the *demand* structure, it is assumed that the total amount of employment (but not the allocation of the labor force) is constant. More precisely, we assume that the supply of labor to each industry is homogeneous of degree zero and that the matrix of partial derivatives of labor supply with respect to real wage rates is symmetric about the diagonal. Output in each industry is a function only of the employment there, with diminishing marginal returns assumed. Market commodity demands are assumed to depend upon real income, real cash balances, and relative prices in the way usually assumed for the individual consumer, and all commodities are consumer goods.

On what conditions will a change in the pattern of demands in this model result in a positive correlation coefficient? I confess I have examined this question only for the case of three commodities, but from the nature of the conditions, I feel sure that the same conditions apply to the case of any number of commodities. The following are sufficient (although unnecessary) conditions for a positive coefficient:

(1) All goods are net substitutes.
(2) All employments are substitutes.

It would be methodologically nice if we could utilize the same model to examine the sign of the correlation coefficient associated with a change in cost conditions, e.g., cost push. Unfortunately, any shift in a labor supply function in this model would necessarily affect real income. This complicates the analysis, as suggested, and it may also be unrealistic if, as some observers believe, the monetary authorities act to restore output and employment to their precost-push levels. Consequently, we need a somewhat different model for cost push.

In this model we assume that the central bank neutralizes the interest and cash balance affects on demand of an increase in prices so as to keep constant the real value of aggregate output. Lest money prices be indeterminate, we assume also that labor is subject to some degree of money illusion. In particular, an equiproportionate increase in all money wage rates and prices is assumed to increase the supply of labor to each industry. The same holds *a fortiori* if prices are held constant.

A change in the supply of labor to an industry in this model will produce a negative correlation coefficient if:

(1) All goods are net substitutes.
(2) All employments are substitutes.
(3) "Diagonal dominance:" The own wage rate effect exceeds the cross effect of any other wage rate on the supply of labor to each industry.

The third condition says essentially that the allocation of labor between two industries depends more upon the two wage rates there than upon any third wage rate. One might wish for less stringent conditions, but it may be that the necessary and sufficient conditions for the desired results are much weaker.

Of course, the changes in relative prices and outputs are attributable to more than cost push and alterations in tastes. Productivities and resource supplies may change for reasons having nothing to do with cost push or taste changes. It has to be assumed that these influences together with taste changes comprise a large number of small independent random forces causing the joint distribution of proportionate price changes and weighted proportionate output changes to be bivariate normal. Moreover, it must be assumed that these "other" forces do not normally cause the correlation coefficient to be so small algebraically that the introduction of cost push into the picture will fail to reduce the observed coefficient. Unless one is willing to make some assumptions about covariances (which assumptions are not entirely unreasonable), this means that the correlation coefficient must be positive in the absence of cost push—all forces acting upon it considered.

We now turn to the application of the test. The first question is the choice of a base period. Hopefully we can choose a base period in which the economy was structurally much the same as it was during the period in which it was suspected of cost push. One of the most important considerations in this respect is probably the degree of unemployment. The response of the correlation coefficient to demand changes and cost changes is unlikely to be the same in a situation of large and widespread unemployment than in a period of tight labor markets and full capacity operation. Since 1955–1957 was a period of high employment, and since the only postwar periods in which employment was about the same (in relation to the size of the labor force) are 1946–1948 and 1950–1952, the base period must be one of these. Many economists feel that cost push was quite strong in 1951 and 1952, however, so that the earlier period seems to be the best candidate for use as base period. Even 1946–1948 is thought by some to have contained some cost push. If there was some cost push during 1946–1948, then our correlation test will determine *not* whether there was *any* cost push, but whether there was *more* cost push in 1955–1957 than in 1946–1948.

The data used in the correlation test are annual real expenditure (rather than output) data and the associated implicit price deflators. Most of this is contained in *U.S. Income and Output* but, in the case of consumer

Year	Correlation for all items except housing
1946–1947	+.092
1947–1948	+.089
1946–1948	+.246
1950–1951	+.140
1951–1952	−.090
1950–1952	+.058
1955–1956	+.066
1956–1957	+.149
1955–1957	−.075

durables, the data are taken from the Bureau of Labor Statistics price series and current-dollar expenditure data in *U.S. Income and Output*. The expenditure data are by type of product, but they are also separated by type of consumer. Hence, automobiles bought by businesses is in a different category from autos bought by households. But the number of such overlaps is small. (The commodity groups are listed in the Appendix.)

Since the behavior of the housing data depends largely upon decisions prior to the current changes in costs and demands, I deem it appropriate to exclude the housing series in computing the correlation coefficients.

Probably the correlation test is sensitive to the degree of cost push only if the intervals over which the price changes and output changes are measured and the interval during which the cost push occurred closely agree. It is possible that the quarterly or annual price changes represent responses to demand changes of much earlier periods (quarters of years, respectively). Likewise, real expenditure changes in the current period may be due to much earlier cost changes. Hence, we do not want to measure the price and expenditure changes over intervals which are too short. On the other hand, if we measure price and output at the start of the expansion and then at the end, the influence of cost push, if any, on relative prices and outputs may be swamped by the larger cyclical changes in demand. Consequently, the best intervals, in my mind, are the 2-year intervals—namely, 1946–1948 and 1955–1957.

Looking at the two-year computations, we find that they are positive for the first two inflations (1946 and 1950). This is important, as we suggested earlier, for if the correlations were normally negative, then the introduction of cost push into an economy would not necessarily reduce the observed value of the coefficient.

Second, we find that the coefficient corresponding to 1955–1957 is indeed smaller than that associated with the base period 1946–1948. However, the statistical significance of the difference depends sensitively upon the choice of the confidence level: The later coefficient is significantly lower at the 90% confidence level, but not so using a 95% confidence level.

Ideally, one chooses the confidence level on the basis of the "costs" of the two types of errors and the power associated with each confidence level. Unfortunately, the probability of a Type II error cannot be specified here since the correlation test is a one-tailed test. However, there is one general principle which I believe deserves to be invoked: If in very large samples it is appropriate to employ a 99% confidence level—because with so many observations and hence power, we can afford to give up some power for better protection against a Type I error—then it seems appropriate in a small sample such as ours to sacrifice some protection against a Type I error in return for greater power.

We are entitled to reject, then, with 90% confidence, the null hypothesis that there was no more cost push in 1955–1957 than in 1946–1948, but we are not so able with 95% confidence.

In the time remaining I would like to make two contrasts between my approach and one which is reminiscent, written by Richard Selden ("Cost-Push versus Demand-Pull" 1955–57) and which appeared in the *Journal of Political Economy* in February 1959. Selden makes some observations about the effects on price and output of shifts in demand and supply curves, from which he concludes that, in the absence of cost push, price and output changes will be positively correlated. He does find a positive correlation, using industrial production data, especially for the interval December 1954–December 1956. He concludes from this that there was little cost inflation during 1955–1957.

I would like to point out, first, that in my approach no significance is attached to the correlation coefficient for 1955–1957 in isolation. Selden's positive coefficient does not clear the period of cost push until we are sure that normally (without cost push) the coefficient is not much greater.

The second contrast I wish to draw concerns the timing of our measurements. Selden's wish to measure from December 1954 (when output was beginning to pick up) reflects, I think, his desire to exclude from the definition of cost push *any* cost pressure induced by demand. This exclusion seems too broad for undoubtedly the degree of cost push exerted in any industry is a function of the employment level there. This close connection between demand-pull and cost push not only makes conceptual distinctions quite intricate, but also makes the empirical detection of cost push difficult.

Appendix: Commodity Groups in the Correlation Test

1. Autos and parts
2. Furniture
3. Kitchen and other household appliances
4. Tableware, etc.
5. Other household furnishings
6. Ophthalmic and orthopedic appliances
7. Toys and sporting goods
8. Books and maps
9. Radios, phonographs, and televisions
10. Jewelry and watches
11. Food
12. Clothing
13. Gasoline and oil
14. Other nondurables
15. Household operation
16. Transportation
17. Other services

18. Residential nonfarm construction
19. Other construction
20. Fabricated metal products
21. Farm machinery
22. Industrial and commercial machinery
23. Laundry and refrigeration equipment
24. Electric apparatus
25. Trucks
26. Aircraft
27. Ship building
28. Railroad equipment
29. Instruments and related products
30. Office fixtures and furniture
31. Business autos
32. Federal government
33. State and local government

STOPOVER MONETARISM: SUPPLY AND DEMAND FACTORS IN THE 1972–74 INFLATION

Our price data and the price statistics constructed from them do not neatly print out historical labels reading "Postwar Inflation Episode No. 5 Begins Here." To limit the time span under analysis, we have to make our own demarcations. In my mind, the resurgence of inflation in the United States begins, just perceptibly, in the second half of 1972—exactly where depends upon one's choice of a price index—and continues up to the time of this writing, April of 1974. By the end of 1972 the twelve-month inflation rate in the consumer price index (CPI) had turned around, reversing the slow decline experienced over 1970 and 1971.[1] Wholesale prices quickened markedly in 1972. In June 1973 the twelve-month CPI inflation rate stood at 5.9 percent, and less than a year later it reached 10 percent.

This paper is addressed to the causes of this episode of inflation. Which supply factors and demand factors together account for the rise in the inflation rate observed over this period? The analysis here, if I may call it that, is qualitative. Implicitly or explicitly, I am ascribing "some influence" to some factors and "little or no influence" to other factors. My interest in several of the possible explanations of the recent inflation goes more to the analytics of the case than to the matter of quantitative importance.

Now that the woefully noneconometric character of this enterprise has been confessed, it will not be misunderstood if I paraphrase the questions I am asking in econometric terms: In which structural equations of our widely accepted international macro-monetary model are the sources of the recent increase in the inflation rate possibly—and likely—to be found? Which disturbance terms, parameter shifts, and predetermined-variable shifts are (together) the culprits? What were their *modi operandi*?

Compare this way of looking at things with the monetarist slogan: Inflation is everywhere and always a monetary phenomenon. Of course, there cannot be a money price of any good without there being money. And the quantity of money prevailing at any moment is an important determinant of the equilibrium money price of meat, oil, and the general money-price level. But it could be said with the same logical status that the goods price of one-dollar bills is always and every-

---

[1] There is a question whether the Phase II controls suppressed inflation more or less in 1972 than Phase I controls set back inflation in 1971.

Reprinted by permission from *The Phenomenon of Worldwide Inflation*, D. I. Meiselman and H. B. Laffers (Eds.). American Enterprise Institute, Washington, D.C., 1975.

where a goods supply phenomenon. The best monetarists are both-blades-of-the-scissors men, however dull their other blade. Milton Friedman, the author of the famous aphorism, explains that the equilibrium money-price level is determined by the stock of money in relation to the "supply of goods." If there should occur a crop failure not fortuitously offset by an exactly compensatory increase in the supply of other goods, then, unless the time path of the money stock is revised downward in such a way as to counteract the crop failure, we should not be surprised to find some (at least temporary) rise of the general price level—relative to what otherwise would have taken place. It is an analytical mistake of some monetarists to suppose that nonagricultural prices are necessarily likely to drop by so much as to leave the general money-price level untouched.

I feel that what the monetarists ought to be saying, and perhaps want to say but never succeed in saying, is that our unbiased prediction of the long-term inflation rate is potentially under social control and that its control is best assigned to the monetary authorities. For example, we might imagine that the price level is subject to a random walk with trend (positive, zero, or negative), while the size of the trend parameter is placed under the control of the monetary authorities. The "expected rate of inflation" over any future interval will approximate this trend rate of inflation (especially expectations of long-term inflation rates) if expectations are "rational." Now the selection of the trend inflation-rate target by the monetary policy planners might or might not be swayed by anticipations of the trend growth rate of real aggregate supply; in the former case, the monetary planners would have to form beliefs about the long-term real growth rate of the economy. In either case, however, one might reasonably say that the *choice* of the *expected inflation rate* (especially long term) belongs to the *monetary authorities*, and one would add that control of the *money stock* is the *chosen instrument*. Yet the *actual* inflation rate over any future interval is the result of the interaction of the ex post growth rates of *both* real aggregate supply and the money supply. Paradoxically, it is precisely when the monetary authorities relinquish their choice of inflation prospects by adopting some rigidly predetermined rule for growth of the money supply, such as Professor Friedman's *k*-percent rule, that it would be semantically anomalous to say that all vicissitudes in the inflation rate were of "monetary" cause.

What in fact tends to be argued by the monetarists, particularly by the more zealous of Professor Friedman's disciples, is that because manipulation of the money supply can ultimately target the economy on any arbitrary money price level (subject to random bombing errors), the behavior of the money stock must be the final cause of any permanent (let alone continuing) rise (or decline) of the price level, and the controllers of the money stock must take the final responsibility for such. Now an econometrician interested in describing what *is* would say, presumably, that what matters in identifying disturbances in the price level is what the monetary authorities habitually do, not what they could do. Perhaps what the monetarists mean is that a permanent rise of the price level is properly to be attributed to "money" when the monetary authorities ought to reverse the price increase but fail to do so. That might be a defensible use of words by any monetarist who favors an endogenous money-supply policy aiming at, say, a constant price level. But those monetarists who favor an exogenous money-supply policy, such as the *k*-percent rule, are in no position to say that money is the final cause of a permanent rise in the price level due to a permanent supply-side disturbance.

Demand Factors

Before completing Table 1, I had the impression that the American money supply was unlikely to have been the prime and exogenous mover of the 1972–1974 increase in the American inflation rate. I was ready to agree that exogenous and

Table 1

LIQUIDITY IN AMERICA

		M_{1_t}	CPI_t	Real M_{1_t}	$(1.01)^t$	m^*_t	V_t
1948	Dec.	111.5	.72	154.9	.844	183.5	4.0
1965	Dec.	171.3	.954	179.6	1.000	179.6	4.0
1966	June	175.4	.970	180.8	1.005	179.9	3.8
	Dec.	175.4	.986	177.9	1.010	176.1	3.8
1967	June	181.1	.996	181.8	1.015	179.1	3.9
	Dec.	186.9	1.016	184.0	1.020	180.4	3.8
1968	June	194.0	1.039	186.7	1.025	182.1	3.7
	Dec.	207.5	1.064	189.5	1.030	184.0	3.4
1969	June	206.9	1.097	188.6	1.035	182.2	3.5
	Dec.	208.8	1.129	184.9	1.041	177.6	3.5
1970	June	216.0	1.163	185.7	1.046	177.5	4.8
	Dec.	221.3	1.191	185.8	1.051	176.8	6.1
1971	June	232.5	1.215	191.4	1.056	181.3	5.8
	Dec.	236.0	1.231	191.7	1.062	180.5	6.0
1972	June	245.1	1.250	196.1	1.067	183.8	5.5
	Dec.	255.5	1.273	200.7	1.072	187.2	5.1
1973	June	265.5	1.324	200.5	1.077	186.2	4.8
	Dec.	270.4	1.385	195.2	1.083	180.2	4.8

Note: The variables are:
M_{1_t} = Money stock in period t;
CPI_t = Consumer price index in period t;
Real M_{1_t} = Real cash balances in period t;
m^*_t = Detrended real cash balances in period t;
V_t = Unemployment rate in period t.

indigenous demand factors, taken together, probably accounted for about half of the increase in the inflation rate and that supply factors, operating independently and also through their inducements to faster ratification of money growth, accounted for the other half. It was my impression that the *real* value of the M_1 money stock (see Table 1), and especially the detrended real value of the M_1 money stock, did not exhibit much of a bulge for any appreciable length of time during 1972 and 1973. It was for that reason that I thought that the money growth occurring over this period was largely induced and that one would have to cast about for other exogenous monetary factors, some of which are touched on later, in order to arrive at a mostly demand-oriented account of the 1972–1974 inflation rise.

Monetary Stimulus. The quasi facts of detrended real cash balances (m^*) do not corroborate that early impression (whatever the final verdict on its falseness). The acceleration of the money stock seems likely to have been the most important demand-side factor.

Table 1 shows that the detrended real money stock was actually back to its pre-game plan high-water mark by June 1972. Indeed the December 1971 figure for m^* marks (a little posthumously) the demise of the game plan and the resuscitation of the detrended real money stock over the preceding months did—as the critics of the prolongation of the game plan said it would—bring the unemployment rate down rapidly. What is most striking in the table, however, is the extraordinary heights to which the monetary authorities had pushed m^* by December 1972. If my simplistic detrending (at a compound rate of 1 percent per annum) or something approximating it is apt, this was a degree of monetary push unprecedented in the years since World War II. The real detrended money stock was maintained at near this peak as late as June 1973.

One reason why the strength of this monetary push may have been underappreciated at the time is that it led to a comparatively small dip of the unemployment rate. The unemployment rate in 1973 averaged around 4.8 percent, a figure that seems quite flabby when put next to the lean figures of 1968 and 1969. This experience suggests the conjecture that the family of Phillips curves—one curve for each expected inflation rate—was steeper in 1972 and 1973 than in the previous inflation episode. In explanation, it might be conjectured that the economy has become more disequilibrium-shy, at least on the boom side of macroeconomic equilibrium. The suppliers of goods and factors may have grown less likely to maintain static expectations about their competitors' asking prices in circumstances where they are being enticed by tight supply conditions to hike up their own prices. What I have just said has to do with the behavior of suppliers' expectations of other suppliers' price *levels*. We might add the possibility that the expected rate of future inflation rose more rapidly in the 1972–1973 period than it did in the gullible days of the late 1960s. Thus the operative Phillips curve of the moment may shift upward more quickly now, after the learning experience of the previous boom. (The role of inflation expectations, considered as an exogenous or at any rate predetermined factor, will be discussed below.)

The above observations and conjectures may shed some light on a puzzle that seems to have received little attention. Why would the Federal Reserve System (Fed) have decided to stimulate the economy to such an extent over the second half of 1972 and most of 1973? It may be that as the unemployment rate neared 5 percent, the Federal Reserve policy makers overestimated the extent to which current monetary growth would express itself in further expansion of output and employment and underestimated the degree to which the stimulus would be expended merely in higher money wage rates and prices. Yet the puzzle will not go away. In the eyes of the Fed, the inflation problem needed licking and had not been licked. So why accept a large risk of a disequilibrium boom, its temporary blessings for output and employment notwithstanding, when that would have increased inflation and the expectations thereof? I imagine that underprediction of the growth of M_1 resulting from the Fed's open-market instructions and underprediction of the equilibrium levels of aggregate output and employment both play some part in the explanation. These days it must seem to the people in the Federal Reserve that its every move makes academic economists bounce to their feet to play counselors of perfection, usually with divergent conceptions of perfection. I should think it is fair to say, however, that the Fed has been operating with too much privacy and insulation, like a monetary Vatican. If it were more open and responsive, the burden of its mistakes would be more widely shared.

Liquidity in General. Before leaving the money supply as a causal factor in the recent upsurge of inflation, we should remember that the monetary theorist's money stock, like the capital theorist's capital stock, is a problematic construct. Liquidity—or, more accurately, the supply of liquidity at each nominal rate of interest—cannot be reliably captured by measurements of a single money-like variable such as my m^* (see Table 1). Friedman's advocacy of his M_2 is well known. The trouble with M_2 as a concept of liquidity is that time deposits and savings accounts are a function of liquidity preference, so that M_2 is not, even potentially, an exogenous or predetermined variable within the period. James Tobin has written of a counter M_2 that would include, with less than unitary dollar-for-dollar weight, the predetermined stocks of government interest-bearing obligations held by the public. But empirical analyses have not been successful in showing that the government debt as a whole is so liquid relative to capital that an increase in it tends to increase the demand for capital (at a given M_1). Finally, Robert Mundell has spoken grandly of an international dollar money supply, say I-M, that would include foreigners' holdings of dollar deposits, Eurodollars, and other "facsimile" dollars. Pentti Kouri has broadened the notion to include all national M_1-type money supplies, converted to dollars at appropriate exchange rates, in a cosmic C-M.

How might we test the hypothesis that there occurred in 1972–1974 a sharp acceleration in the stock of simulated dollars relative to the stock of authentic *ur*-dollars (or maybe *echt* dollars)? In the case of simple counterfeiting, we should expect to observe, between the "before" and the "after" equilibria, a rise of the price level relative to the official money supply, and hence a reduction of measured m^*—that is, if everything else stays "equal." In fact we observe no great fall of detrended real m^*. But this test is not conclusive because other things—like a sharp decrease in the quantity of time deposits owing to their interest-rate ceilings in a time of rising interest rates generally—could have operated to cover the traces of the counterfeiters.

In our "accounting" of the 1972–1974 resurgence of inflation, we have been considering evidence of an outward shift of the money-supply function. Yet the money-supply function never determines anything by itself, such as interest rates or the equilibrium price level or whatever, any more than the marginal-productivity-of-labor function determines in certain models the real wage or employment or whatever. In both theories we need another function as mate to wrap up the determination of one of the unknown variables. This brings us to the demand for money. The Compleat Monetarist must be a both-blades-of-the-scissors man.

I have already mentioned in passing the suggestion that there may have been a significant drop in the demand for M_1 due to the emergence of close or far substitutes. It is an interesting hypothesis, though maybe not a plausible one after close analysis, that goods themselves are becoming more liquid. It must surely be of some importance that the past ten years have been a period of unprecedented stability of real *sales*. Witness the fact that the unemployment rate in this country has hardly risen above 6 percent and hardly fallen below 4 percent. I doubt that one could find another ten-year period in the history of this country over which unemployment and unused capacity have been so stable. What does this portend for liquidity and the demand for goods as against money-like debt instruments? I should suppose, first of all, that firms would tend to want to have fewer liquid assets of the ordinary sort on hand as "precautionary finance" because they are more confident than earlier of being able to run down inventories if the need for more cash should arise. But this hunch does not compel one to venture at the same time that firms will want to hold more inventories relative to normal or expected sales. On the contrary, the less the variance of sales the smaller the quantity of buffer stocks firms will want to hold, very probably. Indeed, a contributing explanation of the sharp rise in prices that accompanied so shallow a plumbing of the unemployment rate (to a mere 4.8 percent) in 1972 and 1973 may be the fact, if it is a fact, that businesses had by then adjusted themselves to a very austere or spare use of inventories and slack (or spare) capacity as compared to the roller-coaster days of William McChesney Martin. Needless to say, I am not sure how much weight to give to this alleged liquification of goods compared to assets which are "liquids" par excellence. And I would add that before we officially designate a new era, the Age of Certainty, we should note the fresh microeconomic uncertainties that have befallen producers since 1972 (not least of which are the potentially mischievous price controls legislated to meet those microeconomic disturbances).

Heightened Expectations. The last demand-side factor I shall discuss is the possibility of an increase in the famous "expected rate of inflation." On the principle that it is better to equivocate in two pages than in five, as in two earlier drafts of this section, I shall be very brief.

I realize that to the extent that expectations are "rational" in the sense of John Muth, the expected rate of inflation is not truly an exogenous factor, and not even a predetermined variable like the capital stock. But if we want to know whether, whatever its cause, an increase in the expected inflation rate did or did not occur, a natural approach to that question is to conduct a thought experiment in which the expected inflation rate is parametrically increased as though it were exogenous.

What are the implications of a *ceteris paribus* increase in the expected inflation rate? Let us start from a situation of full macroeconomic equilibrium with unemployment at its "natural" rate and the actual inflation rate equal to the expected inflation rate. An increase in the latter then shifts upward the *IS* curve in the Hicks-Sargeant money-interest/real-output plane. At the new temporary Keynesian rest point, after multiplier effects but abstracting from the acceleration of the capital stock being induced, the money interest rate is higher approximately by the amount of the increase in the expected inflation rate. The approximation is closer the flatter the *IS* curve. If M_1 is maintained along some predesignated time path, there is little or no fall of m^* at first. (There may be some one-time increase in the price level associated with the rise of output—and, therefore, of marginal costs—induced by the rise of the *IS* curve, but for simplicity let us neglect that.)

In economic terms, producers will want to step up their inventory and other investments when, at the initial money rates of interest, the prices at which future inventories are salable are expected to go up. This effect imparts a tendency toward larger output and real incomes, and thus toward increased transaction demand for real balances at each money rate of interest. This is the mechanism, or one such at any rate, through which the increased expected inflation rate drives up nominal rates of interest. At the new Keynesian rest point, the enlargement of inventory building is not dependent upon a lift in stock prices relative to goods prices (particularly capital-goods prices).

In the longer run of Metzler and Patinkin, output and employment have returned to their macroequilibrium levels and the price level has experienced a one-time rise *relative* to the predesignated time path of M_1. Output is back to normal and m^* is *down* in proportion to the interest elasticity of the demand-for-money function times the rise in the expected inflation rate.

Now we ask: Was there a substantial increase in the expected inflation rate during 1972 and/or 1973? Well, any tendency for m^* to have decreased as a consequence of increased expectations of inflation during 1972 was of course covered up by the sharp acceleration of the money stock—prices being too sluggish to rise quickly in proportion to the rise of M_1 (relative to trend). There was a detectable weakening of m^* during 1973 and it may have been attributable *in part* to the acceleration of prices induced by the expansionary influence of heightened inflationary expectations—that is, the rise of *IS*. (In addition, some of the supply-side pressures upon prices in 1973 may have been fundamentally expectational in origin; a fuller discussion of expectations and supply is given in the second part of the paper.) The larger part of the drop in m^*, which occurs in the second half of 1973, was probably due to acceleration of prices from other causes and to some deceleration of M_1 managed by the monetary authorities. But the December 1973 m^* is *not* so much lower than 1968–1969 as to confirm strongly a major increase in the expected inflation rate.

The stock market performance over 1972–1974 can hardly be called favorable to the hypothesis of increased inflationary expectations. There was a sharp recovery of stock prices in 1972, but some or all of that might have been attributable to the bulge in m^* caused by the monetary authorities. In 1973 and since, stock market prices actually declined relative to goods prices. Should we conclude, then, that expectations of inflation were not on the rise in 1973? I would not. The Federal Reserve tightened the screws sharply in the second half, and in addition there are random disturbances and measurement errors. I would guess that the long-term expected rate of inflation grew very little during 1972–1973, while the *short-term* rates of producers and sophisticated investors were up markedly over the period, especially during the winter of 1973–1974.

Supply Factors

In the previous section, hypotheses of a spurt in money substitutes, money facsimiles, or the moneyness of goods and hypotheses of a spurt in the expected rate of inflation were entertained as supplementary explanatory factors in the accounting of the 1972–1974 rise of inflation. In our agreed-upon neo-Keynesian model, both such hypotheses imply the observation of a fall in m^* at least in conditions of macroequilibrium, other things equal. But the economy is hardly ever, and really never certified to be, in macroequilibrium; and macroequilibrium itself follows an unknown path over time. Eyeballing the data and making certain horseback normalizations of them to allow for macroequilibrium evolution do not yield conclusions that can be confidently maintained.

The same uncertainties beset various hypotheses that certain supply-side disturbances account for some of the 1972–1974 inflation rise. In the terms of standard macrotheory, the equilibrium relation

$$M = p\,L(r + x, Y, \ldots), L_1 < 0, L_2 > 0$$

states that a reduction of the supply of output, Y, in macroequilibrium implies a rise of the equilibrium price level, p, given M (the money stock), the real rate of interest, r, the expected rate of inflation, x, and the other things we usually place in the demand-for-real-balances function, L. An implication of this equation, then, is the presumption that a reduction of Y (relative to trend, of course) spells a reduction of m^* in any new equilibrium. It is a mere presumption, however, because the fall of supply may also alter r or x or both, and do so in nonobvious ways.

The fact that the behavior of actual m^* does not clearly signal important supply-side happenings that pushed up the general price level markedly in 1972–1973 should not, however, cause us to turn a deaf ear to any and all supply-side contributions to the account of the recent inflation. There are after all other kinds of evidence that support, in varying degrees, certain supply-side hypotheses. Anyone who reads newspaper accounts of the rise of ecological consciousness, the fears of a limit to growth from natural-resource barriers, the spectacular run-up of some commodity prices, and the new aggressiveness of the oil-producing countries must be inclined at least to give a hearing to the supply-side hypotheses which these stories suggest. And in that list of newspaper headlines one should not forget to include the depreciation of the dollar.

How can we hope to tell from the ordinary data dealt with by economists whether or not supply-side factors have been acting up significantly at all? One approach to answering that question would involve the use of an econometric model with sectoral supply equations whose residuals could be inspected. Another approach would examine the correlation between price rises and real-expenditure rises over sectors.[2] If price rises were greatest in sectors where increases in expenditures were least, as compared to the usual experience with such a correlation, one would give increased credence to the hypothesis of (differentially exerted or uneven) supply-side pressures—though not to the exclusion of demand factors. My impression is that if such an analysis were carried out today, it would lend some support to the hypothesis of *some* supply-side disturbances. In what follows, it will be taken for granted that supply factors of various sorts may have been at work and, with varying probabilities, were at work. But it is far from certain how forceful any of them were, and some may have been of negligible importance.

[2] Edmund S. Phelps, "A Test for the Presence of Cost Inflation in the U.S. Economy, 1955–57," *Yale Economic Essays*, vol. 1 (January 1961).

I shall be discussing primarily the *how* and the *why* of various kinds of supply-side disturbances rather than the question of *how much*.

Controls, Environmental Restrictions, and Investment Allocation. The other day I came across an explicit statement of a notion that seems to have gained wide currency these days: Environmental restrictions and price controls have reduced plant capacity relative to the size of the labor force. My own impressions of the behavior of plant-and-equipment investment do not confirm this notion. But in any case it is possible that controls and the environmentalists have reduced the efficiency of the allocation of capital—where by efficiency we mean only efficiency at producing GNP, not at producing the good life in a setting of fresh water and greenery. A shortage of capacity in oil refining or power generation is not "offset" by a surplus of capacity in construction or car making or whatever.

As to controls, while their distorting effects may have worsened inflation a little in 1973, they did seem to compress markups in 1972 and thus slowed the growth of the price level that would otherwise have occurred for the same actual growth path of the money stock and other exogenous variables. Whether the controls if maintained would have had a nonvanishing effect on the price level, like a permanent falling behind the original schedule, is probably not worth going into. In fact, as of this writing (April 1974), controls have been successively dismantled with very few exceptions.

Now the crux: is decontrol causing p to rise relative to M? Yes, probably, at least temporarily. But as can easily be checked from our equation, any final rise of equilibrium p for given M, at macroequilibrium Y, must hinge upon an associated rise of the profit rate (given x) and resulting increase in the money rate of interest. I return to this later.

Cartelization, et cetera. There are few things more annoying to the macroeconomic theorist than to be told by laymen and newspaper editorialists, most of whom cannot solve two equations for their two unknowns, that the recent rise of the general price level is due to monopoly, or unions, or some other menacing economic power. Likewise, it is dismaying to hear one's colleagues talk vaguely of a parametric shift in labor militancy or corporate greed or general bloody-mindedness on the occasion of each and every blip of the price level. Still, the boy who cried wolf every time was finally right.

The years 1972–1974 do not strike one as a period of visible aggrandizement by either capital or labor as a whole. While some economists used to think that labor can never be expected to take real wage cuts, least of all when accustomed to real wage growth, labor took a 3 or 4 percent cut in real wage rates in 1973 without a whimper and withstood further real-wage reductions in the first half of 1974. As for "capital," the increase in its relative share of national income is probably attributable entirely to the rise of capacity utilization and the special situation in foods and fuel. It is, in fact, the finding of many students of the

1972–1973 price controls that price markups bore the major brunt of the New Economic Policy.

The oil situation in 1973 seems a natural for the hypothesis of increased cartelization. Some observers suggest that the Arab countries merely increased the tax on the extracting companies to such an extent as to extract the infra-marginal rents accruing to the companies. Perhaps the oil companies seized upon the increase in the tax, or the so-called posted price on which the tax is figured, as the occasion for an increase in the price of crude-oil sales which they wanted to impose anyway. Or perhaps the rise in extraction costs cum tax caused a slowdown in the optimal rate of extraction. Or perhaps there was collusion between oil companies and oil-producing countries to come closer to the joint-revenue maximizing price.

Many economists seem to be instinctively suspicious of any hypothesis of increased monopolization, and maybe properly so: if monopolization and cartelization were so profitable yesterday, why not also the day before? The answer, presumably, is that Rome was not built in a day. Communication, understanding, and trust cannot be established instantly. The hilarious prognostication of a breakfast cartel next—involving international cooperation in the supply of cocoa, coffee beans, bananas, and other morning foods—is not really implausible. It is, as Schumpeter said, only the creative destruction of fresh products—solar energy for heat, seaweed for breakfast—that we can look for (if we are worried about it, for after all the state is the largest beneficiary) to check the tendency to increasing collusive oligopoly profit within and across national borders.

Exhaustible Resource Speculation. The supply prices asked by owners of natural resources of the exhaustible (not Ricardian-indestructible) type depend upon their owners' estimates of the prices that users of these resources will be willing to pay for them in the future. It is only necessary to invoke the name of the late Harold Hotelling, as a kind of code word, in order to summon to mind the capital-theoretic economics of equilibrium competitive prices of natural resources.[3] If timber owners revise upward their estimates of future relative prices of cut timber, given the expected time path of the instantaneous real rate of interest, the time path of real extractions costs, and other such things, then timber owners will reduce their supply offerings at given current prices—or their managers will obediently do it for them—in order to maximize the present value of the cash flow obtainable from current standing timber. This cutback in timber supply will (in the classical analysis) force a rise in the price of timber relative to other current prices, other things equal.

What then of money prices and the general money-price level? The new equilibrium money price of timber, in the example, will be higher while the

[3] Harold Hotelling, "The Economics of Exhaustible Resources," *Journal of Political Economy*, vol. 39 (April 1939), pp. 137–75.

equilibrium money prices of other goods *may* be lower at a given money supply. The *general* money price level will be higher in the new equilibrium. The reason is that, appealing to our equilibrium relation displayed at the beginning of this part of the paper, the macroequilibrium or quasi-full-employment supply of output is reduced because there is less timber cooperating with capital and labor in the production of wooden gross national product. This decline in output and real expenditure reduces the demand for real cash balances at each money rate of interest and thus, presumably, entails a rise in the general price level to re-equate the supply and demand for real cash balances. At the modest level of analysis here, it is possible that there are associated changes in the real rate of interest and in real wealth or other variables entering into the liquidity-demand function that might upset this conclusion, but I leave these possibilities aside. In fact, it should not be hard to show in a more sophisticated model that the money rate of interest must actually rise, thus reinforcing the rise in the equilibrium price level, because it is a rise in the expected real rate of return (on resource holding) that is perturbing the system and such a rise ought to raise the equilibrium real rate of interest (short or medium-term) if it has any effect at all.

What of the short run, before the new equilibrium is approached? The rise in timber prices and of the prices of wood-using products tends to produce an immediate substitution, growing in strength, into other goods, causing their prices to rise also, though not by so much. However, the transitional unemployment of labor and of capital goods which otherwise would have been allocated to wood-using products tends to lower the marginal cost schedules in the other industries, and this works in the opposing direction of lowering prices finally in these other industries. The question of how monetary policy should best respond to this sort of situation is a difficult one even when the facts and theoretical relationships of the situation are clear to the authorities. I shall try to say something about that later.

I have been sketching how a "resource speculation" account of some part of the recent dollar price rise would go. Such an account helps to explain the run-up in the prices of oil, copper, zinc, timber, silver, and so on. I was fortified the other day by remarks of an Iranian economist who was quoted in the *New York Times* as saying that "rightly or wrongly," the Arab oil planners believed that the real rate of return from holding their oil reserves had risen compared to the real rates of interest available in the world to Arab investors. It was straight Wicksell, perhaps via the London School of Economics and the Harvard Business School.

Now the monetarists often remark that no country has to import inflation if it does not want to. If the American authorities had somehow seen the oil price rise coming with six months' warning, should they have appreciated the dollar and reduced the money stock? I do not see how they could have done so without exacerbating most of the resource dislocations, especially the magnitude of the transitional unemployment.

Farm Inflation. Because food costs loom larger in the average consumer's budget than do fuel costs, the rise in farm prices that began in 1972 actually contributed more to the subsequent growth of the consumer price index than did the more dramatic price rises in metals and minerals in 1973 and 1974.

There is direct meteorological and oceanic evidence that suggests that much of the "farm inflation" originated in contracting supplies of livestock and grains. Indeed, the sharp rise in the relative price of agricultural products over 1972–1973 was accompanied by a contraction of world agricultural output. According to a recent analysis by William Nordhaus and John Shoven, the world demand for foodstuffs has been increasing at approximately 4 percent per annum. The world grain crop fell by 4 percent in 1972 and probably did not recover by more than 4 percent in 1973. These figures yield an 8 percent excess demand (at 1971 relative prices) in both 1972 and 1973.[4] An excess demand of such a magnitude might require a 20 or 30 percent rise in the relative price of grains to restore equality of supply and demand.

There is one wrinkle in all this that seems to need some hard thinking. If the world price of anchovies rises, or the world price of oil, then American real income, Y, is presumably lower in the new equilibrium. The reason is that America is a net importer of anchovies and oil. Neglecting the real rate of interest and other esoterica, we then calculate a rise of equilibrium p for given M. But what about wheat, of which America is a net exporter? If real expenditures, Y, on which the demand for money depends are increased, equilibrium m^* must rise and equilibrium p must fall—unless there is a rise in the real rate of interest for which there is no evident reason. It seems possible therefore that if the supply disturbance at home is a rise in the price abroad of export goods, and if the money supply needed to maintain the exchange rate is not much changed as a result of the imported price rise, then there results an excess demand for real cash balances which drives down equity prices and capital-goods prices until the overall dollar price level is finally lower than before.

By a chain of associations one is then led to wonder: can one or two countries—such as Britain, Japan or Italy, alone or coincidentally together—cause a rise in the dollar price of American export goods which will in turn motivate the Federal Reserve to expand its credit, which will bail out the foreign countries and encourage their further monetary expansion, and so on in some converging or diverging multiplier process in terms of the dollar price level? The security blanket that we monetary theorists cling to—America determines the dollar price level while the other countries determine the dollar exchange rates—may be misleading even for the long run in the presence of short-run dynamic interactions among the various central banks.

[4] William Nordhaus and John Shoven, "Inflation 1973: The Year of Infamy," manuscript, February 1974. I am indebted to the authors for permission to refer to their preliminary manuscript.

Dollar Devaluations. The fourth and last putative supply-side factoı I want to discuss is the depreciation of the U.S. dollar. The New Economic Policy announced in August 1971 produced the first devaluation in the fall of that year, and another devaluation followed in February 1973. The dollar slid more in subsequent months—as I well recall, feeling impoverished that summer in Morocco—and some of the recovery later in the year was reversed in 1974.

Part of the depreciation of the dollar may have been the side effect of the metals and minerals situation already discussed; foreign countries rich in these resources may have opted for some currency appreciation vis-à-vis the dollar. It was widely argued that some of the dollar's slide in 1973 was to be attributed to a loss of confidence in the willingness or capacity of the Federal Reserve to hold the rate of dollar inflation down to the range of inflation rates expectable in other countries. A difficulty with this explanation is this: the dollar price of foreign exchange would indeed be bid up by investors insofar as nominal interest rates did not rise by the amount of the increase in the expected dollar inflation rate, and the dollar price of American equities and capital goods would tend to be bid up as well. But, if one regards nominal interest rates in America as having risen to discount fully the prospective increase in American inflation, there is no longer any implication of a stock market boom, and neither is there any implication that the dollar will drop in foreign exchange rates; investors in dollar-denominated assets are being compensated in higher interest for the prospective rise in inflation.

Still another "theory" of the dollar depreciation is that it was the delayed consequence of Federal Reserve expansiveness relative to the expansiveness of foreign central banks. Very roughly, neglecting Treasury currency and Pigou-Metzler effects, an x percent rise of Federal Reserve credit (high-powered money) spells an *eventual* increase in the *dollar* prices of all goods everywhere in the world, traded or nontraded. Whether this development will result eventually in an x percent increase in foreign goods prices denominated in foreign currencies *or* result instead in an x percent appreciation of foreign currencies relative to the dollar—or some linear combination between these two polar outcomes—is in some slightly strained sense "up to the foreign central banks" (hence up to foreign politics).

As long as the foreign central banks maintain their exchange rates with the dollar, the process of dollar price adjustment goes on slowly and is incomplete (less than x percent after any finite time); some of the increase in potential American money supply goes abroad and has to foster increased growth of foreign money supplies before finally coming home when American prices are finally x percent higher.

But suppose that at some moment the foreign central banks relinquish the old exchange rates, appreciating their local currencies against the dollar. Unless the Federal Reserve at that point reverses course, making open market sales to reduce its liabilities to a level somewhat below the x percent augmented level, the result of the foreigners' effective devaluation of the dollar is a one-time inflow of dollars into America that bids American equity prices and goods prices "abruptly" up to the predestined x percent higher level from whatever level they had reached up to that time. A way of understanding that process which my colleague Carlos Rodriguez has suggested to me is that if we take the dollar prices as momentarily given, then the foreign central banks' devaluation of the rate at which they will sell dollars for local currencies must lower the equilibrium price level in those foreign currencies, thus creating excess liquidity and a portfolio adjustment on the part of foreign wealth owners that bids up the dollar prices of bonds, equities, and goods. The Federal Reserve could prevent this only by a one-time open-market sale of Treasury obligations that would satisfy the foreigners' increased demand for earning assets and leave the American money supply and price level unchanged—more specifically, not increased.

Under this "monetarist" theory of the devaluations of the dollar, it is appropriate to say that the rise in Federal Reserve credit was the original cause of the rise in dollar prices associated with the dollar devaluation. The depreciations were exogenous only in the technical jargon of econometric model building. Yet if we want to understand the price rises in some historical episode, we do want to take account of the particular dynamics then operating.

With regard to foreign currency appreciations generally, the above analysis suggests that they will tend to bid up the American price level except in the unlikely event that foresighted Federal Reservists engage beforehand in open-market sales in order to contrive a temporary economic contraction.

What Lessons for Monetary Policy?

I am proud and gleeful to have been in the vanguard of economists who attacked the Federal Reserve in 1970 and 1971 for not seeming to have been aware that inflationary expectations must be met with growing monetary rations if slack capacity and unemployment are not to rise.[5] A decline in the real money stock may signal a failure of the monetary authorities to keep pace with a march of the price level that is actuated by producers' expectations of their competitors' raising their prices and wages. A fall of the real money stock in such circumstances is an antecedent signal (although not a completely timely forewarning) of upward pressure on unemployment.

Now it might be thought by some, and I guess it has been, that this way lies madness. "The fire's worse, boys, so throw on more coal." Not every rise in the price level over all observable situations should prompt the Federal Reserve

[5] For example, see Edmund S. Phelps, "Unreasonable Price Stability," *The Battle Against Unemployment*, ed. A. M. Okun, rev. ed. (New York: Norton, 1972). The real money stock was emphasized in a letter to the *New York Times*, April 29, 1971.

to increase the money supply in the same proportion. If one knew for sure that today's rise in the price level was attributable to yesterday's accidental and regretted rise in the money stock, one would not then feel compelled to continue the mistake into perpetuity by increasing the money stock again today, thus keeping the real stock too large, which would then set up the recurring situation tomorrow and so on ad infinitum. Certainly one no more wants to stabilize the real money stock (or any detrended version) than one wants to fix the unemployment rate or peg the money interest rate.

The ideal response of the money stock to a rise in the price level and to the concomitant changes in other observable variables like inventories, unemployment, and spare capacity depends upon what cause or causes are acting upon these variables. The optimal response in the face of imperfect knowledge of the causes requires inferences about the identity of the disturbances. The period 1972–1974 seems to have raised particularly acute identification problems, for many things were probably happening at once. But that is no ground for counseling the money managers and their advisers and critics to pay no attention to the data at any and all times. One expects and hopes that there will be occasions from time to time in which the causes of price rises or falls are well agreed upon. In that spirit of optimism, however unwarranted, I would like to make the following points.

Suppose the price level rises and m^* falls and we believe that a substantial portion of the fall of m^* is attributable to reduced domestic capacity, be it a matter of misinvestments or domestic crop failures or an adverse movement of the terms of trade (oil, anchovies or the like). To say that M should be increased in order to restore the value of m^* appears to be senseless unless we think that more money can make more anchovies. (It might make more oil if the Arabs wished they had not increased the posted price by so much relative to other goods prices but are embarrased to cut the price.) If the adversity brings a reduction in equilibrium real income, Y, then there has to be a fall of the equilibrium m^* (subject to qualifications discussed earlier). The Fed's sandbox contains alternative disequilibrium paths to play with, but these are all keyed in a certain way to the equilibrium m^* and Y which the Fed cannot do much about.

I am afraid I am unable to resist the temptation to quote from a preliminary draft on just this issue by my friend Robert J. Gordon:

> . . . an increase in the aggregate price *level* in 1974, due to the permanent increases in the prices of oil and food and to the end of the temporary effect of controls, without any accommodating adjustment in the *level* of the nominal money supply, must be accompanied by a reduction in the demand for real money balances, requiring some combination of a reduction in real output below the level, and an increase in the nominal interest rate above the level, which would otherwise be expected.

Perhaps we should pause here to notice that Gordon seems to regard the price rise as the active force which pulls down Y. He seems to describe the process as simply a leftward shift of *LM* along a traditionally negatively sloped *IS* curve and to interpret the *LM* shift as gratuitous and remediable. Continuing, he writes: "The desirable reaction of the Federal Reserve to a one-time-only increase in the structure of prices is a one-time-only increase in the *level* of the money supply. . . . The alternative is an increase in the unemployment rate which comes close to being permanent."[6] If I understand Gordon correctly, he is not facing his own hypothesized fact of a permanent reduction of equilibrium income supply, *Y*, and is thus advocating in effect the institution of a permanent disequilibrium at above-equilibrium levels of real income and real cash balances.

Nevertheless, there may be a case to be constructed from the particulars of the situation at hand for an increase of the money supply to facilitate and hasten the reallocation of workers made structurally unemployed by the supply-side calamity. As this paper has mentioned several times, a reduction in the supply of goods *X* may lead to a decrease in the equilibrium price and money wage in the other industries (though it need not). It may help speed the relocation of labor, therefore, if the monetary authorities step up *M* in order to avert a painful fall of money wage rates in the other sector—though not by so much as to raise money wage rates *generally* and thus cause labor to linger too long in uneconomical disequilibrium activities. I take little or no responsibility for these remarks, as my attitude toward the matter changes weekly. For after all, if the monetary authorities are asked to increase the money supply every time a mudslide or a forest fire breaks out in the land, what then?

My second and last point is that Gordon should stick to his guns. Many supply-side disturbances are only paper tigers that do not really gnaw away at equilibrium *Y*. Consider decontrol once more. The captains of industry push up prices in an endeavor to restore the dividend checks to blue-haired shareholders. But, at a given money stock, they cause a fall in output and employment and may even, in a paradox of greed, cause a fall in profits. Only after a long process of money-wage reduction, in which the blood of many a worker is spilled, will the managers once more find the old equilibrium level of output profitable to produce—at a price level much the same as that prevailing before decontrol.

It is a good question why the Federal Reserve should sit idly by and force us all to watch this gratuitous spectacle. Gordon is right to try to persuade the Fed to ratify *some* portion of the large 1974 price rise by raising the money stock a little relative to trend. The appropriate amount of ratification depends upon estimates not only of the decontrol effect but also of the other causal factors discussed in this paper—exchange rates, disturbances abroad altering the terms of trade, variations in expectations of inflation, and so on.

---

[6] Robert J. Gordon, "The Consequences of Inflation for Monetary Policy," presented at the Conference Board's Fifth Annual Mid-Year Outlook Conference, Chicago, April 10, 1974, manuscript.

If the unemployment rate reaches 6 percent or more by 1975 or earlier, I will feel then that we ratified too little in the spring of 1974. At this moment I am not very certain of much more. I do suspect that the willingness of the Federal Reserve to engage in some ratification in some circumstances will probably improve its performance a little on the average.

Part VI
STABILIZATION THEORY

INTRODUCTION

The four papers in this last group address some recent questions in the theory of economic stabilization by monetary and fiscal policy. There were, of course, quite enough stabilization issues worth analyzing before the arrival of non-Walrasian models of wage and price behavior. Nevertheless, the development of expectational theories of wage and price setting inevitably brought new questions to mind.

There has been a tendency among non-Walrasian models to portray the economy, any market economy, as one not inherently unstable; the potential for wide swings in economic activity of the boom-bust sort, if it exists, is ascribed to the possibilities of random disturbances of peculiar force and timing. Such a conclusion is not deducible from every plausible hypothesis of expectation formation, and there is always a question, in theory, of the very existence of a "full-employment" equilibrium; yet I confess that I incline to that view. Nevertheless it is not a corollary of that position, I would emphasize, that a suitable monetary policy can add nothing to the speed with which employment recovers to its natural level. Nor it is implied that an unsuitable monetary policy (or fiscal policy) could do nothing to counteract the self-stabilizing mechanisms of work.

Unfortunately there have also been unnecessary tendencies to carry the non-Walrasian image of the economy to such extremes that monetary stabilization policy is made to appear useless at best, and harmful only if misused, in the stabilization of employment. One of these tendencies has produced a recrudescence of classical thinking: If wage and price setting is purposive and calculating, not rigidly convention-bound as the Keynesians envisioned, then perhaps labor and product markets are quickly reequilibrated after all—only an unlucky succession of shocks could keep an economy down (or up) for more than a few months. The other tendency I have labeled semiclassical: If the firm is really the remote outpost that non-Walrasian theory represents it to be, it will offer real-wage and employment insurance to prospective employees—a barter-contract model is more descriptive of this economy than any monetary perspective. Either of these views, the classical or the semiclassical, engenders a new dichotomy in which, put crudely, monetary policy impinges only on money wages and prices while fiscal policy affects only capital formation and growth; in the semiclassical view, the trend of employment would depend to a degree on the growth of capital.

The first paper in this section, written with John Taylor, takes up the revival of the classical view, due largely to Robert Lucas, Thomas Sargent, and Neil Wallace. Those authors based their conclusion on the hypothesis of rational expectations. But that conclusion also rested on the extraneous assumption that in each time period all wages and prices are freshly redetermined, as is the money supply, with the same set of information in hand as is possessed by the stabilization authorities.

The purpose of the paper with Taylor is to demonstrate that the choice of a monetary stabilization policy will make a difference for the stochastic behavior of output and employment if it is assumed instead that some or all prices have been *pre*determined in each period on the basis of information antedating the new information available to current transactors and to the central bank. In addition, it is shown that there is a trade-off faced by the monetary authorities in their choice of a stabilization rule between on the one hand, the stability of output, and, on the other, the stability of the price level.

No one would deny us our assumption of a necessary lead time in price setting if one thinks of the "period" as being quite short; but the period of time over which the chosen monetary policy makes a difference following an unanticipated disturbance is equally short. Our resurrection of stabilization policy would have been more impressive had it been based on the more realistic assumption that price setting—or wage setting, or both—is staggered over the economy; then each unanticipated shock would have a long transient which stabilization policy could serve to damp, if desired, at the cost of a resulting displacement of the price level.

The semiclassical line of thought, that wage indexation effectively determines real wages in such a way as to insulate employment from purely monetary forces and thus from central bank operations, is the topic of the second paper in this group. In recent years the work of the contract theorists has threatened to negate the central propositions of Keynes on the consequences of a rise of liquidity preference, a decline in the marginal efficiency of capital, and the corollary benefits of a countercyclical monetary policy—and thus to nullify the efforts of non-Walrasian theorists to make sense of, and to some degree justify, Keynes' position. My paper on indexation is another attempt to shore up the economics of Keynes.

So many issues are addressed in this paper, however glancingly, that I had better let the paper speak for itself. Yet one clarification may be needed. If it is last quarter's price level to which this quarter's money wage is indexed, so that this quarter's money wage is predetermined, current (or recent) monetary stimulus to foreshorten a business slump may be presumed to have some effect on current sales and end-of-quarter inventories, hence on output next quarter, and perhaps on this quarter's output as well. The drawback is that if the boost of the money supply is not repeated, then employment will slip back to its depressed level, there to await the springs of a natural recovery; if monetary stimulus is renewed to secure the gain in output, the rise in this quarter's price level will then build in permanently higher inflation. The former effect is attenuated, and the latter effect lessened, to the extent that this quarter's prices are likewise indexed to last quarter's price level.

The Appendix to that paper is a start toward a theory of less-than-full indexation of money wages in a quasi-contract setting. I hold its coauthor Guillermo Calvo largely responsible for the results. The primary results rest on two postulates: The first is that the prudent worker evaluating the quasi-contractual pledges of various firms will give little credence to any promise of protection from loss of a job for business cycle, as contrasted with other, reasons. Who could certify the firm's predicament and sort out its causes? The worker will assume that he faces a lower risk of being let go the less expensive his employment is. The other postulate is that a rise of the general price level frequently signals an increase of nonwage costs, in which case a contract calling for a proportionate rise of money wages equal to the proportionate rise of the price level would raise unnecessarily the risk of being let go—the whole incidence of the cost rise would fall on job security and none on the real wage. An optimal contract, it is then argued, will not generally contain full indexation against each and every rise of the general price level. And an optimal monetary policy would seize the opportunity to amplify the signal of an employment-threatening rise of nonwage costs.

Seldom have the forces of full indexation and the forces of little or no indexation been better joined than in the period of the sharp rise of prices attributable to the 1973 supply shocks in agriculture and oil. The third essay gives an analysis of the issues in monetary policy during that episode. Full indexationists predicted that real wages would decline, if at all, in relation to trend only through the purge and catharsis of a lengthy depression. The proposal that I and others made for a quantum jump of the quantity of money, in order to reduce real wages without a long recession, was spurned by the semiclassicists on the belief that it would merely add proportionally to the average money wage level on top of the rise of money wages already in store, without any beneficial results for employment.

Experience seems to have differed among countries suffering through this laboratory experiment, and hardly any country took the bold monetary response to the supply shocks that had been proposed. Yet the American data do not appear to bear out even remotely the hypothesis of full indexation: In 1974 and subsequently, following the wave of supply disturbances, real wages decelerated and, in some years, actually fell. Whether a one-time monetary stimulus could have hastened the process of real-wage adjustment was not tested.

The fourth paper in the present group on economic stabilization turns to fiscal policy, particularly to fiscal policy of the balanced-budget type. Being three papers in one, all rather difficult, it is not easy reading. Does a balanced-budget expansion of the public sector in a monetarist climate of unbending money supply tend to raise money wages and (at least transiently) employment over the long pull? If one country expands alone, do all countries' employment levels tend to be affected in the same direction? Is the problem of full-employment fiscal policy one of achieving international coordination or instead a zero-sum game of beggar thy neighbor?

Tens of equations later the main conclusion becomes clear. A balanced-budget stimulus in one large country, while probably hastening recovery in all countries over the near term, is apt in the long run to work against prosperity especially in the rest of the world. In the long run, all countries may return to the natural rate. But in the process the rest of the world will suffer a loss of capital, a decline of real wages, and a dampening of employment. Without the countercyclical use of monetary policy, the world may have to resign itself to the risk of long-lived slumps in economic activity.

STABILIZING POWERS OF MONETARY POLICY UNDER RATIONAL EXPECTATIONS*

The potential of monetary policy to stabilize fluctuations in output and employment is demonstrated in a stochastic rational expectations model in which firms choose, considering average profitability, to set prices in advance of the period when they apply to goods sold. This lead time in pricing decisions increases the fluctuations of output about the normal employment level. But proper use of a feedback monetary policy rule can reduce these fluctuations even though expectations are rational and people know the policy rule. It is noted that use of a rule-dictated policy sometimes requires the monetary authorities to penalize the economy in the short run for the sake of beneficial system effects of the rule upon the relevant steady-state distributions.

The information-based reconstruction of employment and inflation theory, begun in the late sixties, led to the conclusion that the customary Keynesian postulate of sticky wages or prices (or both) could be replaced, at least for some purposes, by the more tractable premise that prices and wages adjust costlessly and instantaneously to changes in perceptions and estimates of the current state of the economy.[1] In particular, the "new microeconomics" argued that an unforeseen disturbance would have "disequilibrating" effects on output and employment to the extent that information is imperfect about the generality of the shock over the economy or about the persistence of the shock over time, the perfect flexibility of prices and wages notwithstanding.

Our paper and the paper by Stanley Fischer (1977), while produced independently, have the same principal theme—the potential of monetary policy, even anticipated policy, for the stabilization of economic activity. But in the structure of the models and the development of other results, the two papers are quite different and usefully so. Some of these differences will be pointed to in the course of our exposition. A National Science Foundation grant is acknowledged.

[1] Many of the ideas can be found in Phelps et al. (1970).

* This paper was written with John B. Taylor.

Reprinted by permission from *The Journal of Political Economy*, Vol. 85(1), January/February 1977.

In the new theory, then, the effects upon output and employment of a change in the supply of money will depend in part upon the informational circumstances surrounding the change. Consider an open-market purchase, one not previously foreseen, about which there is at once perfect information: everyone knows the increase to have just occurred and everyone knows it to be a fact known to all. To simplify, we postulate that money is twice neutral in the sense that employment, saving, and other nonmonetary variables are invariant to both the level and rate of change of the money supply when long anticipated.[2]

Were there a Walrasian economy-wide auctioneer at work in this setting, the monetary disturbance would cause an immediate jump of money wages and prices and, if the increased money were believed temporary, a drop of money interest rates. By the neutrality postulates, these "nominal" adjustments would exactly preserve the levels of production, consumption, employment, and the associated real wage rates and expected real rates of interest.

In the new theory, however, prices and wages are left to noncooperative and imperfectly informed decisions, there being no economy-wide auctioneer. In reaction to the monetary disturbance, each firm or local auctioneer will determine higher prices and wages—*how much higher* depending in part upon its expectations of the price and wage increases going to be made by other firms or auctioneers. But how much higher is that? And will the levels of production and employment be preserved as a result?

Sargent and Wallace (1975) give an answer, invoking the postulate of rational price expectations in the sense of Muth (1961). They show that in their model the money supply for the current period, if correctly estimated from the outset of the period, can have only nominal effects. It cannot alter output and employment, the real wage and the expected real interest rate. Thus money wages and prices, actual and expected, adjust as though guided by an invisible Walrasian auctioneer. Only those monetary disturbances that create a discrepancy between the actual money supply and the currently expected money supply have an effect upon employment.

Making some additional assumptions, the authors draw a disquieting conclusion regarding the power (for good or ill) of monetary policy to influence output and employment. Suppose that the money supply set by the central bank is determined by a policy rule. Suppose further that the public in effect knows (forecasts and takes actions as though it knew) the policy rule. And suppose finally that the public acquires as soon as the bank all the information from which (following its rule) the bank sets

[2] Thus the nonneutral Metzler-Patinkin wealth effects from open-market transactions and the nonneutral Friedman-Mundell income-and-wealth effects from expectations of inflation upon the supplies of saving and effort are all absent.

the money supply. The public can therefore estimate or forecast without bias in each period the money supply currently to be set (or its expected value if the rule should be "noisy"). *Provided* that the wages and prices prevailing in the period and the price-wage expectations they depend on are based on the same current information on which the period's money supply is decided, it follows that the current money interest rate and the current price and wage levels will have "fully discounted" the bank's money-supply intentions for the period. By always adjusting in such a way as to preserve the real wage and the expected real rate of interest, the "nominal" prices effectively neutralize any effect on employment that the rule-dictated movements of the money supply would otherwise have had. Hence the choice of the monetary policy rule, once adapted to by the public, can have no leverage over output and employment. Only some error by the bank or an unexpected change of its rule can affect output in the period.[3]

What then of the old faith that systematic monetary policy matters for the fluctuation of output and employment? This paper will produce a reformulation, if not yet a victorious restoration, of that old doctrine. To do so we depart from Sargent and Wallace in one crucial respect: we postulate that firms choose to set their prices and wage rates *1 period in advance* of the period over which they will apply, hence before the central bank decides on the money supply for that (latter) period. Because the monetary authorities do not want the "lead time" desired by price and wage setters, the information set available at the time of the money supply decision is later and larger than the information set available when current prices and wages were decided, contrary to the aforementioned *proviso*. Our prices and wages are thus "sticky" in the sense of being predetermined from period to period at successive levels generally different from what would have been established had current business conditions been (correctly) anticipated when the current prices and wage rates were decided.[4]

Two questions must spring to mind. For what reasons would a firm choose to decide a period (a quarter, say) in advance the prices and wages at which it would sell and hire? Many a firm may find it advantageous as a device for attracting and keeping customers and employees to save them the trouble of direct inquiry into the firm's price and wage scale, thus

[3] Barro (1976) has shown, building on models by Lucas, that "noise" in the monetary policy rule affects the probability distribution of the real variables by lessening the information value of individual price observations. But the optimal policy rule in his model is noise free. Hence this noise relation is not constructive for *active* stabilization policy, which is our interest here.

[4] In our model, then, all prices and wages are reviewed and reset every period. Hence there are no long-term contracts like those in the model by Fischer. Nor are there purchases or sales for future delivery of goods and labor. (There may be debts and loans, of course.)

removing or reducing their cost of learning the firm's offer and (if the offer is judged satisfactory) reducing their incentive to inquire elsewhere; the publication and dissemination to potential users of this information will in many cases take time.[5] A firm may also regard it as profitable on average, in attracting buyers and workers, to remove the risk of price and wage disappointment—at least if the corresponding risk of quantity unavailabilities is not increased too much. But we do not pretend to have a rigorous understanding of these considerations at this time. In the ancient and honorable tradition of Keynesians past, we take it for granted that there are disadvantages from too-frequent or too-precipitate revisions of price lists and wage schedules.

Have not previous Keynesians already shown (many times) that monetary policy "matters" when prices and wages are "sticky"? Yes, but only by positing laws of adjustment in expectations to current states and events that are invariant to the monetary policy in force. By adopting the framework of rational expectations, we hope to have produced not a new wine but an old wine in a new and more secure bottle.

I. The Rudimentary Model

The setting is a stationary one in which the size of the working-age population, tastes, and technology are unchanging through time. In the "rudimentary" model to which we devote most of our attention, the "full-employment" quantity of output is taken to be a constant, ϕ, totally exogenous and unchanging over time. A "full" model that makes ϕ endogenous is constructed and briefly discussed in the Appendix below.

At the beginning of any period t, $t = 1, 2, \ldots$, the agents of the economy learn (for the first time) the size of the starting stock of (finished) inventories, k_{t-1}, left over at the end of the previous period. At that point the agents also learn (for the first time) the index of consumer prices that were determined earlier to apply to sales of the current period, P_{t-1}. These two variables, (k_{t-1}, P_{t-1}), describe fully the (initial) state in period t. Simultaneously the central bank determines the supply of money, M_t, according to a policy rule that makes M_t some known and stationary function of the current state. For simplicity, we take M_t as observed, like the state variables.

Households and firms then make their various decisions for the period with perfect information about (M_t, k_{t-1}, P_{t-1}) but with imperfect information about the uncoordinated current decisions of one another and thus with imperfect foresight about the results of those decisions for

[5] Far from being a dissonant element, this information-based argument is a natural extension of the approach to price and wage setting taken by some of the authors in Phelps et al. A recent and extensive discussion of this kind of argument is contained in the paper (and comments of Poole and others) by Okun (1975).

the next state, (k_t, P_t). Each firm has to decide early this period both the price it will charge consumers for goods it sells next period and the amount of output it will produce this period for availability next period *before* it knows for sure the amount of its sales this period, the production and sales at other firms, and the average price that other firms will charge in the next period. Firms and households, having rational expectations, base their respective decisions on the expected values of the variables that will subsequently confront them. The actual values of the variables are subject to random (unpredictable) disturbances.

It may therefore happen, perhaps because producers last period underpredicted their own and others' end-of-period inventories or somehow overpredicted the prices their competitors were simultaneously deciding, that either P_{t-1} or k_{t-1} or both are so high in relation to M_t (corresponding to some policy rule) as to cause a probable "deficiency of aggregate demand" in the current period t. Alternatively, the random events of the previous period may have determined a state (k_{t-1}, P_{t-1}) that spells "excess aggregate demand" in period t. What then? Because the price level is stuck for the period at its predetermined level, it cannot function to equate aggregate demand (considered as a function in the price-output plane) to aggregate supply, ϕ. In both cases we suppose that aggregate demand calls the tune, determining the expected value of output in the current period.

The solution for the (expected) demand-determined levels of aggregate output and nominal rate of interest in the current period proceeds along somewhat conventional IS-LM lines, given the expectation of the next period's price level (which producers and consumers need in order to figure the expected real rate of interest). Calculating this expectation is the critical task in the analysis of the model.

Our portrayal of current output as demand-determined calls for a word about labor and money wage rates, which do not appear in the rudimentary model. A tempting interpretation of the model is that wages are revisable within the period in such a way as to clear the labor market, making "voluntary" whatever joblessness results from the demand-determined production.[6] But that interpretation strikes us as unrealistic in a short-run model, and logically uncomfortable besides since the fixity of ϕ in the rudimentary model implies that no decline (rise) in the real wage would reconcile workers to reduced (increased) employment. A more satisfactory interpretation is that, like current prices, current money wage rates have been predetermined early in the previous period. Thus deficient demand raises the volume of involuntary unemployment above the normal ("full-employment") level which is attributable to

[6] That interpretation would be symmetrical to Fischer's model in which goods prices drop within the period so as to make voluntary any slack capacity (idle machines) imposed by deficient aggregate demand.

imperfect knowledge about available workers and jobs; surplus demand lowers the volume of involuntary unemployment (firms hire some workers whom they otherwise would not have found acceptable) and perhaps also raises employees' overtime (which employees may be obligated to supply in such contingencies). However, the explicit introduction of a predetermined real wage, as done in the "full" model (Appendix), adds a third state variable. If that real wage varies little, the rudimentary model can be viewed as a tolerable approximation of the "full" model.[7] Other interpretations have firms hanging on to their spare employees, or the government replacing their wages in periods of slack demand. Some readers may prefer those latter interpretations.

Our algebraic description of the rudimentary model, save for the monetary rule, follows:

$$y_t = \phi + \psi_1(n_t - r_t) + \varepsilon_t^y, \tag{1}$$

$$c_t = -\gamma_1 r_t + \gamma_2 y_t + \gamma_3 \underset{t-1}{E}\, y_t + \varepsilon_t^c, \tag{2}$$

$$i_t = \mu_1(p_{t-1} - m_t) + \mu_2 y_t + \mu_3 \underset{t-1}{E}\, y_t + \varepsilon_t^i, \tag{3}$$

$$k_t = k_{t-1} + y_t - c_t, \tag{4}$$

$$p_t = \underset{t-1}{E}\, p_t + \varepsilon_t^p, \tag{5}$$

$$\underset{t-1}{E}\, y_{t+s} = \phi, \qquad s = 1, 2, \ldots, \tag{6}$$

for all integers t, where

y_t = real output during period t,

c_t = real consumption of output during period t,

m_t = logarithm of the money stock in period t,

p_t = logarithm of the price level decided at the start of t and prevailing in period $t + 1$,

k_t = stock of inventory at the end of period t, resulting from period t decisions,

E_{t-1} = mathematical conditional expectation operator, given information up to the beginning of period t: k_{t-1}, p_{t-1}, m_t,

[7] If workers should aim to stabilize the real wage, as in Fischer's model, and if they should succeed, the real wage is no complication, being a constant. The only complication then is that current full-capacity output is a variable depending (negatively) on the starting stock of inventory. But allowance for that relationship does not alter the fundamental structure of the model nor the qualitative features of its behavior.

i_t = money rate of interest from the start of period t to the start of period $t + 1$,

$r_t = i_t - E_{t-1}\, p_t + p_{t-1}$ = expected real rate of interest for period t,

$n_t = \upsilon_1 - \upsilon_2\, E_{t-1}\, k_t$ = expected natural rate of interest for period t, represented as a linear decreasing function of expected end-of-period inventory stock.

The parameters ϕ, ψ_1, γ_1, γ_2, γ_3, μ_1, μ_2, υ_1, and υ_2 are all positive, and $\gamma_2 + \gamma_3$ is less than one. The random disturbances, $(\varepsilon_t^y, \varepsilon_t^c, \varepsilon_t^i, \varepsilon_t^p)$, are serially independent with mean zero and covariance matrix $\sum$ that is *not* generally diagonal.

Equation (1) is the output-determination equation. The amounts that firms decide to produce are positively related to the difference between the expected natural rate of interest and the expected real rate of interest. The natural rate is defined as the expected marginal efficiency of (inventory) investment and is approximated by a linear decreasing function of the expected end-of-period inventory level.[8] Thus, intended inventory investment is a decreasing function of the expected real rate of interest and of expected end-of-period inventory stocks.

Consumption, in equation (2), depends negatively upon the expected real rate of interest. Consumption also depends upon expected and actual current income (hence upon expected and actual output) with positive, possibly unequal, marginal propensities to consume that add up to less than one.

The money rate of interest equates the quantity of real money balances demanded to the real supply. The logarithm of the former is negatively related to the money interest rate and positively to output and expected output, reflecting two sources of transactions demands for money. This gives equation (3).[9]

Equation (4) states that the excess of output over consumption is added to the stock of inventory, which does not depreciate or obsolesce.

The final two equations determine future price levels, expected and actual. Equation (5) states that the actual price level decided at the start of period t and prevailing over the next period is equal to the *expected* price level, given the information available at the start of period t, plus a random error term. The meaning of (6) is that at the start of each period the price level expected to prevail in any future period is such that the

[8] The rationale is increasing marginal costs of holding inventory (see Phelps 1969).

[9] Equations resembling (2) and (3) were used in a fixed-price model by Pashigian (1969). Note that the functional form connecting real cash demand to output is unusual implying decreasing transactions economies; it serves to preserve the linear parametric structure. (That linear structure should be considered an approximation over small variations around the central tendency of the variables.)

conditional expectation of output in that future period is equal to the full-employment level ϕ.

In our interpretation of (6), a twofold condition is met: first, money wage rates are expected to be just high enough in relation to expected prices next period that, if the price level and starting inventories turn out as expected, the corresponding expected real wage will be just high enough to trim the full-capacity quantity of labor demanded down to the size of the full-employment supply of labor.[10] Second, the price level expected to prevail next period is just low enough, and thus the corresponding expected liquidity is just large enough, that producers will be expected to want next period to accumulate the (algebraic) increase of inventories implied by their producing at full capacity.

These notions, expressed in (6), are implied by rational expectations theory as we understand it. Do they have any plausibility? We can offer a few heuristic remarks in their defense: if the representative firms were generally and regularly expected (in some or all initial states) to set money wage rates so low that on average their eventual demands for labor next period were partially frustrated, such a firm could raise its expected profit by setting a higher money wage for the next period in order to obtain a larger share of workers; there would be a tendency therefore for such wage expectations to be corrected. If firms were habitually setting prices so low as to demand-determine (via unexpectedly low real interest rates) production levels beyond what they had expected, it is likewise plausible that such a firm would adjust its pricing policies in such a way as to expect to sell less at higher prices next period (and to invest in larger inventories); if all firms so revise their policies, the systematic error in expectations about the next period will tend to be corrected.

To begin the analysis, let us now derive "reduced-form" expressions for y_t and k_t in terms of $E_{t-1}\, p_t$, m_t, p_{t-1}, and k_{t-1}. Because m_t is taken to be observed at the start of period t we have $E_{t-1}\, m_t = m_t$. Both m_t and $E_{t-1}\, p_t$ are taken in this section as given. Their levels are determined in the next section where we introduce the monetary policy rule.

Substituting (3) into (2), taking expectations, and solving for $E_{t-1}\, c_t$ results in

$$\underset{t-1}{E}\, c_t = \gamma_1 \underset{t-1}{E}\, p_t - \gamma_1(1 + \mu_1)p_{t-1} + \gamma_1\mu_1 m_t + (\gamma_2 + \gamma_3 - \gamma_1\mu_2 - \psi_1\mu_3) \underset{t-1}{E}\, y_t. \tag{7}$$

[10] The real wage thus determined (and its expectation a period earlier) cannot generally be constant over time because any change in the expected starting inventory next period (due say to above-or-below-average starting inventory this period) will alter the expected demand for labor next period at each real wage. The rudimentariness of the rudimentary model, again, is that it cannot handle real-wage variability over time.

Substituting (3) into (1), taking expectations, and solving for y_t using (7) gives the following reduced-form relation for output:

$$y_t = \alpha_0 + \alpha_1 \underset{t-1}{E} p_t - \alpha_1(1 + \mu_1)p_{t-1} + \alpha_1\mu_1 m_t + \alpha_2 k_{t-1} + v_t^y, \tag{8}$$

where

$$\alpha_0 = \frac{\phi + \psi_1 \upsilon_1}{1 + \psi_1\mu_2 + b} > 0,$$

$$\alpha_1 = \frac{\psi_1(1 + \upsilon_2\psi_1)}{1 + \psi_1\mu_2 + b} > 0,$$

$$\alpha_2 = -\frac{\psi_1\upsilon_2}{1 + \psi_1\mu_2 + b} < 0,$$

$$b = \psi_1[\mu_3 + \upsilon_2(1 - \gamma_2 - \gamma_3 + \gamma_1\mu_2 + \gamma_1\mu_3)] > 0,$$

$$v_t^y = \frac{-\psi_1\varepsilon_t^i + \varepsilon_t^y}{1 + \psi_1\mu_2}.$$

The parameter b (figuring in the α's) is positive because $\gamma_2 + \gamma_3 < 1$. It measures the extent to which expected increases in output tend to be damped by the implied increases in transactions demand for money and expected end-of-period inventories. Consequently, the larger b is the smaller the multipliers of the predetermined variables in (8) are. The reduced-form disturbance term v_t^y is a linear combination of structural disturbances in the output and interest-rate equations. Unexpected increases in the nominal rate of interest have a negative impact on output in the current period. (Output and the interest rate are simultaneously determined; the interest rate is not assumed to be predetermined as is the price of goods.)

To derive a reduced-form expression for k_t, substitute (2), (3), and (8) into (4) using (7) to obtain

$$k_t = \delta_0 + \delta_1 \underset{t-1}{E} p_t - \delta_1(1 + \mu_1)p_{t-1} + \delta_1\mu_1 m_t + \delta_2 k_{t-1} + v_t^k, \tag{9}$$

where

$$\delta_0 = \alpha_0 d > 0,$$

$$\delta_1 = \alpha_1 d - \gamma_1,$$

$$\delta_2 = 1 + \alpha_2 d < 1,$$

$$d = 1 - \gamma_2 - \gamma_3 + \gamma_1\mu_2 + \gamma_1\mu_3 > 0,$$

$$v_t^k = (1 - \gamma_2 + \gamma_1\mu_2)v_t^y - \varepsilon_t^c + \gamma_1\varepsilon_t^i.$$

The sign of d is positive because $\gamma_2 + \gamma_3$ is less than one. Therefore, since higher inventory levels tend to have a negative impact on output ($\alpha_2 < 0$), the coefficient δ_2 is less than one. The sign of δ_1 will be positive provided the stimulus to output from the associated fall of the expected real rate of interest exceeds the stimulus to consumption, taking all monetary and real feedbacks into account. That is, using the definition of α_1 in (8), δ_1 can be written $[\psi_1(1 - \gamma_2 - \gamma_2) - \gamma_1]/(1 + \psi_1\mu_2 + b)$ and therefore has a positive sign if $\psi_1(1 - \gamma_2 - \gamma_3) > \gamma_1$. In a short-run model it is likely that the consumption propensities are relatively small, so that we would expect δ_1 to be positive. An increase in the expected price level tends to increase the end-of-period capital stock. The analysis which follows, however, does not require that δ_1 is positive.

The variable $E_{t-1}\, p_t$ in the reduced-form equations (8) and (9) remains to be determined (next section). Until we specify the class of monetary policy rules we cannot show that $E_{t-1}\, p_t$ is determinate nor that other conditions assuring a solution will obtain. But assume provisionally that a solution does exist for some class of policy rules. Then we may ask: What are the conditional expectations in period t of end-of-period inventory and output *1 period or* s *periods ahead*—given the current information about k_{t-1}, p_{t-1}, m_t, and given some admissible sequence $\{E_{t-1}\, m_{t+s} \mid s = 1, 2, \ldots\}$? The question is apposite for we want to show that the rate at which, say, an "excess" inventory is expected to be worked off over the future is independent of expected future money stocks and thus invariant to the expected policy rule (from the admissible set). For if it were *not* invariant, the output equation would evidently be logically incomplete and misleading.

To answer that let us add s to each subscript in the output and end-of-period inventory equations (8) and (9), take expectations, and use (6) to substitute ϕ for $E_{t-1}\, y_{t+s}$. For simplicity of notation, a conditional expectation like $E_{t-1}\, k_{t+s}$ will be denoted (leaving the index t implicit) by $\hat{k}_s$; correspondingly, the variables $\hat{p}_s$ and $\hat{m}_s$ denote forecasts of decisions taken "s periods ahead." In these terms, we then have for $s \geq 1$

$$\phi = \alpha_1\hat{p}_s - \alpha_1(1 + \mu_1)\hat{p}_{s-1} + \alpha_1\mu_1\hat{m}_s + \alpha_2\hat{k}_{s-1} + \alpha_0, \tag{10}$$

$$\hat{k}_s = \delta_1\hat{p}_s - \delta_1(1 + \mu_1)\hat{p}_{s-1} + \delta_1\mu_1\hat{m}_s + \delta_2\hat{k}_{s-1} + \delta_0. \tag{11}$$

Subtracting δ_1/α_1 times (10) from (11) results in

$$\hat{k}_s = \left(\delta_2 - \frac{\delta_1}{\alpha_1}\alpha_2\right)\hat{k}_{s-1} + \frac{\delta_1}{\alpha_1}(\phi - \alpha_0) + \delta_0 \tag{12}$$

for all $s \geq 1$, independent of the sequence $\{\hat{m}_s, s = 1, 2, \ldots\}$. The coefficient of $\hat{k}_{s-1}$ in (12) can be shown to equal $(1 + \gamma_1 v_2)^{-1}$ which is less than one, indicating the tendency of conditionally expected future inventories to "regress toward the mean." The invariance of this process to monetary policy is an outcome of excluding nonneutral wealth and liquidity effects from the model.

II. Determining Price Expectations for a Class of Policy Rules

The reduced-form expressions for output and inventory, (8) and (9), show how m_t affects those variables for a given expectation of the price level next period—$E_{t-1}\,p_t$ or, equivalently, $\hat{p}_0$ in the abbreviated notation. But as (10) shows, the value of $\hat{p}_0$ that equates expected output next period to ϕ depends upon the expected money supply next period, $\hat{m}_1$, and the conditional expectation now (at t) of the price level that will then be expected to be set for the following period, $\hat{p}_1$. Similarly, $\hat{p}_1$ will depend upon $\hat{m}_2$ and $\hat{p}_2$, and so on. Thus we see that the effects of a monetary policy upon current variables (compared with another monetary policy) depend upon its expected consequences for the supply of money and the level of prices over all future periods, not solely upon its determination of the current money supply.

What would be a reasonable sort of monetary policy in the present model? Consider the "unconditional full-employment" policy of setting m_{t+s} equal to that linear combination of k_{t+s-1}, p_{t+s-1}, and $E_{t+s-1}\,p_{t+s}$ such that $E_{t+s-1}\,y_{t+s}$ in (8) equals ϕ. That policy, omitting again the index t, implies the rule $m_s = (\alpha_1\mu_1)^{-1}[\alpha_1\mu_1 p_{s-1} - \alpha_1(E_{s-1}\,p_s - p_{s-1}) - \alpha_2 k_{s-1} + \phi - \alpha_0]$, for $s = 0, 1, 2, \ldots$. But under that rule, the conditional expectation $\hat{m}_s$ turns (10) into an identity that is satisfied by any value of the price level expected to prevail s periods ahead, $\hat{p}_{s-1}$. A consequence of this indeterminacy is that it threatens to make monetary policy incapable of having any effect on output at all. If the central bank should raise the money rate of interest, in order to reduce expected output to ϕ or some other lower level, firms will feel free to raise the prices they are setting for the next period by enough to nullify the bank's intended effect upon the expected real rate of interest—as long as each firm expects other firms will be similarly passing along the higher nominal interest cost (and why not?).

Consider, second, the unconditional policy to fix the (expected) money rate of interest. By (3) and (8), the implied rule is $m_s = \mu_1^{-1}[\mu_1 p_{s-1} + (\mu_2 + \mu_3)\,E_{s-1}\,y_s - i^*]$, where i^* is the target money interest rate. Upon taking the conditional expectation, m_s, and using $y_s = \phi$, equation (11) gives the following result for the conditional expectation of the price level predeterminedly prevailing s periods ahead: $\hat{p}_{s-1} = \hat{p}_s + \alpha_1^{-1}\alpha_2\hat{k}_{s-1} + (\mu_2 + \mu_3 - \alpha_1^{-1})\phi - i^*$. We could thus calculate, if this solution made sense, the conditional expected value of the sequence of expected inflation rates prevailing next period and beyond; they have to produce the sequence of conditionally expected real rates of interest consistent with the conditionally expected sequence of inventory stocks. But there is never a determinate conditionally expected price level some number of periods in the future, nor some asymptotic future price level, from which we could work backward to determine the expected price *level* next period. Consequently the expected inflation rate in the current period t and the associated expected current output are indeterminate. The success and viability of this monetary policy is thus cast in doubt.

The defect of policy rules that focus myopically on only current desiderata—current output and money interest being the examples—is that they fail to attend to the system effects upon expectations of future price levels that they create or permit; in so doing they jeopardize their own objectives. A reasonable monetary policy evidently must pay heed to the price level or its rate of change.

Here we shall study the class of policy rules that make the money stock (in logs) in any period a linear time-independent function solely of the state variables in that period. Owing to the serial independence of all the random disturbances, our model would be first-order linear under the passive rule of constant money over time; it is a convenient property of the present class of policy rules that they preserve the linear Markov property.

Thus the central bank plans, and is understood by the public to plan, the supply of money s periods ahead of period t according to the contingency rule

$$m_s = g_0 + g_1 p_{s-1} + g_2 k_{s-1}, \qquad s = 0, 1, 2, \ldots, \tag{13}$$

where g_0, g_1, and g_2 are known parameters, independent of s. The particular rule adopted is characterized by the values of these parameters, especially the latter two. A passive (1959) Friedman rule sets both g_1 and g_2 equal to zero while active rules do not. Our (minimum) objective is to show that the choice of g_1 and g_2 makes a difference for the variance of output.

Substitution of this money supply rule into the output and inventory equations, (8) and (9), yields

$$y_t = \alpha_1 \underset{t-1}{E} p_t - \alpha_1[1 + \mu_1(1 - g_1)]p_{t-1} + (\alpha_2\alpha_1\mu_1 g_2)k_{t-1} + \alpha_1\mu_1 g_0 + \alpha_0 + v_t^y, \tag{14}$$

$$k_t = \delta_1 \underset{t-1}{E} p_t - \delta_1[1 + \mu_1(1 - g_1)]p_{t-1} + (\delta_2 + \delta_1\mu_1 g_2)k_{t-1} + \delta_1\mu_1 g_0 + \delta_0 + v_t^k. \tag{15}$$

Equation (15), upon taking expectations, provides a linear equation for $E_{t-1}\, k_t$ as a function of the unknown $E_{t-1}\, p_t$. This relationship is the rising line in figure 1 with slope δ_1^{-1} and intercept depending on the predetermined p_{t-1} and k_{t-1}. To determine $E_{t-1}\, p_t$ we shall now derive an equation for $E_{t-1}\, p_t$ as a function of $E_{t-1}\, k_t$.

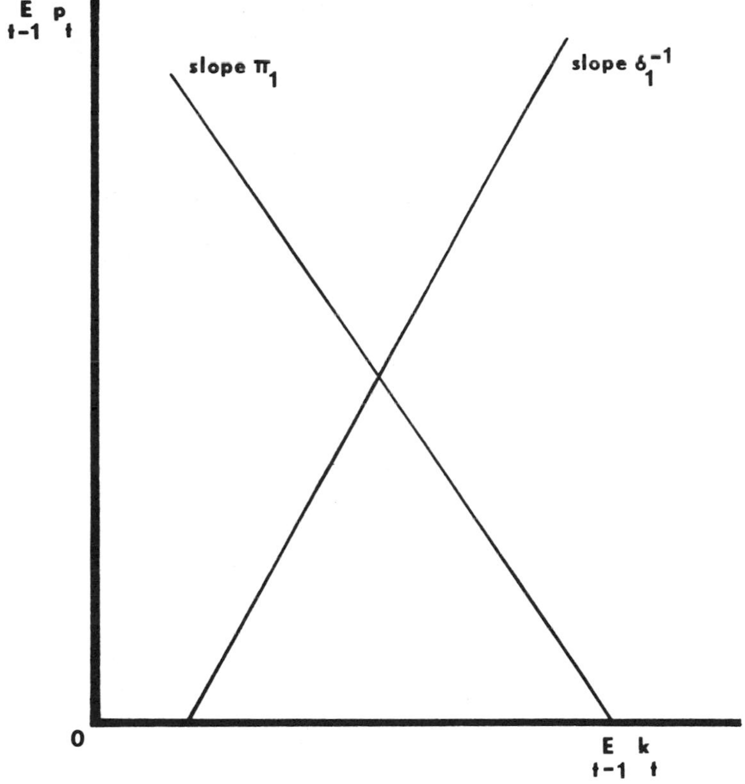

FIG. 1

To do this we use the expected future equilibrium assumption, (6), to obtain the rule-specific analogues to (10) and (11),

$$\phi = \alpha_1\hat{p}_s - \alpha_1[1 + \mu_1(1 - g_1)]\hat{p}_{s-1} + (\alpha_2 + \alpha_1\mu_1 g_2)\hat{k}_{s-1} + \alpha_1\mu_1 g_0 + \alpha_0, \tag{16}$$

$$\hat{k}_s = \delta_1\hat{p}_s - \delta_1[1 + \mu_1(1 - g_1)]\hat{p}_{s-1} + (\delta_2 + \delta_1\mu_1 g_2)\hat{k}_{s-1} + \delta_1\mu_1 g_2 + \delta_0, \tag{17}$$

$s = 1, 2, \ldots,$ where again we use the notation $\hat{p}_s = E_{t-1}\,p_{t+s}$ and $\hat{k}_s = E_{t-1}\,k_{t+s}$ for the period t forecasts of the price level and starting inventory that will prevail s periods ahead.

Recall the argument for (12), which follows again from the above two equations as well as from the more general (10) and (11), according to which the conditional expectation of future money stocks are "neutral" for the conditional forecast of investment s periods ahead, $s \geq 1$. We may thus use (12) in place of (17) and rearrange terms in (16) to obtain

$$\hat{p}_{s-1} = a_1\hat{p}_s + a_2\hat{k}_{s-1} + a_3, \tag{18}$$

$$\hat{k}_s = a_4\hat{k}_{s-1} + a_5, \tag{19}$$

where

$$a_1 = \frac{1}{1 + \mu_1(1 - g_1)},$$

$$a_2 = \frac{\alpha_2 + \alpha_1\mu_1 g_2}{\alpha_1[1 + \mu_1(1 - g_1)]},$$

$$a_3 = \frac{\alpha_1\mu_1 g_0 - \phi + \alpha_0}{\alpha_1[1 + \mu_1(1 - g_1)]},$$

$$a_4 = \frac{1}{1 + \gamma_1 v_2},$$

$$a_5 = \frac{\delta_1}{\alpha_1}(\phi - \alpha_0) + \delta_0.$$

The parameters a_1, a_2, and a_3 are subject to the choice of policy—within limits.

It will be useful here to recall Samuelson's (1947) Correspondence Principle which recognizes that comparative-statics analysis would be anomalous without the added hypothesis of stability, so that the analyst may as well proceed to take advantage of any restrictions on the parameters of his model which such stability would entail. By a methodological parallel, we maintain that one cannot with internal consistency do comparative-policy analysis in a model having a continuum of equilibria or having no equilibrium at all, and consequently we are free to impose, for the purpose of that analysis, such conditions on the parameters as may be implied by such determinateness of the equilibrium path.

It follows that we must bound the parameter so that $a_1 < 1$.[11] Consider (18) and (19) under this assumption. Making repeated use of (18) we can work "backward" from some $\hat{p}_s$ "expected" to be determined during

[11] If $a_1 = 1$, then only the expected inflation rate $\hat{p}_s - \hat{p}_{s-1}$ appears in (31) and (32) so that any arbitrary $\hat{p}_0$ will satisfy these equations. If $a_1 > 1$, then $\hat{p}_0$ is also indeterminate. To see this, consider (31) and (32) as a first-order difference equation in the vector $(\hat{p}_s, \hat{k}_s)$. The two characteristic roots of this system are a_1^{-1} and a_4, so that when $a_1^{-1} < 1$ any arbitrary $\hat{p}_0$ will generate an acceptable stable path of expected (log) price levels, and hence a bounded expected inflation rate. (Note that if $a_1 < 1$, the case considered in the text, then $(\hat{p}_0, \hat{k}_0)$ must lie on the saddle point path given by the characteristic vector associated with the root a_4, in order for $\hat{p}_s$ not to diverge geometrically. Equation [24] is just this saddle point requirement.)

any period $s > 1$. If $s = 2$, for example, $\hat{p}_0 = a_1(a_1\hat{p}_2 + a_2\hat{k}_1 + a_3) + a_2\hat{k}_0 + a_3$. In general, for any $s = 1, 2, \ldots$

$$\hat{p}_0 = a_1^s\hat{p}_s + a_2 \sum_{j=0}^{s-1} a_1^j\hat{k}_j + a_3 \sum_{j=0}^{s-1} a_1^j. \tag{20}$$

By successive "forward" substitutions in (19) we have

$$\hat{k}_s = a_4^s\hat{k}_0 + a_5 \sum_{i=0}^{s-1} a_4^i. \tag{21}$$

Substituting (21) for $\hat{k}_j$ in (20) yields

$$\hat{p}_0 = a_1^s\hat{p}_s + a_2 \sum_{j=0}^{s-1} a_1^j a_4^j\hat{k}_0 + a_2a_5 \sum_{j=0}^{s-1} a_1^j \sum_{i=0}^{j-1} a_4^i + a_3 \sum_{j=0}^{s-1} a_1^j. \tag{22}$$

In analyzing (22) we ought to interpret the present model as a linear approximation to a model in which the counterpart to (3) places both a lower bound (say, zero) and an upper bound on the money rate of interest. (At the lower bound money will not be offered for property claims and at the upper bound goods will not be offered for money.) It can then be argued that the methodological requirements stated above call for the further hypothesis that

$$\lim_{s\to\infty} a_1^s\hat{p}_s = 0. \tag{23}$$

For consider the contrary hypothesis, that $a_1^s\hat{p}_s$ would *not* vanish in the limit. Then the *log* of the price level expected in the future would be either rising or falling geometrically, if not faster, with s and thus (the inflation rate and) the money interest rate would be projected to be either rising or falling *without bound*—until striking some interest-rate boundary. Such expectations would raise one or two anomalies: First, it would make little sense to do comparative policy analysis of an economy projected to be on a collision course with an interest-rate boundary and consequent monetary collapse. Better to ask whether there do not exist some monetary policies that will avert the projected catastrophe! One normally wants the equilibrium one studies not only to exist but to be viable. Second, the very notion of a forecasted path of expected values (or conditional probability distributions) running into a boundary contains some analytical contradictions—much as the aberrant capital-goods paths in the deterministic "Hahn problem" were shown by Shell-Stiglitz (1967) to fail the full test for equilibrium: if the money interest rate were projected to hit the *upper* bound in a finite number of periods, money would be expected to be worthless then; so money would not be expected to be accepted as payment for goods the previous period and would therefore be expected to be worthless then, and so on backward to period $t + 1$; therefore $\hat{p}_0$ would equal plus infinity, and hence money would not be accepted in payment for goods even in the *present* period. This argument is (unrigorous) proof-by-contradiction that no rational expectation equilibrium in the present period exists under such a hyperinflationary projection of the rate of inflation. Now for the other (harder) case. If the money interest rate were projected to hit the *lower* bound in finite time, then the economy would be projected to be heading for an ultra-Keynesian collapse; but it is doubtful that the equations of our model would correctly describe the path of the economy if such a fate were expected. So an assumption contrary to (23) would not be suitable for comparative policy analysis of the model in its present form.

If $a_1^s \hat{p}_s$ vanishes, then (22) converges to

$$\hat{p}_0 = \pi_1 \hat{k}_0 + \pi_0, \tag{24}$$

where

$$\pi_1 = \frac{a_2}{1 - a_1 a_4} = \frac{\alpha_2 + \alpha_1 \mu_1 g_2}{\alpha_1[1 + \mu_1(1 - g_1) - (1 + \gamma_1 \upsilon_2)^{-1}]},$$

$$\pi_0 = \frac{a_1 a_2 a_5}{(1 - a_1)(1 - a_1 a_4)} + \frac{a_3}{1 - a_1}.$$

Recalling that $\hat{p}_0 = E_{t-1}\, p_t$ and $\hat{k}_0 = E_{t-1}\, k_t$, we note that (24) is the other needed relationship for determining $E_{t-1}\, p_t$. It is described by the downward-sloped line in figure 1 with slope π_1 and intercept π_0. With $a_1 < 1$, we have $\pi_1 < 0$ if and only if $g_2 < \upsilon_2 \mu_1^{-1} a_4$. This latter inequality clearly holds when $g_2 = 0$. In that case it can also be shown that $\pi_1 \neq \delta_1^{-1}$ so that the two lines in figure 1 will definitely have an intersection. In order to insure that there is an intersection when $g_2 \neq 0$ we will restrict the admissible values of g_2 to those for which $\pi_1 \neq \delta_1^{-1}$. The resulting intersection of these two lines will then uniquely determine the expected price level next period:

$$\underset{t-1}{E}\, p_t = (1 - \pi_1 \delta_1)^{-1} \times \{-\delta_1 \pi_1 [1 + \mu_1(1 - g_1)] p_{t-1} + \pi_1(\delta_2 + \delta_1 \mu_1 g_2) k_{t-1} + \pi_1(\delta_1 \mu_1 g_0 + \delta_0) + \pi_0\}. \tag{25}$$

III. Operating Characteristics of the Stochastic System

Having derived the unknown $E_{t-1}\, p_t$ implied by the expected future equilibrium assumption, we can deduce a pair of stochastic difference equations in the state variables p_t and k_t. Output can then be written as a function of these two state variables and a random disturbance term to complete the stochastic characterization of the rudimentary model. For ease of notation in the policy analysis which follows we introduce the following four parameters:

$$H_1 = 1 + \mu_1(1 - g_1),$$
$$H_2 = \delta_2 + \delta_1\mu_1 g_2,$$
$$G_1 = H_1 - a_4,$$
$$G_2 = H_2 - a_4.$$

Note that H_1 and G_1 depend only on g_1 and that H_2 and G_2 depend only on g_2. The coefficients of p_{t-1} and k_{t-1} in equation (15) are $-\delta_1 H_2$ and H_2, respectively. The restrictions on these parameters implied by our policy restrictions in Section II are that $H_1 > 1$ and $H_1 \neq H_2$.

Substituting (25) into (5) and (15) yields

$$p'_t = \beta_{11}p'_{t-1} + \beta_{12}k'_{t-1} + \varepsilon^p_t, \tag{26}$$
$$k'_t = \beta_{21}p'_{t-1} + \beta_{22}k'_{t-1} + v^k_t, \tag{27}$$

where $p'_t = p_t - \bar{p}$ and $k'_t = k_t - \bar{k}$ are deviations from the steady-state means, which equal $\bar{k} = (1 - a_4)^{-1}a_5$ and $\bar{p} = (1 - a_1)^{-1}(a_2\bar{k} + a_3)$, and where

$$\beta_{11} = -G_2H_1(G_1 - G_2)^{-1},$$
$$\beta_{12} = G_2H_2\delta_1^{-1}(G_1 - G_2)^{-1},$$
$$\beta_{21} = -G_1H_1\delta_1(G_1 - G_2)^{-1},$$
$$\beta_{22} = G_1H_2(G_1 - G_2)^{-1}.$$

The dynamics of this bivariate first-order difference equation are singular in that the matrix of β coefficients is singular. Hence there is a linear combination of p'_t and k'_t which is serially independent (since the random shocks in the structure of the rudimentary model are serially independent) and is given by

$$u_t \equiv \delta_1G_1p'_t - G_2k'_t = \delta_1G_1\varepsilon^p_t - G_2v^k_t. \tag{28}$$

This singularity is implied by the stability requirement that the 1-period conditional forecasts of p_t and k_t have the time-invariant relationship given in (24). The connection between (28) and (24) is made clear by noting that $\pi_1 = G_2(\delta_1G_1)^{-1}$. Using equation (28), p_t and k_t can be decomposed (by substitution into [26] and [27]) into a pair of univariate first-order autoregressive processes with an additional moving average of u_{t-1} and ε^p_t or v^k_t:

$$p'_t = a_4p'_{t-1} - H_2\delta_1^{-1}(G_1 - G_2)^{-1}u_{t-1} + \varepsilon^p_t \tag{29}$$
$$k'_t = a_4k'_{t-1} - H_1(G_1 - G_2)^{-1}u_{t-1} + v^k_t. \tag{30}$$

An equation for output can be derived from (14) by substituting for $E_{t-1}\, p_t$ and subsequently substituting for p_{t-1} and k_{t-1} using (26) and (27). This results in

$$y_t = \phi - \alpha_1 \delta_1^{-1}(G_1 + a_4)(G_1 - G_2)^{-1} u_{t-1} + v_t^y. \qquad (31)$$

The term involving u_{t-1} in the above three equations represents the impact of sticky prices on the stochastic evolution of inventories, prices, and output. If prices were flexible (à la Sargent-Wallace) then this term would not appear; output would be a serially independent random variable with mean ϕ and variance equal to var (v_t^y). This sticky price-generated noise is a linear combination of the four disturbances ε_{t-1}^y, ε_{t-1}^c, ε_{t-1}^i, and ε_{t-1}^p in the structural equations, so that its variance will depend on variances and covariances of these terms. Since this noise is lagged, there is a lag of shocks from one period to the next. While this 1-period lag may lead to some important dynamic phenomena (especially when mixed with other sources of serial correlation), the fundamental aspect of sticky prices in this model is more noise rather than more dynamics.

More important for policy implications is that the variance of this noise, though not the mean, depends on the policy parameters g_1 and g_2, while the other parameters (a_4 and ϕ) and the variances of ε_t^p, v_t^k, and v_t^y are policy invariant. This indicates not only how monetary policy can be useful for stabilization, but also that its utility arises solely from the inflexibility of prices.

To investigate these stabilization possibilities we will consider the effect of g_1 and g_2 on the steady-state distribution of price and output. As we only examine the variances and covariance of this distribution we are implicitly assuming either normally distributed errors or a quadratic social welfare function in p_t and y_t. Concentration on the steady-state distributions implies an infinite horizon with no discounting, which is a reasonable criterion for stabilization analysis.

In order to derive the steady-state variance of p_t we must consider its joint stationary distribution with k_t as evidenced in (26) and (27). Let Ω, with elements ω_{11}, ω_{22}, ω_{12}, be the variance-covariance matrix of (ε_t^p, v_t^k) which can be derived from $\sum$, and let B be the matrix of β-coefficients in (26) and (27). Then the steady-state variance-covariance matrix of (p_t, k_t) is given by

$$\sum_{i=0}^{\infty} B^i \Omega (B')^i = \Omega + (1 - a_4^2)^{-1} B \Omega B'$$

since $B^{i+1} = a_4^i B$, $i = 0, 1, 2, \ldots$. Letting

$$h = \delta_1^2 H_1^2 \omega_{11} - 2\delta_1 H_1 H_2 \omega_{12} + H_2^2 \omega_{22},$$

we have

$$\text{var}\ (k_t) = \omega_{22} + G_1^2(1 - a_4^2)^{-1}(G_1 - G_2)^{-2}h \tag{32}$$

$$\text{cov}\ (p_t, k_t) = \omega_{12} + G_1G_2\delta_1^{-1}(1 - a_4^2)^{-1}(G_1 - G_2)^{-2}h \tag{33}$$

$$\text{var}\ (p_t) = \omega_{11} + G_2^2\delta_1^{-2}(1 - a_4^2)^{-1}(G_1 - G_2)^{-2}h. \tag{34}$$

Though our main concern is with price variance versus *output* variance, it is illuminating to examine the effect of policy on the joint distribution of price and inventories. There is a scale effect of policy, common to both variances and the covariance, represented by $(G_1 - G_2)^{-2}h$, as well as the relative effects of G_1 and G_2 on real and nominal magnitudes. Setting G_2 to zero (that is, $g_2 = (a_4 - \delta_2)\delta_1\mu_1^{-1}$) will minimize the variance of p_t at ω_{11}. The economics behind this is that m_s is then anticipated to respond to k_{s-1} (in all periods) in such a way that the same expected price level $\hat{p}_s$ is generated for all expected inventory levels. This implies that $\hat{p}_s = \bar{p}$ for all s and therefore that $\hat{p}_t = \bar{p} + \varepsilon_t^p$. Geometrically this policy twists the downward-sloping line in figure 1 to the horizontal.

It may be thought that setting $G_1 = 0$ in order to make this line vertical will bring the variance of k_t to ω_{22}, but this alternative is not feasible because it implies that $g_1 > 1$, which leads to an indeterminate price level. The line will tend to the vertical as $g_2 \rightarrow \infty$, but then the variance of the price level will tend to infinity.

Rather than pursuing a policy to minimize var (k_t), we consider the more relevant real variable y_t, the variance of which can be calculated directly from (31) and is given by

$$E(y_t - \phi)^2 = \alpha_1^2\delta_1^{-2}(G_1 + a_4)^2(G_1 - G_2)^{-2}\ \text{var}\ u_t + \omega_y \tag{35}$$

where $\omega_y = \text{var}\ (v_t^y)$ and where var $u_t = \delta_1^2G_1^2\omega_{11} - 2\delta_1G_1G_2\omega_{12} + G_2^2\omega_{22}$.

As stated in the introduction, our central purpose in this paper is to restore the faith that monetary policy makes a difference for output and employment. That it does make a difference is evident from (35). To take the simplest case, let $G_2 = 0$ so that the variance of the price level is held to its minimum ω_{11}. If $g_1 = 0$, then the variance of output is $\omega_y + \alpha_1^2(1 + \mu_1)^2\omega_{11}$; but as g_1 is increased toward 1 the variance of output is reduced toward $\omega_y + \alpha_1^2\omega_{11}$. So a simple proof by contradiction establishes the theorem that perfectly anticipated monetary policy affects the variance of output and thus employment.

It is possible of course to reduce the variance of output below $\omega_y + \alpha_1^2\omega_{11}$ if we are willing to tolerate an increase in the variance of the price level. Ignoring the constant ω_y, this output variance is the ratio of two quadratic forms in the vector (G_1, G_2) multiplied by $(G_1 + a_4)^2$. The numerator quadratic form is var u_t and the denominator quadratic form (which is not positive definite) is $(G_1 - G_2)^2$; since the ratio is homogeneous of degree zero in G_1 and G_2 only the direction of (G_1, G_2) matters for the minimization of this ratio. That is, if (G_1^*, G_2^*) minimizes the ratio, then so does $(\lambda G_1^*, \lambda G_2^*)$ for arbitrary λ. But since this ratio is multiplied by $(G_1 + a_4)^2$ the minimum of the variance of output occurs when λ is chosen such that $(G_1^* + a_4) = 1$. Since this value of G_1 implies that $g_1 = 1$, a case ruled out in Section II because of the resulting indeterminacy of the price level, it is not possible to reach this minimum, though one can get arbitrarily close.

The minimizing value of G_2/G_1 is given by $(\delta_1^2\omega_{11} - \delta_1\omega_{12})/(\delta_1\omega_{12} - \omega_{22})$, a function of δ_1 and the variance covariance matrix of ε_t^p and v_t^k. The larger is the structural price variance ω_{11}, the larger g_2 will be relative to g_1, the money stock being relatively less dependent on the price level. Conversely, if real disturbances have large variances (ω_{22} is relatively large), then the money stock will depend relatively less on inventories for output variance minimizing policy.

The resulting minimum value of the output variance obtained at $g_1 = 1$ is given by $[\alpha_1^2(\omega_{11}\omega_{22} - \omega_{12}^2)]/(\delta_1^2\omega_{11} - 2\delta_1\omega_{12} + \omega_{22}) + \omega_y$, which is less than $\omega_y + a_1^2\omega_{11}$. However, the variance of the price level will be greater than ω_{11} at this choice of policy. Further, since the output variance is at a minimum, additional increases in the variance of price will not decrease the variance of output. Therefore, the optimal choice of policy for a utility function which weights both variances (at least with this class of policy rules) will give variances which lie somewhere between the minimum price variance and the minimum output variance points given above. Note also that the passive policy for which $g_1 = 0$ and $g_2 = 0$ will not in general be efficient with regard to these two variances, though there may be some model parameter configuration for which this is the case.

Although we have not placed great emphasis here on correlations between output and price at different points in time, it is of interest to ask whether such correlations could lead to a statistical Phillips curve. Suppose that an econometrician attempts to estimate a Phillips curve by regressing the next inflation rate $p_t - p_{t-1}$ on the deviation of current output from full employment $\phi - y_t$ using data on price and output generated by this model. Given a large enough sample, a downward-sloping Phillips curve would appear if $E[(p_t - p_{t-1})(\phi - y_t)]$ were negative. To show that this covariance may well be negative, we will consider the case where ε_t^p is uncorrelated with ε_t^y, ε_t^i, and ε_t^c (such correlation could of course cause a statistical Phillips curve independently of sticky prices). We also assume that $g_1 = g_2 = 0$. The covariance is then given by

$$E[(p_t - p_{t-1})(\phi - y_t)] = -(1 - a_4)\alpha_1 H_1 G_1(G_1 - G_2)^{-1}\omega_{11} - \alpha_1 H_1 H_2 \delta_1^{-2}(G_1 - G_2)^{-2} \operatorname{var} u_t. \tag{36}$$

Both expressions on the right-hand side of (36) are negative, because $G_1 - G_2 = 1 + \mu_1 - \delta_2 > 0$, $G_1 < 0$, and $a_4 < 1$. Therefore, the inflexibility of prices generates a negatively sloped Phillips curve. On average, the greater is the realized rate of inflation from the start of period t to the start of period $t + 1$, the greater is production during period t. Note that suitable choice of policy can reduce this correlation and even reverse the sign. Such action may not, however, be optimal.

IV. Summary and Extensions

The foregoing has presumably made its primary point—the sense in which monetary policy, even systematic and correctly anticipated policy, can make a difference for the stability of output in a rational expectations model with sticky prices and wages. Among the other results obtained, two further conclusions may be recalled: the passive monetary rule in which the money supply does not respond to the state of the economy will not generally be efficient with regard to the variances of output and the price level. In fact, no particular policy rule among the class of rules studied will be undominated in this respect for every configuration of the parameters. It was also shown that hyperactivist rules that attempt to insulate output or interest rates from the state of the economy will leave the expected future price level, and thus current aggregate demand, completely indeterminate.

Nevertheless, the class of policy rules analyzed above and the structure of the model itself have certain limitations and thus point to the desirability of certain extensions, a few of which we would like at least to identify. One of the extensions to be discussed, a variation on the policy rule, is straightforward enough to be sketched here.

The policy rules in (13) may seem general, apart from their linearity, but they are not. They express aversion to a discrepancy of the price level from some desired mean rather than aversion to a deviation of the expected inflation rate from its desired norm. We explore here some consequences of a class of policy rules of the latter type. For expository convenience we take the "desired expected inflation rate" to be zero.

Consider the class of policies constrained to make the conditional expectation of the inflation rate $E_{t-1} p_t - p_{t-1}$ equal to zero for all t. If the central bank sought in every period to choose *current* m_t such that $E_{t-1} p_t = p_{t-1}$, then output and employment would be unnecessarily disrupted. For example, in order to lower the expected price level using m_t it would be necessary to lower expected end-of-period inventories $E_{t-1} k_t$ by reducing expected output (see the downward-sloping relation in fig. 1). The central bank can better satisfy the above constraint by committing itself to a rule with the property that the current expectation of *next* period's money stock $E_{t-1} m_{t+1}$ makes $E_{t-1} p_t = p_{t-1}$, that the current expectation of the money stock 2 periods ahead $E_{t-1}\, m_{t+2}$ makes $E_{t-1}\, p_{t+1} = E_{t-1}\, p_t$ and, in general, that the current expectation of the money stock s periods ahead $E_{t-1}\, m_{t+s}$ makes $E_{t-1}\, p_{t+s} = E_{t-1}\, p_{t+s-1}$. By (10), the value of $E_{t-1}\, m_{t+1}$ which makes $E_{t-1}\, p_t = p_{t-1}$ is $E_{t-1}\, m_{t+1} = (1 + \mu_1)\mu_1^{-1} p_{t-1} - \mu_1^{-1} E_{t-1} p_{t+1} - (\alpha_1\mu_1)^{-1}(\alpha_2 E_{t-1} k_t + \alpha_0 - \phi)$. But since $E_{t-1}\, m_{t+2}$ is expected subsequently to make $E_{t-1}\, p_{t+1}$ equal to $E_{t-1}\, p_t$, which in turn is now equal to p_{t-1}, this expression reduces to

$$\underset{t-1}{E}\, m_{t+1} = p_{t-1} - (\alpha_1\mu_1)^{-1}(\alpha_2 \underset{t-1}{E}\, k_t + \alpha_0 - \phi). \tag{37}$$

The advantage of this type of rule is that actual m_{t+1} need not equal $E_{t-1}\, m_{t+1}$ so that current realizations of the rule can be used to stabilize output and employment. Such a contingency rule that obeys the constraint expressed in equation (37) is a convex combination of $E_{t-1}\, m_{t+1}$ and that level of m_{t+1}, call it m_{t+1}^{ϕ}, which would be necessary for (expected) full employment. This latter quantity of money is given by equating $E_t\, y_{t+1}$ in (8) to ϕ, i.e., $\alpha_0 + \alpha_1(E_t\, p_{t+1} - p_t) + \alpha_1\mu_1 \times (m_{t+1}^{\phi} - p_t) + \alpha_2 k_t = \phi$, and noting that the rule makes $E_t\, p_{t+1}$ equal to p_t. Hence

$$m_{t+1}^{\phi} = p_t - (\alpha_1\mu_1)^{-1}(\alpha_2 k_t + \alpha_0 - \phi). \tag{38}$$

Then the class of rules suggested is describable by

$$m_{t+1} = \underset{t-1}{E}\, m_{t+1} + \theta\,(m_{t+1}^{\phi} - \underset{t-1}{E}\, m_{t+1}), \qquad 0 < \theta < 1. \tag{39}$$

The latter term is the quantity of money in period $t + 1$ that was unanticipated at the beginning of period t. By taking expectations in (38) conditional on information at the start of period t, $E_{t-1}\, m_{t+1}^{\phi}$ can be seen to equal $E_{t-1}\, m_{t+1}$ so that the actual discrepancy, $m_{t+1}^{\phi} - E_{t-1}\, m_{t+1}$, is a white noise random variable from the vantage point of period t, given only k_{t-1}, p_{t-1} and m_t.

Some implications of the rule in (39) emerge if we make the substitutions from (37) and (38):

$$\begin{aligned} m_{t+1} &= p_{t-1} - \alpha_2(\alpha_1\mu_1)^{-1} \underset{t-1}{E}\, k_t + (\alpha_1\mu_1)^{-1}(\phi - \alpha_0) \\ &\quad + \theta\left[p_t - p_{t-1} - \alpha_2(\alpha_1\mu_1)^{-1}\left(k_t - \underset{t-1}{E}\, k_t\right)\right]. \end{aligned} \tag{40}$$

A novelty of this rule, compared with (26), is that both the current price level and the previous period's price level figure in the determination of the current money supply. (The memory of the previously expected starting inventory is also a new determinant.) Although the central bank in period t could not care less about p_{t-2} per se, (40) requires that it set real balances according to

$$\begin{aligned} m_t - p_{t-1} = & -(1 - \theta)(p_{t-1} - p_{t-2}) \\ & - \alpha_2(\alpha_1\mu_1)^{-1}\left[\theta k_{t-1} + (1 - \theta) \underset{t-2}{E}\, k_{t-2}\right] \\ & + (\alpha_1\mu_1)^{-1}(\phi - \alpha_0). \end{aligned} \tag{41}$$

The reason is one of strategy: the bank must penalize the economy for unanticipated inflation in order to support the belief that $E_{t-1}\, p_t = p_{t-1}$. For if it does not penalize now, why should it be expected to do so in future periods? In dynamic "differential" game theory, "bygones" are not all forgotten or forgiven.[12]

Two consequences of the rules belonging to the class (39) are immediate. One is that, since $E_{t-1}\, p_t = p_{t-1}$, the price level takes a random walk:

$$p_t = p_{t-1} + \varepsilon_t^p. \tag{42}$$

The second is that the deviation of output from ϕ is given by

$$\phi - y_t = (1 - \theta)\left[\alpha_1\mu_1(p_{t-1} - p_{t-2}) - \alpha_2\left(k_{t-1} - \underset{t-2}{E}\, k_{t-1}\right)\right] + v_t^y. \tag{43}$$

Both results are disconcerting and point to the desirability of a future alteration of the model. It follows from the former result that the variance of the inflation rate is the variance of ε_t^p, which is independent of the value of θ and thus of the "specifics" of the policy rule. The fact that the variance of the unanticipated inflation rate, $p_t - E_{t-1}\, p_t$, is independent of the parameters g_1 and g_2 for the class of rules (26) is correspondingly bothersome.

It follows from the latter result that the variance of $\phi - y_t$ is a linear combination of the variances of ε_t^p and v_t^k (which are independent of θ), multiplied by $(1 - \theta)^2$, plus the variance of v_t^y (also independent of θ). Hence for every θ however close (but unequal) to one, a closer θ would reduce the variance of output discrepancies from ϕ; indeed it would do so at no visible cost—neither for the variance of the money interest rate nor of the inflation rate. Yet $\theta = 1$ would render $E_{t-1}\, p_t$ indeterminate. An analogous problem arose when, under the class of rules (26), we considered setting g_1 equal to one in order to minimize the output variance studied in Section III.

Our rational expectations are "noisy"—ε_t^p is to be interpreted as reflecting in part the noisiness of price expectations—and this noisiness befits the "noisiness" of the environment. But the noisiness of our expec-

[12] In the "pension game," for example, the old are rewarded with a pension if and only if they had paid a fair pension to their predecessors (see Hammond 1975).

tations is exogenous, independent of the degree of noisiness in the environment. A promising remedy for the above difficulties is to prescribe endogenous noisiness of expectations. For example, if one replaced (5) by $p_t = E_{t-1} p_t + \varepsilon_t^p + u_t$ where u_t is the carryover noise introduced in Section III, then the variance of the inflation rate would depend upon the policy parameters contained in u_t.

A few other extensions of the model that keep within its analytical framework are attractive. In order to generate systematic serial persistence of production over more than 1 period ahead, one might introduce a spectrum of lead times in some wages or prices. If some firms are induced by informational considerations to establish some wages or prices 1 period in advance, may not some of these firms be similarly motivated to set some wages or prices 2 or more periods in advance?

Without departing from rational expectations, one might also introduce information specialization. If the "state" of the economy encompasses a great many variables, it becomes implausible that every agent effectively shares and processes the identical information set; each firm will likely know more about its own situation and its industry's than will generally be known. Then the decisions in an industry or sector may be interpreted as signals from which the rest of the economy draws inferences (correct or not) as to the new information causing those decisions. Some question may then arise over the existence of a (stochastic) equilibrium of self-confirming expectations and decision rules.[13]

Despite this lengthy agenda of further research, we believe the assumptions of sticky prices and of rational expectations are promising for the analysis of monetary stabilization policy.

Appendix

A full model, one that makes ϕ endogenous, can be cast in terms of three state variables: the predetermined average price level, the predetermined starting inventory level, and the *real* value of the predetermined average money wage. Let v_{t-1} denote the logarithm of the real wage prevailing in period t. Then the initial state at the outset of t is fully described by $(p_{t-1}, k_{t-1}, v_{t-1})$.

Normal or full capacity, which appears as the makeshift parameter ϕ in (1) and (6), is now to be regarded as a function of the initial state. Its value in period t will be denoted ϕ_{t-1} because, like k_{t-1} and p_{t-1} and v_{t-1}, it is a consequence of decisions and disturbances in period $t - 1$.

Let w_{t-1} denote the log of the predetermined money wage prevailing in period t. We shall suppose that, analogously to (5),

$$w_t = \underset{t-1}{E} w_t + \varepsilon_t^w, \tag{A1}$$

[13] In this connection we might add that some kinds of disturbances (e.g., structural shifts) will fail to produce a "rational" expectation of their effects, there being inadequate experience and econometric knowledge of them on which to base unbiased forecasts. The response of expectations to such shifts would presumably be similar to the transitional expectations discussed by Taylor (1975).

where ε_t^w is a serially independent random disturbance with mean zero; it may be correlated to $(\varepsilon^p, \varepsilon^y, \varepsilon^c, \varepsilon^i)$. The "money wage" level should be understood as an average over jobs that are normally filled by a "standard" worker. Then, by (A1) and (5), the log of the real wage in period $t + 1$, $w_t - p_t = v_t$, satisfies

$$v_t = \underset{t-1}{E}\, v_t + \varepsilon_t^w - \varepsilon_t^p. \tag{A2}$$

The conditional expectations of capacity and the real wage next period are jointly determined; these conditional expectations plus current random disturbances then determine the actual capacity and real wage.

Consider next period's normal capacity, ϕ_t. It will depend upon next period's starting k_t and prevailing v_t, whatever these turn out to be, and upon nothing else. Actual production next period, however, will exceed or fall short of normal capacity production ϕ_t according to then-prevailing demand factors. In the spirit of (1) we have $y_{t+1} = \phi_t + \psi_1(v_1 - v_2 E_t k_{t+1} - r_{t+1}) + \varepsilon_{t+1}^y$, where the function determining ϕ_t is not of immediate concern. Correspondingly, the t-period conditional expectation of output 1 period or s periods hence ($s = 1, 2, \ldots$) can be expressed by

$$\underset{t-1}{E}\, y_{t+s} = \underset{t-1}{E}\, \phi_{t+s-1} + \psi_1 \left(v_1 - v_2 \underset{t-1}{E}\, k_{t+s} - \underset{t-1}{E}\, r_{t+s}\right). \tag{A3}$$

If we postulate again that $E_{t-1}\, p_{t+s}$ is such as to cause the conditional expectation of equilibrium in future periods, then we have in the role of (6)

$$\underset{t-1}{E}\, y_{t+s} = \underset{t-1}{E}\, \phi_{t+s-1}, \qquad s = 1, 2, \ldots \tag{A4}$$

whence

$$\underset{t-1}{E}\, r_{t+s} = v_1 - v_2 \underset{t-1}{E}\, k_{t+s}. \tag{A5}$$

So producers in period t expect to produce on average next period the output level they plan or intend to have the capacity to produce.

A producer implements his intention to increase his capacity by raising the money wage he sets for next period relatively to the average wage he expects other producers to be setting. The equilibrium money wage has the property that its expected real value is just high enough to limit the aggregate capacity expected to be desired by producers to the capacity level which production functions and the labor supply function imply would be "attainable" at that real wage. With regard to the former capacity level, the quantity "demanded," 1 period or s periods ahead, we write

$$\underset{t-1}{E}\, \phi_{t+s-1} = \lambda_0 - \lambda_1 \underset{t-1}{E}\, k_{t+s-1} - \lambda_2 \underset{t-1}{E}\, r_{t+s} - \lambda_3 \underset{t-1}{E}\, v_{t+s-1}. \tag{A6}$$

And for the average capacity level attainable, the quantity "supplied," we write

$$\underset{t-1}{E}\, \phi_{t+s-1} = \sigma_0 - \sigma_1 \underset{t-1}{E}\, k_{t+s-1} + \sigma_2 \underset{t-1}{E}\, r_{t+s} + \sigma_3 \underset{t-1}{E}\, v_{t+s-1}. \tag{A7}$$

These are quasi-reduced-form demand and supply functions for labor plugged into firms' (identical) production functions. The parameters λ_j, σ_j are all positive, $j = 1, 2, 3$; $\lambda_1 > 0$ because larger k_{t+s-1} at the start of period $t + s$ spells a longer average period of waiting until the last unit of output is sold; $\sigma_1 > 0$ because k_{t+s-1} is a proxy for wealth or lifetime income and leisure is a normal good. We shall suppose that $\lambda_1 > \sigma_1$. Given k_{t+s-1}, a rise of r_{t+s} reduces expected labor demand because future sales from the output produced are discounted more heavily. With regard to σ_2, it could be, we grant, that $\sigma_2 < 0$. (If it were the case that $\lambda_1 = \sigma_1$ and $\sigma_2 = -\lambda_2$, then $E_{t-1}\, v_{t+s-1}$ would be constant, independent of $E_{t-1}\, r_{t+s}$ and $E_{t-1}\, k_{t+s-1}$; if $\varepsilon^w \equiv \varepsilon^p$ for all t, we would then have constant v_t, but not constant ϕ_t.) But it strikes us as more plausible that $\sigma_2 > 0$, given wealth. Presumably $\sigma_3 > 0$ and $\lambda_3 > 0$ raise no problems.

Equations (A6) and (A7) determine $E_{t-1}\, v_{t+s-1}$ as some linear combination of $E_{t-1}\, k_{t+s-1}$ and $E_{t-1}\, r_{t+s}$. We need not show it.

Plugging this result into (A6) and using (A5) to substitute $E_{t-1}\, k_{t+s}$ for $E_{t-1}\, r_{t+s}$ yields

$$\underset{t-1}{E}\, \phi_{t+s-1} = (\sigma_3 + \lambda_3)^{-1} \times [\lambda_0\sigma_3 - \sigma_0\lambda_3 - v_1(\lambda_2\sigma_3 - \sigma_2\lambda_3) - (\lambda_1\sigma_3 + \sigma_1\lambda_3) \times \underset{t-1}{E}\, k_{t+s-1} + v_2(\lambda_2\sigma_3 - \sigma_2\lambda_3) \underset{t-1}{E}\, k_{t+s}]. \tag{A8}$$

Upon replacing ϕ by ϕ_{s-1} in (10) and (11), it is obvious that $E_{t-1}\, k_{t+s}$ is a function of $E_{t-1}\, k_{t+s-1}$ and $E_{t-1}\, \phi_{t+s-1}$ in the manner of (12):

$$\underset{t-1}{E}\, k_{t+s} = (1 + \gamma_1 v_2)^{-1} \underset{t-1}{E}\, k_{t+s-1} + \delta_1\alpha_1^{-1} \underset{t-1}{E}\, \phi_{t+s-1} + \delta_0 - \alpha_1^{-1}\delta_0\delta_1. \tag{A9}$$

We assume that both the coefficient of $E_{t-1}\, k_{t+s}$ in (A8) and the coefficient of $E_{t-1}\, \phi_{t+s-1}$ in (A9) are less than one. Then

$$\underset{t-1}{E}\, \phi_{t+s-1} = q^{-1}(\sigma_3 + \lambda_3)^{-1} \times \{\lambda_0\sigma_3 - \sigma_0\lambda_3 - (\lambda_2\sigma_3 - \sigma_2\lambda_3)[v_1 - v_2\delta_0(1 - \delta_1\alpha_1)^{-1}] + [-(\lambda_1\sigma_3 + \sigma_1\lambda_3) + v_2(\lambda_2\sigma_3 - \sigma_2\lambda_3) (1 + \gamma_1 v_2)^{-1}] \underset{t-1}{E}\, k_{t+s-1}\} \tag{A10}$$

where

$$q \equiv 1 - \delta_1\alpha_1^{-1}v_2 \frac{\lambda_2\sigma_3 - \sigma_2\lambda_3}{\sigma_3 + \lambda_3} > 0.$$

The coefficient of $E_{t-1}\, k_{t+s-1}$ is negative if $\lambda_2\sigma_3$ is not too large. The coefficient would be zero, as in the rudimentary model, if $\sigma_1 = \sigma_2 = \sigma_3 = 0$. An alternative way to keep $E_{t-1}\, \phi_{t+s-1}$ constant over time is to restrict σ_1, σ_2, λ_1, and λ_2 in such a way that, in view of (A5), $E_{t-1}\, k_{t+s-1}$ and $E_{t-1}\, r_{t+s}$ wash out of the supply and demand equations (A6) and (A7).

Note also that from (A9) and (A10)

$$\underset{t-1}{E}\, k_{t+s} = q^{-1}(a_4 + q - 1) \underset{t-1}{E}\, k_{t+s-1} + \text{const}, \tag{A11}$$

indicating, as in the rudimentary model, the tendency for inventories to regress toward the mean, if as is natural to require, the coefficient in (A11), like a_4 in (19), is less than one in absolute value.

Equations (A10) and (A11) have an interesting implication. Suppose that $E_{t-1}\, k_t$ exceeds average $\bar{k}$, owing (say) to a larger-than-average k_{t-1}. If the coefficient in (A10) is negative, then $E_{t-1}\, \phi_{t-1}$ is depressed; and if the coefficient in (A11) is positive, $E_{t-1}\, \phi_{t-1}$ recovers its average value monotonically and asymptotically as $s \to \infty$. This implies the prolongation of booms and slumps that could be explained in the rudimentary model only by appeal to accidental "runs" of the random disturbances.

A further implication is that $E_{t-1}\, v_{t+s-1}$ can now be determined as a linear function of only $E_{t-1}\, k_{t+s-1}$, namely,

$$\underset{t-1}{E}\, v_{t+s-1} = (\sigma_3 + \lambda_3)^{-1} \times \{[\sigma_1 - \lambda_1 + (\sigma_2 + \lambda_2)\upsilon_2 q^{-1}(a_4 + q - 1)] \underset{t-1}{E}\, k_{t+s-1} - (\sigma_2 + \lambda_2)\upsilon_1 - (\sigma_0 - \lambda_0)\}. \tag{A12}$$

The structure of the full model has now been outlined in every essential. Given the initial state $(p_{t-1}, k_{t-1}, v_{t-1})$ in period t and given a normal capacity function $\phi\,(k_{t-1}, v_{t-1})$ for determining current normal capacity output ϕ_{t-1}, one applies the methods of Sections I and II to determine the conditional expectations of the next state. In fact, the calculation of $E_{t-1}\, k_t$ immediately implies the entirety of the sequences of $E_{t-1}\, v_{t+s-1}$ and (given the monetary policy rule) $E_{t-1}\, p_{t+s-1}$ according to the first-order process labeled regression toward the mean. The conditional expectations of the next period's state variables plus the white-noise random disturbances in the current period produce the actual state (p_t, k_t, v_t) that is next realized. It should, of course, be understood that many restrictions on the parameters, some of which have already been noticed, are necessary in order that this system be well behaved in the way that the rudimentary model was shown to be when restricted.

It remains only to specify the ex post reduced-form capacity equation. The most convenient form is the linear one:

$$\phi_{t-1} = \phi_0 - \phi_1 v_{t-1} - \phi_2 k_{t-1}. \tag{A13}$$

This is a locus of points all but one of which are "off the curves" describing the virtual demands and supplies of capacity in equations (A6) and (A7). The only point of contact among them is the logical requirement that, for every s and t, those three equations predict the same $E_{t-1}\, \phi_{t+s-1}$ for given $E_{t-1}\, k_{t+s-1}$, $E_{t-1}\, v_{t+s-1}$, and $E_{t-1}\, r_{t+s}$ (a determinable function of $E_{t-1}\, k_{t+s-1}$). The locus in (A13) may be regarded as a blend of the supply and demand curves and as being closer to the demand curve than to the supply.

A detailed specification and interpretation of this function and of the other functions arising in the full model are not now of primary concern, so we shall not pursue here the operating characteristics of this model. (Some of the above functions, we suspect, contain redundant variables and overlook implied relationships among the coefficients.) This exposition of the full model will have served its purpose if it has clarified the meaning and the restrictiveness of the rudimentary model.

References

Barro, R. J. "Rational Expectations and the Role of Monetary Policy." *J. Monetary Econ.* 2 (January 1976): 1–32.

Fischer, S. "Long-Term Contracts, Rational Expectations, and the Optimal Money Supply Rule." *J.P.E.* 85, no. 1 (February 1977): 191–205.

Friedman, M. *A Program for Monetary Stability*. New York: Fordham Univ. Press, 1959.

Hammond, P. "Charity: Altruism or Cooperative Egoism?" In *Altruism, Morality and Economic Theory*, edited by E. S. Phelps. New York: Basic, 1975.

Muth, J. F. "Rational Expectations and the Theory of Price Movements." *Econometrica* 29 (July 1961): 315–35.

Okun, A. M. "Inflation: Its Mechanism and Welfare Costs." *Brookings Papers Econ. Activity* 2 (1975): 351–401.

Pashigian, B. P. "Growth and Oscillations of Income When Expectations Are Consistent." Mimeographed. Univ. Chicago Bus. School, October 24, 1969.

Phelps, E. S. "A Note on Short-Run Employment and Real Wage Rate under Competitive Commodity Markets." *Internat. Econ. Rev.* 10 (June 1969): 220–32.

Phelps, E. S., et al. *Microeconomic Foundations of Employment and Inflation Theory.* New York: Norton, 1970.

Samuelson, P. A. *Foundations of Economic Analysis.* Cambridge, Mass.: Harvard Univ. Press, 1947.

Sargent, T. J., and Wallace, N. " 'Rational' Expectations, the Optimal Monetary Instrument, and the Optimal Money Supply Rule." *J.P.E.* 83, no. 2 (April 1975): 241–54.

Shell, K., and Stiglitz, J. E. "The Allocation of Investment in a Dynamic Economy." *Q.J.E.* 81 (November 1967): 592–609.

Taylor, J. B. "Monetary Policy during a Transition to Rational Expectations." *J.P.E.* 83, no. 5 (October 1975): 1009–22.

INDEXATION ISSUES

Indexing, I take it, means tying some or all elements of a transaction to one or more contingencies--to events or reports not counted as certain at the initial decision. Bonds that promise to pay future in proportion to the future price level are said to be indexed. Some retirement benefits are indexed to money wage levels. Banks and insurance companies have begun to index their loan rates and premium rates by market interest rates. Some public spending programs are automatically started and shut off by the rise and fall of the unemployment rate. Insurance is the best example of indexation because the "indicator" is typically capable of manipulation or misrepresentation.

I focus here upon recent issues in the positive and normative theory of wage indexation--the voluntary indexing of the money wage rate commitments, or implicit contracts, offered by some or all firms.[1] As the first paragraph tediously suggests, a firm now deciding its money wage commitment over some future period could choose to index that wage to a nearly infinite variety of events between now and then. Hence, those wage commitments which are indexed only to the so-called escalator clause represent just one type of indexation.[2] In respect both to its viability and desirability, that type needs to be compared to more general types of indexation, not merely to no indexation at all.

The agenda of issues to be discussed is prompted by the creeping indexationism of the past few years. In that vision, indexed contracts will soon be sweeping the economy. These contracts will ultimately offer full escalation of

---

*My fixed opinions on this subject were prepared for the January 1975 Sao Paulo Conference on Indexation where I took the solitary position that parties to indexed labor contracts would not freely choose full escalation of wages to the price level and that compulsory full escalation would serve them ill. A grant from the National Bureau of Economic Research is gratefully acknowledged. The present paper ventures to give reasons for these opinions. The Appendix is largely the work of Guillermo Calvo, and both he and John Taylor contributed to the argument at several points.

[1] I shall not have in mind the Brazilian variant in which there is, by fiat, a retroactive "monetary adjustment" of wages for work previously performed. It will be supposed that the contingencies upon which the current money wage depends are known by the firm and its employees by the time the current work performed at that wage takes place; and that such contingent wage commitments are neither mandated nor enforced by the government.

[2] Under the escalator clause the money wage is an increasing function of the price level.

Reprinted by permission from *Stabilization of the Domestic and International Economy,* K. Brunner and A. H. Meltzer (Eds.). Carnegie-Rochester Conference Series on Public Policy—A Supplementary Series to the Journal of Monetary Economics, Vol. 5, 1977, North-Holland Publishing Company.

money wages to the general price level (making the real wage independent of the price level). A dual consequence is the abolition--or, more realistically in view of price data lags, the rapid attenuation--of the employment effects of demand shocks and, as a corollary, the abolition (or rapid attenuation) of the central bank's power to moderate the employment effects of supply shocks (which effects will be magnified by escalation). But, the latter consequence is not a real cost because unemployment brought about by unanticipated supply shocks is "contractual" and the contracts are Pareto-optimal with regard to an individual's ex ante expected utilities.[3]

I think it should be conceded that there are some grains of truth in the models that have generated these conclusions. There is no doubt that the fascinating developments in "contract theory" have opened up a new line of research of great promise. Nevertheless, in perhaps an allergic reaction to those grains of truth, I shall argue that realistic contract theory will not support the conclusions overreached by the indexationists.

1. Where in the economy are there tendencies toward indexation of some kind?

Many firms are so situated that they find it (ultimately) profitable regularly to make and to keep advance commitments regarding the terms on which they will employ certain kinds of workers (if hired). One of the reasons recently glimpsed is that the firm will find a recruiting advantage in having a pre-announced wage scale that reduces the time and trouble of information gathering for the potential employee.[4] If he has to negotiate his wage at one firm but not at others, and then only when he can show the firm he is in earnest, the recruit is apt not to bother with that firm. Another reason for pre-arrangement is that, without it, the prospective employee may worry that the firm will exploit his having distanced himself from alternative employment prospects.[5] The presence of mobility costs tempts every firm to pay its current employees something less than their "going wage."[6]

These remarks, obvious or problematic, leave open the form that wage and employment commitments may take. If a degree of uncertainty about economic conditions during the period of the commitment is added to the above considerations, then it is plausible to expect that such commitments will take

---

[3]As Fischer puts it, " . . . it should be recognized that the professional presumption. . .that private contracts, freely entered into, lead to desirable outcomes in the absence of externalities.

[4]See Okun (1975).

[5]Calvo (conversation).

[6]William Vickrey, in conversation, has noted a similar problem for the existence of equilibrium in the taxi industry.

the form of contingency agreements. If, as I shall suppose, all (or at any rate most) workers are averse to risk, they may be willing to pay for some "insurance" against certain contingencies; and the firm, even the risk-neutral firm, may be willing to pay for contingency clauses allowing it to make employment or wage adjustments.

The tendency toward contingent or indexed commitments appears to be limited to the situations just described. Where the prospective employment is nearly immediate and short-term, it would seem that the firm might as well offer certain employment at a certain money wage. Unless the prospective duration of the job is long, or the job is far in the future, so that substantial uncertainties loom over the horizon, it will not be worth the administrative and evaluational costs to deal in indexed commitments. Where conditions of costless information and costless mobility prevail, the potential worker who can always supply other services at the average wage might welcome fluctuations rather than stability in the wage periodically paid for that service. There may normally exist a dominant arrangement by which the supplier of the service effectively indentures himself to some firm in return for some retainer fee; but, for such an arrangement to exist, the firm must trust the supplier's availability when it is needed and the supplier must trust that the firm will not demand his service when it is not warranted by the firm's true needs.

The nature of the indexation provided by bilaterally optimal contingent commitments, where they exist, is the next question. The implicit contract theories of Azariadis (1975), Baily (1974), and Gordon (1976) appear to imply that optimal commitments will stabilize the real wage--full escalation of the money wage to the price level--and leave workers with some risk of undesired layoffs. Whether or not these conclusions are intended and valid deductions, they are crucially dependent upon the model adopted.

2. Do optimal indexed contracts protect the real wage rate from all shocks?

Azariadis (1975) has constructed a theory of <u>state contingent</u> contracts from a model in which, knowing only the probabilities of each possible "state of the world" before it occurs, risk-neutral firms choose contingent contracts that maximize their expected profits and (homogeneous) risk-averse workers choose the firms at which to locate so as to maximize their expected utilities. This model is subject to the conditions that workers are then immobilized at the firms of their choice for the life of the contracts, so that the firm cannot hire more persons than have come to it and, if it hires fewer, the firm's workers will have an equal probability of not being hired.[7]

The first result pertains to the employment terms of the contract. Given the optimal wage rate to be paid in each state, the firm commits itself to hire generously--beyond the point where marginal value product equals the real wage–when the state is "poor" in order to attract a desirably large pool of workers to be available when the state turns out "good."[8]

A more striking result pertains to the wage terms of the contract. The optimal contract of a firm specifies a wage that is independent of the state (and therefore independent of the employment level corresponding to that state). Given the number of workers who position themselves in advance at the firm, and given the optimal number to be employed (and hence the probability of being hired) in each state, the firm will minimize the expected value of its wage costs while providing workers with the "competitive" level of expected utility only if it ensures the same wage across all states. The following remark may be helpful. Because the probability of being hired in each state is an independent control variable being simultaneously optimized, the problem of wage optimization is reduced, by an envelope theorem, to that of dividing up the total rent (for each state that eventuates) between the risk-averse workers who are hired and the risk-neutral firm.

Is this "wage," which is state-invariant during the contract, the money wage or the real wage? If it is supposed, as Azariadis seems to prefer, that monetary policy holds constant the price level, then the real wage is state-independent at least for that macroeconomically very special case. But, it would not do violence to the model if we stipulate, as most analysts have been inclined to do, that workers' utilities are a function of leisure and the real wage <u>only</u>–at least when product markets and money markets are in equilibrium. Then, stabilizing (across states) the utility from job holding entails stabilizing the real wage. It is this specialized general equilibrium version of the model that most readers have in mind when they infer from Azariadis that his theory (and that of other contract theorists) makes the real wage a "constant" over the life of the contract.

---

[7]The model is outlined in the Appendix. Perhaps the best interpretation of the postulate that workers are perfectly mobile among firms ex ante and perfectly immobile ex post is that, by assumption, every state which turns up after decisions are made is believed to be "temporary," the probability distribution of states being believed to be unchanged. Then, the failure or incapacity of a firm to offer the "competitive" level of <u>expected</u> utility would be a reason for workers not to join it, or to leave it if located there to begin with, if the cost of moving is not too large. But, ex post bad luck at the firm in the current period need not induce workers to leave if it is believed that next period the firm's contract will again offer the previous competitive expected utility to a pool of workers of undiminished size. Add to this the possibility that other firms will give first preference to workers who were original members of their pools.

[8]Fischer neglects this aspect of Azariadis' contracts, but his results are thereby affected only in degree, not in kind.

The fixed real wage solution takes some getting used to. If it seems riskier and therefore less attractive than the auction solution, which at least assures every worker an earning job (save in exceptional cases), then it should be noted that the level of the fixed wage may exceed the expected value of the auction wage. The firm is compensated by the resulting increase in the size of the attracted labor pool which can be employed in states requiring maximum hiring. Keep in mind also that the Azariadis firm hires beyond the cash flow maximizing level (in each state that it can do so) in order to increase the size of the labor pool attracted to it.

Nevertheless, this constancy of the real wage gives way when some of the assumptions are relaxed. The firm's neutrality toward risk is a frequently cited example. As shown by Blinder, the introduction of worker holdings of unindexed wealth would also make a difference. Azariadis himself emphasizes the strong role played by the assumption of total immobility over the life of the implicit contract--an uncomfortable assumption if it is precisely long-run contracts that are the best candidates for indexation. It would be interesting to see contingent wage commitments introduced into an intertemporal model of job search--on-the-job search or out-of-work search.

A crucial assumption is of the workers' trust that the firm will honor the contract. If the workers cannot see that the firm's state requires the number of layoffs that the firm claims, they may distrust a contract expressed in terms of such uncertifiable states. Using employment rather than the underlying state as a variable eligible for wage indexation leads to a different maximization problem. Some results concerning optimal employment contingent contracts are derived in the Appendix.

One of these is that, in cases which I believe to be normal, the real wage is lower (at any given general price level) the larger the unemployment rate at the firm.[9] It is just as we always thought--prior to the advent of state-contingent contract theory! This intuitive finding is based on the belief that the firm will hire a worker (in its predetermined labor pool) with greater probability the lower the real wage; and the proportionate increase in the employment rate induced by a one dollar concession in the real wage, hence the associated proportionate rise in the probability of being hired, is greater the larger the unemployment rate that would occur without any real wage concession.

The assumption (mine, at least) is that while sophisticated contracts will index money wage rates to the money price level (in some way), the most sophisticated of these will index the wage also to various real contingencies both within and without the firm. It is only a very rough approximation to assume,

[9]Another proposition, concerning "escalation," is taken up in the next section.

as Fischer does, that the money wage is indexed only to the money price level in the voluntary "indexed economy."

3. Will equilibrium indexing (once established) nullify monetary policy?

I leave til last the perilous issue of social efficiency and the consequent role for public intervention existing in the kinds of economy under discussion. First, I simply suppose that it would be desirable to call on monetary policy to moderate the employment fluctuations that result from certain unanticipated shocks (for example, supply shocks). The question arises, however, whether monetary policy will be effective in that task when contracts are indexed in the bilaterally optimal way.

Recent discussions, including that by Fischer, presume that optimal contracts will be in "real" terms, making the money wage a linear homogeneous function of the consumer price level. The conclusion drawn from that premise is that changes in the supply of money, even unanticipated ones, will have equiproportional effects on money wages and prices and "consequently" zero effects on output and employment--at least to a satisfactory approximation. Although that thesis may turn out to be passingly accurate as an empirical prediction, it grows out of a projection of the voluntary indexed economy that seems to me to be inappropriate in important respects.

Let us tentatively accept the homogeneity premise of full escalation. It is nevertheless implausible that short-term wage commitments will be so indexed or indeed indexed at all, as I suggest above. Furthermore, many goods prices may similarly be predetermined and unindexed over the selling season to which current price lists apply.[10] Only the longer run commitments regarding wages and prices pose enough risk so that their reduction by indexing is worth the effort and complexity. One would suppose monetary policy to have some leverage over output and employment in an incompletely indexed economy if one supposes it to have such leverage in the same economy when the practice of indexation is not yet widely developed.

Another objection is that those contracts which are, in fact, indexed would be likely to make the money wage in the current quarter a function of the price level (and other nominal magnitudes) in the previous quarter, not in the current one. Most price level indices are at least a month old when first reported, and are then revised a month later. Implementing the consequent wage adjustment also takes time. Furthermore, many firms would not want to collect and process these data and to recalibrate their paychecks each month however "current" or laggard the data. Thus, an increase in the supply of money would

[10] This is the principal point in Phelps and Taylor (1976). Some difficulties in indexing prices to monetary conditions in a neutralizing way are implied below.

not be immediately offset, in the manner of Sargent-Wallace (1975), by an employment-preserving rise of current money wage rates and prices. For some months, wages (and perhaps prices as well) would behave predeterminedly owing to the indexation lags.

A further dispute with this thesis goes to an old theoretical issue. It seems to me that juxtaposing Phelps-Winter (1970) firms, each of which has a market limited by the size of aggregate demand, with the notion of a pool of labor to be called up or laid off at an above-market-clearing wage (indexed or not), as demand prompts, would allow unanticipated changes in the money supply to affect output and employment, despite escalation of money wage rates in proportion to the price level. In such a model, engineering a rise of output by monetary policy does not depend on a rise of money prices relative to money wage rates; it may suffice that the typical firm underestimates the rise in prices by its close competitors. (This may be a tall assumption if the rise in the general price level is immediately known.)

Another point in this brief for monetary policy is that, with workers initially unable to move between the capital goods and consumer goods industries without incurring information gathering and other frictional costs, it seems unnecessary for a rise in employment that the monetary authorities raise consumer goods prices relative to money wage rates. In an indexed economy of this frictional sort, is there any reason why an increase in the money supply (in response to an unanticipated downward shock to aggregate demand), the first impact of which is only to raise (flexible) capital goods prices and not consumer goods prices, will produce a chain effect–via indexation linkages–that raises general money wage rates and the general price level (in relation to expected future prices) by just enough as to nullify the incipient stimulus to production in the capital goods sector? I do not see how the mere escalation of money wage rates to consumer goods prices would block the desired expansion of capital goods sector employment.

I return to the homogeneity premise itself, that optimally indexed contracts will display full (100 percent) escalation to the general price level; that the contracted money wage rate is proportional to the general price level (at least at a constant general real wage level), given the real prices of outputs and inputs "facing" the firm, which are a part of the description of the individual firm's "state" (to which the money wage may also be indexed). Despite Azariadis' request that we take as given the general price level, so we may not ask what would happen if all money prices were raised, it is correctly deduced (by Fischer and others) from the Azariadis equations that if utility depends only upon the real wage and leisure (and literally nothing else), then optimal contracts will specify the real wage to be paid by the firm in each of its states (which are also expressed in real terms).

Regarding the implied escalator clause, Azariadis himself makes the point that in a more general model the expected real rate of interest would figure in the utility function; if that variable, to which the wage is not easily indexed, is positively correlated with the level of money prices, then we should expect less than full escalation to the general price level. Blinder introduces the additional factor of the workers' net position with respect to (unindexed) monetary assets and liabilities; net debtors would want less than full escalation in order to stabilize their real wage plus (expected?) net real capital gains.

There is a general point to be made against the "optimality" of full escalation if indexation must be "second-best" owing to the infeasibility of indexing the money (and therefore real) wage rate to the (real) state in all its dimensions. Suppose that, because of practical difficulties of certifying the true state of the world, money wage rates at a firm are indexable only to easily measurable variables, in particular the general price level and perhaps also the employment level at the individual firm. Then, the general price level might constitute a proxy for certain excluded variables which would call for a lower real wage were the latter indexable to them. In that case, presumably, money wage rates would not be fully escalated to the price level because on average it is desired to have a somewhat reduced real wage rate when the general price level is high.[11]

Even if the foregoing is correct, it still does not follow that monetary policy will make a difference for the fluctuation of employment in response to supply shocks (or, for that matter, to demand shocks). Might not bilaterally optimal implicit contracts index directly to indices of monetary policy in such a way that the employment effect of monetary policy reactions (at least the normal and predicted reactions) to unanticipated shocks was rendered nil?

I think it can be agreed that clever second-best indexers will devise ways to index to monetary indicators which can be seen by workers to provide more dependably the real wage, or, more accurately, the utility that the optimum implicit contract would produce in each "state" (or employment situation) in which workers and firms find themselves. But these indexers will not want to insulate totally real wages and employment from monetary policy insofar as the latter operates to signal (or proxy for) elements of the state that are not easily measured or observed.

Moreover, such neutralizing indexation of wages and prices to monetary indicators, if desired, would encounter several difficulites: the problem of temporary versus permanent changes of the money supply; the distinction

---

[11]This point is developed further in the Appendix.

between "autonomous" and "demand induced" money supply; the distinction between a change of the supply resulting from systematic policy responses and that resulting from random vicissitudes in central bank intentions; and so on. The fallacy of (misplaced) concreteness should warn us against supposing that actors in the real world will dare to experiment with such (perversely) ultra-sophisticated indexation merely because some analyst can devise the optimum contract for a model with a simple structure (M1 or maybe M2, but not more) and all probability distributions known. Therefore, I doubt that such indexing to monetary policy indicators, if it develops at all, will reduce the leverage of monetary policy over output and employment much beyond the reduction caused by (optimal) escalation.

4. Ought the central bank to moderate "contractual" layoffs in some states?

Consider first the state contingent contracts of Azariadis. If we agree to impose "imperfections" in the goods markets, such as predetermined product prices, then some states will be accompanied by layoffs (and new entrants not hired), not because of reduced productivity that might justify a general decline in employment, but, rather, because of reduced aggregate demand. Surely there will exist states in which unemployment is sufficiently large for this reason that ex post profit and expected utility would be increased by a small improvement of the state, the resultant rise of employment being effected, therefore, by monetary policy.[12] It follows, I presume, that a monetary policy which systematically moderates deep slumps in employment attributable to unanticipated shocks to aggregate demand will secure an improvement of ex ante expected utility and expected profits.

Layoffs attributable to supply shocks present a trickier problem in the state contingent framework. Azariadis presupposes that firms (for reasons, if any, requiring examination) pay no private unemployment compensation. Yet his model, taken literally, implies that firms have sufficient incentive to establish their own private unemployment compensation programs. The firm's first-best contract offers private unemployment compensation equal to the real wage, and promises to hire the whole labor pool _or_ to hire up to the point where marginal product of labor when multiplied by every worker's (equal) marginal utility of income equals the disutility of working instead of staying home.[13] There is, in any reasonable sense, full employment in every state; in no state is there possible a Pareto improvement. If there is a supply shock causing layoffs

[12] I specify "expected" utility, even ex post, because the distribution of the total layoffs over persons is determined by a random drawing.

[13] The particulars of these two results obtain if utility is additively separable in leisure and income.

in the contractual amount, then monetary policy would achieve nothing. Note that if leisure is preferred to working, the unemployed are the lucky ones.

These fully optimal contracts appear to be enforceable, free from moral hazard, because anyone refusing to work would be dropped from the firm's pool and would then have to incur the set-up cost of moving to another firm. ("If you were sick, you should have phoned in to relinquish your compensation claim for the day.") Yet almost nowhere do we observe contracts effectively guaranteeing income. That may be because employers have not widely perceived its advantages to them. More likely, the model is in need of extensions.

Pending these alterations, I will offer two thoughts. In the real world, unemployment produces various external diseconomies, including the public unemployment compensation intended to moderate them, while firms making hiring decisions consider mainly the private cost of hiring labor, not the (lesser) social cost. So there is a _prima facie_ case for monetary policies that cushion unemployment from serious supply shocks. Second, is there not something disturbing about contracts which are Pareto-optimal ex ante, with regard to every worker's _expected_ utility, if some workers will suffer unemployment and low utility ex post? Suppose the contracts are for life and the supply shock is recognized to be permanent. Should an individual be permitted to gamble his career for a sufficiently greater expected income?

Now consider the employment contingent contracts studied in the Appendix. The state is unobservable by workers. (Unemployment compensation is omitted.) Contracts index the money wage to the firm's employment rate and to the general price level. In some cases, at least, the real wage is a rising function of employment because, when the firm's demand for labor falls, a fall in the real wage serves to moderate the resulting rise in the probability of being laid off. But, this schedule shifts down with a rise in the price level because, under suitable monetary policies, such a price rise signals supply shocks which, if they had been observed by workers, would have caused them to accept a lower than usual real wage (at each level of employment) in order to moderate the greater than usual probability of being unemployed. The desirability of a monetary policy that allows a rise in the price level in response to an estimated supply shock, and the greater desirability of a policy that magnifies the price rise and thus amplifies the signal is that it accomplishes some appropriate real wage reduction directly, rather than exclusively via reduced employment, and thus it increases both profit and expected utility.

While the analysis of employment contingent contracts is very difficult, the message is simple. Sophisticated contractors will not escalate fully their money wage rates to the general price level if the monetary authorities are known to permit and to encourage a rise in prices when raw material supplies contract. Further, the central bank ought to follow that policy, if contractors will count on it, and accordingly not adopt full escalation.

There is another point that might usefully be made if it might be assumed that firms have static or dynamic monopoly power in product markets. Then, the size of the employment gain from a dollar reduction of the firm's real wage depends both on how steeply the marginal physical product of labor declines with employment and on how steeply the firm's (optimal) relative price must decline with the rise in sales. If all firms and workers were to find themselves in the same boat of high unemployment, they would, if they could, enter into a binding agreement to accept a still lower real wage than each firm's workers would agree to accept if they and the firm were acting alone. For, if they all marched in step, then, at no firm (roughly speaking) would the predictable employment effect be diminished by an associated fall in that firm's relative price. If that is correct, then it can be said that, from a social or collective viewpoint, workers are trapped (or may sometimes be trapped) in a situation of excessive unemployment because of a kind of "prisoners' dilemma" arising from the lack of opportunities for concerted wage policy. The answer to that dilemma is a decision on the part of the central bank to raise the price level in lieu of that wage policy.

These points regarding employment contingent wage behavior are strongly reminiscent of Keynes' cryptic, yet central, remark in his General Theory to the effect that there exist circumstances in which a real wage reduction that no worker nor union of workers would seek through a unilateral reduction of the money wage would be accepted knowingly and gratefully by all if there were a rise in the general price level.

APPENDIX

Employment Contingent Wage Contracts

Guillermo A. Calvo and Edmund S. Phelps

The existing theory of wage and employment contracts postulates perfect information about the possible states of nature and their probability distribution. In this note, we discuss some implications of a contrasting assumption. We show, among other things, that under imperfect information monetary policy may become an effective instrument for economic stabilization.

Let us first briefly recall the elements of Azariadis' (1975) theory. Workers are perfectly mobile between firms ex ante, i. e., before the state is known, but immobile ex post. Each worker positions himself at a firm where the wage and employment prospects give him the highest expected utility. Workers are homogeneous in all respects and the probability of employment at a firm is the same for everyone who has selected that firm. Thus, if m is the size of the firm's labor pool and n (s) is its employment when state s occurs, each worker's probability of being employed in that state is [n (s) / m]. Firms, which are price takers on the product side, offer wage and employment contracts which maximize expected profits subject to the constraint that workers' expected utility be equal to the maximum offered by other firms.

If we denote by v (s) the real wage to be paid in state s, then expected profits is given by

$$(1) \quad \underset{s}{E}\ f\,[\,n(s), s\,] - v(s)\, n(s),$$

where f (·) is the firm's production function multiplied by the relative price of the firm's output in terms of wage goods. The expected utility constraint is given by

$$(2) \quad \underset{s}{E}\ u\,[\,v(s)\,]\ \frac{n(s)}{m} = k\,.$$

The left side of (2) is the representative worker's expected utility under the simplifying assumption that the utility function can be scaled so that the utility derived from being unemployed is zero; function u (·) is a von Neumann-Morgenstern utility index.

If each possible s, once it has occurred, is identifiable, then it makes sense to draw contracts in terms of [n (s) , v (s)], an optimal contract being, therefore, one that maximizes (1) subject to (2), and $0 \leq n(s) \leq m$ for all s. Furthermore, if, as Azariadis assumes, there are "prohibitive" costs in breaking a contract, workers would be assured that those commitments will be honored ex post. The story is consistent.

We turn now to a case of imperfect information. Suppose that, while firms are perfectly informed about s, workers have no direct information about s--they observe only v and n–or, if w is the nominal wage and p the money price of wage goods, that workers can observe w, p, and n. (This is admittedly an extreme example of the class of situations in which the firm is "better" informed than workers.)

In such a setting, workers do not need to know the distribution of s in order to calculate their expected utility. The joint distribution of n and v will suffice; that can, in principle, be calculated once [n (s), v (s)] and m are determined. Thus, Azariadis' optimal contract for the perfect information case would, if adopted by firms, produce the same expected utility calculable on the basis of the induced distribution of n and v, as was calculable under perfect information. Moreover, that contract would be optimal in the case of imperfect information too _if_ firms were bound to honor it ex post. It is at this point that new elements emerge.

How, in this case, would workers discover that a firm is breaking such a contract? Based on his assumptions, Azariadis showed that under perfect information an optimal contract has $v(s) = \bar{v}$, a constant, and n (s) varying with s. But, when the workers are ignorant of s, the firm can change n (s), arguing that the state is s', for example, instead of s. Would it be profitable to do so? The answer is yes, at least in the short run. To see this, let λ be the Lagrange multiplier corresponding to (2), and differentiate the Lagrangian with respect to n (s). The first order condition associated with an optimal contract is then, at an interior optimum,

$$(3) \qquad f_n [n(s), s] - \bar{v} + \frac{\lambda}{m} u(\bar{v}) = 0 ,$$

where $f_n \equiv \partial f / \partial n$; in normal circumstances, $\lambda > 0$. Hence, given $\bar{v}$, the marginal productivity of labor is different ex post from the wage rate (if $u(\bar{v}) > 0$, for instance, $f_n < \bar{v}$). Thus, there is room for the firm to increase its profits by employing a different number of workers from that in Azariadis' contracts. Consequently, if workers cannot find out about s, it would be to the advantage of the firm, in general, to depart from the Azariadis contract.

This argument suggests that a contract would better be drawn up in such a way that it is possible for workers to monitor it ex post. Because they are observable by the workers in the case under analysis, w, n, and p should be the variables in terms of which a contract is expressed. Suppose, first, that the government varies the money supply to hold constant the price level. In this case, contracts might just as well be drawn in terms of v and n.[14] We will analyze the case where v is made a function of n, i. e., v = h (n) for some function h.

We will also assume that for each state s the firm maximizes profits subject to h (n). In other words, n (s) = n*(s; m, h) where[15]

$$(4) \quad f\,[n^*(s;m,h),s] - h\,[n^*(s;m,h)]\,n^*(s;m,h) = \max_{0 \le n \le m} [f(n,s) - h(n)\,n]\,.$$

This assumption would be fully justified if the firm's horizon did not extend beyond one period. With a multiperiod horizon, the impact of present policies on the estimated future joint distribution of v and n would have to be taken into account.

An optimal contract is some function h* (n) such that it solves the following problem:

$$(5) \quad \text{Max}\ \underset{s}{E}\ f\,[n^*(s;m,h),s] - h\,[n^*(s;m,h)]\,n^*(s;m,h)$$

subject to

$$\underset{s}{E}\ u\,[h\,(n^*(s;m,h))]\,\frac{n^*(s;m,h)}{m} = k\,.$$

Thus, the function h (·) is to be optimally chosen, taking into account the firm's resulting ex post employment policy.

The full characterization of h* (·) is not a simple analytical matter. Here we will be content to show that: (i) for every (s,s') such that n*(s; m, h) >

---

[14] It is true that m, the pool of workers, can be entered into the contract, but we prefer to let it be determined by a condition like (2). That is to say, m is determined by the equilibrium condition that expected utility is equal in all firms.

[15] In order to ensure uniqueness of n*, we define it as the highest n among those that solve the maximum problem in (4). Notice that that will be the employment level chosen by the firm in any solution of problem (5) below if the utility attained when employed is always larger for the worker than that when unemployed.

$n^*(s'; m, h) > 0$, $h[n^*(s; m, h)] \geq h[n^*(s'; m, h)]$ if $\partial f_n(n,s)/\partial s \geq 0$ for all n (or $\leq$ for all n); and that (ii) there exist cases where the last inequality is strict (i. e., >) for optimal h (i.e., for h*). Statement (i) says simply that for <u>any</u> function h a larger employment will be associated with a higher or equal real wage if a larger s always "shifts out" (or always "shifts in") the marginal labor productivity schedule. Statement (ii) is the more interesting. It asserts that one can find cases where in an optimal contract a larger employment implies a larger real wage, proving that a constant real wage contract is not optimal in general.

Statement (i) is an immediate consequence of (4). In particular, when $0 < n^* < m$, i. e., when the solution to (4) is interior and h is continuously differentiable, (i) can be verified by implicit differentiation of the first order condition involved in (4).

In order to prove (ii), let us consider the following example. Workers are risk neutral and the technology is

$$\text{(6)} \quad f(n,s) = \begin{cases} A(s)\,n, & 0 \leq n \leq 1 ; \\ A(s), & n \geq 1 , \end{cases}$$

where A (s) is positive and increasing with s. We further suppose that s can take only two values: s_1 and s_2, $s_2 \geq s_1$.

Assume now, contradicting statement (ii), that all optimal contracts have a constant $\bar{v}$, (i. e., $h^*(n) \equiv \bar{v}$). Expected utility would then be $\bar{v} \underset{s}{E}\, n(s)$ and, recalling that the firm maximizes ex post profits,

$$\text{(7)} \quad \text{expected utility} = \begin{cases} \bar{v} & \text{if } \bar{v} \leq A(s_1) ; \\ \bar{v}\,P(s_2) & \text{if } A(s_1) < \bar{v} \leq A(s_2) ; \\ 0 & \text{if } A(s_2) < \bar{v}, \end{cases}$$

where $P(s_2)$ is the probability of state s_2. Thus, if k in equation (2) is set higher than $A(s_1)$, we can ensure, by (7), that $\bar{v} > A(s_1)$; hence, (2) will read

$$\text{(8)} \quad \bar{v}\,P(s_2) = k .$$

Under these circumstances, the firm will be operated $(n > 0)$ in state s_2 if

$$\text{(9)} \quad A(s_2) > \frac{k}{P(s_2)} .$$

Let us assume $A(s_1) < k$ and (9) hold; as argued above, the firm will be operated only if s_2 turns up. Consequently, by (8) and (9), $n = \min(m, 1)$ for $m > 0$ and

$$(10) \quad \text{expected profit} = [A(s_2) - \frac{k}{P(s_2)}] \; P(s_2)\, m \text{ if } 0 < m \leq 1 .$$

By (6), the maximum expected profit in this case is obtained at

$$(11) \quad m = 1 .$$

We will now show that there is some $\underline{v} < \bar{v}$ and $0 < n_o < 1$ such that a contract like the one depicted in Figure 1 yields higher expected utility and profit.

Taking $0 < \underline{v} < A(s_1)$, we ensure positive quasi-rents in state s_1 as long as $n_o > 0$. On the other hand, when s_2 occurs, the firm will not opt for the lower wage if n_o is such that

$$(12) \quad [A(s_2) - \underline{v}] \; n_o < A(s_2) - \bar{v} .$$

Under the present assumptions, there exists $n_o > 0$ satisfying (12) because the right-hand side is positive. It is now straightforward to check that the modified contract is associated with larger expected utility and profit, which contradicts the optimality of having a constant v.

Under the assumptions of the counter example, it can also be shown that there is an optimal contract of the form indicated in Figure 1.

The supposition above is that monetary policy keeps constant the general price level p--by price stabilizing transactions in goods, if necessary. We now turn briefly to the consequences of alternative monetary policies.

It might be thought that the above monetary policy would make the "supply of money" a sufficient indicator of the state s and that, consequently, firms could and would index w (and n) by the money supply instead of by n, thus restoring Azariadis' contract.

Matters of lags and money supply measurement aside, there are two difficulties with that view. One is that, for the above analysis, the state s can be taken to be a _vector_ of real shocks (as measured, for example, by all real materials prices and relative goods prices). Hence, the money supply would not generally disclose variations in s in a way that would reflect adequately their impacts upon every firm's f (n, s). For simplicity, however, we shall restrict the remaining discussion to an economy with a one-dimensional s (such as the real price of some material input).

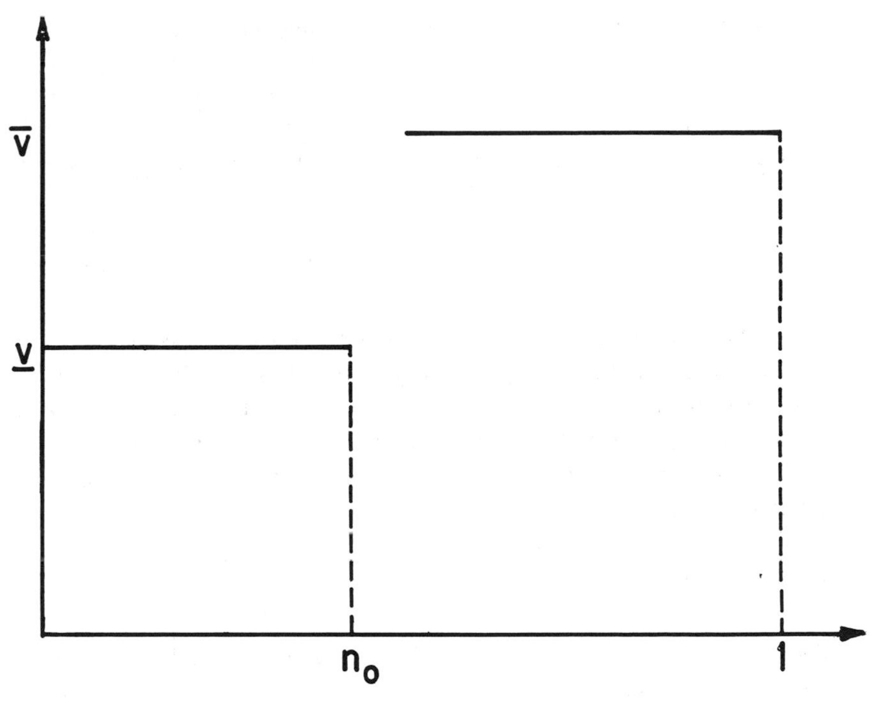

Figure 1

The second difficulty is that changes in the money supply may be attributable to a "velocity shock" (liquidity preference) rather than to the "real shock" measured by s. To take a simple case, let

$$(13a)\quad M = p^{o} L[Y(s), s]\ z, \quad L_{Y} > 0, L_{s} > 0, z > 0;$$

$$(14)\quad Y(s) = \sum_{j} f^{j}[n^{j}(s), s], \quad f^{j}_{n} > 0, f^{j}_{s} > 0, s > 0,$$

where z is the velocity variable and Y (s) is interpretable as aggregate output when (real) state s occurs. Then, the money supply, M, constitutes a "signal" not of s alone but, rather, of L (·) z. The latter contains also the "noise" from z which may vary independently of s.

If money policy fixed M instead and the price level adjusted in such a way that

$$(13b)\quad M^{o} = p L[Y(s), s]\ z,$$

then p would constitute the same noisy signal as did M when p was fixed.

Under either policy, it is likely that contracts specifying v and n will give little weight to M, p, and M/p, as we have modeled them, if the variance of z is sufficiently large and the correlation between z and s sufficiently small.

Suppose now that the central bank can perfectly forecast z and let monetary policy make

$$(15)\quad M = \beta z, \ \beta > 0.$$

If Y (s) is increasing in s, then p will be decreasing in s and will therefore constitute a perfect signal of s. Now, if s is indeed one-dimensional, firms could adopt the Azariadis contract–if they did so, no firm would find it profitable to deviate from it–and the opportunity for a welfare gain (in part from larger employment in poor states) is clear. If the state is in fact multidimensional, Azariadis' contracts are impractical (as we argued above). But, firms could write contracts indexing v by both n <u>and</u> p, so as to take advantage of those elements of s which are signaled by p. To illustrate the nature of this advantage, we refer to the previous two-state example. If the policy in (15) is followed, and firms index v by n in the manner previously analyzed, then p would be a decreasing function of s. Hence, the firm could index w by p instead of by n (for example, by setting $\frac{w}{p} = \bar{v}$ if s_2 and $\frac{w}{p} = \underline{v}$ if s_1) in such a way that, since this variation of v is independent of n, the firm could operate at "full employment" (n = m) in both states and thus increase both expected profits and utility. Previously, the monopsony effect of larger n upon v was a bar to full employment in the poorer state.

It is interesting to note that the usefulness of these monetary policies which (merely) neutralize z does not require that the central bank know s. Suppose now that the bank can perfectly forecast s as well as z. Then, every policy function from the class of functions M (s, z), which makes p a one-to-one function of s, performs no better or worse than the semiactivist policy described by (15). In particular, the choice among activist policy functions

$$(16) \quad M(s, z) = \beta z \mu(s), \quad \mu'(s) < 0$$

makes no difference because $\mu(s)$ only introduces a monotone transformation of the one-to-one relation between p and s.

The choice among such activist monetary policy functions, however, does make a difference if the bank's estimates of z and s are subject to error. It is reasonable conjecture that if z is subject to large errors of forecast and s is not, then, when forecasting small (large) s, the central bank should increase (decrease) M relative to z so as to magnify the expected rise (fall) of p and thus strengthen the ratio of "signal to noise" conveyed by the price level.

REFERENCES

1. Arrow, K. J. Essays in the Theory of Risk-Bearing. Amsterdam: North-Holland Publishing Co., 1970.

2. Azariadis, C., "Implicit Contracts and Underemployment Equilibria," Journal of Political Economy, 83, No. 6, (December 1975), 1183-1202.

3. Baily, M. N., "Wages and Employment under Uncertain Demand," Review of Economic Studies, XLI (1), No. 125, (January 1974), 37-50.

4. Gordon, D. F., "A Neo-Classical Theory of Keynesian Unemployment," in The Phillips Curve and Labor Markets, (eds. K. Brunner and A. H. Meltzer), Carnegie-Rochester Conference Series on Public Policy, Vol. 1, Amsterdam: North-Holland, (1976), 65-97.

5. Okun, A. M., "Inflation: Its Mechanics and Welfare Costs," Brookings Papers on Economic Activity, Washington, D. C.: The Brookings Institution, 6 (1975:2), 351-401.

6. Phelps, E. S., and Taylor, J. B., "Stabilizing Powers of Monetary Policy under Rational Expectations," Journal of Political Economy, 84, No. 6, forthcoming December 1976.

7. Phelps, E. S., and Winter, S. G. Jr., "Optimal Price Policy under Atomistic Competition," in Microeconomic Foundations of Employment and Inflation Theory, (eds. E.S. Phelps, et al.), New York: W.W. Norton, 1970.

8. Sargent, T. J., and Wallace, N., "'Rational' Expectations, the Optimal Monetary Instrument, and the Optimal Money Supply Rule," Journal of Political Economy, 83, No. 2, (April 1975), 241-254.

9. Shavell, S., "Sharing Risks of Deferred Payment," Journal of Political Economy, 84, No. 1, (February 1976), 161-168.

COMMODITY-SUPPLY SHOCK AND FULL-EMPLOYMENT MONETARY POLICY

IF ONE OR MORE unanticipated disturbances should cause the expectation of a lengthy contraction of commodity supplies, what quick adjustment of the money supply—failing a quick adjustment of money wage rates—would be required to maintain the normal volume of employment? Or would the monetarist course be best suited to avoid both the Scylla of underemployment depression and the Charybdis of overemployment wage inflation? This question, first posed by Robert Gordon and me in early 1974 after a succession of supply shocks, became the focal issue in monetary policy over the ensuing slump.[1]

Gordon [3] warned of the recession that would result from the disturbances to food and fuel supplies if the money supply were not stepped up to accommodate the consequent rise of money prices. On the other hand, I observed [5], the appropriate rise of the money supply is unlikely to be proportional

* Portions of this material were presented at the Carnegie-Rochester conference in Pittsburgh, November 14–15, 1975, and at the Barnard-Columbia International Monetary Symposium, December 11–12, 1975. A National Science Foundation grant is acknowledged.

[1] Gordon and I happened to have early opportunities to ponder the problem: Gordon on April 10, 1974, at the annual meeting of the Saving and Loan Association in Chicago, and I at meetings sponsored by the American Enterprise Institute on April 1 and May 1 in Tokyo and Washington, D.C. Some others who addressed the issue are cited below. If the supply shocks produced inadequate professional attention and advice in this country, whatever good it would have done, the shortcoming was institutional more than intellectual.

Of course, had the supply disturbances then observed been as fleeting as was wished, the question could have been neglected at little cost. In fact, though, the oil cartel begun in late 1973 has held up despite the Scylla of depression; droughts which began in 1972–73 have continued intermittenly; even the wayward anchovy has remained so. Nor were the shocks minor in size. Estimates that the full-employment domestic product of the OECD economies fell in 1974 by about one year's growth give some idea, albeit not a full picture, of the scale of the supply shocks experienced.

EDMUND S. PHELPS *is professor of economics, Columbia University.*

0022-2879/78/0578-0206 $00.50/0
JOURNAL OF MONEY, CREDIT, AND BANKING, vol. 10, no. 2 (May 1978)

to the rise of prices: the contraction of full-employment output due to the supply shocks ordains *some* decline of real cash balances in the new full-employment equilibrium—barring an attendant fall of interest rates so large as to offset the contraction of the transactions demand for liquidity. The critical issue was whether the supply shocks would drive up the demand price for the full-employment volume of output—the price level at which the decreased full-employment output could be sold—by *enough* (without a boost to the money supply) to reduce the real value of the pre-existing money wage down to the new and lower real wage level that producers, working with reduced commodity inputs, would require to go on employing the full-employment quantity of labor. *If* not, a slump would follow until wage negotiations finally brought the average money wage down to the point where the supply price that producers asked for the full-employment volume of output no longer exceeded the demand price at which that output could be sold.

Yet I, and perhaps others, had not then thought through the structural conditions under which this recession-spelling "if" would be the empirically applicable one. It was only at the end of 1974, when the price level had risen more than most had expected and indeed every sign pointed to a major recession, that I began urging a "quantum increase" in the quantity of money [4].[2]

The belated objective of this paper is a formal analysis of the theoretical question posed by Gordon and me. Gordon [2] has since performed a similar exercise in the form of a two-sector (food and nonfood) model. Ronald Findlay and Carlos Rodriguez [1] have produced an international model to much the same end. To differentiate my product, I analyze in part 1 a closed economy producing a single final good with attention to traditional matters of capital, inflation, and interest. The abundance of issues raised by this model, especially its treatment of wages, are then taken up in part 2.

1. A MODEL OF MONETARY ACCOMODATION

The supply shock will be represented by a permanent decline in the supply per unit of time, to be denoted σ, of some raw material consumed in the production process. In the simplest story, the material is produced without the assistance of labor and capital. In any case, the quantity of the material is hypothesized to enter into an aggregate production function

$$Y = F(\overset{+}{K}, \overset{+}{N}, \overset{+}{\sigma}), \tag{1}$$

[2] Much else in the way of antirecession advice was then being given. By September 1974, for example, Richard Cooper and Robert Mundell were advocating a massive tax cut to offset the "oil tax" on American consumers and investors. Franco Modigliani expressed concern over the erosion of real cash balances then developing, and James Tobin pleaded for fiscal and monetary expansion. Most professional forecasters were then predicting a large rise of unemployment in 1975. But it is the macrotheoretics of supply shock, especially in relation to monetary policy, not the historical record of forecasts and prescriptions, with which I am concerned here.

where F is strictly quasiconcave and linear homogeneous in capital K, employment N, and σ. The algebraic signs of the three first derivatives are indicated above the respective arguments of the function.

The supply price of this final output, to which the actual price quickly tends, is given by a "mark-up" function homogeneous of degree one in the average money wage w:

$$P^S = P^S(\overset{+}{Y}, \overset{-}{K}, \overset{-}{\sigma}; \overset{+}{w}). \tag{2}$$

Specializing for exactness and simplicity, I shall treat the P^S function as the industry marginal cost curve, so that

$$P^S = w \cdot [F_N(\overset{+}{K}, \overset{-}{N}, \overset{+}{\sigma})]^{-1}. \tag{2'}$$

I shall be assuming, as indicated, that σ and N are "complements" in the sense that, with the given K, the decline of σ reduces labor's marginal product $F_N(\cdot)$ for each N and thus, by (2′), raises P^S for each (N, w). See Figure 1 for the old and new supply-price schedules, corresponding to σ_0 and σ_1 respectively.

We shall be interested particularly in the supply price of final output at the "normal" or "full-employment" level of employment. The full-employment supply of labor $N^S(F_N, F, K, \cdots)$ will not generally be independent of σ. Perhaps it will be decreasing in σ, the income effect outweighing the substitution effect over the relevant range; perhaps it will be increasing in σ. A compromise

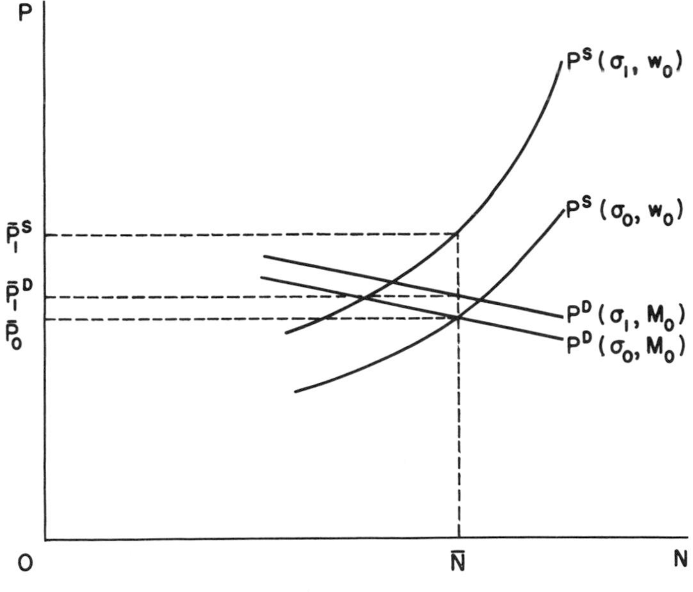

Fig. 1.

assumption is that the full-employment quantity of employment, to be denoted $\bar{N}$, is left unaltered by the particular decline of σ actually experienced:

$$N^S(\sigma_1, K_0) = N^S(\sigma_0, K_0) = \bar{N}, \qquad \sigma_1 < \sigma_0. \tag{3}$$

It remains to specify the behavior of the average money wage that figures in the supply-price function. I assume that the level of the money wage will be substantially unperturbed by the supply shock, at least over the near future. If we let w_o devote the preshock level of the average money wage and w_0 the postshock level—$t = 0$ being the moment of the supply shock—then

$$w_0 = w_o, \qquad w_o = \text{given} > 0. \tag{4}$$

The thrust of (4) is that money wages will not or cannot make the quick adjustment that might be necessary to maintain "full employment" following a supply shock; but by the same token an accommodative monetary policy can obviate the necessity for such a wage adjustment.

One theoretical justification of (4) appeals to the (possible) behavior of labor-market expectations. Suppose that wage setters expect the central bank to *accommodate* the supply shock by adjusting the money supply and thus the price level in such a way as to hold invariant the quantity of labor that will be demanded by firms at the pre-existing money wage w_o. Suppose also that wage setters, anticipating the invariance of the full-employment quantity of labor as postulated in (3), expect no change in the quantity of labor supplied. If they know they hold these beliefs in common, then their "rational expectation" is that the preshock money wage will equilibrate the labor market as it did before the shock. Each firm will expect the other firms to maintain their wages and it will do the same.

Another interpretation of (4) is available in economies where, because of the staggering of money-wage contracts, the average wage is a continuous-state variable like the aggregate capital stock: it can rise or fall only sluggishly in response to disturbances, so that its current *level* at any moment is given by past history. A key proviso here is that these contracts do not effectively "index" money wages to the money supply either directly or indirectly through cost-of-living escalators—at least not in an equiproportionate or unitary-elastic way (full escalation), for in that extreme case monetary policy would be powerless to accommodate the supply shock through its adjustment of aggregate demand and money prices.

A third justification of my wage assumption is possible when the latter is amended to read: $w_0 = w_\sigma$ if $N = \bar{N}$. It might be a feature of the understanding between firm and employees that their money wages will be reduced only if economic forces have in fact driven the firm to impose layoffs. These remarks in defense of (4) will be amplified when consideration is given to others wage theories in part 2.

It follows from the above equations that the supply price of full-employment output, which is defined by

$$\bar{P}^S = w_O \cdot F_N(\bar{N}, K, \sigma)^{-1}, \tag{5}$$

will be driven up by the decline of σ. The full-employment supply price—the final-goods price at which producers must be able to sell if they are to go on employing the quantity $\bar{N}$—is increased from $\bar{P}_0^S$ to $\bar{P}_1^S$ as shown in Figure 1.

Now suppose the economy was operating at full employment until the supply shock. If producers were soon to put their prices up to $\bar{P}_1^S$ and if the current money supply remained at M_0, would there be just enough "aggregate demand" at that price level and money supply to maintain full employment? Too much? Or too little? One's answer depends, of course, on the demand side of one's model. For illustration I adopt the equations of Tobin's [6] aggregative model, extending it later to incorporate the expected rate of inflation and the growth of capital.

A. A Statical Analysis

The *LM* equation is

$$M_0 = P^D \cdot L[F(K, \overset{+}{N}, \sigma), r \overset{-}{+} x], \tag{6}$$

where r is the expected short-term real rate of interest and x, treated as a *parameter* to begin with, is the expected short-term rate of inflation. Hence $r + x \equiv i$ is the short-term money interest rate. Given r, (6) determines for each N the corresponding demand price of final output P^D. The latter is that price level (which if it were set by producers would be) just large enough to bring the demand for money up to equality with the money supply M_0 at a given employment level.

The following *IS* equation determines the expected real interest rate as a function of employment:

$$r = F_K(\overset{-}{K}, \overset{+}{N}, \overset{+}{\sigma}). \tag{7}$$

Note the premise that lower σ spells a lower value of F_K.

Equations (6) and (7) together make the demand price a (single-valued) function of employment. Such a schedule is drawn—one for each σ—in Figure 1. Every point on the demand-price schedule corresponds to a *LM-IS* intersection in the (N, r) plane. At any point on this schedule where the corresponding *IS* curve cuts the *LM* schedule from above, the demand-price schedule is falling (with rising employment). The analysis below is confined to that normal case.

The *full-employment* demand price may now be seen to satisfy

$$\bar{P}^D = M_0 \cdot L[F(K, \bar{N}, \sigma), F_K(K, \bar{N}, \sigma) + x]^{-1}. \tag{8}$$

The maintenance of full employment requires that the right-hand side of equation (8) continue to equal the full-employment supply price given in equation (5). Though the fall of σ was seen to raise $\bar{P}^S$, there is no guarantee from (8) that $\bar{P}^D$ will be raised as much or even raised at all.

Let us calculate the proportionate (algebraic) *rise* of the full-employment demand price per unit of *decline* in σ. It is

$$-\frac{d\bar{P}^D}{d\sigma}\frac{1}{\bar{P}^D}=\frac{\overset{+}{L_Y}F}{L}\cdot\frac{\overset{+}{F_\sigma}}{F}+\frac{\overset{-}{L_i}F_K}{L}\cdot\frac{\overset{+}{F_{K\sigma}}}{F_K} \tag{9}$$

by differentiation of (8). This calculation is to be compared to the proportionate rise of the full-employment supply price which, by differentiation of (5), is

$$-\frac{d\bar{P}^S}{d\sigma}\frac{1}{\bar{P}^S}=\frac{\overset{+}{F_{N\sigma}}}{F_N}. \tag{10}$$

If the right-hand side of (9) is less than the right side of (10), full employment will not be maintainable with unchanged M_0. In all normal cases, where the demand-price schedule cuts the supply-price schedule from above, the result will then be a fall from full employment.[3] The algebraic excess of (10) over (9) is precisely the proportionate increase of the money supply needed to maintain full employment, i.e., $-(1/\bar{M})\,d\bar{M}/d\sigma$.

Consider now a transparent example: $F_\sigma/F = F_{N\sigma}/F_N(>0)$ and $L_i = 0$. Thus, total product and labor's marginal product fall in equal proportion. If the demand for real cash balances $L(\cdot)$ is proportional to real income and insensitive to $i \equiv F_K + x$, then the fall of full-employment output will produce a proportionate rise in the demand price for full-employment output equal to the proportionate fall in the total and marginal product of the full-employment quantity of labor and hence equal to the proportionate rise in the supply price of full-employment output. In this example, therefore, no change of the money supply is needed to maintain full-employment.

It should now be evident that, in this example, the demand price $\bar{P}^D$ rises *less* than the supply price if and only if the income elasticity $L_Y Y/L$ is less than one. In that event, to repeat, "aggregate demand" will be insufficient to sustain full employment; in all normal cases, a recession of employment must occur until the money wage has dropped enough to bring the supply price of full-employment output down to the initially deficient demand price. Most empirical estimates, of course, put the income elasticity at considerably less than one.

A contraction of σ, contrary to the above example, may very well increase its own relative share in (the reduced) full-employment income. Then either F_N or F_K or both must fall in greater proportion than the fall of F. A contraction of σ that reduces full-employment F from 100 to 96 and increases its own share

[3] These are the cases in which the *IS* curve cuts the upward-slopping *LM* curve from above.

from 5 percent to 10 percent would reduce real wage *plus* capital income from 95 to 86.4, a decline of more than 9 percent (of itself). Should F_N decline by the representative 9 percent when F falls by 4 percent (at the full-employment N), the rise of the demand price $\bar{P}^D$ would be at least 5 percent short of the new and (9 percent) higher supply price—if $L_Y Y/L \leqslant 1$ and assuming still that $L_i = 0$. Then maintenance of full employment at the initial money wage would require a one-shot increase in the money stock of at least 5 percent.

Now suppose instead that $L_i < 0$. If $F_{K\sigma} > 0$, the decline of σ reduces F_K which, by (7), reduces r and thus, by (9), makes the new full-employment demand price smaller than it otherwise would be. This profit-rate effect is another element in the possible tendency to insufficient demand for maintenance of full employment.

In the above analysis we have taken $F_{K\sigma}$ and $F_{N\sigma}$ as independent. If instead we take $F_{\sigma\sigma}$ to be given independently, $F_{N\sigma}$ is smaller the larger is $F_{K\sigma}$. The connecting relation among the three derivatives is

$$\frac{F_{K\sigma}}{F_K} \cdot \frac{KF_K}{F} + \frac{F_{N\sigma}}{F_N} \cdot \frac{NF_N}{F} + \frac{F_{\sigma\sigma}}{F_\sigma} \cdot \frac{\sigma F_\sigma}{F} = 0. \tag{11}$$

Hence the excess of the right-hand side of (10) over that of (9), which difference is the proportionate increase of the money supply required for full employment, can be written

$$\frac{\overset{+}{F}_{N\sigma}}{F_N}\left[1 + \frac{\overset{-}{L}_i r}{L} \cdot \frac{\bar{N}\overset{+}{F}_N}{KF_K}\right] - \frac{\overset{+}{L}_Y F}{L}\,\frac{\overset{+}{F}_\sigma}{F} + \frac{\overset{-}{L}_i F_K}{L}\,\frac{\overset{-}{F}_{\sigma\sigma}}{F_\sigma}\,\frac{\sigma \overset{+}{F}_\sigma}{KF_K} = -\frac{\bar{M}_\sigma}{\bar{M}}. \tag{12}$$

$\bar{M}$, being the full-employment money supply, is that value of M which equates $\bar{P}^D$ (a function of M) to $\bar{P}^S$ (a function of w). Assuming as before that $F_{N\sigma}/F_N > (YL_Y/L)F_\sigma/F(>0)$, the above expression is unambiguously positive if $0 > \bar{N}F_{N\sigma} + \sigma F_{\sigma\sigma} = -KF_{K\sigma}$, which was already implied. However (12) shows that even when $F_{N\sigma} < 0$ an increase of the money supply may well be required; for if $L_i < 0$, smaller $F_{N\sigma}$ is (at least partially) offset by larger $F_{K\sigma}$.

B. *Dynamical Analyses*

The remaining problem in calculating the change of the money supply required for maintenance of full employment is to release the expected inflation rate, x in our notation, from the pound of ceteris paribus. I shall use here the hypothesis of rational expectations: The expected inflation rate correctly forecasts the actual rate. Absent further shocks, the future path of inflation will be determined by the ensuing growth in the supplies of money and capital.

Three scenarios will be considered. In each, the money supply has been jumped to the new level initially required for full employment. And in each, the average money wage, though perhaps sluggish, is assumed to be moving (if necessary) in relation to the path of the money supply in such a way as will maintain full employment thereafter. The implied path of the average money wage will, of course, depend upon the accompanying paths of capital and money. These full-employment scenarios are not equally plausible or desirable. They are intended mainly as reference points.

Imagine that the economy was in a full-employment, zero-inflation stationary state until the supply shock occurred. By hypothesis, $\bar{N}$ and the technology remain constant over the future, but K does not. I postulate that the fall of σ reduces consumption by less than output at each K, so that K must begin to decline along the (new) full-employment path.[4] I shall further suppose that the ensuing decline is monotonic, smooth, and asymptotic to some new stationary level $K^* < K_0$. These assumptions about the full-employment path of capital are amply captured by

$$\dot{K} = S(K; \sigma), \quad S_K < 0, \quad S_\sigma > 0; \qquad S(K^*, \sigma) = 0, \tag{13}$$

where $\dot{K}$ is net investment. In general, a dotted variable such as $\dot{Z}$ will denote the first time derivative of the variable. Also, since $\bar{N}$ is going to be treated as fixed through time, I shall supress it from the notation where possible, so that the production function, for example, will be written $F(K, \sigma)$.

1. In the first scenario considered, the money supply is continuously varied, following whatever initial adjustment was needed at $t = 0$ to accommodate the supply shock, so as to hold steady the *average money wage* level throughout the future at the same level that prevailed up to $t = 0$. The logic of this sequence is just a reiteration of equation (4). The central bank promises and delivers that growth of the money supply which will precisely and indefinitely underwrite continued "full employment" in the (desired) event that wage setters will maintain money wage rates—which wage setters then have every incentive to do.[5]

Accordingly the full-employment price level is given by $w_o F(K(t), \sigma_1)^{-1}$, where w_o is now a constant throughout time. Because K will be declining toward K^*, and $F_{NK} > 0$, the full-employment price level will be rising toward P^*, say. This transient after-inflation is the mechanism by which real wages decline to match the decline of the full-employment marginal product of labor that is entailed by the decline of the capital stock. The rate of inflation at any moment during this adjustment process is evidently $-(F_N)^{-1} F_{NK} \dot{K}/K$. Using (13), therefore, we obtain

$$\bar{M}(t) = w_o F_N(K(t), \sigma_1)^{-1} L[F(K(t), \sigma_1), F_K - F_N^{-1} F_{NK} K^{-1} S(K(t), \sigma_1)] \tag{14'}$$

[4] Possibly a society might produce *increasing* K to "make up" for the fall of σ. The analysis of that symmetrical story is left to the reader.

[5] If the monetary authorities are believed, and if our earlier assumptions (on behalf of uniqueness) are satisfied, any other wage trajectory would have to be based on mistaken wage expectations. But what would inspire a speculative bubble, say, in a setting where the equilibrium trajectory is so conspicuous?

for the path of the money supply necessary for continuing full employment at a "level" money wage. Plausibly, this money supply will be rising in the transition to a lower capital stock.

In this constant-wage scenario, then, the expected rate of inflation, zero by hypothesis before the supply shock, turns (transiently) positive afterwards in rational anticipation of the subsequent capital-shallowing postulated in (13). But it does not appear that the magnitude of the prospective inflation would be large enough to overturn the presumption reached in the previous section: that the money supply must jump up when the supply shock strikes if money wages will not jump down.

2. The second scenario has the money supply adjusting so as to keep the *price level* constant over time following its initial rise. Accordingly, rational expectations make $x = 0$ over the entire future. In this scenario, then, no expectation of subsequent inflation arises which might alter (reduce) the demand for money and thus lessen the required increase of the money supply at $t = 0$; there is only the unanticipated one-time jump of the price level attributable to the drop of σ. The expected rate of inflation x is thus constant—as it was treated in the statical exercise.[6]

The necessary path of the money supply for full employment with zero inflation is given by

$$\bar{M}(t) = \bar{P} \cdot L[F(K(t), \sigma_1), F_K(K(t), \sigma_1)], \tag{14''}$$

where, of course, $\bar{P}$ as well as σ_1 are constants. If, as postulated, K will move downward following the supply shock, and in so doing reduce the demand for real cash balances, then $\bar{M}(t)$ must decline following its initial jump in order to avoid inflation and its anticipation over the future.

3. The final scenario to be considered is monetarist. Here the *money supply* remains constant, following its initial adjustment at $t = 0$, and is announced and forecasted to be so:

$$\bar{M}(t) = \text{constant for all } t > 0. \tag{14'''}$$

If we suppose, as in the second scenario, that wages adjust to maintain full employment, so that $N = \bar{N} = \text{constant}$, then differentiation of (5) gives

$$(\overset{+}{L}_Y \overset{+}{F}_K + \overset{-}{L}_i \overset{-}{F}_{KK})\dot{K} + \overset{-}{L}_i \dot{x} = -xL, \tag{15}$$

where we have used $x = \dot{P}/P$, $M/P = L$, and hence $\dot{L} = -xL$. Therefore $x = 0$ in any stationary state with $L > 0$. In the neighborhood of such a state, then,

[6] The behavior of x would complicate the conduct of the full-employment monetary policy if, because some or all prices were sticky, the price level took some time to reach the new full-employment supply-price level $\bar{P}^S(\sigma_1)$; then the money supply might have to adjust along a J-curve rather than rise abruptly. However, the analysis of a sticky-price system is beyond the scope of this paper.

(15) implies

$$\dot{x} = J(K, x, \sigma_1), \quad J_K < 0, \quad J_x > 0, \quad J_\sigma > 0. \tag{16}$$

The phase diagram in the (K, x) plane of the system (13) and (16), which the reader is invited to draw, discloses saddle-point stability; there exists a unique trajectory to the stationary state along which x initially jumps to a positive level and then declines, like K, monotonically to the rest point (where $K = K^*, x = 0$).

A brief word on the comparative merits of these three monetary strategies: the second scenario requires a (gradual) decline of money wage rates—a fall away from the previous trend path of wages if the economy is accustomed to secular inflation or productivity growth. So too does the third scenario, though to a necessarily lesser extent, if the decline of the capital stock (like the fall of σ) reduces the full-employment real wage proportionately more than it reduces the full-employment demand for cash balances. The neoclassical presumption, to overwork the familiar adjective, has been that a central bank can engineer the second (or the third) scenario as easily as the first: if money wages have to adjust, it is "rational" for them to do it, and so they will. But, if I am right, that outcome is the exception rather than the rule; the first scenario is the only one truly consistent with continuous full employment for the same reasons given in defense of equation (4).

2. WHY POLICY WAS UNACCOMMODATING

If the above macroeconomic model is not misleading, a monetary policy of supply-shock accommodation was both necessary and sufficient to forestall or foreshorten the post-1974 slump in aggregate employment. From that perspective it is striking and disturbing to observe that there was no effort at accommodation though the 1974–75 downturn was the deepest one since the Great Depression. This paper would be frustratingly incomplete without a consideration of the reasons for this surprising turn in monetary policy.

Current discussions offer a wealth of hypotheses in the political economy of government policy-making and central-bank policy in particular. In new-left theory, for example, recessions are occassionally inflicted on the work force to put an end to rising strikes and sagging worker efficiency. Yet sociological studies find that recessions produce mental illness and subsequent health problems, not a renewal of efficiency. (There is, however, a more influential hypothesis that strikes much the same note, so I shall be returning to the new-left perspective.)

In recent electoral theories, an electorate that is enjoying job security at election time will reciprocate the favor by rewarding the incumbent administration with reelection; such job security can be engineered by depressing employment before election year and restoring it during election year so that employment is rising and the chance of layoff is small on election day. Most of the evidence on behalf of this theory comes from the 1930s. But the Democrats then had a double advantage; they could take credit for raising employment and blame the Republicans for the prior downturn. Incumbents might hesitate to create their own downturn without a promising excuse—would blaming the Arabs have been judged good enough in 1975? They might also fear the risk that recovery would be too little and too late. In any case, the Federal Reserve provided little or no stimulus to aid reelection of the Republicans in 1976.

Another theory observes that an unanticipated rise of the price level is hard on lenders, pensioners, and those living out their careers on outdated wage agreements; if the governors of the Federal Reserve meet that description, their bread must be buttered on the side of a temporary slump rather than a rise of the price level. But surely the normal person prizes his self-respect more than his "goods" and wants also the esteem of his community. This theory takes too narrow a view of self-interest.

A more plausible hypothesis starts from the political theory of concentrated benefits: Each agency of government becomes the captive of the pressure group that has the comparative advantage and comparative interest in dominating it. If the political equilibrium allocates monetary policy to "banking interests" hostile to unanticipated inflation, leaving trade and immigration to the labor unions, then the monetary accommodation of supply shocks has little chance of adoption. It is not obvious, however, that monetary policy should become the special preserve of a single interest group, nor why that group should be the banks. A few decades ago it was labor's capture of the central bank that was said to explain monetary policy.

A limitation of these hypotheses is their incomplete view of human motivations. When low-income voters seemed ready to spurn McGovern's 1972 plan for a $1,000 demogrant, I asked, "Whatever happened to the theory that people vote their self-interests?" My colleague Albert Hart shot back, "Their ideas are their interests." Government officials are presumably no exception to this observation and indeed they often complain of the pecuniary sacrifies they have to make in order to work for their beliefs. The concentrated-benefits hypothesis in particular overlooks the role played by "theory." To hold sway over monetary policy, vested interests may find it necessary to persuade the public (and perhaps themselves) that their policy is harmless or benevolent. The advent of new theories may tip the balance in the determination of public policy.

In the area of monetary economics, one need not look far to find a new belief. Monetarism, the doctrine of inflexible monetary policy, is in the ascendant. It is entirely possible that the rise of monetarism predisposed the Federal Reserve against accommodation of the recent supply shocks; the emphasis upon monetary aggregates instead of interest rates must have worked in that direction. Yet the original argument for monetarism could hardly have been very influential—the argument that fine tuning might be worse than no tuning, worse for the stability of employment as well as the stability of the price level.

It is hard to believe that the economics profession and the Federal Reserve could have worried that a small jump of the money supply in the winter of 1974–75 would have risked a boom and thus *de*stabilized employment. One wonders, therefore, what new arguments might have justified the Fed's stance against accommodation of the recent supply shocks.

The answer, I suggest, is that the Federal Reserve, and with it much of the profession, has come to operate on new or rehabilitated conceptions of money-wage behavior quite unlike that prevailing early in this decade: a *classical* theory according to which a policy of monetary accommodation was dispensable, because employment would recover quickly enough without it; and a *semiclassical* theory according to which accommodation would have been ineffective. Although these two theories are mutually exclusive, they share the implication that nonaccommodation is virtually harmless. Since both theories differ so from the wage theory underlying my own analysis of supply-shock accommodation, a critical survey of them seems in order.

A. Alternative Models of Nonaccommodation

In the *classical* theory, the prospect of unaccommodating monetary policy toward a supply shock will elicit a fall of money wage rates—in lieu of the rise of the money supply—large enough to maintain or soon restore full employment. If all firms' money-wage rate commitments for the next interval are perfectly synchronous, the temporary slump of employment caused by the the unanticipated supply shock will persist only until the date at which the new and lower wage rates can be established. If firms' wage commitments are nonsynchronous, full recovery will be reached on the expiration of the last surviving wage commitment made prior to the supply shock. In an economy where most wage and salary commitments run for one year and union agreements typically two or three, therefore, employment might recover about half its lost ground within one year and nearly all the ground within two.

One of the more precarious assumptions of the theory is its hypothesis of rational expectations based on *public* knowledge of the correct (in this case classical) econometric model. Suppose, contrariwise, that each firm, whatever its own certainty about the size of the general reduction of money wage rates needed to restore full-employment equilibrium, is uncertain about the estimates being made by other firms. Then each firm may reduce its own money-way scale insufficiently for full employment within the time span predicted by the classical theory if, for one reason or another, it would prefer its own wages to err on the high side rather than the low side of the market average. Uncertainty about the adjustment of their employees' expectations of wages elsewhere might also be a cause for caution.

An assumption in the theory regarding the terms of wage commitments is also crucial: that all or most such commitments specify a moving money-wage rather than a fixed money-wage over the contract period. In fact, long-term union agreements apart, the most common arrangement is a flat wage or salary reviewed and revised every twelve months. If wage commitments are predominantly of that latter form and if their starting dates are staggered evenly over the calender year—half the firms revising wages every January and half every July, for example—then it can be argued that the average money wage will merely approach but never reach the reduced level predicted for it by the classical theory. Barring help from some new economic disturbance or some other adjustment mechanism (not envisioned by the classical theory), recovery to full employment will proceed asymptotically in a long dragged-out process.

Another difficulty for the classical theory is the matter of credibility. If firms chose not to cut their wages, wouldn't the central bank abandon its sincere and avowed intentions not to accommodate? If firms so believe won't they in fact decide to maintain their money wage rates, figuring that other firms will do the same and the central bank will consequently accommodate? It is a little like the familiar problem of deterrence in which the side aiming to deter is known to prefer not to carry out its threat if and when the threat fails and the damage is done.

The analogy is inexact though, because, unlike the decision to launch a nuclear strike, the decision of the central bank not to accommodate can be revised at any future moment. That reversibility may cut both ways. By refusing to accommodate at first, no matter what money wages do, the central bank can presumably establish in the minds of wage setters the riskiness of assuming that the bank will decide to accommodate in the future; in the case of synchronous wage setting this risk seems to be all the central bank requires to motivate wage cuts (though they may be insufficient at first to restore full employment for the reasons suggested earlier). On the other hand, the bank's problem may be made worse if wages are set nonsynchronously: firms currently revising wages may wonder whether the bank will not eventually settle for half a loaf, accommodating the remaining part of the supply shock if and when wages have fallen enough to satisfy the central bank. Then the decline of wages and the recovery of employment would proceed more slowly than if nonaccommodation were thought to be total and irrevocable.

A deep problem for classical theory arises if the year-to-year revisions in wage and salary commitments are manifestations of some much longer-lived "implicit contracts" between firm and employees. In the classical theory, a firm reduces its money wages in anticipation that other firms will be doing the same (concurrently or in the future when their turn for wage adjustments comes up) and hence in the anticipation that failure to reduce money wages would cause it to lose sales. It is possible, however, that the individual firm has an obligation, and will abide by the obligation for the sake of its long-range interests, not to reduce money wages except in response to a realized decline of the general wage level or a realized decline of employment. Then the classical theory of anticipatory money-wage reductions that preserve or quickly restore the level of employment evidently falls to the ground. Though each firm's money wage rates might fall with the decline of its employment level, and fall further if its wage rates were tied to other firms' similarly lower wages, these wage reductions would be erased if employment were fully to be restored—since such contracts warrant lower wages only as long as employment and other wages remain lower. It may very well be that these quasicontractual constraints would gradually recede as the slump continued. Yet they might seriously retard the downward adjustment of money wage rates on which a full and prompt recovery of employment depends.

The notion that long-running implicit contracts or norms place confining limitations on wage and salary behavior leads conveniently to a discussion of what I called the *semiclassical* theory of wage behavior. This theory accepts only portions of the classical contentions: A permanent change of the money supply would cause all money wages and prices ultimately to change equiproportionately over what they would otherwise ultimately be, and thus it would have no lasting effects on output and employment. Any permanent shock that reduced only the demand price for the original level of output, not the supply price, would cause prices and money wages to fall to such an extent as to restore the original level of output. Yet the mechanism is not the classical one in which money wage rates tend to equilibrate the labor market and money prices the goods markets—thus working always toward *full* employment—with whatever independence they may need for that task. The semiclassical mechanism is, instead, the alleged tendency of labor contracts to tie money wage rates equiproportionately to the cost of living.

Some unclassical consequences of that mechanism emerge when the disturbance to equilibrium is a commodity supply shock. Suppose, for simplicity, that the impact of the shock leaves the full-employment demand price of output unchanged but raises the full-employment supply price. This reduces the real wage required to induce firms to continue producing at the full-employment level; but the real wage actually paid at full employment is stuck, money wages being tied to money prices. Barring new structural changes, policy-made or other, a slump of employment will result and persist as long as the real wage that goes with the full-employment level of activity stays fixed—as long as money wages wait for prices to fall and prices wait for wages from their newly elevated levels. We may think of the economy as coming to rest at the employment level where the marginal product of labor schedule, shifted downward by the supply shock, interesects an unchanged real wage schedule that shows contractual real wages as some (nondecreasing) function of the level of employment. From this semiclassical rest point, monetary policy can do nothing to hasten or assure the recovery of employment; any acceleration of employment achieved would raise prices in the process, and the ensuing catch-up of wages to prices would drive prices still higher until output and employment had slid back to where they otherwise would have been. A self-correcting mechanism will come into play, tending to restore full employment, only if and when firms are permitted (with the lapse of contracts) or compelled (by new entrants) to revise downwards the real wages they offer their employees.

An empirical appraisal of this theory might concede that the failure of money wage rates to fall or even to decelerate much in 1975 and beyond lends some support to the semiclassicists; however, the objections and qualifications to the classical theory registered earlier provide alternative explanations of the disappointing behavior of wages. The most telling evidence so far seems to be against the semiclassical theory. Real wages were not maintained following the recent supply shocks—they fell relative to their trend and over some of the recent period they fell absolutely. A plausible and preliminary verdict based on United States data is that the semiclassical theory is at best half-right. A policy to accommodate an 8 percent rise in the full-employment supply price of output might have provoked a 4 percent extra rise of money wages and, hence, an additional 4 percent rise of prices, and so on; the process would then have ended with a 16 percent rise of the price level and an 8 percent rise of wages.

A theoretical examination of the semi-classical theory would also greatly weaken its argument. There is, first of all, the obvious point that wage "contracts," implicit or explicit, do not prevail in much of the labor market (the market for day labor and for piecework, for examples). There is also the point that wage-contract theory, where applicable, reaches the conclusion that money wages will be indexed *in proportion* to the price level by reasoning from a questionable (though fascinating) model. The model assumes that workers and firms alike know the exact character of each economic disturbance; they not only read the observable economic variables, they also know the true model and the present state of the world. From a different kind of model, in which workers have incomplete information, it can be argued that a rise of the price level will *not* cause money wage rates to be escalated in equal proportion. The rise of the price level serves as a signal of the appropriateness, on average, of accepting a reduction of real wages as a trade-off for lesser contraction of employment. A corrolary is that a monetary policy of accommodating supply shocks serves the useful function of amplifying that "signal" and, thus, lowering further the real wage that goes with a given level of employment. Escalator clauses and cola agreements there may be—but not full escalation.

These brief remarks on semiclassical theory are all that a wide-ranging survey will permit. The theory warrants the most intensive analysis, both theoretical and empirical. For, though the worst of the post-1974 slump is behind us in the United States, several economies, including the American one, are not yet out of the woods and, in any case, supply shocks will surely strike again. So the question of their monetary accommodation will be recurring, whether or not it is in abeyance at this moment. It is to be hoped, therefore, that we will soon be better able to appraise the semiclassical view of supply-shock accommodation than we have been to date.

LITERATURE CITED

1. Findlay, Ronald, and Carlos A. Rodriguez. "Intermediate Imports and Macroeconomic Policy under Flexible Exchange Rates." *Canadian Journal of Economics*, 10 (May 1977), 208–17.

2. Gordon, Robert J. "Alternative Responses of Policy to External Shocks." *Brookings Papers on Economic Activity*, 6 (1:1975), 183–204.

3. ———. "The Consequences of Inflation for Monetary Policy." The Conference Board's Fifth Annual Midyear Outlook Conference. Chicago, Illinois, April 10, 1974.

4. Phelps, Edmund S. "Creating the Money for Tax Rebates." *New York Times*, January 26, 1975.

5. ———. "Stopover Monetarism: Supply and Demand Factors in the 1972–74 Inflation." In *The Phenomenon of Worldwide Inflation*, edited by David I. Meiselman and Arther B. Laffer, pp. 183–200. Washington, D.C.: American Enterprise Institute, 1975.

6. Tobin, James. "A Dynamic Aggregative Model." *Journal of Political Economy*, 63, (April 1955), 103–15.

TRANSNATIONAL EFFECTS OF FISCAL SHOCKS IN A TWO-COUNTRY MODEL OF DYNAMIC EQUILIBRIUM

What are the effects upon a large country, such as the United States, of a permanent fiscal shock occurring abroad? How is the Opportunity Set, available through the use of ordinary fiscal tools, altered in that country over the short and long run? If employment can be maintained at home, what else can be stabilized and what cannot be? Can all government generally reach and secure "full" employment through domestic fiscal policies? These questions are studied here from the vantage point of a dynamic macromodel of a two-country world with "monetarist" central banks and a freely floating exchange rate.

The most distinctive feature of this model is its treatment of capital stocks and national savings as endogenous state variables. The focus throughout is on the equilibrium path along which, by definition, expectations are continuously fulfilled—as if there were "perfect foresight" or "rational expectations" with regard to prices, profit, and exchange rates. Also new to international economics, although not a novelty in macroeconomics, is the model's one-product character—the aggregation assumptions of identical production functions and shiftable capital stocks within national borders. Unusual too is the assumption of "equities only" instead of the more customary "bonds only."

Less cheerfully I postulate that world goods markets are perfectly competitive—not just atomistic, but frictionless. The hope is that this assumption will not be seriously misleading (for the issues at hand) save over some very short run. I also pretend that no national ever holds another nation's money, which is surely an idealization, and no investor holds equities from both countries unless they have the same expected rate of return. The jarring assumption in the present context is the fixity of money wage rates. Yet, it can be argued that constancy of money wage rates is a tenable assumption (in some circumstances) when the question is the existence of full-employment fiscal policies in both countries.

A word about the organization of this paper. Section I lays out the model and contains some preliminary remarks on its behavior in the short run. Section II studies the determinants of the model's *stationary* equilib-

Reprinted by permission from *Public Policies in Open Economies*, K. Brunner and A. H. Meltzer (Eds.). Carnegie-Rochester Conference Series on Public Policy—A Supplementary Series to the Journal of Monetary Economics, Vol. 9, 1978, North-Holland Publishing Company.

rium with principal attention to the effects upon the home country of a fiscal shift abroad. Section III takes up the dynamics of the equilibrium path from arbitrary initial conditions. (This latter material might be skipped in a first reading.) The concluding section recapitulates some findings of the analysis regarding the maintenance of full employment by means of balanced-budget fiscal policy. The bearing of these results on Continental skepticism that fiscal stimulus at home would be beneficial abroad is noticed.

My apologies go to the readers for demanding of them more than their normal share of the work and to authors in the field for omitting comparisons of my findings to theirs. I take refuge in Wilde's advice that a job worth doing is worth doing badly. The reader can find several references to the recent literature and an analysis of a two-country dynamic model strikingly similar to mine in many respects in the paper (which has since come to my attention) by Aoki and Canzoneri in *Annals of Economic and Social Measurement* (May 1978).

I. The Model

There is a single neoclassical production function, good for both countries, and for both consumer good and capital good production. Gross domestic product in "our" country, call it "Home," is therefore a familiar function $F(N, K)$ of employment N and capital K existing there. Net domestic product is given by $F(N, K) - \mu K \equiv f(N, K)$, $\mu > 0$. The marginal product of labor is $f_N(N, K)$ and the net marginal product of capital is $f_K(N, K)$. Employment and capital in the other country, call it "Star," are denoted N^* and K^*, respectively. With perfect competition and our aggregation assumptions, any equilibrium path requires that employment in each country equate labor's marginal product to the real wage at every instant:

$$\bar{W} = Pf_N(N, K), \tag{1.1}$$

$$\bar{W}^* = P^*f_N(N^*, K^*); \quad f_N > 0, f_{NN} < 0, f_{KN} > 0, f_{KK} < 0, \text{ etc.} \tag{1.2}$$

Here W denotes the money wage and P the money price level in Home. Likewise, W^* and P^* denote the money wage and price level in Star. Throughout this paper I shall take W and W^* as fixed at the levels $\bar{W}$ and $\bar{W}^*$. Terms like $f_N(N^*, K^*)$ will often be denoted by $f_N{}^*$ although it should be kept in mind that the functions f and f^* are identical.

Is the real rate of interest in a country likewise equal to the net marginal product of its capital? Not generally. The real rates of return on money invested in *shares,* to which the real rates of interest are equal, are generally given by

$$r = \frac{Pf_K(N,K)}{P_K} + \frac{P_K - P}{P_K} \cdot \frac{\dot{K}}{K} + \frac{\dot{P}_K}{P_K} - \frac{\dot{P}}{P}, \tag{1.3}$$

$$r^* = \frac{P^*f_K(N^*,K^*)}{P_K^*} + \frac{P_K^* - P^*}{P_K^*} \frac{\dot{K}^*}{K^*} + \frac{\dot{P}_K^*}{P_K^*} - \frac{\dot{P}^*}{P^*}. \tag{1.4}$$

The sum of the second and third terms would equal the rate of appreciation in the price of shares if the stock of shares held by households and the central bank were constant. Since I suppose that each firm continuously splits its stock (when necessary) to keep the number of its shares held by the public equal to the size of its capital stock, the aforementioned gain is divided between the growth rate of the price of such shares *and* the own-rate of return on equity paper that results from stock splitting; the latter arises if either $P_K/P \equiv q > 1$ and firms are issuing new shares to make $\dot{K} > 0$ *or* $q < 1$ and firms are buying back their shares, instead of replacing their capital, so that $\dot{K} < 0$.[1] We may think of (1.3) and (1.4) as the outcomes of taking the time derivative of the equations for the levels of P_K and P_K^*:

$$P_K = \int_t^\infty Pf_K \cdot \exp\left[\int_t^u \left(\frac{P_K - P}{P_K} \frac{\dot{K}}{K} - r - \frac{\dot{P}}{P}\right) dv\right] du, \tag{1.3'}$$

$$P_K^* = \int_t^\infty P^*f_K^* \cdot \exp\left[\int_t^u \left(\frac{P_K^* - P^*}{P_K^*} \frac{\dot{K}^*}{K^*} - r^* - \frac{\dot{P}^*}{P^*}\right) dv\right] du. \tag{1.4'}$$

In the Yale theory of investment of Fisher and Tobin, firms engage in capital transactions so as to maximize the P_K, or q, enjoyed by their stockholders. Hence firms would attempt infinite $\dot{K}$ if $q > 1$ and will make $\dot{K} = -\mu K$ when $q < 1$. (More about this soon.)

Now let S denote the amount of capital, wherever located, to which residents of Home and its central bank have ownership claims. S is therefore the number of shares owned in Home (other than the holdings of their own shares by Home firms). Let S^* denote the amount of world capital owned by Star. I shall assume that Home happens to be the net creditor,

$$S - K = K^* - S^* > 0, \tag{1.5}$$

where $S^* > 0$ and $K > 0$ by assumption, so that S and K^* are also positive. I also assume Home is the only gross creditor, being the sole owner of the capital there. Nevertheless, investors "follow the flag" only in a lexicographic manner. The rate of return is prior to the nationality of shares.

Suppose that a Home-dollar's worth of Home and Star shares are perfect portfolio substitutes, at least for the cosmopolitan wealth owners

[1] I am indebted to John B. Taylor for discussions.

at Home. Then if the Star shares not held in Star are to be held in Home, the Home-dollar rate of return from holding Home shares must be matched by the "covered" dollar rate of return from holding Star shares. Let the former rate, which is the money interest rate in Home, be denoted i; let i^* denote the money interest rate in Star, the local-money rate of return on Star shares; and let E denote the exchange rate, the Home-dollar cost of one Star mark. In this notation, then, $i = i^* + \dot{E}/E$. But $P = EP^*$ by commodity arbitrage, so $\dot{E}/E = \dot{P}/P - \dot{P}^*/P^*$. Therefore $i - \dot{P}/P = i^* - P^*/\dot{P}^*$, i.e.,

$$r = r^*. \tag{1.6}$$

Assume that asset markets clear in the two countries along any equilibrium or anticipated path, so that the demand for real money balances continuously equals the supply in each country. The LM equations to be used here are

$$\begin{aligned} \bar{M} = PL\Bigg[&N\frac{\bar{W}}{P} - \bar{G} + r\hat{S}_b + \left(K - \frac{P}{P_K}\hat{S}_b\right)f_K \\ &+ (S - K)f_K{}^*, r + \frac{\dot{P}}{P}, \frac{P_K}{P}K - \hat{S}_b + \frac{P_K{}^*}{P^*}(S - K) + \frac{\bar{M}}{P}\Bigg], \end{aligned} \tag{1.7}$$

$$\begin{aligned} \bar{M}^* = P^*L^*\Bigg[&N^*\frac{\bar{W}^*}{P^*} - G^* + r^*\hat{S}_b{}^* \\ &+ \left(S^* - \frac{P^*}{P_K{}^*}S_b{}^*\right)f_K{}^*, r^* + \frac{\dot{P}^*}{P^*}, \frac{P_K{}^*}{P^*}S^* - \hat{S}_b{}^* + \frac{\bar{M}^*}{P^*}\Bigg], \\ &L_1, L_1{}^* > 0; \quad L_2, L_2{}^* < 0; \quad 0 < L_3, L_3{}^* < 1. \end{aligned} \tag{1.8}$$

By virtue of Walras' law and the aforementioned substitutability of shares, the equations of demand and supply in the shares markets may be omitted.

The third argument of each real-balance demand function is the real market value of private wealth. S_b denotes the shares owned by the national bank in Home and $\hat{S}_b$ their real market valuation, i.e., $P_K S_b/P$ or qS_b. These shares were acquired in the process of creating the money supply—now fixed at $\bar{M}$. Using analogous notation, $S^*P_K{}^*/P^* - \hat{S}_b{}^* + \bar{M}^*/P^*$ is evidently the real market value of privately held wealth in Star. The real value of private wealth in Home is obtained by deflating nominal private wealth, $P_K K - P\tilde{S}_b + EP_K{}^*(S - K) + M$, by the price level P and substituting P/P^* for E.

The second arguments of the functions L and L^* are the money rates of interest in Home and Star, respectively. One may think of these rates as being the expected nominal rates of return on shares figured in the local currencies along an equilibrium path.

The first arguments of L and L^* are take-home real wage receipts plus dividends. All taxes are on wage income, with full withholding, and government budgets are balanced in a sophisticated accounting sense. Wage taxes equal government expenditures less the real returns on the national bank's holdings of securities: $r\ P_K S_b/P = r\ \tilde{S}_b$ in Home, for example. This implies that the real value of bank holdings stays constant over time. Since the bank also holds the money supply constant, the bank may therefore have to surrender shares to the fisc, or the fisc acquire shares for the bank through extra taxes. (Of all the awkward modeling choices available, the postulate of fixed $\tilde{S}_b$ and $\tilde{S}_b{}^*$ seems to be the most tractable.) We have now discussed disposable real-wage income. To that we add the real value of cash dividends received by households. In Star, the easier case, real dividends are just $(S^* - S_b{}^*)f_K = [S^* - \tilde{S}_b{}^*(1/q^*)]f_K{}^*$. Note that I have excluded business demands for money; but see Section II for an analysis of an alternate model emphasizing firms' cash balances.

Taking stock: At this juncture we have 8 equations of the 12 necessary to determine the 12-dimensional path $\{N, N^*, P, P^*, P_K, P_K{}^*, r, r^*, K, K^*, S, S^* \mid t \geq 0\}$, where $S(t)$ and $S^*(t)$ are predetermined at $t = 0$, and so, too, are $K(t)$ and $K^*(t)$. We shall need 4 additional equations to determine the dynamics of S, S^*, K, and K^*. Until these equations have been added, there is no way to calculate even the short-run behavior of the world economy: One has to determine the future to work back to the present.

Nevertheless there is an irresistible temptation to make a few heuristic observations about the short run in a simple case: $\tilde{S}_b = \tilde{S}_b{}^* = 0$, $L_2 = L_2{}^* = 0$, and over some near term at least, $q^* = 1$ and $\dot{q}^* = 0$. Then, by (1.4), $f_K{}^*(N^*, K^*) = r^*$ yields the upward-sloping IS^* curve in the (N^*, r^*) plane of Figure 1. Upon substituting marginal cost $\bar{W}^*/f_N(N^*, K^*)$ for P^*, we may use (1.8) to obtain $\bar{M}^* f_N{}^* = \bar{W}^* L^*[N^* f_N{}^* + S^* f_K{}^* - G^*, i^*, S^* - S_b{}^* + f_N{}^*\ \bar{M}^*/\bar{W}^*]$. The solution for N^*, which is independent of i^* if $L_2{}^* = 0$, gives a vertical LM^* curve in the (N^*, r^*) plane. That curve determines N^* while IS^* determines r^*. An increase of G^*, by reducing take-home pay and hence the demand for money, must increase N^* until the money demand again equals the money supply—provided the fiscal shift leaves $q^* = 1$ and $\dot{q}^* = 0$ over the near term. On the same proviso, N^* is independent of events in Home, notably the behavior of G. Now assume also that $q = 1$ and $\dot{q} = 0$. *If* the corresponding IS and LM curves in the (N, r) plane perchance determine N such that $f_K(N, K)$ equals the r^* previously determined, we have hit upon one candidate for the momentary equilibrium. In any event, our task is to find the right pair $(q, \dot{q})$ among the many pairs such that $r = r^*$.

To close the model, we turn now to the dynamics of the state variables: S, S^*, K, and K^*. Consider first the accumulation of S and S^*. Let $\hat{S}$ denote $qK + q^*(S - K)$ and let $\hat{S}^*$ denote q^*S^*. Then, as a matter of accounting, $\dot{\hat{S}} = Nf_N + r\hat{S} - C - G$, and similarly for Star, where C denotes consumption in Home and C^* denotes consumption in Star.

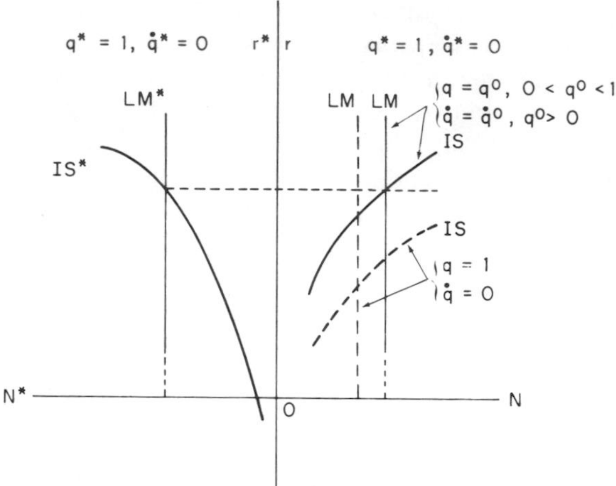

Figure 1

Our consumption functions are in the spirit of life-cycle saving theory much simplified. The first argument of these functions is real disposable income including capital gains; the second argument is the real rate of interest; and the third argument is the real value of private wealth, $\tilde{S} - \tilde{S}_b + \bar{M}/P$ at Home.

A compact version of our accumulation equations is thus

$$\dot{\tilde{S}} = Nf_N + r\tilde{S} - \bar{G} - C(Nf_N - \bar{G} + r\tilde{S}, r, \tilde{S} - \tilde{S}_b + (\bar{M}/P)), \quad (1.9')$$

$$\dot{\tilde{S}}^* = N^*f_N^* + r^*\tilde{S}^* - \bar{G}^* - C^*(N^*f_N^* - \bar{G}^* + r^*\tilde{S}^*, r^*,$$
$$S^* - \tilde{S}_b^* + (M^*/P^*)), \quad 1 > C_1, C_1^* > 0; \quad C_3, C_3^* > 0. \quad (1.10')$$

Of course, these equations do not add up to $\dot{K} + \dot{K}^*$. If we want equations that do so add up we have to use (1.3) and (1.4) in substitution for r and r^*, use $\dot{q}^*S^* + q^*\dot{S}^*$ in place of $\dot{\tilde{S}}^*$, and do likewise for $\dot{\tilde{S}}$. Then

$$\dot{S} = \frac{P^*}{P_K^*}[Nf_N + Kf_K + (S - K)f_K^* - C(\cdot) - \bar{G}]$$
$$+ \frac{P_K^* - P^*}{P_K^*} \cdot \left[\frac{\dot{K}}{K}K + \frac{\dot{K}^*}{K^*}(S - K)\right], \quad (1.9)$$

$$\dot{S}^* = \frac{P^*}{P_K^*}[N^*f_N^* + S^*f_K^* - C^*(\cdot) - \bar{G}^*] + \frac{P_K^* - P^*}{P_K^*}\frac{\dot{K}^*}{K^*}S^*. \quad (1.10)$$

We are adding to purchases of shares the share accruals that come from the own-returns on shares discussed in connection with Eq. (1.3) and (1.4). The right-hand sides can be seen to add up to $\dot{K} + \dot{K}^*$.

We need finally to determine the rates of capital formulation—as distinct from the rates of capital–goods output—in each country. It is clear, given *intra*national shiftability of capital goods between consumer-good and capital–good production, that no firm in either country will produce capital goods for sale in Home if $P_K < P$ because a firm can then earn more revenue (for the same cost) by instead producing consumer goods for sale in Home; similarly, gross capital formation in Star will be nil if $P_K^* < P^*$. Hence, if firms are buying new capital, they must be paying at least the going price for consumer goods.

It is also clear that no firm in either country would sell consumer goods in the Home market if $P_K > P$ because it could then increase its revenue by instead selling claims to additional capital put into operation in Home; similarly, sales of consumer goods would be nil in Star's market if $P_K^* > P^*$. But we shall want to assume that $C + G > 0$ and $C^* + G^* > 0$ always. Hence $P_K \leq P$ and $P_K^* \leq P^*$.

Recalling that $\dot{K} \geq -\mu K$ and $\dot{K}^* \geq -\mu K^*$, we therefore have

$$P \begin{cases} \geq P_K \text{ always} \\ = P_K \text{ if } \dot{K} + \mu K > 0 \end{cases} \Rightarrow \dot{K} + \mu K \begin{cases} = 0 \text{ if } P_K < P \\ \geq 0 \text{ if } P_K = P \end{cases} \quad (1.11)$$

$$P^* \begin{cases} \geq P_K^* \text{ always} \\ = P_K^* \text{ if } K^* + \mu K^* > 0 \end{cases} \Rightarrow \dot{K}^* + \mu K^* \begin{cases} = 0 \text{ if } P_K^* < P^* \\ \geq 0 \text{ if } P_K^* = P^* \end{cases}. \quad (1.12)$$

What if *both* $P_K = P$ and $P_K^* = P^*$? In that case, world investment is determinate, being equal to world saving, but its national distribution is not—at least not apparently. It will turn out, however, that when both $q = 1$ and $q^* = 1$ the motion of N/K and N^*/K^* is uniquely determined.

II. Stationary Equilibrium

In a normal stationary state, the state variables are positive constants to be determined: $\bar{K}, \bar{K}^*, \bar{S}, \bar{S}^*$. From (1.11), (1.12), and associated reasoning it follows that $q = q^* = 1$. It is intuitively clear that the state variables will not stay constant unless r also is a constant, $\bar{r}$. Therefore $f_K(N, \bar{K}) = f_K(N^*, \bar{K}^*) = \bar{r}$ and hence the employment levels are also constant, $\bar{N}$ and $\bar{N}^*$. The employment–capital ratios and therefore the real-wage rates must be equal owing to the linear homogeneity of the identical production functions. Letting V denote the stationary real wage, we have $f_N(\bar{N}/\bar{K}, 1) = f_N(\bar{N}^*/\bar{K}^*, 1) = V(\bar{r})$, where $V'(\bar{r}) = -k < 0$, $k \equiv K/N$. The respective money-price levels are therefore $\bar{W}/V(\bar{r})$ and $\bar{W}^*/V(\bar{r})$. Hence $\bar{E} = \bar{W}/\bar{W}^*$.

Because even the stationary-state equations of our model are relatively complicated, and the underlying functions contain a few novelties, it may be useful to study first a simpler model before attacking the one in Section I. This alternate model differs only with respect to Eq. (1.7) and (1.8). It emphasizes the business demands for money rather than the household demands and adopts the textbook real-balance demand functions $L(F(N, K), r)$ and $L^*(F(N^*, K^*), r)$. The following equations, with the bars suppressed, can then be understood as a subsystem of the equations describing any stationary state in the alternate model:

$$M = (W/V(\mathrm{r}))L\{N[V(r) + (r + \mu)\, k(r)], r\}, \tag{2.1 alt}$$

$$M^* = (W^*/V(r))L^*\{N^*[V(r) + (r + \mu)\, k(r)], r\}, \tag{2.2 alt}$$

$$r = f_K[(N + N^*)/(S + S^*), 1]. \tag{2.3}$$

Here $V(r) + (r + \mu)\, k(r)$ represents wages plus profits plus depreciation per unit of labor, so the expression in the square bracket equals gross domestic product per unit of labor (equal across countries). The third equation reminds us that, in a stationary state, capital is so located as to equalize its net marginal product and thus equate the national employment–capital ratios to the "world ratio" $N + N^*/S + S^*$.

Two exercises with this alternate model suggest themselves. One of them takes S and S^* as exogenous—as if each were the target of national fiscal policy in the corresponding country. We might imagine that each country has so controlled the size of its public sector, and the resulting flow of national saving, as to reach some desired stock of national savings.

A geometrical representation of the above system is shown in Figure 2. It is a diagram in the World–*IS*–*LM* plane, with r on the vertical axis and employment (in either or both countries) on the horizontal. The first *LM* equation gives the steady-state N that can be supported at a given r; the corresponding curve is labeled $\mathscr{L}$ and its abscissa is denoted $\mathscr{L}(r)$. The second *LM* equation gives the stationary N^* that can be similarly supported; the corresponding curve, not drawn, is labeled $\mathscr{L}^*$ and its abscissa is denoted $\mathscr{L}^*(r)$. The horizontal sum of the two curves is the World *LM* curve giving world employment $N + N^*$ as a function of r; its abscissa is $\mathscr{L}(r) + \mathscr{L}^*(r)$. The third equation serves as a World–*IS* curve giving r as an increasing function of world employment–given the world capital stock $S + S^*$.

Even in this easiest of exercises, ambiguities in the results may turn up. If there were no intersection between World *IS* and World *LM*, it would mean that $S + S^*$ was unreachable—the targets too large for the existence of any corresponding stationary state; we may as well focus on attainable targets for present purposes. There may then, however, exist more than one intersection point. I shall invoke two conditions that are necessary for the uniqueness of the equilibrium path toward the stationary

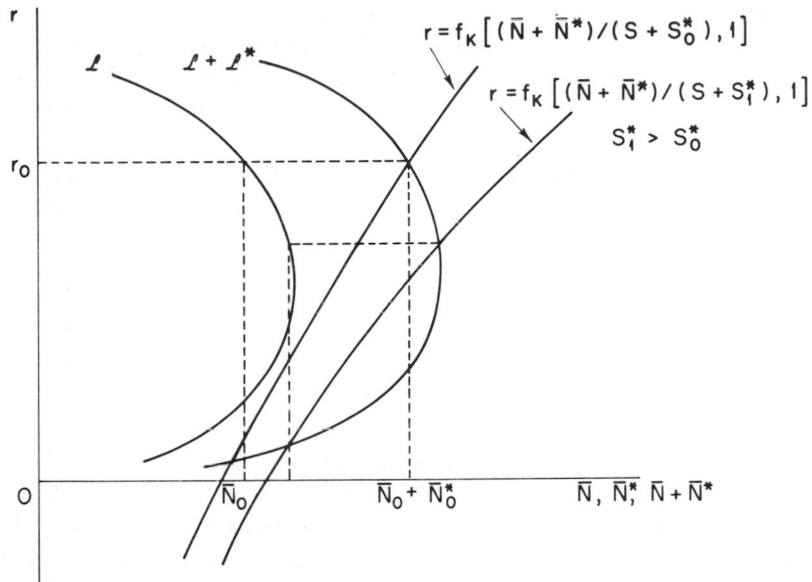

Figure 2

state, namely, the stationary state corresponding to our S and S^* is one where the upward sloping World *IS* curve is flatter than the World *LM* curve, hence cutting the latter "from above," and there is just one such stationary state.[2] Then, and only then, a downward shift of the World *IS* curve drives down the unique stationary-equilibrium value of r.

Consider now an increase of the targer S^*. (Notice that the effects upon N and N^* will be no different from those of an equal increase of S instead because those effects work only through r.) The increase of S^* shifts the World *IS* curve to the right, hence downward, because more world employment would be needed for the same r, and consequently, for the same world ratio of employment to capital. The curves $\mathscr{L}$ and $\mathscr{L}^*$ do not shift. Therefore r falls, and the direction of the effects upon N and N^* depends only upon the signs of the slopes of the curves $\mathscr{L}$ and $\mathscr{L}^*$, respectively. Take $\mathscr{L}$ for example. In the ultra-Keynesian range where r is small, we have $L_2 \ll 0$ so that $\mathscr{L}$ is positively sloped in that neighborhood at least—like the textbook *LM* curve. In that range the fall of r is likely to *reduce N*. But in the neo-Keynesian range where r is not small (but not critically

[2] I am indebted to Guillermo A. Calvo for informal discussions.

large either), L_2 may be close to zero so that the lower price level, i.e., $W/V(r)$, resulting from the fall of r is likely to be the dominant effect, causing $\mathscr{L}$ to be negatively sloped in the range of r. In that range the fall of r will *expand* N. The corresponding analysis applies to $\mathscr{L}^*$. *If* r is in the neo-Keynesian range of *both* countries, for example, *both* N and N^* will *increase* with the increase of S^*. (But there are three other evident possibilities.)

The second exercise takes S and S^* as the steady-state outcomes of public-expenditure targets G and G^*. In the stationary state we have

$$0 = V(r)N + rS - G - C[V(r)N + rS - G, r, S - \tilde{S}_b + (M/W)V(r)], \quad (2.4)$$

$$0 = V(r)N^* + rS^* - G^* - C^*[V(r)N^* + rS - G^*, r, S^* - \tilde{S}_b{}^* + (M^*/W^*)V(r)]. \quad (2.5)$$

Hence the stationary-state S is an implicit function, say $\mathscr{S}$, of the variables r and N and the parameters G, $\tilde{S}_b$, and M/W. S^* is given by an analogous function $\mathscr{S}^*$. These functions $\mathscr{S}$ and $\mathscr{S}^*$ are decreasing in G and G^* because $C_1 < 1$ and $C_3 > 0$; the greater disposable income from lower G would generate saving until the accumulated stock of savings had *risen* enough to generate a higher consumption by the old, large enough to offset the lessened total of expenditures by the government and by the young. The functions $\mathscr{S}$ and $\mathscr{S}^*$ are increasing in N and N^* for the same reason; larger employment generates more saving until the accumulated stock of savings finally encourages consumption of the whole increase of income. To keep the increase of S finite we suppose also that $C_3 + C_1 r > r$, hence $C_3 > r(1 - C_1)$, which is entirely natural to posit in a life-cycle theory of saving. As a matter of notation, we write the values of the two functions as $\mathscr{S}(N, r; G, \tilde{S}_b, m)$ and $\mathscr{S}^*(N^*, r; G^*, \tilde{S}_b{}^*, m^*)$ where $m \equiv M/W$ and $m^* \equiv M^*/W^*$; the latter are the money supplies in Keynes' wage units, and they are fixed.

The stationary equilibrium corresponding to given G and G^* is then determinable as follows. For any trial value of r we may again calculate the corresponding Home employment level $\mathscr{L}(r)$ that satisfies Home's *LM* equation (2.1 alt). Likewise, we may calculate the corresponding $\mathscr{L}^*(r)$ from (2.2 alt). We then use the corresponding $\mathscr{S}(\mathscr{L}(r), r; G)$ and $\mathscr{S}^*(\mathscr{L}^*(r), r; G^*)$ to substitute for $S + S^*$ in (2.3). This gives the new World *IS* curve, the locus of points $(N + N^*, r)$ where

$$r = f_K\{(N + N^*)/[\mathscr{S}(\mathscr{L}(r), r; G, \tilde{S}_b, m) + \mathscr{S}^*(\mathscr{L}^*(r), r; G^*, \tilde{S}_b{}^*, m^*)], 1\}. \quad (2.3 \text{ alt})$$

This curve represents the world employment level needed to equate f_K to r when the other equations are simultaneously satisfied. If this world employment level equals $\mathscr{L}(r) + \mathscr{L}^*(r)$, then we have a candidate for a stationary solution. We shall assume again that there exists just one intersection where the new World *IS* curve is flatter then the World *LM* curve, and that this intersection marks the unique stationary equilibrium.

Consider now a decrease of G^*. The curves $\mathscr{L}$ and $\mathscr{L}^*$ do not shift, but at every r, $\mathscr{S}^*$ $(\mathscr{L}^*(r), r; G^*, \tilde{S}_b^*, M^*/W^*)$ is *increased* while $\mathscr{S}(\cdot)$ is unaffected. Therefore the World *IS* curve must shift to the right. The effect is thus broadly similar to the effect of increased S^* found in the former exercise. The world interest rate must fall. *If* the equilibrium r is in the neo-Keynesian range where the price-level effect of lower r dominates the L_2 effect in *both* countries, so that $\mathscr{L}'(r)$ and $\mathscr{L}^{*\prime}(r)$ are negative, then *both* N and N^* are *increased* by the decrease of G^*.

To neutralize the effect upon its stationary employment level of the reduction of G^*, what must Home do? Home must increase its G by an amount such that, at the initial rate of interest, Home's stock of national savings is decreased in the amount by which Star's stock of savings was increased by the reduction of its G^*. In so doing, Home will prevent the rate of interest from declining and thereby insulate the levels of employment and capital in both countries. Home's residents will thus suffer higher taxes, hence smaller private consumption and lesser life-cycle saving. On the other hand, they will enjoy a larger public sector from which they may have been deterred earlier (before Star reduced G^*) since, absent Star's move, increased G would have cost Home a reduction of long-run employment in the neo-Keynesian case. The requirements of employment stabilization at Home will be observed to be quite different from that in the original model.

We turn now to the more complex model of Section I. Still letting m denote M/W, letting m^* denote M^*/W^*, and still dropping the bars, we can describe its stationary state by the following system:

$$mV(r) = L[V(r)N + rS - G, r, S - \tilde{S}_b + mV(r)], \tag{2.1}$$

$$m^*V(r) = L^*[V(r)N^* + rS^* - G^*, r, S^* - \tilde{S}_b^* + m^* V(r)], \tag{2.2}$$

$$r = f_K[(N + N^*)/(S + S^*), 1], \tag{2.3}$$

$$0 = V(r)N + rS - G - C[V(r)N + rS - G, \quad r, \quad S - \tilde{S}_b + mV(r)], \tag{2.4}$$

$$0 = V(r)N^* + rS^* - G^* - C^*[V(r)N^* + rS^* - G^*, r, S^* - \tilde{S}_b^* + m^*V(r)] \tag{2.5}$$

In complete analogy to the previous exercise, we shall use (2.4) to derive a function $\mathscr{S}(N, r; G, S, mV(r))$ which may be substituted for S where the latter appears, namely, in (2.1) and (2.3). Likewise, using (2.5) we substitute $\mathscr{S}^*(\cdot)$ for S^* where it appears in (2.2) and (2.3). But the surprising feature of this system is that when the level of N dictated by the LM equation, that level now denoted $\mathscr{L}(r; G)$ because dependent on G, is substituted for N in $\mathscr{S}$, the resulting $\mathscr{S}(\mathscr{L}(r, G), r; G, S_b, mV(r))$ is independent of G; likewise, $\mathscr{S}^*(\cdot)$ is independent of G^*. Hence the World IS curve is not shifted by a change of public expenditures. This will now be shown.

It is clear that (2.1) and (2.4) constitute a pair of equations, with r as a parameter, in two composite variables: disposable national income $Y \equiv V(r)N + rS - G$, and real private wealth $\sigma \equiv S - \tilde{S}_b + mV(r)$. Equation (2.1) makes Y decreasing in σ because L_1 and L_3 are positive. Equation (2.4) makes σ increasing in Y because $C_1 < 1$. The intersection between the corresponding two curves, labeled λ and Σ, respectively, determines $Y(r)$ and $\sigma(r)$ uniquely as shown in Figure 3. Therefore $\sigma(r)$ is independent of G at any r. Consequently $\mathscr{S}(\mathscr{L}(r, G), r; G, S_b, mV(r)) = \sigma(r) + S_b - mV(r)$ is likewise independent of G at any r. If G is decreased *while r remains stationary,* so that take-home pay and money demanded would increase at unchanged real wages, then real wages before tax must fall offsettingly to maintain real balances demanded equal to the amount supplied, $mV(r)$; this means that employment must fall in an amount such that $V(r)dN = dG$. Very loosely speaking, the defense workers losing their jobs are not absorbed elsewhere, the other workers retain their jobs, and the excess capital is ultimately reincarnated abroad—provided r does not change; with disposable income ultimately unchanged, the level of private wealth accumulated is ultimately unchanged too. The same mechanism works in the other country, as described by (2.2) and (2.5).

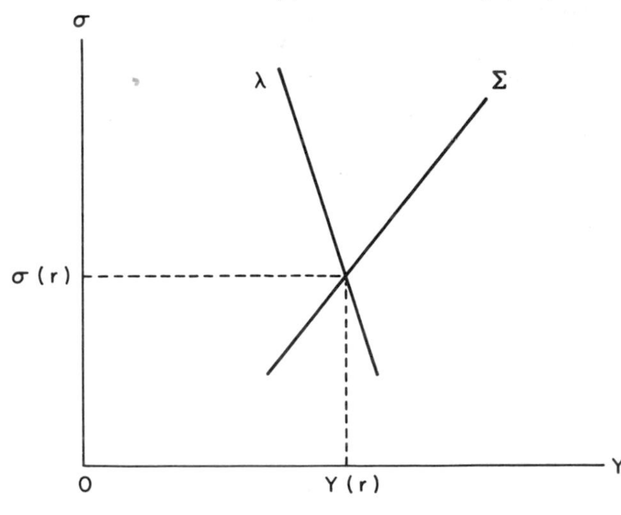

Figure 3

Our reduced-form system is therefore expressible as

$$mV(r) = L\{V(r)N + r\,[\sigma(r) + S_b - mV(r)] - G,\ r,\ \sigma(r)\}, \tag{2.6}$$

$$m^*V(r) = L^*\{V(r)N^* + r[\sigma^*(r) + S_b^* - m^*V(r)] - G^*,\ r,\ \sigma^*(r)\}, \tag{2.7}$$

$$r = f_K\,\{(N + N^*)/[\sigma(r) + S_b - mV(r) + \sigma^*(r) + S_b^* - m^*V(r)], 1\} \tag{2.8}$$

As in the practice exercise, for each trial r we are to calculate $\mathscr{L}(r, G)$ and $\mathscr{L}^*(r, G^*)$ from (2.6) and (2.7) to obtain the corresponding point $(N + N^*, r)$ on the World *LM* curve. We use (2.8) to obtain the corresponding point on the World *IS* curve. Once more we demand of the model's functions that they produce just one intersection of the type where the World *IS* curve cuts the World *LM* curve "from above": If the latter makes $N + N^*$ rise with r then the former makes $N + N^*$ rise faster, and if the latter makes $N + N^*$ fall with r, then the former makes $N + N^*$ rise with r or else fall more slowly. That type of intersection alone satisfies the presumed "stability condition": A small rise of world employment raises the *excess* of the "*LM* interest rate" over the "*IS* interest rate." This intersection will be termed *the* stationary equilibrium (see Figure 4).

Consider again a decrease of G^*. The World *IS* and $\mathscr{L}$ curves do not shift. But the $\mathscr{L}^*$ curve, and hence the World *LM* curve, shifts leftward. It

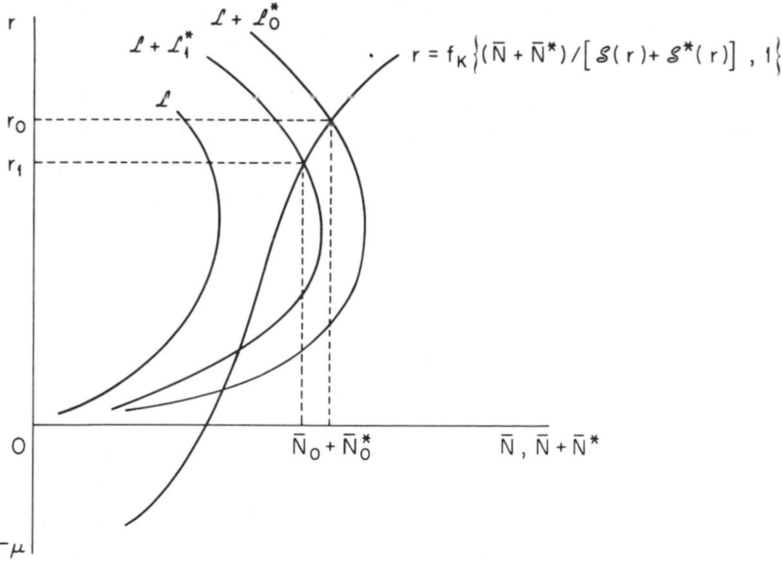

Figure 4

follows from the above stability condition that r falls. World employment therefore falls as well if and only if the World *IS* curve is upward sloping. Is it?

Because $f_{KN}(\cdot) > 0$, the World *IS* curve must be positively sloped if the denominator of the first argument—i.e., world savings, $\mathcal{S}(r) + \mathcal{S}^*(r)$—is independent of r or, *a fortiori,* increasing in r. Evidently the terms $mV(r)$ and $m^*V(r)$, taken with their negative signs, work in the latter direction because $V'(r) < 0$; since real balances would be reduced by higher r, a given $\sigma + \sigma^*$ would then correspond to a larger $S + S^*$. The remaining question is the behavior of $\sigma(r) + \sigma^*(r)$. Figure 3 illustrated the case where $C_2 < 0$ so that a rise of r would shift Σ upward; taken alone that shift would raise σ. But a rise of r would shift λ downward if the neo-Keynesian $V'(r)$ effect on the quantity of real balances in excess supply dominates Keynes' L_2 effect on the quantity of real balances demanded; taken alone, that shift would reduce σ. Because I want to keep this dominance of $V'(r)$ over L_2 open, I shall assume provisionally that $S + S^*$, if indeed decreasing in r, is not so strongly decreasing in r as to upset the technological force tending to keep the World *IS* curve positively sloped. Then *world* employment is decreased.

Whatever the effect on world employment, Home's stationary equilibrium employment level $\mathcal{L}(r, G)$ is increased if and only if $\partial\mathcal{L}(r, G)/\partial r < 0$; i.e., Home was on a backward-bending stretch of its $\mathcal{L}$ curve where the $V'(r)$ effect dominates the L_2 effect of a change of r upon the excess supply of real balances. The result is identical to the finding in the simpler model that Home employment rises if and only if $\mathcal{L}'(r) < 0$. The latter finding depended upon an increase of $\mathcal{S}(\mathcal{L}(r), r, G) + \mathcal{S}^*(\mathcal{L}^*(r), r, G^*)$ with the decrease of G^*; the present result depends on the decrease of $\mathcal{L}^*(r, G)$. In the present model, Home employment will increase, whether or not world savings should fall, if the fall of r, through the real balance effect associated with $V'(r) < 0$, is strong enough to attract to Home some of the capital made "redundant" in Star by its reduction of G^*. (If this $V'(r)$ effect is dominant, net investment turns positive at Home; a falling dollar-price level and rising real balances result; Home's *short-run LM* curve in Fig. 1 therefore moves rightward and fast enough to produce rising employment while both r and N/K are falling because Home's falling *IS* curve is moving rightward faster.)

If N is increased because $\partial\mathcal{L}(r, G)/\partial r < 0$, and $N + N^*$ is decreased because the World *IS* curve is upward sloping, then N^* is decreased by the reduction of G^*. Since $\mathcal{L}^*(r, G^*)$ shifts to the left with the decrease of G^*, there is a presumption that N^* decreases. How could N^* increase? This is possible only if the $V'(r)$ effect in Star is strong enough to offset the shift of $\mathcal{L}^*$. Then either N is down, which would be most odd, or $N + N^*$

is up, which (with our stability condition) would imply that $S + S^*$ rose even more; hence, the World *IS* curve is negatively sloped, presumably because $V'(r)$ is so strong. In the latter case we have a set of results like those of the simpler model examined earlier when the World *LM* curve is negatively sloped around the stationary equilibrium.

Does the foregoing analysis of stationary equilibrium have any direct usefulness for answering the question with which this paper began? It does if the world economy was resting in stationary equilibrium until the reduction of G^*.

Since the effects of reduced G^* on stationary equilibrium employment in Home work only through r, one might think that Home can neutralize those effects by increasing G enough to keep the World *LM* and World *IS* curves intersecting at the same r. That proposition is correct, we saw, within the *simpler* model which focuses on firms' demands for money. Home can shift the World *IS* curve back to where it was before Star shifted it out. With the stationary-equilibrium interest rate thus unchanged, the stationary-equilibrium employment level at Home is unchanged because Home's $\mathscr{L}$ curve is unaffected by the changes of G and G^*. But σ and S will then be shrinking, while σ^* and S^* will be growing, toward their respective new stationary levels. So Home has paid a price. Of course, it is not implied that this response by the Home government will *immediately* neutralize the effects of lower G^* on employment; but it will tend to do so, at least in the long run. The anticipation of that ultimate neutralization may be guessed to dampen any disturbances to capital spending in the short run.

In our *basic* model, however, the increase of G needed to restore the stationary-equilibrium level of r would shift the $\mathscr{L}(r, G)$ curve rightward to offset the leftward shift of $\mathscr{L}^*(r, G)$. This restoration of r would serve to restore each country's disposable national income and its private wealth to their original levels; but those variables are not major objectives of national fiscal policies. The net employment effects of the reduced G^* and the increased G would be an increase of N and a decrease in N^* in the new stationary equilibrium. In fact both the increase of G and the reduction of G^* may very well work in the direction of raising employment at Home.

For the maintenance of stationary-equilibrium employment at Home, the following reactions by Home to a small reduction of G^* are *necessary*. If $\partial\mathscr{L}(r, G)/\partial r < 0$, so that $\mathscr{L}(r, G)$ would be up in the absence of a reaction, reduce G *unless* the resulting additional fall of r would increase $\mathscr{L}(r, G)$ by more than the leftward shift from reduced G would decrease it; in that letter case, raise G by more than enough to restore r and hence by more than G^* was reduced. If $\partial\mathscr{L}(r, G)/\partial r = 0$, leave G unchanged. If $\partial\mathscr{L}(r, G)/\partial r > 0$, so that $\mathscr{L}(r, G)$ would be down absent any reaction, increase G but not by so much as to restore r, hence by less than the reduction of G^*.

The above reactions are necessary but *not sufficient* for the insulation of Home employment from the reduction of G^*. What Home controls is the location of its $\mathscr{L}$ curve. Its opportunity locus may be called the "excess *IS* curve"—the abscissa of World *IS minus* $\mathscr{L}^*(r, G)$. That locus is shifted rightward by the leftward shift of Star's $\mathscr{L}^*$ curve. There may fail to exist any point on the shifted locus, and thus available to Home, that gives the same employment level Home had chosen before.

Perhaps the most interesting lesson to be drawn is the following: Suppose that Star, having in mind the *alternate* model and wishing to raise its employment, chooses to reduce G^*. According to the present model, it may very well be that Star's move will ultimately cost itself some employment (and possibly even some of its national savings). The employment rise, if any, may turn up in Home. If, to restore employment to normal, Home must reduce G and chooses to do just that, world employment, and therefore Star's employment, will be lower than it was originally if the World *IS* curve is positively sloped. If Star wants to raise its own employment, given G, it may need instead to raise G^*. But a rise of G^* may reduce employment in Home. If Home must raise G to restore its own employment and if that move lowers employment abroad, Star will need to raise G^* again. If the World *IS* curve is positively sloped, this process will converge with higher employment for Star, as desired, and unchanged employment at Home. But if not, an unstable contraction in Star may result.

III. Equilibrium Paths

This section addresses two questions: First, it is *possible*, when initial conditions are close enough to the stationary equilibrium of Section II, that the model will generate a unique equilibrium path leading (acyclically or not) toward that stationary state? And if such a unique path may indeed emerge, how is it disturbed—especially in the short run—by a change of public spending in Star? It should be admitted that the following discussion offers only some plausible arguments, not a definitive answer, in regard to the first question. An entirely rigorous analysis is made difficult by the extraordinary dimensionality of our dynamic system and the aggravating nonlinearity presented by the two inequalities $P \geq P_K$ and $P^* \geq P_K^*$.

To begin with, we may reduce the number of variables and equations of the model as follows.[3] Let us define $p \equiv P/\bar{W}$ and $p^* \equiv P^*/\bar{W}^*$. Also let $p_K \equiv P_K/\bar{W}$, $p_K^* \equiv P_K^*/\bar{W}^*$. Recall, too, that $m \equiv M/\bar{W}$ and $m^* \equiv M^*/\bar{W}^*$. So, for example, Home's real balances are m/p, its rate of inflation is $\dot{p}/p$, and its real wage is p^{-1}. Equation (1.1) implicitly makes N/K an increasing function of p, say $\phi(p)$. Likewise (1.2) implies $N^*/K^* = \phi(p^*)$, $\phi'(p^*) > 0$. Making these respective substitutions for N and N^* everywhere, we eliminate (1.1) and (1.2). Then (1.7) and (1.8), for example, may be written

$$m = pL\left\{Kf(\phi(p),1) + \bar{S}_b\left[r - f_K(\phi(p),1)\frac{p}{p_K}\right] + (S - K)f_K^*(\phi(p^*),1) - G, r + \frac{\dot{p}}{p}, \frac{p_K}{p}K - \bar{S}_b + \frac{p_K^*}{p^*}(S - K) + \frac{m}{p}\right\}, \tag{1.7'}$$

$$m^* = p^*L^*\left\{K^*\phi(p^*)f_N(\phi(p^*),1) + S^*f_K(\phi(p^*),1) + \bar{S}_b^*\left[r^* - f_K(\phi(p^*),1)\frac{p^*}{p_K^*}\right] - G, r^* + \frac{\dot{p}^*}{p^*}, \frac{p_K^*}{p^*}S^* - \bar{S}_b^* + \frac{m^*}{p^*}\right\}. \tag{1.8'}$$

To simplify matters a bit, I shall restrict attention to the case where $\bar{S} = \bar{S}_b^* = 0$. Note also that we may use (1.6) to substitute r for r^* throughout. So the original 12-equation system can thus be reduced to 9 equations.

Equations (1.3) and (1.4) may be replaced as follows in view of (1.11) and (1.12):

$$\frac{\dot{p}_K}{p_K} = \frac{\dot{p}}{p} + (r + \mu) - \frac{p}{p_K}[f_K(\phi(p),1) + \mu], \tag{1.3'}$$

$$\frac{\dot{p}_K^*}{p_K^*} = \frac{\dot{p}^*}{p^*} + (r + \mu) - \frac{p^*}{p_K^*}[f_K(\phi(p^*),1) + \mu]. \tag{1.4'}$$

Certainly (1.3′) is valid when $p > p_K$ because $\dot{K}/K$ appearing in the original (1.3) must then equal $-\mu$ according to (1.11); when $p = p_K$, $\dot{K}/K$ drops out of (1.3) as does μ from (1.3′); $p \geq p_K$ always, as stated in (1.11). So (1.3′) captures (1.3) in all relevant cases. Equation (1.4′) has the same generality.

The above observations suggest the following reduction of the

[3] I am grateful to Duncan K. Foley for some suggestions as well as for reading an earlier draft.

original system, with the qualifications arising from $p \geq p_K$ and $p^* \geq p_K^*$ left inexplicit:

$$\dot{p} = p\hat{L}(p, p_K, p^*, p_K^*; S, K; m, G) - r, \tag{3.1}$$

$$\dot{p}^* = p^*\hat{L}^*(p^*, p_K^*; S^*, K^*; m^*, G^*) - r, \tag{3.2}$$

$$\dot{p}_K = p_K \left\{\frac{\dot{p}}{p} + (r + \mu) - \frac{p}{p_K}\,[f_K(\phi(p), 1) + \mu]\right\}, \tag{3.3}$$

$$\dot{p}_K^* = p_K^* \left\{\frac{\dot{p}^*}{p^*} + (r + \mu) - \frac{p}{p_K}\,[f_K(\phi(p^*), 1) + \mu]\right\}, \tag{3.4}$$

$$\dot{S} = U(p, p_K, p^*, p_K^*, r; S, K; m, G), \tag{3.5}$$

$$\dot{S}^* = U^*(p^*, p_K^*, r; S^*, K^*; m^*, G^*), \tag{3.6}$$

$$\dot{K} \begin{cases} = -\mu K & \text{if } p_K < p \\ \geq -\mu K & \text{if } p_K = p \end{cases} \tag{3.7}$$

$$\dot{K}^* \begin{cases} = -\mu K & \text{if } p_K^* < p^* \\ \geq -\mu K & \text{if } p_K^* = p^* \end{cases} \tag{3.8}$$

$$K + K^* = S + S^*. \tag{3.9}$$

These are nine equations in the four state variables (S, S^*, K, K^*), four "prices" (p, p^*, p_K, p_K^*), and r. The first two equations come from inverting (1.7′) and (1.8′). It is unambiguous that $\partial\hat{L}/\partial p_K > 0$ and $\partial\hat{L}^*/\partial p_K^* > 0$ since $L_3, L_3^* > 0$ and $L_2, L_2^* < 0$. I shall also assume that $\partial\hat{L}/\partial p > 0$ and $\partial\hat{L}^*/\partial p^* > 0$ in any neighborhood where $\hat{L} = 0$ at least; only outsized values of L_3 and L_3^* could reverse these latter inequalities.

A noteworthy feature of this reduced system is that the four "prices" appear *perfectly unstable,* given any vector of the variables S, S^*, K, K^*, and r. In any neighborhood where $\dot{p}_K = 0$, we have $\partial\dot{p}_K/\partial p_K > 0$ because $\partial\hat{L}/\partial p_K > 0$ and $f_K + \mu = F_K > 0$ everywhere; moreover, assuming $\partial\dot{p}_K/\partial p > -1$, we have $\partial\dot{p}_K/\partial p_K + (\partial p/\partial p_K)\,(\partial\dot{p}_K/\partial p) > 0$ when the constraint $p \geq p_K$ is binding so that $\partial p/\partial p_K = 1$; likewise, $\partial\dot{p}_K^*/\partial p_K^* > 0$. As already noted, we also have $\partial\dot{p}/\partial p > 0$ and $\partial\dot{p}^*/\partial p^* > 0$. The motion of the four prices is entirely centrifugal—given arbitrary and exogenous behavior of the other variables. If, contrariwise, the prices were to display stability, even saddle-path stability, that would be a disaster for the desired uniqueness of prices in the model; then there would be (at least) a whole schedule or *continuum* of current prices corresponding to each vector of state variables (and the associated r), while one wants instead a corresponding *point* in the price plane.[4]

This instability is illustrated by Figure 5, a phase diagram in the (p_K, p) plane based on (3.1) and (3.3). Formerly the world economy, and Home in particular, was in stationary equilibrium with $p_K = p = \bar{p}$, $S = \bar{S}$, and

[4] I am indebted to Pentti Kouri for this observation.

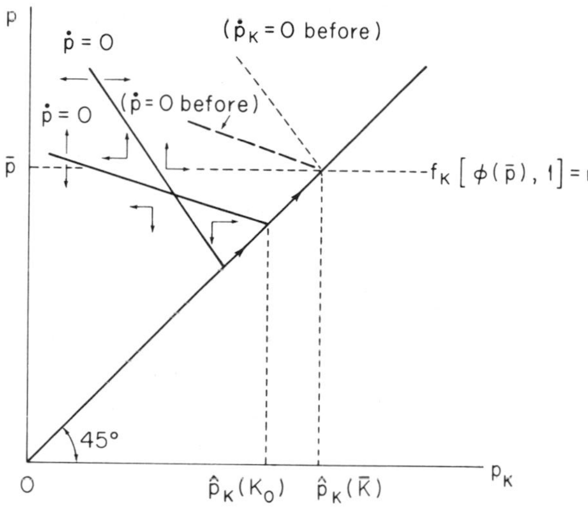

Figure 5

$K = \bar{K}$. Now Home finds itself mysteriously endowed with small equal increments of S and K; for simplicity we imagine that Star remains undisturbed in the following respects: $p_K{}^* = p^* = \bar{p}^*$ and therefore $r = f_K(\phi(\bar{p}^*), 1) =$ constant. Consequently the locus of points where $\hat{L}(\cdot) = 0$, which locus is the line labeled $\dot{p} = 0$, is shifted to the left by the increase of K; for the same p, e.g., $\bar{p}$, a reduction of p_K is needed by (3.1) to achieve $\dot{p} = 0$. The point $(p_K, \bar{p})$ at which $\dot{p}_K = 0$ is also shifted to the left; by (2.2), a lesser reduction of p_K would be necessary to offset the upward effect upon $\dot{p}_K$ of higher $\dot{p}/p$. The new $\dot{p}_K = 0$ locus necessarily intersects the new $\dot{p} = 0$ locus at some $p < \bar{p}$. The diagram illustrates the case where the new intersection lies above the 45° line, so that $p_K < \hat{p}_K(K_0) < p$. As the arrows indicate, the motion of p_K and p is everywhere away from this intersection point.

For a simple illustration of the possible uniqueness of prices, consider again the above displacement of K and S while, by assumption, $p_K{}^* = p^* = \bar{p}$ and $r = \bar{r}$. But suppose, for simplicity, that $L_2 = 0$. Then p must lie on the $\dot{p} = 0$ locus whenever $p_K < p$, more accurately, whenever $p_K \leq \hat{p}_K(K)$, as shown in Fig. 5. Using (1.7′), we may write $p = \pi(p_k, K)$, $p_K < \hat{p}_K(K)$. The function π has the properties $\pi_1 < 0$ and $\pi_2 < 0$. (I am imagining here that $S - K$, which appears in (1.7′), remains constant.) Then (3.3) yields

$$\dot{p}_K = p_K \left\{ \frac{\pi_1 \dot{p}_K + \pi_2 \dot{K}}{\pi(p_K, K)} + (r + \mu) - \frac{\pi}{p_K} [f_K(\phi(\pi), 1) + \mu] \right\} \quad (3.10)$$

or, as long as $p_K < p$,

$$\dot{p}_K = \frac{\pi p_K}{\pi - p_K \pi} \left\{ \frac{-\mu K \pi_2}{\pi} + (r + \mu) - \frac{\pi}{p_K} [f_K(\phi(\pi), 1) + \mu] \right\}. \quad (3.11)$$

It is again the case that $\partial \dot{p}_K / \partial p_K > 0$, at least if the second derivative π_{22} is close to zero. On the same assumption, $\partial \dot{p}_K / \partial K > 0$. These considerations yield the negatively sloped locus labeled $\dot{p}_K = 0$ in Figure 6. For every K and corresponding $\hat{p}_K(K)$, this locus is defined for all $p_K \leq \hat{p}_K(K)$; it is only for such p_K that p is not constrained away from the $\dot{p} = 0$ locus of the previous figure (Fig. 5). I omit discussion of the region in which $p_K > \hat{p}_K(K)$.

To complete the two-dimensional system (still imagining that $S - K$ stays constant) we use (3.7) to write

$$\dot{K} \begin{cases} = -\mu K & \text{if } p_K < \hat{p}_K(K), \quad \text{whence } p > p_K. \\ \geq -\mu K & \text{if } p_K \geq \hat{p}_K(K), \quad \text{whence } p = p_K \end{cases} \quad (3.12)$$

Thus we have downward pointed arrows to the left of the locus marked $p_K = \hat{p}_K(K)$ in Fig. 6. This locus must be negatively sloped since, as Fig. 5 illustrated, higher K reduces $\hat{p}_K(K)$ because it shifts the $\dot{p} = 0$ locus leftward.

Figure 6 displays the well-behaved case in which the $p_K = \hat{p}_K(K)$ locus is steeper than the $\dot{p}_K = 0$ locus. Then K declines monotonically toward $\bar{K}$, from which level it had been disturbed; p_K is uniquely deter-

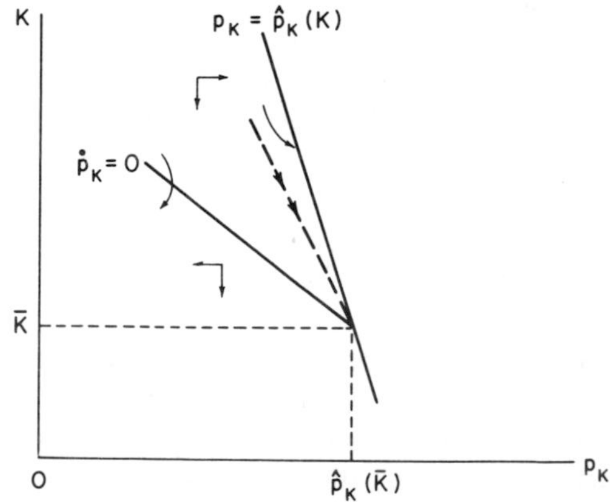

Figure 6

The fall of q is not so large that, through its easing of the demand for Home money and thus its stimulus to Home employment, $f_K(N, K)$ is raised above $f_K(N^*, K^*)$; for if $f_K > f_K^*$ then $q^* < 1$, which is a contradiction. Nor is it the case that f_K is raised equally, except perhaps transiently; for if $f_K^* = f_K$, then $q < 1$ would require $\dot{q} < 0$ in order that $r = f_K^*$; but clearly this could occur only momentarily, if at all, since the immediate decline of K at rate μ must restore q to 1 and so produce $\dot{q} > 0$ in the process. Besides all of this, q is not *able* to raise f_K up to f_K^*, were q to fall even to near-zero, if L_3 is small. I conclude, therefore, that the increase of G^* causes $f_K^* > f_K$ in the short run.

There are several alternative cases to be considered. If an increase of G^* *raises* the stationary equilibrium $\bar{S} + \bar{S}^*$, then the initial point (K_0, K_0^*), being the *old* stationary equilibrium, lies on a lower 135° line than the one passing through the new stationary equilibrium at E. The initial point is then like Q (where $K_0 \gtreqless \bar{K}$). From Q the motion is north–northwest since $K + \dot{K}^* > 0$—we are left of the $\dot{S} + \dot{S}^* = 0$ locus if the latter is convex (as shown) and leftward in any case if $K_0 < \bar{K}$—while $\dot{K} = -\mu K < 0$. If an increase of G^* *reduces* $\bar{S} + \bar{S}^*$, then the initial point may be like R in which case the motion is also north– northwest; the initial point may instead be like X where the motion is west–northwest since $\dot{K} + \dot{K}^* < 0$ while $\dot{K}^* > 0$. From R it is necessary and from Q it is possible (only if $K_0 > \bar{K}$) that the trajectory will cut through the $\dot{S} + \dot{S}^* = 0$ locus after which it is in the region of X whereupon its motion is west–northwest. The points Y and Z are also possible; the trajectory from such points leads to the region of X.

From the region of X all trajectories first reach the $f_K = f_K^*$ locus at a point above E, like point A. From there on, the motion must be *down that locus* toward E. It is impossible to leave the locus without going against the arrows; yet, at A, $\dot{S} + \dot{S}^* < 0$ so the motion must be toward E.

From Q is it possible that the trajectory will proceed, always north–northwest, straight to E. It is also possible that the trajectory will stay inside the $\dot{S} + \dot{S}^* = 0$ locus and reach the $f_K = f_K^*$ locus at a point below E, like point B. From there onward, the motion must be *up the* $f_K = f_K^*$ *locus* because, short of E, $\dot{S} + \dot{S}^* > 0$. But, as mentioned, the motion from Q could also lead into the region of X, then to a point like A, and finally down the $f_K = f_K^*$ locus.

IV. Conclusions and Comments

Let me attempt now to draw together and to explicate the principal implications of the above analysis for the consequences of a foreign fiscal

mined as a decreasing function of K. As K declines, p_K rises—moving down the dashed-line *saddle path* along which, at each step of the way, $p_K < \hat{p}_K(K)$ until p_K reaches $\hat{p}_K(K)$.

One might want to extend the above example to the three-variable system comprised of $\dot{S}$, $\dot{K}$, and $\dot{p}_K$. The saddle path, in those cases where it exists, will lie on a hyperplane slicing through the rest point at $(\bar{S}, \bar{K}, \hat{p}_K(\bar{K}))$; the path itself, however, is apt to be cyclical because K and S are unlikely to reach their stationary values simultaneously. In any case, the above remarks will have served their purpose if they have proved suggestive of the possibility that the four prices are uniquely determined for each K, K^*, S, S^*, and r.

In analyzing the dynamic system (3.1)–(3.9), one wants a convenient way to determine whether $q < 1$ (hence zero gross investment at Home) and whether $q^* < 1$ (hence zero gross investment in Star).[5] To that end we may first establish that

$$q < 1 \quad \text{if} \quad f_K < r; \qquad q^* < 1 \quad \text{if} \quad f_K^* < r. \tag{3.13}$$

The first of these propositions is easily shown from rewriting (1.3′) as

$$r - f_K = (\dot{q}/q) + ((1/q) - 1)(f_K + \mu). \tag{3.14}$$

Since $f_K + \mu \equiv F_K > 0$ and, of course, $\dot{q} \leq 0$ if $q = 1$, $q < 1$ is implied by $r - f_K > 0$. Likewise, $r - f_K^* > 0$ implies $q^* < 1$.

We may also argue, not without difficulty, that

$$r = \max(f_K, f_K^*) \quad \text{when } \dot{K} + \mu K + \dot{K}^* + \mu K^* > 0. \tag{3.15}$$

With world gross investment positive, as it must be in the neighborhood of the stationary equilibrium, either Home or Star or both must be doing positive gross investment; so either $q = 1$ or $q^* = 1$ or both.[6] Further, $q(t)$ and $q^*(t)$ are continuous functions of time or else there would be a (foreseen) capital gain or loss at some future moment presenting an unbounded rate of return (positive or negative) as that moment is approached; so either (a) $q = 1$ *and* $\dot{q} = 0$ or (b) $q^* = 1$ *and* $\dot{q}^* = 0$ or both—for every t and some subsequent interval $(t, t + \Delta(t))$. Hence, by (1.3′) and (1.4′) $r^* = r = f_K$ if (a) and $r = r^* = f_K^*$ if (b); if both, then $r = f_K = f_K^* = r^*$. Is it possible that $f_K^* > f_K$ when (a), thus refuting (3.15)? Only if $\dot{q}^* < 0$, for if $\dot{q}^* \geq 0$ then (since $q^* \leq 1$) $r^* > r$; yet $r^* = r$, a contradiction. It remains to argue, then, that $\dot{q}^* < 0$ and $q^* < 1$ simultaneously are inconsistent *when*

[5] The argument below has benefited from conversations with Guillermo Calvo.

[6] It follows immediately, using (3.13), that *either* $q = 1$ and $q^* < 1$, hence $r \leq f_K$ and either $f_K^* < r \leq f_K$ or $r \leq (f_K, f_K^*)$; or $q^* = 1$ and $q < 1$, hence $r \leq f_K^*$ and either $f_K < r \leq f_K^*$ or $r \leq (f_K^*, f_K)$; *or* $q = q^* = 1$, hence $r \leq (f_K, f_K^*)$. Therefore $r \leq \max(f_K, f_K^*)$. But (3.15) is stronger. We need to argue in effect, that $r \geq \max(f_K, f_K^*)$ as well.

$f_K^* > f_K$. One line of argument is that, with $q^* < 1$, K^* would be declining—which might make N^* decline too but presumably not as fast (especially with q falling), so that f_K^* would be growing larger indefinitely and $f_K^* > f_K$ perpetuated; but then q^* would reach zero, which cannot happen along an equilibrium path. Another line of argument is that when $\dot{K}^* < 0$ we will have $\dot{q}^* > 0$, not $\dot{q}^* < 0$; figs. 5 and 6 illustrated the *rise* of p_K *and* p_K/p with the decline of K. It seems, therefore, that $f_K^* \leq f_K$ if (a), and similarly $f_K \leq f_K^*$ if (b); hence that (3.15) holds along an equilibrium path.

Equations (3.13) and (3.15) yield

$$\dot{K} = -\mu K \quad \text{if } f_K < f_K^*; \qquad \dot{K}^* = -\mu K^* \quad \text{if } f_K^* < f_K. \tag{3.16}$$

Of course, when world gross investment is zero, then gross investment in both countries is nil.

Collecting our theorems, propositions, and surmises, we are led finally to the reduced-form phase diagram in Figure 7. The diagram displays a locus of points (K, K^*) along which $f_K^*[K^*, N^*, K, K^*, K + K^* - S^*, S^*)] = f_K[K, N(K, K^*, K + K^* - S^*, S^*)]$. There is such a locus for every S^*, but for simplicity I shall neglect that dependence; in defense of that, I would argue that S^* may vary little in the thought experiment to be described. The locus is upward sloping on the argument, discussed earlier, that any decline of K^* or increase of K would raise $f_K^* - f_K$. Accordingly, when (K, K^*) lies below the locus, $f_K < f_K^*$, and hence $\dot{K} < 0$; when (K, K^*) lies above the locus, $f_K^* < f_K$ and $\dot{K}^* < 0$. The leftward and downward arrows signify these motions.

Another curve in Figure 7 is the locus of points (K, K^*) at which $\dot{S} + \dot{S}^* = 0$. This locus too is possibly some function of S^*, because of "distribution effects"; however we have boldly assumed that S^* shows little variation in the interest of using the two-dimensional diagram. I take this locus to be negatively sloped, at least around the stationary equilibrium, at point E. Then convergence to stationary equilibrium requires that northeast of this locus $\dot{S} + \dot{S}^* < 0$, so that $K + K^*$ is declining, and southwest of this locus $\dot{S} + \dot{S}^* > 0$, so that $K + K^*$ is rising. Hence, when $\dot{K} = -\mu K$, $\dot{K}^* = \dot{S} + \dot{S}^* + \mu K > 0$ if (K, K^*) lies southwest of this locus *or* not so far northeast of the locus as to make $\dot{S} + \dot{S}^* \leq -\mu K$. Similarly, when $\dot{K}^* = -\mu K^*$, $\dot{K} = \dot{S} + \dot{S}^* + \mu K > 0$ if (K, K^*) lies southwest or not too far northeast of this locus.

Now suppose that initial conditions differ from those in stationary equilibrium. In particular, suppose that the economy *was* in a stationary equilibrium and that now G^* is permanently *increased*. For the purposes of analysis, it suffices to consider the case in which (K_0, K_0^*) lies below the new and current $f_K = f_K^*$ locus. It can be argued, however, that the new locus—the one shown in the figure—does indeed lie above the old one;

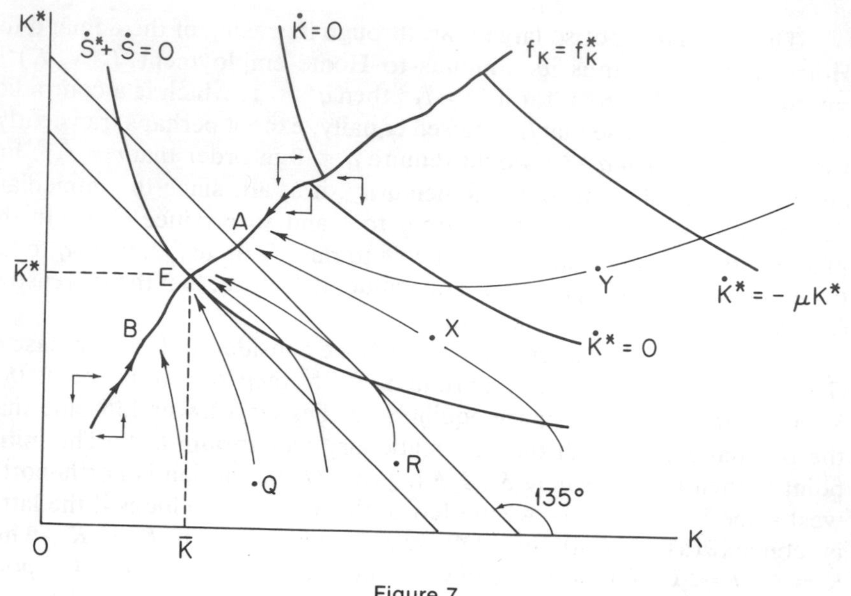

Figure 7

higher G^* makes $f_K^* - f_K$, formerly zero, a positive number at (K_0, K_0^*). The next two paragraphs sketch one line of argument for this proposition, making use again of the simplifying assumption that $L_2 = L_2^* = 0$.

Prior to the rise of G^*, $q^* = 1$, and $\dot{q}^* = 0$ in Star as well as $q = 1$ and $\dot{q} = 0$ in Home. These two patterns prevailed simultaneously because the economy was in stationary equilibrium with $f_K = f_K^*$. Assuming gross world investment stays positive, at least *one* of these patterns must continue, either in Home or Star, after the fixed disturbance. But after the shock it is impossible that both q and q^* equal one. If both were equal to one, then $f_K^* > f_K$: The rise of G^* shifts Star's LM^* curve outward and thus raises both N^* and $f_K(N^*, K^*)$, while the resulting rise of $(S - K)f_K^*$ shifts Home's LM curve inward and thus reduces both N and $f_N(N, K)$; but $f_K < f_K^*$ implies $q < 1$, a contradiction. What must happen is that the pattern $q^* = 1$ and $\dot{q}^* = 0$ survives the disturbance, so f_K^* indeed rises owing to the outward shift of Star's LM^* curve; and q *falls* below one to permit r, as given by (3.14), to match the higher f_K^* caused by the rise of G^*. If it were the case instead that $q = 1$ then $q^* < 1$ by the previous argument; but a reduction of q^* from one tends to increase f_K^* further through the terms q^*S^* and $(-S_b^*/q^*)$ in L^* function, and thus to decrease f_K further. Although the term $q^*(S - K)$ in the L^* function operates in the opposite direction, it is reasonable to suppose that this effect is too weak to carry the others.

disturbance—with special attention to employment effects in the short run. I consider a balanced-budget increase of public expenditures by the foreign country, Star, when the world has been in stationary equilibrium prior to the disturbance.

Section II argued, *mutatis mutandis,* that an increase of G^* will in the long run leave the world rate of interest higher, hence leave higher the employment–capital *ratio* in both countries. (Necessary, and plausible, conditions for these effects upon the stationary equilibrium were spelled out.) World employment will be left higher unless the supply of tangible world savings $(\bar{S} + \bar{S}^*)$ is strongly reduced by the rise of the rate of interest; a reduction of the world capital stock tends, by itself, to reduce world employment via real balance effects.

The presumption is that employment in Star is left higher because, at an unchanged rate of interest, the contraction of the demand for Star's money induced by the increase of G^* would create an excess supply of money if there were no increase of employment in Star. The consequent rise of the interest rate raises several complications but if the relevant interest elasticities are small, which is a reasonable empirical judgement, then employment in Star will indeed be left higher in the long run.

The effect upon employment at Home will depend only upon those interest elasticities. The supply of real cash balances is reduced by the fall of the real wage which is associated with the rise of the rate of interest, since the money wage is constant; this real balance effect tends to reduce employment at Home. So does the rise in the rate of return on private wealth owned by Home money holders. Only the Keynesian "L_2 effect" of a higher interest rate on the quantity of real balances demanded offers a clear basis for hoping that employment at Home will be left higher in the new stationary equilibrium; but this effect may be quite small at interest rates well away from zero.

The short-run effects of higher G^* were analyzed in Section III on two simplifying assumptions. One is that world gross saving, $\dot{S} + \dot{S}^* + \mu K + \mu K^*$, which was formerly equal to $\mu(K + K^*)$, does not drop to zero following the increase of G^*. (Gross saving *is* positive in the regions of Q, R, X, and Y in Figure 7, and zero only in the region of Z.) The other assumption is that L_2 and L_2^* are small enough to be neglected; however these Keynesian effects will be reintroduced shortly. Then our economy is the one pictured, but not wholly determined, by Figure 1.

We argued that the increase of G^* shifts outward Star's short-run LM^* curve, producing a rise of both N^* and $f_K^*(N^*, K^*)$ and thereby a fall of both N and $f_K(N, K)$ due to the rise in the demand for Home money caused by the rise of foreign dividend income. The results are an immediate rise of the real interest rate, since $r = \max(f_K, f_K^*)$ and f_K^* is up; a consequent fall of Home's q from its predisturbance value of 1 in order that the real rate of return on Home shares $f_K + (q^{-1})(f_K + \mu) + \dot{q}/q$ be reequated to the now higher rate of return on Star shares, namely f_K^*, and a continuation of the pattern $q^* = 1$ and $\dot{q}^* = 0$ in Star. The drop of q tends to raise N and $f_K(N, K)$, because the reduction of its wealth valuation reduces Home's demand for money, so these two variables need not fall on balance; indeed, f_K may rise but not more than f_K^* rises and not that much—not for long and almost certainly not at all.

Since f_K rises less (if it rises at all) then f_K^*, N/K rises less (if at all) than N^*/K^*; since these employment–capital ratios were equal before the fiscal disturbance to the former stationary situation, employment at Home can rise only in smaller proportion than employment in Star—and may actually fall.

Over the near-term future, then, the collapse of q will cause gross investment at Home to be zero; while gross investment in Star will stay positive and, eventually if not immediately, exceed capital depreciation. As a result, the price level tends to rise at Home, and to fall (or briefly rise less) in Star. Employment at Home is thereby pulled down, although not as fast as Home's capital is falling, and (eventually if not immediately) employment in Star is pushed up, although not as fast at Star's capital is rising. At some time in the future, Home's rising employment–capital ratio reaches equality with Star's falling ratio. That juncture is either the nadir for capital at Home or the zenith for capital in Star. If there is too much world capital in relation to stationary equilibrium, both capital stocks will thereupon shrink; if too little, both stocks will grow. The former process is likely to produce falling employment in both countries, and the latter to cause rising employment in both countries.

What are the consequences of reintroducing the Keynesian effects, $L_2, L_2^* < 0$? Leaving aside $\bar{S}_b$ and $\bar{S}_b^*$, the curves LM^* and LM then have the customary positive slope; that in itself seems to make no interesting difference for the results. However, since $f_K^* > f_K$ following the fiscal disturbance, Home's price level is up less (if at all) than Star's price level. Yet these price levels must ultimately rise in the same proportion, because the real wage ratio must ultimately be equal again at a lower level. Hence Home's price level must be *rising faster,* following its initial jump, than Star's price level or else *falling* more *slowly* than Star's price level. That means that Home's LM curve must *shift downward* by *more* than Star's or else *shift upward* by *less* than Star's. The anticipation of positive relative inflation at Home, owing to the expectation of quickly shrinking capital there, boosts N and $f_K(N, K)$ or moderates the rise of N^* and $f_K(N^*, K^*)$. It is clear, however, that f_K cannot find itself above f_K^*; for then it would be Home with $q = 1$, and Star with $q < 1$, so Home would be expecting relative deflation. Yet the moderation of the rise in $f_K^* - f_K$ helps to slow the rate of relative inflation at Home subsequent to the initial jump of Home's price level; more of the *total* rise of Home's price level is front-loaded onto the initial jump *or* less of the total rise in Star's price level is front-loaded—or both. Presumably, this price-ratio or exchange-rate mechanism also moderates the drop of Home's q.

A principal conclusion from my analysis, therefore, is that a balanced-budget increase of public expenditures abroad may *increase* employment at Home—in which case Home can reduce its own public expenditures to offset that effect—or *decrease* employment at Home—in which case public expenditures at Home will need to be increased if employment is to be maintained. In the long run, there are important interest-rate and real-balance mechanisms tending to depress employment at Home below what it otherwise would have been. *If* these mechanisms prevail, and if it is to support Home employment, the home country will need higher public expenditures in the long run—on the assumption that higher spending ultimately increases domestic employment. In that case, the rest of the world will need still higher public expenditures if, as a result of the home country's reaction, employment abroad suffers and the foreigners desire the employment gain that would otherwise have resulted. Higher employment in Star *is* sustainable through such fiscal stimulus if the long-run World *IS* is positively sloped. But if it is vertical or backward-bending, because higher public spending just raises prices and lowers the world's capital stock, then the countries abroad cannot gain higher employment through greater public spending unless the home country acquiesces through lower public spending. Then the world is confronted with an anguishing control problem—as long as money supplies and money wages are fixed, and some country wants more employment.

The pertinence of these findings for the present-day disagreements between West Germany and Japan, on the one hand, and America on the other, can hardly have escaped the reader's notice. Some spokesmen for the former group claim that their fiscal austerity is beneficial for the rest of the world—in the long run, whether or not in the short run. They appear to believe that, by exporting capital, they are tending to promote the cessation of inflation in the rest of the world and a recovery of employment there. They also seem to believe that their own interests are served tolerably well by this austerity, apparently on the theory that increased public spending on their part—while beneficial to themselves in the short run—would ultimately damage employment abroad and thus induce added public spending abroad, with worldwide consequences of declining capital, rising prices, and falling employment.

If I am not mistaken, that pessimistic policy position is not internally inconsistent; it is at least not inconsistent with the model studied here. However, it is equally *possible* in my theory that an increase of balanced-budget public spending by the Europeans would stimulate recovery there in both the short and long run; that America could respond with greater fiscal stimulus of its own if American employment would otherwise be contracted; and that the Europeans could counter with further stimulus, and so on, until ultimately employment would stabilize at a higher level in all countries desiring that outcome. This optimistic scenario is equally consistent with my model.

I happen to share the prevailing belief that market-driven money wages tend ultimately to drive every money economy back toward the normal "full employment" operating level. I also believe that the tools of monetary policy are best suited for hastening that stabilization process. Neither consideration, however, detracts from the conclusion I would draw from this study: There are theoretical grounds for worrying that, in a monetarist world caught in a general slump, the balanced-budget fiscal stimulus of one country may finally act as a depressant to other countries—so much so, possibly, that reciprocal fiscal stimuli will be mutually defeating beyond the short run. If so, the Finance Ministers' dilemma is a poor game to play.

ACKNOWLEDGMENTS

I thank Dale Henderson for his comments on an incomplete draft presented at the November 1977 Carnegie–Rochester conference and several colleagues at Columbia University for their advice and corrections. A National Science Foundation grant is acknowledged.

Part VII
TOWARD JUST CRITERIA IN STABILIZATION POLICY

INTRODUCTION

One motive for studying the determination and control of employment and inflation is the belief that the behavior of these economic variables bears on social welfare or, to use a term that has been brought back to favor, economic justice. But the justice, or injustice, of a given stabilization or nonstabilization policy will generally depend upon the particular conception of justice adopted. In matters of social choice, most economists are born utilitarians. One thinks of Bentham, Mill, and Sidgwick, of the rule utilitarianism of Harrod, and the *ex ante* utilitarianism of Vickrey and Harsanyi.

In the concluding paper of this volume I attempt to apply to matters of stochastic social choice, stabilization policy being one instance of such a choice, the conception of justice advanced by Rawls. The undertaking requires a perilous extension of Rawls because there is more than one kind of "minimum" utility that could be maximized. Yet Rawls has left enough hints of how to proceed. A Rawlsian macroeconomic policy, whatever it might look like, would not be ultraconservative, shying from risk to the maximum.

SOCIAL POLICY AND UNCERTAIN CAREERS: BEYOND RAWLS'S PARADIGM CASE

"I'm fed up with symmetry."
from Buñuel's *Le Fantôme de la Liberté*

This chapter begins as a commentary on the neo-utilitarians' "reaction" against John Rawls.[a] One theme is the difference between the underlying concepts of justice from which Rawls and the neo-utilitarians start. Rawls's theory is addressed to the just division of the fruits of economic cooperation among productive persons, not to the wider problems of justice tilted at by utilitarianism from Bentham to the present. Another theme is the distinction between their views of the good life. Rawls takes the opportunities and chances for self-realization and personal growth to be the desiderata for justice, not the lifetime intake of commodities. The main task here has been to explain, as Rawls and other Rawlsians have tried to do, why the neo-utilitarians' solution to the problem of redistributive social policy does not fit the choice problem that is Rawls's paradigm case: In that case, individuals are born into adulthood with predeterminedly differing advantages; given the setting of social policy and institutions, their subsequent lives are then laid out deterministically and foreseeably before them. It is therefore hard to see how the neo-utilitarians, with their axioms on behavior toward risk, provide a natural principle for the selection of redistributive measures.

But in the end this chapter succumbs to a far more intriguing question: How would neo-utilitarianism fare against "Rawls" on the neo-utilitarians' own home ground? In *their* paradigm case, all young persons from any generation begin economic life with the same endowment and tastes; in their ultimate success and enjoyment, however, there is a large element of luck. I shall argue that it is a misreading or mis-extrapolation of Rawls to impute to him, as do Samuelson and

---

My understanding of "Rawls" owes much to Columbia colleagues with whom "it" has been a chronic topic of conversation for three years. The present chapter has benefited from additional discussions with David Colander, Thomas Nagel, and Janusz Ordover.

[a]I refer particularly to the recent papers and reviews by Arrow, Harsanyi and Samuelson listed in the references.

By the term *neo-utilitarianism* I mean the use of "expected utility" for social choice as advocated first by William Vickrey in 1945, 1960, and 1961, and later expounded by J.C. Harsanyi and P.A. Samuelson.

Reprinted by permission from *Public and Urban Economics: Essays in Honor of William S. Vickrey*, R. E. Grieson and D. C. Heath (Eds.). Lexington, Mass., 1976.

some others, the advocacy of redistributive policies that would maximize the minimum realized lifetime utility–the ex post maximin criterion–in this setting of intra-life uncertainty. Yet a Rawlsian cannot go along with the unbridled ex-ante-ism of the neo-utilitarians even in their paradigm case. We need to follow the fortunes of people through their working lives to keep track of their conditional expectations. A 1973 research prospectus of mine glimpses the idea:

> . . . [A] n *unconditional ex ante* notion of social welfare, one which looks from the vantage point of his date of birth solely at the *expected* lifetime utility of each individual, would fail to capture some important aspects of our intuitive feelings about any society's achievement of justice or social welfare. . . . An extreme [approach] would identify social welfare with the worst (lowest) lifetime utility that will be turned into the scorekeeper as the individuals now living (and maybe their descendants) reach death. Such an ex post facto notion of minimum utility would be maximized by a *posterioristic* Rawlsian. An *a prioristic* Rawlsian might maximize the (either subjective or actual) *conditional* expectation of lifetime utility of the persons having the worst such expectation. [first and last italics added.]

The second half of this chapter is an attempt to develop the latter idea in Rawlsian terms, and to define the circumstances in which such an ex ante conditional maximin criterion would be applicable.

Rawlsian Theory in Its Paradigm Case

For simplicity we may usually assume that there are just two sorts of individuals, those born more productive and those born less–top dogs and bottom dogs.

The neo-utilitarians would engage the members of this society in a thought-experiment in which each person (1) accepts the assumption that he had as much chance of being a top dog as anyone else had, and (2) calculates for each redistributive social policy, in view of the relative frequency of top dogs and his attitudes toward risk, the mathematical expectation of the von Neuman-Morgenstern utilities he assigns to each of the two outcomes.

Whatever their full position, the neo-utilitarians then claim that redistribution should not go so far as to reduce everyone's hypothetical "expected utility" so calculated; that would obviously be Pareto inoptimal with regard to these expected utilities. Consider, in particular, that redistributive policy–we may call it the maximin policy with regard to "ex post utilities"–which goes so far as to maximize the realized well-being of actual bottom dogs (their ex post utility level). That policy clearly causes the hypothetical expected utility of any person engaging in the thought-experiment, whether the person is a top or bottom dog, to be smaller than it would be under some more mildly redistributive policy. An "exception" occurs if the person is completely risk-phobic, behaving as though he were fated to be a bottom dog; but that exception is ruled out by the neo-utilitarians' continuity axiom, according to which one will risk crossing the street for a gain on the other side if the chance of accident is sufficiently small.

The Rejection of Neo-Utilitarianism

I shall cite four objections that Rawlsians raise to this neo-utilitarian construction.

1. One objection Rawlsians raise is that the references to "expected utility" suffer from a considerable amount of logical incoherence. If I have an actuarial chance of being a top dog or a bottom dog, then whose utility function and implied risk aversion do I use in calculating "my" expected utility? The notion of averaging top dogs' and bottom dogs' respective risk aversions seems unintelligible; the idea of my entertaining the probability that I will have each person's life prospects cum *my* risk aversion (and other tastes?) seems equally fraught with difficulty. What if I opt *for* special state X on the ground that it is good for you (and I might have turned out to be you) while you oppose X on the ground that it is bad for me (and you might have been me)? Would *these* "ethical preferences" of ours merit any attention? The incapacity to deal persuasively with the diversity of attitudes toward risk has always appeared to be a serious limitation of the neo-utilitarian approach.[b]

The above difficulties over the meaning of "expected utility" notwithstanding, neo-utilitarians are still inclined evidently to pit their approach against Rawls's in the special case where every person's attitude toward risk and implied cardinal utility function is identical to every other person's over the same domain of hypothetical choices. What is said below under points 2, 3, and 4 is compatible with that specialization to identical tastes for risk (though often the assumptions are not couched so as to require that specialization).

2. Another point against neo-utilitarianism is that the willingness or unwillingness of someone (or everyone) to risk his status quo cannot realistically be regarded as independent of his position in the socioeconomic setting.

One of the industrial barons of the '20s remarked that he didn't take risks because he was rich enough not to have to. I suppose he meant relative wealth.

[b]A similar difficulty comes up in connection with intergenerational neo-utilitarianism. The beneficiaries of our generation's decision to make positive net investment in favor of the next generation ("we might equally have been in their shoes, so our 'expected utility' is thereby increased") might not have been willing to make such an investment themselves were they us. The next generation may be more risk-averse than we or they may be intergenerational egalitarians.

Accordingly, it is possible that the willingness of a person–hypothetically–to risk greater hardship to bottom dogs on the chance that he will turn out a top dog with still *greater* benefits is attributed in part to the value he places on additional "relative" income rather than "absolute" income. (Recall the Friedman-Savage hypothesis in this connection.)

Now it is one thing for some disinterested party to suggest that half the population sacrifice themselves so that another half could "make something" of themselves. But insofar as the utility gain to the latter group springs from the aversion to having a low *relative* living standard, the appeal to a sporting attitude seems unjustified.

3. The major Rawlsian objection is to the postulate of prenatal choice with symmetrical probabilities. Suppose the bottom dogs each ask for the maximum feasible utility–which will be less than (or equal to) the utility that top dogs are going to get. It would seem like dubious metaphysics to say to them, and a self-serving rationalization for top dogs to say, that each bottom dog had the same chance to be a top dog as each of the top dogs. It is one thing to ask a person to imagine being another person or persons. It is another thing to ask a person to suppose that in fact he might actually have been someone else with equal probability. It's a commonplace that we don't choose our parents. It is equally true that we don't select a lottery determining who our parents will be.

Note first that the particular specification according to which the equal-probabilities-for-all are *estimated* by the observable relative frequencies of top dogs and bottom dogs is totally non-operational (not that every axiom and injunction can be operational). There is no way whatever of testing it, no evidence on its behalf. The assumption seems to be motivated by the desired result. We might just as well employ the postulate that the true probabilities of being an individual of type t, $t = 1, 2, \ldots, T$, are given by $(p_1, p_2, \ldots, p_T)$, not by the relative frequencies, $(f_1, f_2, \ldots, f_T)$ appearing in a *particular sample*. We could invent more than one model in terms of which to estimate those true probabilities, but I can't see clearly which of those models is best or most natural. True, while not really knowing the true probabilities, I can always formulate my subjective probabilities. Perhaps I do this when *I have to make a decision*, in Bayesian fashion. But who I'm going to be, my birth, is not a decision to be made by me. So how can Bayesian prior probability be imputed to me?

4. Yet suppose, arguendo, we were to agree that the true probabilities are none other than the observed relative frequencies, $(f_1, f_2, \ldots, f_T)$. Thus the probability of being a bottom dog is f_b, the proportion in the current generation, and the probability of being a top dog is $1 - f_b$. A crucial question at this point seems to be: What does the willingness of anyone to gamble signify, if anything, for the distribution of utilities over persons that he would accept? Nothing, Rawlsians say.

Imagine that a teacher were to hand out special rewards and offices to those pupils whose last names were highest in the alphabetical order. To a student who complained of the injustice, would it be adequate for the teacher to reply that the pupil had as much chance of a surname beginning A as any other? Might the student not feel that "equiprobability" was irrelevant?

To quote from my earlier, 1971 NSF research proposal:

> . . . recall the problem of the two men and the cake. They agree that it would be unfair if the man who has the advantage of choosing which piece to eat–we assume non-satiation–were also allowed to cut the cake. So the other man cuts the cake, and of course he divides it equally (thus insuring himself half the cake). In the Rawls model, there are incentive effects from redistribution so that (over the interesting range) the cake is bigger the more unequally the first man cuts it. There is assuredly some sense in which it is only fair if the cutter cuts in such a way as to maximize the absolute size of the smaller piece. After all the other man will have the advantage of choosing the larger piece.
>
> Now some neo-utilitarians such as Harsanyi and Vickrey have said to the disadvantaged cake cutter, "Look, you ought to take a larger view, ontologically speaking. When God rolled the dice, you might have been selected to reap the advantage of choosing the larger piece of cake. Had you not known "who you were going to be," your role in the cake business, then surely you would have sought to maximize your *expected* utility by agreeing with the likewise ignorant second man that whoever turns out to be the cake cutter will cut the cake somewhat more unequally [thus shrinking the smaller piece] . . . rather than [to maximize] *ex post* cake-cutter's utility.
>
> To this the cake cutter might well reply, "What dice? What God? I know for a fact that the other fellow has the advantage, the opportunity to take the larger share of the cake. The probability that it is the other way around looks like zero to me."

Let me try again to dispel the alleged connection between acceptance of dispersion in one's own utilities and acceptance of the same dispersion in utilities across different persons. Suppose that I am a risk-lover to the extent that, in preference to the certainty of having the maximin level of utility, I would *if given the choice* opt for the probability mixture of grinding poverty, of quasi-starvation, with probability f_b and the associated improved level of well-being of top dogs with probability $1 - f_b$. By what additional postulates and argumentation is it implied that I would accept as just or satisfactory that a proportion of the people equal to f_b who are bottom dogs, through no choice of gamble of their own, should suffer quasi-starvation for the sake of the associated gain of the remaining proportion $1 - f_b$? It would not seem that the mere fact that I (and every bottom dog) would *risk* the comfort afforded by maximum minimum utility for the probability $1 - f_b$ of having a better-than maximin level of top-dog utility should signal our willingness to impose this level of misery with certainty on the persons who are predetermined to have the bottom-dog position. The chance that bottom dogs would be willing to take to have a top-dog well-being hardly seems to be a justification for making bottom dogs more miserable than they actually need be (*would* be under maximin).

Rawls's Conception and the Neo-utilitarians' Reaction

Rawls's position, of course, is that the relative number of top dogs ought to have nothing to do with the degree to which the welfare of any single bottom dog is traded off, if at all, for that of a top dog. The maximin allocation displays precisely that invariance to relative numbers. Consider two economies in which the maximin level of utility is equal, but in economy A the relative number of top dogs, $1 - f_b^A$, exceeds that in economy B, $1 - f_b^B$. Rawls asks why the bottom dogs in the two economies should be accorded different utilities, when the maximin allocation of utilities would be identical, merely because of the natural accident and irrelevant detail that they are, say, a smaller minority in economy A. To argue otherwise smacks of "numerical superiority makes right."

To aid in deciding what is a just redistributive arrangement, Rawls argues, a person will want to ascend figuratively to the "original position" where "behind the veil of ignorance" he does not know which type of person ($t = 1, 2, \ldots, n$) he is cast to play in the society below. Of course, the idea of the original position, with its dramatization of the notion of impartiality, Rawls has taken from the neo-utilitarians, but he takes little else. In particular, neither the respective probabilities of being of each type nor any information about the relative frequencies of each type at any particular place and moment are divulged to occupants of the Rawlsian original position. In this way it is insured that reflections on the degree to which one type's utility will be traded off for another type's will not be contaminated by information of relative numbers.

Rawls then asserts that most or all individuals, if placed in that original position of actuarial ignorance, would in fact select a *maximin* strategy. They would agree to be bound by a Constitution requiring that the institutions, laws, and social policies in the society they will actually inhabit be dedicated to maximizing the well-being or opportunities of those persons who are least advantaged—who will have "least utility" in utilitarian terms. Some readers remain "non-Rawlsian" because they balk, or hesitate, over this last step. There is no a priori way to *decide*—as distinct from *illuminate*—this issue.

But the neo-utilitarians stubbornly remain non-Rawlsian because they refuse to play his game. They are irrepresible about saying to Rawls what they have been saying for quite some time, as though they had not been heard before, namely: An occupant of the original position ought to consider being a non-bottom type and maximize some corresponding "expected utility." And Rawls will say again that the occupant cannot be expected to know the true probabilities of being of this or that type and that, even if the probabilities were known, one's willingness and everyone else's to exchange one distribution of own-utilities for another riskier one does not justify exchanging the *maximin* distribution of sure-thing utilities over persons for a more *unequal* distribution of sure-thing utilities when people's relative advantages at earning utility in any social state are in fact predetermined and thus not actually the first-stage outcome of some super-lottery purchased by people who were initially equals.

However, the neo-utilitarians rebut, one in the original position must acknowledge *some* positive probability of being of each type $t = 1, 2, \ldots, n$, hence some positive chance of being of non-bottom type under the maximin policy; for otherwise to what end were we to imagine being of each type there in the original position? Why not then "take a chance" that one will not be a bottom type? Why be "so pessimistic" as to opt for the maximin redistributive social policy? So demand Arrow, Harsanyi, and Samuelson.

One answer to that, I should think, is that no particular counterproposal to the maximin strategy has so far been proposed. It is true, however, that one might imagine each person taking a degree of chance according to his "optimism," "sunniness," or whatever. So we must finally let the issue be decided "behaviorally," by whatever risks people do decide to take in choice situations of total ignorance. But until we have more evidence of choice-behavior in such situations it remains plausible, as it seemed to Rawls, that a person, or most persons, would choose the maximin position.

A related quarrel of the neo-utilitarians with the maximin point is based on cases where the utility-feasibility-curve is smooth. In the two-dimensional top-dog/bottom-dog case, one thinks of the point of maximum minimum utility as being fairly "flat." Hence a tiny sacrifice by bottom dogs would reap a much larger gain by the already better-off top dogs in the maximin position. That situation is illustrated by the diagram in figure 10–1 used by Rawls himself. With some assumption about the proportion of the population who are top dogs one can represent the classical utilitarian solution, at W, and the maximin solution, at R. The utilitarians' average utility is measured along the vertical axis along with minimum (bottom-dog) utility. The latter is at a maximum at R and the former achieves a maximum at W.

In a moment I will respond to this quarrel with Rawls in its above, rather unspecific or general form. But let me first deal with a special version of the quarrel that has sometimes been brought up by way of an example. I quote first from Arrow:

> . . . [the maximin theory] . . . implies that any benefit, no matter how small, to the worst-off member of society will outweigh any loss to a better-off individual, provided it does not reduce the second below the level of the first. Thus, there can easily exist medical procedures which serve to keep people barely alive but with little satisfaction and which

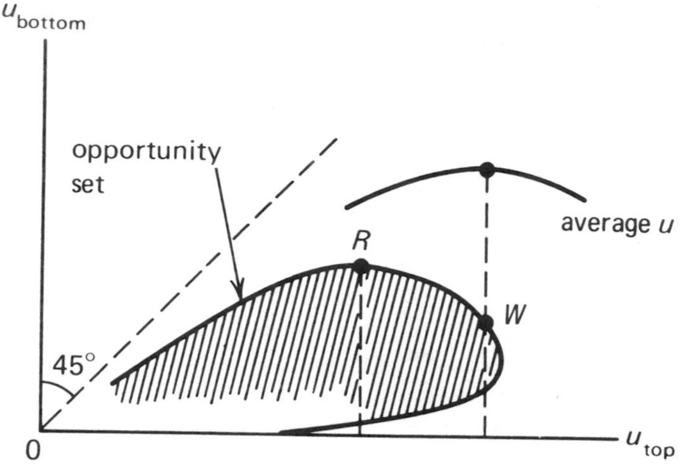

Figure 10–1. Utilitarian and Rawlsian Solutions

> are yet so expensive as to reduce the rest of the population to poverty. A maximin principle would apparently imply that such procedures be adopted.

Harsanyi makes the same criticism:

> Even more disturbing is the fact that the difference principle [meaning the maximin principle (*au.*)] would require us to give *absolute* priority to the interests of the worst-off individual, *no matter what,* even under the most extreme conditions. Even if his interests were affected only in a very minor way, and all other individuals in society had opposite interests of the greatest importance, his interests would always override anybody else's. For example, let us assume that society would consist of a large number of individuals, of whom one would be seriously mentally retarded. Suppose that some extremely expensive treatment would become available which could slightly improve the retarded individual's condition; but the costs would be so high that this treatment could be financed only if some of the most brilliant individuals were deprived of all higher education. The difference principle would require that the retarded individual should all the same receive this very expensive treatment at any event—*no matter how many* people would have to be denied a higher education, and *no matter how strongly* they would desire to obtain one (and no matter how great the satisfaction they would obtain from it).

Actually Harsanyi nearly undermines his case with overstatement. First, a maximin strategy by the state must give a wide amount of latitude to people's ambitions, must allow them nourishing mouthfuls from the invisible hand, if the state is to come up with enough tax revenue to provide maximum support to the bottom groups; unlike the earlier egalitarians, Rawls would harness inequalities and ambition in the name of the least advantaged in that competitive race. Second, if talented scientists and artists were in fact frustrated from acting upon their drives for realization and success, it might very well be them who would be recognized the least favored, most blocked, bottom group; I am sure that Rawls does not mean to fill up the mental wards for the sake of an increase in the motor skills of retardates.

Yet everyone reading Rawls must have wondered at some point or other how he would treat persons whose functioning in and contribution to society are precluded by physical and emotional handicaps. And there is the stickier question of how to treat persons whose impairments place them at the margin of participation in society and its economic activity. Does Rawls envision a state in which the catastrophically disadvantaged are a sink draining off most of available government revenue save for what is deemed necessary to provide incentives for the productive? And if not, how is his position consistent with his endorsement of maximin?

Rawls's oft-cited direct answer rests on the appeal to Kant's principle that people should "treat one another not as means only but as ends in themselves" (p. 179). The answer, couched in the code-words of Kant, has proved too epigrammatic for us economists to understand. But there are enough clues elsewhere in the book for us to be able to figure out Rawls's position.

Rawls's book does not present a general theory of justice, whatever that might mean. It is a theory of social justice, not of justice in all interpersonal transactions. And it is a *special* theory of social justice at that, for it presents only a notion of "economic justice" toward the members of society who can contribute productively to society's "income"—to the vector of satisfactions, achievements, growth of the persons belonging to society.

That this is Rawls's concern and not some wider one embracing unproductive humans, other sentient beings, or indeed even foreigners is made explicit early in the book:

> Let us assume that a society is a more or less self-sufficient association of persons who in their relations to one another recognize certain rules of conduct as binding and who for the most part act in accordance with them. Suppose further that these rules specify a system of cooperation designed to advance the good of those taking part in it. Then, although a society is a cooperative venture for mutual advantage, it is typically marked by a conflict as well as by an identify of interests . . . since persons are not indifferent as to how the greater benefits produced by their collaboration are distributed, for in order to pursue their ends they each prefer a larger to a lesser share. A set of principles is required for choosing among the various social arrangements which determine this division of advantages and for underwriting an agreement on proper distributive shares. These principles are the principles of social justice: they provide a way of assigning rights and duties in the basic institutions of society

> and they define the appropriate distribution of the benefits and burdens of social cooperation (p. 4).
>
> I shall be satisfied if it is possible to formulate a reasonable conception of justice for the basic structure of society conceived for the time being as a closed system isolated from other societies. The significance of this special case is obvious and needs no explanation (p. 8).
>
> Justice as fairness is not a complete contract theory. For it is clear that the contractarian idea can be extended to the choice of more or less an entire ethical system, that is, to a system including principles for all the virtues and not only for justice. Now for the most part I shall consider only principles of justice. . . . Obviously, if justice as fairness succeeds reasonably well, a next step would be to study the more general view suggested by the name 'rightness as fairness'. But even this wider theory fails to embrace all moral relationships, since it would seem to include only our relations with other persons and to leave out of account how we are to conduct ourselves toward animals and the rest of nature (p. 17).

Later in the book, Rawls repeatedly nominates the unskilled worker and his representative expectations as our referent in thinking about the least favored or bottom group (pp. 78, 96, 98). Never does Rawls identify the least-favored as consisting of those who are critically impaired from contributing to society, particularly its economy.

So we are to consider a closed society in which a type like the Beatles have a contribution to social product to make. Less dependably, so does a type like the Fellows of the Econometric Society. Strong-back types contribute who only haul their trash. Provided that a manual-labor type can contribute more to total product when cooperating with the other types of persons in the organized economy (the market sector, if you like) than that type can produce in isolation from the organized economy, his utility is one of those utilities which is qualified for maximin treatment. If there be persons whose faculties are so limited that their "cooperation" in the organized economy would fail to give rise to a gain from trade, so that their participation could not make either themselves or others better off, then those persons are evidently not eligible for "economic" justice and, in particular, for maximin treatment. These dependents of society certainly have our moral concern; but their claim is to our sympathy or pity or some wider sense of right, not to economic justice.

It is an essential feature of this view that no type of person will be expected to receive less than what that type could produce and consume, that is, achieve, on its own, without benefit of social cooperation. Indeed, Rawls envisions that each person will maximize his utility from 9 to 5, subject only to some self-enforced constraints on law-abidingness and other civic and business ethics.

A difficulty that appears in this respect is that as soon as an individual edges over the threshold to participation in the social economy, he is at once likely to be the recipient of substantial support by the state. Because of this unwelcome discontinuity, it becomes important where the line is drawn between contributors and non-contributors to society's production. The line becomes hard to draw if the state's heavy redistribution of the gains of trade in favor of the least favored has the unavoidable side-effect of actually inducing some of the beneficiaries to withdraw their labor from the organized economy. Rawls regards the problem of defining the least-favored group or groups—at any degree of redistributiveness, let us say—as a "serious difficulty" (p. 98). But evidently Rawls does not regard that problem as a fatal weakness of the difference principle, that is, the maximin criterion.

It would not seem, however, that various types of people would be allowed to form coalitions against other types. To do so would be to permit the coalition to appropriate to itself some of the producers' surplus, or gains from trade, in a way that seems close to their expelling the others from the society; but perhaps it can sometime be shown that federations within a larger society, if only for consideration in some hypothetical reasoning, would be of ethical interest.

In this connection one thinks of international justice. If a rich country should discover a poorer country with which it can profitably trade, is the former then obligated to *maximin* over each individual utility within the two societies as if they were now one society? Or is the richer country obliged only to give away the gains from the trade to the poorer country—which it would do if the poor country is too small to affect the larger country's relative prices, and the large country does not think to play monopolist with the terms of trade—as if the rich country were like a type of person in the closed society? Perhaps a national coalition is permissible provided it is not exploitive toward others.

Rawls's position seems to be that taken earlier by Koopmans—that the principles of social choice cannot be established completely independently of the structure of the choices available. Every principle may be found to have tough sledding over some terrain or other. Presumably neo-utilitarians stand ready to amend their criterion in the event it implies enslavement for a few individuals or a national dividend for cats and dogs. If the neo-utilitarians turn a deaf ear to the possibility that the last inch toward *their* optimum—say, maximum average utility or the maximum of some quasi-concave social welfare function of individual utilities—would cause substantial suffering to the least well-off, then how can they fairly turn the same "paradox" against the Rawlsian extreme under which at least it can be said that the sufferers are those better off than the gainers?

Toward a Rawlsian Theory for the Neo-Utilitarians' Case

I have been discussing my understanding of Rawls's theory with reference to the paradigm case for which it was designed. In that case, given the social structure with its various institutions and governmental redistributions, one sees one's whole opportunity set laid out before one at the outset of adulthood. At that age, one's fate is predetermined and known. There is no mid-life lottery, either optional or mandated. However, there are some hints in Rawls's *Justice* of how certain kinds of risks or uncertainties might be treated, and we are free to venture our own extrapolations.

The most logical exposition would deal first with the neo-utilitarians' paradigm case, where every young adult's ex ante lifetime prospects is like every other's and only the ex post experiences differ, and thence on to the mixed or general case where both ex ante and ex post well-being (to use the old shorthand) are heterogeneous. However there is another dimension—whether the mid-life hazards are unavoidable, inescapable uncertainties or whether they are voluntarily assumed.

Inescapable Hazards

It might seem at first that it should make no difference for Rawls's theory whether a person's natural disadvantages are known at the beginning of adulthood or whether they occur with a delay. Better to be partially paralyzed later than sooner, a "Rawlsian" might reflect, but no issue of principle is affected. If those handicapped at birth deserve a certain type of aid by the state to assist them in leading productive lives, then those handicapped later in life deserve the same aid—with minor allowance perhaps for the relatively fulfilled youths of the latter.

But neo-utilitarians who conceded that Rawls had a point when dealing with his paradigm case—the configuration of natural disadvantages were not actually insured against in acts of pre-natal choice, so it seems misplaced to inject the rhetoric of tolerance toward risks—might balk at the suggestion that young people must pay the full *maximin* insurance premiums against mid-life calamities when each young person, knowing the risks, would rather take a greater chance that he will be among the lucky ones.

Rawls's *Justice* does not give any clear evidence of how he would come out on this question. The repeated references to the "representative person" among less-favored groups and to the "representative expectations" of various types of people seem intended to evoke the notion of average ex ante lifetime prospects of the members in the group. I know of no passage in the book suggesting that unskilled manual workers, for example, are to define their prospects as those of the unluckiest persons among them. If every type of person in Rawls's scheme can point to one or more victims of some future calamity, though it is not known which member of the type will be a victim, then the purpose of the typing in terms of the "unskilled worker" and so on seems to be lost; every socio-economic group will have its catastrophic cases, which are much alike.

Let me give one example of an economic model to which it is quite doubtful that Rawls would apply the maximin criterion to ex post lifetime utilities. All people in society live for just one period. They till the soil at the beginning of the period and harvest the crops and consume at the end. There is no carryover of people or capital into the next period. We take the symmetrical case where every person has the same opportunity set and same tastes, hence the same expected (lifetime) utility. Yet it is predictable that bad luck, in the form of floods and drought, will strike some producers, causing an ultimate inequality in ex post before-redistribution incomes across producers. To take an extreme case, corresponding to every allocation of labor in the (identical) "islands" of this society there is a *known* frequency distribution of crop yields across the islands—as if Nature were sampling without replacement. For example, it is known that one-tenth the islands will have half the crops of the other nine-tenths, but it is not known of course which islands will comprise the unlucky tenth.

I find nothing in Rawls's *Justice* to imply that these islanders would, upon original-position reflection, contract to redistribute the aggregate harvest in such a way as to maximize the minimum after-redistribution consumption across islands. These islanders don't need the original position, they are already in it. They all start out as equals, so there is no problem of partiality, and the probabilities of bad luck are actually known (by hypothesis) and can in actual fact be acted upon before the luck of the draw. The probabilities do not have to be postulated retrospectively and imagined to have been acted upon in a hypothetical prior choice.

So it seems to me to be tenably Rawlsian to say that maximin justice has already by accident been realized in this society and it is up to the islanders to decide on the degree of redistribution of ex post harvests in whatever way they (unanimously) prefer; in particular, if they want to maximize expected utility and are not risk phobic (thus, satisfy the continuity axiom), and hence make a compact for less-than-maximin-redistribution to islands with bad crops, it is not unjust toward those who turn out to be unlucky that they do so. Provided that drought would not reduce his well-being below some "social minimum," a person's bad luck would not have prevented him for living the "good life." There is no call to fuss over how the aggregate harvest is divided.

What say the neo-utilitarians? They would advocate that people "insure" against low ex post utility by the payment of premiums—up to the point dictated by their risk-aversion. And they would "prove" that the maximin criterion goes too far. Yet it might be doubted that each islander would *necessarily* have preferences toward frequency distributions of ex post utility across persons that are identical to (and hence derivable simply from) his preferences toward probability distributions of his own utility—even if he knew that all other persons had his preferences toward own-utility distributions. Neo-utilitarianism does not prove the connection between the two sets of preferences, it postulates the connection. I see nothing contradictory about people's being inequality-averse (concave SWFs) while not being risk-averse. So it would not be *irrational,* I believe, if the islanders of the above model *were* to opt for maximin with regard to ex post utilities if that is what they felt like doing.

People's expected utilities are in part a function of the processes, morals, and manners they learn and select among. They may take (utility-enhancing) pride in the cultivation and practice of these traits independently of the terminal consumption of bundles of goods which it gains them or costs them. In this respect, then, the neo-utilitarian theory of the compact which would be made by the islanders—at least the theory in its standard form with egoistic utility functions—is not likely to be descriptive of the social insurance and contingent redistribution compacts that real societies are observed to make. The neo-utilitarian theory is best regarded as an analytical device for rather special situations, such as the model I have just been discussing, in which one would like to be able to say (possibly for some prescriptive purpose), "Even a society of rugged individualists would contract for redistribution of this kind and amount. . . ." It is less effective as a device for deriving propositions like "Rugged individualists who are not risk-phobic would not redistribute by more than that."

Various other modifications of the above model further undermine the neo-utilitarian approach to ex post utilities—where, by that approach, I mean the viewpoint that a person should prefer the "progressive" tax legislation which maximizes his "expected utility."

First, the above model makes the proportion of islands which are going to have a bad harvest a certain fraction which is known universally and deterministically. What if the proportion of islands that will be struck by hurricanes at harvest time is not deterministic but is instead "determinable" only statistically "up to a random white-noise variable with zero mean and other known moments"? If the incidence of hurricanes is above-average, should the islands which are spared send no more food to the unlucky islands than is stipulated by the income-tax legislation which all risk-averting islands agreed upon at the beginning of the period? True, the islanders could draw up redistributive contracts which have contingency clauses to allow for deviations from the mean experience. But such contingent compacts are not a part of neo-utilitarianism.

Second, the problem becomes more Rawlsian once we grant that there is a great variety of catastrophes that can befall us, and the incidence of each tends to rise or fall in ways that were not predicted. So it is grossly unrealistic to say to victims that they could have insured themselves when young, either privately or through public legislation.

Here the neo-utilitarians might reply that the possibility of some unanticipated disasters (or unanticipatable probability of distributions of disaster) does not prevent us from making distinctions according to the degree of insurability. There are certain kinds of risks which, being well-known and presumably constant from year or to, people ought to be left free to insure against by less than the maximin amount; while no island should have to suffer a reduction of its terminal consumption below the maximin level because of a Krakatoa-like explosion or something else never witnessed before. But whatever a neo-utilitarian might feel intuitively about the right way for these islanders to treat Krakatoa-like events whose probabilities are inestimable, I believe it is fair to say that neo-utilitarian theory does not present us with a solution to this problem that is agreed upon by the neo-utilitarians themselves.

Let me now turn to a different model: Overlapping generations have different mid-life fortunes. In view of Rawls's strictures that justice in his sense is owed only to productive, potentially working individuals, let us focus our attention on the coexistence of workers of two ages, disregarding ex-workers now in retirement. For simplicity I maintain at this point our stipulation that all *young* workers have the same ex ante lifetime prospects—in the sense that no young worker is predictably better advantaged than another at the outset of their respective working lives.

Imagine that all thirty-year-olds, though they had the same ex ante prospects as twenty-year olds, have suffered some serious privation owing to a natural disaster, an unprovoked invasion, an economic depression, or whatnot. As a result, let us suppose, the thirty-year-olds are less productive than the twenty-year-olds' expectation of *their* productivity when *they* reach thirty. The question I raise is how the redistributive compacts made by a society of these twenty-year-olds and thirty-year-olds ought to take account of the bad luck of thirty-year-olds.[c]

Now the twenty-year-olds might reply to the thirty-year-old petitioners: "Why didn't you enact (or continue) legislation providing social insurance against misfortunes such as you have experienced? Where are the public entitlements to the state aid that you now claim?" But that position would surely be unjust.[d]

A rejoinder that I have been outlining to this point is that misfortunes come in such varied and novel guises that a generation cannot be expected to anticipate all the contingencies that may befall their members and to enact social insurance programs appropriate to each one of them. Even after the event, we

[c]I am not conjuring up a case in which current thirty-year-olds have suffered a loss of first-decade candy, pure and simple. However much a neo-utilitarian might fret over such a problem, it is doubtful that Rawls would worry much over it. The problem posed is that by natural or social accident the thirty-year-olds have suffered a setback in their productivity, their opportunities for achievement and self-realization in relation to the normal projection. After some reasonable correction for their different stages in the life cycle, the thirty-year-olds now find themselves to be disadvantaged relative to twenty-year-olds.

[d]The twenty-year-olds might also be tempted to demand, "What did you thirty-year-olds do for thirty-year-olds when *you* were twenty?". But if each generation of twenty-year-olds refused to do justice to survivors from earlier generations simply because there was no precedent for it, each such generation would find itself in the same boat later. Justice to older generations would never get off the ground. (In some situations the younger generations may have a game-theoretic motive to start the ball rolling, whatever the "requirements" of their conception of justice to the old.)

sometimes do not know "what hit us"—which contingency to ascribe our condition to. There is some element of uninsurability, therefore. Moreover, the existence of public entitlements on the books could hardly be a sufficient condition for meeting the thirty-year-olds' petitions—they could easily have legislated themselves onto easy street at the expense of twenty-year-olds if their legislated entitlements were sure to be paid out—and this even if the thirty-year-olds could demonstrate that they had treated their elders, allowing for different circumstances, in the "same way" they were asking to be treated now.

There is a second rejoinder, once we admit that each fresh generation consists of members with heterogeneous lifetime prospects. I come back to a point I emphasized earlier: What if those persons, particularly new entrants, who are least advantaged within their generation tend to be least risk-averse (or most risk-seeking) precisely because of their unfavorable socioeconomic position? These least advantaged among the young might prefer to take certain chances, but does that give them the right to deny assistance to older persons who, owing to their same disadvantaged situation, took similar gambles and lost? Current thirty-year-olds are actual people, not just hypothetico-probabilistic thirty-year-olds that twenty-year-olds reckon they may possibly become.

What, the reader must be demanding impatiently, is the "Rawlsian" approach to the problem of intergeneration justice that I posed? Of course, I cannot speak for all Rawlsians, let alone Rawls himself, nor for that matter any Rawlsian other than myself. And the solution "for me" I see now only in hazy outline.

One Rawlsian principle that ought, presumably, to remain intact is this: In deciding upon the program of public assistance to be accorded to twenty-year-olds and the (unlucky) thirty-year-olds, the way we trade off between aid to a person from one group and aid to a person from the other group ought not to depend upon the relative numbers of persons belonging to the two groups. A twenty-year-old should not count for more in relation to a thirty-year-old merely because population is booming (or, even, is optimally booming) so there are more of the former types than the latter.

Second, Rawls's maximin principle also retains considerable appeal if what counts in the "min function" is not the duration of time over which one feels "realized" or "successful" but, rather, the opportunity to achieve "self-realization" or "personal success," the chances of reaching it, and the actuality of reaching it. In that case, the maximin principle does not "favor" the old on the ground that they have so little time left just as it does not "favor" the young merely on the ground that they have a longer life-span ahead of them. *Maximin* means maximizing the smaller of the two probabilities of success—those of twenty- and thirty-year-olds, given appropriate provision for future generations. Thus, the probability of success offered twenty-year-olds should be increased by age-free government programs only up to the point that there is also a gain in the probability of success thereby offered to thirty-year-olds, assuming that the thirty-year-olds will have the lesser chance under the maximin social policy. And insofar as middle-aged-favoring policies are feasible which pull the probability of success of the thirty-year-olds toward the success-probability of twenty-year-olds, these programs should be adopted up to the point of equality.[e]

Discretionary Gambles

Consider first some symmetrical cases beloved of neo-utilitarians. Everyone has identical productivities and identical preferences at least with regard to sure-thing commodity bundles. Whatever this society's economic policy, sure-thing prospects are equal over persons and, if attitudes toward risk are also identical, so are persons' expected utilities.

Some or all individuals in this society will want to take certain risks—climb a mountain, speculate on the bourse, plant a riskier crop for a higher average yield, and so on. What is a "just" social policy toward such risk-takings and their outcomes? Should the government share in the gains and losses? Rescue gamblers from all losses? Prohibit some or all risk-taking?

Rawls's position, to repeat my understanding of it, involves his notion of the good life, his emphasis upon the opportunities for self-realization as distinct from the realization of some final bundle of commodities. One's ex post utility in the neo-utilitarians' sense had little or no significance. It is hard to say what minimizing the worst misfortune would mean in a model of any generality; there is no way for the state to guarantee continued life nor continued productivity, thus guarantee any *deterministic* lifetime utility. The prospect of achieving self-realization may require the individuals' acceptance of certain risks that ought not to be removed by the state. If the government were to tax so heavily the rewards from successful explorations and risk-taking as to maximize the floor below which the unsuccessful outcomes would not fall, then there might result such a decline of risk-taking that people would feel their lives to be meaningless, with insufficient challenge and chances, *win or lose.* There is nothing in Rawls's *Justice* to suggest that his conception of the just society boils down to choosing that social policy which maximizes the smallest realized individual income after governmental transfers.

It should be mentioned too that even if Rawls's criterion *were* the ex post maximin utility criterion, that would not imply that Rawls's society would tax away the total winnings from the acceptance of risks, thus killing off the incentives to take risks. People's willingness to take some risks, like their willingness to work or save, are like resources potentially for the benefit of all. If the least fortunate got only their national dividends, their lump-sum demogrants, and

[e] Age-specific transfer programs are easily instituted; there is no reason why demogrants should be equalized for persons of all ages. But age-specific expenditure programs to develop skills might often be cumbersome to legislate and administer.

minimum ex post utility were a function of only those poll subsidies, then a society bent on maximizing minimum ex post utility would not want to discourage the taking of all business risks; to do so would cost the society some national income and cost the government some of the revenue with which to pay the national dividend.

But while Rawls's conception of justice countenances certain kinds of risk-taking, and does not maximize ex post utility in the neo-utilitarians' sense of that term, there are some respects in which, I suppose, Rawls would differ from the neo-utilitarians over the matter of ex post eventualities. Some of these differences I have already raised in the previous section: Not all misfortunes are like business risks, the probability distributions being known; hence some misfortunes are more like natural accidents, unanticipatable and uninsurable, than ordinary bad luck. Some misfortunes leave the productivities and remaining lifetime prospects of survivors impaired, so that social policy must confront a particular set of present actualities, not simply prepare for certain future possibilities; my grappling with this problem will be recalled.

There are, in addition, some distinctive attitudes usually shown toward voluntary gambles that should be considered. Let us try to abstract from those kinds of voluntary risks which are in some sense socially productive and which the state wishes to a degree to encourage. There remain a variety of other risks like swimming without lifeguards, traveling great distances for vacations by car or plane, using tobacco or alcohol or other drugs, and so on. An attitude sometimes displayed toward the casualties of such risk-taking is, "You made your bed, now lie in it." Of course, it is not always clear that a strategy or life-style followed by a person is really riskier for him than another strategy, given his particular emotional makeup. To frighten a person from taking certain risks might be riskier for him than to sanction his taking those risks. But let that pass.

It seems fairly clear, however, that that attitude is inappropriate except in regard to behavior toward risk which is in some sense aberrant. Obviously it would be somehow ill-becoming for the parents of a normal child to say to the parents of a defective child that the latter should not have taken the chance when the former took the same chance. It is a little more understandable that those persons who have shied away from taking a certain risk should complain at being taxed for the benefit of those who took the risk and got themselves into trouble as a result: Let those who gambled and won pay the tax, if any must pay. But political arrangements of such a contractarian nature may be too complicated to enact—there are too many contingencies, some unimagined, and too great a variety or risks accepted. Further, everyone has his particular vices; more precisely, there are few persons who could show that their risk-avoidance was greater than another person's across the board. So the fact that some persons can show they have not and will not run the particular risk in question is of doubtful significance for their just obligations toward those who are the casualties of that risk.

Concluding Remarks

I have tried to explain, in the first half of this chapter, why neo-utilitarianism is not relevant to the problem of distributive justice upon which Rawls focused. The neo-utilitarians seem to do their interesting idea a disservice when they try to stretch its application to Rawls's problem.

The harder question, struggled with in the second half of this chapter, is what Rawls's insights have to suggest for the solution to the problem that the neo-utilitarians presumably had in mind—homogeneous prospects plus luck. My suggestion, that something like the maximin criterion with regard to *chances* for self-realization holds good in the neo-utilitarians' setting, is a quite tentative, rather wooly, and not fully-worked idea. One worries that, insofar as some discretionary gambles are available, the institution of that criterion might be abused by excessive risk-taking of certain kinds. But I am not sure that the "costliness" of the maximin criterion—in terms of average well-being maybe—should be decisive against it, just as the "disincentive effects" (dead-weight loss) of maximin taxation is not decisive. Perhaps the best answer, and I do mean "perhaps," to moral hazard is moral restraint.

I stipulated earlier that these latter suggestions of mine are extrapolations from Rawls, not explicit in his work. I suspect the same will be true of most thoughts in welfare theory for a decade or more. Rawls should not be held responsible for them, yet in a sense he is responsible. The mark of a great book is that it is a source-book for new ideas and a provocation for further ideas. I doubt that we shall see, and doubt that we could digest, another like it for quite some time.

References

Arrow, K.J. "Some Ordinalist-Utilitarian Notes on Rawls's Theory of Justice." *The Journal of Philosophy* 70 (1973): 245–263.

Harsanyi, J.C., "Cardinal Utility in Welfare Economics and in the Theory of Risk-Taking." *Journal of Political Economy* 61 (1953): 434–435.

Harsanyi, J.C. "Cardinal Welfare, Individualistic Ethics, and Interpersonal Comparisons of Utility." *Journal of Political Economy* 63 (1955): 309–321.

Harsanyi, J.C. "Can the 'Maximin' Principle Serve as a Basis for Morality?" *American Political Science Review* (1974).

Rawls, J. *A Theory of Justice,* Harvard University Press, Cambridge, Mass., 1971.

Samuelson, P.A. "A.P. Lerner at 60." *Review of Economic Studies* 31 (1964): 169–178.

Samuelson, P.A. "Optimal Compacts for Redistribution," in R.E. Grieson, ed., *Public and Urban Economics: Essays in Honor of William S. Vickrey* (Lexington Books, Lexington, Mass. 1976), pp. 179–190.

Vickrey, W.S. "Measuring Marginal Utility by Reactions to Risk." *Econometrica* 13 (1945): 319–333.
Vickrey, W.S. "Utility, Strategy, and Social Decision Rules." *Quarterly Journal of Economics* 74 (1960): 507–535.
Vickrey, W.S. "Risk, Utility, and Social Policy." *Social Research*, 1961.

ECONOMIC THEORY, ECONOMETRICS, AND MATHEMATICAL ECONOMICS

Consulting Editor: Karl Shell

UNIVERSITY OF PENNSYLVANIA
PHILADELPHIA, PENNSYLVANIA

Franklin M. Fisher and Karl Shell. **The Economic Theory of Price Indices: *Two Essays on the Effects of Taste, Quality, and Technological Change***

Luis Eugenio Di Marco (Ed.). **International Economics and Development: *Essays in Honor of Raúl Presbisch***

Erwin Klein. **Mathematical Methods in Theoretical Economics: *Topological and Vector Space Foundations of Equilibrium Analysis***

Paul Zarembka (Ed.). **Frontiers in Econometrics**

George Horwich and Paul A. Samuelson (Eds.). **Trade, Stability, and Macroeconomics: *Essays in Honor of Lloyd A. Metzler***

W. T. Ziemba and R. G. Vickson (Eds.). **Stochastic Optimization Models in Finance**

Steven A. Y. Lin (Ed.). **Theory and Measurement of Economic Externalities**

David Cass and Karl Shell (Eds.). **The Hamiltonian Approach to Dynamic Economics**

R. Shone. **Microeconomics: *A Modern Treatment***

C. W. J. Granger and Paul Newbold. **Forecasting Economic Time Series**

Michael Szenberg, John W. Lombardi, and Eric Y. Lee. **Welfare Effects of Trade Restrictions: *A Case Study of the U.S. Footwear Industry***

Haim Levy and Marshall Sarnat (Eds.). **Financial Decision Making under Uncertainty**

Yasuo Murata. **Mathematics for Stability and Optimization of Economic Systems**

Alan S. Blinder and Philip Friedman (Eds.). **Natural Resources, Uncertainty, and General Equilibrium Systems: *Essays in Memory of Rafael Lusky***

Jerry S. Kelly. **Arrow Impossibility Theorems**

Peter Diamond and Michael Rothschild (Eds.). **Uncertainty in Economics: *Readings and Exercises***

Fritz Machlup. **Methodology of Economics and Other Social Sciences**

Robert H. Frank and Richard T. Freeman. **Distributional Consequences of Direct Foreign Investment**

Elhanan Helpman and Assaf Razin. **A Theory of International Trade Under Uncertainty**

Edmund S. Phelps. **Studies in Macroeconomic Theory, Volume 1: *Employment and Inflation***

In preparation

Marc Nerlove, David M. Grether, and José L. Carvalho. **Analysis of Economic Time Series: *A Synthesis***

Thomas J. Sargent. **Macroeconomic Theory**

Michael J. Boskin (Ed.). **Economics and Human Welfare: *Essays in Honor of Tibor Scitovsky***